The Daily Telegraph

CONCISE WORLD ATLAS

Published by The Daily Telegraph in association
with Pan Books Limited, Cavaye Place,
London SW 10 9 PG

First published in Great Britain 1988.
This edition published 1989.
9 8 7 6 5 4 3 2 1

ISBN 0 330 31230 8

Printed and bound in Yugoslavia

The Daily Telegraph

CONCISE WORLD ATLAS

Pan Books
London, Sydney and Auckland

STATISTICS

The World 6- 7
Europe 8-15
Asia 16-25
Australia 24-27
Africa 28-38
North-America 38-42
South-America 42-47

READER INFORMATION

Reader information 48
Legend 49

EUROPE

Europe, flags 50-51
British Isles and Central Europe 52-53
Belgium, Czechoslovakia, Federal Republic of Germany, German Democratic Republic, Luxembourg, Netherlands, Poland
Northern Europe 54-55
Denmark, Finland, Iceland, Norway, Sweden
Spain, Italy, France 56-57
The Balkans 58-59
Bulgaria, Cyprus, Greece, Hungary, Romania, Turkey
The Middle East 60-61
Bahrain, Iran, Iraq, Israel, Jordan, Kuwait, Lebanon, Qatar, Syria, United Arab Emirates
Western Soviet Union 62-63
European USSR, Western Siberia

ASIA

Asia, flags 64-65
South West Asia 66-67
Afghanistan, Iran, Pakistan
Eastern Soviet Union 68-69
Eastern Siberia, Mongolia
China and Japan 70-71
incl. Mongolia, North Korea, South Korea, Taiwan
India and South East Asia 72-73
incl. Bangladesh, Bhutan, Burma, Kampuchea, Laos, Nepal, Sri Lanka, Thailand, Vietnam
The East Indies 74-75
Brunei, Indonesia, Malaysia, Philippines

AUSTRALIA

Australasia, flags 76-77
Australia 78-79
New Guinea and New Zealand 80-81
Oceania 82-83
Melanesia, Micronesia, Polynesia

AFRICA

Africa, flags 84-85

North-West Africa 86-87
Algeria, Libya, Morocco, Mauretania, Niger, Tunisia

The Nile Valley and Arabia 88-89
Bahrain, Egypt, Iraq, Israel, Jordan, Kuwait, Lebanon, Oman, Qatar, Saudi-Arabia, Southern Yemen, Sudan, Syria, United Arab Emirates, Yemen

West Africa 90-91
Benin, Burkina, Cameroon, Chad, Congo, Equatorial Guinea, Gabon, Ghana, Guinea, Guinea-Bissau, Ivory Coast, Liberia, Mali, Niger, Nigeria, São Tomé and Príncipe, Senegal, Sierra Leone, The Gambia, Togo

East Africa 92-93
Central Africa, Ethiopia, Kenya, Sudan, Tanzania, Uganda, Zaire

Southern Africa 94-95
Angola, Botswana, Comores, Madagascar, Malawi, Mauritius, Mozambique, Namibia, Lesotho, South Africa, Swaziland, Zambia, Zimbabwe

NORTH AMERICA

North America, flags 96-97

Alaska and Western Canada 98-99
incl. the Aleutian islands

Eastern Canada 100-101

The United States 102-103
incl. Mexico

Central America and the West Indies 104-105
Belize, The Caribbean Archipelago, Costa Rica, Cuba, El Salvador, Guatemala, Honduras, Mexico, Nicaragua

SOUTH AMERICA

South America, flags 106-107

South America, northern part 108-109
Brazil, Colombia, Ecuador, Guyana, Panama, Peru, Surinam, Venezuela

South America, central part 110-111
Bolivia, Brazil, Chile, Peru

South America, southern part 112-113
Argentina, Bolivia, Brazil, Chile, Paraguay, Uruguay

POLAR REGIONS

The Arctic 114

The Antarctica 115

THE WORLD

The World, 116-117

The World, political 118-119

The World, Time Zones 120-121

Animals on the Edge of Extinction 122-123

INDEX

Index 125-184

THE WORLD'S longest, greatest, highest, largest

Area: 150.243.000 km²
(Land: 26%, Water: 71%, Ice: 3%)
Population: 4,025,281,000

Greenland

Mount McKinley

Great Br

NORTH AMERICA

Lake Superior

Milwaukee Depth

Amazon

SOUTH AMERICA

Lago Titicaca

Cerro Aconcagua

Grande de Tierra del Fuego

World's Longest Rivers

1. Nile (Africa)	6.690 km
2. Amazon (South America)	6.570 km
3. Mississippi-Missouri (North America)	6.020 km
4. Yangtze (Asia)	5.980 km
5. Yenisey (Asia)	5.870 km

Greatest Depth in each ocean

Arctic: North Polar Basin	5.500 m
Atlantic: Milwaukee Depth (Puerto Rico Trench)	9.219 m
Indian: Java Trench	7.450 m
Pacific: Challenger Deep (Mariana Trench)	11.034 m

Highest Mountain in each continent

Africa: Kilimanjaro	5.895 m
(Antarctica Vinson Massif)	5.140 m
Asia: Mt. Everest	8.848 m
Europe: Mont Blanc	4.810 m
North America: Mount McKinley	6.194 m
Oceania: Puncak Jaya	5.030 m
South America: Cerro Aconcagua	6.959 m

Largest Island in each continent

Africa: Madagascar	587.000 km²
(Antarctica: Alexander 1)	43.200 km²
Asia: Borneo	737.000 km²
Europe: Great Britain	219.000 km²
North America: Greenland	2.131.000 km²
Oceania: New Guinea	790.000 km²
South America: Grande de Tierra del Fuego	48.000 km²

Ladoga
EUROPE
ASIA
Yenisey
Mont Blanc
Caspian Sea
Yangtze
Mt. Everest
AFRICA
Nile
Challenger Deep
Borneo
Lake Victoria
Kilimanjaro
New Guinea
Puncak Jaya
Java Trench
AUSTRALIA
Madagascar
Lake Eyre

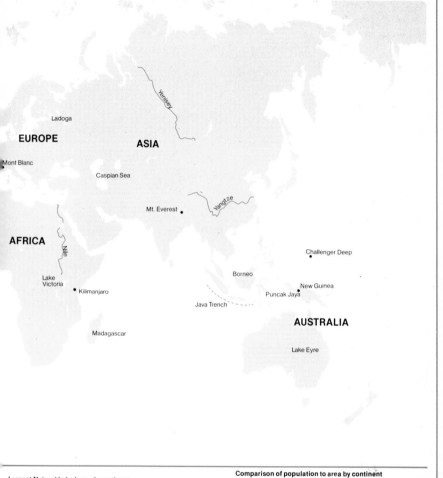

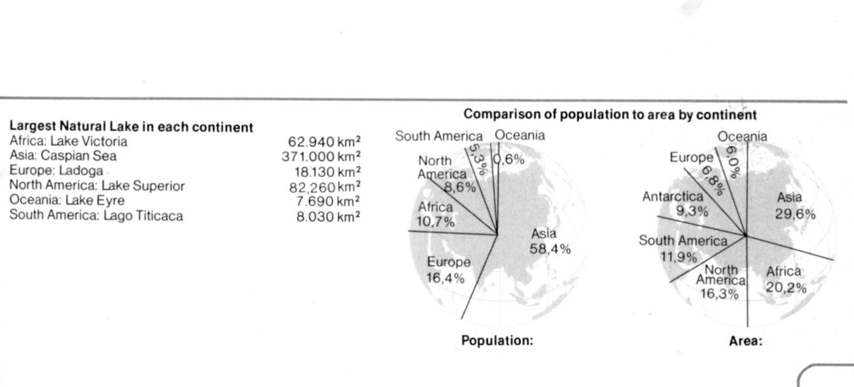

Largest Natural Lake in each continent

Africa: Lake Victoria	62.940 km²
Asia: Caspian Sea	371.000 km²
Europe: Ladoga	18.130 km²
North America: Lake Superior	82,260 km²
Oceania: Lake Eyre	7.690 km²
South America: Lago Titicaca	8.030 km²

EUROPE

Area: 10,245,000 km²
Population: 660,476,000
Density of population per km²: 64

The North Atlantic West Wind Drift together with prevailing westerly winds gives Northern Europe a climate about 5° C. warmer than the average for these latitudes.
The European mainland's most northerly point is Nordkinn at 71° 8′ N. latitude. North Cape is an impressive rocky promontory on the neighbouring island of Mageröy which has its most northerly point at Knivskjellodden.
① ICELAND
All the world's geysers are named after Geysir in Haukadalur, Europe's largest geyser which at irregular intervals, but usually once a day, throws a column of boiling water some 30 m. in the air (maximum height 70m.)
Vatnajökull is Europe's largest glacier with an area of about 8,400 km²
② NORWAY
Sognefjorden (220 km. in length) is Europe's longest inlet.
④ FINLAND
Ladoga with an area 18,130 km² is Europ largest lake.
③ SWEDEN
Europe's largest island is Great Britain which, with an area of 219,000 km², ranks seventh in the world.
⑧ UNION
⑤ REPUBLIC OF IRELAND
⑦ DENMARK
Agricultural land covers 40% of Europe. No other continent is so intensively utilized.
⑥ UNITED KINGDOM
Europe lies on the Prime Meridian, which divides the earth into Eastern and Western hemispheres.
⑨ NETHERLANDS
⑩ FEDERAL REPUBLIC OF GERMANY
⑪ GERMAN DEMOCRATIC REPUBLIC
⑫ POLAND
⑬ BELGIUM
⑭ LUXEMBOURG
⑮ CZECHOSLOVAKIA
At St. Malo the difference between ebb and flow is 15 m., the greatest tidal range in Europe.
⑲ LIECHTENSTEIN
⑳ AUSTRIA
⑰ FRANCE
⑱ SWITZERLAND
HUNGARY ⑯
Cabo da Roca at 9° 31′ W. longitude is the westernmost point on the European mainland.
Mont Blanc is Europe's highest mountain.
㉔ ROMANIA
㉓ YUGOSLAVIA
PORTUGAL ㉕
ANDORRA ㉗
㉑ MONACO
㉘ SAN MARINO
BULGARIA ㉛
㉖ SPAIN
㉙ VATICAN STATE
㉒ ITALY
TURKEY ㉜
㉚ ALBANIA
Europe's highest temperature, 51° C., has been recorded at Sevilla.
㉞ GREECE
Punta Marroqui at 36° O′ N. latitude is the most southerly point on the European mainland.
The highest active volcano in Europe is Etna which last erupted in 1984.
㉝ MALTA

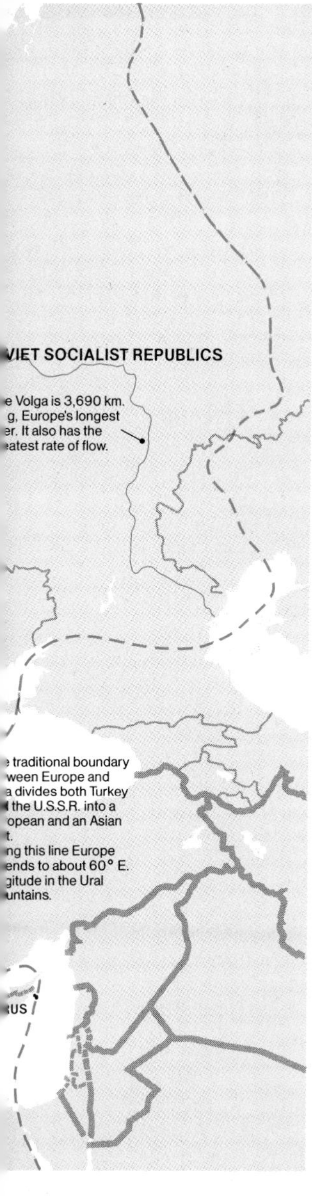
VIET SOCIALIST REPUBLICS
e Volga is 3,690 km.
g, Europe's longest
er. It also has the
eatest rate of flow.
traditional boundary
ween Europe and
a divides both Turkey
the U.S.S.R. into a
opean and an Asian
t.
ng this line Europe
ends to about 60° E.
gitude in the Ural
untains.
US

(30) ALBANIA
(27) ANDORRA
(20) AUSTRIA
(13) BELGIUM
(31) BULGARIA
(35) CYPRUS
(15) CZECHOSLOVAKIA
(7) DENMARK
(10) FEDERAL REPUBLIC OF GERMANY
(4) FINLAND
(17) FRANCE
(11) GERMAN DEMOCRATIC REPUBLIC
(34) GREECE
(16) HUNGARY
(1) ICELAND
(22) ITALY
(19) LIECHTENSTEIN
(14) LUXEMBOURG
(33) MALTA
(21) MONACO
(9) NETHERLANDS
(2) NORWAY
(12) POLAND
(25) PORTUGAL
(5) REPUBLIC OF IRELAND
(24) ROMANIA
(28) SAN MARINO
(26) SPAIN
(3) SWEDEN
(18) SWITZERLAND
(32) TURKEY
(8) UNION OF SOVIET SOCIALIST REPUBLICS
(6) UNITED KINGDOM AND NORTHERN IRELAND
(29) VATICAN STATE
(23) YUGOSLAVIA

① ICELAND

Lýðveldið Island
(Republic of Iceland)

Area: 102,819 km²
Population: 240,000
Population growth per annum: 1.1%
Life expectancy at birth: males 73 years, females 79 years
Literacy: 99,9%
Capital with population: Reykjavik 87,000
Other important cities with population: Akureyri 14,000
Language: Icelandic
Religion: Protestant
Currency: Króna = 100 aurar

The Island of the Norse sagas, Iceland's "althingi" claims to be the world's oldest parliament, enacting laws since 930. The Icelanders kept the old Norse myths and sagas alive by oral tradition until Snorri Sturluson collected them in his epic Edda. A sight to be seen is the world famous Geysir. Independent 930, JUN 17, 1944.

② NORWAY

Kongeriket Norge
(Kingdom of Norway)

Area: 386,974 km² (including Svalbard and Jan Mayen)
Population: 4,130,000
Population growth per annum: 0.4%
Life expectancy at birth: males 72 years, females 78 years
Literacy: 99%
Capital with population: Oslo 447,000
Other important cities with population: Bergen 207,000, Trondheim 134,000
Language: Norwegian
Religion: Protestant
Currency: Norwegian krone = 100 öre

Norway, proclaimed 'The land of the Midnight Sun" might rather be called the Land of Fiords. These spectacular inlets between vertical mountain walls dissect Norway, and have made the Norwegians a people who sail and fish. The Sogne Fiord is 220 km. long — the Europe's longest bay. Independent 1905.

③ SWEDEN

Konungariket Sverige
(Kingdom of Sweden)

Area: 449,964 km²
Population: 8,350,000
Population growth per annum: 0.2%
Life expectancy at birth: males 72 years, females 79 years
Literacy: 99%
Capital with population: Stockholm 651,000 (metropolitan area 1,409, 000)
Other important cities with population: Göteborg 424,000 Malmö 230,000
Language: Swedish
Religion: Protestant
Currency: Swedish krona = 100 öre

The metallurgical industry that gave the world "Swedish steel" has traditions that reach beyond the Viking Age. The world's oldest company, Stora, chartered in 1280, is still working the mine of Falun, that produced the copper that once made Sweden a great power.

④ FINLAND

Suomen Tasavatta — Republiken Finland
(Republic of Finland)

Area: 337,032 km²
Population: 4,870 000
Population growth per annum: 0.6%
Life expectancy at birth: males 69 years, females 77 years
Literacy: 99%
Capital with population: Helsinki (Helsingfors) 484,000
Other important cities with population: Tampere (Tammerfors) 170.000, Turku (Åbo) 165,000
Language: Finnish, Swedish
Religion: Protestant
Currency: Markka (mark) = 100 penniä (penni)

The "land of a thousand lakes" (actually almost a hundred thousand) has also become known as "the land that pays its debts" — by repaying not only U.S. loans but also a huge war indemnity to the Soviet Union after World War II. Exporting high quality manufactured goods to East and West has brought prosperity to the Finns. Independent DEC 6, 1917

⑤ REPUBLIC OF IRELAND

Poblacht na L'Éireann
(Eire)

Area: 70,283 km²
Population: 3,440,000
Population growth per annum: 1.1%
Life expectancy at birth: males 70 years, females 75 years
Literacy: 99%
Capital with population: Dublin 526,000
Other important cities with population: Cork 150,000, Limerick 76,000
Language: Irish, English
Religion: Roman Catholic
Currency: Irish pound (punt Eirenmach) = 100 pighne

"The Emerald Isle" is perhaps most famous for its people — for boisterous bards, for poets and playwrights and Irish Eyes — but also for Irish coffee, whiskey and Guinness beer. Ireland justly prides itself also on the Book of Kells — and maybe more reluctantly for the Blarney Stone, kissed by many. Independent 1916, 1922.

⑥ THE UNITED KINGDOM OF GREAT BRITAIN AND NORTHERN IRELAND

Area: 244,104 km²
Population: 56,780,000
Population growth per annum: — 0.1%
Life expectancy at birth: males 70 years, females 76 years
Literacy: 99%
Capital with population: London 6,755,000
Other important cities with population: Birmingham 1,013,000, Leeds 714,000, Sheffield 543,000
Language: English
Religion: Protestant, Roman Catholic, Moslem
Currency: British pound = 100 pence

Britannia ruled the waves for over three hundred years, and finally gracefully resigned from the role of "peacekeeper" after the Pax Britannica had been broken by two world wars. The sun may have set over the Empire, but it still shines on the Union Jack in many places all over the world.

⑦ DENMARK

Kongeriget Danmark
(Kingdom of Denmark)

Area: 43,069 km²
Population: 5,112,000
Population growth per annum: 0.2%
Life expectancy at birth: males 71 years, females 77 years
Literacy: 99%
Capital with population: Köbenhavn (Copenhagen) 483,000, (Greater Copenhagen 1,400,000)
Other important cities with population: Aarhus 250,000, Odense 170,000
Language: Danish
Religion: Protestant (Lutherans)
Currency: Danish krone = 100 øre

Danish kings have ruled not only all of Scandinavia but also England. Today no other country has larger overseas territories. They include the world's largest island, Greenland. Friendly Denmark now serves as an important link between the Nordic countries and the rest of Europe, especially the E.E.C.

⑧ UNION OF SOVIET SOCIALIST REPUBLICS

Soyuz Sovyetskikh
Sotsialisticheskikh Respublik

Area: 22,402,200 km²
Population: 276,300,000
Population growth per annum: 0.9 %
Life expectancy at birth: males 65 years, females 74 years
Literacy: 99%
Capital with population: Moskva (Moscow) 8,537,000
Other important cities with population: Leningrad 4,800,000, Baku 1,660,000, Kuybyshev 1,250,000
Language: Slavic (Russian, Ukrainian, Byelorussian, Polish), Altaic (Turkish , etc.) Other Indo-European, Uralian, Caucasian.
Religion: Orthodox, Moslem
Currency: Rubel = 100 kopek

The U.S.S.R. is a country that is almost a continent not only in size, but also in diversity. It covers 1/6 of the Earth's land area, and is larger than South America. 75% is traditionally considered to be part of Asia, but 75% of its people live in the European part. In comprises 120 different peoples, dominated by the Russians.

⑨ NETHERLANDS

Koninkrijk der Nederlanden
(Kingdom of the Netherlands)

Area: 41,548 km²
Population: 14,395,000
Population growth per annum: 0.6%
Life expectancy at birth: males 72 years, females 78 years
Literacy: 99%
Capital with population: Amsterdam 994,000
Other important cities with population: Rotterdam 1,025,500, S-Gravenhage (The Hague) (672,000)
Language: Dutch
Religion: Roman Catholic (40%), Protestant (35%)
Currency: Guilder = 100 cents

More than one third of the country lies below sealevel. Some Dutch say that 'God created the world, except the Netherlands, which we had to create ourselves'. This task was begun in the 15th century, when they learned to reclaim their slowly sinking land from the encroaching sea. Independent APR 19, 1839.

⑩ FEDERAL REPUBLIC OF GERMANY

Bundesrepublik Deutschland

Area: 248,687 km²
Population: 61,420,000
Population growth per annum: — 0.3 %
Life expectancy at birth: males 69 years, females 75 years
Literacy: 99%
Capital with population: Bonn 293,000
Other important cities with population: Berlin 1,860,000, Hamburg 1,620,000, Munich 1,285,000
Language: German
Religion: Protestant (49%), Roman Catholic (45%)
Currency: D-mark = 100 pfennig

Like the mythical Phoenix, West Germany has miraculously sprung from the pyre of total defeat and destruction since 1945. In economic and industrial importance the western half of divided Germany now ranks fourth in the world. The Grand Tour must include the Rhine valley with its castles and vineyards. Independent SEP 6, 1949.

⑪ GERMAN DEMOCRATIC REPUBLIC

Deutsche Demokratische Republik

Area: 108,333 km²
Population: 16,700,000
Population growth per annum: 0%
Life expectancy at birth: males 69 years, females 75 years
Literacy: 99%
Capital with population: Berlin 1,185,000
Other important cities with population: Leipzig 560,000, Dresden 525,000, Karl-Marx-Stadt 320,000
Language: German
Religion: Protestant (80%)
Currency: Mark (of the GDR) = 100 pfennig

The republic is divided nation with a divided capital. The fears and the rivalries of the victorious powers after World War II prevented the reestablishment of a German "Reich". Thus part of the old capital, Berlin, is now a West German enclave, by road and railway over 150 km. (100 miles) inside East Germany. Independent OCT 7, 1949.

⑫ POLAND

Polska Rzeczpospolita Ludowa
(Polish Peoples Republic)

Area: 312,683 km²
Population: 36,400,000
Population growth per annum: 1.0 %
Life expectancy at birth: males 67 years, females 75 years
Literacy: 98%
Capital with population: Warszawa (Warsaw) 1,630,000
Other important cities with population: Lódź 850,000 Kraków 725,000
Language: Polish
Religion: Roman Catholic
Currency: Zloty = 100 groszy

The Polish people do not give up. Time and again conquering armies have swept over Poland and divided the spoils. After World War II the Soviet Union pushed the land westwards over former German land, annexing 1/3 of pre-war Poland in the east. Independent 966, NOV 10, 1918.

⑬ BELGIUM

Royaume de Belgique —
Koninkrijk België
(Kingdom of Belgium)

Area: 30,519 km²
Population: 9,850 000
Population growth per annum: 0.1%
Life expectancy at birth: males 69 years, females 75 years
Literacy: 98%
Capital with population: Bruxelles 980,000 (Brussels)
Other important cities with population:
Antwerpen 490,000, Gent 240,000
Language: Flemish (Dutch), French, German
Religion: Roman Catholic
Currency: Belgian franc = 100 centimes

The country at "the crossroads of Western Europe" is dominated by the capital Brussels, Brussels is also the capital of the E.E.C. The difficulties in uniting Europe are mirrored in the Belgian nation. The Dutch-speaking Flemings and French-speaking Walloons stick together against others, but often quarrel amongst themselves. Independent OCT 4, 1830.

⑭ LUXEMBOURG

Grand-Duché Luxembourg
(Grand Duchy of Luxembourg)

Area: 2,586 km²
Population: 366,000
Population growth per annum: —0.04%
Life expectancy at birth: males 68 years, females 75 years
Literacy: 100%
Capital with population: Luxembourg 79,000
Other important cities with population: none
Language: Luxemburgish, French, German
Religion: Roman Catholic (94%)
Currency: Luxembourg franc = 100 centimes

Historically Luxembourg has always had strong ties with one or another of its neighbours while maintaining independence in form if not in fact. It also formed some sort of a nucleus for the Coal and Steel Union that evolved into the E.E.C. Indep. 1866.

⑮ CZECHOSLOVAKIA

Československá Socialistická
Republika
(Czechoslovak Socialist Republic)

Area: 127,869 km²
Population: 15,400 000
Population growth per annum: 0.7%
Life expectancy at birth: males 67 years, females 74 years
Literacy: 99%
Capital with population: Praha (Prague) 1,185,000
Other important cities with population: Bratislava 395,000, Brno 380,000
Language: Czech, Slovak
Religion: Roman Catholic (55%), Protestant (10%)
Currency: Koruna = 100 haléřu

Haseks fictionary "Good soldier Schweik" in many ways epitomizes the survival instincts of his fellow citizens. Both Czechs and Slovaks have always striven for freedom, but throughout the centuries have been forced to bow to foreign rule. Mining and manufacturing have a long history in Czechoslovakia. Independent OCT 28, 1918.

⑯ HUNGARY

Magyar Nepköztársaság
(Hungarian People's Republic)

Area: 93,032 km²
Population: 10,680,000
Population growth per annum: 0.4%
Life expectancy at birth: males 67 years, females 73 years
Literacy: 98%
Capital with population: Budapest 2,064,000
Other important cities with population:
Debrecen 205,000, Miskolc 212,000
Language: Hungarian (Magyar)
Religion: Roman Catholic (65%), Protestant (25%)
Currency: Forint = 100 fillér

Hungary is in many ways an enclave in Eastern Europe — a Finno-Ugric nation surrounded by Slav neighbors, a land of plains, the famous puszta, and rolling hills, encircled by higher mountain lands — and, within limits, more prosperous and "capitalistic" than the other Soviet satellites. Independent 1001.

⑰ FRANCE

République Française
(French Republic)

Area: 547,026 km²
Population: 54,539,000
Population growth per annum: 0.3%
Life expectancy at birth: males 70 years, females 78 years
Literacy: 99%
Capital with population: Paris 2,320,000 (Greater Paris 8,550,000)
Other important cities with population: Marseille 915,000, Lyon 465,000
Language: French
Religion: Roman Catholic (90%) Islam (4%)
Currency: French franc = 100 centimes

France is one of the great powers of the world. The French language is still the language of diplomacy. France is culturally the world's leading nation, and most former French colonies remain members of the French Commonwealth. France is also the leading European nation on the space frontier. National day: JULY 14, (1789)

⑱ SWITZERLAND

Schweiz - Suisse - Svizzera
(Swiss Confederation)

Area: 41,293 km²
Population: 6,400,000
Population growth per annum: 0.2 %
Life expectancy at birth: males 72 years, females 78 years
Literacy: 99%
Capital with population: Bern 144,000
Other important cities with population: Zürich 363,000, Basel 180,000
Language: German, French, Italian, Romansch
Religion: Roman Catholic (49%), Protestant (48%)
Currency: Swiss franc = 100 centimes (rappen)

The Financial Pole of the world is claimed to be in situated in some undefined spot in Zürich. Through centuries of neutrality and economic stability, Switzerland has grown into a global center of banking. Besides quality watches, tourism somehow seems to have been invented in this land of few natural resources. Independent AUG 1, 1291.

⑲ LIECHTENSTEIN

Fürstentum Liechtenstein
(Principality of Liechtenstein)

Area: 160 km²
Population: 27,000
Population growth per annum: 7.0%
Life expectancy at birth: not available
Literacy: 100 %
Capital with population: Vaduz 5,000
Other important cities with population: none
Language: German
Religion: Roman Catholic
Currency: Swiss franc = 100 centimes

Liechtenstein epitomizes the notion "postage stamp state" — because of its size and its fame among collectors of stamps. It is also an anomaly surviving principality from the times when Europe was divided among many princes and kings, before their realms were united into nations. Independent MAY 3, 1342.

⑳ AUSTRIA

Republik Österreich
(Republic of Austria)

Area: 83,853 km²)
Population: 7,550,000
Population growth per annum: —0.1%
Life expectancy at birth: males 68 years, females 75 years
Literacy: 98%
Capital with population: Wien (Vienna) 1,530,000
Other important cities with population: Graz 243,000, Linz 200,000
Language: German
Religion: Roman Catholic (89%), Protestant (6%)
Currency: Schilling = 100 groschen

Austria is the only state pledged both by law and treaties to neutrality. Vienna, for centuries the capital of the "Holy Roman Empire", the seat of the Habsburg Emperors, still bears the imprint of bygone greatness, and remains the cultural capital of Central Europe. Indep. 1276, 1804, 1918, APR 27, 1945.

㉑ MONACO

Principauté de Monaco
(Principality of Monaco)

Area: 1,95 km²
Population: 27,000
Population growth per annum: —3.0%
Life expectancy at birth: males 70 years, females 78 years
Literacy: 99%
Capital with population: Monaco-Ville 1,700
Other important cities with population: none
Languages: French, Monegasque
Religion: Roman Catholic
Currency: French-or Monegasque franc = 100 centimes

Monaco proves that gambling can pay provided you run the bank! The Monte Carlo Casino has been the Mecca of gamblers since 1858 and also made Monaco a fashionable tourist resort. The citizens of microscopic Monaco do not pay income tax. Independent 1297.

㉒ ITALY

Repubblica Italiana
(Italian Republic)

Area: 301,268 km²
Population: 56,930,000
Population growth per annum: 0.4%
Life expectancy at birth: males 70 years, females 76 years
Literacy: 98%
Capital with population: Roma (Rome) 2,830,000
Other important cities with population: Milano 1,500,000, Napoli 1,200,000
Language: Italian
Religion: Roman Catholic
Currency: Lira = 100 centesimi

All roads lead to Rome, still the Eternal City — the city of the Pope, of the Sistine Chapel, of the Colosseum and innumerable monuments of Imperial Rome. But Italy is also the land of Saint Francis and Leonardo, of Pisa, Venice and Florence — and today of Milan, Torino and Cortina d'Ampezzo. Independent FEB 18, 1861.

㉓ YUGOSLAVIA

Socijalistička Federativna Republika Jugoslavija
(Socialist Federal Republ. of Yogoslavia)

Area: 255,804 km²
Population: 22,850,000
Population growth per annum: 0.9%
Life expectancy at birth: males 67 years, females 72 years
Literacy: 85%
Capital with population: Beograd (Belgrade) 1,407,000
Other important cities with population: Zagreb 1,175,000, Skopje 507,000, Ljubljana 305,000
Language: Serbo-Croatian, Macedonian, Slovenian, Albanian
Religion: Orthodox (41%), Roman Catholic (32%), Moslem (12%)
Currency: Yugoslavian dinar = 100 para

Few would in 1918 have placed any money on the survival of any country in the Balkan Peninsula and least of them all Yugoslavia with its mosaic of quarrelling religions — three — and combative peoples — five — speaking four different languages. Independent DEC 1, 1918.

㉔ ROMANIA

Republica Socialistâ România
(Socialist Republic of Romania)

Area: 237,500 km²
Population: 22,600,000
Population growth per annum: 0.9%
Life expectancy at birth: males 68 years, females 73 years
Literacy: 98%
Capital with population: Bucuresti (Bucharest) 1,835,000
Other important cities with population: Constanța 285,000, Cluj-Napoca 271,000
Language: Romanian
Religion: Orthodox (70%), Roman Catholic (14%)
Currency: Leu = 100 bani

A land that is still Roman after almost two thousand years! Rome sett-led fertile Dacia and made an everlasting imprint. In spite of that, the frontier province was lost less than two centuries after conquest. The people today speak a language based on Latin. Transylvania is known for fictitious Count Dracula. Independent 1877.

㉕ PORTUGAL

República Portuguesa
(Republic of Portugal)

Area: 92,082 km²
Population: 9,930,000
Population growth per annum: 0.9%
Life expectancy at birth: males 66 years, females 74 years
Literacy: 80%
Capital with population: Lisboa (Lisbon) 818,000
Other important cities with population: Porto 330,000
Language: Portuguese
Religion: Roman Catholic
Currency: Escudo = 100 centavos

In spite of its small size, Portugal managed to become one of the world's great powers, and to acquire and retain a global empire for half a millennium. Portugal produces famous wines, such as madeira and port (from Oporto), and every second wine bottle in the world is sealed with Portuguese cork.

㉖ SPAIN

Reino de España
(Kingdom of Spain)

Area: 504,782 km²
Population: 38,220,000
Population growth per annum: 1.0 %
Life expectancy at birth: males 70 years, females 76 years
Literacy: 97%
Capital with population: Madrid 3,188,000
Other important cities with population:
Barcelona 1,755,000, Sevilla 654,000,
Zaragoza 600,000
Language: Spanish, Catalan, Basque
Religion: Roman Catholic
Currency: Spanish peseta = 100 céntimos

Proud Spain, once one of the world's great powers that sent the Great Armada to England in a bid to become master of the oceans, is today still the cultural leader in the Iberic World. It gave the world people such as Cervantes, Loyola, Goya, and Picasso.

㉗ ANDORRA

Principat d'Andorra
(Principality of Andorra)

Area: 453 km²
Population: 41,600
Population growth per annum: not available
Life expectancy at birth: males 70 years, females 76 years
Literacy: 100%
Capital with population: Andorra la Vella 10,500
Other important cities with population: none
Language: Catalan
Religion: Roman Catholic
Currency: French franc, Spanish peseta

Conducting trade between Spain and France is and has been the main business of this Pyrenean principality, jointly ruled by the Spanish Bishop of Urgel and the Head of State of France. Outside Andorra some call it smuggling. Tourism also benefits from the absence of customs duties. Independent 1278.

㉘ SAN MARINO

Repubblica di San Marino
(Republic of San Marino)

Area: 61 km²
Population: 22,000
Population growth per annum: not available
Life expectancy at birth: not available
Literacy: not available
Capital with population: San Marino 5,000
Other important cities with population: none
Language: Italian
Religion: Roman Catholic
Currency: Italian lira = 100 centesimi

The only surviving city state of medieval Italy, San Marino is still governed by two Capitani Reggenti, democratically elected for a period of only six months. Sale of postage stamps was an important industry, but is now dwarfed by the tourist trade. Over 3.5 million visit San Marino each year. Independent 1263.

㉙ VATICAN CITY STATE

Stato della Citta del Vaticano

Area: 0,44 km²
Population: 1,000
Population growth per annum: —
Life expectancy at birth: —
Literacy: —
Capital with population: —
Other important cities with population: —
Language: Italian
Religion: Roman Catholic
Currency: Vatican City lira, Italian lira = 100 centesimi

The spiritual importance of the Pope is inversely proportionate to the size of his worldly domains, the world's smallest state. Relative to its size it certainly contains greater treasures of art than any other state in the world, such as the Sistine Chapel and the Pietà. Independent FEB 11, 1929.

㉚ ALBANIA

Rebublika Popullore
Socialiste e Shqipërisë

Area: 28,748 km²
Population: 2,850 000
Population growth per annum: 2.4%
Life expectancy at birth: males 68 years, females 71 years
Literacy: 75%
Capital with population: Tirana 198,000
Other important cities with population: Shkodra 63,000
Language: Albanian
Religion: Religions are not allowed since 1967
Currency: Lek = 100 qindarka

A desire for self-sufficiency has turned Albania into a virtually unknown "white spot" on the map. This nation is Europe's only Moslem country, but has declared itself "the world's first atheist state". It is so dogmatically communist, that it has broken all ties with other communist countries. Independent NOV 11,1912.

㉛ BULGARIA

Narodna Republika Bâlgarija
(Peoples Republic of Bulgaria)

Area: 110,912 km²
Population: 8,930,000
Population growth per annum: 0.6%
Life expectancy at birth: males 69 years, females 75 years
Literacy: 95%
Capital with population: Sofiya 1,080,000
Other important cities with population: Plovid 310,000, Varna 260,000
Language: Bulgarian
Religion: Orthodox (85%), Moslem (13%)
Currency: Lev = 100 stótinki

The Bulgarians do not forget that Russia helped to liberate their country from Turkish rule that lasted for over five centuries. Today it is counted among the most loyal allies of the Soviet Union. Europe's "vegetable and fruit garden" is also the tourist "Riviera" of Eastern Europe. Independent SEPT 22, 1908.

㉜ TURKEY

Türkiye Cumhuriyeti
(Republic of Turkey)

Area: 779,452 km²
Population: 48,000,000
Population growth per annum: 2.5%
Life expectancy at birth: males 58 years, females 63 years
Literacy: 70%
Capital with population: Ankara 1,877,000
Other important cities with population: Istanbul 2,773,000, Izmir 758,000,
Language: Turkish
Religion: Moslem
Currency: Turkish lira = 100 kuruş

The land that for centuries served as a link between Europe and Asia now also provides the two continents with a physical link, the huge bridge over the Bosporus. The world famous cathedral of Hagia Sofia, built by emperor Justinian 532-537, was turned into a mosque after the fall of Constantinople in 1453.

㉝ MALTA

Repubblika ta'Malta
(Republic of Malta)

Area: 316 km²
Population: 330,000
Population growth per annum: 0.9%
Life expectancy at birth: males 69 years, females 73 years
Literacy: 83%
Capital with population: Valletta 14,000
Other important cities with population: none
Language: Maltese, English
Religion: Roman Catholic
Currency: Lira Maltija (Maltese Lira) = 100 cents = 1000 mils

For unprecedented valour during World War II the people of Malta were collectively awarded the George Cross, Britaini's highest civilian decoration. Malta still proudly carries the cross in its national flag. From 1530 to 1798 Malta was ruled by the Knights Hospitallers — since Known as the Knights of Malta. Independent SEP 21, 1964.

㉞ GREECE

Elleniki Dimokratia
(Hellenic Republic)

Area: 131,944 km²
Population: 9,750,000
Population growth per annum: 0.6%
Life expectancy at birth: males 71 years, females 75 years
Literacy: 95%
Capital with population: Athínai (Athens) 900,000 (Greater Athens 3,000,000)
Other important cities with population: Thessaloníki 400,000, Pátrai 140,000
Language: Greek
Religion: Greek Orthodox (97%)
Currency: Drachma = 100 lepta

The cradle of European civilization is now a member of the E.E.C. and thus takes an active part in shaping the Europe of the future. Greece may well have the world's largest merchant fleet — even if few sail under Greek flag. Venerable Parthenon, temple of Pallas Athena, still crowns Athen's Acropolis. Independent FEB 3, 1830.

㉟ CYPRUS

Kypriaki Dimokratia —
Kibris Cumhuriyeti
(Republic of Cyprus)

Area: 9,251 km²
Population: 655,000
Population growth per annum: 0.4%
Life expectancy at birth: males 70 years, females 74 years
Literacy: 89%
Capital with population: Nicosia 161,000
Other important cities with population: Limassol 107,000, Famagusta 40,000
Language: Greek, Turkish
Religion: Orthodox (77%)
Currency: Cyprus pound = 100 cents

The very name of the metal copper is derived from the island's original name, Kypros, as it in ancient times was the world's leading producer of copper. The Greek goddess of love, Aphrodite, was said to have been born here out of the surf. Actually Cyprus itself is a child of the sea, a part of former deep ocean crust lifted high above sealevel. Indep. AUG 16, 1960.

ASIA

Area: 44,493,000 km²
Population: 2,349,048,000
Density of population per km²: 53

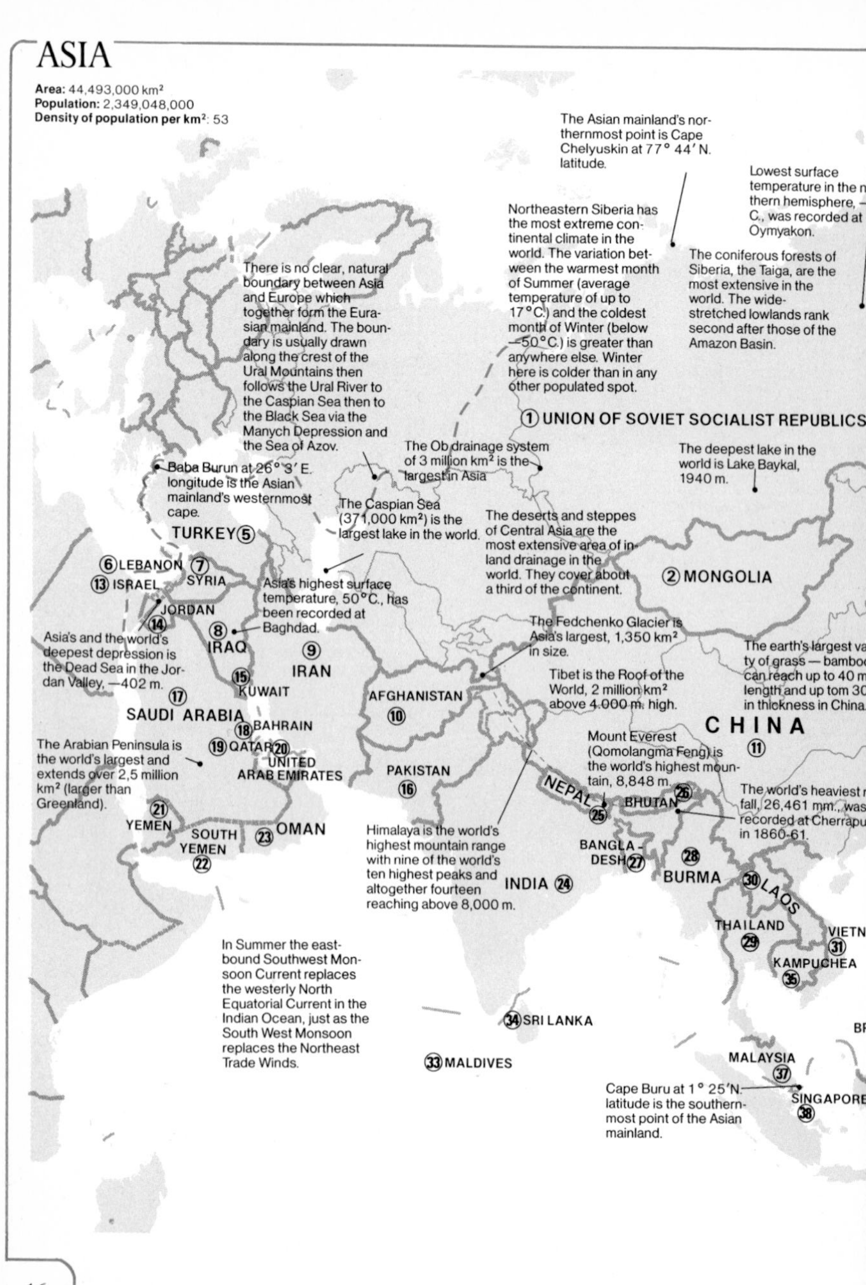

The Asian mainland's northernmost point is Cape Chelyuskin at 77° 44′ N. latitude.
Lowest surface temperature in the no
thern hemisphere, —
C., was recorded at Oymyakon.
Northeastern Siberia has the most extreme continental climate in the world. The variation between the warmest month of Summer (average temperature of up to 17°C.) and the coldest month of Winter (below —50°C.) is greater than anywhere else. Winter here is colder than in any other populated spot.
The coniferous forests of Siberia, the Taiga, are the most extensive in the world. The wide-stretched lowlands rank second after those of the Amazon Basin.
There is no clear, natural boundary between Asia and Europe which together form the Eurasian mainland. The boundary is usually drawn along the crest of the Ural Mountains then follows the Ural River to the Caspian Sea then to the Black Sea via the Manych Depression and the Sea of Azov.
① UNION OF SOVIET SOCIALIST REPUBLICS
The Ob drainage system of 3 million km² is the largest in Asia
The deepest lake in the world is Lake Baykal, 1940 m.
Baba Burun at 26° 3′ E. longitude is the Asian mainland's westernmost cape.
The Caspian Sea (371,000 km²) is the largest lake in the world.
The deserts and steppes of Central Asia are the most extensive area of inland drainage in the world. They cover about a third of the continent.
TURKEY ⑤
⑥ LEBANON
⑦ SYRIA
⑬ ISRAEL
JORDAN ⑭
Asia's highest surface temperature, 50°C., has been recorded at Baghdad.
② MONGOLIA
⑧ IRAQ
The Fedchenko Glacier is Asia's largest, 1,350 km² in size.
Asia's and the world's deepest depression is the Dead Sea in the Jordan Valley, —402 m.
⑨ IRAN
⑮ KUWAIT
Tibet is the Roof of the World, 2 million km² above 4.000 m. high.
The earth's largest var
ty of grass — bamboo
can reach up to 40 m i
length and up tom 30
in thickness in China.
⑰ SAUDI ARABIA
AFGHANISTAN ⑩
⑱ BAHRAIN
CHINA ⑪
The Arabian Peninsula is the world's largest and extends over 2,5 million km² (larger than Greenland).
⑲ QATAR
⑳ UNITED ARAB EMIRATES
Mount Everest (Qomolangma Feng) is the world's highest mountain, 8,848 m.
PAKISTAN ⑯
NEPAL ㉕
BHUTAN ㉖
The world's heaviest ra
fall, 26,461 mm., was recorded at Cherrapun
in 1860-61.
㉑ YEMEN
SOUTH YEMEN ㉒
㉓ OMAN
Himalaya is the world's highest mountain range with nine of the world's ten highest peaks and altogether fourteen reaching above 8,000 m.
BANGLADESH ㉗
㉘ BURMA
INDIA ㉔
㉚ LAOS
THAILAND ㉙
VIETNA
㉛
KAMPUCHEA ㉟
In Summer the eastbound Southwest Monsoon Current replaces the westerly North Equatorial Current in the Indian Ocean, just as the South West Monsoon replaces the Northeast Trade Winds.
㉞ SRI LANKA
BR
㉝ MALDIVES
MALAYSIA ㊲
Cape Buru at 1° 25′N. latitude is the southernmost point of the Asian mainland.
SINGAPORE ㊳

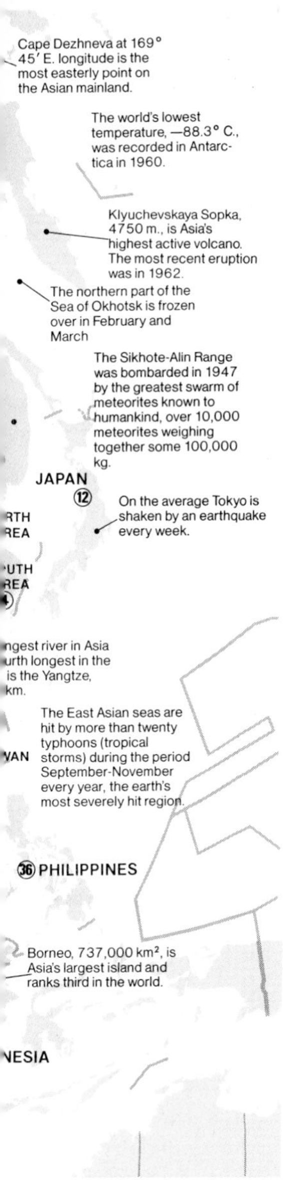

Cape Dezhneva at 169° 45′ E. longitude is the most easterly point on the Asian mainland.

The world's lowest temperature, —88.3° C., was recorded in Antarctica in 1960.

Klyuchevskaya Sopka, 4750 m., is Asia's highest active volcano. The most recent eruption was in 1962.

The northern part of the Sea of Okhotsk is frozen over in February and March

The Sikhote-Alin Range was bombarded in 1947 by the greatest swarm of meteorites known to humankind, over 10,000 meteorites weighing together some 100,000 kg.

JAPAN
⑫

On the average Tokyo is shaken by an earthquake every week.

RTH
REA

UTH
REA

ngest river in Asia
urth longest in the
is the Yangtze,
km.

The East Asian seas are hit by more than twenty typhoons (tropical storms) during the period September-November every year, the earth's most severely hit region.

VAN

㊱ PHILIPPINES

Borneo, 737,000 km², is Asia's largest island and ranks third in the world.

NESIA

⑩ AFGHANISTAN
⑱ BAHRAIN
㉗ BANGLADESH
㉖ BHUTAN
㊴ BRUNEI
㉘ BURMA
⑪ CHINA
㉔ INDIA
㊵ INDONESIA
⑨ IRAN
⑧ IRAQ
⑬ ISRAEL
⑫ JAPAN
⑭ JORDAN
㉟ KAMPUCHEA
⑮ KUWAIT
㉚ LAOS
⑥ LEBANON
㊲ MALAYSIA
㉝ MALDIVES
② MONGOLIA
㉕ NEPAL
③ NORTH KOREA
㉓ OMAN
⑯ PAKISTAN
㊱ PHILIPPINES
⑲ QATAR
⑰ SAUDI ARABIA
㊳ SINGAPORE
④ SOUTH KOREA
㉒ SOUTH YEMEN
㉞ SRI LANKA
⑦ SYRIA
㉙ THAILAND
㉜ TAIWAN
⑤ TURKEY
① UNION OF SOVIET SOCIALIST REPUBLICS
⑳ UNITED ARAB EMIRATES
㉛ VIETNAM
㉑ YEMEN

① UNION OF SOVIET SOCIALIST REPUBLICS

Soyuz Sovyetskikh Sotsialisticheskikh Respublik

Area: 22,402,200 km²
Population: 276,300,000
Population growth per annum: 0.9%
Life expectancy at birth: males 65 years, females 74 years
Literacy: 99%
Capital with population: Moskva (Moscow) 8,537,000
Other important cities with population: Leningrad 4,800,000, Baku 1,660,000, Kuybyshev 1,250,000
Language: Altaic (Turkish etc.), other Indo-European, Uralian Caucasian
Religion: Orthodox, Moslem
Currency: Rubel = 100 kopek

The U.S.S.R. is a country that is almost a continent not only in size, but also in diversity. It covers 1/6 of the Earth's land area, and is larger than South America. 75% is traditionally considered to be part of Asia, but 75% of its people live in the European part. In comprises 120 different peoples, dominated by the Russians.

② MONGOLIA

Bügd Nayramdakh Mongol Ard Uls
(Mongolian People's Republic)

Area: 1,565,000 km²
Population: 1,820,000
Population growth per annum: 2.9%
Life expectancy at birth: males 61 years, females 65 years
Literacy: 80%
Capital with population: Ulaanbaatar (Ulan Bator) 400,000
Other important cities with population: Darkhan 52,000
Language: Mongol, Russian, Chinese
Religions: Buddhist
Currency: Tugrik = 100 möngö

The home of Genghis Khan is now as then a land of unbroken horizons where trees are as rare as people on the windswept grasslands. The Mongols have now exchanged their horses for motor bikes and so only disappear faster out of view. One third of Mongolia is part of the mighty Gobi Desert. Independent JAN 5, 1946.

③ NORTH KOREA

Chosun Minchu-chui Inmin Konghwa-guk
(Democratic People's Republic of Korea)

Area: 122,098 km²
Population: 18,490,000
Population growth per annum: 3.2%
Life expectancy at birth: males 70 years, females 78 years
Literacy: 85%
Capital with population: P'yŏngyang 1,280,000
Other important cities with population: Hamhŭng 420,000, Ch'ŏngjin 265,000
Languages: Korean
Religion: Buddhist (activities discouraged)
Currency: Won = 100 chon

Korea is a victim of the 20th century. During the scramble for colonies it was annexed by Japan, and after the Japanese capitulation in 1945 it was divided into two zones of occupation by the U.S.A. and the U.S.S.R. along 38° N lat. The cold war began here and grew into a real war 1950-53. Korea remains divided. Independent NOV 9, 1948.

④ SOUTH KOREA

Han Kook
(Republic of Korea)

Area: 98,992 km²
Population: 39,950,000
Population growth per annum: 1.6%
Life expectancy at birth: 68 years
Literacy: 92%
Capital with population: Sŏul (Seoul) 8,367,000
Other important cities with population: Pusan 3,160,000, Taegu 1,607,000
Language: Korean
Religion: Buddhist, Confucianist, Christian
Currency: Won = 100 chon

In the shadow of China, the Korean people have managed to maintain a national identity — and true independence during most of their history — and also to achieve great cultural feats of their own. Here books were being printed as early as a thousand years ago. Independent AUG 15, 1948.

⑤ TURKEY

Türkiye Cumhuriyeti
(Republic of Turkey)

Area: 779,452 km²
Population: 48,000,000
Population growth per annum: 2.5%
Life expectancy at birth: males 58 years, females 63 years
Literacy: 70%
Capital with population: Ankara 1,877,000
Other important cities with population: Istanbul 2,773,000, Izmir 758,000
Language: Turkish
Religion: Moslem
Currency: Turkish lira = 100 kurş

The land that for centuries served as a link between Europe and Asia now also provides the two continents with a physical link, the huge bridge over the Bosporus. The world famous cathedral of Hagia Sofia, built by emperor Justinian 532-537, was turned into a mosque after the fall of Constantinople in 1453.

⑥ LEBANON

Al-Jumhouriya al-Lubnaniya
(Republic of Lebanon)

Area: 10,452 km²
Population: 3,500,000
Population growth per annum: 0.8%
Life expectancy at birth: males 63 years, females 67 years
Literacy: 75%
Capital with population: Bayrût (Beirut) 702,000
Other important cities with population: Tarâbulus (Tripoli) 175,000
Language: Arabaic
Religion: Moslem (50%), Christian (50%)
Currency: Lebanese pound = 100 piastres

Since Phoenician times international trade has been the blood of life here at the crossroads of the Levant, populated by fiercely proud clans from all over the Middle East. The lone cedar tree of the flag is almost the last remnant of the mighty forests that once covered Mt. Lebanon. Independent JUN 1, 1944.

⑦ SYRIA

Al-Jamhouriya al Arabia as-Souriya
(Syrian Arab republic)

Area: 185,180 km²
Population: 9,840,000
Population growth per annum: 3.8%
Life expectancy at birth: males 63 years, females 66 years
Literacy: 65%
Capital with population: Dimashq (Damascus) 1,251,000
Other important cities with population:
Halab (Aleppo) 1,525,000 Hims (Homs) 630,000
Language: Arabic
Religion: Moslem (88%), Christian
Currency: Syrian pound = 100 piaster

Long before Rome was founded all caravan trails and trade routes "of the world" converged on the capital of Syria, Damascus. Herod, St. Paul and Ibn Battuta as well as Alexander the Great, Julius Caesar and Genghis Khan have all passed through Damascus. Independent JAN 1, 1944.

⑧ IRAQ

Al Jumhouriya al 'Iraqia
(Republic of Iraq)

Area: 434,924 km²
Population: 14,000,000
Population growth per annum: 3.4%
Life expectancy at birth: males 54 years, females 57 years
Literacy: 70%
Capital with population: Baghdad 3,200,000
Other important cities with population: Al Basrah 400,000, Al Mawsil (Mosul) 350,000
Language: Arabic, Kurdish
Religion: Moslem (95%)
Currency: Iraqi dinar = 20 dirham = 1000 fils

The ancient "Land Between the Rivers", Mesopotamia, is today known as Iraq. The name is said to be derived from a word meaning "origin", a very apt name. Here the wheel and the plow were invented. Here the oldest maps and written records have been found as well as the oldest Codes of Law. Independent 1932.

⑨ IRAN

Jomhori-e-Islami-e-Irân
(Islamic Republic of Iran)

Area: 1,648,100 km²
Population: 43,830,000
Population growth per annum: 3.0%
Life expectancy at birth: males 53 years, females 54 years
Literacy: 48%
Capital with population: Tehrān 4,500,000
Other important cities with population: Esfahān 700,000, Mashhad 700,000
Language: Farsi (persian), Turkic languages, Kurdish
Religion: Shiá Moslems (93%)
Currency: Rial = 100 dinars

Through milennia Iran previously called Persia — has influenced the history and culture of all people. Iran has nurtured Cyrus, Darius and Xerxes, Zoroaster, Firdawsi and Omar Khayyam — and ayatollah Khomeini. Iranians invented polo and developed chess.

⑩ AFGHANISTAN

De Afghanistan Democrateek
Jamhuriat
(Democratic Republic of Afganistan)

Area: 647,497 km²
Population: 17,500,000 (of which 23% are refugees outside the country)
Population growth per annum: 2.5%
Life expectancy at birth: males 40 years, females 41 years
Literacy: 10%
Capital with population: Kabul 900,000
Other important cities with population: Kandahar 180,000 Herat 140,000
Language: Pushtu, Dari (Persian)
Religion: Islam (90% Sunni Moslems)
Currency: Afghani = 100 puls

The crossroads of Asia — and once more, a theater of war. Throughout history, conquering armies have marched through the green valleys beneath Afghanistan's forbidding mountains, but no one has ever been able to subjugate its warlike tribes, so fiercely independent, that they were not even united into an emirate before 1747. Independent 1747.

⑪ CHINA

(Peoples Republic of China)

Area: 9,561,000 km²
Population: 1,008,175,000
Population growth per annum: 1.4%
Life expectancy at birth: males 62 years, females 69 years
Literacy: 75%
Capital with population: Beijing (Peking) 5,550,000
Other important cities with population: Shanghai 6,300,000, Tianjin 5,200,000, Shenuang 4,000,000
Language: Mandarin Chinese, Shanghai-, Canton-, Fukien-, Hakka- dialects, Tibetan, Vigus (Turkic)
Religion: Officially atheist, Confucanist, Buddhist, Taoist.
Currency: Yuan = 10 jiap = 100 fen

The length of the historical records of China are paralleled only by the Great Wall one of the greatest human-made structures 4,000 kms, 2,500 miles). China is the world's most populous nation, human-made, and will without doubt be one of the superpowers of the future. Independent OCT 1, 1949.

⑫ JAPAN

Nippon (or Nihon)

Area: 377,765 km²
Population: 119,500,000
Population growth per annum: 0.9%
Life expectancy at birth: males 73 years, females 78 years
Literacy: 99%
Capital with population: Tōkyō 8,150,000
Other important cities with population:
Yokohama 2,870,000 Nagoya 2,060,000, Kyōto 1,460,000
Language: Japanese
Religion: Buddhist, Shinto, Roman Catholic
Currency: Yen = 100 sen

Japan has learned to live with earthquakes. Minor tremors are registered more than twice a day, and on average the earth here trembles perceptibly once a week. Only a few cause damage to buildings, as houses here are either very light structures or built to resist even severe shocks.

⑬ ISRAEL

Medinat Israel — State of Israel

Area: 20,770 km²
Population: 4,150,000
Population growth per annum: 2.6%
Life expectancy at birth: males 71 years, females 73 years
Literacy: 88%
Capital with population: Yerushalayim (Jerusalem) 430,000
Other important cities with population: Tel Aviv-Yafo 330,000, Hefa (Haifa) 226,000
Language: Hebrew, Arabic
Religion: Judaism (85%), Moslem (11%)
Currency: Shekel = 100 agorot

The unprecedented rebirth of a land and a language after almost two thousand years must be considered a miracle. This fulfillment of an cient prophecies is due to the tenacity and spirit of the Jewish people. A majority of human kind considers Jerusalem Holy. Independent MAY 14, 1948.

⑭ JORDAN

Al Mamlaka al Urduniya al Hashemiyah (The Hashemite Kingdom of Jordan)

Area: 97,740 km² (incl. 5,880 km² on the West Bank)
Population: 3,500,000
Population growth per annum: 3.7%
Life expectancy at birth: males 58 years, females 62 years
Literacy: 58%
Capital with population: 'Ammān 1,230,000
Other important cities with population: Az Zarqā' 270,000, Irbid 140,000
Language: Arabic
Religion: Moslem (80% Sunni Moslems)
Currency: Jordan dinar = 1000 fils

Once the rulers of the arid lands east of River Jordan controlled the trade routes across the desert, and accumulated wealth from the incense trade, as can be seen from the glory of the rose-red ruins of Petra. Independent MAR 22, 1946.

⑮ KUWAIT

Dowlat al Kuwait (State of Kuwait)

Area: 17,818 km²
Population: 1,910,,000
Population growth per annum: 6.0%
Life expectancy at birth: males 67 years, females 72 years
Literacy: 71%
Capital with population: Al Kuwayt (Kuwait) 280,000
Other important cities with population: none
Language: Arabic
Religion: Moslem (70% Sunni Moslems)
Currency: Kuwait dinar = 1000 fils

The name Kuwait today associates with oil and wealth. Once sturdy dhows sailing to far away African and East Indian ports brought renown to Kuwait. The real Sindbad the Sailor may have lived here. Independent JUN 19, 1961.

⑯ PAKISTAN

(Islamic Republic of Pakistan)

Area: 887,747 km²
Population: 89,000,000
Population growth per annum: 2.8%
Life expectancy at birth: males 52 years, females 50 years
Literacy: 23%
Capital with population: Islamabad 201,000
Other important cities with population: Karachi 5,103,000, Lahore 2,920,000, Faisalabad 1,092,000
Language: Urdu, Punjabi
Religion: Moslem (sunni Moslems)
Currency: Pakistani rupie = 100 paisa

By peaceful agreement, but through tumultuous upheaval the Islamic nation of Pakistan was created out of parts of former British India. Until 1971 it also comprised Bangladesh 2,000 km. away, then known as East Pakistan. Independent AUG 14, 1947.

⑰ SAUDI ARABIA

Al-Mamlaka-al-Arabiya as-Sa'udiya (Kingdom of Saudi Arabia)

Area: 2,149,690 km²
Population: 10,970,000
Population growth per annum: 4.2%
Life expectancy at birth: males 53 years, females 56 years
Literacy: 25%
Capital with population: Ar Riyád (Riyadh) 1,250,000
Other important cities with population: Jiddah 1,300,000, Makkah (Mecca) 550,000
Language: Arabic
Religion: Moslem
Currency: Rial = 100 halalas

Like the genie released from Aladdin's oil lamp, the wealth of oil released from the rocks of the desert have brought fabulous palaces and gardens to its owners. Modern cities, industries, universities and motorways have been created overnight. Independent SEP 20, 1932.

⑱ BAHRAIN

Mashyaka al Bahrayn (State of Bahrain)

Area: 622 km²
Population: 380,000
Population growth per annum: 2.8%
Life expectancy at birth: males 64 years, females 68 years
Literacy: 40%
Capital with population: Al Manāmah 122,000
Other important cities with population: Al Muharraq 62,000
Language: Arabic
Religion: Islam (Sunni Moslems)
Currency: Bahrain dinar = 100 fils

The popular joke, that Bahrain gas stations should give free fuel to every buyer of water for coolant, is of course not true. It reflects the lack of water that troubles oil-rich Bahrain. It will be solved by a pipeline following the giant causeway to the mainland. Independent AUG 15, 1971.

⑲ QATAR
Dawlat Qatar
(State of Qatar)

Area: 11,437 km²
Population: 260 000
Population growth per annum: 6.5%
Life expectancy at birth: males 55 years, females 58 years
Literacy: 40%
Capital with population: Ad Dawhah 190,000
Other important cities with population: none
Language: Arabic
Religion: Moslem
Currency: Riyal = 100 dirham

A black underground sea of oil has become the source of wealth to Qatar, instead of the Gulf's warm blue waters and its pearl oysters. Independent SEP 1, 1971.

⑳ UNITED ARAB EMIRATES
Al Imarat al Arabiya al Muttahida

Area: 92,100 km²
Population: 1,175,000
Population growth per annum: 7.3%
Life expectancy at birth: males 60 years, females 74 years
Literacy: 53%
Capital with population: Alu Zaly (Abu Dhabi) 240,000
Other important cities with population: Dubayy 278,000
Language: Arabic
Religion: Islam
Currency: UAE dirham = 100 fils

Pearl-fishing and clandestine trade (by some called smuggling) sustained the people on the Trucial Coast after the more lucrative slave trade was abolished by the Perpetual Maritime Truce Treaty, signed by Great Britain and the seven sheiks 1853. Oil has now brought prosperity. Independent DEC 2, 1971.

㉑ YEMEN
Al Jamhuriyah al Arabiya al Yamaniya
(Yemen Arab Republic)

Area: 195,000 km²
Population: 7,160,000
Population growth per annum: 2.3%
Life expectancy at birth: males 37 years, females 39 years
Literacy: 12%
Capital with population: San'a 278,000
Other important cities with population: Hodeida 130,000, Taż 120,000
Language: Arabic
Religion: Moslem
Currency: Yemen paper riyal = 100 rial

The Roman name for Yemen "Arabia Felix" or Lucky Arabia was more apt then than today. The old great dams filled up with silt and were destroyed by floods, and incense no longer fetches its weight in silver or gold.

㉒ SOUTH YEMEN
Jumhurijah al-Yemen al Dimuqratiya al Sha'abijah
(Peoples Democratic)

Area: 287,682 km²
Population: 2,030,000
Population growth per annum: 1.8%
Life expectancy at birth: males 40 years, females 42 years
Literacy: 25%
Capital with population: Baladıyat 'Adan (Aden) 295,000
Other important cities with population: Al Mukallá 100,000
Language: Arabic
Religion: Moslem
Currency: South Yemen dinar = 1000 fils

This is the land of ancient skyscrapers. The high-rise buildings that form the skyline of Hadramaut are mainly built of mud bricks. They are 6-7 stories high, but seem higher as every story has 2 rows of windows.

㉓ OMAN
(Sultanate of Oman)

Area: 212,457 km²
Population: 1,500 000
Population growth per annum: 3.0%
Life expectancy at birth: males 46 years, females 48 years
Literacy: 20%
Capital with population: Masqat 50,000
Language: Arabic
Religion: Moslem
Currency: Rial = 1000 biazas

Like his rival, the King of Portugal, the Sultan of Oman once ruled over a far-flung transocean empire. The red flag of the Sultan flew over forts and trading posts on Asian and African coasts, such as Mombasa and Zanzibar.

㉔ INDIA
Bharat
(Republic of India)

Area: 3,184,290 km²
Population: 683,810,000
Population growth per annum: 2.0%
Life expectancy at birth: males 50 years, females 49 years
Literacy: 36%
Capital with population: Delhi 5,720,000
Other important cities with population:
Bombay 8,230,000, Calcutta 9,170,000,
Madras 4,280,000
Language: Hindi, English
Religion: Hindu (83%), Moslem (11%)
Currency: Rupee = 100 Paise

Like the images of Hindu gods that have several eyes, heads and arms (symbolizing their paradoxical nature), the subcontinent and nation of India has many diverse and contradictory features. India is the serene Taj Mahal in cool white marble, and Calcutta with its teeming millions, holy cows and also nuclear power. Independent JAN 26, 1950.

㉕ NEPAL
Sri Nepala Sarkar
(Kingdom of Nepal)

Area: 145,391 km²
Population: 16,100,000
Population growth per annum: 2.3%
Life expectancy at birth: males 43 years, females 44 years
Literacy: 20%
Capital with population: Katmandu 195,000
Other important cities with population: Patan 50,000
Language: Nepali, Indian Languages
Religion: Hindu (90%), Buddist (7%)
Currency: Nepalese Rupee = 2 mohur = 100 paisa

By avoiding involvement in the affairs of the outside world the mountain kingdom of Nepal has like Switzerland managed to remain independent. Nepal shares with China the world's highest peak, Chomolungma, the "Goddess Mother of the World" to the Tibetans, since 1865 also known as Mt. Everest.

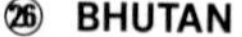

㉖ BHUTAN
Druk Gaykhab
(Kingdom of Bhutan)

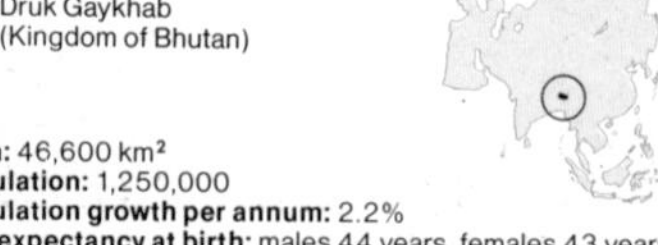

Area: 46,600 km²
Population: 1,250,000
Population growth per annum: 2.2%
Life expectancy at birth: males 44 years, females 43 years
Literacy: 5%
Capital with population: Thimphu 21,000
Other important cities with population: none
Language: Dzongka, Nepali
Religion: Buddhist (70%), Hindu
Currency: Ngultrum = 100 chetrums (Indian rupee also used)

Bhutan's official name Druk Yul translates Land of the Dragon. This is an apt name, as the mountainous former hermit kingdom has many fairy-tale qualities . The only real dragons to be found are those on the national flags.

㉗ BANGLADESH
(Peoples Republic of Bangladesh)

Area: 143,998 km²
Population: 96,000,000
Population growth per annum: 2.8%
Life expectancy at birth: males 46 years, females 46 years
Literacy: 25%
Capital with population: Dakha 3,500,000
Other important cities with population:
Ghittagong 1,390,000, Khulna 650,000
Language: Bengali, English
Religion: Islam (80%), Hindu
Currency: Taka = 100 poisha

The fertile delta lands of Ganges and Brahmaputra, created by floods, have long been more than overpopulated. Troubled by alternating droughts and torrential rains, poor Bangladesh is frequently plagued by hurricanes and devastating tidal floods. Independent DEC 20, 1971.

㉘ BURMA
Pyidaungsu Socialist Thammada Myanma Naingngandaw
(Socialist Republic of the Union of Burma)

Area: 676,552 km²
Population: 35,310,000
Population growth per annum: 2.4%
Life expectancy at birth: males 51 years, females 54 years
Literacy: 78%
Capital with population: Rangoon 2,460,000
Other important cities with population: Mandalay 420,000, Bassein 360,000
Language: Burmese
Religions: Buddhist (85%)
Currency: Kyat = 100 pyas

Burma is still the land of the gilded pagodas, where time flows as slowly as the mighty Irrawaddy. In this land of yesterday veteran cars are in everyday use, and elephants haul teak logs to the rivers. Burma's socialists have governed the country since 1948. Independent JAN 4, 1948.

㉙ THAILAND
Prathes Thai
(Kingdom of Thailand)

Area: 514,000 km²
Population: 50,000,000
Population growth per annum: 2.3%
Life expectancy at birth: males 58 years, females 63 years
Literacy: 84%
Capital with population: Krung Thep (Bangkok) 5,470,000
Other important cities with population: Chiang Mai 105,000
Language: Thai
Religion: Buddhist (93%), Moslem (4%)
Currency: Baht = 100 Satang

Thailand has throughout history managed to survive and maintain independence by deft diplomacy and careful observation of prevailing wind directions. Internally the king retains power in much the same way.

㉚ LAOS
(The Lao People's Democratic Republic)

Area: 236,800 km²
Population: 3,500,000
Population growth per annum: 2.4%
Life expectancy at birth: males 42 years, females 45 years
Literacy: 28%
Capital with population: Vientiane 120,000
Other important cities with population:
Luang Prabang 45,000
Language: Lao
Religion: Buddhist
Currency: Kip = 100 at

Reverence for royalty has always transcended life in Laos. A royal prince led the communists to victory in 1975 and abolished monarchy. Several hundred huge carved burial urns, presumably containing royal remains from prehistoric times, still dot the Plain of Jars. Independent JUN 20, 1954.

㉛ VIETNAM

Công Hòa Xã Hôi Chu Nghĩa Viêt Nam
(Socialist Republic of Vietnam)

Area: 329,566 km²
Population: 60,000,000
Population growth per annum: 2.3%
Life expectancy at birth: males 51 years, females 54 years
Literacy: 73%
Capital with population: Hanoi 2,570,000
Other important cities with population:
Ho Chi Minh 3,500,000, Hai Phong 1,300,000
Language: Vietnamese, French, English
Religion: Buddhist
Currency: Dong = 10 hao = 10 xu

The proud and martial Vietnamese of the Red River basin have been called the Prussians of Indo-China. With military aid from the U.S.S.R and captured U.S. arms they have now become the strongest military power of South East Asia. Independent JUL 20, 1954.

㉜ TAIWAN

(Republic of China)

Area: 36,174 km²
Population: 18,800,000
Population growth per annum: 1.8%
Life expectancy at birth: males 70 years, females 75 years
Literacy: 89%
Capital with population: Taipei 2,400,000
Other important cities with population:
Kaohsiung 1,260,000
Language: Chinese
Religion: Confucianist, Buddist, Taoist
Currency: New Taiwan dollar = 100 cents

The Chinese governments in Peking and Taipei do agree in one important respect: There is only one China, and Taiwan is no more than a Chinese province. The main difference is that the authority of the rulers in Taipei does not extend to any part of ancient, mainland China proper.

㉝ MALDIVES

Divehi Jumhuriya
(Republic of Maldives)

Area: 298 km²
Population: 168,000
Population growth per annum: 2.9%
Life expectancy at birth: not available
Literacy: 36%
Capital with population: Malé 40,000
Other important cities with population: none
Languages: Divehi
Religion: Moslem (Sunni Moslems)
Currency: Rufiyaa = 100 laaris

In the days when the dhows carried carpets, ivory and slaves over the Indian Ocean, the thousand coral islands of the Maldives lay at the crossroads of the ocean. Now even the names of the atolls, Tiladummati, Fadiffolu, Miladummadulu sound of long lost fame and tales of far away lands. Independent NOV 11, 1968.

㉞ SRI LANKA

(Democratic Socialist
Republic of Sri Lanka)

Area: 65,610 km²
Population: 14,850,000
Population growth per annum: 1.7%
Life expectancy at birth: males 64 years, females 67 years
Literacy: 84%
Capital with population: Colombo 586,000
Other important cities with population:
Dehiwela-Mt. Lavinia 175,000, Moratuwa 136,000
Language: Sinhala, Tamil
Religion: Buddhist (70%), Hindu (17%), Christian, Moslem
Currency: Sri Lanka rupee = 100 cents

Ceylon is even today a land of legends. On the top of Adam's Peak there is a 1.5 m. (5 ft.) long foot print, claimed to be left in the rock by Adam (or by Buddha, or Sheva, or St. Thomas according to preference). Independent 1947.

㉟ KAMPUCHEA

(Cambodian People's Republic)

Area: 181,035 km²
Population: 6,680,000
Population growth per annum: 2.9%
Life expectancy at birth: males 44 years, females 47 years
Literacy: 48%
Capital with population: Phnom Penh 500,000
Other important cities with population:
Battambang 50,000
Language: Khmer
Religion: Buddhist
Currency: Riel = 100 sen

Clashing radical ideologies have once more made life only worse for everyone. Pleasant Kampuchea now lies in ruins like mighty remains from its glorious past. Famous Angkor, for over 500 years the capital of all Indochina, has so far been spared further destruction. Independent OCT 9, 1970.

㊱ PHILIPPINES

República de Filipinas -
Republika ng Pilipinas
(Republic of the Philippines)

Area: 300,000 km²
Population: 53,350,000
Population growth per annum: 2.7%
Life expectancy at birth: males 59 years, females 62 years
Literacy: 88%
Capital with population: Manila 1,600,000
Other important cities with population:
Quezon City 1,200,000, Davao 620,000, Cebu 500,000
Language: Pilipino, English, Spanish
Religion: Roman Catholic (80%), Islam (7%)
Currency: Philippine pesó = 100 centavos

East and west meet in this island nation, east of the Asian mainland, yet west of the Pacific. The people of this fomer colony of Spain (1521-1899) and the United States (1899-1942) are of Malayo-Polynesian stock but speak Spanish, English and Pilipino. Most are Roman Catholics but some are Moslems. Independent JUL 4, 1946.

㊲ MALAYSIA

Area: 329,749 km²
Population: 15,070,000
Population growth per annum: 2.5%
Life expectancy at birth: males 62 years, females 65 years
Literacy: 75%
Capital with population: Kuala Lumpur 450,000
Other important cities with population:
George Town 300,000, Ipoh 250,000
Language: Bahasa Malaysia, Chinese
Religion: Moslem 50%, Buddhist (26%), Hindu (9%)
Currency: Ringgit = 100 sen

In this land reigning rajahs (and sultans) each in turn serve five years as 'Supreme Head of State'. This unusual system of royal rotation has brought unity and stability to the geographically divided nation. In Sarawak the world's largest cave (700×300 m.) has been found. Independent SEP 16, 1963.

㊳ SINGAPORE

(Republic of Singapore)

Area: 618 km²
Population: 2,530,000
Population growth per annum: 1.2%
Life expectancy at birth: males 69 years, females 73 years
Literacy: 84%
Capital with population: Singapore 2,350,000
Other important cities with population: none
Language: Chinese, Malay, Tamil, English
Religion: Buddhist, Taoist, Moslem, Hindu, Christian
Currency: Singapore-dollar = 100 cents

A modern City state, living off free entrepot trade and local manufacturing industries requiring skilled labour, Singapore survives without hinterland. Independent AUG 9, 1965.

AUSTRALIA

Area: 8,945,000 km²
Population: 23,446,000
Density of population per km²: 2,6

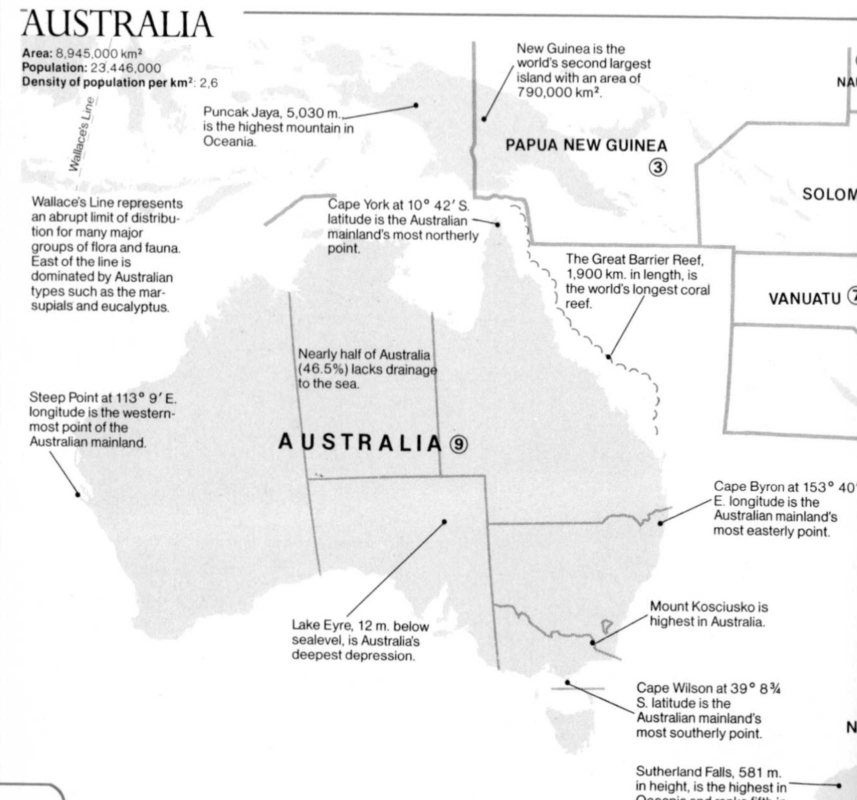
Wallace's Line
Puncak Jaya, 5,030 m., is the highest mountain in Oceania.
New Guinea is the world's second largest island with an area of 790,000 km².
PAPUA NEW GUINEA ③
SOLOM
VANUATU
Wallace's Line represents an abrupt limit of distribution for many major groups of flora and fauna. East of the line is dominated by Australian types such as the marsupials and eucalyptus.
Cape York at 10° 42′ S. latitude is the Australian mainland's most northerly point.
The Great Barrier Reef, 1,900 km. in length, is the world's longest coral reef.
Nearly half of Australia (46.5%) lacks drainage to the sea.
Steep Point at 113° 9′ E. longitude is the westernmost point of the Australian mainland.
AUSTRALIA ⑨
Cape Byron at 153° 40′ E. longitude is the Australian mainland's most easterly point.
Mount Kosciusko is highest in Australia.
Lake Eyre, 12 m. below sealevel, is Australia's deepest depression.
Cape Wilson at 39° 8¾ S. latitude is the Australian mainland's most southerly point.
Sutherland Falls, 581 m. in height, is the highest in Oceania and ranks fifth in the world.

(39) BRUNEI

Area: 5,765 km²
Population: 213,000
Population growth per annum: not available
Life expectancy at birth: not available
Literacy: not available
Capital with population: Bandar Seri Begawan 51,000
Other important cities with population: none
Language: Malay, English
Religion: Moslem (64%), Buddhist, Christian
Currency: Brunei dollar = 100 cents

A land flowing with oil — where the citizens can use their own money to buy "milk and honey" — as they do not have to pay any income taxes! No wonder the Sultan of Brunei can continue to rule — with broad popular support. Independent DEC 31, 1983.

(40) INDONESIA

Republik Indonesia
(Republic of Indonesia)

Area: 1,919,400 km²
Population: 158,000,000
Population growth per annum: 1.7%
Life expectancy at birth: males 46 years, females 49 years
Literacy: 64%
Capital with population: Jakarta 6,500,000
Other important cities with population: Surabaya 2,000,000 Bandung 1,500,000, Medan 1,400,000
Language: Bahasa Indonesia
Religion: Moslem (92%)
Currency: Rupiah = 100 sen

Panta rei (all flows) ought to be the motto of this nation of over 13,000 islands. No other state has so many active volcanoes. On Java alone there are 27. Here the island volcano of Krakatoa, 1,800 m. (6,000 ft.) high, disintegrated in 1883 in the most catastrophic eruption in history. Independent AUG 17, 1945.

KIRIBATI (2)

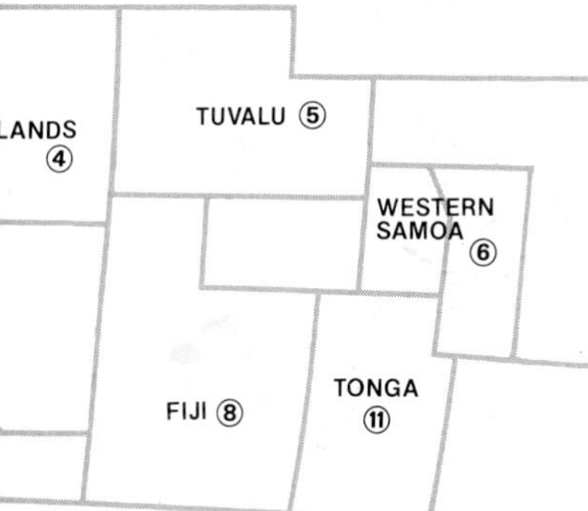

The area around Lake Taupo is a unique landscape of volcanic features such as bubbling mud cauldrons, hot springs, solfataras and fumaroles. The geyser Waimangu used to be the world's greatest, the column of water could reach as high as 450 m.

ALAND (10)

- (9) AUSTRALIA
- (8) FIJI
- (2) KIRIBATI
- (1) NAURU
- (10) NEW ZEALAND
- (3) PAPUA NEW GUINEA
- (4) SOLOMON ISLANDS
- (11) TONGA
- (5) TUVALU
- (7) VANUATU
- (6) WESTERN SAMOA

① NAURU
(Republic of Nauru)

Area: 21,3 km^2
Population: 8,400
Population growth per annum: 1.5%
Life expectancy at birth: not available
Literacy: 99%
Capital with population: Yaren
Other important cities with population: none
Language: Nauruan, English
Religion: Protestant (60%), Roman Catholic (30%)
Currency: Australian dollar = 100 cents

It is easy to drive around all of Nauru in a car in less time that it takes for an astronaut to circle the Earth, as the total circumference is only 34 km. (21 miles). Independent JUN 31, 1970.

② KIRIBATI
(Republic of Kiribati)

Area: 886 km^2
Population: 60,000
Population growth per annum: not available
Life expectancy at birth: not available
Literacy: not available
Capital with population: Bairiki 20,000
Other important cities with population: none
Language: Kiribati, English
Religion: Protestant (50%), Roman Catholic (50%)
Currency: Australian dollar = 100 cents

No other nation is spread so thinly as Kiribati, with land size — smaller than New York City scattered over an area wider than the contiguous United States! Kiribati always has two days, as it is divided by the dateline. Independent JUL 12, 1979.

③ PAPUA NEW GUINEA

Area: 461,691 km^2
Population: 3,260,000
Population growth per annum: 2.7%
Life expectancy at birth: males 51 years, females 50 years
Literacy: 32%
Capital with population: Port Moresby 124,000
Other important cities with population: Lae 62,000
Language: English, numerous, local languages
Religions: Animist, Protestant, Roman Catholic
Currency: Kina = 100 toe

The official "Pidgin English" developed here during the last hundred years is quite a new language, using mainly English words. E.g. "Ars bilong diwai" means "roots" (Diwai is a melanesian word for tree, belong equals of — and ars is just the very bottom of anything. Independent SEP 16, 1975.

④ SOLOMON ISLANDS

Area: 29,785 km^2
Population: 258,000
Population growth per annum: 3.0%
Life expectancy at birth: not available
Literacy: not available
Capital with population: Honiara 24,000
Other important cities with population: none
Language: English, numerous local languages
Religion: Protestant (75%), Roman Catholic (19%)
Currency: Solomon Island dollar = 100 cents

The Solomon Islands suffered heavily during World War II during the battles of Guadalcanal and the Coral Sea. Yet some islands still profit from the spoils of war by exporting scrap iron. Independent JUL 7, 1978.

⑤ TUVALU

Area: 24,6 km^2
Population: 7,300
Population growth per annum: 1.6%
Life expectancy at birth: males 57 years, females 59 years
Literacy: not available
Capital with population: Funafuti 2,100
Other important cities with population: none
Language: Samoan, English
Religion: Protestant
Currency: Australian dollar = 100 cents

Tuvalu comprises nine low coral atolls (formerly also called Lagoon or Ellice islands) in the very centre of the island world of the South Pacific. In spite of the fact that an atoll can measure 10-20 km. across its land area is almost negligible. Independent OCT 1, 1978.

⑥ WESTERN SAMOA
Samoa i Sisifo
(Independent State of Western Samoa)

Area: 2,831 km^2
Population: 156,000
Population growth per annum: 1.3%
Life expectancy at birth: 63%
Literacy: 90%
Capital with population: Apia 33,200
Other important cities with population: none
Language: Samoan, English
Religion: Protestant (75%), Roman Catholic (22%)
Currency: Tala = 100 sene

Truly Polynesian Samoa is in many ways an incarnation of the South Sea Islands — complete with beaches and palms and friendly people, but it is at the same time a modern society with TV, colleges, and all the rest. Independent JAN 1, 1962.

⑦ VANUATU
(Republic of Vanuatu)

Area: 14,763 km²
Population: 117,000
Population growth per annum: 2.7%
Life expectancy at birth: not available
Literacy: not available
Capital with population: Vila 14,000
Other important cities with population: none
Language: Bislama, English, French
Religion: Protestant (68%), Roman Catholic (16%)
Currency: Vatu

Two colonial powers, France and Great Britain ruled the former Condominium of the New Hebrides in quaint harmony with strict and sometimes silly division of authority 1906-80. Independent JUL 30, 1980.

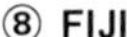

⑧ FIJI
(Dominion of Fiji)

Area: 18,376 km²
Population: 670,000
Population growth per annum: 1.8%
Life expectancy at birth: males 70 years, females 73 years
Literacy: 75%
Capital with population: Suva 71,000
Other important cities with population: Lautoka 26,000
Language: English, Fijian, Hindustani
Religion: Christian (49%), Hindu (40%)
Currency: Fijian dollar = 100 cents

Volcanic soil, tropical sunshine and gentle trade winds bringing regular rainfall favour sugar cane cultivation. Sugar has become the major product of Fiji. Independent OCT 10, 1970.

⑨ AUSTRALIA
(Commonwealth of Australia)

Area: 7,686,848 km²
Population: 15,450,000
Population growth per annum: 1.2%
Life expectancy at birth: males 70 years, females 76 years
Literacy: 99%
Capital with population: Canberra 256,000
Other important cities with population: Sydney 3,281,000, Melbourne 2,804,000, Brisbane 1,090,000
Language: English, aboriginal languages
Religion: Christian Protestant (61%), Catholic (27%)
Currency: Australian dollar = 100 cents

The only land that is quite different, Australia comprises an entire continent with a quite different fauna and flora — eucalyptus trees and kangaroos, egg-laying mammals and koalas, the living teddy bears. The 1,900 km. long Great Barrier Reef is the world's longest coral reef. Independent JAN 1, 1901.

⑩ NEW ZEALAND

Area: 268,704 km²
Population: 3,200,000
Population growth per annum: 1.1%
Life expectancy at birth: males 70 years, females 76 years
Literacy: 99%
Capital with population: Wellington 342,000
Other important cities with population: Auckland 864,000, Christchurch 322,000
Language: English, Maori
Religion: Protestant
Currency: New Zealand dollar = 100 cents

Far from being the opposite of England, green and civilized New Zealand is at the Antipodes seen from Britain — that is exactly at the other side of the Earth. New Zealand England is rich in beautiful scenery. Independent 1931.

⑪ TONGA
(Kingdom of Tonga)

Area: 748 km²
Population: 99,000
Population growth per annum: not available
Life expectancy at birth: not available
Literacy: not available
Capital with population: Niku'alofa 20,000
Other important cities with population: none
Language: English
Religion: Protestant (85%), Roman Catholic (15%)
Currency: Pa'anga = 100 seniti

The "Friendly Islands", Captain Cook's name for Tonga, are not easy to reach due to lack of good harbours. The island of Niuafo'ou has become known among philatelists as "Tin Can Island" because of the method used to collect and deliver mail. Independent JUN 4, 1970.

AFRICA

Area: 30,293,000 km²
Population: 431,209,,000
Density of population per km²: 14

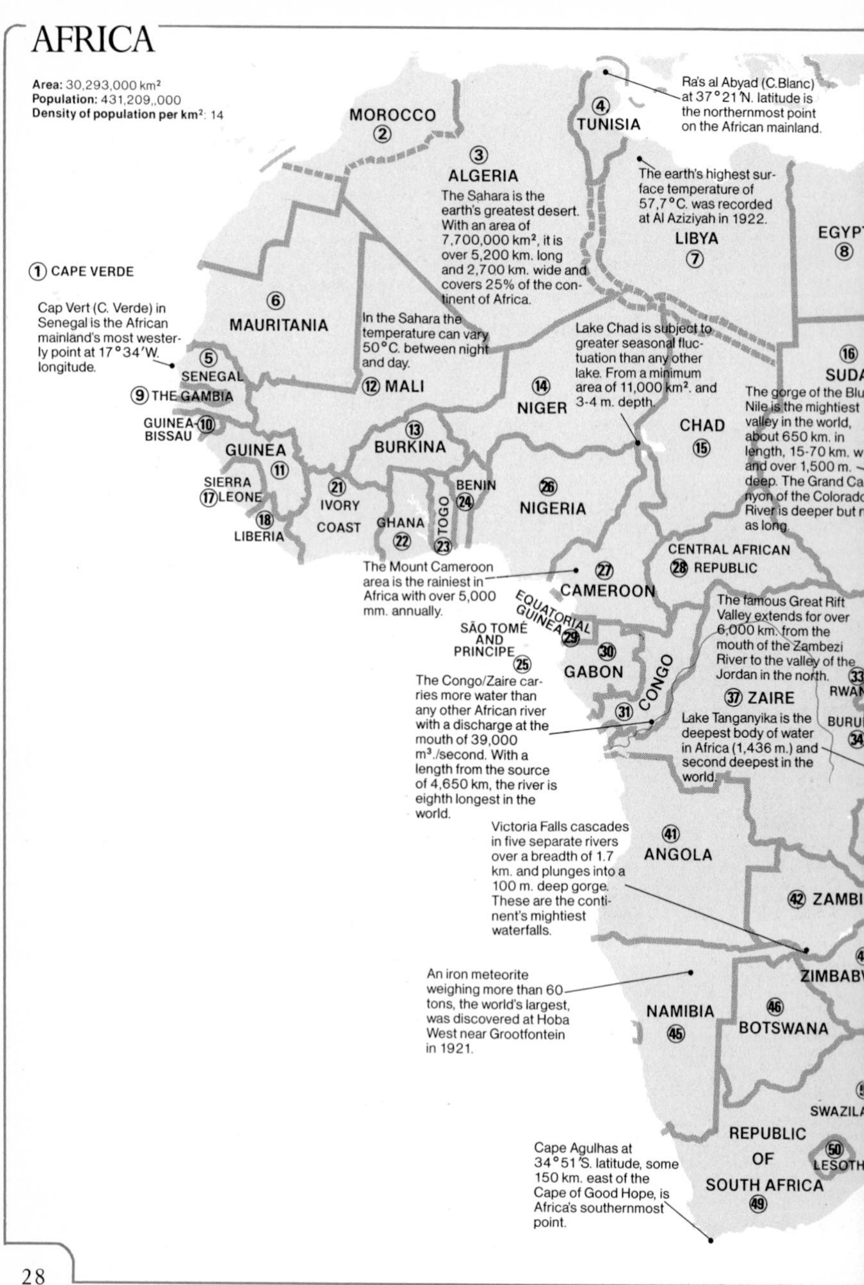

① CAPE VERDE
Cap Vert (C. Verde) in Senegal is the African mainland's most westerly point at 17°34′W. longitude.
MOROCCO ②
③ ALGERIA
The Sahara is the earth's greatest desert. With an area of 7,700,000 km², it is over 5,200 km. long and 2,700 km. wide and covers 25% of the continent of Africa.
④ TUNISIA
Ra's al Abyad (C.Blanc) at 37°21′N. latitude is the northernmost point on the African mainland.
The earth's highest surface temperature of 57,7°C. was recorded at Al Aziziyah in 1922.
LIBYA ⑦
EGYP ⑧
⑥ MAURITANIA
In the Sahara the temperature can vary 50°C. between night and day.
Lake Chad is subject to greater seasonal fluctuation than any other lake. From a minimum area of 11,000 km². and 3-4 m. depth.
⑤ SENEGAL
⑨ THE GAMBIA
GUINEA-⑩ BISSAU
⑫ MALI
⑭ NIGER
CHAD ⑮
⑯ SUDA
The gorge of the Blu Nile is the mightiest valley in the world, about 650 km. in length, 15-70 km. w and over 1,500 m. deep. The Grand Ca nyon of the Colorado River is deeper but n as long.
GUINEA ⑪
⑬ BURKINA
SIERRA ⑰ LEONE
⑱ LIBERIA
㉑ IVORY COAST
GHANA ㉒
TOGO ㉓
BENIN ㉔
㉖ NIGERIA
CENTRAL AFRICAN ㉘ REPUBLIC
The Mount Cameroon area is the rainiest in Africa with over 5,000 mm. annually.
㉗ CAMEROON
EQUATORIAL GUINEA ㉙
SÃO TOMÉ AND PRINCIPE ㉕
㉚ GABON
CONGO ㉛
The famous Great Rift Valley extends for over 6,000 km. from the mouth of the Zambezi River to the valley of the Jordan in the north.
㊲ ZAIRE
RWAN
BURU
The Congo/Zaire carries more water than any other African river with a discharge at the mouth of 39,000 m³./second. With a length from the source of 4,650 km, the river is eighth longest in the world.
Lake Tanganyika is the deepest body of water in Africa (1,436 m.) and second deepest in the world.
Victoria Falls cascades in five separate rivers over a breadth of 1.7 km. and plunges into a 100 m. deep gorge. These are the continent's mightiest waterfalls.
㊶ ANGOLA
㊷ ZAMBI
ZIMBAB
An iron meteorite weighing more than 60 tons, the world's largest, was discovered at Hoba West near Grootfontein in 1921.
NAMIBIA ㊺
㊻ BOTSWANA
SWAZIL
REPUBLIC OF SOUTH AFRICA ㊾
㊿ LESOTH
Cape Agulhas at 34°51′S. latitude, some 150 km. east of the Cape of Good Hope, is Africa's southernmost point.

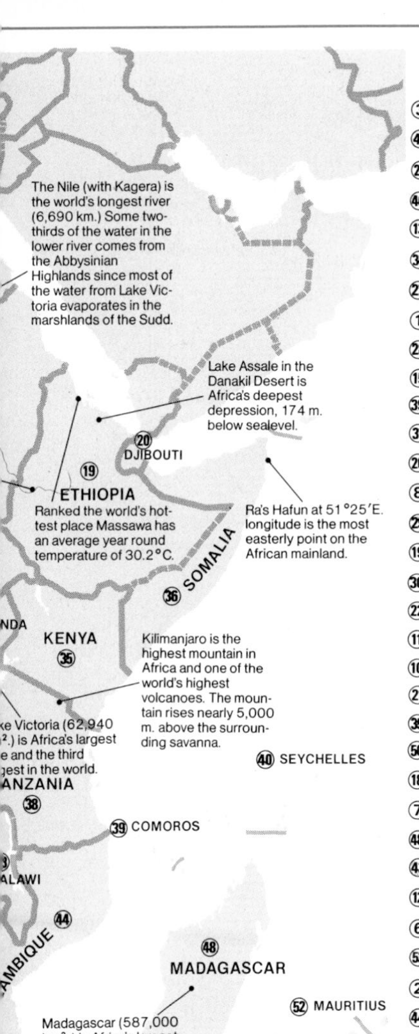

The Nile (with Kagera) is the world's longest river (6,690 km.) Some two-thirds of the water in the lower river comes from the Abbysinian Highlands since most of the water from Lake Victoria evaporates in the marshlands of the Sudd.
Lake Assale in the Danakil Desert is Africa's deepest depression, 174 m. below sealevel.
⑳ DJIBOUTI
⑲ ETHIOPIA
Ranked the world's hottest place Massawa has an average year round temperature of 30.2°C.
Ra's Hafun at 51°25′E. longitude is the most easterly point on the African mainland.
SOMALIA ㊱
KENYA ㉟
Kilimanjaro is the highest mountain in Africa and one of the world's highest volcanoes. The mountain rises nearly 5,000 m. above the surrounding savanna.
㊵ SEYCHELLES
㊴ COMOROS
㊽ MADAGASCAR
Madagascar (587,000 km².) is Africa's largest island and ranks fourth in the world.
52 MAURITIUS

③ ALGERIA
㊶ ANGOLA
㉔ BENIN
㊻ BOTSWANA
⑬ BURKINA
㉞ BURUNDI
㉗ CAMEROON
① CAPE VERDE
㉘ CENTRAL AFRICAN REP.
⑮ CHAD
㊴ COMOROS
㉛ CONGO
⑳ DJIBOUTI
⑧ EGYPT
㉙ EQUATORIAL GUINEA
⑲ ETHIOPIA
㉚ GABON
㉒ GHANA
⑪ GUINEA
⑩ GUINEA-BISSAU
㉑ IVORY COAST
㉟ KENYA
㊿ LESOTHO
⑱ LIBERIA
⑦ LIBYA
㊽ MADAGASCAR
㊸ MALAWI
⑫ MALI
⑥ MAURITANIA
52 MAURITIUS
② MOROCCO
㊹ MOZAMBIQUE
㊺ NAMIBIA
⑭ NIGER
㉖ NIGERIA
㊾ REPUBLIC OF SOUTH AFRICA
㉝ RWANDA
㉕ SÃO TOMÉ AND PRINCIPE
⑤ SENEGAL
㊵ SEYCHELLES
⑰ SIERRA LEONE
㊱ SOMALIA
⑯ SUDAN
51 SWAZILAND
㊳ TANZANIA
⑨ THE GAMBIA
㉓ TOGO
④ TUNISIA
㉜ UGANDA
㊲ ZAIRE
㊷ ZAMBIA
㊼ ZIMBABWE

① CAPE VERDE

República de Cabo Verde
(Republic of Cape Verde)

Area: 4,033 km²
Population: 296,000
Population growth per annum: 1.7%
Life expectancy at birth: males 58 years, females 62 years
Literacy: 37%
Capital with population: Praia 38,000
Other important cities with population: Mindelo 40,000
Language: Portuguese, Crioulo
Religion: Roman Catholic
Currency: Escudo = 100 centavos

Heat and drought are two words that characterize the volcanic islands, named after a cape on the mainland, 580 km. to the east. Salt is produced by evaporation an industry with good natural prospects. Independent JUL 5, 1975.

② MOROCCO

Al-Mamlaka al-Maghrebia
(Kingdom of Morocco)

Area: 458,730 km²
Population: 21,160,000
Population growth per annum: 3.2%
Life expectancy at birth: males 54 years, females 57 years
Literacy: 24%
Capital with population: Rabat 440,000
Other important cities with population: Dar el Beida (Casablanca) 1,400,000, Marrakech 330,000
Language: Arabic, Berber
Religion: Moslem, (Sunni Moslems)
Currency: Dirham = 100 centimes

East and West meet in Morocco. For the "western" world it is a land of the Near East — and for the "eastern", Islamic world it is a land of the Maghreb, The West. The mosques and palaces of cities such as Marrakech and Fez are famous in the west as well as in the east. Independent MAR 28, 1956.

③ ALGERIA

al-Jumhuriya al -Jazairia
ad-Dimuqratiya ash-Shabiya
(Democratic and Popular Republ. of Algeria)

Area: 2,381,740 km²
Population: 21,460,000
Population growth per annum: 3.3%
Life expectancy at birth: males 54 years, females 56 years
Literacy: 46%
Capital with population: Al Jazair (Algiers) 2,500,000
Other important cities with population: Oran 630,000, Constantine 385,000
Language: Arabic
Religion: Islam (Sunni Moslems)
Currency: Algerian dinar = 100 centimes

Four-fifths of the land is desert. The prosperous and fertile coastal area is just a thin gilt edge along the northern rim of the majestic Sahara. Covering 7.7 million km². (5,200 by 2,700 km.), the Sahara is the world's greatest desert, so that the barren wastes of Algeria comprise only 25% of the Sahara! Independent JUL 3, 1962.

④ TUNISIA

Al-Djoumhouria Attunisia
(Republic of Tunisia)

Area: 164,150 km²
Population: 6,970,000
Population growth per annum: 2.5%
Life expectancy at birth: males 57 years, females 58 years
Literacy: 62%
Capital with population: Tunis 557,000
Other important cities with population: Sfax 232,000, Sousse 85,000
Language: Arabic
Religion: Moslem
Currency: Tunisian dinar = 100 millimes

A nation with many ties. Ties of history and culture link it forever to all its Mediterranean neighbours, and very strongly to France. Ties of language and blood bind it to the Arabic West, Maghreb. This is also the land of Carthage, that fought Rome for the hegemony of "the world". Independent MAR 20, 1956.

⑤ SENEGAL

République du Sénégal
(Republic of Senegal)

Area: 196,192 km²
Population: 6,270,000
Population growth per annum: 2.6%
Life expectancy at birth: males 41 years, females 44 years
Literacy: 10%
Capital with population: Dakar 800,000
Other important cities with population: Thies 130,000 Kaolack 116,000
Language: French, Tribal languages
Religion: Moslem (80%), Christian (10%), Animist
Currency: CFA-franc = 100 centimes

The Gateway to West Africa. The leading metropolis of the area, Dakar, is favoured by a magnificent natural harbour. The location near Cap Vert, the most westerly point of the mainland made Dakar the natural staging post for transatlantic flights to South America until the 1960's. Independent AUG 20, 1960.

⑥ MAURITANIA

République Islamique de Mauritanie
(Islamic Republic of Mauritania)

Area: 1,030,700 km²
Population: 1,830,000
Population growth per annum: 2.8%
Life expectancy at birth: males 41 years, females 44 years
Literacy: 17%
Capital with population: Nouakchott 135,000
Other important cities with population: none
Language: French, Arabic
Religion: Moslem
Currency: Ouguiya = 5 khoum

For the Arabs and the Islamic World, Mauretania is the Far West, the Land of the Sunset. Only a fraction of the vast country is habitable, and the lack of water is a severe handicap to any development. Independent NOV 28, 1960.

⑦ LIBYA

Al-Jamahiriya Al-Arabiya-Al Libya
Al-Shabiya Al-Ishitrakiya
(Socialist People's Libyan Arab jamahiriya)

Area: 1,759,540 km²
Population: 3,500,000
Population growth per annum: 4.1%
Life expectancy at birth: males 54 years, females 57 years
Literacy: 40 %
Capital with population: Tripoli (Tarabulus) 860,000
Other important cities with population: Beghasi 300,000
Language: Arabic
Religion: Moslem
Currency: Libyan dinar = 1000 dirham

Elusive Libya retains in our times some of the enigmatic features of Africa. The central volcanic area, the Black Hills that are clearly visible on space images of Africa, were recently mapped with the aid of satellite photos.

⑧ EGYPT

Jumhuriyat Misr al-Arabiya
(Arab Republic of Egypt)

Area: 1,001,449 km²
Population: 46,000,000
Population growth per annum: 2.6%
Life expectancy at birth: males 54 years, females 56 years
Literacy: 40%
Capital with population: Al Qahirah (Cairo)9,000,000
Other important cities with population: Al Iskandariyah (Alexandria) 3,000,000, Al Jızah (Giza) 2,000,000
Language: Arabic
Religion: Islam (Sunni Moslems 90%)
Currency: Egyptian pound = 100 piastres

The whole of inhabitable Egypt is nothing but an oasis — totally dependent on the water of the Nile. In general the width of the cultivated and settled land is only 3-15 km. Of the seven wonders of the ancient world, Egypt had two, and even if the Pharos has been destroyed, the Pyramids still stand. Independent FEB 28. 1922.

⑨ THE GAMBIA

(Republic of The Gambia)

Area: 11,295 km²
Population: 700,000
Population growth per annum: 2.8%
Life expectancy at birth: males 39 years, females 43 years
Literacy: 12 %
Capital with population: Banjul 45,000
Other important cities with population: none
Language: English, Mandinka, Wolof
Religion: Moslem (85%), Christian, Animist
Currency: Dalasi = 100 bututs

The land that is a river. This former British colonial enclave inside Senegal is now joined with Senegal in the Confederation of Senegambia. Here Alex Haley found his roots, as described in his bestseller. Independent FEB 18, 1965.

⑩ GUINEA-BISSAU

(Republic of Guinea-Bissau)

Area: 36,125 km²
Population: 830,000
Population growth per annum: 1.7%
Life expectancy at birth: males 39 years, females 43 years
Literacy: 9%
Capital with population: Bissau 110,000
Other important cities with population: none
Language: Portuguese, Criolo
Religion: Tribal (50%), Moslem (38%), Christian (5%)
Currency: Guinea-Bissau peso = 100 centavos

A new name heralds a new era. For more than 500 years this land was known as Portuguese Guinea. No other land has been a colony for so many years. Guinea Bissau has an exceptional un-African archipelago coast. Independent SEP 24, 1973.

⑪ GUINEA

République populaire
et révolutionnaire de Guinée
(Republic of Guinea)

Area: 245,857 km²
Population: 5,410,000
Population growth per annum: 2.5%
Life expectancy at birth: males 42 years, females 45 years
Literacy: 48 %
Capital with population: Conakry
Other important cities with population: Kankan 100,000
Language: French, tribal languages
Religion: Moslems (75%), Tribal
Currency: Syli = 100 cauris

The name Guinea rings with a chink of gold — since 1663, when coins were struck in England out of pure 22 carat gold from Guinea. In Britain prices can still be quoted in guineas. Guinea still has natural resources that could bring prosperity to this very poor country. Independent OCT 2, 1958.

⑫ MALI

République du Mali
(Republic of Mali)

Area: 1,240,142 km²
Population: 7,720,000
Population growth per annum: 2.7%
Life expectancy at birth: males 44 years, females 44 years
Literacy: 10%
Capital with population: Bamako 405,000
Other important cities with population: Ségou 65,000
Language: French, Bambara
Religion: Moslem (65%), Animist (30%), Christian (5%)
Currency: Mali franc = 100 centimes

Half Sahara and half Sahel, half desert and half savanna land, Mali has been hard hit by years of drought. Once the kings of Mali controlled the trade routes of the Sahara and the minarets of fabled Timbuktu attracted both traders and adventurers to cross the sand seas. Independent SEP 22, 1960.

⑬ BURKINA

République de Burkina Faso
(People's Democratic Republic of Burkina)

Area: 274,122 km²
Population: 6,700,000
Population growth per annum: 2.6%
Life expectancy at birth: males 42 years, females 45 years
Literacy: 7%
Capital with population: Ouagadougou 286,000
Other important cities with population: Bobu Dioulasso 165,000
Language: French, Sudanic tribal languages
Religion: Animist (50%), Moslem (20%)
Currency: CFA-franc = 100 centimes

A land at the mercy of the winds. The dreaded dry Harmattan blowing from Sahara is a harbinger of death — the blessed Guinea Monsoon from the south an angel of life with its seasonal rain. The savanna lands here depend on a precarious balance between precipitation and evaporation. Independent AUG 5, 1960.

⑭ NIGER

République du Niger
(Republic of Niger)

Area: 1,267,000 km²
Population: 6,270,000
Population growth per annum: 2.9%
Life expectancy at birth: males 41 years, females 44 years
Literacy: 5%
Capital with population: Niamey 225,000
Other important cities with population: Zinder 60,000,
Language: French, Hausa, Djerma
Religion: Moslem (85%), Animist
Currency: CFA-franc = 100 centimes

A name that is more of an incantation than a description. This is a land-locked, dry and infertile part of Sahara, and the mighty Niger crosses only a narrow corner. The Tuaregs still cross the desert with salt caravans. Independent AUG 3, 1960.

⑮ CHAD

République du Tchad
(Republic of Chad)

Area: 1,284,000 km²
Population: 5,120,000
Population growth per annum: 2.0%
Life expectancy at birth: males 39 years, females 41 years
Literacy: 15%
Capital with population: N'djamena 303,000
Other important cities with population: Moundou 66,000
Language: French, Arabic, Sudanese languages
Religion: Animist, Moslem (45%), Christian (5%)
Currency: CFA-franc = 100 centimes

Land-locked Chad can be called a coastal land, as it is part of the Sahel, "the coast" of the sand sea of Sahara. It is drained to the shallow central basin of Lake Chad, the ever changing lake that varies from 10,000-50,000 km². and from 1 to 4 m. in average depth. Independent AUG 11, 1960.

⑯ SUDAN

Jamhuryat es-Sudan Al Democratia
(The Democratic Republic of Sudan)

Area: 2,505,813 km²
Population: 21,440,000
Population growth per annum: 2.8%
Life expectancy at birth: males 46 years, females 48 years
Literacy: 20 %
Capital with population: Al Khartum (Khartoum) 476,000, (Metropolitanarea 1,350,000)
Other important cities with population: Bur Sudan 207,000
Language: Arabic, various tribal languages
Religion: Moslem (70%) Christian, Animist
Currency: Sudanese pound = 100 piaster

In Sudan there are two countries in one. There are the Islamic, Arabic-speaking northern desert lands, and there are the Christian, Nilotic southern savanna lands. In spite of the name, most of the world's gum arabic comes from the acacia forests of Sudan. Independent JAN 1, 1956.

⑰ SIERRA LEONE

(Republic of Sierra Leone)

Area: 73,326 km²
Population: 3,350,000
Population growth per annum: 2.6%
Life expectancy at birth: males 44 years, females 48 years
Literacy: 15 %
Capital with population: Freetown 300,000
Other important cities with population: Makeni 1,000,000, Kenema 775,000
Language: English, Tribal languages
Religion: Animist, Moslem (30%)
Currency: Leone = 100 cents

A new homeland for freed slaves. Under British protection repatriated slaves from Great Britain founded Freetown at one of the few good natural harbours of West Africa back in 1787. Later it was used as a settlement for Africans rescued from slaveships. Sierra Leone became independent in APR 27, 1961.

⑱ LIBERIA

(Republic of Liberia)

Area: 111,369 km²
Population: 1,900,000
Population growth per annum: 3.5%
Life expectancy at birth: males 52 years, females 54 years
Literacy: 24%
Capital with population: Monrovia 425,000
Other important cities with population: none
Language: English
Religion: Moslem (21%), Christian (35%), Traditional (43%)
Currency: Liberian dollar = 100 cents

As the name implies, Liberia is a free nation, and has been since it was established in 1822 for freed slaves from the USA. In 1847 it became the continent's first independent republic and remained so during the days of the "Scramble for Africa" when this was divided into colonies.

⑲ ETHIOPIA

Hebretesbawit Ityopia
(Socialist Ethiopia)

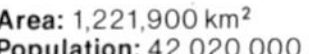

Area: 1,221,900 km²
Population: 42,020,000
Population growth per annum: 1.8%
Life expectancy at birth: males 38 years, females 41 years
Literacy: 8%
Capital with population: Addis Ababa 1,400,000
Other important cities with population: Asmara 45,000, Gondar 80,000
Language: Amharic, other Semitic and Hamitic languages, Arabic, English
Religion: Orthodox Christian (40%), Moslem (40%)
Currency: Ethiopian birr = 100 cents

The nation that is an archipelago on dry land. For centuries Ethiopia was a Christian island in a Moslem sea. It is still an archipelago of densely populated islands of high plateaus, separated by deep river gorges and hot lowlands — and a linguistic archipelago of over 70 ethnic groups.

⑳ DJIBOUTI

Jumhouriyya Djibouti
(Republic of Djibouti)

Area: 23,000 km²
Population: 340,000
Population growth per annum: 2.2%
Life expectancy at birth: 50 years
Literacy: 20%
Capital with population: Djibouti 150,000
Other important cities with population: Tadjourah
Language: French, Arabic
Religion: Islam
Currency: Djibouti franc = 100 centimes

The nation is a railway terminal — and vice versa. The entrepôt port would not and could not exist as an independent unity without the railway to Addis-Ababa. This railway was built in 1915 and has since served as the major link between central Ethiopia and the world. Independent JUN 27, 1977.

㉑ IVORY COAST

République de la Côte d'Ivoire
(Republic of Ivory Coast)

Area: 322,464 km²
Population: 8,500,000
Population growth per annum: 3.5%
Life expectancy at birth: males 44 years, females 48 years
Literacy: 24%
Capital with population: Abidjan 1,850,000
Other important cities with population: Bouaké 640,000, Man-Danané 450,000
Language: French, tribal languages
Religion: Moslem (15%), Christian (12%), Indigenous (63%)
Currency: CFA-franc = 100 centimes

The Cocoa Coast would be more apt but less poetic name for this land. Cocoa and coffee long ago replaced ivory and slaves as the staples of the Ivory Coast. No nation produces more cocoa. Other agricultural products are pineapples, bananas and palm oil. Independent AUG 7, 1960.

㉒ GHANA

(Republic of Ghana)

Area: 238,305 km²
Population: 12,210,000
Population growth per annum: 3.1%
Life expectancy at birth: males 47 years, females 50 years
Literacy: 30%
Capital with population: Accra 750,000
Other important cities with population: Sekondi-Takoradi 300,000,
Language: English, 50 tribal languages
Religion: Christian (42%), Traditional beliefs, Moslem (12%)
Currency: Cedi = 100 pesewas

The former Gold Coast is at the same time a historic truth and a fitting description. One man and his dreams brought first independence and then financial ruin to his once — prosperous country. Many foreign flags have flown over Gold Coast — Portuguese, Swedish, Danish, Dutch and British. Independent MAR 6, 1957.

㉓ TOGO

République Togolaise
(Republic of Togo)

Area: 56,785 km²
Population: 2,890,000
Population growth per annum: 2.7%
Life expectancy at birth: males 44 years, females 48 years
Literacy: 10%
Capital with population: Lomé 283,000
Other important cities with population: none
Language: French, Tribal languages
Religion: Animist, Christian (25%), Moslem (10%)
Currency: CFA-franc = 100 centimes

An artificial nation. During the scramble for Africa, the Germans, like all other colonial powers just grabbed as much land as they could regardless of tribal, linguistic and other natural boundaries. Part of their colonial patchwork finally emerged as free Togo. Independent APR 27, 1960.

㉔ BENIN

République Populaire du Benin
(Peoples Republic of Benin)

Area: 112,622 km²
Population: 3,830 000
Population growth per annum: 3.0%
Life expectancy at birth: males 44 years, females 48 years
Literacy: 20%
Capital with population: Porto Novo 105,000
Other important cities with population: Cotonou 490,000
Language: French, local dialects
Religion: Roman Catholic, Islam, Animist
Currency: CFA-franc = 100 centimes

Coastal Benin is a country apart island — studded lagoons that are neither sea nor land. Here the fishing villages were built on stilts to escape occasional floods and to give some protection against slavers. Independent AUG 1, 1960.

25 SÃO TOMÉ AND PRINCIPE

São Tomé e Principe
(Democratic Republic of Sao Tome and Principe)

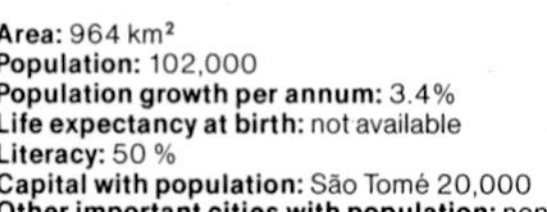

Area: 964 km²
Population: 102,000
Population growth per annum: 3.4%
Life expectancy at birth: not available
Literacy: 50 %
Capital with population: São Tomé 20,000
Other important cities with population: none
Language: Portuguese
Religion: Roman Catholic
Currency: Dobra = 100 centimos

These tropical islands in the cool Benguela current are favoured by fertile volcanic soil. At the turn of the century they were the world's leading producers of cocoa — but now others produce more. Coconuts and coffee are also grown. Independent JUL 12, 1975.

26 NIGERIA

(Federal Republic of Nigeria)

Area: 923,768 km²
Population: 82,390,000
Population growth per annum: 3.2%
Life expectancy at birth: males 46 years, females 49 years
Literacy: 25%
Capital with population: Lagos 1,061,000
Other important cities with population: Ibadan 850,000, Ogbomosho 435,000, Kano 400,000
Language: English, Hausa, Yoruba, Ibo
Religion: Moslem (55%), Christian (25%)
Currency: Naira = 100 kobo

Nigeria is Africa's most populous country in more than one sense. No other can match its over 80 millions and its over 250 linguistic groups (and tribes). It is hard to believe that this prosperous nation once was justly called "The White Man's Grave" (due to the coastal malaria swamps). Independent OCT 1, 1960.

27 CAMEROON

République du Cameroun
(United Republic of Cameroon)

Area: 475,442 km²
Population: 9,060,000
Population growth per annum: 2.3%
Life expectancy at birth: males 44 years, females 48 years
Literacy: 34%
Capital with population: Yaoundé 314,000
Other important cities with population: Douala 460,000
Language: English, French, Bantu, Sudanic
Religion: Moslem (25%), Roman Catholic (20%), Protestant (15%), Animist
Currency: CFA-franc = 100 centimes

An ethnic kaleidoscope, the country was a German colony, then two separate League of Nations mandates (French and British) before becoming a unitary republic. There are some two hundred different African ethnic groups. The famous Mt. Cameroon, that rises 4,070 m. up from the sea, serves at times as a natural lighthouse. The volcano erupted as recently as 1959. Indep.JAN 1, 1960.

28 CENTRAL AFRICAN REPUBLIC

République Centralafricaine

Area: 622,984 km²
Population: 2,520 000
Population growth per annum: 2.7%
Life expectancy at birth: 44 years
Literacy: 20%
Capital with population: Bangui 390,000
Other important cities with population: Berbérati 95,000
Language: French, local dialects
Religion: Animist (57%), Roman Catholic (20%), Protestant (15%)
Currency: CFA-franc = 100 centimes

At this crossroads of Africa the savannas meet the rain forests and the Bantu peoples mingle with the nilo-saharan groups and others. Even the rivers are running in opposite directions: the Ubangi towards Congo, the Shari to Lake Chad. Indep. AUG 13, 1960.

29 EQUATORIAL GUINEA

República de Guinea Ecuatorial
(Republic of Equatorial)

Area: 28,051 km²
Population: 398,000
Population growth per annum: 2.3%
Life expectancy at birth: males 44 years, females 48 years
Literacy: 20%
Capital with population: Malabo 27,000
Other important cities with population: none
Language: Spanish, Fang, English
Religion: Roman Catholic (60%)
Currency: Ekuele = 100 céntimos

As an antithesis, a part of the mainland of Africa belongs to the main island of Equatorial Guinea. On Bioko the lingua franca has been pidgin English and on Pagalu Portuguese patois in spite of the fact that Spanish was the official language! Indep. OCT 12, 1968.

30 GABON

République Gabonaise
(Gabonese Republic)

Area: 267,667 km²
Population: 1,370,000
Population growth per annum: 1.0%
Life expectancy at birth: males 42 years, females 45 years
Literacy: 65%
Capital with population: Libreville 350,000
Other important cities with population: Port Gentil 78,000
Language: French, Bantu dialects
Religion: Roman Catholic (42%), Animist, Protestant
Currency: CFA-franc = 100 centimes

Like some brand names Gabon has become almost a household word, because of the widespread use of mahogany plywood for furniture and doors. In addition to timber, Gabon produces oil, manganese and uranium. Independent AUG 17, 1960.

㉛ CONGO

République Populaire du Congo
(Peoples Republic of the Congo)

Area: 342,000 km²
Population: 1,740 000
Population growth per annum: 2.6%
Life expectancy at birth: males 44 years, females 48 years
Literacy: 80%
Capital with population: Brazzaville 422,000
Other important cities with population:
Pointe Noire 185,000
Language: French, bantu dialects
Religion: Animist (47%), Roman Catholic (40%), Protestant (12%)
Currency: CFA-franc = 100 centimes

Without the Congo River there wouldn't be any Congo. The sole reason for establishing the French colony north of the great river was to explore and exploit as much as possible of the basin (in competition with the Belgians). The name of the capital still honours the founding explorer de Brazza. Independent AUG 15, 1960.

㉜ UGANDA

(Republic of Uganda)

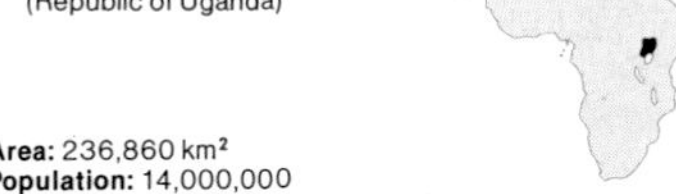

Area: 236,860 km²
Population: 14,000,000
Population growth per annum: 3.0%
Life expectancy at birth: males 51 years, females 54 years
Literacy: 25%
Capital with population: Kampala 340,000
Other important cities with population: none
Language: English, Swahili, Tribal languages
Religion: Roman Catholic (35%), Protestant (25%), Moslem (10%), Animist
Currency: Uganda shilling = 100 cents

Once and future Pearl of Africa? Here people has demonstrated once more that they are their own worst enemy in their lust for power. The setting of the gem remains: fertile lands wity an abundance of water, and magnificent scenery: The fabled Mountains of the Moon, the Ruwenzori, and the source lakes of the Nile. Independent SEP 9, 1962.

㉝ RWANDA

Republika y'u Rwanda
(Republic of Rwanda)

Area: 26,338 km²
Population: 5,650,000
Population growth per annum: 3.0%
Life expectancy at birth: males 44 years, females 48 years
Literacy: 37%
Capital with population: Kigali 157,000
Other important cities with population: none
Language: French, Kinyarwandu, Swahili
Religion: Animist, Roman Catholic (40%)
Currency: Rwanda franc = 100 centimes

This tiny nation contains some spectacular features: some of the true sources of the Nile, some of the last mountain gorillas and some active volcanoes in the Virunga Mountains. Independent JUL 7, 1962.

㉞ BURUNDI

(Republic of Burundi)

Area: 27,834 km²
Population: 4,560 000
Population growth per annum: 2.2%
Life expectancy at birth: males 39 years, females 43 years
Literacy: 25%
Capital with population: Bujumbura 160,000
Other important cities with population: none
Language: French, Kirundi
Religion: Roman Catholic 78%
Currency: Burundi franc = 100 centimes

A free colony. The hamitic Tutsi established colonial rule over the Hutu — the Bantu majority of the people as early as the 17th century. The Europeans came over two hundred years later and left after seventy years. The Tutsi still rule Burundi. Independent JUL 1, 1962.

㉟ KENYA

Jamhuri ya Kenya
(Republic of Kenya)

Area: 582,646 km²
Population: 19,500,000
Population growth per annum: 4.0%
Life expectancy at birth: males 51 years, females 56 years
Literacy: 40 %
Capital with population: Nairobi 1,200,000
Other important cities with population: Mombasa 340,000, Kisumu 155,000
Language: Swahili, English
Religion: Protestant (37%), Roman Catholic (22%), Moslem (5%), Others
Currency: Kenya Shilling = 100 cents

If there is a Safari Land in the world, it must be Kenya. The word safari (from the Arabic word for travel) rings with adventure. Here the adventurer's dreams may still be realized. In parks such as famous Amboseli close-ups of lions can be taken against the background of snow-capped Kilimanjaro. Independent DEC 12, 1963.

㊱ SOMALIA

Jamhuryadda Dimugradiga Somaliya
(Somali Democratic Republic)

Area: 637,657 km²
Population: 3,860,000
Population growth per annum: 7.9%
Life expectancy at birth: males 41 years, females 45 years
Literacy: 5%
Capital with population: Muqdisho 600,000
Other important cities with population: Hargeysa 150,000
Language: Somali
Religion: Moslem
Currency: Somali shilling = 100 centesimi

The land of frankincense and myrrh — today as in the days of ancient Egypt. Incense resins and carvings of aromatic resinous wood are still an important product of this droughtridden land of semideserts and dry savannas. Some of its proud camel herders now farm irrigated lands. Independent JUL 1, 1960.

37 ZAIRE

République du Zaïre
(Republic of Zaire)

Area: 2,344,885 km²
Population: 31,940,000
Population growth per annum: 2.8%
Life expectancy at birth: males 44 years, females 48 years
Literacy: males 40%, females 15%
Capital with population: Kinshasa 2,450,000
Other important cities with population: Kananga 705,000, Lubumbashi 455,000
Language: French, Bantu-an Sudan dialects
Religion: Roman Catholic 48%, Animist, Protestant (12%)
Currency: Zaire = 100 makuta

The heart of Africa. Within Zaire (former Belgian Congo) can be found sophisticated Kinshasa and rain forests with pygmy tribes, uranium and diamond mines as well as leaking river steamers, steaming rain forests but also prosperous farmland — and some 200 different ethnic groups. Independent JUN 30, 1960.

38 TANZANIA

(United Republic of Tanzania)

Area: 945,050 km²
Population: 19,730,000
Population growth per annum: 2.9%
Life expectancy at birth: 52 years
Literacy: 66%
Capital with population: Dar es Salaam 757,000
Other important cities with population: Zanzibar (Town) 111,000, Mwanza 111,000
Language: Swahili, English, local dialects
Religion: Animist, Christian (30%), Moslem (30%)
Currency: Tanzanian shilling = 100 cents

Arid Tanzania is full of natural wonders: The snow-capped, perfect volcanic cone on Mt Kilimanjaro, highest in Africa; Lake Victoria, third largest in the World; Lake Tanganyika, second deepest; the Serengeti Plains with the last prim of eval herds wild animals; the serene Ngorongoro Crater.

39 COMOROS

Republique fédérale islamique
des Comores
(Federal Islamic Republic of the Comoros)

Area: 1,862 km²
Population: 370,000
Population growth per annum: 2.2%
Life expectancy at birth: males 47 years, females 45 years
Literacy: 15%
Capital with population: Moroni 25,000
Other important cities with population: none
Language: French, Arabic
Religion: Islam
Currency: CFA-franc = 100 centimes

Essence is the very essence of the economy of the Comoro Islands that produce exotic ilang-ilang, citronella and jasmine essences as well as vanilla extract and cloves. Independent JUL 6, 1975.

40 SEYCHELLES

(Republic of Seychelles)

Area: 443 km²
Population: 65,000
Population growth per annum: 3.1%
Life expectancy at birth: 66 years
Literacy: 60%
Capital with population: Victoria 14,000
Other important cities with population: none
Language: English, French, Creole
Religion: Roman Catholic (91%), Protestant (8%)
Currency: Seychelles rupee = 100 cents

The islands of the love fruit — the world's largest, the sea (or double) coconut. This gigantic fruit, that may weigh 20-25 kg. (50 pounds), contains 3-4 smooth bilobed nuts with unavoidable associations to the human body. They grow only on the Seychelles, and their origin was long a mystery. Independent JUN 29, 1976.

41 ANGOLA

República Popular de Angola
(People's Republic of Angola)

Area: 1,246,700 km²
Population: 7,770,000
Population growth per annum: 2.5%
Life expectancy at birth: males 40 years, females 43 years
Literacy: 20 %
Capital with population: Luanda 475,000
Other important cities with population: Huambo 62,000
Language: Portuguese, various Bantu languages
Religion: Roman Catholic, Animist
Currency: Kwanza = 100 lwei

Accessibility shaped the destiny of Angola. In contrast to other parts of Africa there are good harbours here and neither forbidding deserts nor feverish swamps bar the routes to the interior. Thus Angola became one of the first European colonies on the African mainland. Independent NOV 11, 1975.

42 ZAMBIA

(Republic of Zambia)

Area: 752,620 km²
Population: 6,240,000
Population growth per annum: 3.2%
Life expectancy at birth: males 47 years, females 50 years
Literacy: 54%
Capital with population: Lusaka 538,000
Other important cities with population: Kitwe 315,000, Ndola 285,000
Language: English, Bantu dialects
Religion: Christian (60%), Animist
Currency: Kwacha = 100 ngwee

A colony for less than 40 years! Here colonial rule was not established until 1924 (as the result of Cecil Rhode's dream of extending British rule from the Cape to Cairo) but by 1964 the winds of change brought freedom to Zambia. The Victoria Falls are Zambia's most famous sight. Independent OCT 24, 1964.

43 MALAWI

(Republic of Malawi)

Area: 118,484 km²
Population: 6,100 000
Population growth per annum: 3.2%
Life expectancy at birth: males 44 years, females 48 years
Literacy: 25%
Capital with population: Lilongwe 103,000
Other important cities with population: Blantyre 220,000
Language: English, Chichewa
Religion: Animist, Christian (30%), Moslem (15%)
Currency: Kwacha = 100 tambala

A self-sufficient land of farmers, striving to build a better future. This is expressed also in their names for the units of currency. One kwacha (dawn) is divided into 100 tambalas (cockerels).

44 MOZAMBIQUE

República Popular de Moçambique
(People's Republic of Mozambique)

Area: 799,380 km²
Population: 13,140,000
Population growth per annum: 2.6%
Life expectancy at birth: males 44 years, females 48 years
Literacy: 14%
Capital with population: Maputo 755,000
Other important cities with population: Nampula 156,000
Beira 230,000
Language: Portuguese, Bantu languages
Religion: Roman Catholic (18%), Moslem (10%), Animist
Currency: Metical = 100 centavos

Geographical facts force "all-black" Mozambique to live in an uneasy partnership with "all-white" South Africa. Mozambique has water-power (Cabora Bassa, 1.4 GW.) and people-power but few minerals. South Africa needs contract workers and electricity in its mines. Independent JUN 15, 1975.

45 NAMIBIA (SOUTH-WEST AFRICA)

Namibia (Suidwes-Afrika)
(U.N. trusteeship, ruled by South Africa)

Area: 823,168 km²
Population: 1,040,000
Population growth per annum: not available
Life expectancy at birth: not available
Literacy: not available
Capital with population: Windhoek 89,000
Other important cities with population: none
Language: Afrikaans, English, German
Religion: Protestant (40%)
Currency: South African rand = 100 cents

Poor but potentially rich, a nation but yet kept in colonial bondage, Namibia awaits full freedom. This former German colony was given as a mandate under the auspices of the League of Nations in 1919. South Africa refuses to set Namibia free.

46 BOTSWANA

(Republic of Botswana)

Area: 600,372 km²
Population: 940,000
Population growth per annum: 2.8%
Life expectancy at birth: males 47 years, females 50 years
Literacy: 30%
Capital with population: Gaborone79,000
Other important cities with population:
Francistown 36,000
Language: English, Setswana
Religion: Indigenous beliefs (majority), Christian (15%)
Currency: Pula = 100 thebe

Land-locked Botswana lies in the center of the mountainbowl of southern Africa. Here lies the Kalahari desert and here the Cubango River loses itself in a maze of salt swamps and shallow lakes without outlet, such as famed Lake Ngami. Independent SEP 30, 1966.

47 ZIMBABWE

Area: 390,308 km²
Population: 7,530,000
Population growth per annum: 3.4%
Life expectancy at birth: males 52 years, females 55 years
Literacy: 45 %
Capital with population: Harare 656,000
Other important cities with population: Bulawayo 414,000, Chitungwiza 175,000
Language: English, Bantu dialects
Religion: Christian, Animist
Currency: Zimbabwe dollar = 100 cents

A nation with well-deserved pride. Zimbabwe is named after the impressive ruin-city that also is the firm foundation of the national spirit. These massive stone walls and towers were built more than a thousand years ago by Bantu kings — ancestors to the people of today's Zimbabwe. Independent APR 18, 1980.

48 MADAGASCAR

Repoblika Demokratika n'i Madagascar
(Democratic Republic of Madagascar)

Area: 587,041 km²
Population: 9,740,000
Population growth per annum: 2.6%
Life expectancy at birth: males 44 years, females 48 years
Literacy: 53%
Capital with population: Antananarivo 500,000
Other important cities with population: Toamasina 60,000
Language: Merina, French
Religion: Animist, Christian (40%), Moslem (10%)
Currency: Malagasy franc = 100 centimes

The fourth largest island of all — and in most aspects an Asian island. Geologically it is a segment of the same block as India, and the population is of Indo-Melanesian stock. The endemic wildlife comprises rare species, such as the bug-eyed aye-aye and the hedgehog-like tenrec.

㊾ REPUBLIC OF SOUTH AFRICA

Area: 1,225,824 km²
Population: 31,850,000
Population growth per annum: 2.8%
Life expectancy at birth: males 59 years, females 62 years
Literacy: Whites 98%, Asians 85%, Coloureds 75%
Capital with population: Cape Town 1,108,000
Pretoria 528,000
Other important cities with population:
Johannesburg 1,540,000 Durban 506,000
Language: Afrikaans, English
Religion: Protestant, Roman Catholic
Currency: Rand = 100 cents

Humans are their own enemies in rich South Africa. The original natives, the bushmen, fled into the Kalahari desert at the arrival of the Bantu tribes and the original Dutch Boers. The peoples of South Africa are now torn apart by worsening racial conflicts, aggravated by the in famous Apartheid ideology. Independent MAY 31, 1910, 1931.

㊿ LESOTHO
(Kingdom of Lesotho)

Area: 30,355 km²
Population: 1,470,000
Population growth per annum: 2.4%
Life expectancy at birth: males 49 years, females 51 years
Literacy: 55%
Capital with population: Maseru 45,000
Other important cities with population: none
Language: Sesotho, English
Religion: Roman Catholic (40%), Protestant (40%)
Currency: Lote = 100 lisente

An encircled nation, but not a subjugated land. This free black enclave in "white" South Africa is a reminder to its neighbours that all people are created equal. Independent OCT 4, 1966.

NORTH AMERICA

Area: 24,454,000 km²
Population: 346,418,000
Density of population per km²: 14

Cape Prince of Wales at 168° 4′ W. longitude is the North American mainland's most westerly point.

Mount McKinley is North America's highest peak, 6,194 m.

The Malaspina Glacier, covering an area of 3,8 km², is the largest on t North American mainla

The United States bou Alaska from Russia in 1867 for $ 7,200,00C

Snake River Canyon (Hell's Canyon) on the boundary between Ida and Oregon is the wo deepest ravine, 2,40C in depth.

The world's loftiest trees — up to 111 m. tall — gro in the redwood forests o California.

Death Valley is the co nent's deepest depre sion, 86 m. below sealevel, and also its test place (highest re ed temperature of 56 C.).

⑩ BELIZE
① CANADA
⑭ COSTA RICA
⑤ CUBA
⑧ DOMINICAN REPUBLIC
⑪ EL SALVADOR
⑨ GUATEMALA
⑦ HAITI
⑫ HONDURAS
⑥ JAMAICA
③ MEXICO
⑬ NICARAGUA
⑮ PANAMA
④ THE BAHAMAS
② UNITED STATES

51 SWAZILAND
(Kingdom of Swaziland)

Area: 17,365 km²
Population: 630,000
Population growth per annum: 2.8%
Life expectancy at birth: males 44 years, females 48 years
Literacy: 65%
Capital with population: Mbabane 23,000
Other important cities with population: none
Language: Swazi, English
Religion: Protestant (60%), Roman Catholic, Animist
Currency: Lilangeni = 100 cents

The proud Swazi people claim a history of five hundred years, but in their country their 'rights' are not older than those of their white neighbours on the other side of the Drakensberg Mountains. British protection kept Swaziland out of the Boer's hands. Independent SEP 6, 1968.

52 MAURITIUS

Area: 2,045 km²
Population: 990,000
Population growth per annum: 1.6%
Life expectancy at birth: males 61 years, females 67 years
Literacy: 61%
Capital with population: Port-Louis 150,000
Other important cities with population: Beau-Bassin (Rose Hill) 90,000
Language: English, French, Creole
Religion: Hindu (53%), Roman Catholic (25%), Moslem (16%)
Currency: Mauritius rupee = 100 cents

In relation to size no land on Earth has as many different languages — spoken by so many diverse ethnic groups: English (official), Hindi, Creole, Urdu, Tamil, French, Chinese, Arabic and a few African languages. Indep. MAR 12, 1968.

Cape Murchison on the Boothia Peninsula at 71° 59′ N. latitude is the northernmost point on the continent's mainland.
Greenland, with an area of 2,131,000 km², is the world's largest island. Only 341,700 km² is ice-free land. Measurement of the icecap has revealed that Greenland is in fact a number of separate islands covered by ice that in places is up to 4,000 m. thick.
North America's lowest temperature, —78°C., was recorded in the valley of the MacKenzie River.
Chubb Crater on the Ungava Peninsula is the world's largest meteorite crater, 3.5 km. in diameter and more than 400 m. deep.
Four of the world's ten largest lakes are found in North America.
Cape Charles at 55° 39′ W. longitude is the North American mainland's easternmost point.
CANADA
①
Lake Superior, with an area of 82,260 km², is the world's largest fresh water lake and ranks as the world's second largest lake after the Caspian Sea.
Yellowstone is the world's oldest national park, founded 1872. The park is well known for its teeming animal life and for more than a hundred splendid geysers including The Giant, the biggest in the world.
The tidal range in the Bay of Fundy is the largest in the world, 19.6 m. between ebb and flow.
The strongest wind ever to be recorded at the earth's surface, 103 m./sek., was measured in New Hampshire in 1934.
North America's highest waterfall and third highest in the world is Yosemite Falls, 739 m.
②
UNITED STATES
The Mississippi-Missouri is North America's longest river and with a length of 6,020 km. is third longest in the world.
Mammoth Cave in Kentucky is the world's longest with 240 km. of passages on five levels, two lakes, three rivers and eight waterfalls below ground.
The world's mightiest flow of water is the Gulf Stream, 30-40 km. wide with a flow of 55 million m³ per second at a rate of 3-5 knots.
y the gorge of the Blue is bigger than the nd Canyon on the Col- do River which is 350 long, up to 21 km. e and reaches a depth ,800 m.
Between June and November the Gulf of Mexico and Caribbean Sea are hit by destructive tropical storms, hurricanes, with torrential rainfall and wind forces up to 100 m./second.
④
THE BAHAMAS
MEXICO
③
CUBA
⑤
HAITI
⑦
⑧
DOMINICAN REPUBLIC
⑥
JAMAICA
BELIZE ⑩
⑨
HONDURAS
GUATEMALA
⑫
⑬
⑪
NICARAGUA
EL SALVADOR
The Isthmus of Panama is generally considered to be the boundary between North and South America. The southernmost point on the North American mainland is Punta Naranjas at 8° 13′ N. latitude.
⑭ COSTA RICA
⑮
PANAMA

① CANADA

Area: 9,976,139 km²
Population: 25,130,000
Population growth per annum: 1.5%
Life expectancy at birth: males 70 years, females 77 years
Literacy: 99%
Capital with population: Ottawa 295,000
Other important cities with population:
Montréal 1,000,000, Toronto 600,000, Calgary 595,000
Language: English, French
Religion: Roman Catholic (46%), Protestant (36%)
Currency: Canadian dollar = 100 cents

A nation that spans a continent, Canada is the world's second largest country. Halifax on the Atlantic is closer to Great Britain than to Vancouver on the Pacific. When the sun rises over Newfoundland it is still midnight in Yukon. The 19.6 m (55 ft) tides in the Bay of Fundy are the world's greatest. Independent JUL 1, 1867.

② UNITED STATES OF AMERICA

Area: 9,363,123 km²
Population: 234,250,000
Population growth per annum: 0.9%
Life expectancy at birth: males 69 years, females 77 years
Literacy: 99%
Capital with population: Washington 638,000
Other important cities with population:
New York 7,100,000, Chicago 3,000,000, Los Angeles 3,000,000
Language: English
Religion: Protestant (33%),Roman Catholic (23%), Judaism (3%)
Currency: US dollar = 100 cents

U.S.A. is a powerful nation. The economic strength and military might of the nation can hardly be overestimated. It is the world's leading producer of most important commodities: oil, gas, coal, steel, paper. It is also found at the top of most lists of world records and extremes — and especially those of engineering feats. Independent JUL 4, 1776.

③ MEXICO
Estados Unidos Mexicanos
(United Mexican States)

Area: 1,972,547 km²
Population: 76,790,000
Population growth per annum: 3.0%
Life expectancy at birth: males 62 years, females 67 years
Literacy: 74 %
Capital with population: Mexico City 13,000,000
Other important cities with population:
Guadalajara 2,300,000, Monterrey 2,000,000
Language: Spanish
Religion: Roman Catholic
Currency: Mexican peso = 100 centavos

The centre of power in Central America lies as before in Mexico. In the early 19th century, the Spanish viceroy ruled half of Northern America from here, and today the nation is ranked high among the powers of the Third World. The famous pyramids of Teotihuacán manifest the greatness of Mexico. Independent SEP 16, 1810.

④ THE BAHAMAS
(Commonwealth of the Bahamas)

Area: 13,935 km²
Population: 230,000
Population growth per annum: 3.7%
Life expectancy at birth: males 64 years, females 69 years
Literacy: 89 %
Capital with population: Nassau 139,000
Other important cities with population: Freeport 16,000
Language: English
Religion: mainly Protestant
Currency: Bahamian dollar = 100 cents

A thousand coral reefs and not one but 700 coral islands in the sun. For the industrial eastern USA the beaches of the Bahamas are conveniently close — as Mediterranean shores are to northwestern Europe. Blue underwater caves attract scuba divers. Independent JUL 10, 1973.

⑤ CUBA
República de Cuba
(Republic of Cuba)

Area: 121,046 km²
Population: 10,000 000
Population growth per annum: 0.8%
Life expectancy at birth: males 71 years, females 74 years
Literacy: 96%
Capital with population: La Habana (Havana) 1,950,000
Other important cities with population:
Santiago de Cuba 565,000, Camagüey 480,000
Language: Spanish
Religion: Roman Catholic
Currency: Cuban peso = 100 centavos

The Sugar Island. Sugar and Cuba are now almost synonymous words, but it is a fact that the sugar cane was imported to Cuba from the Old World by the Spaniards. The Cubans themselves are also descendants of immigrants from the Old World: the Spaniards and their negro slaves. Independent DEC 10, 1898.

⑥ JAMAICA

Area: 10,991 km²
Population: 2,310,000
Population growth per annum: 1.4%
Life expectancy at birth: males 68 years, females 73 years
Literacy: 82%
Capital with population: Kingston 650,000
Other important cities with population:
St. Catherine 220,000, Clarendon 195,000
Language: English
Religion: Protestant (75%), Roman Catholic
Currency: Jamaica dollar = 100 cents

Pirate Island has become Island in the Sun and Land of the Rasta — as Fifteen men on a dead man's chest has been replaced by the inspired music of the Rastafarians. The bottle of rum is still available. Only scuba divers can today visit infamous Port Royal on the bottom of Kingston Bay. Independent AUG 6, 1962.

⑦ HAITI

République d'Haiti
(Republic of Haiti)

Area: 27,750 km²
Population: 5,200,000
Population growth per annum: 2.4%
Life expectancy at birth: males 49 years, females 52 years
Literacy: 23%
Capital with population: Port-au-Prince 460,000
Other important cities with population: Cap Haïtien 55,000
Language: French, Creole
Religion: Roman Catholic (66%), Protestant (11%)
Currency: Guorde = 100 centimes

Historically the land of voodo, of mystery and magic. Officially all are Roman catholics, but the undercurrent of ancient African religions is still strong here. Slaves who won their freedom against Spanish, British and French armies created here the world's first Negro republic. Independent JAN 1, 1804.

⑧ DOMINICAN REPUBLIC

Repblica Dominicana

Area: 48,442 km²
Population: 5,980,000
Population growth per annum: 2.6%
Life expectancy at birth: males 58 years, females 62 years
Literacy: 62%
Capital with population: Santo Domingo 1,300,000
Other important cities with population: Santiago (de los Caballeros) 280,000, La Romana 90,000
Language: Spanish
Religion: Roman Catholic
Currency: RD peso = 100 centavos

This is in all but name Columbu's country. Here lie his mortal remains in a lead casket in the cathedral of Santo Domingo. The city that he founded is the oldest European city in the New World, and the island itself carries the name he gave it, Hispaniola — "the Spanish (Island)". Independent FEB 27, 1844.

⑨ GUATEMALA

República de Guatemala
(Republic of Guatemala)

Area: 108,889 km²
Population: 6,580,000
Population growth per annum: 3.0%
Life expectancy at birth: males 57 years, females 59 years
Literacy: 47%
Capital with population: Guatemala 1,300,000
Other important cities with population: Quezaltenango 66,000
Language: Spanish, Indian dialects
Religion: Roman Catholic
Currency: Quetzal = 100 centavos

A land of awe inspiring ruins and memories of its brilliant past during the reign of the Mayas — of once glorious cities like Tikal and Uaxactún. It is also a land of melodious place names like Chichicastenango (a famous market town) and Sololá. Independent 1821, 1839.

⑩ BELIZE

Area: 22,965 km²
Population: 158 000
Population growth per annum: not available
Life expectancy at birth: 60 years
Literacy: 80%
Capital with population: Belmopan 2,900
Other important cities with population: Belize City 40,000
Language: English, Spanish
Religion: Roman Catholic (60%), Protestant
Currency: Belize dollar = 100 cents

Belize is an anomaly — the only British enclave in Latin America. The forests yield valuable timber — mahogany and rosewood — and chicle latex, the original "gum" used for making chewing gum before the development of synthetic gum. Independent SEP 21, 1981.

⑪ EL SALVADOR

República de El Salvador
(Republic of El Salvador)

Area: 21,393 km²
Population: 5,300,000
Population growth per annum: 2.9%
Life expectancy at birth: males 60 years, females 65 years
Literacy: 40%
Capital with population: San Salvador 884,000
Other important cities with population: Santa Ana 210,000, San Miguel 160,000
Language: Spanish
Religion: Roman Catholic
Currency: Colón = 100 centavos

This is truly the land of volcanoes. The average distance between active volcanoes here is less than 30 km. (19 miles)! Politically the nation is disrupted by even more serious eruptions of violence, aggravated by outside interference. Independent 1839, 1841.

⑫ HONDURAS

República de Honduras
(Republic of Honduras)

Area: 112,088 km²
Population: 4,090,000
Population growth per annum: 3.8%
Life expectancy at birth: males 55 years, females 59 years
Literacy: 47%
Capital with population: Tegucigalpa 534,000
Other important cities with population: San Pedro Sula 398,000, El Progreso 105,000
Language: Spanish
Religion: Roman Catholic
Currency: Lempira = 100 centavos

The word banana republic must have been coined with Honduras in mind. Bananas thrive in the fertile volcanic soil and the warm, humid climate of the tropical coastlands. The forest covers impressive Maya ruins, such as Copán. Independent 1821, NOV 5, 1838.

⑬ NICARAGUA

República de Nicaragua
(Republic of Nicaragua)

Area: 148,000 km²
Population: 2,910,000
Population growth per annum: 3.3%
Life expectancy at birth: males 54 years, females 57 years
Literacy: 87%
Capital with population: Managua 615,000
Other important cities with population: León 160,000
Language: Spanish
Religion: Roman Catholic
Currency: Córdoba = 100 centavos

Nicaragua could be called a land of turmoil. Plagued by earthquakes, revolutions, and counter-revolutions the people today are certainly longing for peace and quiet. Lake Nicaragua is said to contain people-eating sharks, trapped there when the former bay became a fresh water lake. Indep. 1821, 1838.

⑭ COSTA RICA

República de Costa Rica

Area: 50,700 km²
Population: 2,450,000
Population growth per annum: 2.4%
Life expectancy at birth: males 68 years, females 72 years
Literacy: 90%
Capital with population: San José 245,000
Other important cities with population: Alajuela 35,000
Language: Spanish
Religion: Roman Catholic
Currency: Colón = 100 céntimos

Costa Rica is known as the country that has no army, but the police are one of the world's best equipped! The lack of generals and colonels is in any case not the only cause for the peaceful, democratic development of the country during the last twenty-five years. Independent 1821, 1838.

⑮ PANAMA

República de Panamá
(Republic of Panamá)

Area: 78,046 km²
Population: 1,970,000
Population growth per annum: 2.5%
Life expectancy at birth: males 68 years, females 72 years
Literacy: 85%
Capital with population: Panamá 389,000
Other important cities with population: Colón 80,000
Language: Spanish
Religion: Roman Catholic
Currency: Balboa = 100 centimes

Panama is known all over the Seven Seas. Few know that the word means 'abundance of fish' but many know the quartered tricolor flag that is flown over many ships (as a flag of 'convenience') — and all know of the Canal that every year carries over 10,000 large ships between the Atlantic and the Pacific. Independent 1819, NOV 3, 1903.

SOUTH AMERICA

Area: 17,838,000 km²
Population: 214,684,000
Density of population per km²: 12

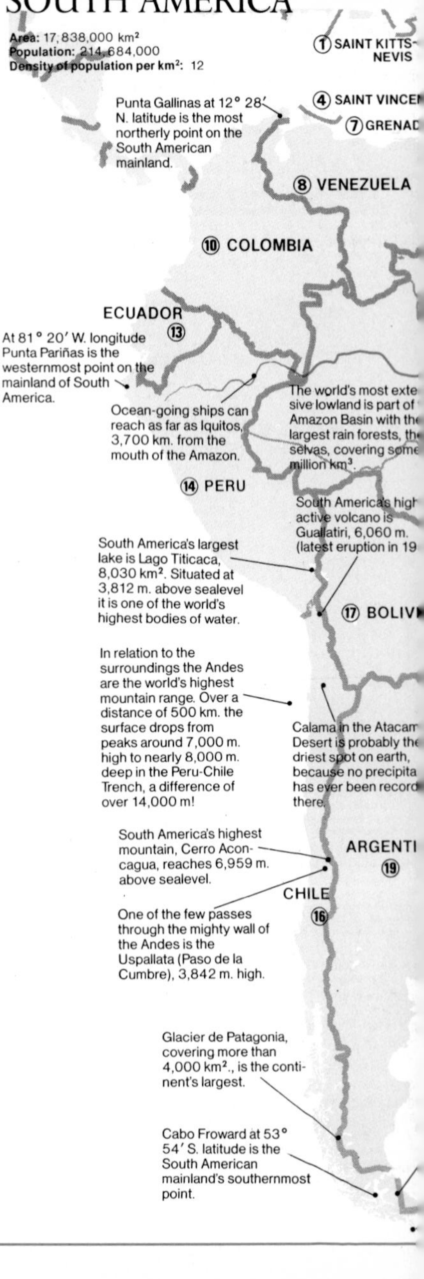

① SAINT KITTS-NEVIS
④ SAINT VINCE
⑦ GRENAD
⑧ VENEZUELA
⑩ COLOMBIA
ECUADOR ⑬
⑭ PERU
⑰ BOLIV
ARGENTI ⑲
CHILE ⑯

Punta Gallinas at 12° 28′ N. latitude is the most northerly point on the South American mainland.

At 81° 20′ W. longitude Punta Pariñas is the westernmost point on the mainland of South America.

Ocean-going ships can reach as far as Iquitos, 3,700 km. from the mouth of the Amazon.

The world's most exte sive lowland is part of Amazon Basin with th largest rain forests, th selvas, covering some million km³.

South America's high active volcano is Guallatiri, 6,060 m. (latest eruption in 19

South America's largest lake is Lago Titicaca, 8,030 km². Situated at 3,812 m. above sealevel it is one of the world's highest bodies of water.

In relation to the surroundings the Andes are the world's highest mountain range. Over a distance of 500 km. the surface drops from peaks around 7,000 m. high to nearly 8,000 m. deep in the Peru-Chile Trench, a difference of over 14,000 m!

Calama in the Atacam Desert is probably th driest spot on earth, because no precipita has ever been record there.

South America's highest mountain, Cerro Aconcagua, reaches 6,959 m. above sealevel.

One of the few passes through the mighty wall of the Andes is the Uspallata (Paso de la Cumbre), 3,842 m. high.

Glacier de Patagonia, covering more than 4,000 km²., is the continent's largest.

Cabo Froward at 53° 54′ S. latitude is the South American mainland's southernmost point.

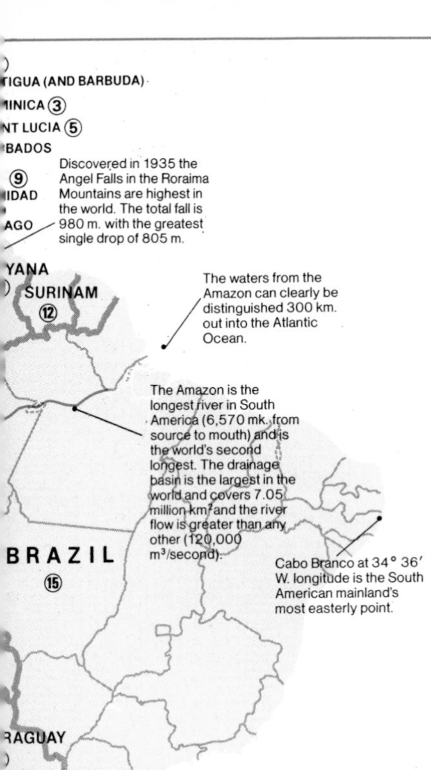
TIGUA (AND BARBUDA)
INICA ③
NT LUCIA ⑤
BADOS
⑨
IDAD
AGO
Discovered in 1935 the Angel Falls in the Roraima Mountains are highest in the world. The total fall is 980 m. with the greatest single drop of 805 m.
YANA
SURINAM
⑫
The waters from the Amazon can clearly be distinguished 300 km. out into the Atlantic Ocean.
The Amazon is the longest river in South America (6,570 mk. from source to mouth) and is the world's second longest. The drainage basin is the largest in the world and covers 7.05 million km² and the river flow is greater than any other (120,000 m³/second).
BRAZIL
⑮
Cabo Branco at 34° 36′ W. longitude is the South American mainland's most easterly point.
RAGUAY

The Iguazu Falls are the mightiest in South America. The falls are divided by forested islands over a width of 3.5 km. with two falls totalling a height of 70 m.

⑳
URUGUAY

e deepest depression
South America is
inas Grandes on
ninsula Valdes, 35 m.
ow sealevel.

Grande de Tierra del
go is the continent's
est island (48,400

Most southerly point in South America is Cape Horn at 55° 59′s. latitude.

② ANTIGUA (AND BARBUDA)

⑲ ARGENTINA

⑥ BARBADOS

⑰ BOLIVIA

⑮ BRAZIL

⑯ CHILE

⑩ COLOMBIA

③ DOMINICA

⑬ ECUADOR

⑦ GRENADA

⑪ GUYANA

⑱ PARAGUAY

⑭ PERU

① SAINT KITTS-NEVIS

⑤ SAINT LUCIA

④ SAINT VINCENT

⑫ SURINAM

⑨ TRINIDAD AND TOBAGO

⑳ URUGUAY

⑧ VENEZUELA

① SAINT KITTS-NEVIS

Federation of Saint Christopher and Nevis

Area: 261 km²
Population: 45,000
Population growth per annum: not available
Life expectancy at birth: not available
Literacy: not available
Capital with population: Basseterre 15,000
Other important cities with population: none
Language: English
Religion: Protestant (76%), Roman Catholic (8%)
Currency: EC-dollar = 100 cents

St. Kitts cultivates tourists and sugar. The pleasant climate in the trade wind tropics favours both of the main industries. Palms and beaches correspond to the common "image" of the Caribbean. Independent SEP 19, 1983.

② ANTIGUA (AND BARBUDA)

Area: 442 km²
Population: 79,000
Population growth per annum: not available
Life expectancy at birth: not available
Literacy: not available
Capital with population: Saint Johns 25,000
Other important cities with population: none
Language: English
Religion: Christian (predominantly Church of England)
Currency: East Caribbean dollar = 100 cents

Antigua and Barbuda are names known to collectors of stamps, to naval strategy planners, some students of colonial history and a few in the sugar trade, and of course, to the proud and independent islanders of the Lesser Antilles. Ind. NOV 1, 1981.

③ DOMINICA

(Commonwealth of Dominica)

Area: 751 km²
Population: 82,000
Population growth per annum: 2.7%
Life expectancy at birth: males 57 years, females 59 years
Literacy: not available
Capital with population: Roseau 20,000
Other important cities with population: none
Language: English, French patois
Religion: Roman Catholic
Currency: French franc = 100 centimes

Dominica can be called the only Caribbean country among all the Caribbean lands. Only here still lives a sizeable remnant of the once dreaded Carib Indians — whose name is perpetuated in the equally dreadful word cannibal. Indep. NOV 3, 1978.

④ SAINT VINCENT (AND THE GRENADINES)

Area: 389 km²
Population: 123,000
Population growth per annum: 5.9%
Life expectancy at birth: males 59 years, females 60 years
Literacy: 95 %
Capital with population: Kingstown 33,000
Other important cities with population: none
Language: English
Religion: Protestant (75%), Roman Catholic (13%)
Currency: EC-dollar = 100 cents

Many different kinds of fruit are grown on the islands — coconuts, mangoes, avocados, guavas just to mention a few, but not the pomegranates used for making grenadine syrup (an ingredient of many cocktails). Most of the 600 volcanic Grenadine Islands belong to St. Vincent. Ind. OCT 27, 1979.

⑤ SAINT LUCIA

Area: 616 km²
Population: 127,000
Population growth per annum: 1.8%
Life expectancy at birth: males 65 years, females 70 years
Literacy: 78%
Capital with population: Castries 45,000
Other important cities with population: none
Language: English, French patois
Religion: Roman Catholic
Currency: EC-dollar = 100 cents

Bananas, cocoa and coconuts are the chief products of St. Lucia instead of sugar as on most other Antillean Islands. A growing number of tourists are discovering the pleasant beaches of St. Lucia. Independent FEB 22, 1979.

⑥ BARBADOS

Area: 431 km²
Population: 250,000
Population growth per annum: 1.4%
Life expectancy at birth: males 68 years, females 73 years
Literacy: 97%
Capital with population: Bridgetown 7,500
Other important cities with population: none
Language: English
Religion: Protestant
Currency: Barbados dollar = 100 cents

Tourists and sugar cane thrive here on the most easterly of the Windward Islands. The gentle trade winds blow with a constant 5-6 m./s. to keep the surf rolling in and the sky clear of clouds. Independent NOV 30, 1966.

⑦ GRENADA
(State of Grenada)

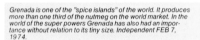

Area: 344 km²
Population: 115,000
Population growth per annum: 1.0%
Life expectancy at birth: 69 years
Literacy: 85%
Capital with population: Saint George's 7,500
Other important cities with population: none
Language: English
Religion: Roman Catholic
Currency: E C dollar = 100 cents

Grenada is one of the "spice islands" of the world. It produces more than one third of the nutmeg on the world market. In the world of the super powers Grenada has also had an importance without relation to its tiny size. Independent FEB 7, 1974.

⑧ VENEZUELA
República de Venezuela
(Republic of Venezuela)

Area: 912,050 km²
Population: 15,260,000
Population growth per annum: 3.5%
Life expectancy at birth: males 64 years, females 69 years
Literacy: 86%
Capital with population: Caracas 2,700,000
Other important cities with population:
Maracaibo 845,000, Barquismeto 459,000
Language: Spanish
Religion: Roman Catholic
Currency: Bolívar = 100 céntimos

Venice has been called a floating city, and Venezuela — "little Venice" — a land floating on oil. Over 4,000 oil drilling derricks stand now in the shallow waters of the Maracaibo lagoon like the houses on stilts that gave the country its name. In the southeast the Angel Falls, highest in the world, plunge 980 m. down (805 m. uninterrupted). Independent 1821, 1830.

⑨ TRINIDAD AND TOBAGO

Area: 5,128 km²
Population: 1,160,000
Population growth per annum: 1.5%
Life expectancy at birth: males 66 years, females 72 years
Literacy: 92%
Capital with population: Port of Spain 56,000
Other important cities with population:
San Fernando 40,000
Language: English, Spanish
Religion: Roman Catholic (31%), Protestant (26%), Hindu (23%), Moslem (6%)
Currency: Trinidad and Tobago dollar = 100 cents

A melting pot where everything is transformed. Cultures traditions, and people from five continents have been mixed and combined under the sun of Trinidad. A different melting pot an "inexhaustible" lake of asphalt, Pitch Lake, is unique in the world. Independent AUG 31, 1962.

⑩ COLOMBIA
República de Colombia
(Republic of Colombia)

Area: 1,141,748 km²
Population: 27,410,000
Population growth per annum: 2.1%
Life expectancy at birth: males 60 years, females 65 years
Literacy: 82%
Capital with population: Bogotá 4,900,000
Other important cities with population:
Medellin 1,800,000, Cali 1,200,000, Barranquilla 900,000
Language: Spanish
Religion: Roman Catholic
Currency: Colombian peso = 100 centavos

Colombia may have been the legendary land of El Dorado — the gold-covered king. Today it could be called the land of green gold — as 90% of all emeralds in the world come from mines in Colombia. However high quality coffee is the country's main export product. Independent DEC 17, 1819.

⑪ GUYANA
(Cooperative Republic of Guyana)

Area: 215,000 km²
Population: 830,000
Population growth per annum: 2.2%
Life expectancy at birth: males 67 years, females 72 years
Literacy: 85%
Capital with population: Georgetown 187,000
Other important cities with population: none
Language: English, Hindi, Creole
Religion: Hindu (37%), Protestant (32%), Roman Catholic (13%), Islam (9%)
Currency: Guyana dollar = 100 cents

Guyana is an East Indian country in the West Indies, as the major part of the inhabitants are descendants of immigrants from India. Of all the world's waterfalls only nine are higher than the near 500 m. high uninterrupted cascades of the King George VI Falls, north of the Roraima Plateau. Indep. MAY 26, 1966.

⑫ SURINAM

Area: 163,820 km²
Population: 370,000
Population growth per annum: 1.3%
Life expectancy at birth: males 65 years, females 70 years
Literacy: 80%
Capital with population: Paramaribo 68,000
Other important cities with population: none
Language: Dutch
Religion: Hindu (29%), Protestant (20%), Moslem (19%), Roman Catholic (18%)
Currency: Suriname guilder or florin = 100 cents

A country för $ 24? In a deal with Britain in the 15th century the Dutch acquired this British colony in exchange for New Amsterdam — later better known as the city of New York — in turn bought for $24. 90% of today's Surinam is covered with dense rainforest. Independent NOV 25, 1975.

⑬ ECUADOR
República del Ecuador
(Republic of Ecuador)

Area: 283,561 km²,
(disputed area 190,807 km² not included)
Population: 8,810,000
Population growth per annum: 3.0%
Life expectancy at birth: males 58 years, females 62 years
Literacy: 84%
Capital with population: Quito 920,000
Other important cities with population:
Guaqaquil 1,300,000, Cuenca 270,000
Language: Spanish, Quechuan, Jivaroan
Religion: Predominantly Roman Catholic
Currency: Sucre = 100 centavos

A "heavy" item in Ecuador's export statistics is featherweight balsa timber. The Spanish word balsa denotes both raft and the timber, lighter than cork. The Indians used it for building sailing rafts as early as prehistoric times. The logs for Heyerdahl's famous Kon-Tiki were cut in Ecuador in 1947. Independent MAY 13, 1830.

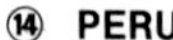

⑭ PERU
República del Perú
(Republic of Peru)

Area: 1,285,216 km²
Population: 18,300,000
Population growth per annum: 2.7%
Life expectancy at birth: males 56 years, females 59 years
Literacy: 72%
Capital with population: Lima 3,100,000
Other important cities with population: Callao 300,000
Language: Spanish, Quechua, Aymará
Religion: Roman Catholic
Currency: Sol = 100 centavos

The Inca's land of gold and silver was turned into a land of guano and fishmeal. The conquistadores stripped the land of its immense treasures of golden artwork. The stone buildings of Machu Picchu's breath-taking eagle's nest-city still remain — hidden and forgotten for five centuries until discovered by Hiram Bingham in 1911. Independent JUL 28, 1821.

⑮ BRAZIL
República Federativa do Brasil
(Federative Republic of Brazil)

Area: 8,511,965 km²
Population: 120,000,000
Population growth per annum: 2.4%
Life expectancy at birth: males 60 years, females 64 years
Literacy: 68%
Capital with population: Brasília 410,000,
(Federal district 1,200,000)
Other important cities with population:
São Paulo 7,000,000, Rio de Janeiro 5,100,000
Language: Portuguese
Religion: Roman Catholic (89%), Protestant (7%)
Currency: Cruzeiro = 100 centavos

Only four countries in the world are larger than Brazil, The mighty Amazon carries more water than any other river (120 000 m²/s at the mouth) and is navigable for ocean-going ships up to Iquitos, 3 700 km from the sea. Brasília, created by president Kubitscheck and architects Oscar Niemeyer and Lúcio Costa, became capital in 1960. Independent SEP 7, 1822.

⑯ CHILE
República de Chile
(Republic of Chile)

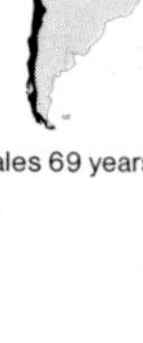

Area: 756,945 km²
Population: 11,490,000
Population growth per annum: 1.7%
Life expectancy at birth: males 62 years, females 69 years
Literacy: 90%
Capital with population: Santiago 3,450,000
Other important cities with population:
Viña del Mar 300,000, Varpariso 270,000
Language: Spanish
Religion: Predominantly Roman Catholic
Currency: Chilean peso = 100 centavos

The "narrowest" country in the world, Chile, is nearly twenty-five times longer than it is wide (175 by 4 300 km) and stretches from the tropics down to the stormy Cape Horn in the "Furious Fifties". At Calama in the Atacama Desert no rainfall has ever been recorded. Independent SEP 18, 1810.

⑰ BOLIVIA
República de Bolivia
(Republic of Bolivia)

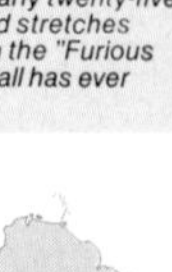

Area: 1,098,580 km²
Population: 5,900 000
Population growth per annum: 2.6%
Life expectancy at birth: males 47 years, females 51 years
Literacy: 75%
Capital with population: La Paz 650,000 and Sucre 65,000
Other important cities with population:
Santa Cruz 260,000, Cochabamba 200,000
Language: Spanish, Quechua (34%), Aymará (25%)
Religion: Roman Catholic
Currency: Bolivian peso = 100 centavos

Tin mining is the main source of wealth in land-locked Bolivia. Most of the population live on the dry, cold tablelands, higher than many peaks in the European Alps. Lake Titicaca, shared with Peru, is the, worlds highest (3 812 m) navigable body of water. Independent AUG 6, 1825.

⑱ PARAGUAY
República del Paraguay
(Republic of Paraguay)

Area: 406,752 km²
Population: 3,000,000
Population growth per annum: 3.3%
Life expectancy at birth: males 62 years, females 66 years
Literacy: 82%
Capital with population: Asunción 460,000
Other important cities with population: Caaguazu 73,000
Language: Spanish, Guarani (90%)
Religion: Roman Catholic
Currency: Guarani = 100 céntimos

Here one man's will is, and has been, law — by unbroken tradition from Jesuit times. The pope was replaced by the King of Spain, he in turn by the founding dictator "El Supremo" and so on. General Alfredo Stroessner seized power in 1954. The Iguaçu falls of the Parana cascade 82 m. over a width of four km. between hundreds of forest islands. Independent MAY 14, 1811.

19 ARGENTINA

República Argentina
(Argentine Republic)

Area: 2,777,815 km²
Population: 27,950,000
Population growth per annum: 1.3%
Life expectancy at birth: males 66 years, females 73 years
Literacy: 94 %
Capital with population: Buenos Aires 2,900,000, (Greater Buenos Aires 9,900,000)
Other important cities with population: Córdoba 970,000, Rosario 880,000, Mendoza 600,000
Language: Spanish
Religion: Roman Catholic
Currency: Arg. peso = 100 centavos

The home of the tango and the gaucho, Argentina is a Europe in miniature. It is situated on southern latitudes, and it, was populated by settlers from all over Europe. It has the continents highest peak, Aconcagua, and its lowest spot, Salinas Grandes on the Peninsula Valdés, 35 m. below sea level. Independent MAR 25, 1810.

20 URUGUAY

República Oriental del Uruguay
(Oriental Republic of Uruguay)

Area: 186,926 km²
Population: 2,990,000
Population growth per annum: 0.6%
Life expectancy at birth: males 66 years, females 73 years
Literacy: 94%
Capital with population: Montevideo 1,362,000
Other important cities with population: Salto 80,000, Paysandá 80,000
Language: Spanish
Religion: Roman Catholic
Currency: Nuevo peso (new peso) = 100 centésimos

A country of rolling grasslands with grazing cattle and cultivated fields. As in other agricultural lands, more people live in the capital than in all the other towns put together. Independent AUG. 25, 1825.

READER INFORMATION

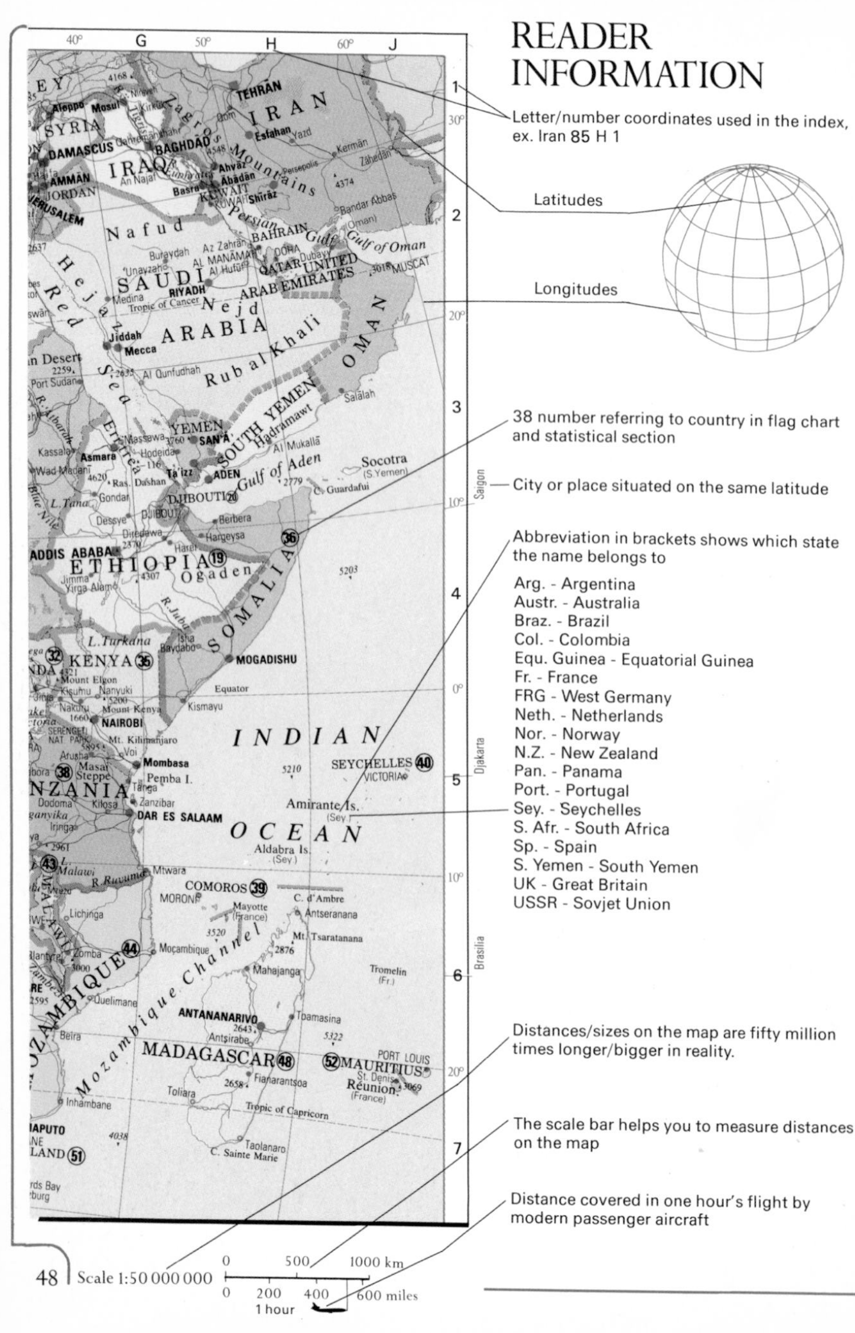

Letter/number coordinates used in the index, ex. Iran 85 H 1
Latitudes
Longitudes
38 number referring to country in flag chart and statistical section
City or place situated on the same latitude
Abbreviation in brackets shows which state the name belongs to
Arg. - Argentina
Austr. - Australia
Braz. - Brazil
Col. - Colombia
Equ. Guinea - Equatorial Guinea
Fr. - France
FRG - West Germany
Neth. - Netherlands
Nor. - Norway
N.Z. - New Zealand
Pan. - Panama
Port. - Portugal
Sey. - Seychelles
S. Afr. - South Africa
Sp. - Spain
S. Yemen - South Yemen
UK - Great Britain
USSR - Sovjet Union
Distances/sizes on the map are fifty million times longer/bigger in reality.
The scale bar helps you to measure distances on the map
Distance covered in one hour's flight by modern passenger aircraft
Scale 1:50 000 000
0 500 1000 km
0 200 400 600 miles
1 hour

Symbols Scale 1:10 000 000, 1:20 000 000

Bombay	More than 5 000 000 inhabitants
Milano	1 000 000-5 000 000 inhabitants
Zürich	250 000-1 000 000 inhabitants
Dijon	100 000-250 000 inhabitants
Dover	25 000-100 000 inhabitants
Torquay	Less than 25 000 inhabitants
Tachiumet	Small sites
WIEN	National capital
Atlanta	State capital

Major road
Other road
Road under construction
Railway
Railway under construction
Train ferry
National boundary
Disputed national boundary
State boundary
Disputed state boundary
Undefined boundary in the sea

4807	Height above sea-level in metres
3068	Depth in metres
	National park
Niniveh	Ruin
	Pass
KAINJI DAM	Dam
	Wadi
	Canal
	Waterfalls
	Reef

Symbols Scale 1:30 000 000 1:50 000 000 1:54 000 000 1:60 000 000 1:75 000 000

Shanghai	More than 5 000000 inhabitants
Barcelona	1 000000-5 000000 inhabitants
Venice	250 000-1 000 000 inhabitants
Aberdeen	50 000-250 000 inhabitants
Beida	Less than 50 000 inhabitants
Mawson	Scientific station
CAIRO	National capital

Major road
Railway
Railway under construction
National boundary
Disputed national boundary
State boundary
Disputed state boundary
Undefined boundary in the sea

8848	Height above sea-level in metres
11034	Depth in metres
2645	Thickness of ice cap
Thebes	Ruin
	Dam
	Wadi
	Canal
	Waterfalls
	Reef

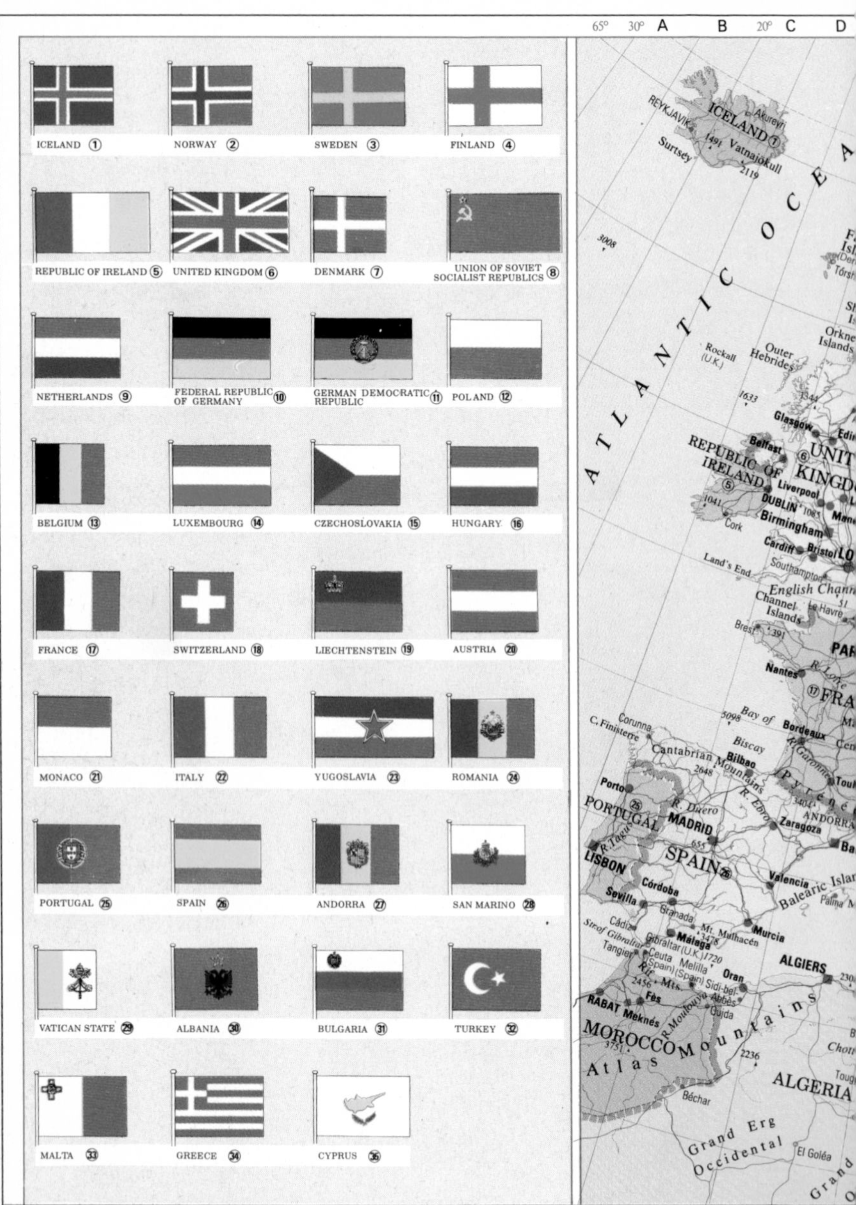

ICELAND 1
NORWAY 2
SWEDEN 3
FINLAND 4
REPUBLIC OF IRELAND 5
UNITED KINGDOM 6
DENMARK 7
UNION OF SOVIET SOCIALIST REPUBLICS 8
NETHERLANDS 9
FEDERAL REPUBLIC OF GERMANY 10
GERMAN DEMOCRATIC REPUBLIC 11
POLAND 12
BELGIUM 13
LUXEMBOURG 14
CZECHOSLOVAKIA 15
HUNGARY 16
FRANCE 17
SWITZERLAND 18
LIECHTENSTEIN 19
AUSTRIA 20
MONACO 21
ITALY 22
YUGOSLAVIA 23
ROMANIA 24
PORTUGAL 25
SPAIN 26
ANDORRA 27
SAN MARINO 28
VATICAN STATE 29
ALBANIA 30
BULGARIA 31
TURKEY 32
MALTA 33
GREECE 34
CYPRUS 35
65° 30° A B 20° C D
REYKJAVIK
ICELAND 1
Akureyri
1491
Vatnajökull
2119
Surtsey
3008
ATLANTIC OCEA
Rockall (U.K.)
Outer Hebrides
1633
1344
Glasgow
Belfast
REPUBLIC OF IRELAND 5
6
Liverpool
DUBLIN
1041
1085
Cork
Birmingham
Cardiff
Bristol
Land's End
Southampton
Channel Islands
Le Havre
Brest
391
Nantes
R. Loire
17
Bay of Biscay
5098
Bordeaux
R. Garonne
Corunna
C. Finisterre
Cantabrian Mountains
2648
Bilbao
Porto
R. Duero
R. Ebro
PORTUGAL 25
MADRID
655
3404
ANDORRA
Zaragoza
R. Tagus
LISBON
SPAIN 26
Córdoba
Valencia
Sevilla
Granada
Mt. Mulhacén
3478
Murcia
Cádiz
Str. of Gibraltar
Gibraltar (U.K.)
1720
Málaga
Tangier
Ceuta (Spain)
Melilla (Spain)
Oran
ALGIERS
Rif Mts.
2456
Fès
Sidi-bel-Abbès
RABAT
Meknès
R. Moulouya
Oujda
MOROCCO
3751
Atlas Mountains
2236
ALGERIA
Béchar
Grand Erg Occidental
El Goléa

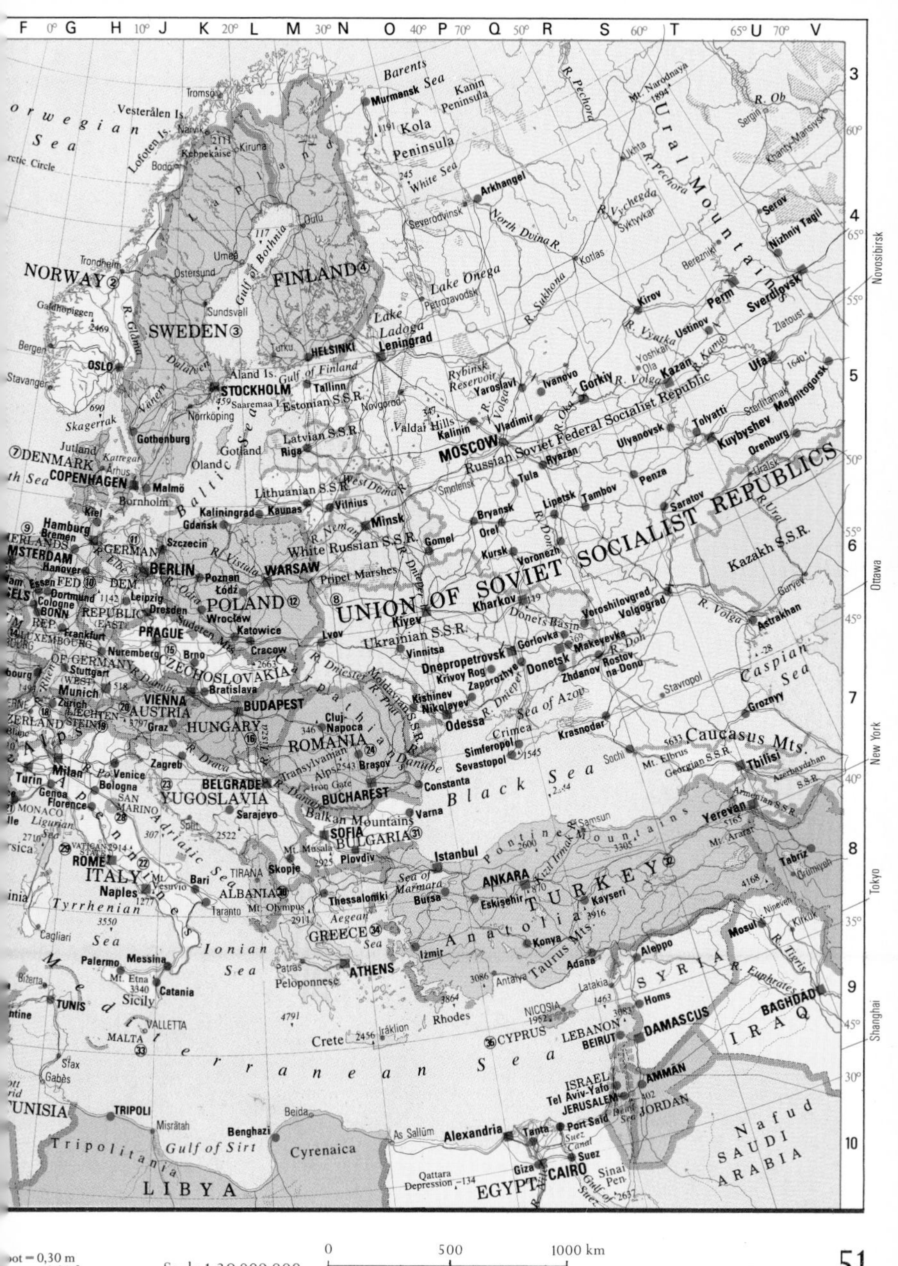

oot = 0,30 m
neter = 3,28 feet

Scale 1:30 000 000

0 500 1000 km
0 250 500 miles
1 hour

A
B
C
D
1
3
4
5
62°
55°
50°
Faeroe Is
(Denmark)
Norðoyar
Streymoy
Vàgar
Eysturoy
Sandoy
Tuðroyri
Suðuroy
Unst
Shetland Is
(U.K.)
Mainland
Lerwick
Sumburgh Head
Fair Isle
Mainland
Orkney
Islands
Hoy
Kirkwall
John o' Groats
Wick
Butt of Lewis
Cape Wrath
Stornoway
Lewis
Outer Hebrides
North Uist
South Uist
Barra
Barra Head
Skye
Portree
Kyle of Lochalsh
Ullapool
North Minch
North West Highlands
Moray Firth
Inverness
Kinnaird's Head
Ben Macdui
1309
Aberdeen
Mallaig
Fort William
Ben Nevis
1344
Grampian Mountains
Inner Hebrides
Mull
Oban
Jura
Islay
Scotland
Perth
Dundee
Loch Lomond
Glenrothes
Firth of Forth
Greenock
Glasgow
Paisley
Edinburgh
Kilmarnock
Arran
Ayr
Southern Uplands
UNITED
KINGDOM
Dumfries
Newcastle-upon-Tyne
South Shields
Sunderland
Hartlepool
Teesside
Pennine Chain
Carlisle
Whitehaven
977
Scafell Pike
Isle of Man
Douglas
Darlington
Scarborough
Lancaster
Blackpool
Bradford
York
Preston
Leeds
Kingston-upon-Hull
Bolton
Manchester
Birkenhead
Grimsby
Sheffield
Liverpool
Anglesey
Holyhead
Snowdon
1085
Stoke-on-Trent
Derby
Lincoln
The Wash
Wales
Shrewsbury
Stafford
Nottingham
Leicester
Wolverhampton
Dudley
Birmingham
Coventry
Norwich
Lowestoft
England
Cambridge
Northampton
Hereford
Worcester
Ipswich
Gloucester
Oxford
Luton
Swansea
Newport
Rhondda
Cardiff
Bristol
Reading
Southend-on-Sea
LONDON
Ramsgate
Dover
Guildford
Folkestone
Taunton
Southampton
Brighton
Exeter
Portsmouth
Poole
Bournemouth
Isle of Wight
Dartmoor
Torbay
Plymouth
St. Austell
Falmouth
Land's End
Lizard
Isles of Scilly
Bristol Channel
Cambrian Mts
Cardigan Bay
Aberystwyth
Fishguard
Milford Haven
St George's Channel
Irish Sea
North Channel
Malin Head
Londonderry
Donegal Mountains
Donegal Bay
Northern Ireland
Ulster
Larne
Lisburn
Newtownabbey
Bangor
Belfast
Lough Neagh
852
Mullet Peninsula
722
Mountains of Mayo
Sligo
Monaghan
Dundalk
Dundalk Bay
Connaught
Carrick-on-Shannon
REPUBLIC OF IRELAND (EIRE)
(Gaillimh) Galway
DUBLIN (BAILE ATHA CLIATH)
Dún Laoghaire
Port Laoise
Shannon
Boyne
Mouth of the Shannon
Munster
Limerick
(Luimneach)
Arklow
Killarney
Barrow
Boggeragh Mts.
Waterford
(Port Láirge)
Rosslare
Cork
(Corcaigh)
Mizen Head
Celtic Sea
120
2300
1600
2487
294
140
15
10
150
Great Fisher Bank
North Sea
Dogger Bank
Strait of Dover (Pas de Calais)
English Channel
(La Manche)
Cap de la Hague
Cherbourg
Guernsey
Jersey
Channel Islands
(U.K.)
Golfe de Saint-Malo
Ile d'Ouessant
Brest
Saint-Brieuc
Saint-Malo
Bretagne
Quimper
Pointe de Penmarch
Rennes
Bassin de Rennes
Lorient
Vannes
Belle-Ile
Saint-Nazaire
Nantes
Ile de Ré
Ile d'Yeu
Rezé
Bocage Vendéen
La Roche-sur-Yon
Cholet
Angers
Laval
Fougères
Forêt d'Ecouves
Alençon
Le Mans
Normandie
Caen
Le Havre
Lisieux
Rouen
Seine
Collines du Perche
Dreux
Evreux
Saint-Denis
Versailles
PARIS
Chartres
Orléans
Blois
Tours
Loire
Anjou
Touraine
Châtellerault
Châteauroux
Vierzon
Bourges
Nevers
FRANCE
Ile de France
Picardie
Amiens
Abbeville
Dieppe
Beauvais
Creil
Compiègne
Laon
Reims
Marne
Meaux
Épernay
Châlons-sur-Marne
Melun
Troyes
Sens
Auxerre
Yonne
Champagne
Saint-Dizier
Chaumont
Bourgogne
Dijon
Chalon-sur-Saône
Calais
Boulogne
Béthune
Plaine des Flandres
Arras
Somme
Cambrai
Saint-Quentin
Maubeuge
Fourmies
Sedan
Ardennes
Lille
Tourcoing
Dunkerque
BRUXELLES
BELGIUM
Brugge
Oostende
Gent
Antwerpen
Mons
Charleroi
Namur
Liège
Maastricht
Vlissingen
Breda
Tilburg
Dordrecht
Rotterdam
s-Gravenhage
(The Haag)
Leiden
Haarlem
AMSTERDAM
Utrecht
Apeldoorn
Arnhem
Nijmegen
Den Helder
Leeuwarden
NETHERLANDS
Frisian
Bergen
Sotra
Voss
Korsfj
Stord
Haugesund
Karmøy
Bokna
Stavanger
Sandnes
Bryne
Egersund
Fensfjorden
NORWAY
Hardangerfj
ATLANTIC OCEAN

1 foot = 0,30 m
1 meter = 3,28 feet

Scale 1:10 000 000

0 100 200 300 400 500 km
0 100 200 300 miles
1/2 hour

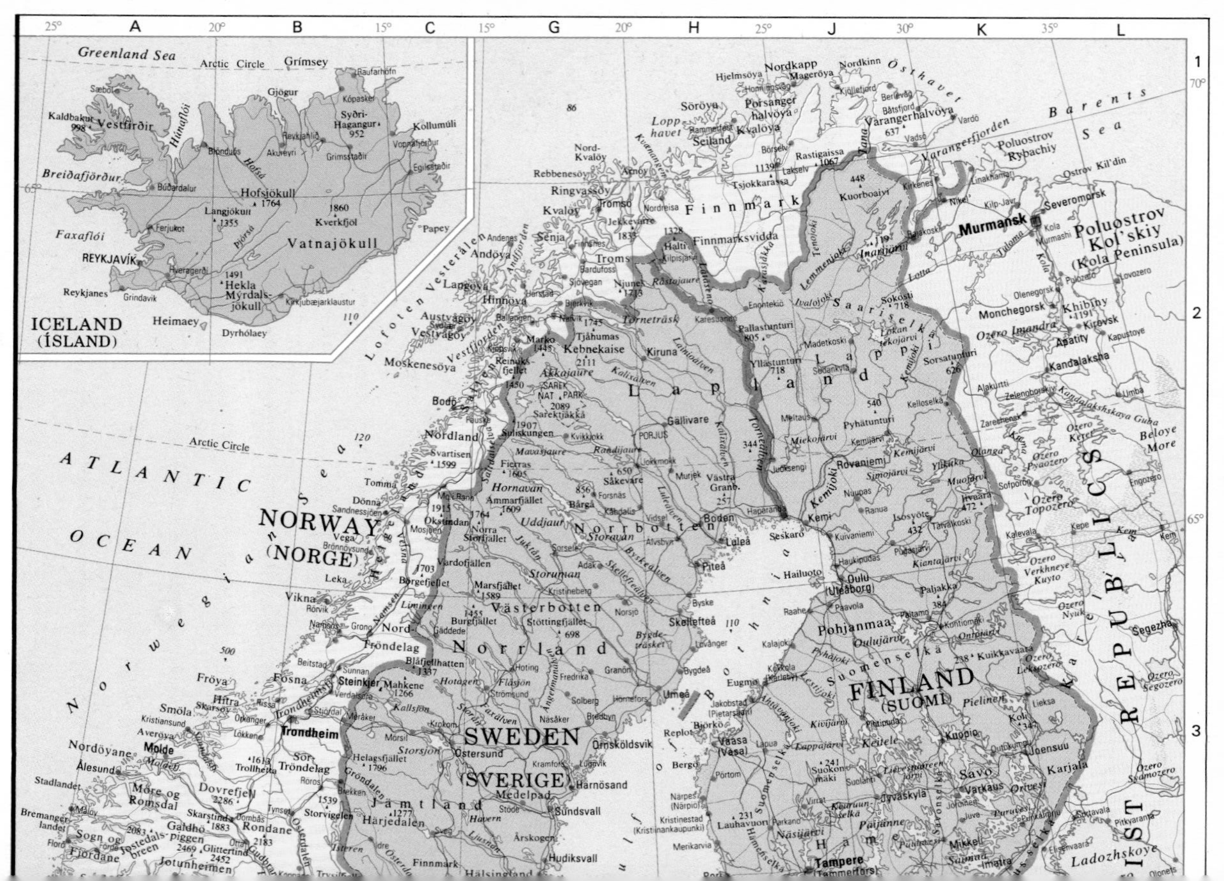
ICELAND
(ÍSLAND)
REYKJAVÍK
Vatnajökull
Hofsjökull
Greenland Sea
Arctic Circle
Grímsey
Heimaey
NORWAY
(NORGE)
SWEDEN
(SVERIGE)
FINLAND
(SUOMI)
ATLANTIC
OCEAN
Barents
Sea
Murmansk
Severomorsk
Poluostrov
Kol'skiy
(Kola Peninsula)
Finnmark
Lappland
Norrbotten
Västerbotten
Norrland
Jämtland
Nordkapp
Tromsø
Kiruna
Bodø
Trondheim
Molde
Ålesund
Östersund
Sundsvall
Umeå
Luleå
Oulu
(Uleåborg)
Vaasa
(Vasa)
Tampere
Kuopio
Joensuu
Savo
Karjala
Lofoten
Vesterålen
Senja
Kvaløy
Sörøya
Jotunheimen
Dovrefjell
Kebnekaise
2111

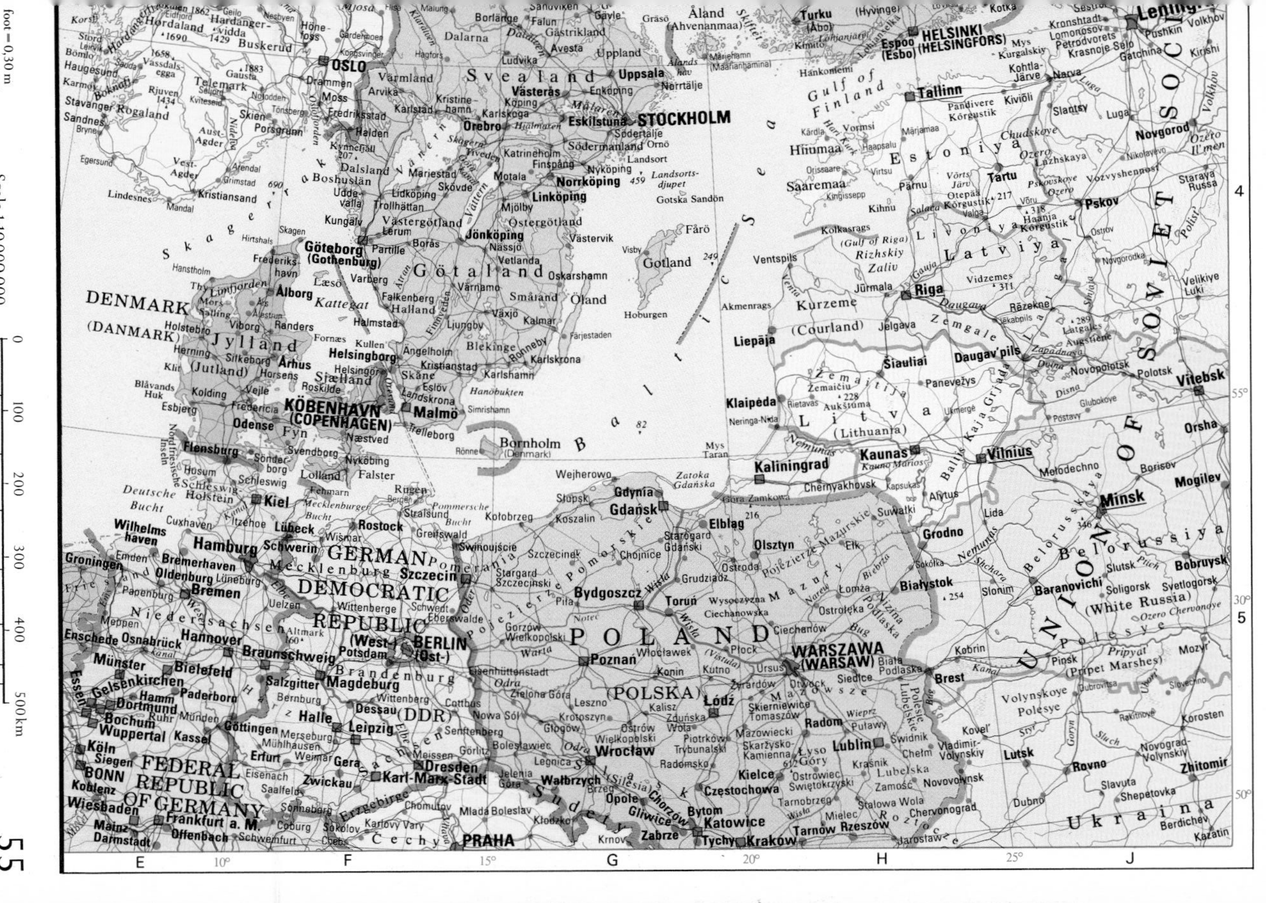

foot = 0,30 m
meter = 3,28 feet

Scale 1:10 000 000

0 100 200 300 400 500 km

0 100 200 300 miles

1/2 hour

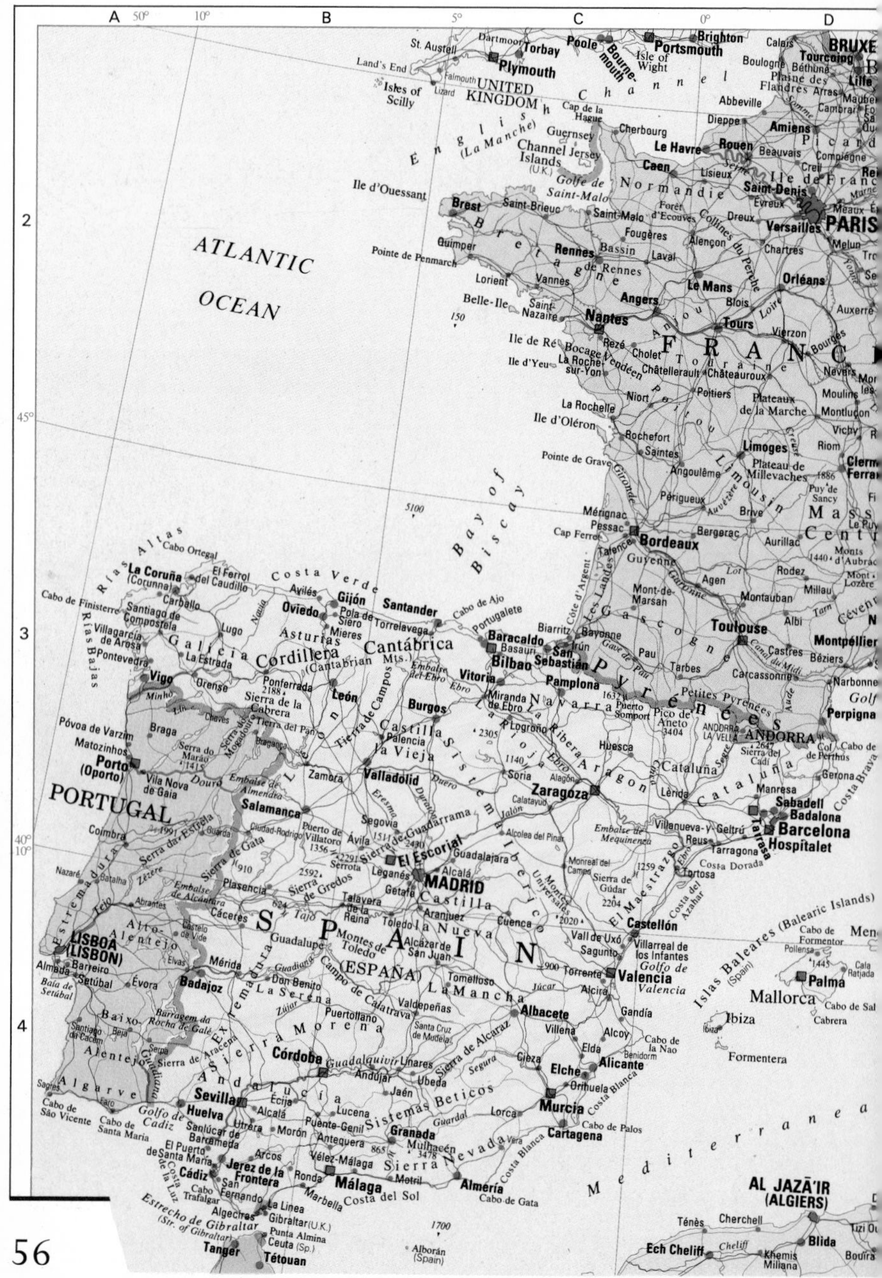
A
B
C
D
2
3
4
50°
10°
5°
0°
45°
40°
ATLANTIC
OCEAN
Bay of Biscay
English Channel
(La Manche)
UNITED
KINGDOM
Land's End
St. Austell
Dartmoor
Torbay
Plymouth
Poole
Bournemouth
Portsmouth
Isle of Wight
Brighton
Isles of Scilly
Falmouth
Lizard
Channel Islands
(U.K.)
Guernsey
Jersey
Cap de la Hague
Cherbourg
Ile d'Ouessant
Brest
Saint-Brieuc
Golfe de Saint-Malo
Saint-Malo
Quimper
Pointe de Penmarch
Bretagne
Rennes
Bassin de Rennes
Lorient
Vannes
Belle-Ile
Saint-Nazaire
Nantes
Ile de Ré
Ile d'Yeu
La Roche-sur-Yon
Bocage Vendéen
Rezé
Cholet
Normandie
Le Havre
Rouen
Caen
Lisieux
Forêt d'Ecouves
Collines du Perche
Fougères
Laval
Alençon
Le Mans
Angers
Anjou
Tours
Blois
Loire
Orléans
Chartres
Dreux
Evreux
Versailles
PARIS
Saint-Denis
Meaux
Melun
Beauvais
Creil
Compiègne
Amiens
Abbeville
Dieppe
Calais
Boulogne
Béthune
Plaine des Flandres
Arras
Lille
Tourcoing
BRUXE
Cambrai
Picardie
Ile de France
FRANCE
Touraine
Châtellerault
Châteauroux
Vierzon
Bourges
Nevers
Poitiers
Poitou
Niort
La Rochelle
Ile d'Oléron
Rochefort
Saintes
Pointe de Grave
Gironde
Angoulême
Limoges
Limousin
Plateaux de la Marche
Plateau de Millevaches
Montluçon
Moulins
Vichy
Riom
Puy de Sancy
1886
Massif Central
Périgueux
Brive
Bergerac
Aurillac
Mérignac
Pessac
Bordeaux
Cap Ferret
Talence
Côte d'Argent
Les Landes
Guyenne
Agen
Lot
Garonne
Mont-de-Marsan
Montauban
Rodez
Millau
Gascogne
Biarritz
Bayonne
Pau
Tarbes
Toulouse
Albi
Castres
Carcassonne
Canal du Midi
Béziers
Montpellier
Narbonne
Perpignan
Golfe du Lion
Pyrénées
Petites Pyrénées
Pic de Aneto
3404
ANDORRA
ANDORRA LA VELLA
Col de Perthus
Cabo de Creus
Costa Brava
Girona
Manresa
Sabadell
Badalona
Barcelona
Hospitalet
Tarrasa
Cataluña
Lérida
Segre
Villanueva-y-Geltrú
Reus
Tarragona
Costa Dorada
Tortosa
Ebro
Rías Altas
Cabo Ortegal
La Coruña
(Corunna)
El Ferrol del Caudillo
Carballo
Cabo de Finisterre
Santiago de Compostela
Rías Bajas
Villagarcía de Arosa
Pontevedra
Vigo
Lugo
Galicia
La Estrada
Orense
Miño
Costa Verde
Avilés
Gijón
Oviedo
Pola de Siero
Mieres
Asturias
Santander
Torrelavega
Cordillera Cantábrica
(Cantabrian Mts.)
Cabo de Ajo
Portugalete
Baracaldo
Basauri
Bilbao
San Sebastián
Irún
Vitoria
Pamplona
Navarra
Embalse del Ebro
Ponferrada
2188
Sierra de la Cabrera
León
Tierra de Campos
Burgos
Miranda de Ebro
Logroño
La Rioja
2305
Puerto Somport
Huesca
Aragón
Castilla la Vieja
Palencia
Sistema Ibérico
Póvoa de Varzim
Matozinhos
Braga
Chaves
Serra do Marão
1415
Porto
(Oporto)
Vila Nova de Gaia
Douro
Bragança
Tierra del Pan
Zamora
Valladolid
Duero
Soria
1140
Zaragoza
Calatayud
Jalón
PORTUGAL
Coimbra
1991
Serra da Estrela
Guarda
Ciudad-Rodrigo
Salamanca
Embalse de Almendra
Puerto de Villatoro
1356
Ávila
Segovia
Sierra de Guadarrama
El Escorial
Guadalajara
Alcolea del Pinar
Embalse de Mequinenza
Nazaré
Batalha
Zêzere
Sierra de Gata
Plasencia
Sierra de Gredos
2592
Serrota
Leganés
MADRID
Alcalá
Getafe
Monreal del Campo
Sierra de Gúdar
2204
1259
El Maestrazgo
Costa del Azahar
Estremadura
Tejo
Abrantes
Embalse de Alcántara
Cáceres
Talavera de la Reina
Tajo
Toledo
Aranjuez
Castilla la Nueva
Cuenca
Montes Universales
2020
Castellón
SPAIN
(ESPAÑA)
LISBOA
(LISBON)
Alto Alentejo
Castelo de Vide
Elvas
Mérida
Guadalupe
Montes de Toledo
Alcázar de San Juan
Vall de Uxó
Sagunto
Villarreal de los Infantes
Golfo de Valencia
Valencia
Torrente
Almada
Barreiro
Setúbal
Baía de Setúbal
Évora
Badajoz
Guadiana
Don Benito
La Serena
Campo de Calatrava
Tomelloso
La Mancha
Júcar
Alcira
Albacete
Gandía
Valdepeñas
Puertollano
Santiago do Cacém
Beja
Baixo Alentejo
Barragem da Rocha de Galé
Serpa
Sierra de Aracena
Sierra Morena
Santa Cruz de Mudela
Sierra de Alcaraz
Villena
Alcoy
Elda
Alicante
Cabo de la Nao
Benidorm
Córdoba
Guadalquivir
Andújar
Linares
Ubeda
Segura
Cieza
Elche
Orihuela
Costa Blanca
Murcia
Algarve
Sagres
Faro
Cabo de São Vicente
Cabo de Santa Maria
Golfo de Cadiz
Huelva
Sevilla
Ecija
Alcalá
Lucena
Jaén
Andalucía
Sistemas Beticos
Guadal
Lorca
Cartagena
Cabo de Palos
Sanlúcar de Barrameda
Utrera
Morón
Puente-Genil
Antequera
Granada
Mulhacén
3478
865
El Puerto de Santa María
Costa de la Luz
Arcos
Jerez de la Frontera
Vélez-Málaga
Sierra Nevada
Vera
Cádiz
San Fernando
Cabo Trafalgar
Ronda
Málaga
Motril
Almería
Cabo de Gata
Marbella
Costa del Sol
Algeciras
La Linea
Gibraltar (U.K.)
Estrecho de Gibraltar
(Str. of Gibraltar)
Punta Almina
Ceuta (Sp.)
Tanger
Tétouan
1700
Alborán
(Spain)
5100
150
Islas Baleares (Balearic Islands)
(Spain)
Cabo de Formentor
Pollensa
1445
Cala Ratjada
Palma
Mallorca
Cabo de Salinas
Cabrera
Ibiza
Formentera
Menorca
Mediterranean
AL JAZĀ'IR
(ALGIERS)
Ténès
Cherchell
Ech Cheliff
Cheliff
Khemis Miliana
Blida

5°
E
10°
F
15°
G
20°
H
50°
2
3
4
45°
20°
40°
Ottava
New York
FEDERAL REPUBLIC OF GERMANY
(BUNDESREPUBLIK DEUTSCHLAND)
Köln
Siegen
BONN
Koblenz
Wiesbaden
Aachen
Liège
Namur
Frankfurt a. M.
Offenbach
Mainz
Darmstadt
Ludwigshafen
Mannheim
Heidelberg
Kaiserslautern
Saarbrücken
Karlsruhe
Pforzheim
Heilbronn
Stuttgart
Baden-Baden
Würzburg
Nürnberg (Nuremberg)
Fürth
Regensburg
Bayern (Bavaria)
Augsburg
München (Munich)
Freiburg
Schwenningen
Biberach
Memmingen
Kaufbeuren
Schaffhausen
Konstanz
Bodensee
Lindau
Garmisch-Partenkirchen
Zugspitze
2963
Eisenach
Saalfeld
Zwickau
Sonneberg
Coburg
Sokolov
Cheb
Bayreuth
Weiden
Schweinfurt
Aalen
Heidenheim
Landshut
Passau
Erzgebirge
Chomutov
Karlovy Vary
Mladá Boleslav
Kłodzko
PRAHA (PRAGUE)
Pardubice
Čechy (Bohemia)
Plzeň
Příbram
Písek
Tábor
České Budějovice
Šumava
Böhmerwald
Straubing
Česká země
CZECHOSLOVAKIA
Morava
Brno
Znojmo
Šumperk
Krnov
Ostrava
Olomouc
Zabrze
Rybnik
Tychy
Jastrzębie Zdrój
Bielsko-Biała
Nowy Sącz
Beskidy Zachodnie
Tatry
Vsetín
Žilina
Ružomberok
Uherské Hradiště
Trenčín
Banská Bystrica
Zvolen
Piešťany
Trnava
Nitra
Lučenec
Ozd
Miskolc
Mátra 1015
Gyöngyös
Bratislava
Esztergom
Vác
Komárno
Győr
BUDAPEST
Jászberény
Szolnok
Tatabánya
Pápa
Bakony
Érd
Székesfehérvár
HUNGARY (MAGYARORSZÁG)
Dunaújváros
Szentes
Szombathely
Sopron
Balaton
Dunántúl
Zalaegerszeg
Szekszárd
Szeged
Kaposvár
Baja
Pécs
Senta
Nagykanizsa
WIEN (VIENNA)
Wiener Neustadt
2075
980 Semmering
Kapfenberg
Sankt Pölten
Linz
Wels
Steyr
Traun
Inn
Salzburg
Rosenheim
Kufstein
AUSTRIA
Niedere Tauern
Graz
Raab
Zell am See
Innsbruck
3797
Grossglockner
Tirol
1375 Brenner
Lienz
Klagenfurt
Villach
Maribor
Mura
Drau
1368 Ljubelj
Luxembourg
LUXEMBOURG
Trier
Ardennes
Eifel
Mosel
Metz
Verdun
Marne
Nancy
Lorraine
Saint-Dizier
Épinal
Strasbourg
Vosges
Schwarzwald
Rhein
Donau
Mulhouse
Belfort
Montbéliard
Basel
Winterthur
Zürich
St Gallen
VADUZ
LIECHTENSTEIN
Biel
Luzern
Neuchâtel
BERN (BERNE)
SWITZERLAND
Chur
Dijon
Besançon
Dole
Saône
Jura
Lausanne
L. Léman
Genève
Montreux
Berner Alpen
2108 Sankt Gotthard Pass
Rhône
St Moritz
4049 Bernina
Matterhorn 4478
Locarno
Lugano
L. Maggiore
Thonon
Bourg
Annecy
Villefranche
Lyon
Vienne
Mont Blanc 4810
Aosta
Chambéry
Grenoble
Massif du Pelvoux
4103
Romans-sur-Isère
Dauphiné
Gap
Ivrea
Chivasso
Rivoli
Pinerolo
Torino (Turin)
The Alps
Alpi
Dolomitiche
3736
Merano
3902
Bolzano
Adige
Belluno
Alpi Carniche
Udine
Kranj
Celje
Ljubljana
Slovenija
Monfalcone
Trieste
Vittorio Veneto
Trento
Rovereto
Lago di Garda
Treviso
San Donà di Piave
Venezia (Venice)
Padova
Vicenza
Verona
Brescia
Bergamo
Como
Monza
Milano (Milan)
Varese
Legnano
Novara
Vigevano
Cremona
Legnago
Chioggia
Rovigo
Mantova
Ferrara
Po
Piacenza
Parma
Vercelli
Voghera
Alessandria
Novi Ligure
Reggio nell' Emilia
Modena
Bologna
Ravenna
Foci del Po
Gulf of Venice
Rt Kamenjak
Istra
Pula
Cres
Krk
Rijeka
Lošinj
Karlovac
Zagreb
Bilo Gora
Hrvatska (Croatia)
Osijek
Drava
Sisak
Novi Sad
Vukovar
Vinkovci
Dilj
Slavonski Brod
Sremska Mitrovica
Sava
Brčko
Bijeljina
Šabac
Tuzla
507 Petrova Gora
Bihać
Banja Luka
Grmeč
Borja 1077
Kvarner
Pag
Gračac
Zadar
YUGOSLAVIA
Bosna
Zenica
Sarajevo
Dinara Planina
2116
Jablanica
Vran
Bjelašnica
1533
Kovač
Mostar
Velež 1969
Ploče
Viduša
Nikšić
Šibenik
Split
Dugi Otok
Rt Ploča
Brač
Hvar
Korčula
Pelješac
Mljet
Dubrovnik
Alba
Fossano
Cuneo
Mont Pelat
1908
Mont Ventoux 1909
Avignon
Durance
Salon-de-Provence
Provence
Monte Carlo
MONACO
San Remo
Nice
Cannes
Côte d'Azur
Fréjus
Aix-en-Provence
Marseille
Toulon
La Seyne-sur-Mer
Îles d'Hyères
Cap Camarat
Genova (Genoa)
Chiavari
Riviera di Ponente
Riviera di Levante
Golfo di Genova
Ligurian Sea
La Spezia
Sassuolo
2165
Appennino Tosco-Emiliano
Faenza
Forlì
Rimini
SAN MARINO
Pesaro
Prato
Pisa
Firenze (Florence)
Livorno
Arezzo
Siena
Toscana
Fabriano
Ancona
Civitanova Marche
Macerata
Marche
Assisi
Perugia
Umbria
Ascoli Piceno
Teramo
Grosseto
Elba
L. di Bolsena
Tevere (Tiber)
Gran Sasso d'Italia
2914
L'Aquila
Pescara
Montesilvano
Abruzzo
Lanciano
Vasto
Terni
Adriatic Sea
Cap Corse
Bastia
Calvi
Monte Cinto 2710
Corse (Corsica)
(Fr.)
Monte d'Oro 2391
Aléria
Ajaccio
Porto-Vecchio
Strait of Bonifacio
Capo Testa
Giglio
Montecristo
Civitavecchia
CITTÀ DEL VATICANO
ROMA (ROME)
ITALY (ITALIA)
Sora
Albano Laziale
Nettuno
Terracina
Gaeta
Cassino
Caserta
Benevento
Capo Circeo
Isole Ponziane
Mondragone
Napoli (Naples)
Ischia
Vesuvio 1277
Pompei
Capri
Salerno
Golfo di Salerno
Eboli
Lucera
Foggia
Promontorio del Gargano
San Severo
Manfredonia
Barletta
Canosa
Bari
Gioia
Fasano
Brindisi
Gravina
Matera
Massafra
Taranto
Penisola Salentina
Lecce
Galatina
Golfo di Taranto
Potenza
Sirino 2005
Appennino Lucano
Lauria
2248
Corigliano
Capo Santa Maria di Leuca
Capo Palinuro
Calabro
Rossano
Acri
1928
Cosenza
Crotone
Calabria
Lamezia Terme
Catanzaro
Golfo di Squillace
Vibo Valentia
Appennino Calabro
Siderno
Isole Eolie o Lipari
Lipari
Messina
Milazzo
Barcellona
Stretto di Messina
Reggio di Calabria
Tyrrhenian Sea
3500
Asinara
Tavolara
Olbia
Sassari
1259 Monti di Ala
Alghero
Sardegna (Sardinia) (Italia)
Tirso
Nuoro
Oristano
La Marmora 1834
Arbatax
Capo San Marco
Campidano
Quartu Sant' Elena
Iglesias
Carbonia
Cagliari
Sant' Antioco
Capo Spartivento
Capo Carbonara
Sicilia (Sicily)
Capo Gallo
Palermo
Trapani
Segesta
Marsala
Castelvetrano
Caltanissetta
Etna 3340
Adrano
Catania
Selinunte
Sciacca
Agrigento
Salso
Lentini
Siracusa
Licata
Gela
Avola
Scicli
Capo Passero
Canale di Sicilia
Canale di Malta
Pantelleria
San Dimitri Point
Gozo
MALTA
VALLETTA
Linosa
Sea
Jālitah
Ra's al Abyaḑ
Banzart (Bizerta)
Ra's at Tīb
Manzil Bū Ruqaybah
Cap de Fer
Skikda
Annaba
Jijel
Bejaïa
Azzaba
Bājah
TŪNIS
Nābul
Guelma
Souk Ahras
Sétif
Constantine
El Eulma
Zaghwān

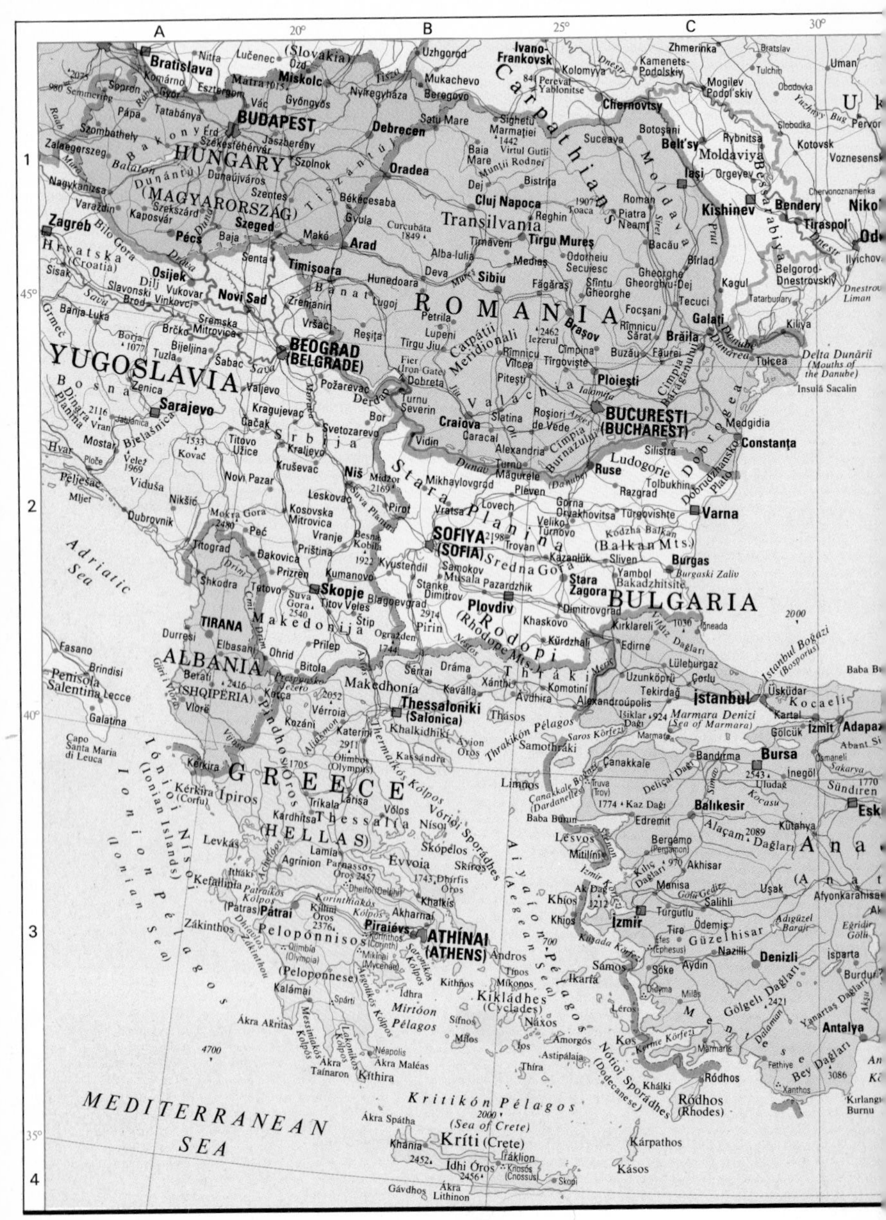

THE BALKANS

1 foot = 0,30 m
1 meter = 3,28 feet

Scale 1:10 000 000

0 100 200 300 400 500 km

0 100 200 300 miles

1/2 hour

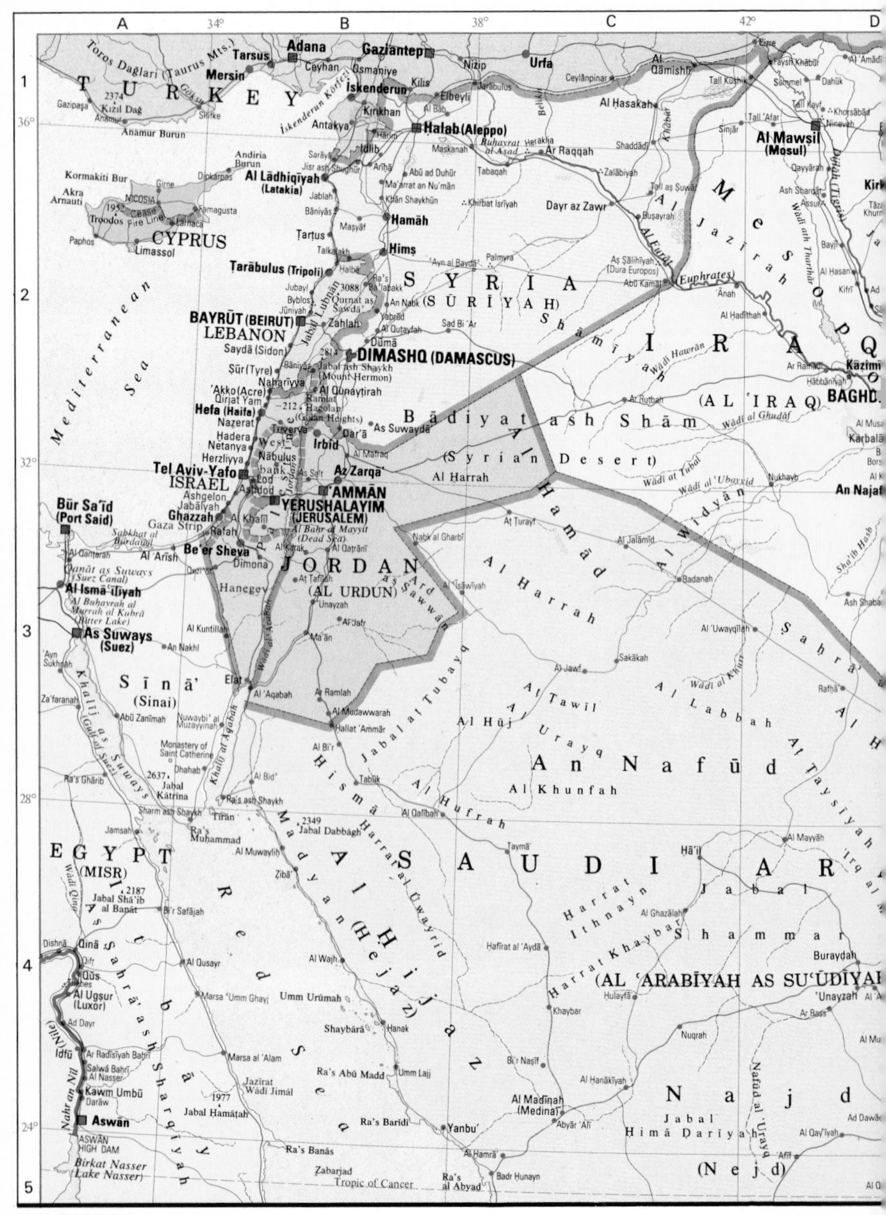

 THE MIDDLE EAST

1 foot = 0,30 m
1 meter = 3,28 feet

Scale 1:10 000 0

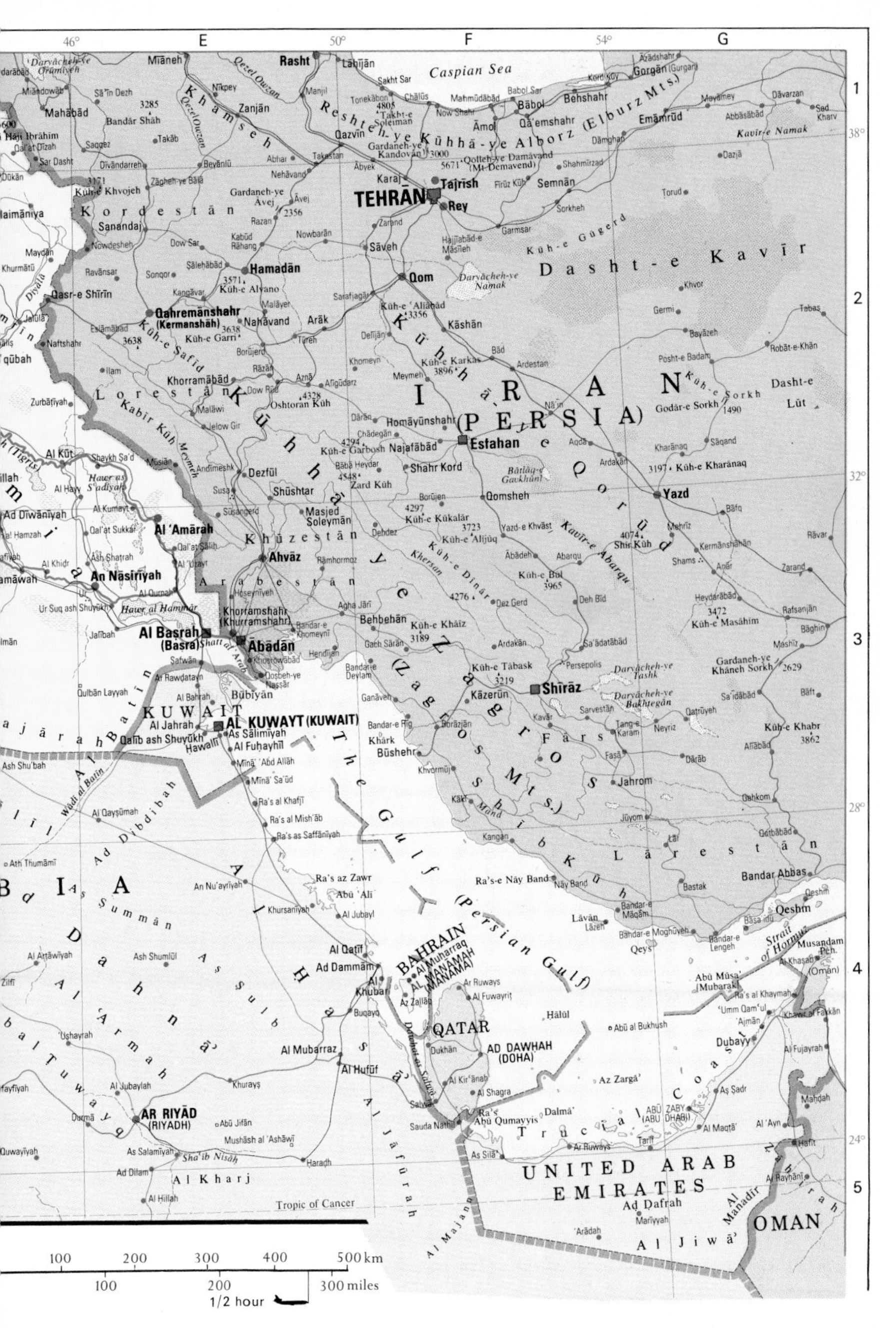
46°
E
50°
F
54°
G
1
2
3
4
5
38°
32°
28°
24°
Caspian Sea
Rasht
Lāhījān
Mīāneh
Gorgān
Behshahr
Bābol
Āmol
Qā'emshahr
Emāmrūd
Semnān
Dāmghān
Mahābād
Zanjān
Qazvīn
Karaj
Tajrīsh
TEHRĀN
Rey
Kavīr-e Namak
Reshteh-ye Kūhhā-ye Alborz (Elburz Mts.)
Qolleh-ye Damāvand (Mt Demavend)
5671
Khamseh
Kordestān
Sanandaj
Hamadān
Sāveh
Qom
Dasht-e Kavīr
Daryācheh-ye Namak
Kūh-e Gūgerd
Qasr-e Shīrīn
Qahremānshahr (Kermanshāh)
Nahāvand
Arāk
Kāshān
Kūhrūd
Khorramābād
Lorestān
Kabīr Kūh
Dezfūl
Shūshtar
Masjed Soleymān
Khūzestān
Ahvāz
Arabestān
Esfahān
Najafābād
Shahr Kord
Zard Kūh
Homāyūnshahr
Qomsheh
IRAN (PERSIA)
Yazd
Dasht-e Lūt
Kūh-e Sorkh
Kūh-e Dīnār
Al Kūt
Al 'Amārah
An Nāsirīyah
Ad Dīwānīyah
Hawr al Hammār
Al Basrah (Basra)
Khorramshahr (Khurramshahr)
Ābādān
Shatt al 'Arab
Bubīyān
KUWAIT
AL KUWAYT (KUWAIT)
Al Jahrah
Behbehān
Bandar-e Deylam
Khārk
Būshehr
Kāzerūn
Persepolis
Shīrāz
Fārs
Jahrom
Zagros Mts.
Lārestān
Bandar 'Abbās
Qeshm
Strait of Hormuz
Kermān
Rafsanjān
Kūh-e Masāhim
Kūh-e Khabr
Āb Khvorān
The Gulf (Persian Gulf)
Ras az Zawr
Al Jubayl
Al Qatīf
Ad Dammām
BAHRAIN
AL MANĀMAH (MANAMA)
Al Khubar
QATAR
AD DAWHAH (DOHA)
Dukhān
Al Hufūf
Al Mubarraz
Al Hasā
Ad Dahnā
As Summān
ARABIA
AR RIYĀD (RIYADH)
Al Kharj
Tropic of Cancer
Trucial Coast
Dubayy
ABŪ ZABY (ABU DHABI)
'Ajmān
Ra's al Khaymah
Musandam Pen. (Oman)
Al Fujayrah
UNITED ARAB EMIRATES
Ad Dafrah
Al Jiwā'
OMAN
100 200 300 400 500 km
100 200 300 miles
1/2 hour

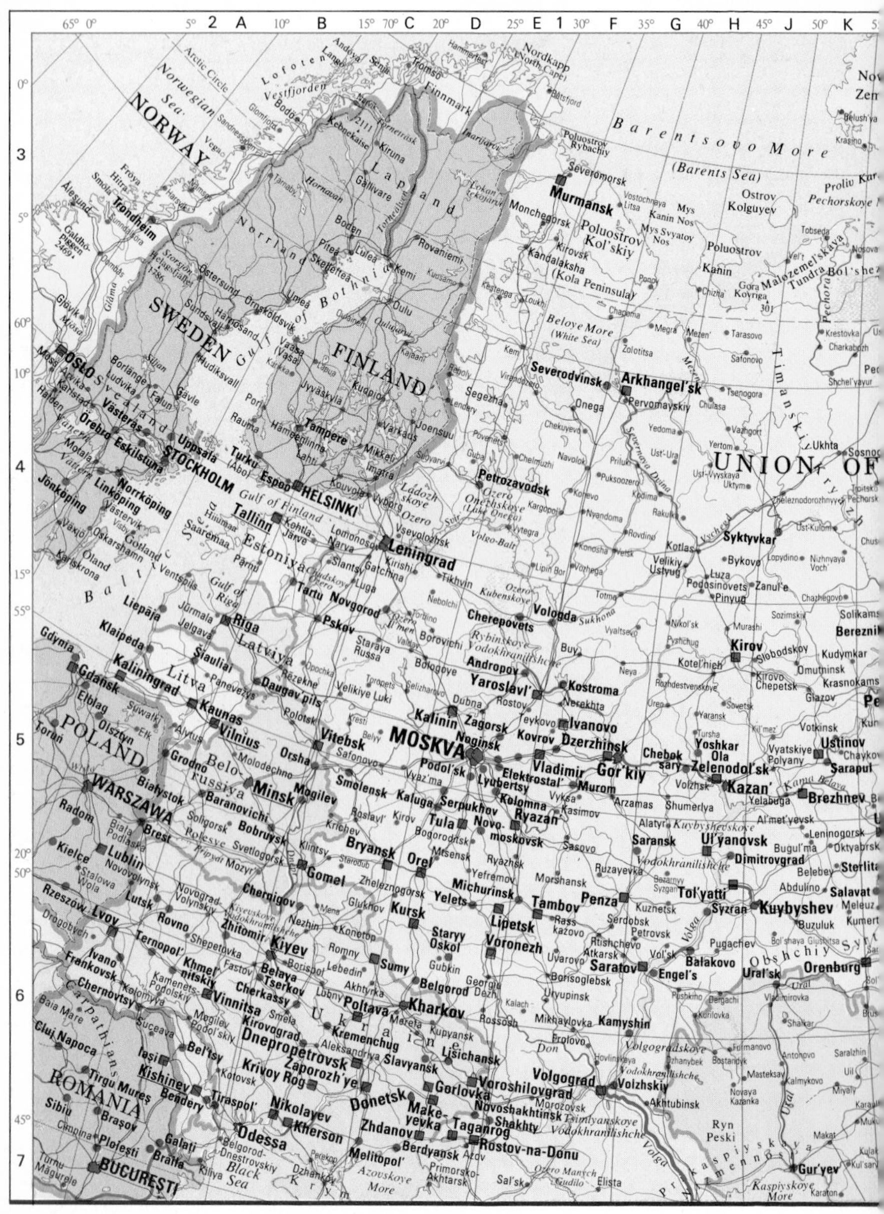

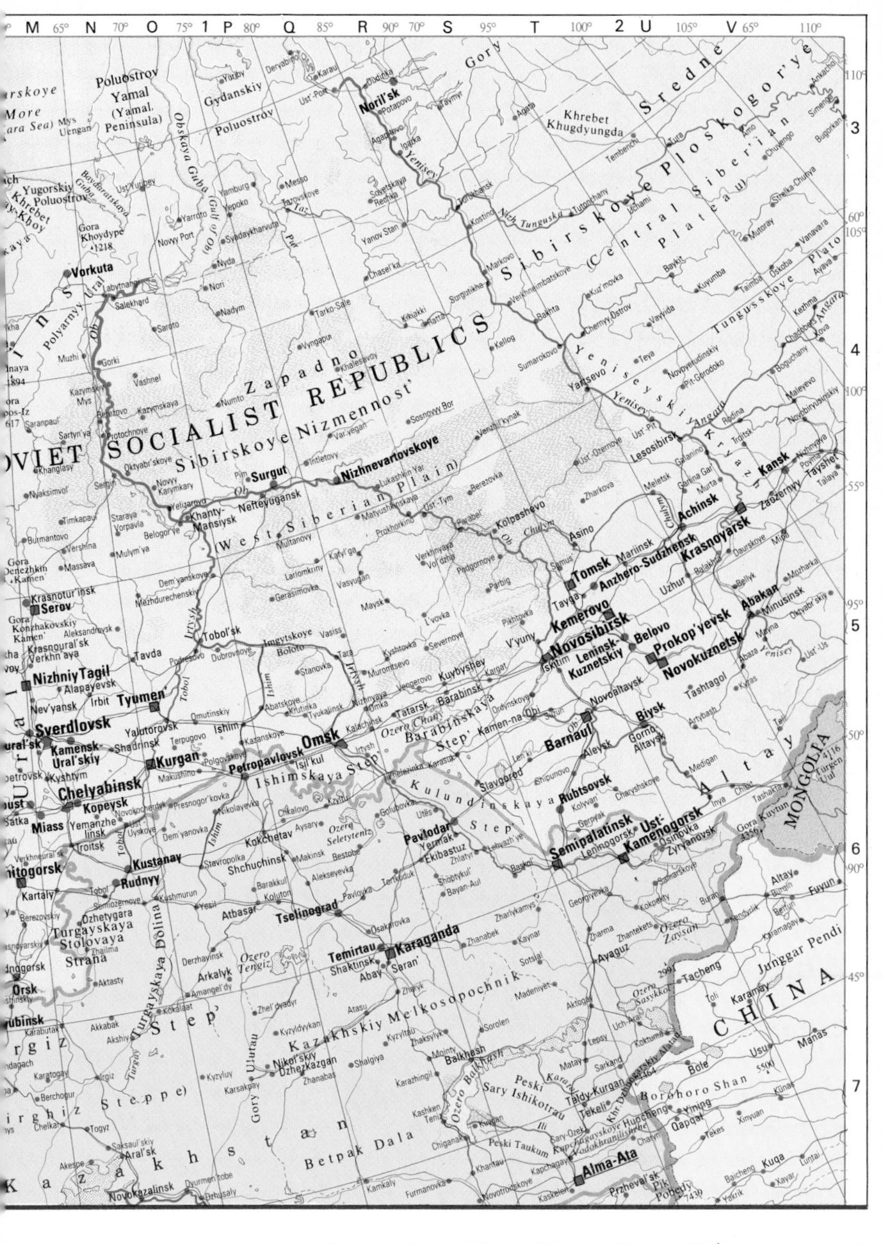

foot = 0,30 m
meter = 3,28 feet

Scale 1:20 000 000

0 200 400 600 800 1000 km
0 200 400 600 miles
1 hour

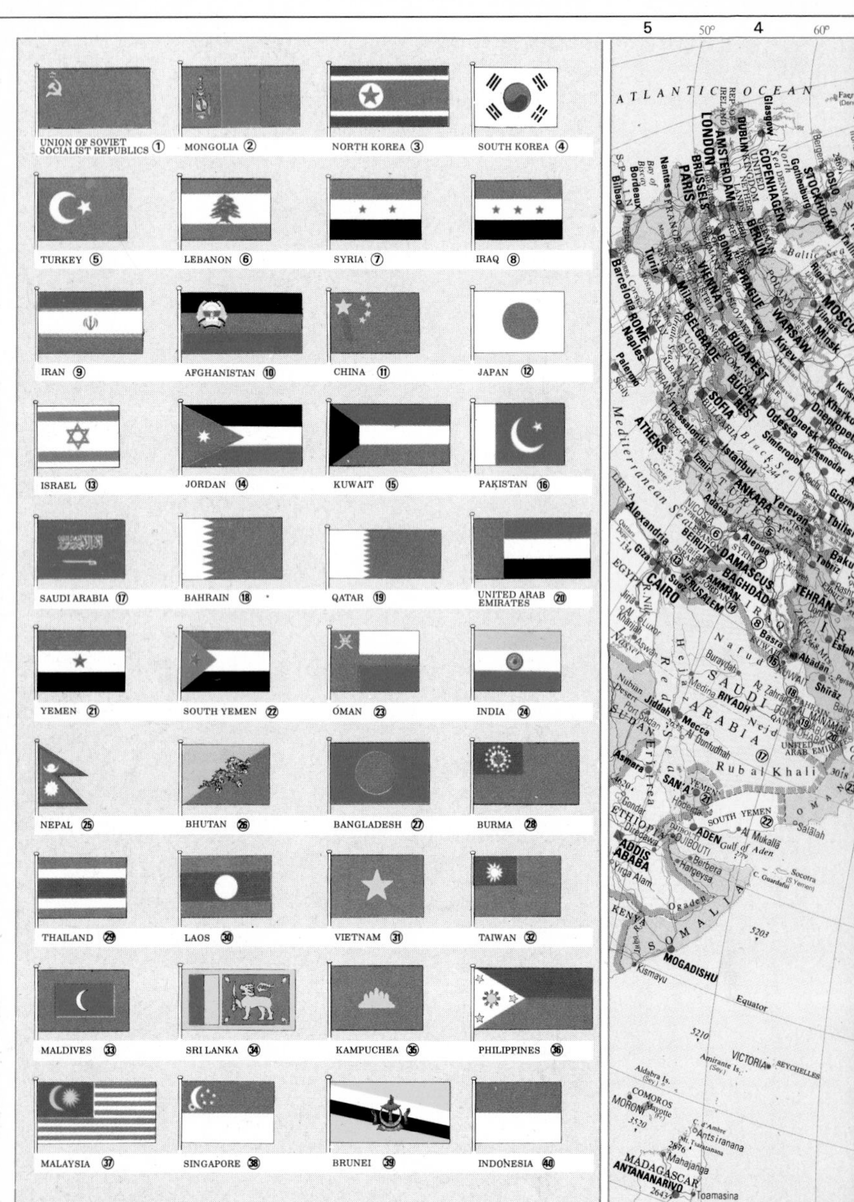

UNION OF SOVIET SOCIALIST REPUBLICS ①
MONGOLIA ②
NORTH KOREA ③
SOUTH KOREA ④
TURKEY ⑤
LEBANON ⑥
SYRIA ⑦
IRAQ ⑧
IRAN ⑨
AFGHANISTAN ⑩
CHINA ⑪
JAPAN ⑫
ISRAEL ⑬
JORDAN ⑭
KUWAIT ⑮
PAKISTAN ⑯
SAUDI ARABIA ⑰
BAHRAIN ⑱
QATAR ⑲
UNITED ARAB EMIRATES ⑳
YEMEN ㉑
SOUTH YEMEN ㉒
OMAN ㉓
INDIA ㉔
NEPAL ㉕
BHUTAN ㉖
BANGLADESH ㉗
BURMA ㉘
THAILAND ㉙
LAOS ㉚
VIETNAM ㉛
TAIWAN ㉜
MALDIVES ㉝
SRI LANKA ㉞
KAMPUCHEA ㉟
PHILIPPINES ㊱
MALAYSIA ㊲
SINGAPORE ㊳
BRUNEI ㊴
INDONESIA ㊵
5
50°
4
60°
ATLANTIC OCEAN
LONDON
PARIS
BRUSSELS
AMSTERDAM
COPENHAGEN
STOCKHOLM
BERLIN
PRAGUE
VIENNA
WARSAW
BUDAPEST
BELGRADE
ROME
ATHENS
SOFIA
Istanbul
ANKARA
NICOSIA
BEIRUT
DAMASCUS
BAGHDAD
TEHRAN
AMMAN
JERUSALEM
CAIRO
Alexandria
RIYADH
Mecca
Jiddah
SAUDI ARABIA
Rub al Khali
SAN'A
ADEN
SOUTH YEMEN
Gulf of Aden
ADDIS ABABA
ETHIOPIA
DJIBOUTI
SOMALIA
MOGADISHU
KENYA
Equator
VICTORIA
SEYCHELLES
COMOROS
MORONI
MADAGASCAR
ANTANANARIVO
Toamasina
Mahajanga
Antsiranana

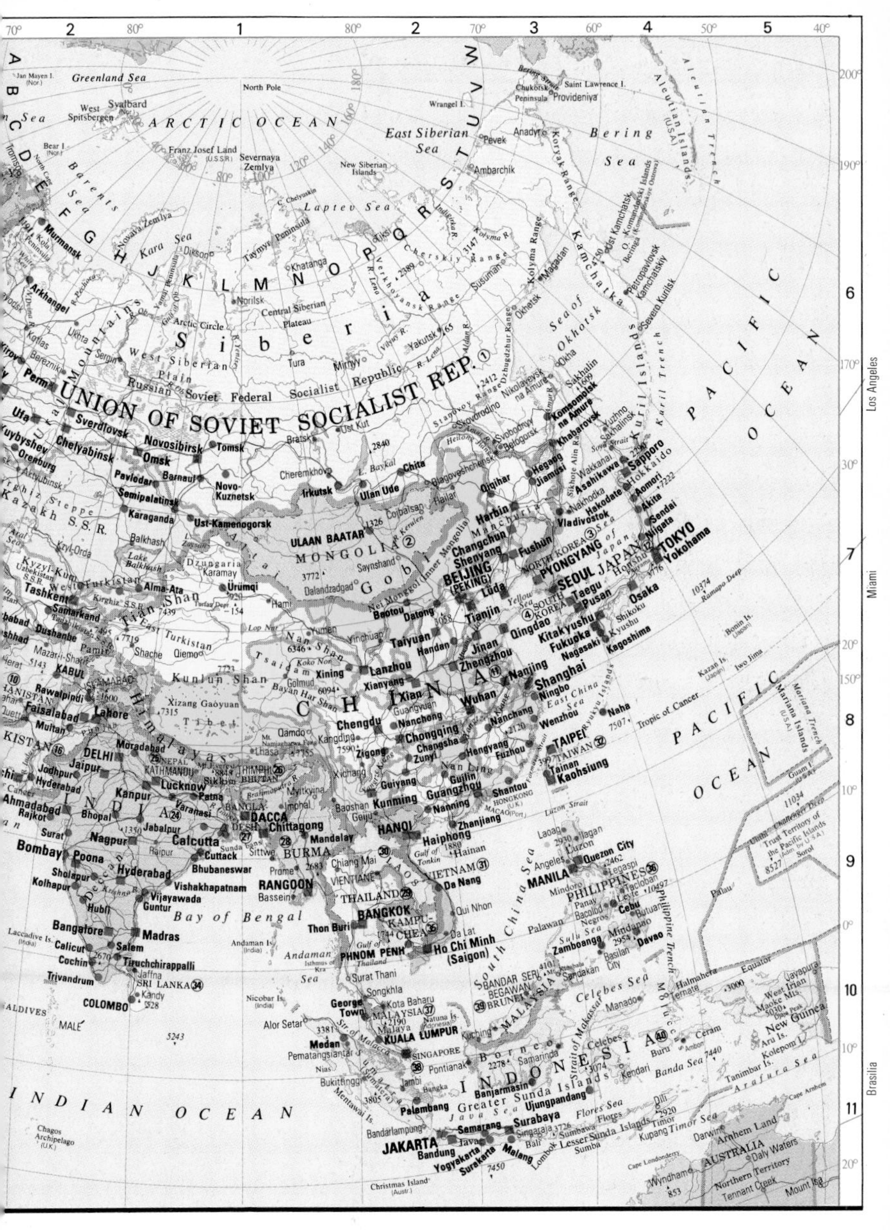

oot = 0,30 m
neter = 3,28 feet

Scale 1:75 000 000

0 1000 2000 km
0 400 800 1200 miles
1 hour

30°
A
35°
B
40°
C
45°
D
50°
E
55°
F
1
2
3
4
5
6
Galati
Brăila
Odessa
Nikolayev
Kherson
Donetsk
Gorlovka
Makeyevka
Zhdanov
Voroshilovgrad
Volgograd
Volzhskiy
Taganrog
Novoshakhtinsk
Shakhty
Rostov-na-Donu
Melitopol'
Berdyansk
Constanța
Sevastopol'
Simferopol'
Kerch
Krasnodar
Novorossiysk
Armavir
Maykop
Stavropol'
Astrakhan
Gur'yev
Aktyubinsk
Black Sea
Azovskoye More
Kaspiyskoye More
Elista
Sochi
Pyatigorsk
Sukhumi
Nal'chik
Ordzhonikidze
Groznyy
Makhachkala
Batumi
Kutaisi
Tbilisi
Rustavi
Kirovabad
Leninakan
Kirovakan
Yerevan
Sumgait
Baku
Krasnovodsk
Shevchenko
UNION OF SOVIET
Gruziya
Armeniya
Azerbaydzhan
Bol'shoy Kavkaz (Caucasus Mts.)
Caspian Sea
Plato Ustyurt
Zaliv Kara-Bogaz Gol
Turkmeni
ANKARA
Samsun
Trabzon
Erzurum
Kayseri
Konya
Malatya
Elazığ
Diyarbakır
Urfa
Gaziantep
Kahramanmaraş
Adana
Tarsus
Mersin
İskenderun
TURKEY
Van Gölü
Halab (Aleppo)
Al Lādhiqīyah
Ḥamāh
Ḥimṣ
Ṭarābulus
BAYRŪT (BEIRUT)
LEBANON
SYRIA (SŪRĪYAH)
DIMASHQ (DAMASCUS)
Tel Aviv-Yafo
YERUSHALAYIM (JERUSALEM)
'AMMĀN
JORDAN (AL URDUN)
Al Mawṣil (Mosul)
Kirkūk
BAGHDĀD
IRAQ
Mesopotamia
An Najaf
Al 'Amārah
An Nāṣirīyah
Al Baṣrah (Basra)
Abādān
KUWAIT
AL KUWAYT
Tabrīz
Orūmīyeh
Rasht
TEHRĀN
Qom
Hamadān
Eṣfahān
Shīrāz
Yazd
Kermān
Mashhad
IRAN (PERSIA)
Dasht-e Kavīr
Dasht-e Lut
Khorāsān
Kūhhā-ye Alborz (Elburz Mts.)
Kūhhā-ye Zāgros (Zagros Mts.)
Khūzestān
SAUDI ARABIA (AL 'ARABĪYAH AS SU'ŪDĪYAH)
An Nafūd
Al Hijāz (Hejaz)
Najd (Nejd)
Al Ḥasā
Ad Dahnā
AR RIYĀD (RIYADH)
Al Madīnah
Yanbu'
Tropic of Cancer
Red Sea
BAHRAIN
AL MANĀMAH
QATAR
AD DAWḤAH (DOHA)
Trucial Coast
UNITED ARAB EMIRATES
ABŪ ẒABY
Dubayy
OMAN
Strait of Hormuz
Gulf of Oman
The Gulf

ot = 0,30 m
eter = 3,28 feet

Scale 1:20 000 000

0 200 400 600 800 1000 km
0 200 400 600 miles
1 hour

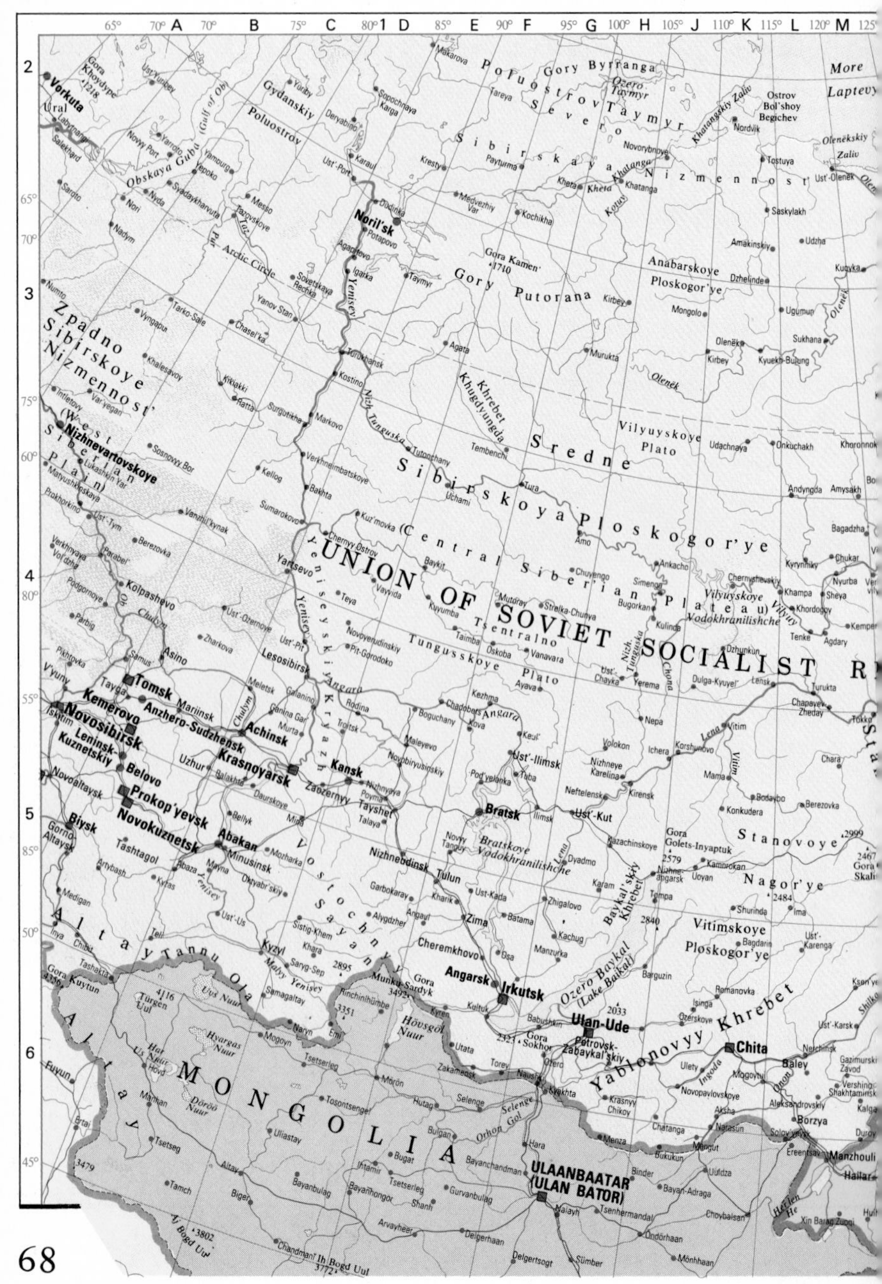
UNION OF SOVIET SOCIALIST R
MONGOLIA
Sredne Sibirskoya Ploskogor'ye (Central Siberian Plateau)
Zpadno Sibirskoye Nizmennost' (West Siberian Plain)
Poluostrov Taymyr
Severo Sibirskaya Nizmennost'
Gory Byrranga
Gory Putorana
Anabarskoye Ploskogor'ye
Vilyuyskoye Plato
Tungusskoye Plato
Vostochnyy Sayan
Altay
Tannu Ola
Stanovoye Nagor'ye
Vitimskoye Ploskogor'ye
Yablonovyy Khrebet
Ozero Baykal (Lake Baikal)
Arctic Circle
Obskaya Guba (Gulf of Ob)
More Laptevy
Vorkuta
Noril'sk
Tomsk
Kemerovo
Novosibirsk
Leninsk-Kuznetskiy
Belovo
Prokop'yevsk
Novokuznetsk
Biysk
Nizhnevartovskoye
Anzhero-Sudzhensk
Achinsk
Krasnoyarsk
Kansk
Abakan
Bratsk
Angarsk
Irkutsk
Ulan-Ude
Chita
ULAANBAATAR (ULAN BATOR)
Manzhouli

135° P 140° Q 145° R 150° S 155° T 1 160° U 165° V 170° W 175° 2 X 180° 65° Y
3
4
5
6
180°
175°
60°
170°
165°
55°
160°
50°
155°
45°
Ostrov Kotel'nyy
O. Malyy Lyakhovskiy
Ostrov Bol'shoy Lyakhovskiy
Lyakhovskiye Ostrova
Mys Svatoy Nos
Mys Buorkhaya
Yanskiy Zaliv
Guba Buorkhaya
Yano-Indigirskaya Nizmennost
Indigirka
Khrebet Cherskogo (Cherskiy Range)
Kolymskaya Nizmennost
Indigirskaya Nizmennost
Gora Khil'mi 914
Kolyma
Omolon
Severnyy Anyuyskiy Khrebet
Anadyrskoye Ploskogor'ye
Arctic Circle
Anadyrskaja Nizmennost
Anadyrskiy Zaliv
Mys Navarin
Yukagirskoye Ploskogor'ye
Oloyskiye Gory
Kolymskiy Khrebet (Kolyma Range)
Penzhinskiy Khrebet
Koryakskiy Khrebet
Kryazh Kula
Gora Syuge-Khaya 1059
Momskiy Khrebet
Gora Pobeda 3147
Verkhoyanskiy Khrebet (Verkhoyansk Range)
Verkhoyansk
Batagay-Alyta
2389
Gora Ezop 2038
Kolymskoye Nagor'ye
Penzhinskaya Guba
Gizhiginskaya Guba
Mys Taygonos
Bering Sea
Mys Olyutorskiy
Gora Nelkuchan 1627
Gora Taklaun 2341
Khrebet Suntar Khayata
Zaliv Shelikhova
Mys Tolstoy
Sredinnyy Khrebet
Sopka Shiveluch 3283
Mys Kronotskiy
Khandyga
Aldan
Yakutsk
Magadan
Ostrov Zav'yalova
Poluostrov Koni
Mys Yuzhnyy
Khr. Sette Daban
Mys Duga-Zapadnaya
Okhotsk
Ichinskaya Sopka 3621
Kronotskaya Sopka 3528
BLICS
Amga
Khrebet Dzhugdzhur (Dzhugdzhur Range)
1402 Nitiya
Okhotskoye More (Sea of Okhotsk)
Poluostrov Kamchatka
Petropavlovsk-Kamchatskiy
Yelizovo
Mys Shipunskiy
Aldanskoye Nagor'ye
Gora Golets Skalistyy 2482
Ayan
Shantarskiye Ostrova
Ostrov Bol'shoy Shantar
Ostrov Feklistova
Mys Yelizavety
Kambal'naya Sopka 2156
Mys Lopatka
Stanovoy Khrebet
Tynda
Zaliv Akademii
Sakhalinskiy Zaliv
Okha
Ostrov Paramushir
Khrebet Dzhagdy
Nikolayevsk-na-Amure
Ostrov Onekotan
Ostrov Shiashkotan
Zeya
Khrebet Turana
Khrebet Bureinskiy
Khrebet Chayatyn
Amur
Proliv Nevel'skogo
Sakhalin
Kuril'skiye Ostrova (Kuril Is) (USSR)
O. Matua
O. Rasshua
O. Ketoy
Ostrov Simushir
Ostrova Chernyye Brat'ya
Heilong Jiang
Komsomol'sk-na-Amure
Svobodnyy
Belogorsk
Blagoveshchensk
Zaliv Terpeniya
Mys Terpeniya
Xiao Hinggan Ling
Sikhote Alin
Tatarskiy Proliv
Birobidzhan
Khabarovsk
Ostrov Urup
Yuzhno-Sakhalinsk
Kholmsk
Korsakov
Mys Aniva 720
Mys Kril'on
CHINA
Nenjiang
Nehe
Bei'an
Yichun
Hegang
Jiamusi
Fujin
Qiqihar
Gora Medvezh'ya 1556
Ostrov Iturup

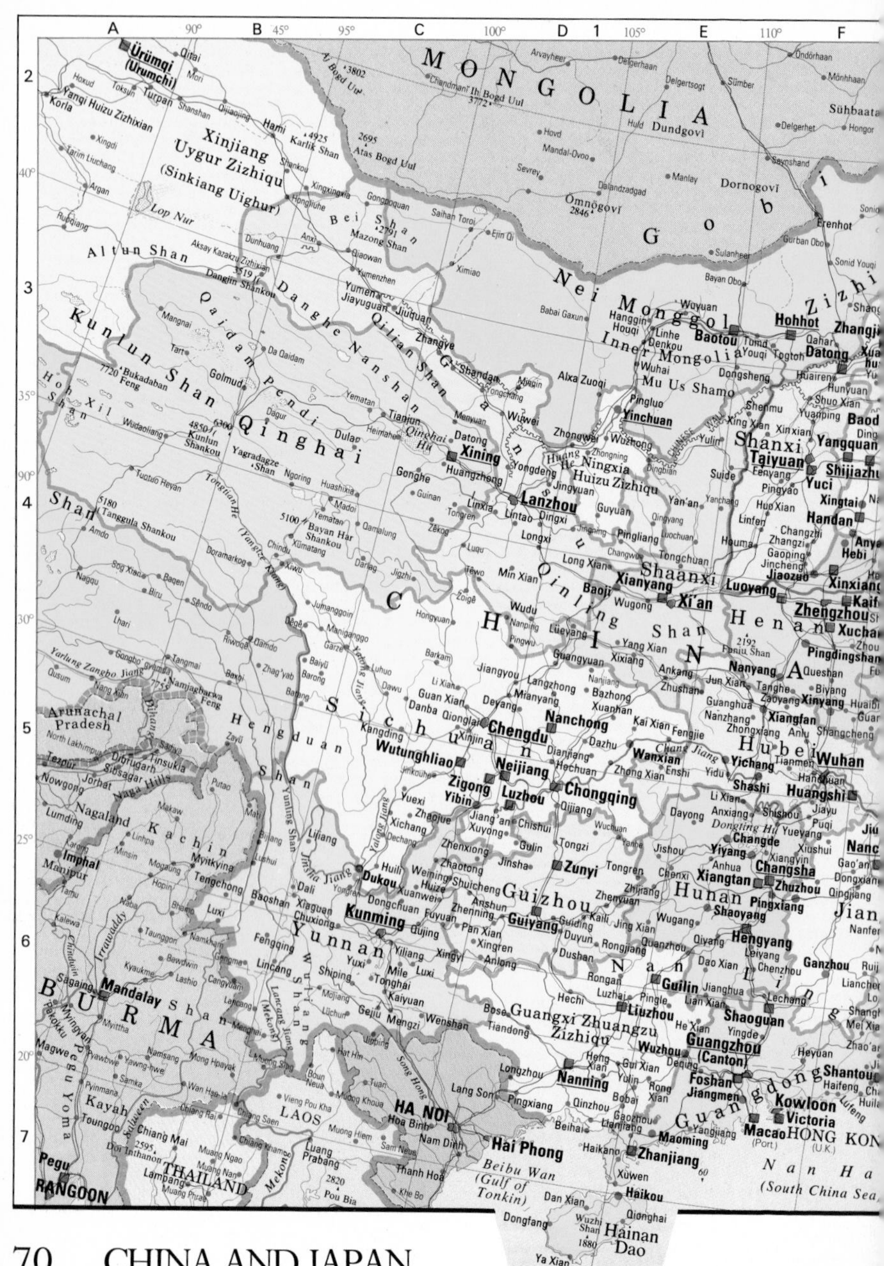
A
B
C
D
E
F
90°
95°
100°
105°
110°
45°
1
2
3
4
5
6
7
40°
35°
30°
25°
20°
MONGOLIA
Ürümqi (Urumchi)
Qitai
Turpan
Korla
Hami
Xinjiang Uygur Zizhiqu (Sinkiang Uighur)
Lop Nur
Altun Shan
Kunlun Shan
Qaidam Pendi
Qinghai
Golmud
Dunhuang
Anxi
Yumen
Jiayuguan
Jiuquan
Zhangye
Qilian Shan
Danghe Nanshan
Bei Shan
Mazong Shan
Atas Bogd Uul
Karlik Shan
Gobi
Nei Mongol
Inner Mongolia
Dundgovi
Dornogovi
Ömnögovi
Hohhot
Baotou
Datong
Zhangjiakou
Yinchuan
Mu Us Shamo
Ningxia Huizu Zizhiqu
Lanzhou
Xining
Qinghai Hu
Shanxi
Taiyuan
Shijiazhuang
Handan
Shaanxi
Xianyang
Xi'an
Baoji
Qinling Shan
Luoyang
Zhengzhou
Henan
Kaifeng
Pingdingshan
Nanyang
CHINA
Sichuan
Chengdu
Nanchong
Neijiang
Zigong
Luzhou
Yibin
Chongqing
Wanxian
Yichang
Shashi
Hubei
Wuhan
Huangshi
Changde
Changsha
Xiangtan
Zhuzhou
Hunan
Hengyang
Shaoyang
Guizhou
Guiyang
Zunyi
Kunming
Yunnan
Dukou
Hengduan Shan
Guilin
Liuzhou
Nan Ling
Guangxi Zhuangzu Zizhiqu
Nanning
Guangzhou (Canton)
Guangdong
Foshan
Jiangmen
Shaoguan
Shantou
Kowloon
Victoria
HONG KONG (U.K.)
Macao (Port)
Zhanjiang
Maoming
Haikou
Hainan Dao
Beibu Wan (Gulf of Tonkin)
Nan Hai (South China Sea)
HA NOI
Hai Phong
LAOS
THAILAND
BURMA
RANGOON
Pegu
Mandalay
Shan
Kachin
Nagaland
Imphal
Manipur
Arunachal Pradesh
Yarlung Zangbo Jiang
Tanggula Shankou
Bayan Har Shankou
Mekong
Irrawaddy
Salween
Chiang Mai

foot = 0,30 m
meter = 3,28 feet

Scale 1:20 000 000

0 200 400 600 800 1000 km

0 200 400 600 miles

1 hour

65° A 70° B 75° C 80° D 85° E
1
2
3
4
5
6
30°
25°
20°
15°
10°
AFGHANISTAN
Tarin Kowt
Tarakki
Zurmat
Gardez
Zadran
Khakriz
Kharoti
Qalat
Lashkar Gah
Kandahar
Registan
Quetta
Zarghun 3593
Toba Kakar Range
Sulaiman Range
Bolan Pass
Nushki
Peshawar
Wah
Bannu
Rawalpindi
ISLAMABAD
Salt Range
Dera Ismail Khan
Jhelum
Gujrat
Gujranwala
Sargodha
Faisalabad
Jhang Sadar
Lahore
Sahiwal
Okara
Multan
Bahawalpur
Khairpur
Khanpur
Rahimyar Khan
PAKISTAN
Punjab
Jacobabad
Shikarpur
Larkana
Sukkur
Khairpur
Nawabshah
Sind
Hyderabad
Karachi
Mouths of the Indus
Indus
Thar Desert (Great Indian Desert)
Rann of Kutch
Kutch
Gulf of Kutch
Tropic of Cancer
Mandvi
Jamnagar
Rajkot
Dwarka
Porbandar
Kathiawar
Dhoraji
Junagadh
Veraval
Gujarat
Bhavnagar
Gulf of Khambhat
Surat
Daman
Sopur
Baramula
Srinagar
Jammu and Kashmir
Banihal Pass 2832
Jammu
Sialkot
Pathankot
Himachal Pradesh
Amritsar
Jullundur
Ludhiana
Simla
Chandigarh
Ambala
Dehra Dun
Bhatinda
Sirsa
Patiala
Haryana
Rohtak
DELHI
Meerut
Saharanpur
Muzaffarnagar
Moradabad
Rampur
Bareilly
Aligarh
Shahjahanpur
Bikaner
Ratangarh
Churu
Shekhawati
Rewari
Alwar
Rajasthan
Jodhpur
Ajmer
Jaipur
Mathura
Agra
Firozabad
Fatehgarh
Mallani
Barmer
Pali
Godwar
Beawar
Tonk
Bhilwara
Aravalli Range
Abu Road
Udaipur
Chittaurgarh
Kota
Gwalior
Shivpuri
Datia
Jhansi
Palanpur
Patan
Mahesana
Ahmadabad
Nadiad
Dohad
Ratlam
Ujjain
Indore
Bhopal
Vadodara
Bharuch
Vindhya Range
Narmada
Satpura R.
Khandwa
Itarsi
Betul
Jalgaon
Dhule
Burhanpur
Bhusawal
Nagpur
Amravati
Akola
Nasik
Malegaon
Manmad
Thana
Ulhasnagar
Bombay
Kalsubai 1646
Aurangabad
Ahmadnagar
Maharashtra
Pune
Nander
Konkan
Western Ghats
Arabian Sea
Ratnagiri
Dapoli
Janjira
Barsi
Udgir
Osmanabad
Pandharpur
Sholapur
Sangli
Bijapur
Gulbarga
Kolhapur
Belgaum
Bagalkot
Panaji
Goa
Dharwar
Karnataka
Gadag
Raichur
Bellary
Hubli
Hospet
Karwar
Honavar
Shimoga
Davangere
Bhadravati
Udipi
Mangalore
Bangalore
Hassan
Cannanore
Mysore
Amindivi Islands
Lakshadweep (Laccadive Islands)
Malabar Coast
Calicut
Kerala
Trichur
Cochin
Alleppey
Quilon
Trivandrum
Nagercoil
Cape Comorin
MALDIVES
4000
1900
INDIA
Gangdisê Shan
Himalaya
Qing Zang Gaoyuan (Plateau of Tibet)
Xizang Zizhi (Tibet)
Zaskar Mts
Nanda Devi 7817
Kamet 7756
NEPAL
Dhaulagiri 8172
Annapurna 8078
Siwalik Range
KATMANDU
Mt. Everest 8848
Sikkim
Lucknow
Kanpur
Uttar Pradesh
Faizabad
Gorakhpur
Allahabad
Varanasi (Benares)
Mirzapur
Patna
Bihar
Gaya
Monghyr
Bhagalpur
Muzaffarpur
Darbhanga
Sagar
Jabalpur
Madhya Pradesh
Satna
Kaimur Range
Ranchi
Chotanagpur
Jamshedpur
Asansol
Durgapur
Burdwan
Howrah
Calcutta
Bilaspur
Korba
Raurkela
Kharagpur
Raigarh
Sambalpur
Orissa
Raipur
Durg
Bhandara
Gondia
Chandrapur
Hinganghat
Adilabad
Cuttack
Bhubaneshwar
Berhampur
Balasore
Bhadrakh
Palmyras Point
Nizamabad
Warangal
Hyderabad
Deccan
Godavari
Eastern Ghats
Jagdalpur
Jeypore
Srikakulam
Vizianagaram
Vishakhapatnam
Anakapalle
Rajahmundry
Kakinada
Eluru
Vijayawada
Machilipatnam
Guntur
Tenali
Andhra Pradesh
Krishna
Kurnool
Nandyal
Ongole
Anantapur
Cuddapah
Nellore
Gudur
Tirupati
Chittoor
Kolar
Vellore
Madras
Kanchipuram
Ambur
Tiruvannamalai
Pondicherry
Cuddalore
Salem
Tamil Nadu
Erode
Coimbatore
Kumbakonam
Karikal
Thanjavur
Tiruchchirappalli
Anaimalai Hills 2670
Dindigul
Madurai
Rajapalaiyam
Aruppukkottai
Tirunelveli
Tuticorin
Coromandel Coast
Palk Strait
Adams Bridge
Gulf of Mannar
Kankesanturai
Jaffna
Mullaittivu
Trincomalee
Anuradhapura
Kurunegala
Negombo
COLOMBO
Kandy
Pidurutalagala
Badulla
SRI LANKA (CEYLON)
Moratuwa
Ratnapura
Yala
Galle
Matara
Dondra Head
Bay of
INDIAN OCEAN
1500
3900
3600

CHINA
BURMA
LAOS
THAILAND
KAMPUCHEA (CAMBODIA)
VIETNAM
MALAYSIA
Sichuan
Yunnan
Guizhou
Hunan
Hubei
Guangxi Zhuangzu Zizhiqu
Chengdu
Chongqing
Kunming
Guiyang
Nanning
Guangzhou (Canton)
Wuhan
Changsha
HA NOI
Hai Phong
VIENTIANE
KRUNG THEP (BANGKOK)
PHNOM PENH
Ho Chi Minh (Saigon)
RANGOON
Mandalay
Chittagong
Da Nang
Hue
Gulf of Thailand
South China Sea
Andaman Sea
Beibu Wan (Gulf of Tonkin)
Hainan Dao
Andaman Islands (India)
Nicobar Islands (India)
Paracel Islands (China)
1 foot = 0,30 m
1 meter = 3,28 feet
Scale 1:20 000 000

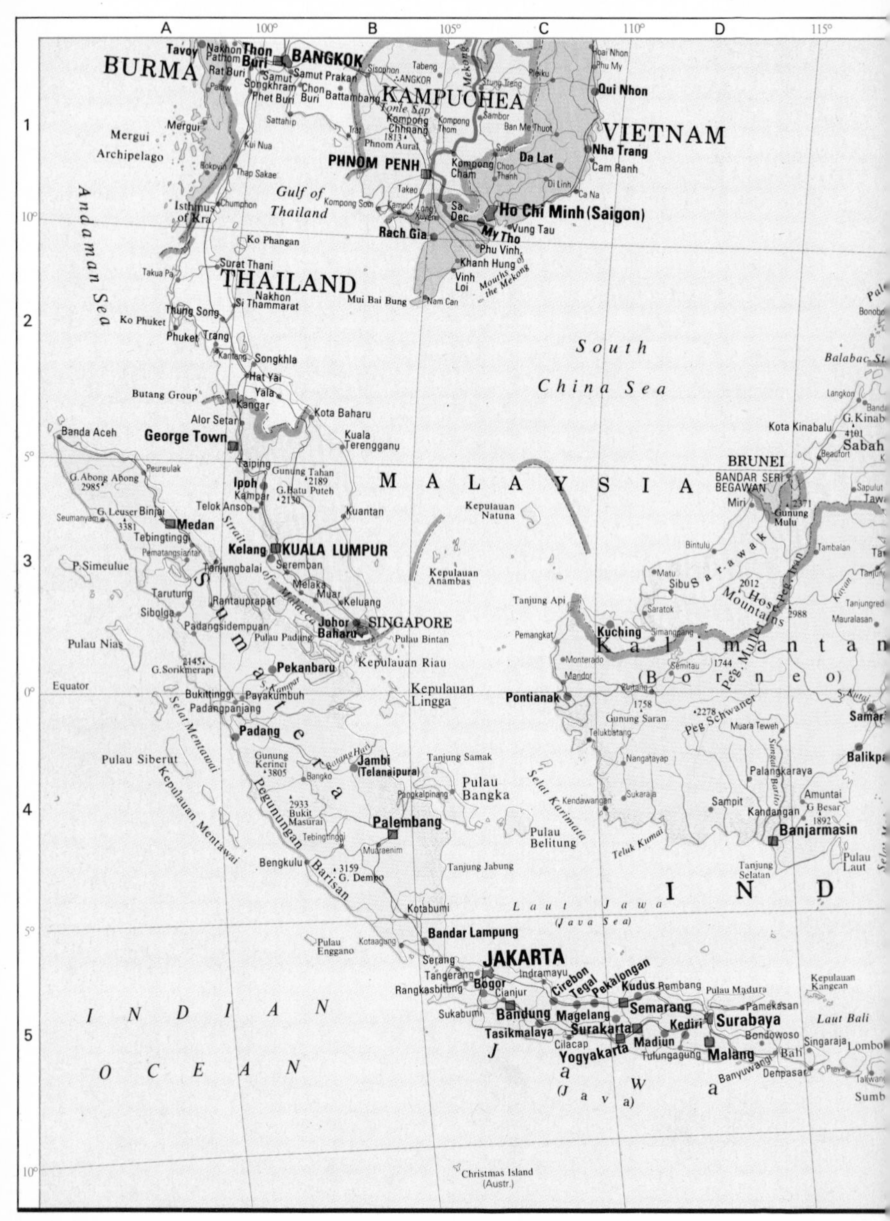
BURMA
THAILAND
KAMPUCHEA
VIETNAM
MALAYSIA
BANGKOK
PHNOM PENH
Ho Chi Minh (Saigon)
KUALA LUMPUR
SINGAPORE
JAKARTA
South China Sea
Andaman Sea
Gulf of Thailand
Strait of Malacca
INDIAN OCEAN
Laut Jawa (Java Sea)
Sumatera
Kalimantan (Borneo)
Jawa (Java)
BRUNEI
BANDAR SERI BEGAWAN
Equator
Christmas Island (Austr.)

1 foot = 0,30 m
1 meter = 3,28 feet

Scale 1:20 000 000

0 200 400 600 800 1000 km
0 200 400 600 miles
1 hour

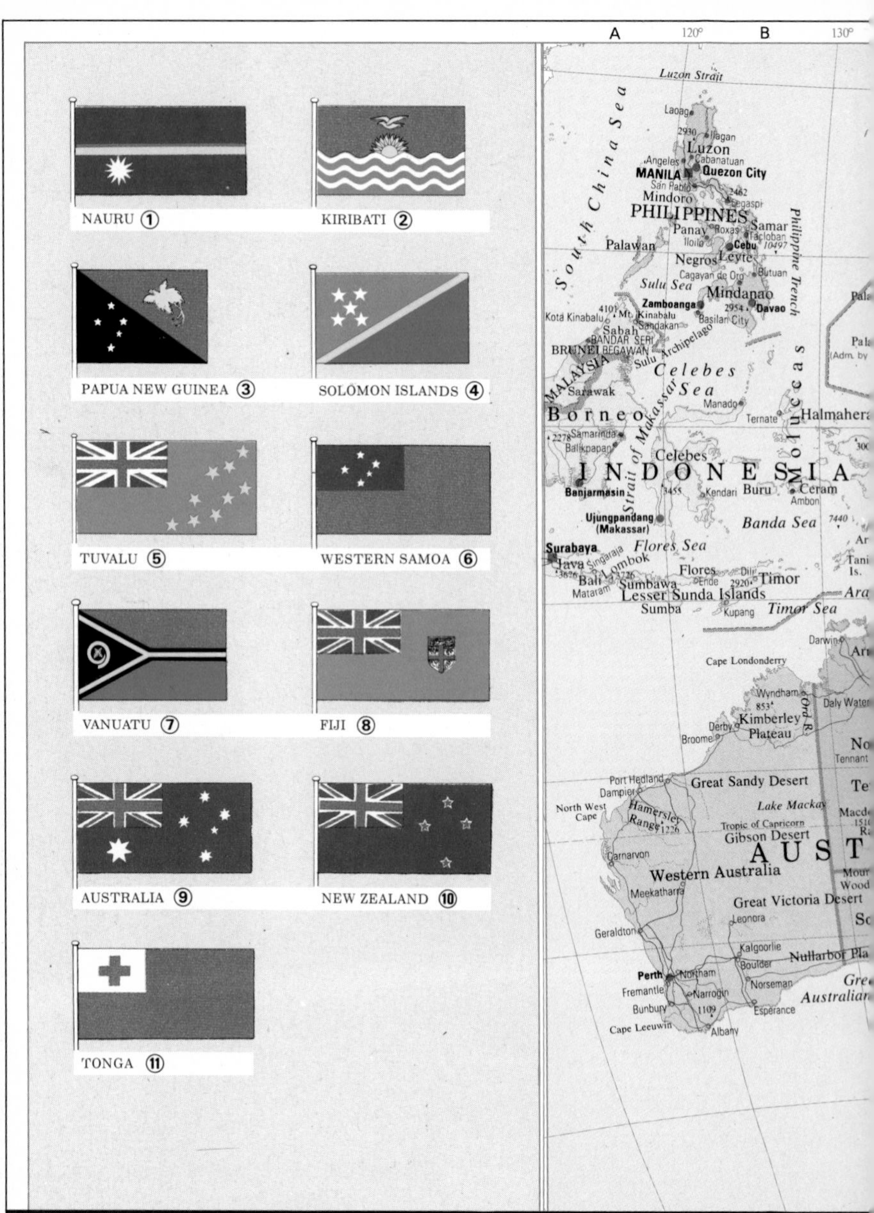
NAURU ①
KIRIBATI ②
PAPUA NEW GUINEA ③
SOLOMON ISLANDS ④
TUVALU ⑤
WESTERN SAMOA ⑥
VANUATU ⑦
FIJI ⑧
AUSTRALIA ⑨
NEW ZEALAND ⑩
TONGA ⑪
A
120°
B
130°
Luzon Strait
South China Sea
Laoag
Ilagan
Luzon
Cabanatuan
Angeles
MANILA
Quezon City
San Pablo
Mindoro
Legaspi
PHILIPPINES
Samar
Panay
Roxas
Tacloban
Palawan
Iloilo
Cebu
Philippine Trench
Negros
Leyte
Cagayan de Oro
Butuan
Sulu Sea
Zamboanga
Mindanao
Davao
Kota Kinabalu
Mt. Kinabalu
Sandakan
Basilan City
Sabah
BANDAR SERI BEGAWAN
BRUNEI
Sulu Archipelago
MALAYSIA
Celebes Sea
Sarawak
Manado
Borneo
Ternate
Halmahera
Moluccas
Samarinda
Balikpapan
Celebes
Strait of Makassar
INDONESIA
Banjarmasin
Kendari
Buru
Ceram
Ambon
Ujungpandang (Makassar)
Banda Sea
Surabaya
Flores Sea
Java
Lombok
Flores
Dili
Timor
Bali
Sumbawa
Ende
Mataram
Lesser Sunda Islands
Sumba
Kupang
Timor Sea
Darwin
Cape Londonderry
Wyndham
Ord R.
Daly Waters
Kimberley Plateau
Derby
Broome
Tennant
Port Hedland
Great Sandy Desert
Dampier
North West Cape
Hamersley Range
Lake Mackay
Tropic of Capricorn
Gibson Desert
Carnarvon
AUST
Western Australia
Meekatharra
Great Victoria Desert
Leonora
Geraldton
Kalgoorlie
Boulder
Nullarbor Pla
Perth
Northam
Fremantle
Narrogin
Norseman
Bunbury
Esperance
Cape Leeuwin
Albany

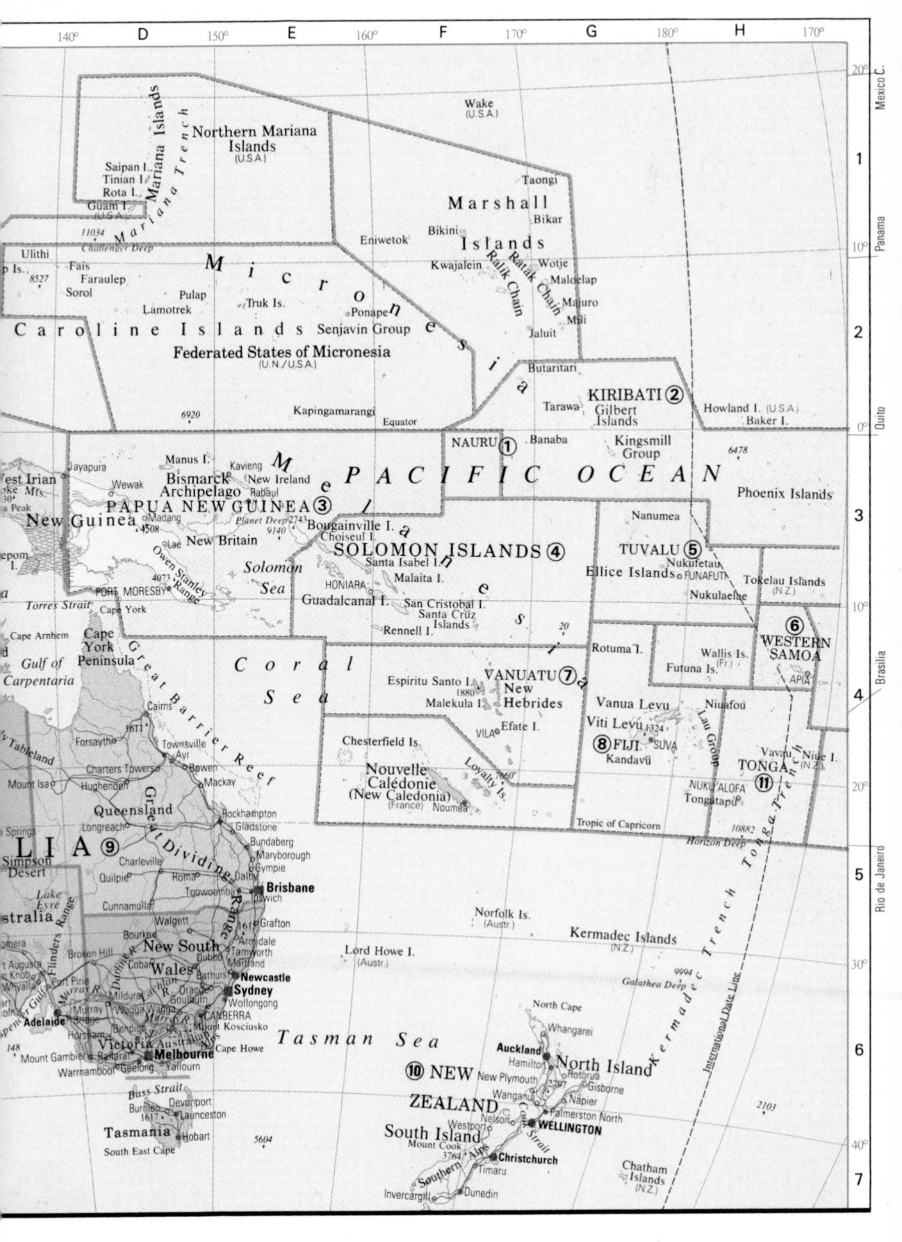

foot = 0,30 m
meter = 3,28 feet

Scale 1:50 000 000

0 500 1000 km
0 200 400 600 miles
1 hour

A 115° B 120° C 125° D 130° E 135°

1 2 3 4 5 6

INDONESIA
Kupang
Pulau Roti
Baing
Timor Sea
INDIAN OCEAN
Cape Van Diemen
Bathurst Island
Melville Island
Cape Croker
Croker Island
Van Diemen Gulf
Port Darwin
Darwin
Arnhem Land
Cape Scott
Cape Londonderry
Joseph Bonaparte Gulf
Scott Reef
Bonaparte Archipelago
Kalumburu
DRYSDALE RIVER NATIONAL PARK
Wyndham
Kimberley
Port Keats
Daly River
KATHERINE GORGE N.P.
Katherine
Mataranka
Roper R.
Legune
Kununurra
Newry
Bradshaw
Victoria River
Willeroo
Collier Bay
Cape Lévêque
King Sound
Derby
Dampier Land
King Leopold Ranges
Mount Ord 936
Kimberley Plateau
Durack Range
Ord R.
Lake Argyle
Montejinnie
Daly Waters
Dunmarra
Yeeda River
Broome
Roebuck Bay
Thangoo
Fitzroy River
Fitzroy Crossing
Halls Creek
Wave Hill
Newcastle Waters
Elliot
Northern Territory
Gordon Downs
Tanami Desert
Bohemia Downs
Eighty Mile Beach
Anna Plains
Canning Basin
Great Sandy Desert
Larrey Point
Port Hedland
Goldsworthy
Tanami
Tennant
The Granites 436
TANAMI DESERT WILDLIFE SANCTUARY
Barrow Island
Dampier
Roebourne
North West Cape
Exmouth
Onslow
Hamersley Range
Mount Bruce 1235
RUDALL RIVER NATIONAL PARK
AUSTRALIA
Barrow Cr.
Lake Mackay
Roy Hill
HAMERSLEY RANGE NATIONAL PARK
Newman
Lake Disappointment
Narwietooma
Mount Br.
1128
Alice Springs
Macdonnell Ranges
Western Australia
Gibson Desert
FINKE GORGE NATIONAL PARK
Lake Amadeus
Henbury
Lake McLeod
Mount Augustus 1106
KENNEDY RANGE N.P.
Carnarvon
Gascoyne Junction
COLLIER RANGES NATIONAL PARK
Mount Essendon 910
Milgun
BROWNE RANGE NATURE RESERVE
Mount Deering 1219
Giles
AYERS ROCK - MOUNT OLGA NATIONAL PARK
Kulgera
Shark Bay
Macadam Plains
Carnegie
Wooramel
Dirk Hartog Island
Byro
Mount Hale 732
Karalundi
Warburton Mission
Tomkinson Ranges
Musgrave Ranges
Hamelin Pool
Edel Land
Meekatharra
Lake Carnegie
Birksgate Range 773
South Australia
KALBARRI NATIONAL PARK
Murchison R.
Lake Austin
Mount Shenton 594
Great Victoria Desert
Yalgoo
Mount Magnet
Mullewa
Geraldton
Morava
Dongara
Paynes Find
Lake Barlee
Leonora
Lake Carey
Lake Ballard
Lake Moore
Menzies
Lake Rebecca
GREAT VICTORIA DESERT NATURE RESERVE
Lake Maurice
Watheroo
Dalwallinu
Mount Jackson
Kalgoorlie
Boulder
Cook
Ooldea
Wynbring
1186 Mount
Jurien Bay
Koridut
Southern Cross
Zanthus
Rawlinna
Forrest
Nullarbor Plain
Lake Lefroy
Gingin
Northam
Merredin
Cocklebiddy
Wilson Bluff
Colona
Fowlers Bay
Penong
Perth
York
Brookton
The Johnston Lakes
Hyden
Norseman
Eyre
Streaky Bay
Darling Range
Mandurah
Jarrahdale
Kondinin
Narrogin
658 Charles Peak
Balladonia
Point Culver
Great Australian Bight
Bunbury
Wagin
Cape Naturaliste
FITZGERALD RIVER N.P.
Esperance Bay
CAPE ARID NATIONAL PARK
Cape Arid
Cape F
Margaret River
Bridgetown
STIRLING RANGE N.P. 1042
Bluff Knoll
Hood Point
Cranbrook
Cape Leeuwin
Albany
Point D'Entrecasteaux
Bald Head

15° 20° 25° 30° 35°

 Scale 1:20 000 000

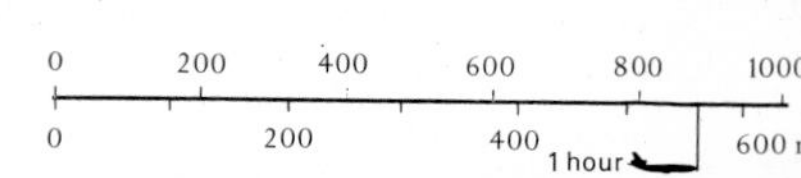

1 foot = 0,30 m
1 meter = 3,28 feet

Halmahera
Bukit Sulat
Pulau Waigeo
Equator
Laut Halmahera
3000 Gunung Kwoka
Cendrawasih
P. Salawati
Pulau Biak
Pulau Misool
Pulau Yapen
Teluk Cendrawasih
Laut Seram
Teluk Berau
Bomberai
Irian Jaya
3055 Gunung Binaiya
Seram
Ambon
New Guinea
Pegunungan Maoke
5030 Puncak Jaya
INDONESIA
Kepulauan Kai
P. Kai Besar
Kepulauan Aru
Pulau Wokam
Pulau Kobroor
Pulau Trangan
Laut Banda (Banda Sea)
Tenggara
Pulau Yamdena
Kepulauan Tanimbar
Kepulauan Babar
Pulau Selaru
Kepulauan Leti
Laut Arafura (Arafura Sea)
Pulau Jos Sodarso
Tanjung Vals
Laut Timor (Timor Sea)
AUSTRALIA
Cape Van Diemen
Bathurst Island
Melville Island
Van Diemen Gulf
Cape Croker
Croker Island
Cape Wessel
Buckingham Bay
Admiralty Islands
Manus
Bismarck
Schouten Islands
Sepik River
PAPUA
Karkar
Long Island
Umboi
Vitiaz Strait
Bismarck Range
Centra Range
Mount Wilhelm 4508
Doma Peaks 3962
Mount Bangeta 4107
Huon Gulf
NEW GUINEA (NIUGINI)
Owen Stanley Range
Fly River
Gulf of Papua
PORT MORESBY
Mulgrave Island
Banks Island
Torres Strait
Prince of Wales Island
Cape York
JARDINE RIVER NATIONAL PARK
Coral Sea
Sydney
Wollongong
Shellharbour
Lachlan River
Murrumbidgee R.
Riverina
Wagga Wagga
CANBERRA
Australian Capital Territory
Batemans Bay
Mount Kosciusko 2230
Australian Alps
Mount Feathertop 1922
Albury
Shepparton
Bendigo
Ballarat
Melbourne
Geelong
Cape Howe
Ninety Mile Beach
Wilsons Promontory
Cape Otway
King
Bass Strait
North Point
Furneaux Group
Banks Strait
Cape Grim
Launceston
Saint Marys
Mount Ossa 1617
Freycinet Peninsula
HARTZ MOUNTAINS NATIONAL PARK
Hobart
Port Arthur
South East Cape
Tasmania
Tasman Sea
5604
Mount Aspiring 3036
FIORDLAND NATIONAL PARK
Cape Providence
Invercargill
Foveaux Strait
Stewart Island
Southwest Cape

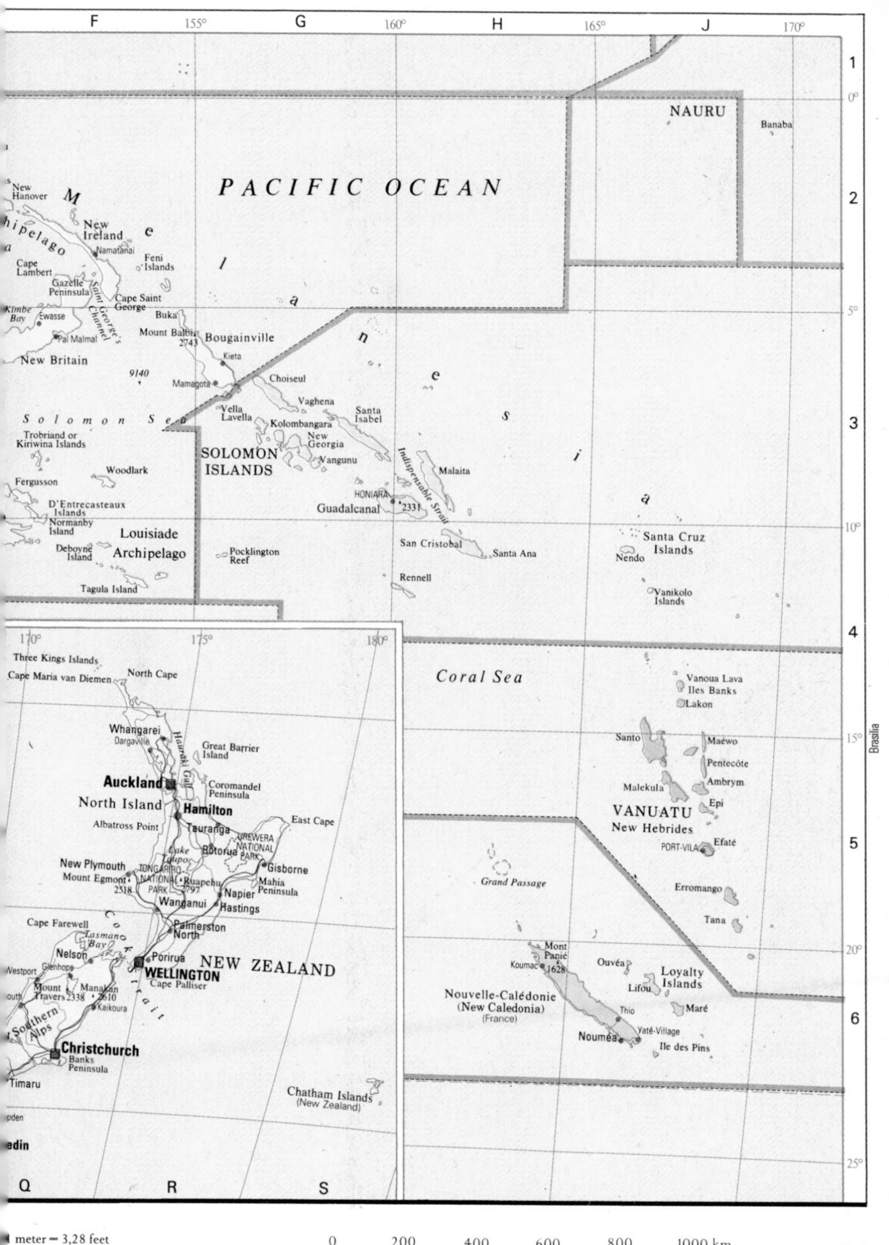

meter = 3,28 feet

Scale 1:20 000 000

0 200 400 600 800 1000 km

0 200 400 1 hour 600 miles

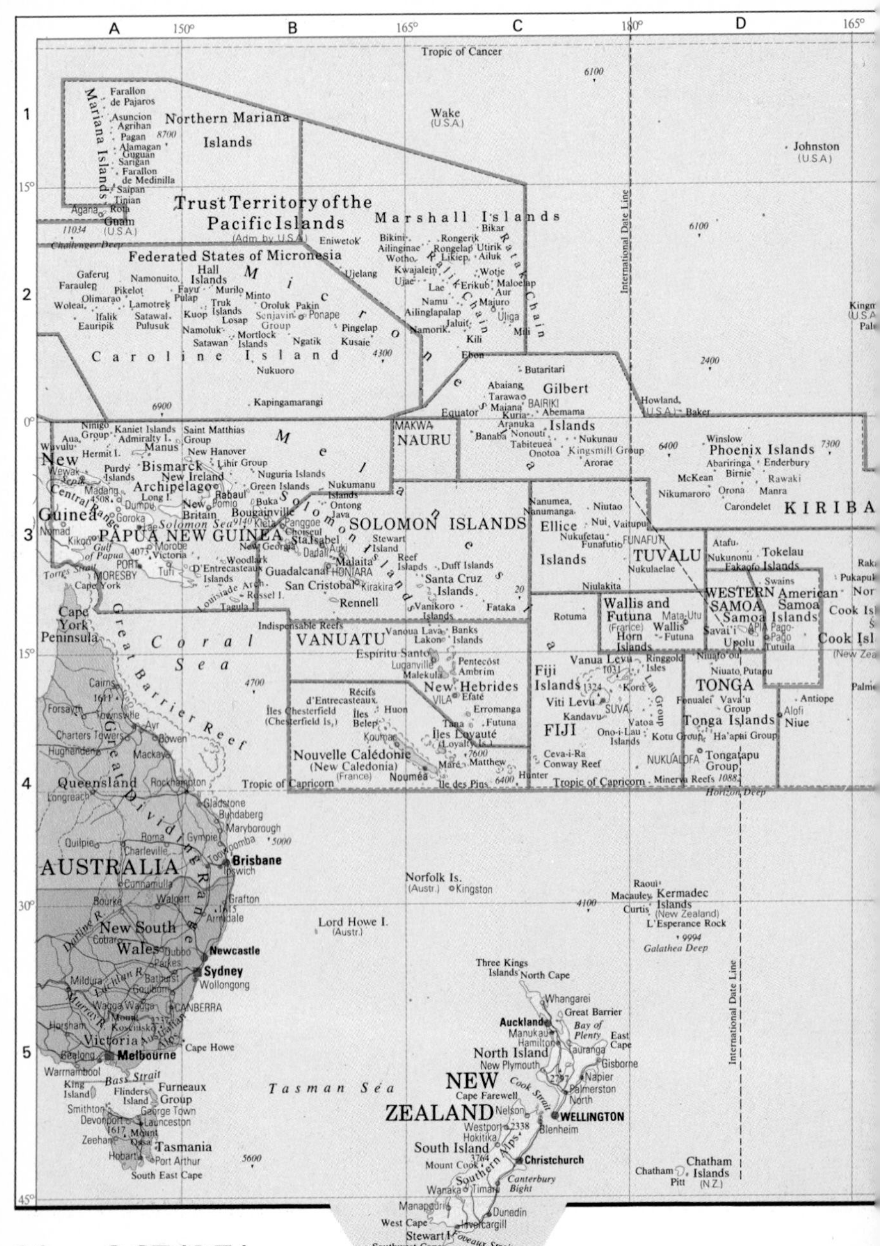

Northern Mariana Islands
Trust Territory of the Pacific Islands
Federated States of Micronesia
Marshall Islands
Caroline Island
Micronesia
Melanesia
Gilbert Islands
NAURU
Phoenix Islands
KIRIBATI
PAPUA NEW GUINEA
SOLOMON ISLANDS
TUVALU
Tokelau
Wallis and Futuna
WESTERN SAMOA
American Samoa
Cook Islands
VANUATU
Fiji Islands
FIJI
TONGA
Niue
Nouvelle Calédonie (New Caledonia) (France)
Coral Sea
Great Barrier Reef
AUSTRALIA
Queensland
New South Wales
Victoria
Tasmania
Brisbane
Newcastle
Sydney
CANBERRA
Melbourne
Norfolk Is.
Lord Howe I.
Kermadec Islands
Tasman Sea
NEW ZEALAND
North Island
South Island
Auckland
WELLINGTON
Christchurch
Chatham Islands
Tropic of Cancer
Tropic of Capricorn
International Date Line

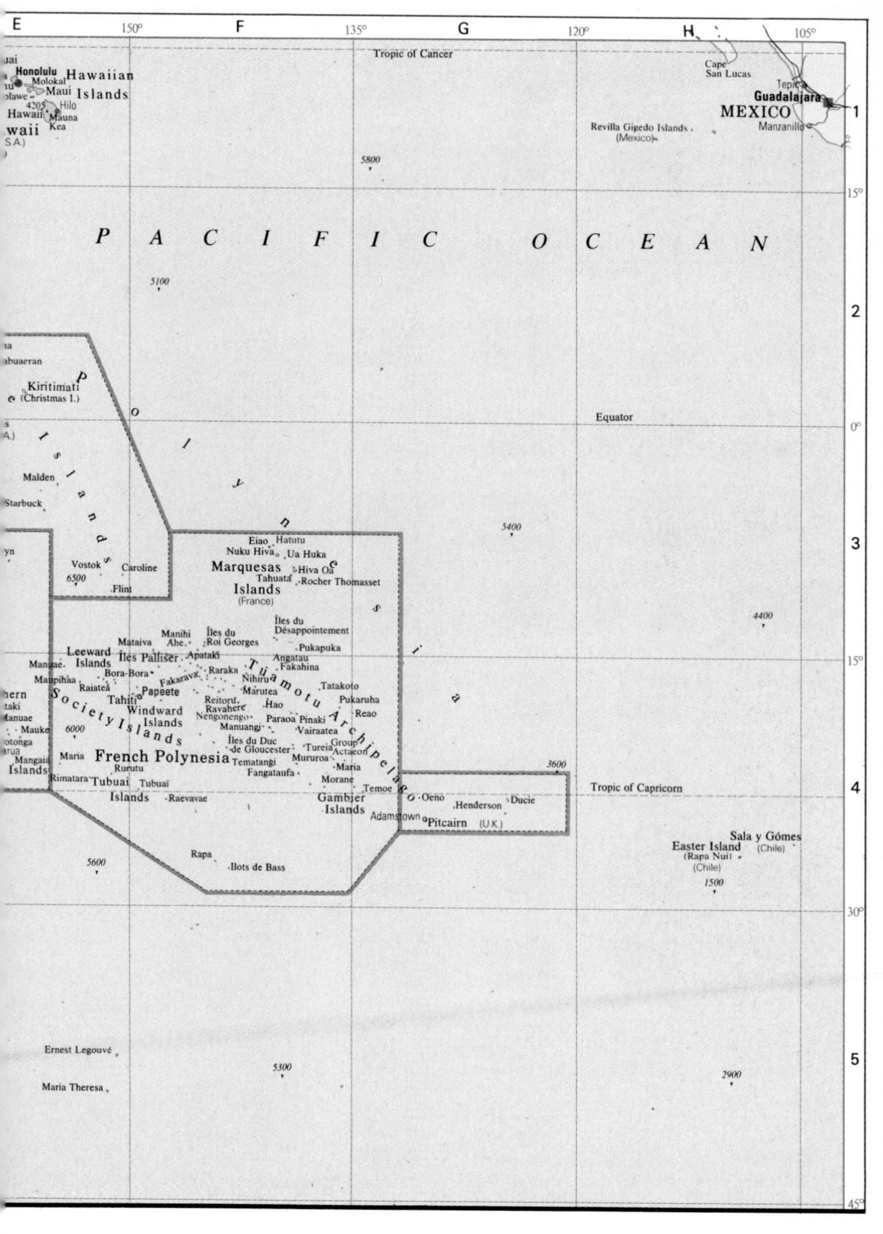

1 foot = 0,30 m
1 meter = 3,28 feet

Scale 1:54 000 000

0 1000 2000 km
0 400 800 1200 miles
1 hour

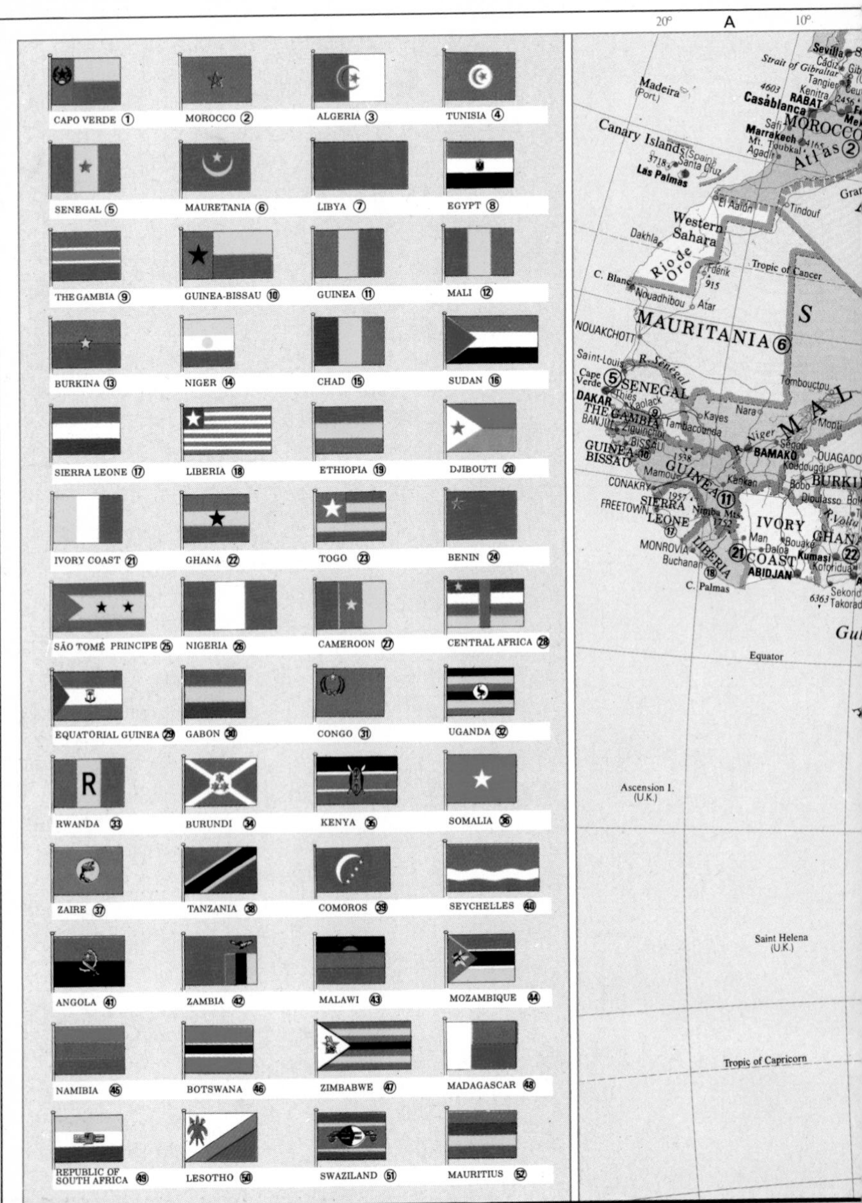
CAPO VERDE ①
MOROCCO ②
ALGERIA ③
TUNISIA ④
SENEGAL ⑤
MAURETANIA ⑥
LIBYA ⑦
EGYPT ⑧
THE GAMBIA ⑨
GUINEA-BISSAU ⑩
GUINEA ⑪
MALI ⑫
BURKINA ⑬
NIGER ⑭
CHAD ⑮
SUDAN ⑯
SIERRA LEONE ⑰
LIBERIA ⑱
ETHIOPIA ⑲
DJIBOUTI ⑳
IVORY COAST ㉑
GHANA ㉒
TOGO ㉓
BENIN ㉔
SÃO TOMÉ PRINCIPE ㉕
NIGERIA ㉖
CAMEROON ㉗
CENTRAL AFRICA ㉘
EQUATORIAL GUINEA ㉙
GABON ㉚
CONGO ㉛
UGANDA ㉜
RWANDA ㉝
BURUNDI ㉞
KENYA ㉟
SOMALIA ㊱
ZAIRE ㊲
TANZANIA ㊳
COMOROS ㊴
SEYCHELLES ㊵
ANGOLA ㊶
ZAMBIA ㊷
MALAWI ㊸
MOZAMBIQUE ㊹
NAMIBIA ㊺
BOTSWANA ㊻
ZIMBABWE ㊼
MADAGASCAR ㊽
REPUBLIC OF SOUTH AFRICA ㊾
LESOTHO ㊿
SWAZILAND 51
MAURITIUS 52
20°
A
10°
Strait of Gibraltar
Madeira (Port.)
Casablanca
RABAT
MOROCCO ②
Marrakech
Mt. Toubkal
Agadir
Canary Islands (Spain)
Santa Cruz
Las Palmas
El Aaiún
Tindouf
Western Sahara
Dakhla
Rio de Oro
Tropic of Cancer
C. Blanc
Nouadhibou
Atar
MAURITANIA ⑥
NOUAKCHOTT
Saint-Louis
R. Sénégal
Cape Verde
SENEGAL
DAKAR
Kaolack
THE GAMBIA
BANJUL
Ziguinchor
Tambacounda
Kayes
Nara
Tombouctou
R. Niger
Ségou
BAMAKO
Mopti
OUAGADOUGOU
GUINEA-BISSAU
BISSAU
GUINEA ⑪
Mamou
Kankan
CONAKRY
FREETOWN
SIERRA LEONE
Nimba Mts.
IVORY COAST
Man
Daloa
Bouaké
MONROVIA
LIBERIA
Buchanan
C. Palmas
ABIDJAN
Kumasi
Sekondi Takoradi
Equator
Ascension I. (U.K.)
Saint Helena (U.K.)
Tropic of Capricorn

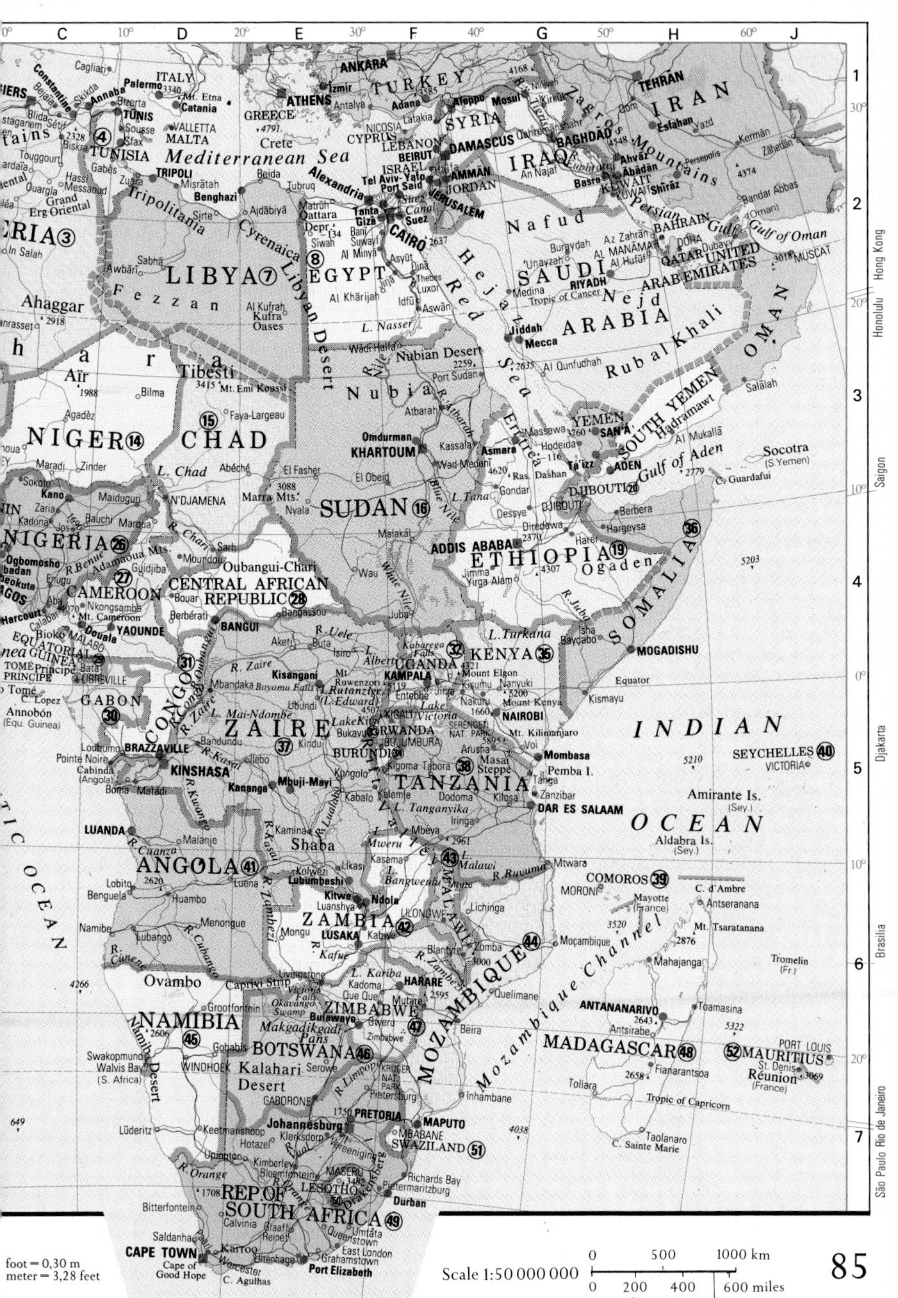

foot = 0,30 m
meter = 3,28 feet

Scale 1:50 000 000
0 500 1000 km
0 200 400 600 miles
1 hour

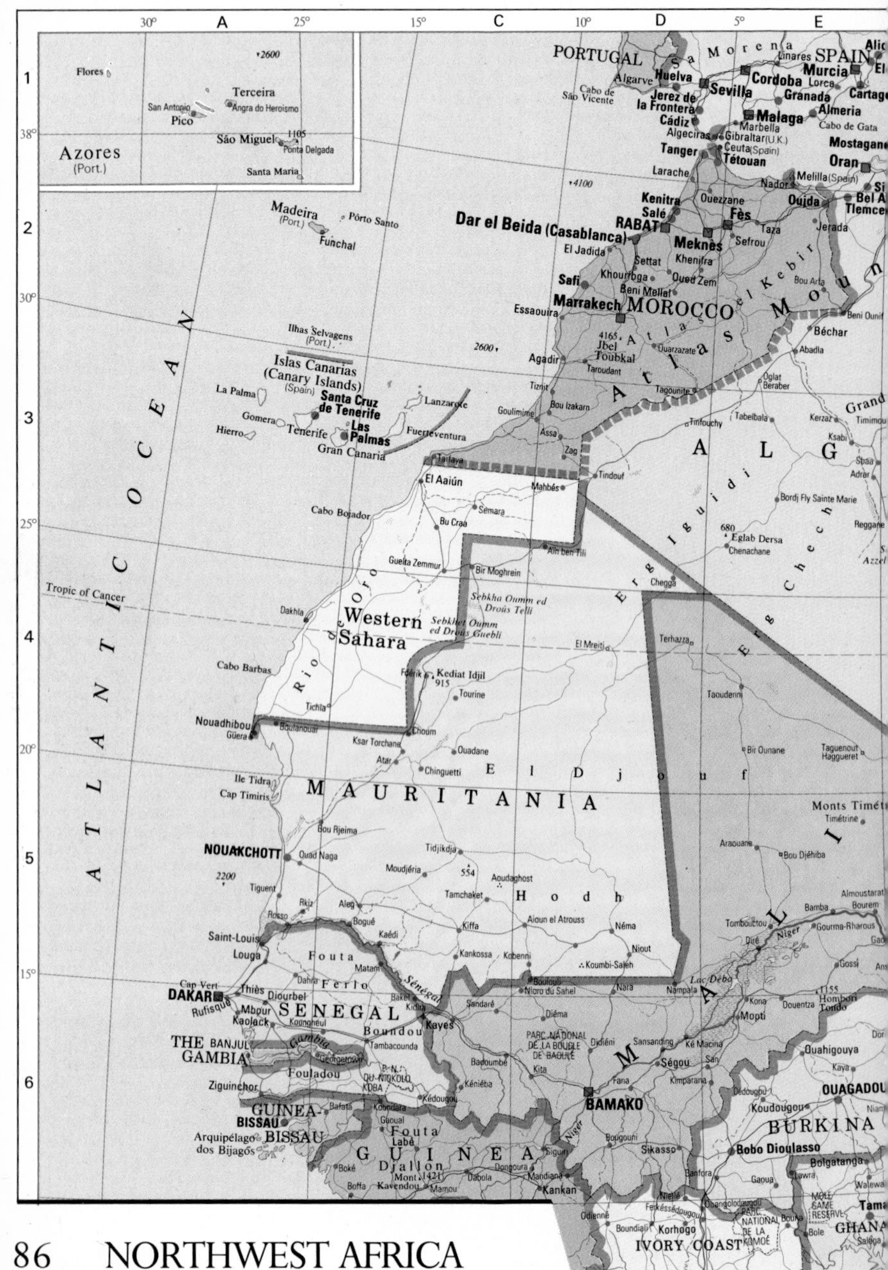

30°
A
25°
15°
C
10°
D
5°
E
Azores
(Port.)
Flores
Terceira
Angra do Heroismo
San Antonio
Pico
São Miguel
Ponta Delgada
Santa Maria
1105
2600
38°
PORTUGAL
Algarve
Cabo de São Vicente
Sa Morena
Linares
SPAIN
Huelva
Sevilla
Cordoba
Murcia
Lorca
Jerez de la Frontera
Granada
Cádiz
Malaga
Almeria
Marbella
Cabo de Gata
Algeciras
Gibraltar (U.K.)
Ceuta (Spain)
Tanger
Tétouan
Mostagan
Oran
Larache
Melilla (Spain)
Nador
4100
Kenitra
Salé
RABAT
Ouezzane
Fès
Oujda
Bel A
Tlemce
Madeira
(Port.)
Pôrto Santo
Funchal
Dar el Beida (Casablanca)
Meknès
Sefrou
Taza
Jerada
El Jadida
Settat
Khenifra
Safi
Khouribga
Oued Zem
Beni Mellal
Bou Arfa
30°
Marrakech
MOROCCO
Essaouira
Beni Ounif
Béchar
Ilhas Selvagens
(Port.)
2600
4165
Jbel Toubkal
Ouarzazate
Abadla
Agadir
Taroudant
Islas Canarias
(Canary Islands)
(Spain)
La Palma
Santa Cruz de Tenerife
Lanzarote
Gomera
Hierro
Tenerife
Las Palmas
Fuerteventura
Gran Canaria
Tiznit
Tagounite
Oglat Beraber
Goulimime
Bou Izakarn
Tabelbala
Kerzaz
Grand
Timimoun
Tinfouchy
Assa
Ksabi
Zag
Atlas Mountains
A L G
Tarfaya
Tindouf
Sbaa
Adrar
El Aaiún
Mahbès
Semara
Cabo Bojador
Bordj Fly Sainte Marie
Bu Craa
Reggane
25°
Iguidi
680
Eglab Dersa
Chenachane
Guelta Zemmur
Aïn ben Tili
Bir Moghrein
Erg Chech
Chegga
Tropic of Cancer
Sebkha Oumm ed Droûs Telli
Dakhla
Western Sahara
Sebkhet Oumm ed Droûs Guebli
Terhazza
El Mreiti
Rio de Oro
Cabo Barbas
Fdérik
Kediat Idjil
915
Tourine
Taoudenni
Tichla
Nouadhibou
Güera
Boulanouar
Choum
Ksar Torchane
20°
Bir Ounane
Taguenout Haggueret
Ouadane
Atar
Chinguetti
El Djouf
Ile Tidra
Cap Timiris
MAURITANIA
Monts Timét
Timétrine
Bou Rjeima
NOUAKCHOTT
Ouad Naga
Tidjikdja
Araouane
Bou Djébiha
2200
Moudjéria
554
Aoudaghost
Tiguent
Tamchaket
Hodh
Almoustarat
Rkiz
Aleg
Bamba
Bourem
Rosso
Bogué
Tombouctou
Gourma-Rharous
Kaédi
Kiffa
Aioun el Atrouss
Néma
Diré
Niger
Saint-Louis
Louga
Fouta
Kankossa
Kobenni
Niout
Matam
Koumbi-Saleh
Gossi
15°
Dahra
Ferlo
Sénégal
Cap Vert
DAKAR
Thiès
Diourbel
Boulouli
Nioro du Sahel
Nara
Nampala
Lac Debo
1155
Hombori Tondo
Rufisque
Mbour
SENEGAL
Bakel
Kidira
Sandaré
Kona
Douentza
Kaolack
Koungheul
Kayes
Diéma
Mopti
THE GAMBIA
BANJUL
Gambia
Georgetown
Boundou
Tambacounda
PARC NATIONAL DE LA BOUCLE DE BAOULÉ
Didiéni
Sansanding
Ké Macina
Ouahigouya
Badoumbé
Ségou
San
Kaya
Fouladou
Kita
Ziguinchor
P.N. DU NIOKOLO KOBA
Kéniéba
Fana
Kimparana
MALI
GUINEA-BISSAU
Bafata
Koundara
Kédougou
BAMAKO
Dedougou
OUAGADOU
Koudougou
Gaoual
Fouta
Niger
BURKINA
Arquipélago dos Bijagós
BISSAU
Labé
Bougouni
Sikasso
Bobo Dioulasso
Siguiri
GUINEA
Djallon
Dinguiraye
Bolgatanga
Boké
Mont 1421
Dabola
Mandiana
Banfora
Gaoua
Lawra
Walewa
Boffa
Kavendou
Mamou
Kankan
MOLE GAME RESERVE
Tama
Niellé
Ouangolodougou
Ferkéssédougou
Bouna
Bole
Odienné
Boundiali
Korhogo
PARC NATIONAL DE LA KOMOÉ
GHANA
IVORY COAST
Salaga

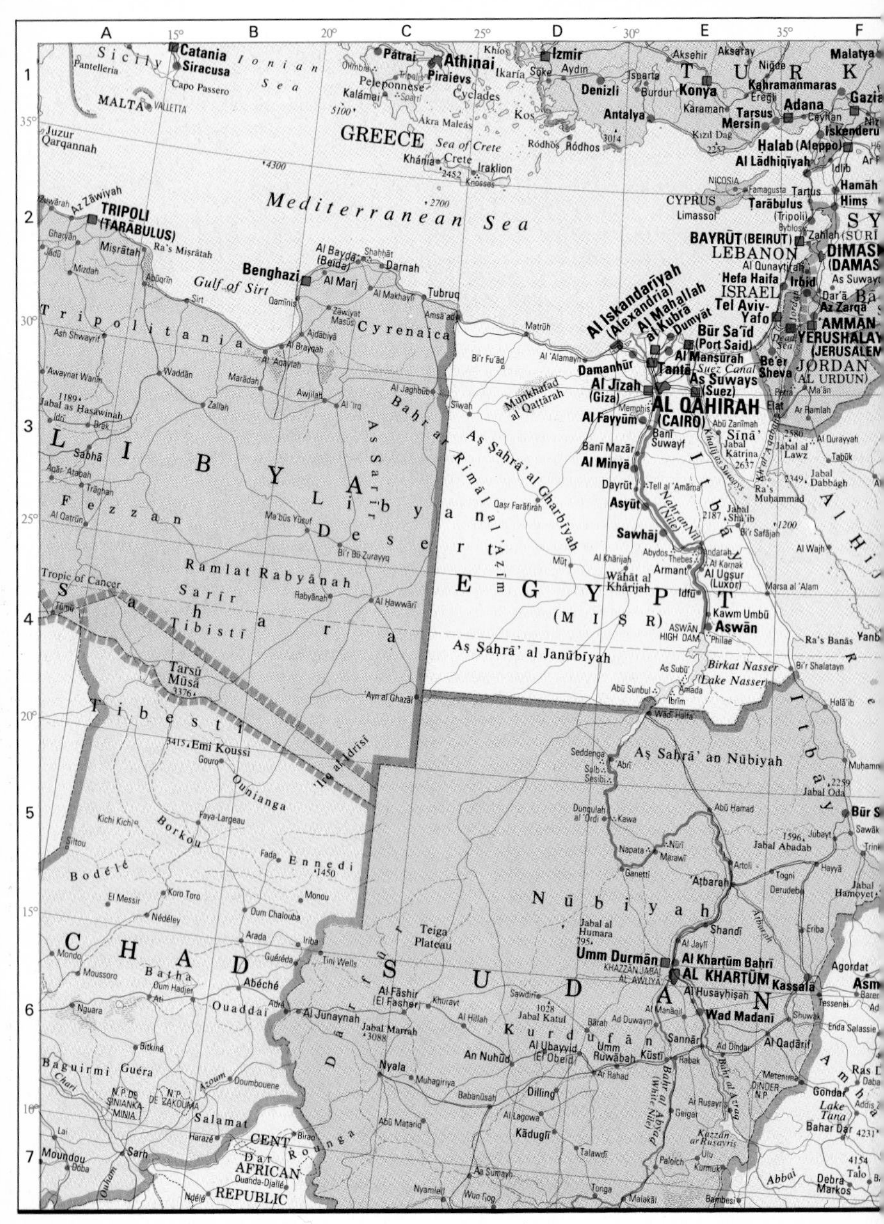

A
B
C
D
E
F
1
2
3
4
5
6
7
15°
20°
25°
30°
35°
Sicily
Catania
Siracusa
Capo Passero
Pantelleria
MALTA
VALLETTA
Ionian Sea
Pátrai
Athinai
Piraievs
Peloponnese
Kalámai
Cyclades
Ikaría
Khios
Izmir
Aydın
Söke
Kos
Ródhos
GREECE
Sea of Crete
Ákra Maleás
Khánia
Crete
Iraklion
Knossos
2452
4300
2700
5100
TURKEY
Aksehir
Aksaray
Niğde
Malatya
Isparta
Denizli
Burdur
Konya
Kahramanmaras
Ereğli
Adana
Karaman
Tarsus
Mersin
Antalya
3014
Kızıl Dag
2257
Iskenderun
Halab (Aleppo)
Al Lādhiqīyah
Idlib
Hamāh
Tartus
Hims
NICOSIA
Famagusta
CYPRUS
Limassol
Tarābulus
(Tripoli)
Byblos
Zahlah
BAYRŪT (BEIRUT)
LEBANON
Al Qunaytirah
Hefa Haifa
Irbid
ISRAEL
Tel Aviv-Yafo
Dar'ā
Az Zarqa
'AMMĀN
YERUSHALAYIM
(JERUSALEM)
Be'er Sheva
JORDAN
(AL URDUN)
Ma'ān
Elat
Petra
Al Ramlah
Juzur Qarqannah
Mediterranean Sea
Az Zāwiyah
Zuwārah
TRIPOLI
(TARĀBULUS)
Gharyān
Misrātah
Ra's Misrātah
Mizdah
Abūqrīn
Gulf of Sirt
Sirt
Benghazi
Al Bayḍā (Beida)
Shaḥḥāt
Darnah
Al Marj
Tubruq
Qamīnis
Al Makhaylī
Zāwiyat Masūs
Amsā'ad
Tripolitania
Cyrenaica
Ash Shwayrif
Ajdābiyā
Al Brayqah
Al 'Aqaylah
'Awaynat Wanīn
Waddān
Marādah
Al Jaghbūb
Awjilah
Al 'Irq
Zallah
1189
Jabal as Ḥasāwinah
Idrī
Brāk
Sabhā
Agār 'Atabah
Trāghan
Fezzan
Al Qaṭrūn
LIBYA
Libyan Desert
Ma'būs Yūsuf
Bi'r Bū Zurayyq
As Sarīr
Baḥr ar Rimāl al 'Aẓīm
Ramlat Rabyānah
Rabyānah
Sarīr Tibistī
Sahara
Al Hawwārī
Tropic of Cancer
Tümmo
Tarsū Mūsā
3376
'Ayn al Ghazāl
Tibesti
3415 Emi Koussi
Gouro
'Irq al Idrīsī
Ounianga
Kichi Kichi
Faya-Largeau
Borkou
Siltou
Bodélé
Fada
Ennedi
1450
El Messir
Koro Toro
Monou
Nédéley
Oum Chalouba
Arada
Iriba
Tini Wells
Guéréda
CHAD
Mondo
Moussoro
Batha
Oum Hadjer
Ati
Abéché
Adré
Ouaddaï
Nguara
Bitkiné
Baguirmi
Guéra
Chari
Azoum
Doumbouene
N.P. DE SINIANKA-MINIA
N.P. DE ZAKOUMA
Salamat
Harazé
Lai
Moundou
Doba
Sarh
Ouham
CENT. AFRICAN REPUBLIC
Dar Rounga
Birao
Ouanda-Djallé
Ndélé
Matrūḥ
Bi'r Fu'ād
Al 'Alamayn
Munkhafaḍ al Qaṭṭārah
Siwah
Al Iskandarīyah (Alexandria)
Al Maḥallah al Kubrā
Dumyāṭ
Būr Sa'īd (Port Said)
Al Manṣūrah
Damanhūr
Ṭanṭā
Suez Canal
As Suways (Suez)
Al Jīzah (Giza)
Memphis
AL QĀHIRAH (CAIRO)
Al Fayyūm
Abū Zanīmah
Sīnā'
Banī Suwayf
Banī Mazār
Al Minyā
Jabal Kātrīna
2637
Khalīj as Suways
As Ṣaḥrā' al Gharbīyah
Qaṣr Farāfirah
Dayrūṭ
Tell al 'Amārna
Asyūṭ
Nahr an Nīl (Nile)
Ra's Muḥammad
2349 Jabal Dabbāgh
2580
Jabal al Lawz
Al Qurayyah
Tabūk
Jabal Shā'ib
2187
Bi'r Safājah
1200
Sawhāj
Abydos
Thebes
Dandarah
Al Karnak
Al Wajh
Mūṭ
Al Khārijah
Wāḥāt al Khārijah
Armant
Al Uqṣur (Luxor)
Idfū
Marsa al 'Alam
EGYPT
(MIṢR)
Kawm Umbū
ASWĀN HIGH DAM
Aswān
Philae
Ra's Banās
Aṣ Ṣaḥrā' al Janūbīyah
As Subū'
Birkat Nasser (Lake Nasser)
Bi'r Shalatayn
Abū Sunbul
Amada
Ibrīm
Wādī Ḥalfā'
Ḥalā'ib
Seddenga
'Abrī
Sulb
Sesibi
Aṣ Ṣaḥrā' an Nūbiyah
Muḥammad Qol
2259 Jabal Oda
Dunqulah al 'Ordi
Kawa
Abū Ḥamad
Būr Sūdān
Nūrī
Napata
Marawī
1596 Jabal Abadab
Jubayt
Sawākin
Ganettī
Artoli
'Aṭbarah
Togni
Derudeb
Hayyā
Jabal Hamoyet
Nūbiyah
Teiga Plateau
Jabal al Humara
795
Shandī
Eriba
Umm Durmān
KHAZZAN JABAL AL AWLIYA'
Al Jaylī
Al Khartūm Baḥrī
AL KHARTŪM
Kassalā
Agordat
Tessenei
SUDAN
Al Fāshir (El Fasher)
Khurayt
Sawdirī
1028 Jabal Katul
Al Ḥusayḥiṣah
Al Manāqil
Wad Madanī
Shuwak
Al Junaynah
Jabal Marrah
3088
Al Ḥillah
Bārah
Ad Duwaym
Sannār
Ad Dindar
Al Qaḍārif
Kurdufān
Al Ubayyid (El Obeid)
Umm Ruwābah
Kūstī
Rabak
An Nuhūd
Nyala
Muhagiriya
Ar Rahad
Metenima
DINDER N.P.
Gondar
Lake Tana
Bahar Dar
4231
Babanūsah
Dilling
Al Lagowa
Abū Maṭāriq
Kāduglī
Al Rusayri
Geigar
Kazzān ar Ruṣayriṣ
Baḥr al Abyaḍ (White Nile)
Baḥr al Azraq
Ulu
Kurmuk
Talawdī
Paloich
Aa Sumayḥ
Tonga
Malakāl
Bambesi
Nyamlell
Wun Rog
Abbai
Debra Markos
4154
Talo
Darfur
Amhara
Itbāy
Al Ḥijāz

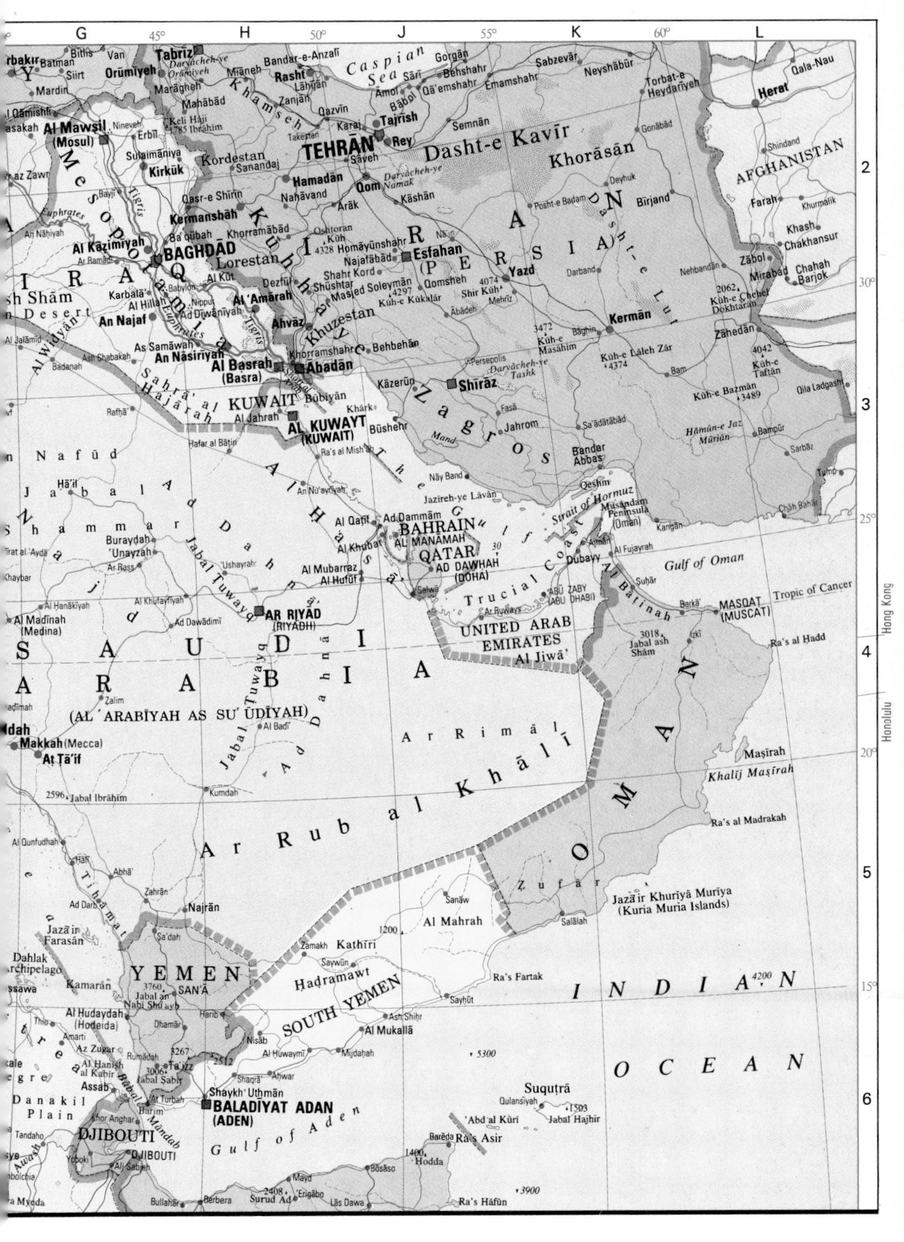

foot = 0,30 m
meter = 3,28 feet

Scale 1:20 000 000

0 200 400 600 800 1000 km

0 200 400 600 miles

1 hour

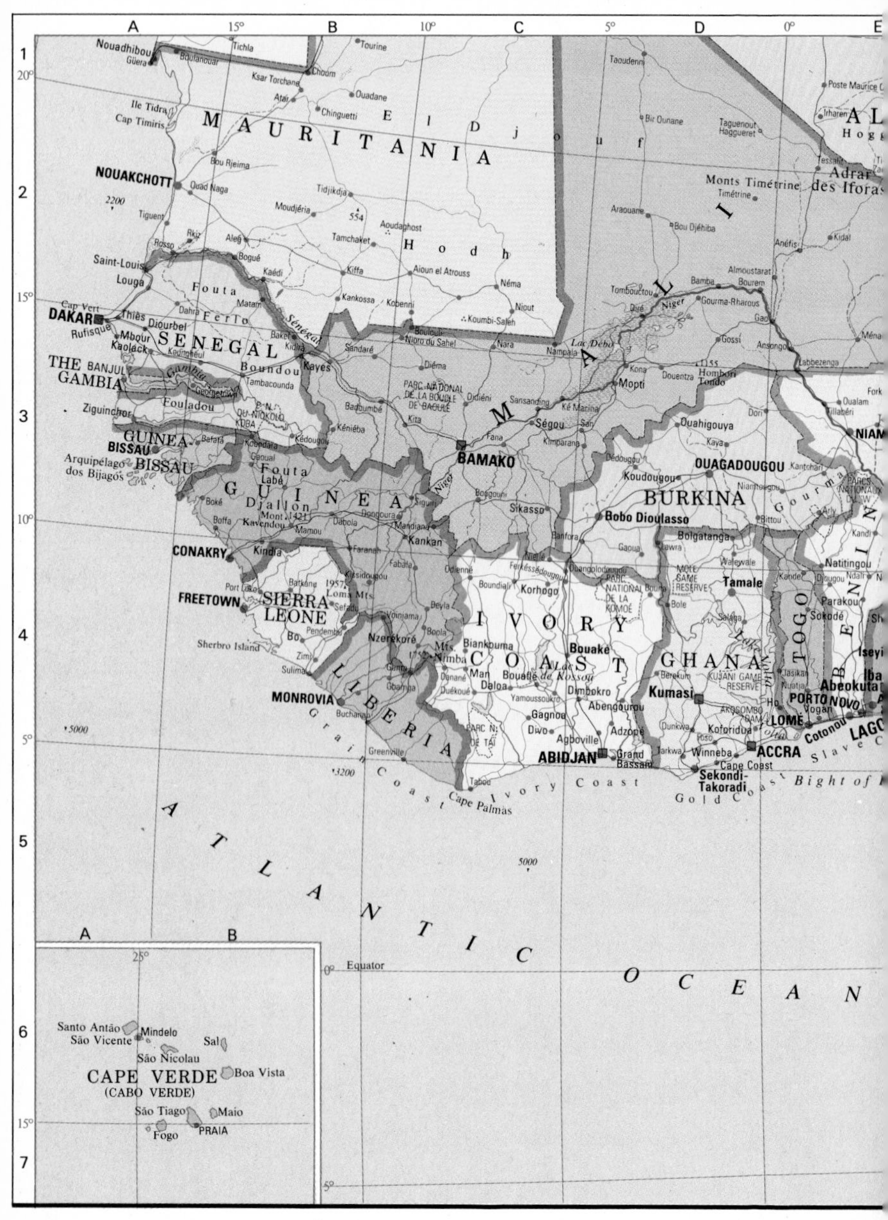
MAURITANIA
El Djouf
Hodh
NOUAKCHOTT
Nouadhibou
Ile Tidra
Cap Timiris
Saint-Louis
DAKAR
Cap Vert
SENEGAL
THE GAMBIA
BANJUL
Ziguinchor
GUINEA-BISSAU
BISSAU
Arquipélago dos Bijagós
GUINEA
Fouta Djallon
CONAKRY
FREETOWN
SIERRA LEONE
Sherbro Island
MONROVIA
LIBERIA
Grain Coast
Cape Palmas
IVORY COAST
Ivory Coast
ABIDJAN
Lac de Kossou
MALI
BAMAKO
Niger
Sénégal
Lac Débo
Mopti
Ségou
Tombouctou
BURKINA
OUAGADOUGOU
Bobo Dioulasso
Koudougou
Ouahigouya
GHANA
ACCRA
Kumasi
Tamale
Sekondi-Takoradi
Cape Coast
Gold Coast
TOGO
LOMÉ
BENIN
PORTO NOVO
Cotonou
Bight of
Monts Timétrine
Adrar des Iforas
NIAMEY
ATLANTIC OCEAN
Equator
CAPE VERDE
(CABO VERDE)
Santo Antão
São Vicente
Mindelo
Sal
São Nicolau
Boa Vista
São Tiago
Maio
Fogo
PRAIA

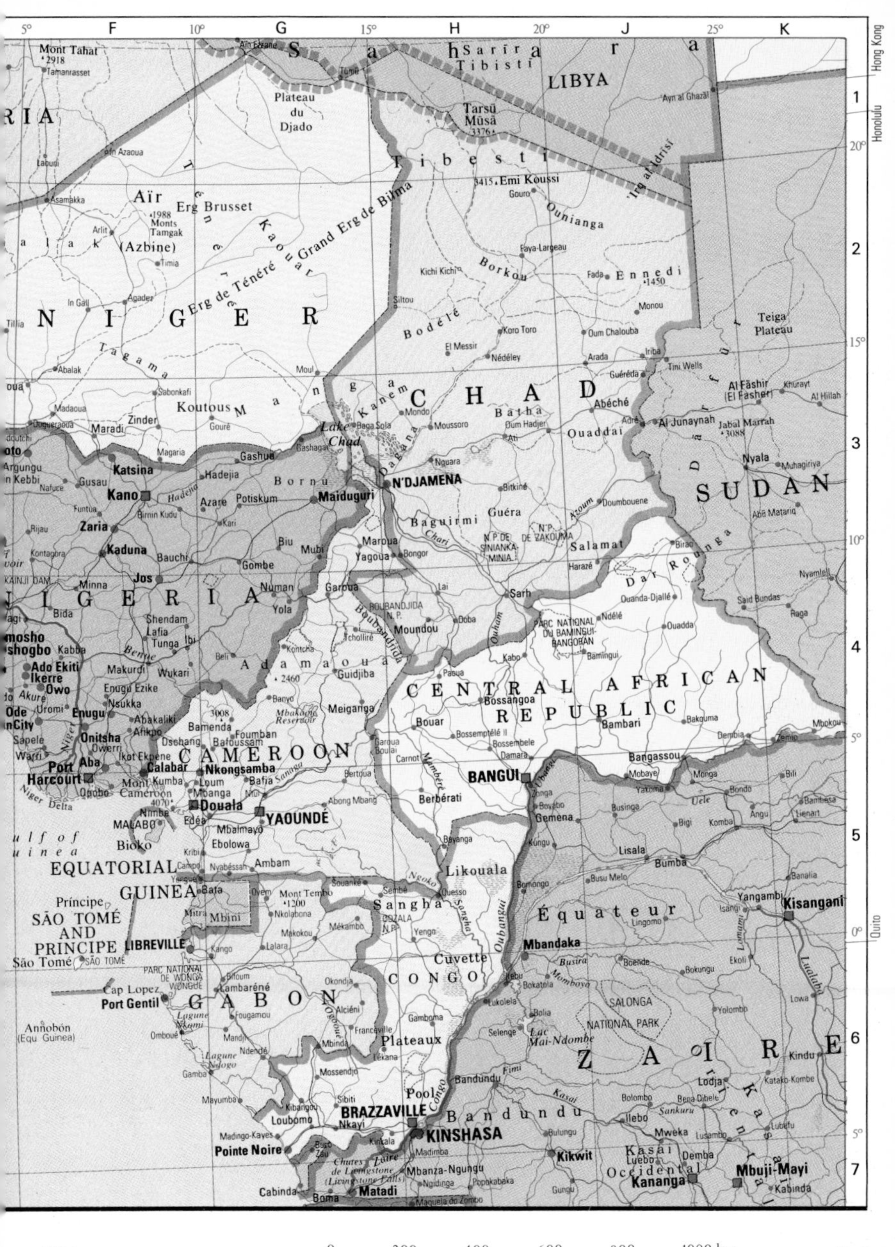

ıeter = 3,28 feet
ıeter = 3,28 feet

Scale 1:20 000 000

0 200 400 600 800 1000 km

0 200 400 600 miles

1 hour

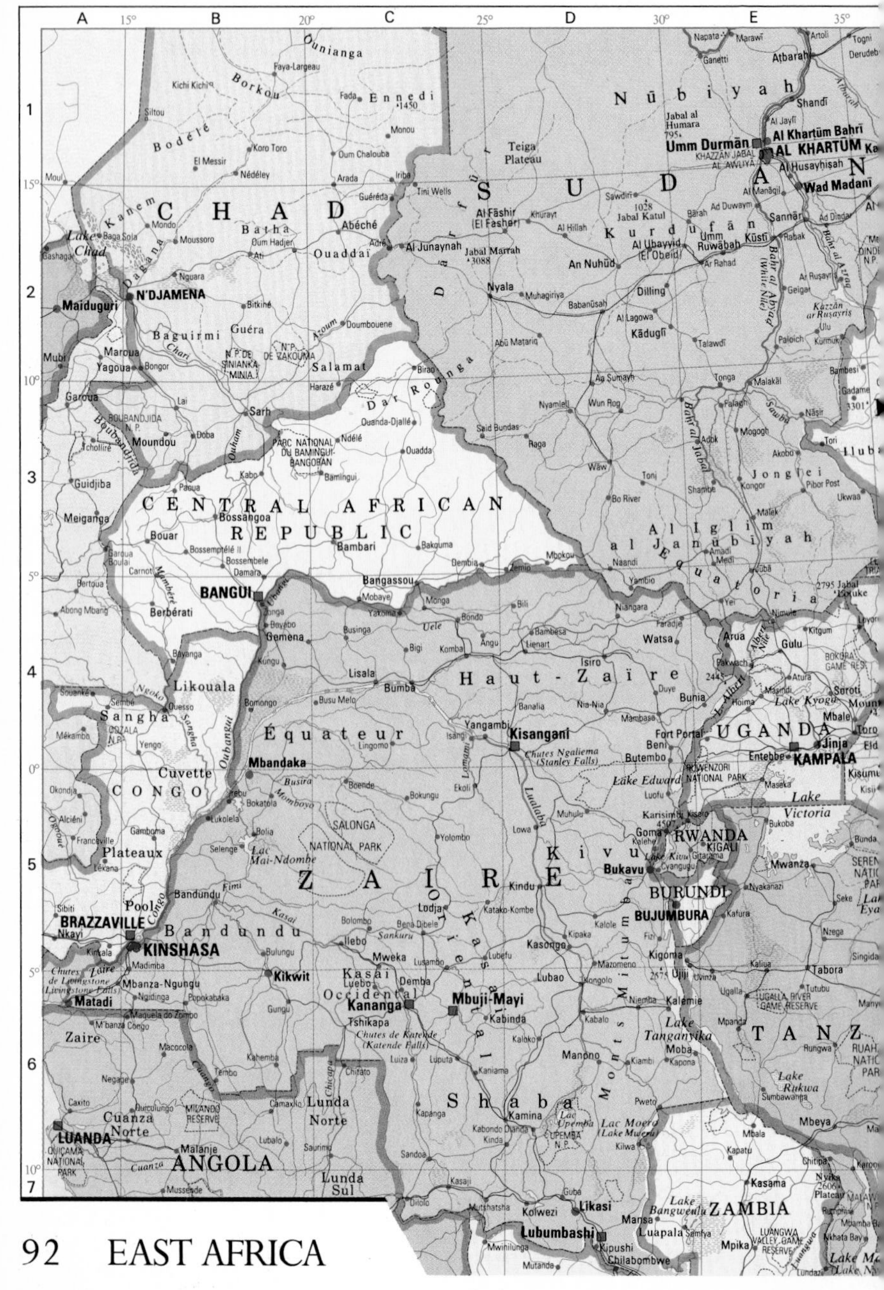
A
B
C
D
E
15°
20°
25°
30°
35°
1
2
3
4
5
6
7
CHAD
SUDAN
CENTRAL AFRICAN REPUBLIC
ZAIRE
CONGO
ANGOLA
UGANDA
RWANDA
BURUNDI
ZAMBIA
TANZ
N'DJAMENA
BANGUI
KINSHASA
BRAZZAVILLE
LUANDA
KAMPALA
KIGALI
BUJUMBURA
AL KHARTŪM
Al Khartūm Bahrī
Umm Durmān
Nūbiyah
Kurdufān
Darfūr
Teiga Plateau
Al Fāshir (El Fasher)
Al Junaynah
Jabal Marrah 3088
Nyala
An Nuhūd
Al Ubayyid (El Obeid)
Kūstī
Wad Madanī
Sannār
Atbarah
Shandī
Dilling
Kāduglī
Malakāl
Jonglei
Al Iqlīm al Janūbiyah
Al Istiwā'iyah
Juba
Wāw
Bahr al Jabal
Bahr al Abyad (White Nile)
Bahr al Azraq
Kanem
Batha
Abéché
Ouaddaï
Borkou
Ennedi 1450
Ounianga
Faya-Largeau
Bodélé
Lake Chad
Baguirmi
Guéra
Salamat
Sarh
Moundou
Maiduguri
Dar Rounga
PARC NATIONAL DU BAMINGUI-BANGORAN
Bossangoa
Bambari
Bangassou
Berbérati
Likouala
Sangha
Cuvette
Plateaux
Pool
Gemena
Lisala
Bumba
Haut-Zaïre
Équateur
Mbandaka
Kisangani
Chutes Ngaliema (Stanley Falls)
Isiro
Bunia
Arua
Gulu
Lake Kyoga
Jinja
Entebbe
Fort Portal
Lake Edward
RUWENZORI NATIONAL PARK
Lake Victoria
Goma
Bukavu
Kivu
Lake Albert
SALONGA NATIONAL PARK
Lac Mai-Ndombe
Bandundu
Kikwit
Kasai Occidental
Kasai Oriental
Kananga
Mbuji-Mayi
Tshikapa
Chutes de Katende (Katende Falls)
Kindu
Kasongo
Kalemie
Lake Tanganyika
Kigoma
Tabora
Mwanza
Shaba
Kamina
Lac Upemba
Lac Moero (Lake Mweru)
Likasi
Lubumbashi
Kolwezi
Lake Bangweulu
Kasama
Mbeya
Lake Rukwa
Lunda Norte
Lunda Sul
Cuanza Norte
Matadi
Malanje
Zaire
Chutes de Livingstone (Livingstone Falls)
Monts Mitumba
Lualaba
Ubangi
Congo
Kasai
Uele

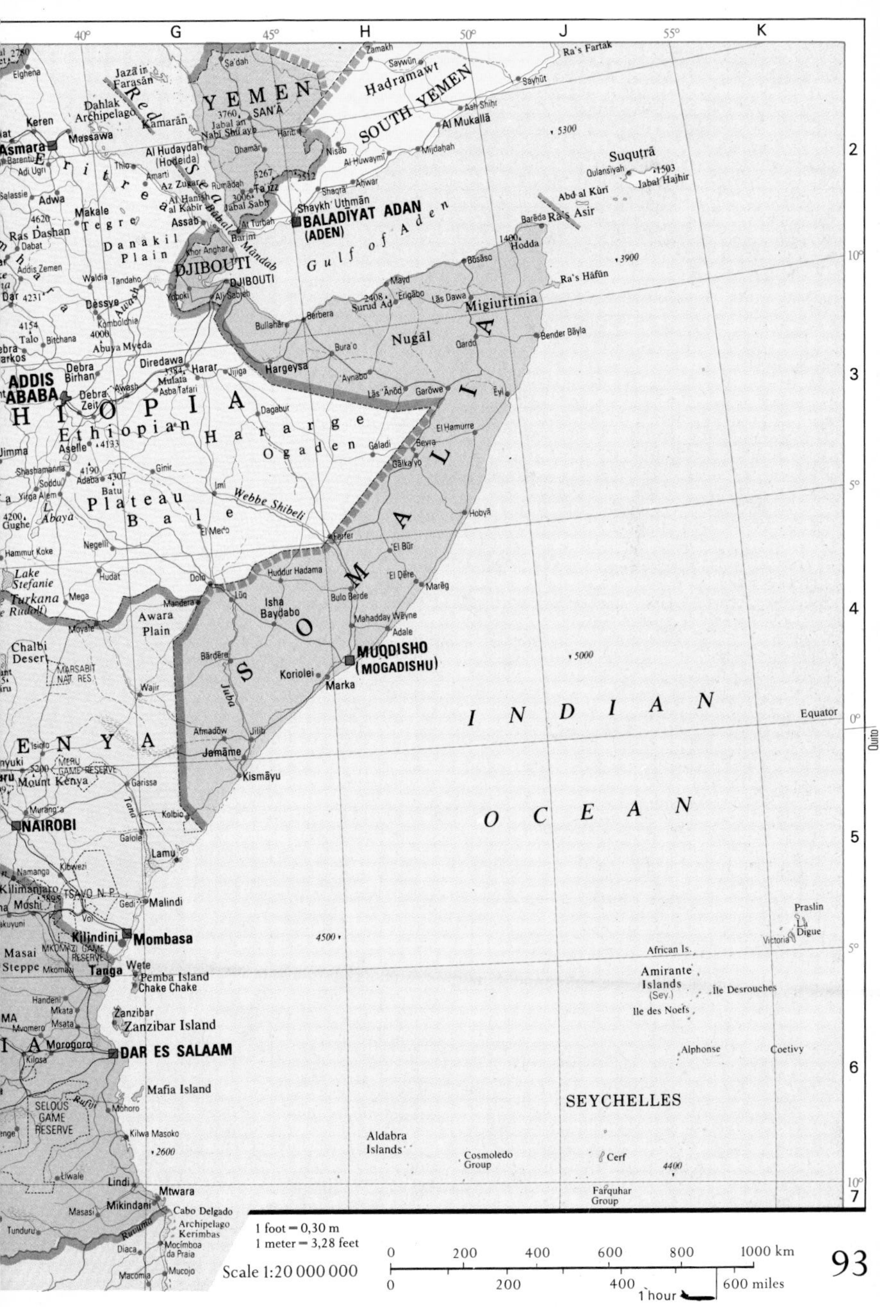
YEMEN
SAN'Ā
SOUTH YEMEN
Hadramawt
Al Mukallā
Suqutrā
BALADIYAT ADAN
(ADEN)
Gulf of Aden
DJIBOUTI
Red Sea
Bab al Māndab
Eritrea
Asmara
Massawa
Dahlak Archipelago
Danakil Plain
ADDIS ABABA
ETHIOPIA
Ethiopian Plateau
Bale
Hararge
Ogaden
Webbe Shibeli
SOMALIA
Nugāl
Migiurtinia
Hargeysa
Berbera
MUQDISHO
(MOGADISHU)
Kismāyu
Juba
KENYA
NAIROBI
Mount Kenya
Mombasa
Tanga
Pemba Island
Zanzibar Island
DAR ES SALAAM
Mafia Island
INDIAN OCEAN
Equator
SEYCHELLES
Amirante Islands
Aldabra Islands
Cosmoledo Group
Farquhar Group
Praslin
La Digue
Victoria
Ras Asir
Ras Hāfūn
Lake Turkana (Lake Rudolf)
Chalbi Desert
Awara Plain
1 foot = 0,30 m
1 meter = 3,28 feet
Scale 1:20 000 000
0 200 400 600 800 1000 km
0 200 400 600 miles
1 hour

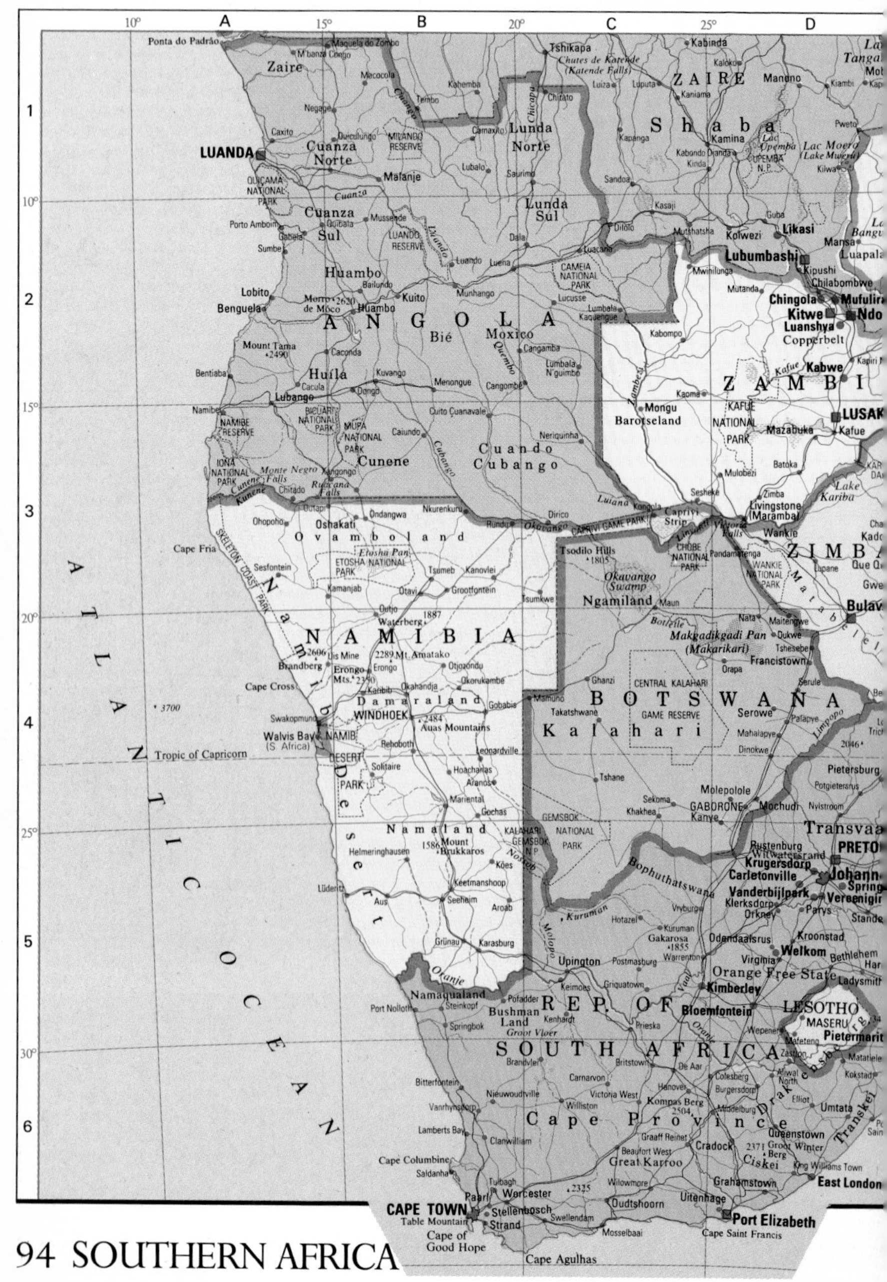

94 SOUTHERN AFRICA

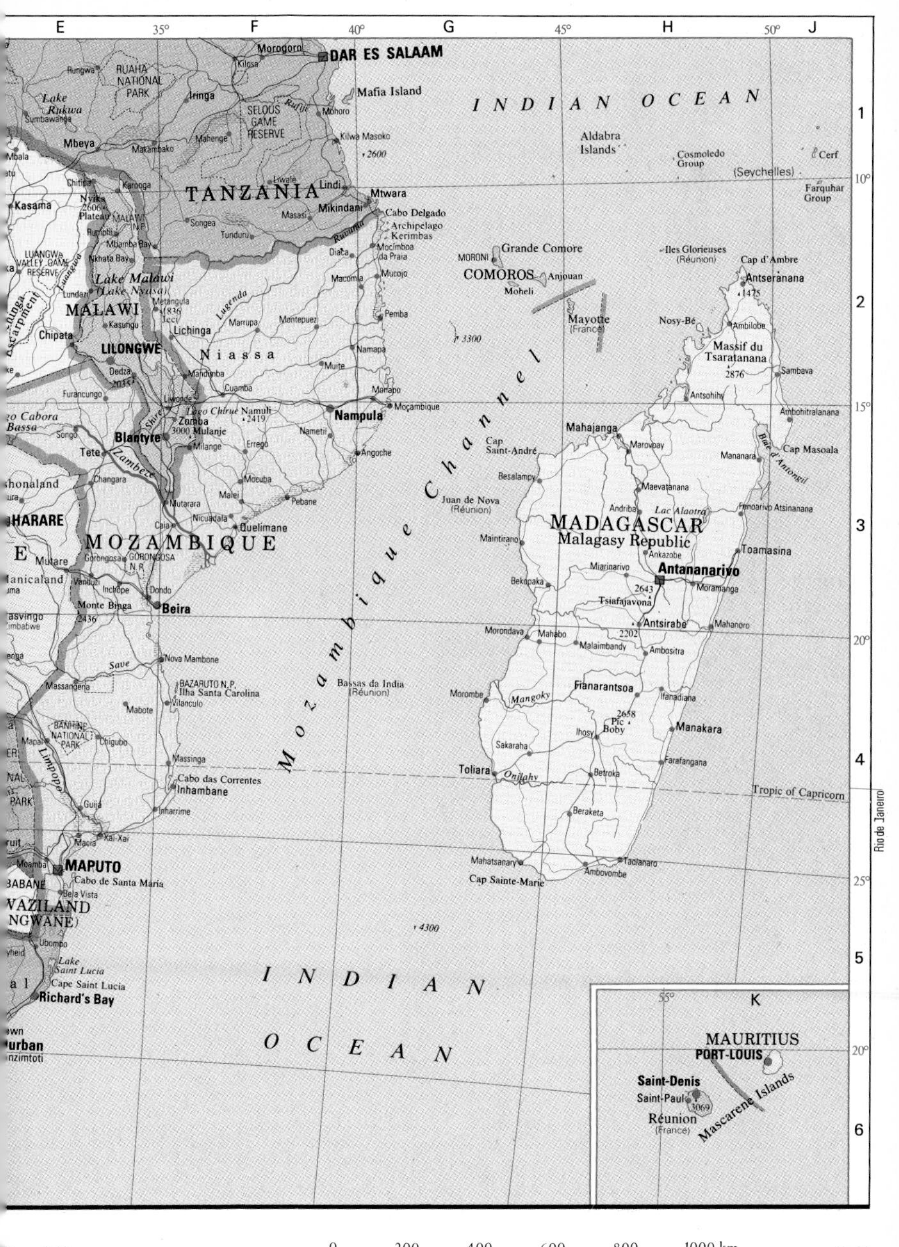

1 foot = 0,30 m
1 meter = 3,28 feet

Scale 1:20 000 000

0 200 400 600 800 1000 km
0 200 400 600 miles
1 hour

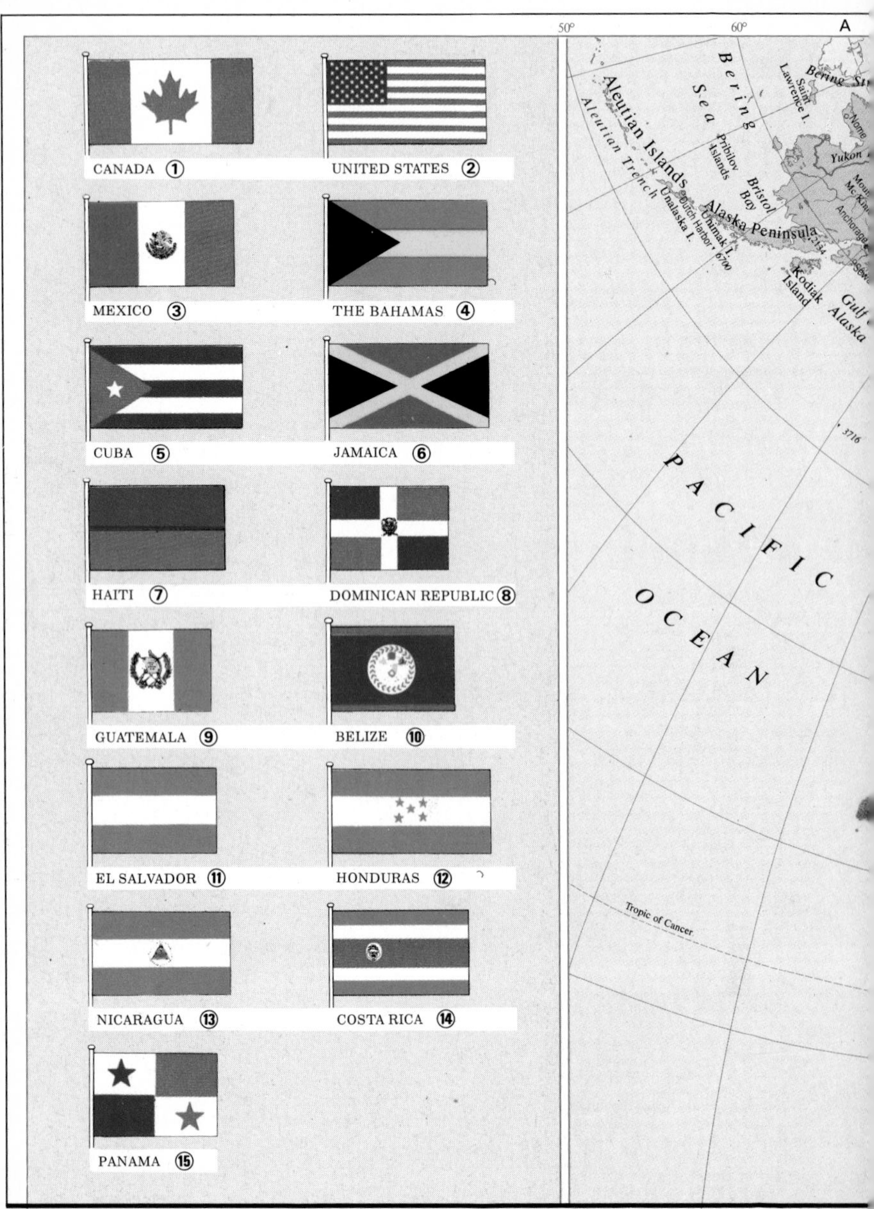

1 foot = 0,30 m
1 meter = 3,28 feet

Scale 1:50 000 0

Greenland
(Denmark)
Thule
Upernavik
Umanak
Jakobshavn
Disko
Egedesminde
Angmagssalik
Godthåb
Frederikshåb
Julianehåb
C. Farewell
Ellesmere Island
Sverdrup Islands
Queen Elizabeth Islands
Prince Patrick Island
Parry Islands
Melville Island
Area of Magnetic N. Pole
Devon Island
Somerset Island
Prince of Wales Island
Banks Island
Victoria Island
Boothia Pen.
Melville Peninsula
Baffin Bay
Davis Strait
Baffin Island
Foxe Basin
Beaufort Sea
Barrow
Prudhoe Bay
Aklavik
Inuvik
Dawson
Yukon
Mackenzie Mountains
Mackenzie R.
Great Bear Lake
Northwest Territories
Echo Bay
Arctic Circle
Back R.
Whitehorse
Skagway
Yellowknife
Great Slave Lake
Hay River
Liard
Southampton Island
Hudson Strait
Cape Chidley
Ungava Bay
Ungava Peninsula
Hudson Bay
Kazan R.
Labrador Sea
Newfoundland and Labrador
Schefferville
Goose Bay
Labrador
Peace R.
Lake Athabasca
Churchill
Reindeer Lake
Mc Murray
CANADA
Dawson Creek
Lynn Lake
Nelson R.
Port Nelson
Belcher Islands
British Columbia
Prince George
Alberta
Edmonton
Saskatchewan
Manitoba
Severn R.
James Bay
Quebec
Gagnon
Sept-Îles
Anticosti I.
Gulf of Saint Lawrence
Corner Brook
St. John's
St. Pierre and Miquelon (Fr.)
Vancouver
Kamloops
Calgary
Saskatoon
Lake Winnipeg
Albany R.
Moosonee
Port Cartier
Sydney
Cape Breton Island
Seattle
Regina
Brandon
Lake Manitoba
Winnipeg
Ontario
Québec
St. Lawrence R.
New Brunswick
Nova Scotia
Halifax
Mt. Rainier
Columbia River
Spokane
Thunder Bay
Trois-Rivières
Saint John
Missouri R.
Yellowstone R.
Bismarck
Billings
L. Superior
Duluth
Montreal
OTTAWA
Portland
Columbia Plateau
ROCKY MOUNTAINS
Coast Mountains
Cascade Range
L. Huron
L. Michigan
L. Ontario
Toronto
Hamilton
Rochester
Buffalo
Boston
Cape Cod
Boise
Minneapolis
St. Paul
Milwaukee
Detroit
Niagara Falls
Snake R.
Pierre
Sioux Falls
Madison
Cleveland
Newark
New York
Great Salt Lake
Salt Lake City
Cheyenne
Omaha
Chicago
Toledo
Pittsburgh
Philadelphia
Baltimore
WASHINGTON
Reno
Sacramento
Oakland
San José
Great Basin
Sierra Nevada
Denver
Lincoln
Des Moines
Indianapolis
Columbus
Mount Elbert
Colorado Springs
UNITED STATES (USA)
Richmond
Norfolk
Death Valley
Mount Whitney
Las Vegas
Colorado R.
Wichita
Kansas City
St. Louis
Louisville
Ohio R.
Grand Canyon
Nashville
Mount Mitchell
Charlotte
Cape Hatteras
Santa Fe
Albuquerque
Oklahoma City
Tulsa
Memphis
Appalachian Mountains
Bermuda Islands (U.K.)
Phoenix
Tucson
Lubbock
Red River
Little Rock
Atlanta
Charleston
Savannah
Mississippi R.
Birmingham
Jackson
Fort Worth
Dallas
Long Beach
San Diego
Tijuana
Mexicali
Rio Grande
El Paso
Ciudad Juárez
Mobile
Jacksonville
Lower California
Gulf of California
Hermosillo
Austin
Beaumont
New Orleans
Houston
Galveston
Cape Canaveral
Florida
Tampa
St. Petersburg
San Antonio
Chihuahua
Western Sierra Madre
Eastern Sierra Madre
Corpus Christi
Miami
NASSAU
THE BAHAMAS
Tropic of Cancer
Gulf of Mexico
Key West
Straits of Florida
Torreón
Saltillo
Monterrey
Matamoros
West Indies
Puerto Rico Trench
HAVANA
Santa Clara
Culiacán
MEXICO
C. San Lucas
Mazatlán
San Luis Potosí
Aguascalientes
Tampico
Yucatán Channel
CUBA
Guantánamo
Santiago de Cuba
HAITI
DOMINICAN REPUBLIC
San Juan
Puerto Rico (U.S.A.)
PORT-AU-PRINCE
SANTO DOMINGO
Greater Antilles
León
Guadalajara
Santiago R.
Mérida
Chichén Itzá
Bay of Campeche
MEXICO CITY
Veracruz
Revilla Gigedo Is. (Mexico)
Morelia
Mt. Popocatepetl
Puebla
JAMAICA
KINGSTON
BELIZE
BELMOPAN
Aruba I. (Neth.)
Curaçao I. (Neth.)
Bonaire I. (Neth.)
Southern Sierra Madre
Isthmus of Tehuantepec
Acapulco
Mt. Tajamulco
GUATEMALA
HONDURAS
TEGUCIGALPA
Caribbean Sea
P. Gallinas
Maracaibo
Barquisimeto
CARACAS
Middle America Trench
EL SALVADOR
SAN SALVADOR
NICARAGUA
Lake Nicaragua
Barranquilla
Cartagena
Mt. Cristóbal Colón
Valencia
VENEZUELA
MANAGUA
COSTA RICA
SAN JOSÉ
Panama Canal
Colón
Pan (U.S.A.)
PANAMA
San Cristóbal
Bucaramanga
COLOMBIA
Medellín
Manizales
BOGOTÁ
Moscow
Rome
Athens
Cairo
Al Kharțum
500 1000 km
200 400 600 miles
1 hour

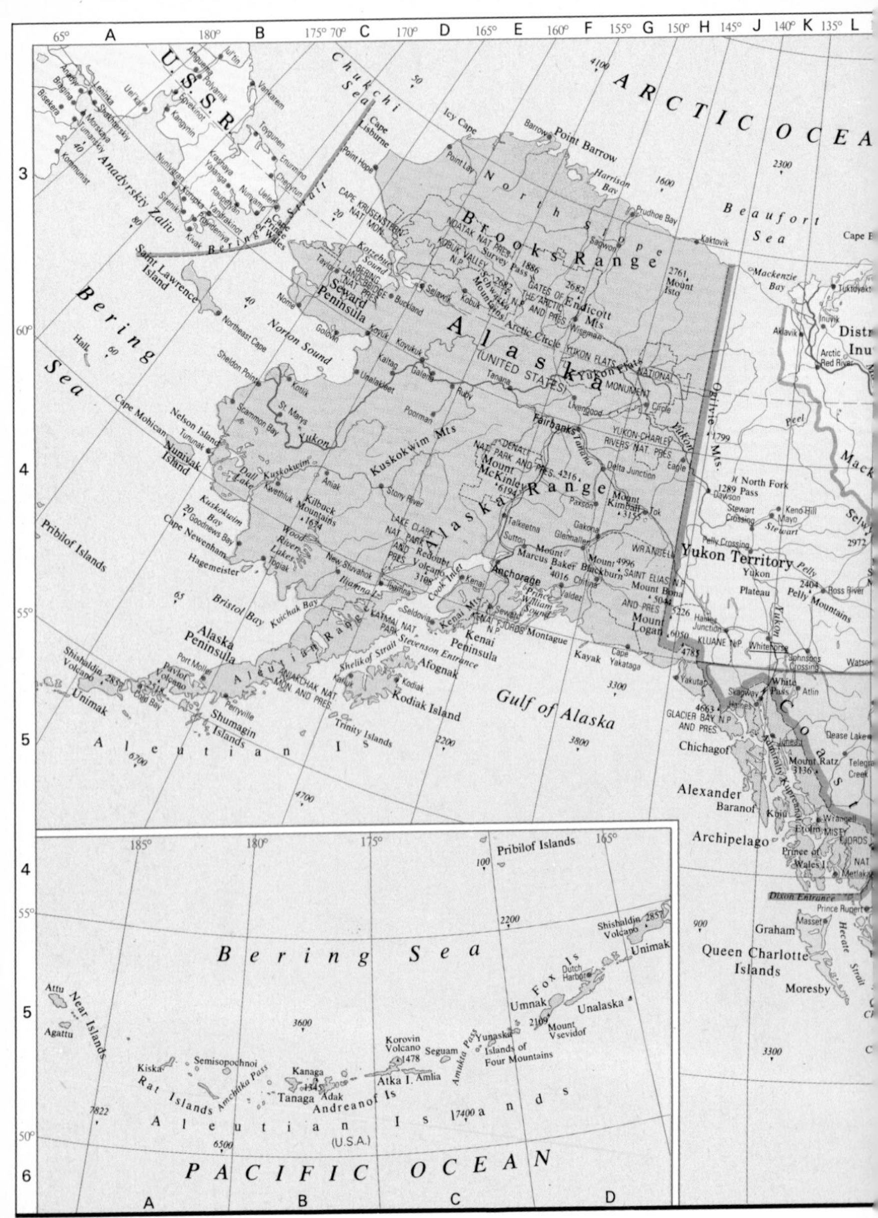
ARCTIC OCEAN
Chukchi Sea
Beaufort Sea
Bering Sea
Bering Strait
Anadyrskiy Zaliv
U.S.S.R.
Cape Lisburne
Point Hope
Icy Cape
Point Lay
Barrow
Point Barrow
Harrison Bay
Prudhoe Bay
Kaktovik
North Slope
Brooks Range
Mount Isto
Mackenzie Bay
Saint Lawrence Island
Seward Peninsula
Kotzebue Sound
Nome
Norton Sound
Alaska
(UNITED STATES)
Yukon Flats
Arctic Circle
Endicott Mts
Fairbanks
Tanana
Yukon
Kuskokwim Mts
Nelson Island
Nunivak Island
Kuskokwim Bay
Cape Newenham
Pribilof Islands
Kilbuck Mountains
Alaska Range
Mount McKinley
6194
Mount Kimball
Mount Marcus Baker
Mount Blackburn
Anchorage
Cook Inlet
Prince William Sound
Kenai Peninsula
Mount Logan
Bristol Bay
Alaska Peninsula
Aleutian Range
Shelikof Strait
Kodiak Island
Afognak
Gulf of Alaska
Shumagin Islands
Unimak
Aleutian Is
Yukon Territory
Ogilvie Mts.
Pelly Mountains
Yukon Plateau
Whitehorse
Juneau
Chichagof
Alexander Archipelago
Baranof
Prince of Wales I.
Dixon Entrance
Prince Rupert
Queen Charlotte Islands
Graham
Moresby
Hecate Strait
Pribilof Islands
Bering Sea
Near Islands
Attu
Agattu
Kiska
Semisopochnoi
Rat Islands
Amchitka Pass
Kanaga
Tanaga
Adak
Andreanof Is
Atka I.
Amlia
Korovin Volcano
Seguam
Amukta Pass
Yunaska
Islands of Four Mountains
Umnak
Fox Is
Dutch Harbor
Unalaska
Mount Vsevidof
Shishaldin Volcano
Aleutian Islands
(U.S.A.)
PACIFIC OCEAN

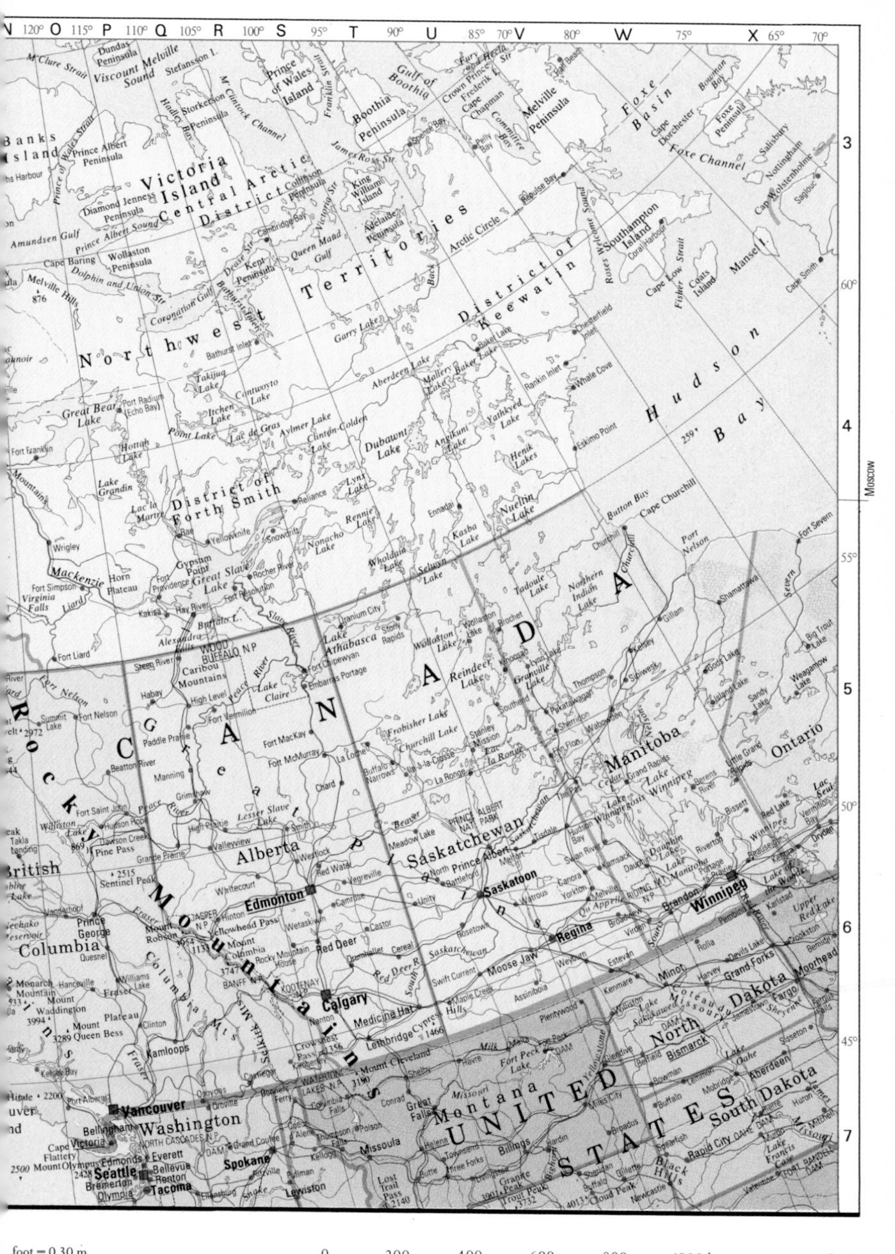

foot = 0,30 m
meter = 3,28 feet

Scale 1:20 000 000

0 200 400 600 800 1000 km
0 200 400 600 miles
1 hour

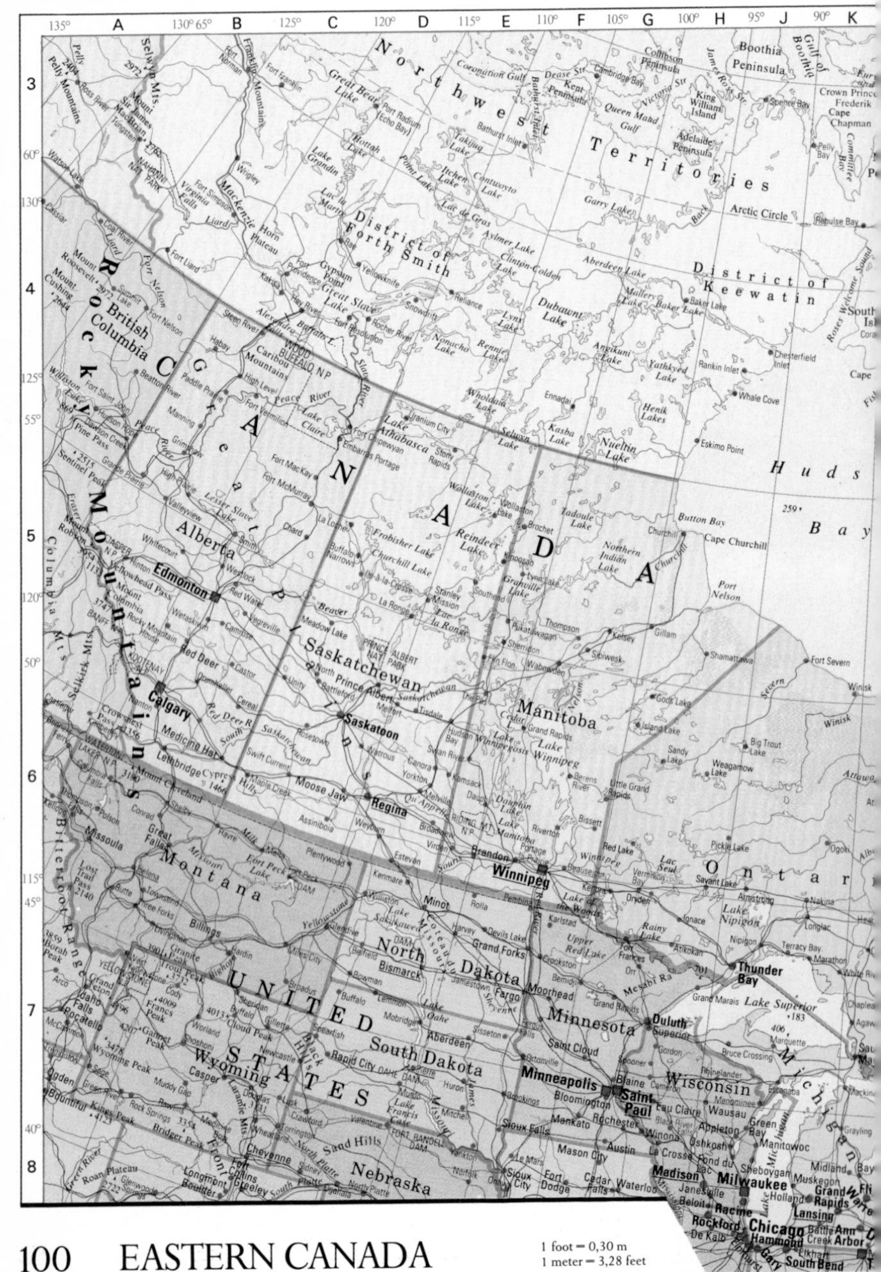

1 foot = 0,30 m
1 meter = 3,28 feet

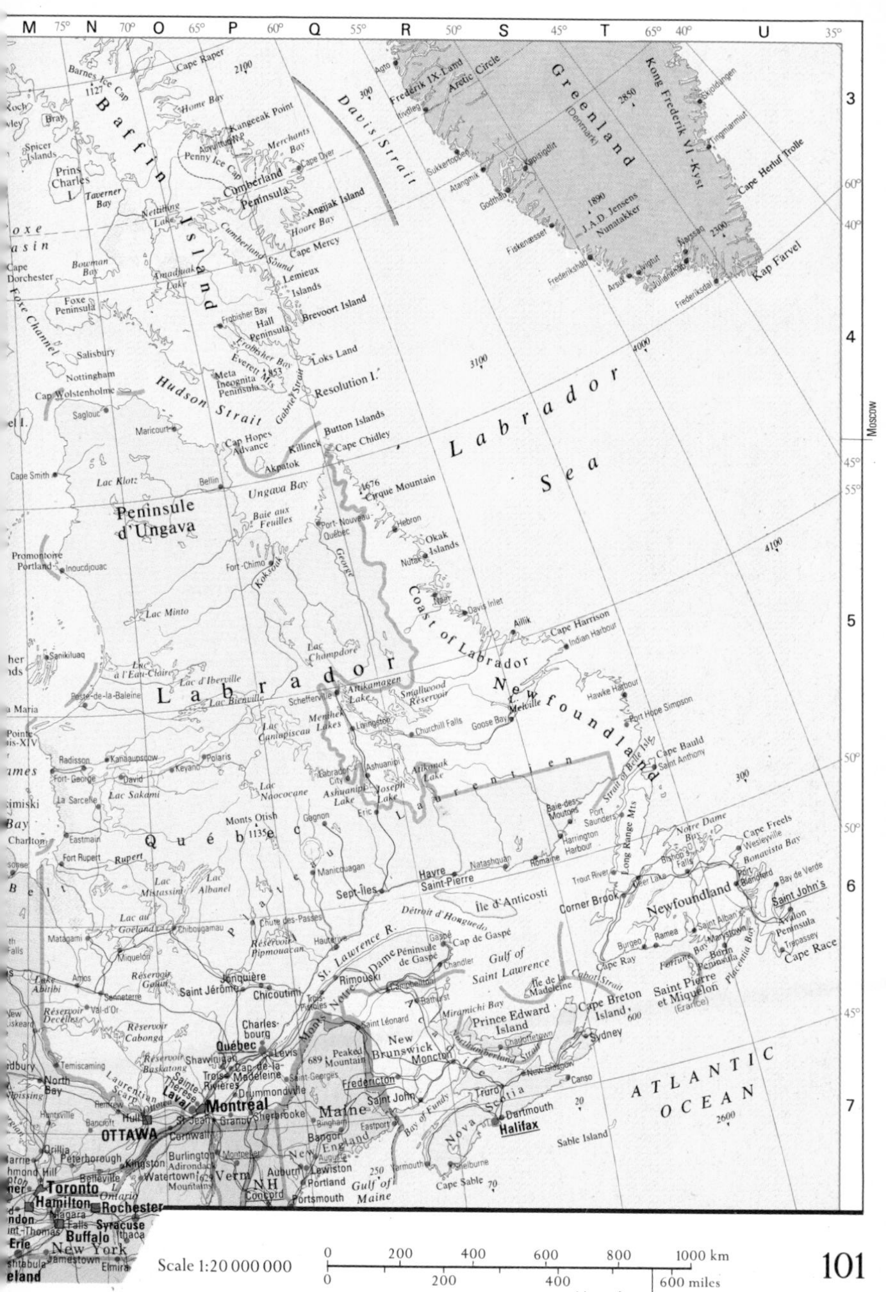

Scale 1:20 000 000

0 200 400 600 800 1000 km

0 200 400 600 miles

1 hour

1 foot = 0,30 m
1 meter = 3,28 feet

Scale 1:20 000 00

95°
H
90°
J
85°
K
80°
L
50°
75°
M
70°
N
65°
2
3
4
5
6
7
45°
40°
35°
30°
25°
70°
Rome
Cairo
Delhi
Ontario
CANADA
Québec
New Brunswick
Moncton
Fredericton
Saint John
Bay of Fundy
Red Lake
Lac Seul
Savant Lake
Armstrong
Nakina
Hearst
Lake Nipigon
Nipigon
Terrace Bay
Marathon
White River
Kenora
Dryden
Rainy Lake
Atikokan
Upper Red Lake
Fort Frances
Thunder Bay
Lake Superior
Mesabi Ra
Duluth
Superior
Grand Marais
Marquette
Sault Sainte Marie
Chapleau
Sudbury
North Bay
Timmins
Kapuskasing
Réservoir Decelles
Réservoir Cabonga
Réservoir Gouin
Saint Jérôme
Jonquière
Chicoutimi
Charlesbourg
Québec
Shawinigan
Trois Rivières
Drummondville
Sherbrooke
Laval
Montreal
OTTAWA
Laurentian Scarp
Lake Nipissing
Georgian Bay
Huntsville
Cornwall
Kingston
Burlington
Watertown
Adirondack Mountains
Maine
Bangor
Lewiston
Portland
Portsmouth
Auburn
Eastport
Gulf of Maine
New England
Vermont
NH
Concord
Gloucester
Cambridge
Boston
Cape Cod
Lowell
Worcester
Mass
New Bedford
Fall River
Providence
Springfield
Hartford
New Haven
Bridgeport
Stamford
Yonkers
Waterbury
Paterson
New York
Newark
Trenton
Philadelphia
Atlantic City
NJ
Delaware
Dover
Wilmington
Annapolis
Baltimore
WASHINGTON
Arlington
Alexandria
Maryland
Accomac
Cape Charles
CHESAPEAKE BAY BRIDGE-TUNNEL
Richmond
Norfolk
Virginia Beach
Portsmouth
Charlottesville
Petersburg
Lynchburg
Danville
Virginia
Greensboro
Rocky Mount
Wilson
Durham
Raleigh
Goldsboro
Pamlico Sound
Cape Hatteras
New Bern
Cape Lookout
Winston-Salem
Kannapolis
Charlotte
Fayetteville
Wilmington
Cape Fear
Rock Hill
Spartanburg
Greenville
Sumter
Columbia
Myrtle Beach
South Carolina
Charleston
Beaufort
Savannah
Augusta
Athens
Macon
Georgia
Columbus
Albany
Valdosta
Waycross
Jacksonville
Tallahassee
Lake City
Gainesville
Daytona Beach
Ocala
Titusville
Cape Canaveral
Merritt Island
Melbourne
Orlando
Tampa
Lakeland
Palm Bay
Fort Pierce
Clearwater
Saint Petersburg
Bradenton
Sarasota
Florida
Lake Okeechobee
West Palm Beach
Boca Raton
Fort Lauderdale
Hollywood
Fort Myers
The Everglades
Hialeah
Miami
Miami Beach
EVERGLADES NAT PARK
Cape Sable
Key West
Florida Keys
Straits of Florida
Toronto
Hamilton
Rochester
Syracuse
Utica
Schenectady
Albany
Amsterdam
Ithaca
Binghamton
Elmira
Buffalo
Niagara
Lake Ontario
Oshawa
Barrie
Orillia
Peterborough
Belleville
Kitchener
Brampton
London
Saint Thomas
Chatham
Windsor
Sarnia
Lake Huron
Lake Erie
Erie
Jamestown
New York
Newburgh
Pennsylvania
Williamsport
Wilkes-Barre
Allentown
Lebanon
Harrisburg
York
Johnstown
Pittsburgh
McKeesport
Youngstown
Cleveland
Ashtabula
Canton
Akron
Ohio
Mansfield
Marion
Toledo
Lima
Findlay
Columbus
Dayton
Xenia
Cincinnati
Steubenville
Wheeling
Zanesville
Newark
Parkersburg
Clarksburg
Fairmont
Cumberland
West Virginia
Charleston
Huntington
Portsmouth
Shenandoah
Alpena
Michigan
Lake Michigan
Grayling
Bay City
Saginaw
Flint
Midland
Port Huron
Warren
Detroit
Ann Arbor
Lansing
Grand Rapids
Muskegon
Holland
Battle Creek
Monroe
South Bend
Elkhart
Fort Wayne
Marion
Kokomo
Muncie
Anderson
Indiana
Indianapolis
Lafayette
Bloomington
Columbus
Covington
Frankfort
Louisville
New Albany
Lexington
Kentucky
Owensboro
Evansville
Bowling Green
Paducah
Cumberland Plateau
Appalachian Mountains
Blue Ridge
Kingsport
Knoxville
Oak Ridge
Asheville
Nashville
Tennessee
Clarksville
Jackson
Chattanooga
Huntsville
Memphis
West Memphis
Florence
Decatur
Marietta
Atlanta
Gadsden
Birmingham
Tuscaloosa
Alabama
Montgomery
Selma
Phenix City
Dothan
Mobile
Pensacola
Panama City
Cape San Blas
Gulfport
Biloxi
Pascagoula
Hattiesburg
Mississippi
Meridian
Jackson
Vicksburg
Greenville
Columbus
Tupelo
Natchez
Baton Rouge
Metairie
New Orleans
Lafayette
New Iberia
Houma
Mississippi Delta
Lake Charles
Beaumont
Port Arthur
Orange
Houston
Baytown
Texas City
Galveston
Palacios
Matagorda Island
Corpus Christi
Padre Island
Kingsville
Brownsville
Matamoros
Wisconsin
Rhinelander
Wausau
Eau Claire
Green Bay
Appleton
Oshkosh
Manitowoc
Sheboygan
Fond du Lac
La Crosse
Winona
Madison
Milwaukee
Racine
Janesville
Beloit
Rockford
Chicago
Hammond
Gary
De Kalb
Dubuque
Cedar Rapids
Waterloo
Cedar Falls
Davenport
Rock Island
Moline
Galesburg
Peoria
Pekin
Illinois
Decatur
Springfield
Quincy
Alton
Granite City
Belleville
Saint Louis
Minnesota
Saint Cloud
Minneapolis
Saint Paul
Bloomington
Rochester
Mankato
Austin
Mason City
Sioux Falls
Fort Dodge
Ames
Marshalltown
Iowa City
Iowa
Des Moines
Ottumwa
Burlington
Council Bluffs
Sioux City
Kirksville
Saint Joseph
Kansas City
Independence
Columbia
Jefferson City
Missouri
Lake of the Ozarks
Springfield
Joplin
Ozark Plat
UNITED STATES
Cape Girardeau
Tulsa
Bartlesville
Muskogee
Fayetteville
Fort Smith
Arkansas
Little Rock
North Little Rock
Pine Bluff
Hot Springs
Ouachita Mts
Texarkana
El Dorado
Monroe
Shreveport
Bossier City
Longview
Tyler
Alexandria
Dallas
Paris
Red River
Louisiana
ATLANTIC OCEAN
Gulf of Mexico
Tropic of Cancer
Little Abaco Island
Grand Bahama Island
Abaco Island
Marsh Harbour
Northeast Providence Channel
Eleuthera Island
THE BAHAMAS
NASSAU
New Providence I.
Andros Island
Kemps Bay
Cat Island
San Salvador (Watling I.)
Bahama Islands
Great Exuma Island
Long Island
Crooked Island Passage
Acklins Island
Old Bahama Channel
LA HABANA (HAVANA)
San Miguel del Padrón
Marianao
Artemisa
Pinar del Río
Cabo San Antonio
Nueva Gerona
Isla de la Juventud
Güines
Colón
Cárdenas
Sagua la Grande
Caibarién
Santa Clara
Cienfuegos
Placetas
Sancti Spíritus
Trinidad
Morón
Ciego de Ávila
Florida
Camagüey
CUBA
Victoria de las Tunas
Holguín
Banes
Manzanillo
Bayamo
Palma Soriano
Santiago de Cuba
Guantánamo
Naval station (USA)
Cayman Islands (U.K.)
0 200 400 600 800 1000 km
0 200 400 600 miles
1 hour

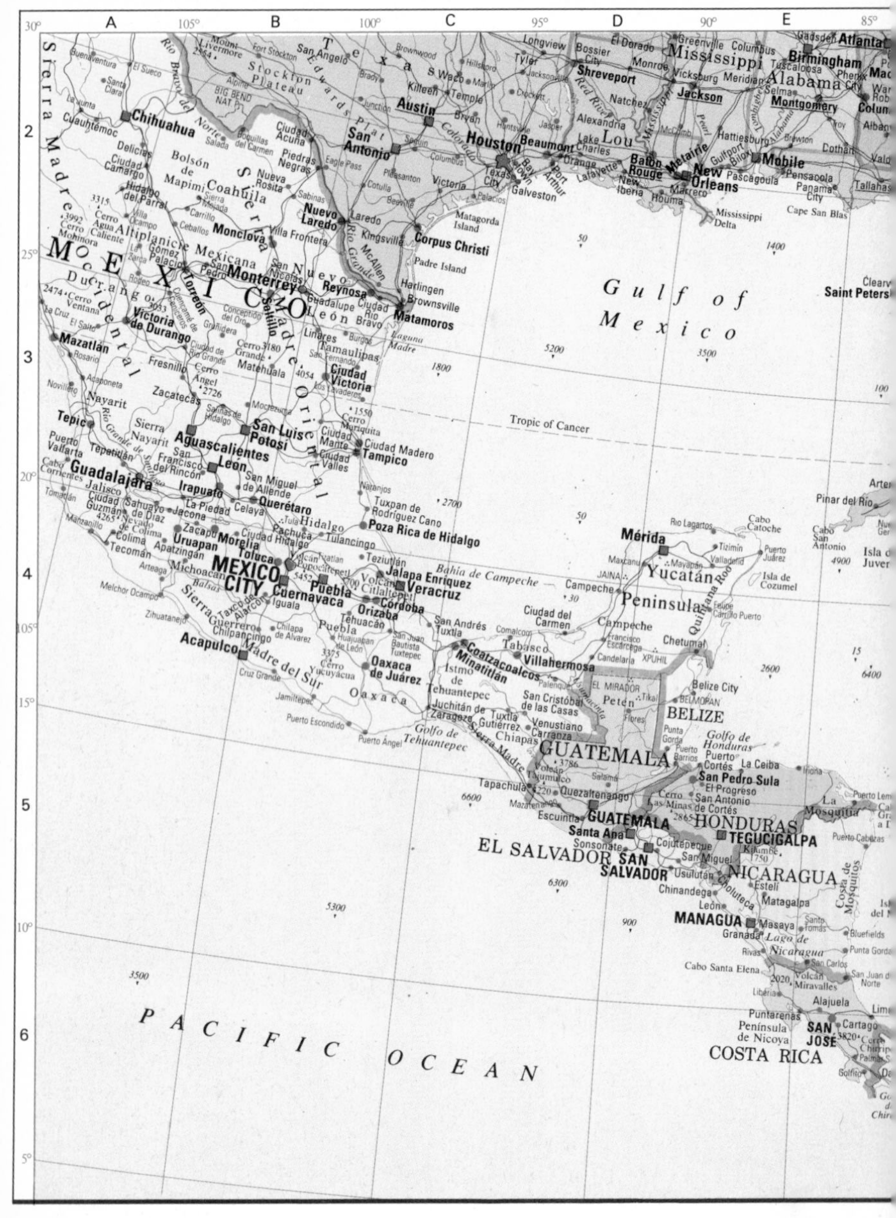

A
B
C
D
E
105°
100°
95°
90°
85°
30°
25°
20°
15°
10°
5°
2
3
4
5
6
Texas
Mississippi
Alabama
Louisiana
Atlanta
Birmingham
Montgomery
Mobile
Jackson
Shreveport
Austin
San Antonio
Houston
Beaumont
Baton Rouge
New Orleans
Galveston
Corpus Christi
Laredo
Nuevo Laredo
Brownsville
Matamoros
Reynosa
Chihuahua
Monclova
Monterrey
Saltillo
Torreón
Victoria de Durango
Mazatlán
Ciudad Victoria
Tampico
San Luis Potosí
Aguascalientes
León
Guadalajara
Irapuato
Querétaro
Poza Rica de Hidalgo
Morelia
Uruapan
Toluca
MEXICO CITY
Puebla
Cuernavaca
Jalapa Enríquez
Veracruz
Córdoba
Orizaba
Acapulco
Oaxaca de Juárez
Coatzacoalcos
Minatitlán
Villahermosa
Mérida
Campeche
Chetumal
Tepic
Zacatecas
MEXICO
Sierra Madre Occidental
Sierra Madre Oriental
Sierra Madre del Sur
Altiplanicie Mexicana
Bolsón de Mapimí
Gulf of Mexico
Bahía de Campeche
Tropic of Cancer
Yucatán Peninsula
Istmo de Tehuantepec
Golfo de Tehuantepec
GUATEMALA
BELIZE
Belize City
HONDURAS
TEGUCIGALPA
San Pedro Sula
EL SALVADOR
SAN SALVADOR
Santa Ana
NICARAGUA
MANAGUA
Lago de Nicaragua
COSTA RICA
SAN JOSÉ
Golfo de Honduras
Quezaltenango
Tapachula
Saint Petersburg
Pinar del Río
PACIFIC OCEAN

1 foot = 0,30 m
1 meter = 3,28 feet

Scale 1:20 000 000

0 200 400 600 800 1000 km
0 200 400 600 miles
1 hour

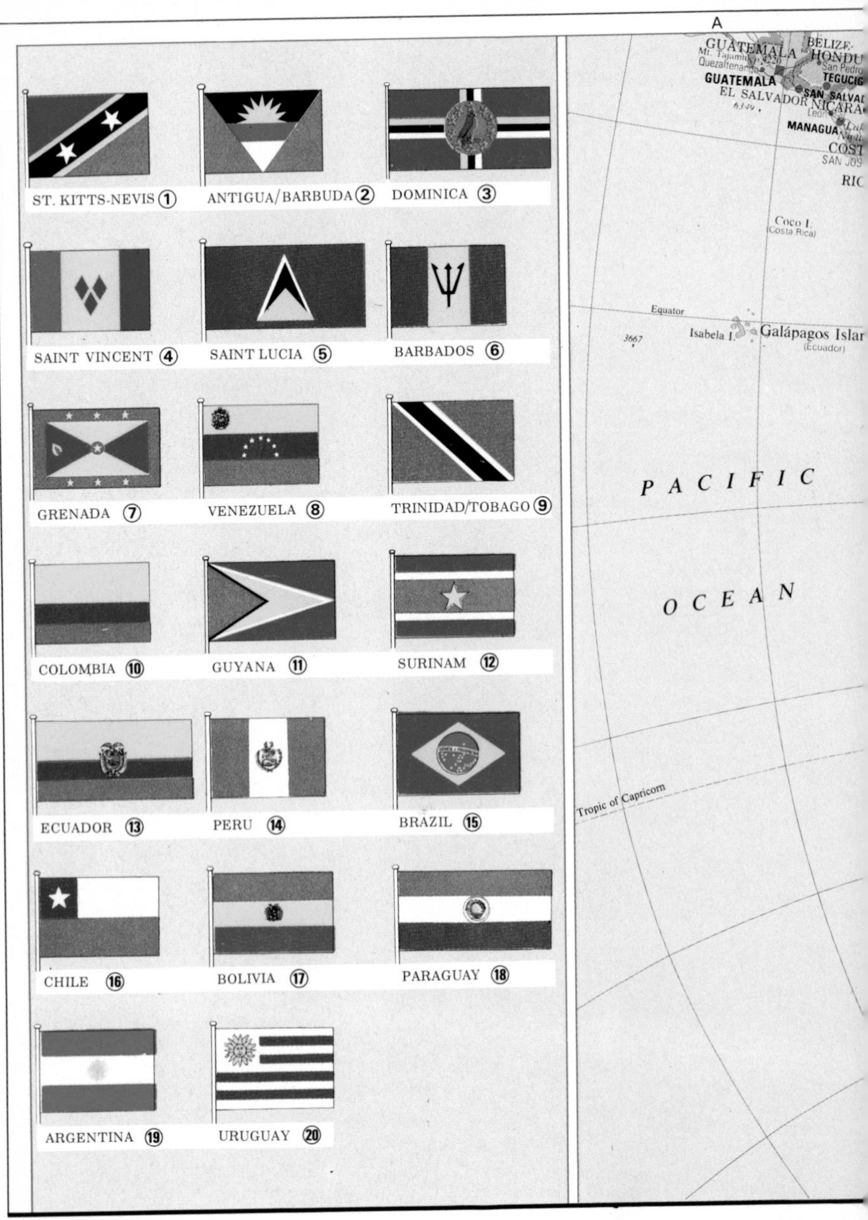
ST. KITTS-NEVIS ①
ANTIGUA/BARBUDA ②
DOMINICA ③
SAINT VINCENT ④
SAINT LUCIA ⑤
BARBADOS ⑥
GRENADA ⑦
VENEZUELA ⑧
TRINIDAD/TOBAGO ⑨
COLOMBIA ⑩
GUYANA ⑪
SURINAM ⑫
ECUADOR ⑬
PERU ⑭
BRAZIL ⑮
CHILE ⑯
BOLIVIA ⑰
PARAGUAY ⑱
ARGENTINA ⑲
URUGUAY ⑳
A
GUATEMALA
BELIZE
GUATEMALA
EL SALVADOR
MANAGUA
Coco I.
(Costa Rica)
Equator
Isabela I.
Galápagos Islar
(Ecuador)
3667
PACIFIC
OCEAN
Tropic of Capricorn

1 foot = 0,30 m
1 meter = 3,28 feet

Scale 1:50 000

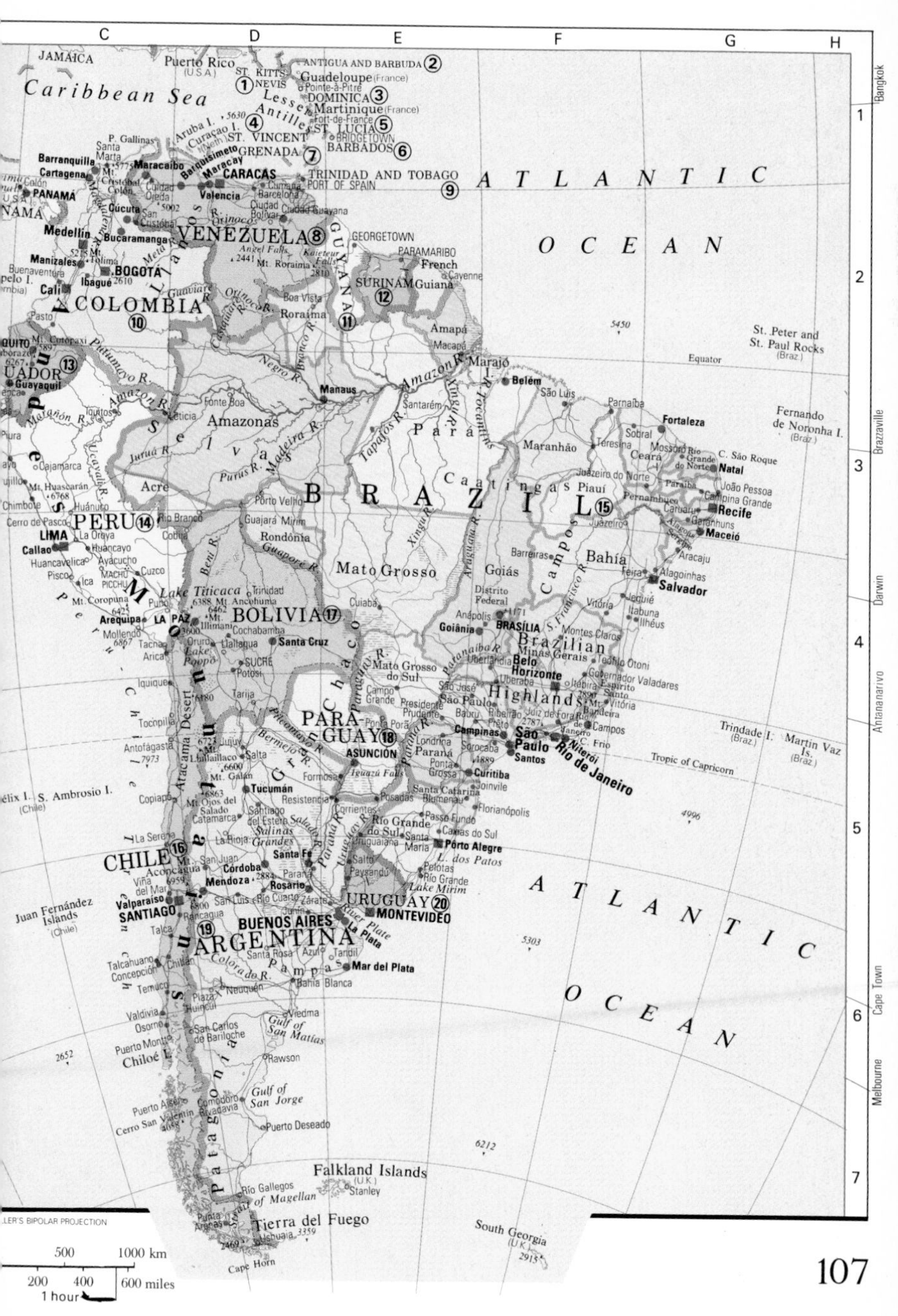
C
D
E
F
G
H
1
2
3
4
5
6
7
Bangkok
Brazzaville
Darwin
Antananarivo
Cape Town
Melbourne
JAMAICA
Puerto Rico (U.S.A.)
ANTIGUA AND BARBUDA ②
ST. KITTS-NEVIS ①
Guadeloupe (France)
Pointe-à-Pitre
DOMINICA ③
Caribbean Sea
Lesser Antilles
Martinique (France)
Fort-de-France
ST. LUCIA ⑤
Aruba I.
Curaçao I. (Neth.)
ST. VINCENT ④
BRIDGETOWN
BARBADOS ⑥
GRENADA ⑦
TRINIDAD AND TOBAGO ⑨
PORT OF SPAIN
ATLANTIC
OCEAN
Barranquilla
Cartagena
Maracaibo
Barquisimeto
Maracay
CARACAS
Valencia
Cumaná
Barcelona
Ciudad Bolívar
Ciudad Guayana
PANAMA
Cúcuta
Medellín
Bucaramanga
VENEZUELA ⑧
GEORGETOWN
PARAMARIBO
French Guiana
Cayenne
Angel Falls
Mt. Roraima
Kaieteur Falls
GUYANA ⑪
SURINAM ⑫
Manizales
BOGOTÁ
Ibagué
Cali
COLOMBIA ⑩
Orinoco R.
Guaviare R.
Boa Vista
Roraima
Amapá
Macapá
Marajó I.
Belém
São Luís
St. Peter and St. Paul Rocks (Braz.)
Equator
Pasto
QUITO
Mt. Cotopaxi
ECUADOR ⑬
Guayaquil
Putumayo R.
Negro R.
Branco R.
Manaus
Amazon R.
Xingu R.
Tocantins R.
Santarém
Parnaíba
Fortaleza
Fernando de Noronha I. (Braz.)
Iquitos
Marañón R.
Amazon R.
Fonte Boa
Leticia
Amazonas
Selva
Tapajós R.
Madeira R.
Pará
Maranhão
Teresina
Sobral
Ceará
Mossoró
Rio Grande do Norte
C. São Roque
Natal
Cajamarca
Mt. Huascarán
Chimbote
Huánuco
Juruá R.
Purus R.
Acre
Porto Velho
BRAZIL ⑮
Caatingas
Juazeiro do Norte
Piauí
Paraíba
João Pessoa
Campina Grande
Pernambuco
Recife
Caruaru
Garanhuns
Alagoas
Maceió
Sergipe
Aracaju
Juazeiro
Cerro de Pasco
PERU ⑭
Rio Branco
Cobija
Guajará Mirim
Rondônia
Guaporé R.
Mato Grosso
Goiás
Campos
Bahía
Barreiras
Feira
Alagoinhas
Salvador
LIMA
Callao
La Oroya
Huancayo
Huancavelica
Ayacucho
Pisco
Ica
Machu Picchu
Cuzco
Beni R.
Lake Titicaca
Trinidad
Mt. Coropuna
Puno
Mt. Ancohuma
Mt. Illimani
Arequipa
LA PAZ
BOLIVIA ⑰
Cochabamba
Cuiabá
Distrito Federal
Anápolis
Goiânia
BRASÍLIA
Vitória
Jequié
Itabuna
Ilhéus
Mollendo
Tacna
Arica
Oruro
Lake Poopó
Uyuni
Santa Cruz
SUCRE
Potosí
Chaco
Paranaíba R.
Uberlândia
Brazilian Highlands
Minas Gerais
Montes Claros
Belo Horizonte
Teófilo Otoni
Governador Valadares
Espírito Santo
Vitória
Mato Grosso do Sul
Uberaba
Itabira
Iquique
Tarija
Campo Grande
São José
São Paulo
Presidente Prudente
Bauru
Ribeirão Preto
Juiz de Fora
Rio de Janeiro
Campos
Trindade I. (Braz.)
Martin Vaz Is. (Braz.)
Tocopilla
Atacama Desert
PARAGUAY ⑱
Ponta Porã
Campinas
Sorocaba
São Paulo
Santos
Niterói
C. Frio
Rio de Janeiro
Antofagasta
Jujuy
Mt. Llullaillaco
Salta
Bermejo R.
Pilcomayo R.
ASUNCIÓN
Paraná R.
Londrina
Paraná
Ponta Grossa
Curitiba
Joinvile
Tropic of Capricorn
Mt. Galán
Félix I.
S. Ambrosio I. (Chile)
Copiapó
Mt. Ojos del Salado
Tucumán
Resistencia
Formosa
Iguazú Falls
Posadas
Santa Catarina
Blumenau
Florianópolis
Catamarca
Santiago del Estero
Salinas Grandes
Corrientes
Río Grande do Sul
Passo Fundo
Caxias do Sul
Salado R.
Uruguay R.
Uruguaiana
Santa Maria
Pôrto Alegre
L. dos Patos
La Serena
La Rioja
Santa Fe
Salto
Paysandú
Pelotas
Río Grande
Lake Mirim
CHILE ⑯
San Juan
Mt. Aconcagua
Córdoba
Paraná
Viña del Mar
Mendoza
Rosario
Valparaíso
SANTIAGO
San Luis
Río Cuarto
Zárate
URUGUAY ⑳
MONTEVIDEO
Juan Fernández Islands (Chile)
Rancagua
BUENOS AIRES
River Plate
La Plata
Talca
ARGENTINA ⑲
Santa Rosa
Azul
Tandil
Pampas
Mar del Plata
Talcahuano
Concepción
Chillán
Colorado R.
Temuco
Neuquén
Bahía Blanca
Plaza Huincul
Valdivia
Osorno
Viedma
San Carlos de Bariloche
Gulf of San Matías
Puerto Montt
Chiloé I.
Rawson
Patagonia
Puerto Aisén
Comodoro Rivadavia
Gulf of San Jorge
Cerro San Valentín
Puerto Deseado
Falkland Islands (U.K.)
Stanley
Río Gallegos
Strait of Magellan
Punta Arenas
Tierra del Fuego
Ushuaia
South Georgia (U.K.)
Cape Horn
ATLANTIC
OCEAN
MILLER'S BIPOLAR PROJECTION
500
1000 km
200
400
600 miles
1 hour

A
B
C
D
E
85°
80°
75°
70°
10°
5°
0°
1
2
3
4
5
6
NICARAGUA
Estelí
Matagalpa
León
MANAGUA
Masaya
Granada
Rivas
Lago de Nicaragua
Cabo Santa Elena
Islas del Maíz
San Andrés (Col.)
Bluefields
Punta Gorda
San Carlos
San Juan del Norte
San Juan
Liberia
COSTA RICA
Puntarenas
Alajuela
SAN JOSÉ
Limón
Cartago
Cerro Chirripó
3820
Palmar Sur
Golfito
David
Golfo de Chiriquí
Santiago
Las Tablas
Punta Mariato
Golfo de los Mosquitos
Panama Canal
Colón
La Chorrera
PANAMA
Aguadulce
Golfo de Panamá
Darién
La Palma
Caribbean Sea
4000
Neth. Autilles
Aruba
Curaçao
Willemstad
Punta Gallinas
Carrizal
Uribia
Puerto Estrella
Punta Fijo
Barranquilla
Ciénaga
Santa Marta
Pico Cristóbal Colón
5775
Puerto Colombia
Sabanalarga
Cartagena
Soledad
Valledupar
Arjona
San Jacinto
San Onofre
Sincelejo
El Difícil
Magangué
El Banco
Montería
Sahagún
Nicoclí
Turbo
Chigorodó
Riosucio
Caucasia
Golfo de Venezuela
Coro
Maracaibo
Cabimas
Barquisimeto
Lago de Maracaibo
Valera
Trujillo
San Carlos del Zulia
Puerto Villamizar
Mérida
La Fría
Cúcuta
San Cristóbal
Ocaña
Bucaramanga
Floridablanca
Barrancabermeja
Puerto Wilches
Yarumal
Bello
Medellín
Itagüí
Envigado
Caldas
Quibdó
Jurado
Cupica
El Valle
Cabo Corrientes
Atrato
Cord. Occidental
Cord. Central
Cord. Oriental
Duitama
Sogamoso
Tunja
La Dorada
Manizales
Pereira
Armenia
Tolima
5215
BOGOTÁ
Fusagasuga
Buenaventura
Tuluá
Ibagué
Espinal
Buga
Cali
Palmira
Villavicencio
San Martín
Puerto Limón
Neiva
Huila
5750
Popayán
Santander
Guapí
Mosquera
Pitalito
Florencia
Belén
Bolívar
El Diviso
Tumaco
San Lorenzo
Esmeraldas
Pasto
Ipiales
Cumbal
4764
Tulcán
Puerto Asís
Tres Esquinas
COLOMBIA
San José del Guaviare
Calamar
Santa Rita
Vaupés
Mitú
Yari
Lérida
Caquetá
Apaporis
Putumayo
Puerto Leguízamo
El Encanto
Arica
Tame
Puerto Rondón
Arauca
Meta
Puerto Nuevo
Trinidad
Campo Corrai
Orocué
San Pedro de Arimena
Vichada
Llanos
Guaviare
Inírida
Puerto Carreño
Puerto Ayacucho
Orinoco
Puerto Páez
Cerro Yumari
San Fernando de Atabapo
Maroa
San Felipe
Río Negro
Brazo Casiquiare
Taracuá
Uaupés
Içana
Japurá
Puerto Cumarebo
San Luis
Churuguara
San Felipe
Morón
Puerto Cabello
Maracay
CARACAS
Petare
Higuerote
Guarenas
Los Teques
Valencia
San Juan
Acarigua
Valle de la Pascua
Guanare
Barinas
Calabozo
Guayabal
San Fernando de Apure
Apure
Mantecal
Cabruta
VENE
Rojas
Cojimies
Jama
QUITO
Otavalo
Ibarra
Lago Agrio
Francisco de Orellana
Napo
Cotopaxi
5897
Tena
Nuevo Rocafuerte
Bahía de Caráquez
Manta
Portoviejo
Jipijapa
Quevedo
6267
Ambato
Puyo
ECUADOR
Chimborazo
Riobamba
Babahoyo
Salinas
Santa Elena
Milagro
Guayaquil
Macas
Cuenza
Golfo de Guayaquil
Machala
Zaruma
Tumbes
Zorritos
Máncora
Loja
Macará
Zamora
Ayabaca
Borja
Posto Cunambo
Santa Clotilde
Francisco de Orellana
Maynas
Pebas
Iquitos
Amazonas
Parinari
Nauta
Yapura
Caxias
Loreto
Leticia
Benjamin Constant
Tabatinga
Punta Pariñas
Talara
Negritos
Paita
Sullana
Piura
Sechura
Castilla
Huancabamba
Bayovar
Punta Negra
Desierto de Sechura
Naupe
Olmos
Bagua
Barranca
Nazareth
Marañón
Maipuco
Requena
Elvira
Lagunas
Yurimaguas
Chachapoyas
Rioja
Moyobamba
Lamas
Tarapoto
Mendoza
Ucayali
Lambayeque
Chiclayo
Chepen
Pacasmayo
Puerto Chicama
Cajamarca
Chilete
Moreno
Trujillo
Salaverry
Andes
PERU
Pachiza
Contamana
Chimbote
Nepeña
Casma
Huarmey
6768
Nevado Huascarán
Huaraz
Huánuco
6634
Nevado Yerupajá
Huallaga
Pucallpa
La Montaña
Pativilca
Barranca
Huacho
Huaral
Oyón
Huayllay
Cerro de Pasco
Tarma
Jauja
Satipo
La Oroya
Callao
LIMA
Chosica
Huancayo
Huancavelica
Ayacucho
Chincha Alta
Apurímac
Fitzcarrald
Manú
Quillabamba
Machupicchu
Pisac
Anta
Cuzco
Cord. Occidental
Cord. Central
Cord. Oriental
6200
Northern Perimeter Highway
Solimões
Tonantins
Fonte Boa
Içá
Santo Antônio do Içá
Belém
São Paulo de Olivença
Amazonas
Jutaí
Carauari
Juruá
Renascença
Concórdia
Eirunepé
Ipixuna
Envira
Cruzeiro do Sul
Tarauacá
Pôrto Valter
Feijó
Manuel Urbano
Bôca do Acre
Samaúma
Floriano Peixoto
Acre
Sena Madureira
Taumaturgo
Foz do Breu
Puerto Portillo
Puerto Padilla
Río Branco
Xapuri
Brasiléia
Cobija
Riberalta
Villa Bella
Guajará Mirim
Abunã
Madre de Dios
Beni
Holanda
Puerto Maldonado
Puerto Heath
BOLIVIA
Lago Rogagua
Ixiamas
Malpelo (Col.)
PACIFIC OCEAN
Archipiélago de Colón (Galápagos Islands)
(Ecuador)
90°
Isabela
Santa Cruz
Puerto Baquerizo Moreno
San Cristóbal

1 foot = 0,30 m
1 meter = 3,28 feet

Scale 1:20 000 000

0 200 400 600 800 1000 km
0 200 400 600 miles
1 hour

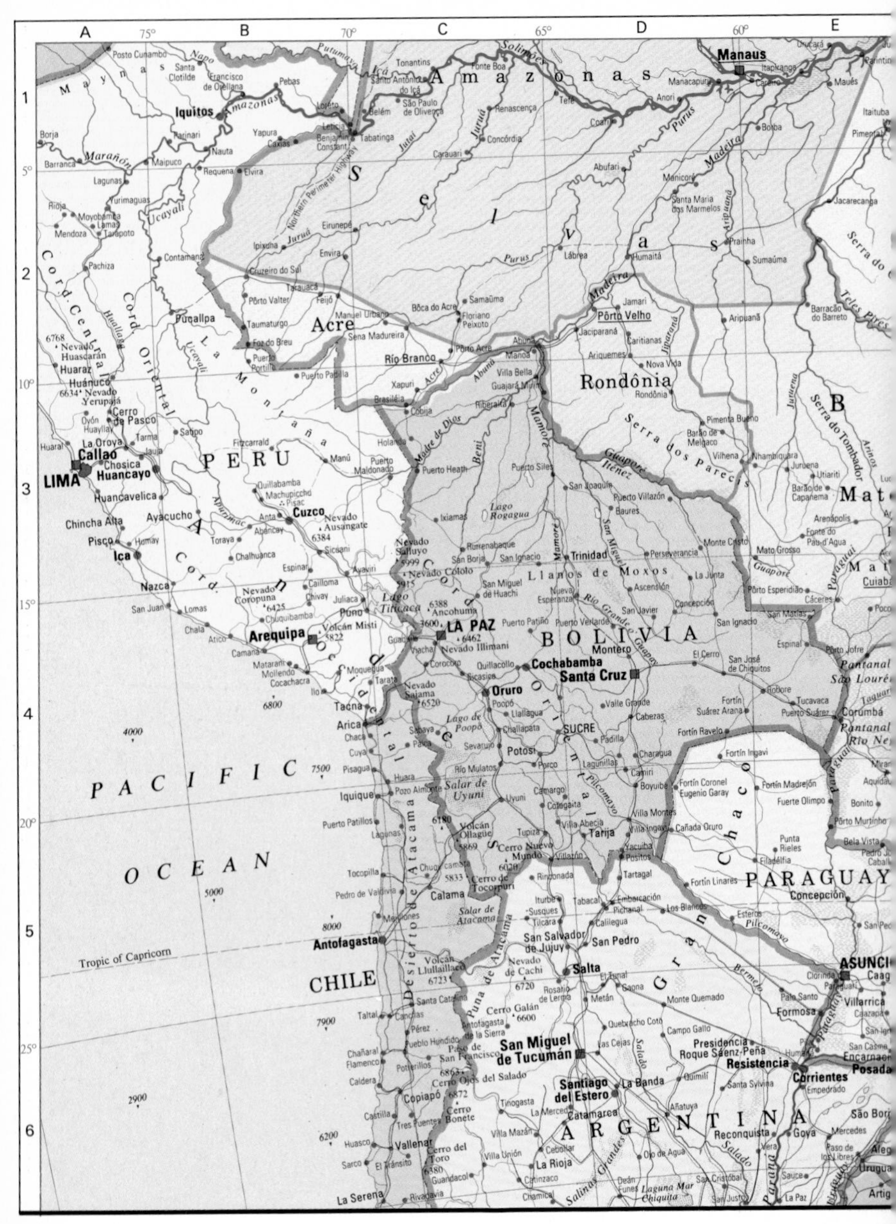

Manaus
Iquitos
Amazonas
Acre
Rio Branco
Rondônia
Pôrto Velho
PERU
LIMA
Callao
Huancayo
Cuzco
Arequipa
BOLIVIA
LA PAZ
Cochabamba
Santa Cruz
Oruro
SUCRE
Potosí
Tarija
PACIFIC OCEAN
CHILE
Antofagasta
Iquique
Arica
Calama
Copiapó
PARAGUAY
ASUNCIÓN
Concepción
ARGENTINA
Salta
San Miguel de Tucumán
Santiago del Estero
Corrientes
Resistencia
Tropic of Capricorn

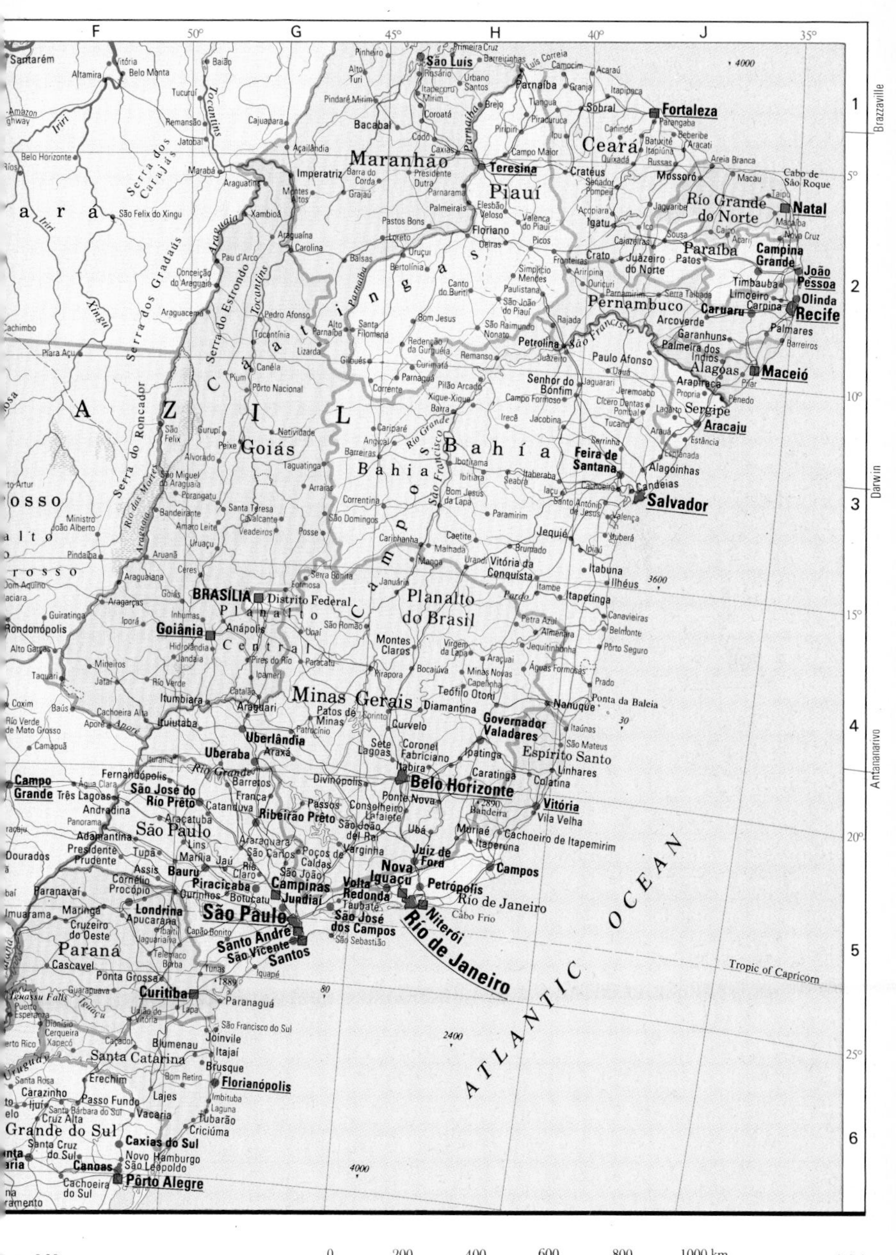

F
50°
G
45°
H
40°
J
35°
1
2
3
4
5
6
5°
10°
15°
20°
25°
Brazzaville
Darwin
Antananarivo
4000
Santarém
Altamira
Vitória
Belo Monte
Baião
Tucuruí
Tocantins
Remansão
Jatobal
Cajuapara
Açailândia
Marabá
Serra dos Carajás
Iriri
Imperatriz
Araguatins
Xambioá
São Felix do Xingu
Araguaína
Carolina
Pau d'Arco
Conceição do Araguaia
Xingu
Araguacema
Serra dos Gradaús
Serra do Estrondo
Pedro Afonso
Tocantínia
Lizarda
Canéla
Pôrto Nacional
Pium
Serra do Roncador
São Felix
Gurupi
Peixe
Goiás
Natividade
Alvorado
São Miguel do Araguaia
Porangatu
Bandeirante
Santa Teresa
Cavalcante
Amaro Leite
Veadeiros
Uruaçu
Aruanã
Ceres
Araguaiana
Aragarças
Goiás
BRASÍLIA
Distrito Federal
Planalto Central
Anápolis
Goiânia
Iporá
Guiratinga
Rondonópolis
Alto Garças
Hidrolândia
Jandaia
Pires do Rio
Paracatu
Ipameri
Mineiros
Jataí
Rio Verde
Taquari
Catalão
Itumbiara
Araguari
Coxim
Baús
Cachoeira Alta
Aporé
Ituiutaba
Rio Verde de Mato Grosso
Camapuã
Uberlândia
Patrocínio
Uberaba
Araxá
Iturama
Rio Grande
Campo Grande
Fernandópolis
Água Clara
Três Lagoas
São José do Rio Prêto
Andradina
Panorama
Adamantina
São Paulo
Presidente Prudente
Tupã
Lins
Marília
Jaú
Assis
Bauru
Cornélio Procópio
Ourinhos
Botucatu
Piracicaba
Campinas
Jundiaí
Dourados
Paranavaí
Maringá
Londrina
Apucarana
Cruzeiro do Oeste
Umuarama
Paraná
Cascavel
Ponta Grossa
Guarapuava
Curitiba
Iguaçu Falls
União do Vitória
Lapa
Paranaguá
São Francisco do Sul
Joinville
Blumenau
Itajaí
Brusque
Santa Catarina
Florianópolis
Caçador
Dionísio Cerqueira
Xapecó
Uruguay
Santa Rosa
Erechim
Carazinho
Passo Fundo
Lajes
Bom Retiro
Imbituba
Laguna
Tubarão
Criciúma
Ijuí
Santa Bárbara do Sul
Cruz Alta
Vacaria
Grande do Sul
Caxias do Sul
Santa Cruz do Sul
Novo Hamburgo
São Leopoldo
Canoas
Cachoeira do Sul
Pôrto Alegre
São Paulo
Capão Bonito
Ibaiti
Jaguariaíva
Telêmaco Borba
Tunas
Iguape
1889
Santo André
São Vicente
Santos
São José dos Campos
São Sebastião
Taubaté
Volta Redonda
Nova Iguaçu
Petrópolis
Rio de Janeiro
Niterói
Cabo Frio
Río de Janeiro
Juiz de Fora
Campos
Ubá
Muriaé
Itaperuna
Cachoeiro de Itapemirim
Vitória
Vila Velha
Bandeira
2890
Ponte Nova
Conselheiro Lafaiete
São João del Rei
Varginha
Poços de Caldas
São João da Boa Vista
Passos
Ribeirão Prêto
Franca
Barretos
Catanduva
Araçatuba
Araraquara
São Carlos
Rio Claro
Divinópolis
Belo Horizonte
Itabira
Sete Lagoas
Coronel Fabriciano
Ipatinga
Caratinga
Governador Valadares
Espírito Santo
Linhares
Colatina
São Mateus
Itaúnas
Nanuque
Ponta da Baleia
Minas Gerais
Patos de Minas
Curvelo
Diamantina
Teófilo Otoni
Capelinha
Minas Novas
Araçuaí
Águas Formosas
Jequitinhonha
Almenara
Petra Azul
Pôrto Seguro
Belmonte
Canavieiras
Prado
Pirapora
Bocaiúva
Montes Claros
Virgem da Lapa
Planalto do Brasil
Januária
Serra Bonita
Formosa
São Romão
Unaí
Manga
Malhada
Carinhanha
Urandi
Vitória da Conquista
Itambe
Pardo
Itapetinga
Itabuna
Ilhéus
3600
Jequié
Ubaitaba
Ubaíra
Ipiaú
Brumado
Caetité
Paramirim
Bom Jesus da Lapa
Ibitiara
Seabra
Itaberaba
Iaçu
Santo Antônio de Jesus
Valença
Cachoeira
Feira de Santana
Salvador
Candeias
Alagoinhas
Esplanada
Estância
Aracaju
Sergipe
Lagarto
Itabaiana
Propriá
Penedo
Arapiraca
Alagoas
Maceió
Pilar
Palmeira dos Índios
Garanhuns
Palmares
Barreiros
Recife
Olinda
Carpina
Limoeiro
Caruaru
Arcoverde
Pernambuco
Timbauba
João Pessoa
Campina Grande
Paraíba
Patos
Sousa
Cajazeiras
Juàzeiro do Norte
Crato
Icó
Iguatu
Acopiara
Jaguaribe
Rio Grande do Norte
Natal
Macaíba
Nova Cruz
Caicó
Acari
Mossoró
Macau
Areia Branca
Cabo de São Roque
Taipu
Russas
Aracati
Beberibe
Batujité
Itapiúna
Quixadá
Ceará
Fortaleza
Parangaba
Canindé
Sobral
Itapipoca
Acaraú
Camocim
Granja
Tianguá
Piracuruca
Ipu
Crateús
Senador Pompeu
Piripiri
Campo Maior
Parnaíba
Luís Correia
Barreirinhas
Primeira Cruz
São Luís
Rosário
Itapecuru Mirim
Urbano Santos
Pinheiro
Alto Turi
Pindaré Mirim
Bacabal
Coroatá
Codó
Caxias
Brejo
Maranhão
Teresina
Piauí
Barra do Corda
Presidente Dutra
Parnarama
Palmeirais
Elesbão Veloso
Valença do Piauí
Montes Altos
Grajaú
Pastos Bons
Floriano
Oeiras
Picos
Loreto
Uruçui
Balsas
Bertolínia
Fronteiras
Simplício Mendes
Paulistana
São João do Piauí
Canto do Buriti
Araripina
Ouricuri
Parnamirim
Serra Talhada
Santa Filomena
Alto Parnaíba
Bom Jesus
Redenção da Gurguéia
São Raimundo Nonato
Rajada
Petrolina
Juàzeiro
São Francisco
Paulo Afonso
Uauá
Jeremoabo
Cícero Dantas
Pombal
Tucano
Ribeira do Pombal
Remanso
Curimatá
Gilbués
Parnaguá
Corrente
Pilão Arcado
Xique-Xique
Barra
Senhor do Bonfim
Jaguarari
Campo Formoso
Irecê
Jacobina
Serrinha
Araúá
Cariparé
Angical
Barreiras
Rio Grande
Bahía
Ibotirama
Taguatinga
Arraias
Correntina
São Domingos
Posse
Campos
Catingas
Pará
Amazon
Belo Horizonte
Píara Açu
Cachimbo
Rio das Mortes
Araguaia
Mato Grosso
Ministro João Alberto
Pindaíba
Rio Verde
Tropic of Capricorn
ATLANTIC OCEAN
30
80
2400
4000

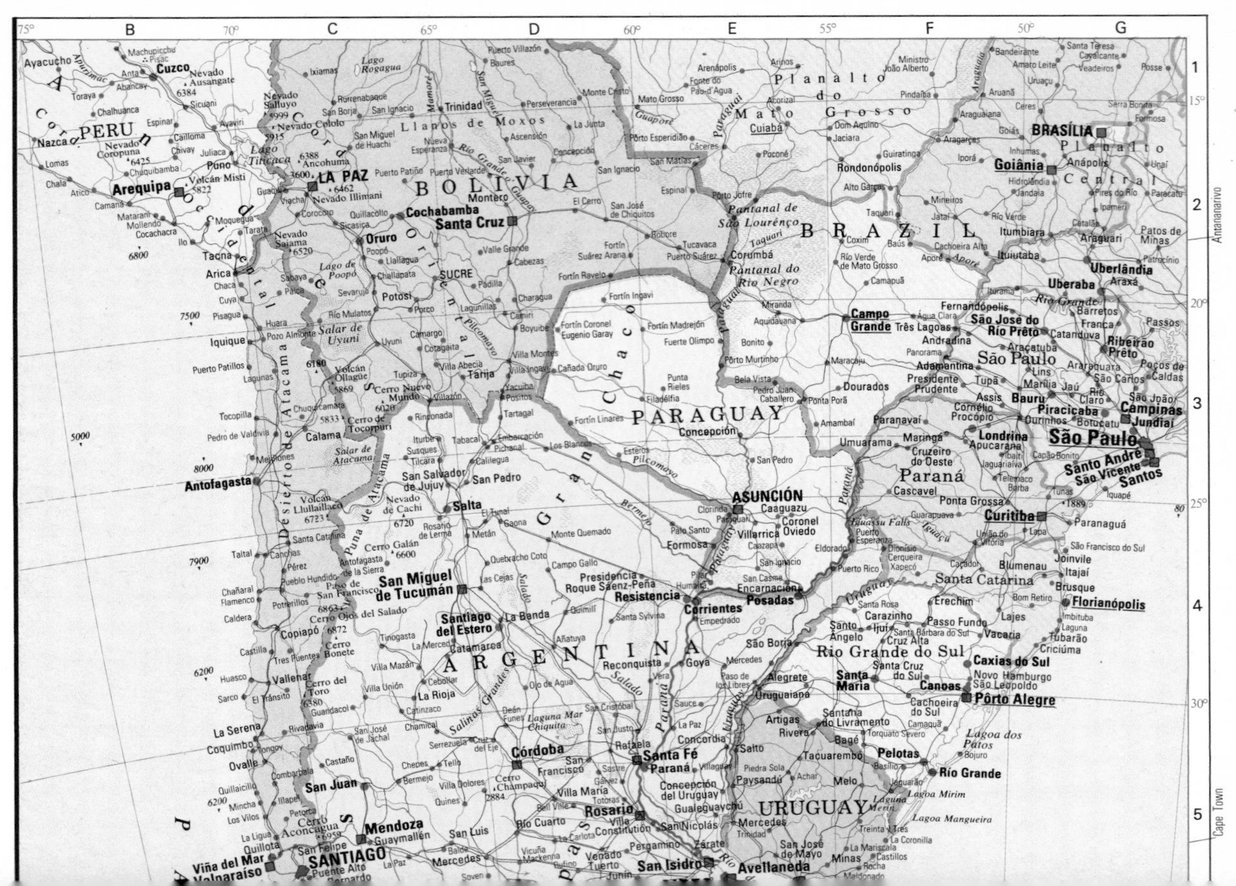

PERU
BOLIVIA
BRAZIL
PARAGUAY
ARGENTINA
URUGUAY
BRASÍLIA
LA PAZ
SUCRE
ASUNCIÓN
SANTIAGO
Cuzco
Arequipa
Cochabamba
Santa Cruz
Oruro
Potosí
Tarija
Cuiabá
Goiânia
Uberlândia
Uberaba
Campo Grande
São Paulo
Santo André
São Vicente
Santos
Campinas
Jundiaí
Londrina
Curitiba
Florianópolis
Pôrto Alegre
Caxias do Sul
Pelotas
Rio Grande
Arica
Iquique
Antofagasta
Calama
Salta
San Miguel de Tucumán
Santiago del Estero
Resistencia
Corrientes
Posadas
Córdoba
Santa Fé
Paraná
Rosario
San Juan
Mendoza
Viña del Mar
San Isidro
Avellaneda
Antananarivo
Cape Town

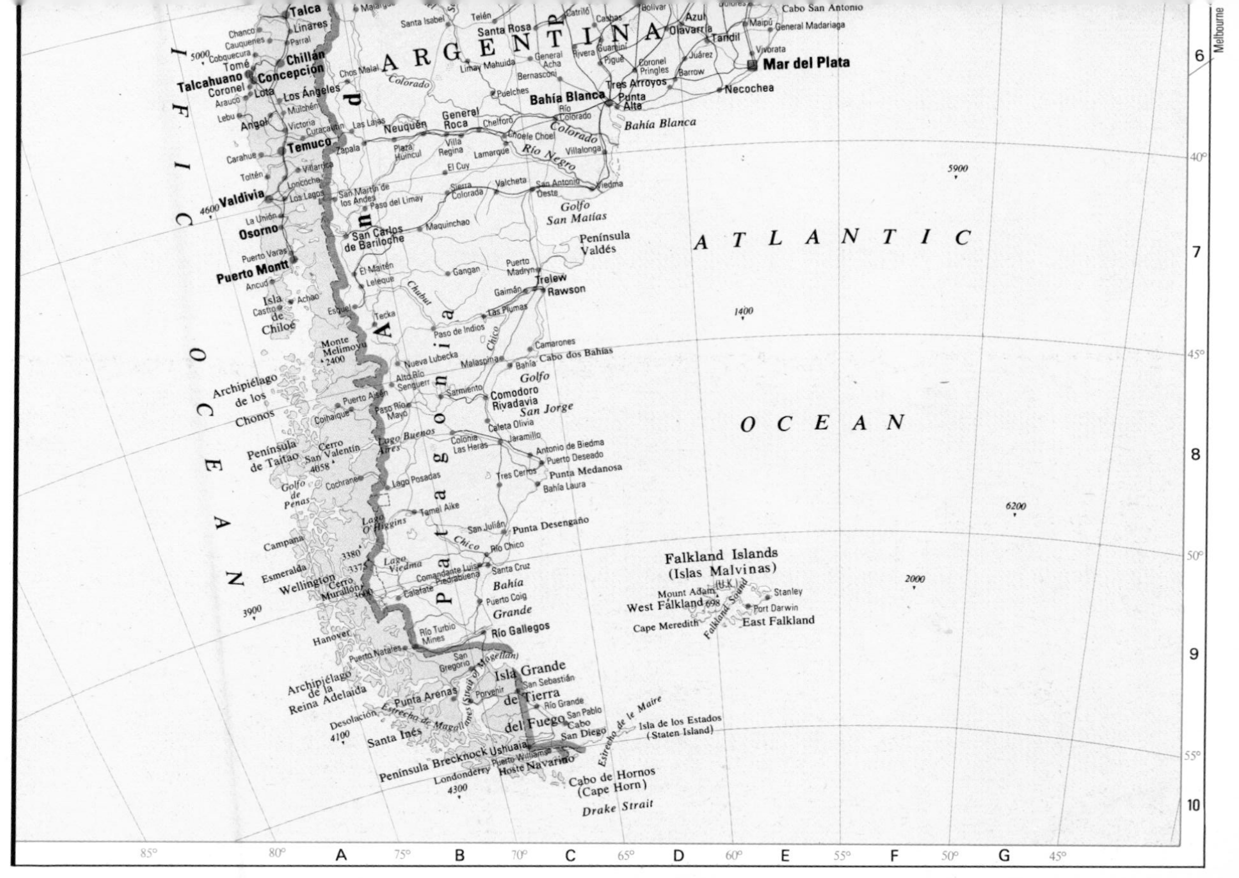

1 foot = 0,30 m
1 meter = 3,28 feet

Scale 1:20 000 000

0 200 400 600 800 1000 km
0 200 400 600 miles
1 hour

1 foot = 0,30 m
1 meter = 3,28 feet

Scale 1:60 000 000

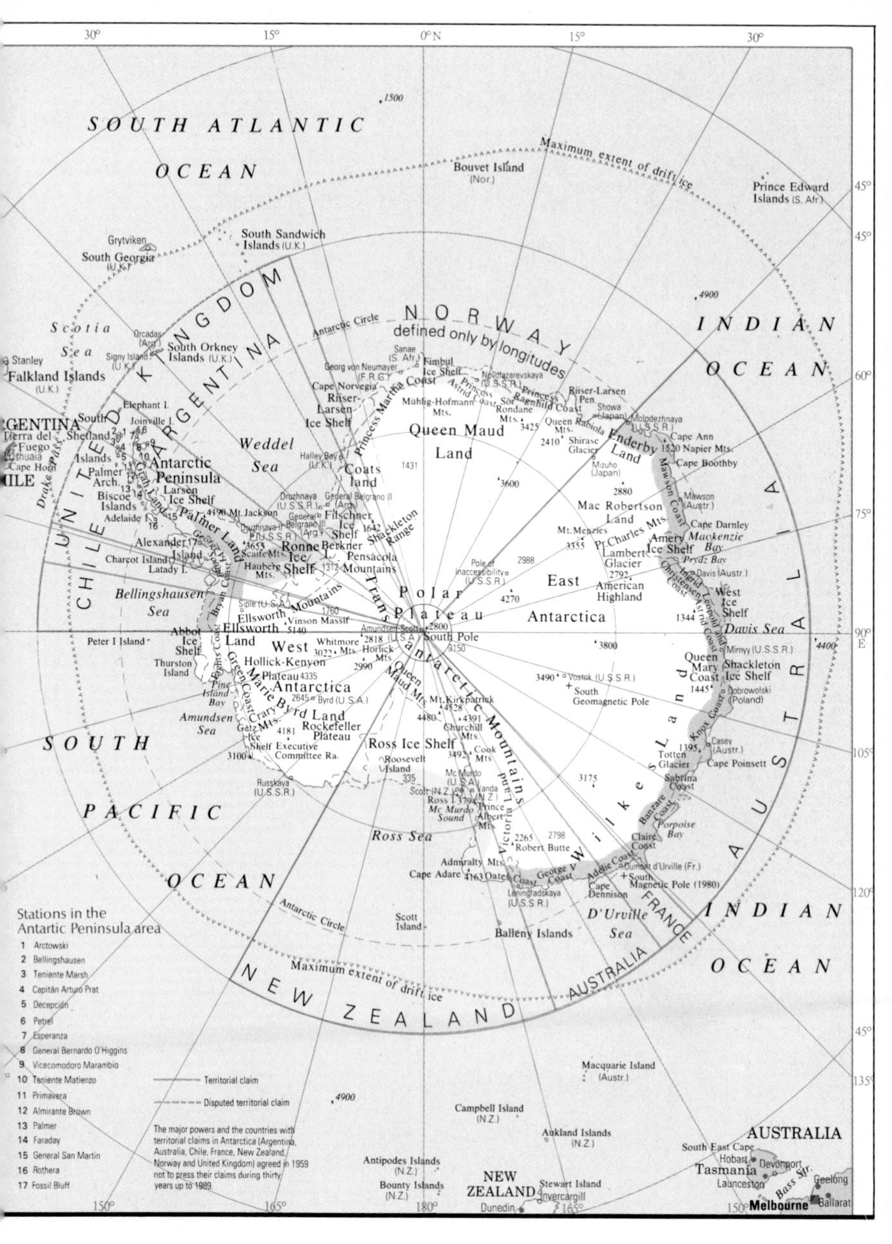

1000 2000 km
1 hour 500 1000 miles

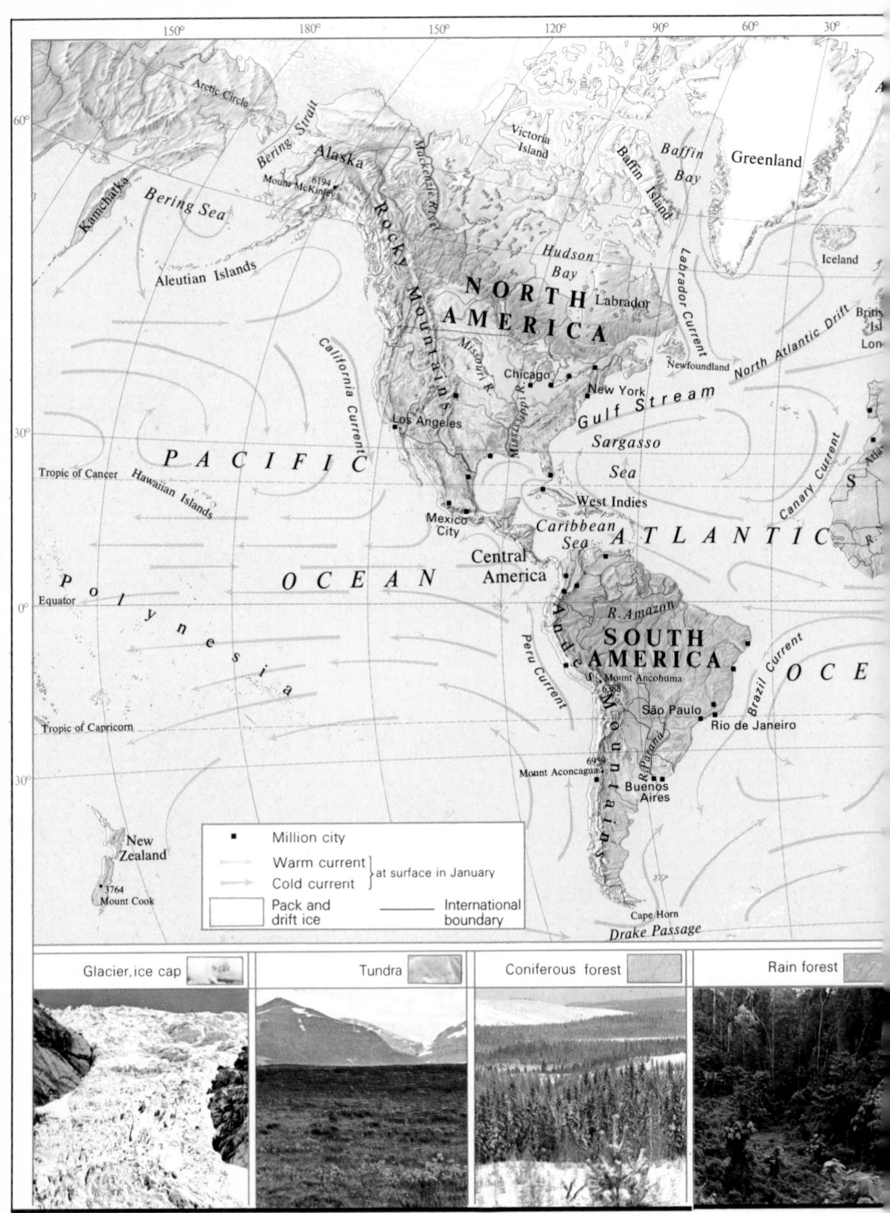

1 foot = 0,30 m
1 meter = 3,28 feet

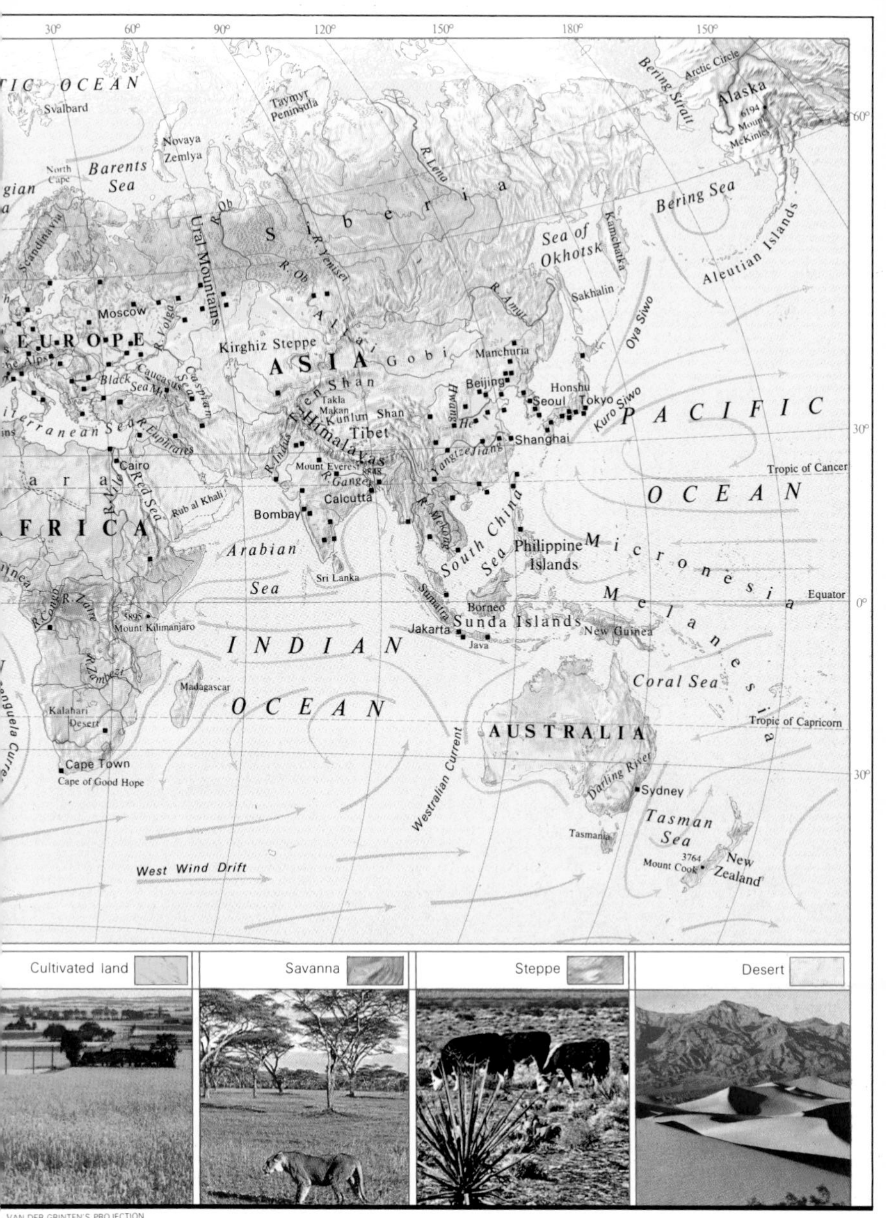

VAN DER GRINTEN'S PROJECTION

Scale 1:180 000 000
at the equator

0° 0 400 800 km
30°
60° 200 600 1000 km

0° 0 200 600 miles
30°
60° 100 300 500 miles

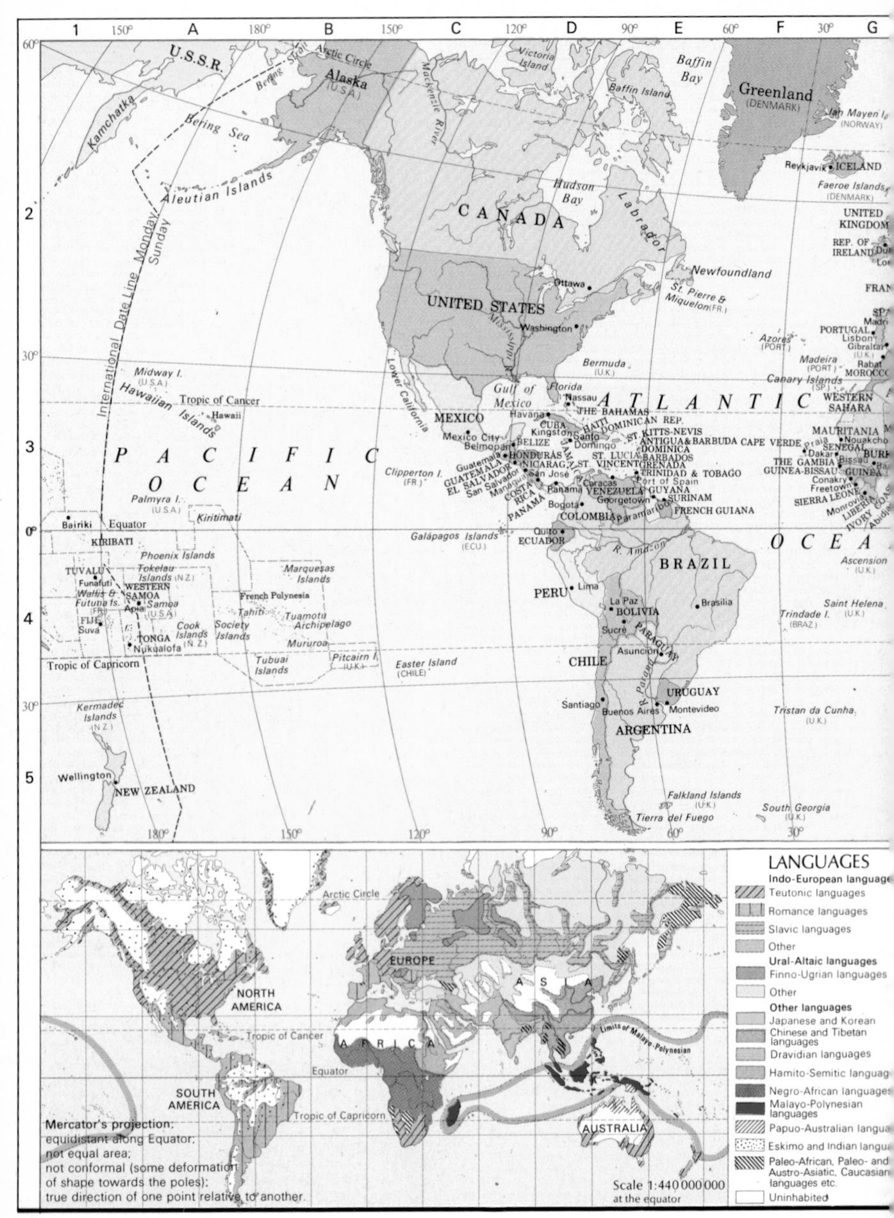

1
A
B
C
D
E
F
G
150°
180°
120°
90°
60°
30°
60°
30°
0°
2
3
4
5
U.S.S.R.
Kamchatka
Bering Strait
Arctic Circle
Alaska
(U.S.A.)
Bering Sea
Aleutian Islands
Mackenzie River
Victoria Island
Baffin Bay
Baffin Island
Greenland
(DENMARK)
Jan Mayen Is.
(NORWAY)
Reykjavik
ICELAND
Faeroe Islands
(DENMARK)
UNITED KINGDOM
REP. OF IRELAND
Hudson Bay
Labrador
CANADA
International Date Line
Monday
Sunday
Newfoundland
St. Pierre & Miquelon (FR.)
Ottawa
UNITED STATES
Mississippi
Washington
Azores
(PORT.)
PORTUGAL
Lisbon
Gibraltar
(U.K.)
Madeira
(PORT.)
Rabat
Bermuda
(U.K.)
Midway I.
(U.S.A.)
Hawaiian Islands
Hawaii
Tropic of Cancer
Lower California
Gulf of Mexico
Florida
Nassau
THE BAHAMAS
Havana
CUBA
HAITI
DOMINICAN REP.
Canary Islands
(SP.)
WESTERN SAHARA
MAURITANIA
Nouakchott
ATLANTIC
MEXICO
Mexico City
Belmopan
BELIZE
Kingston
Santo Domingo
ST. KITTS-NEVIS
ANTIGUA & BARBUDA
DOMINICA
CAPE VERDE
Praia
SENEGAL
Dakar
Bissau
THE GAMBIA
GUINEA-BISSAU
GUINEA
Conakry
Freetown
SIERRA LEONE
Monrovia
LIBERIA
IVORY COAST
PACIFIC
OCEAN
Guatemala
GUATEMALA
EL SALVADOR
San Salvador
HONDURAS
NICARAGUA
Managua
COSTA RICA
San José
PANAMA
Panama
ST. LUCIA
ST. VINCENT
BARBADOS
GRENADA
TRINIDAD & TOBAGO
Port of Spain
Caracas
VENEZUELA
GUYANA
Georgetown
SURINAM
Paramaribo
FRENCH GUIANA
Bogotá
COLOMBIA
Clipperton I.
(FR.)
Palmyra I.
(U.S.A.)
Kiritimati
Bairiki
Equator
KIRIBATI
Galápagos Islands
(ECU.)
Quito
ECUADOR
R. Amazon
OCEA
BRAZIL
Ascension
(U.K.)
Phoenix Islands
TUVALU
Funafuti
Tokelau Islands
(N.Z.)
Marquesas Islands
Wallis & Futuna Is.
WESTERN SAMOA
Apia
Samoa
(U.S.A.)
French Polynesia
PERU
Lima
Brasilia
Saint Helena
(U.K.)
FIJI
Suva
Tahiti
Tuamotu Archipelago
La Paz
BOLIVIA
Sucre
Trindade I.
(BRAZ.)
TONGA
Nukualofa
Cook Islands
(N.Z.)
Society Islands
Mururoa
PARAGUAY
Asunción
Tropic of Capricorn
Tubuai Islands
Pitcairn I.
(U.K.)
Easter Island
(CHILE)
CHILE
Paraná
Kermadec Islands
(N.Z.)
URUGUAY
Santiago
Buenos Aires
Montevideo
Tristan da Cunha
(U.K.)
ARGENTINA
Wellington
NEW ZEALAND
Falkland Islands
(U.K.)
South Georgia
(U.K.)
Tierra del Fuego
Arctic Circle
EUROPE
ASIA
NORTH AMERICA
Tropic of Cancer
AFRICA
Limits of Malayo-Polynesian
Equator
SOUTH AMERICA
Tropic of Capricorn
AUSTRALIA
Mercator's projection;
equidistant along Equator;
not equal area;
not conformal (some deformation of shape towards the poles);
true direction of one point relative to another.
Scale 1:440 000 000
at the equator
LANGUAGES
Indo-European languages
Teutonic languages
Romance languages
Slavic languages
Other
Ural-Altaic languages
Finno-Ugrian languages
Other
Other languages
Japanese and Korean
Chinese and Tibetan languages
Dravidian languages
Hamito-Semitic languages
Negro-African languages
Malayo-Polynesian languages
Papuo-Australian languages
Eskimo and Indian languages
Paleo-African, Paleo- and Austro-Asiatic, Caucasian languages etc.
Uninhabited

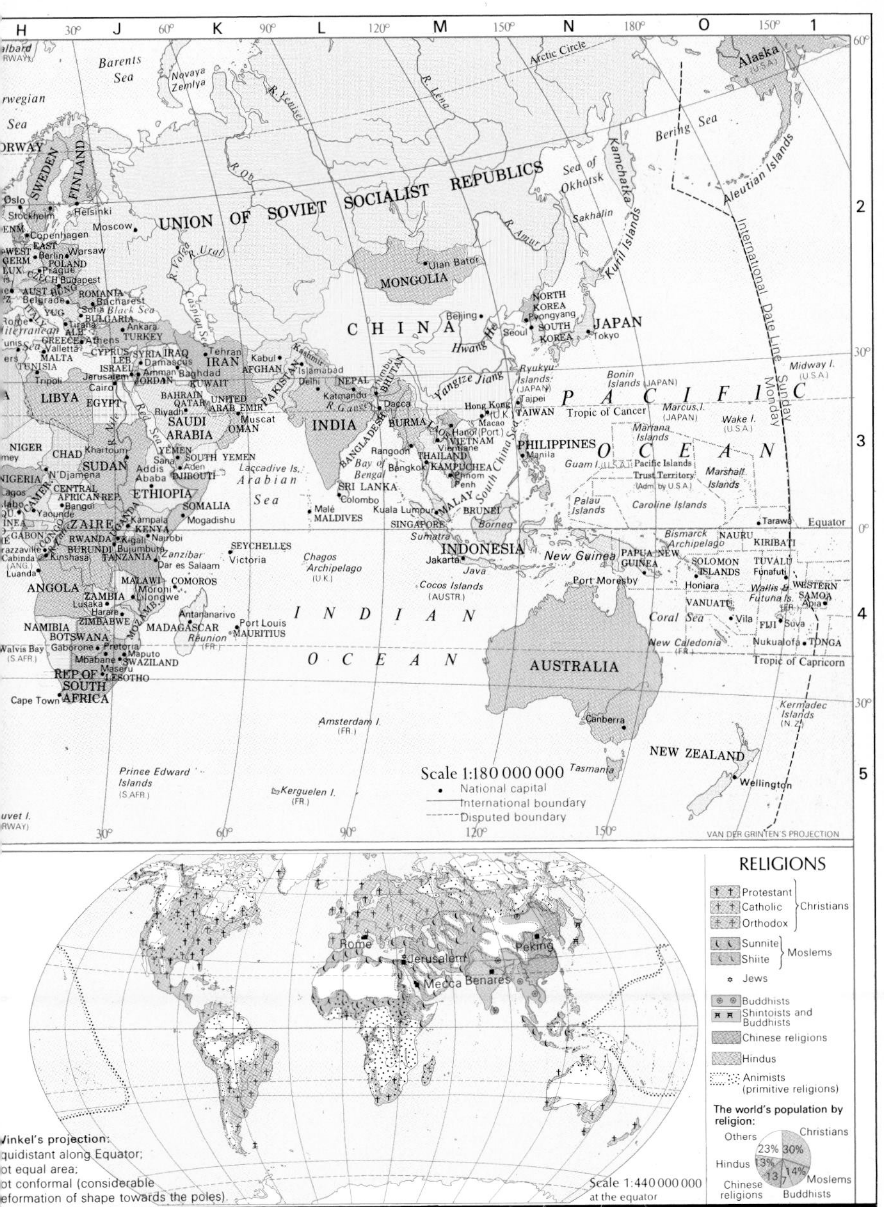

H
J
K
L
M
N
O
1
2
3
4
5
Barents Sea
Novaya Zemlya
Arctic Circle
Alaska (U.S.A.)
Bering Sea
Aleutian Islands
R. Yenisei
R. Lena
R. Ob
Sea of Okhotsk
Kamchatka
UNION OF SOVIET SOCIALIST REPUBLICS
SWEDEN
FINLAND
Oslo
Stockholm
Helsinki
Copenhagen
Moscow
EAST
Berlin
Warsaw
POLAND
Prague
Budapest
ROMANIA
Bucharest
Belgrade
YUG
Sofia
Black Sea
BULGARIA
Tirana
ALB
Rome
Ankara
TURKEY
GREECE
Athens
Valletta
MALTA
TUNISIA
Tripoli
CYPRUS
SYRIA
IRAQ
LEB.
Damascus
ISRAEL
Amman
Baghdad
Jerusalem
JORDAN
KUWAIT
Tehran
IRAN
Kabul
AFGHAN
Islamabad
PAKISTAN
Kashmir
Delhi
NEPAL
Katmandu
Thimbu
BHUTAN
Dacca
BANGLADESH
INDIA
Bay of Bengal
Calcutta
Cairo
LIBYA
EGYPT
BAHRAIN
QATAR
UNITED ARAB EMIR.
Riyadh
Muscat
OMAN
SAUDI ARABIA
R. Nile
Red Sea
Khartoum
SUDAN
CHAD
NIGER
NIGERIA
Lagos
N'Djamena
CENTRAL AFRICAN REP.
Bangui
Yaoundé
CAMEROON
GABON
ZAIRE
Kinshasa
Brazzaville
Cabinda (ANG.)
Luanda
ANGOLA
YEMEN
Sana
Aden
SOUTH YEMEN
DJIBOUTI
Addis Ababa
ETHIOPIA
SOMALIA
Mogadishu
UGANDA
Kampala
KENYA
Nairobi
RWANDA
Kigali
BURUNDI
Bujumbura
TANZANIA
Zanzibar
Dar es Salaam
MALAWI
Lilongwe
ZAMBIA
Lusaka
Harare
ZIMBABWE
MOZAMB.
Moroni
COMOROS
NAMIBIA
BOTSWANA
Gaborone
Pretoria
Maputo
Mbabane
SWAZILAND
Maseru
LESOTHO
REP. OF SOUTH AFRICA
Cape Town
Walvis Bay (S.AFR.)
Antananarivo
MADAGASCAR
Port Louis
MAURITIUS
Réunion (FR.)
SEYCHELLES
Victoria
Laccadive Is.
Arabian Sea
Malé
MALDIVES
SRI LANKA
Colombo
Chagos Archipelago (U.K.)
Caspian Sea
R. Volga
R. Ural
Ulan Bator
MONGOLIA
CHINA
Beijing
Hwang He
Yangtze Jiang
R. Amur
Sakhalin
Kuril Islands
NORTH KOREA
Pyongyang
Seoul
SOUTH KOREA
JAPAN
Tokyo
Ryukyu Islands (JAPAN)
Taipei
TAIWAN
Hong Kong (U.K.)
Macao
Bonin Islands (JAPAN)
Hanoi (Port)
VIETNAM
Vientiane
LAOS
BURMA
Rangoon
THAILAND
Bangkok
KAMPUCHEA
Phnom Penh
South China Sea
PHILIPPINES
Manila
MALAY
Kuala Lumpur
SINGAPORE
BRUNEI
Borneo
Sumatra
INDONESIA
Jakarta
Java
Cocos Islands (AUSTR.)
New Guinea
PAPUA NEW GUINEA
Port Moresby
Bismarck Archipelago
SOLOMON ISLANDS
Honiara
VANUATU
Vila
Coral Sea
New Caledonia (FR.)
AUSTRALIA
Canberra
Tasmania
NEW ZEALAND
Wellington
Kermadec Islands (N.Z.)
PACIFIC OCEAN
Tropic of Cancer
Marcus I. (JAPAN)
Wake I. (U.S.A.)
Midway I. (U.S.A.)
Mariana Islands
Guam I. (U.S.A.)
Pacific Islands Trust Territory (Adm. by U.S.A.)
Marshall Islands
Palau Islands
Caroline Islands
Tarawa
Equator
NAURU
KIRIBATI
TUVALU
Funafuti
Wallis & Futuna Is. (FR.)
WESTERN SAMOA
Apia
FIJI
Suva
Nukualofa
TONGA
Tropic of Capricorn
International Date Line
Sunday
Monday
INDIAN OCEAN
Amsterdam I. (FR.)
Prince Edward Islands (S.AFR.)
Kerguelen I. (FR.)
Scale 1:180 000 000
National capital
International boundary
Disputed boundary
VAN DER GRINTEN'S PROJECTION
RELIGIONS
Protestant
Catholic
Orthodox
Christians
Sunnite
Shiite
Moslems
Jews
Buddhists
Shintoists and Buddhists
Chinese religions
Hindus
Animists (primitive religions)
The world's population by religion:
Others
Christians
23%
30%
Hindus
13%
14%
Moslems
13
7
Chinese religions
Buddhists
Rome
Jerusalem
Mecca
Benares
Peking
Winkel's projection:
equidistant along Equator;
not equal area;
not conformal (considerable
deformation of shape towards the poles).
Scale 1:440 000 000
at the equator

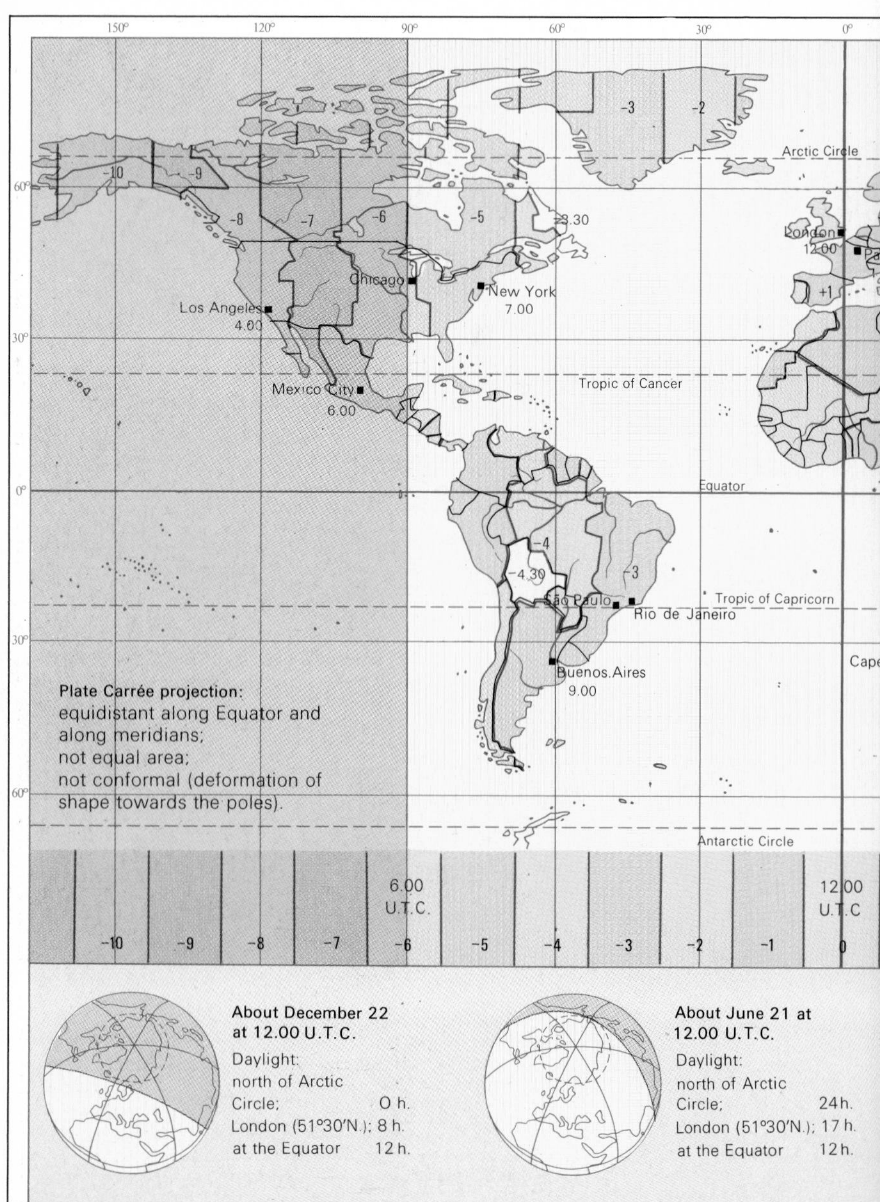
150°
120°
90°
60°
30°
0°
-3
-2
Arctic Circle
-10
-9
-8
-7
-6
-5
-3.30
London
12.00
+1
Chicago
New York
7.00
Los Angeles
4.00
Mexico City
6.00
Tropic of Cancer
Equator
-4
-4.30
-3
São Paulo
Rio de Janeiro
Tropic of Capricorn
Buenos Aires
9.00
Plate Carrée projection:
equidistant along Equator and
along meridians;
not equal area;
not conformal (deformation of
shape towards the poles).
Antarctic Circle
6.00
U.T.C.
12.00
U.T.C
-10
-9
-8
-7
-6
-5
-4
-3
-2
-1
0
About December 22
at 12.00 U.T.C.
Daylight:
north of Arctic
Circle; 0 h.
London (51°30′N.); 8 h.
at the Equator 12 h.
About June 21 at
12.00 U.T.C.
Daylight:
north of Arctic
Circle; 24 h.
London (51°30′N.); 17 h.
at the Equator 12 h.

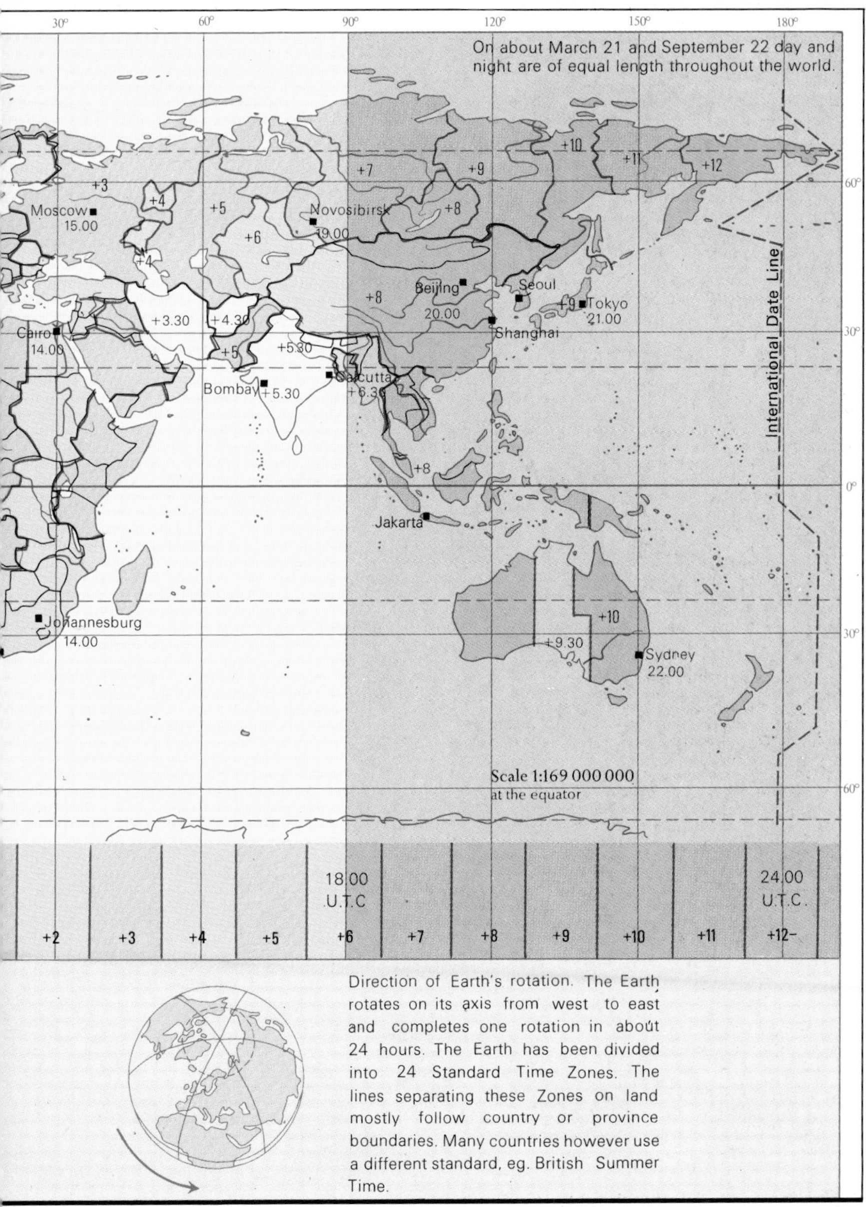

Direction of Earth's rotation. The Earth rotates on its axis from west to east and completes one rotation in about 24 hours. The Earth has been divided into 24 Standard Time Zones. The lines separating these Zones on land mostly follow country or province boundaries. Many countries however use a different standard, eg. British Summer Time.

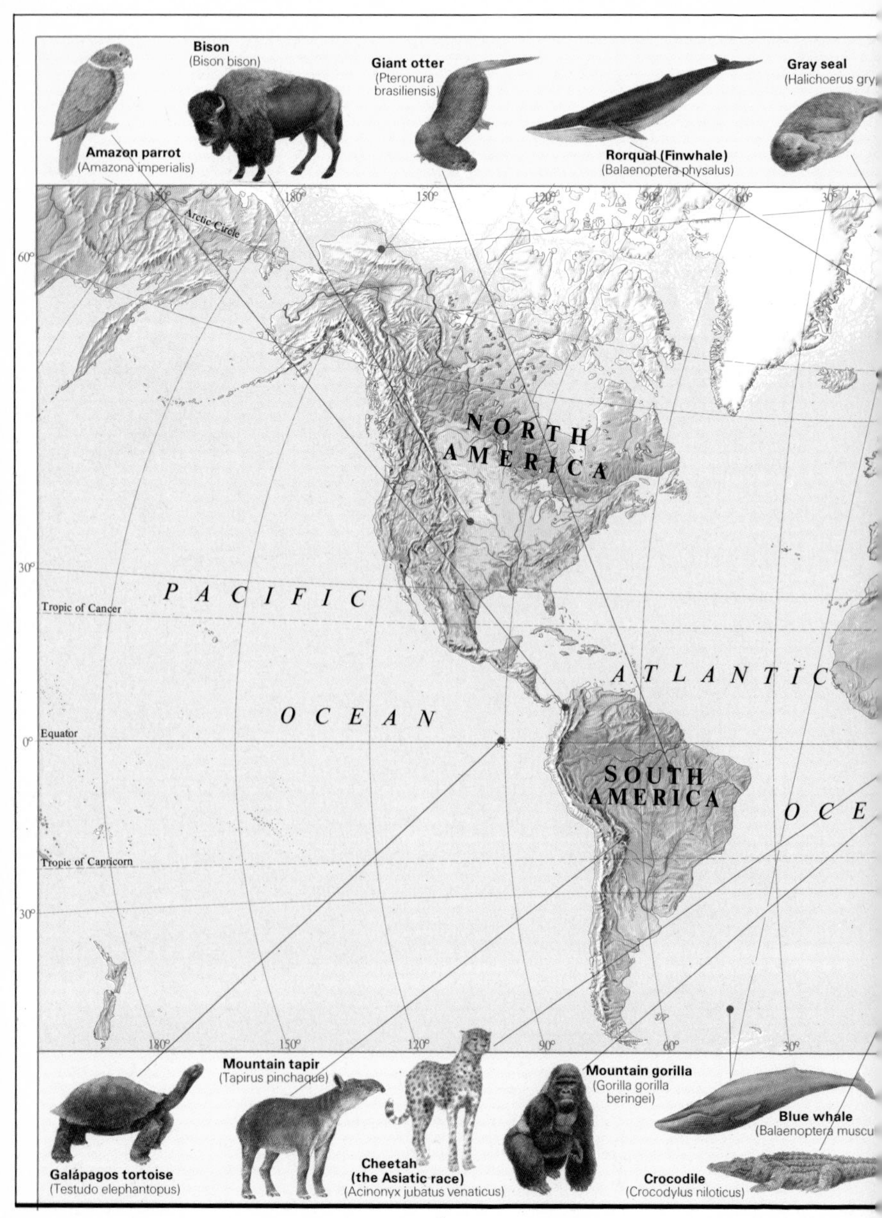

Bison
(Bison bison)
Giant otter
(Pteronura brasiliensis)
Gray seal
(Halichoerus gry
Amazon parrot
(Amazona imperialis)
Rorqual (Finwhale)
(Balaenoptera physalus)
Arctic Circle
NORTH AMERICA
PACIFIC
OCEAN
ATLANTIC
OCE
SOUTH AMERICA
Tropic of Cancer
Equator
Tropic of Capricorn
60°
30°
0°
30°
180°
150°
120°
90°
60°
30°
Mountain tapir
(Tapirus pinchaque)
Mountain gorilla
(Gorilla gorilla beringei)
Blue whale
(Balaenoptera muscu
Galápagos tortoise
(Testudo elephantopus)
Cheetah
(the Asiatic race)
(Acinonyx jubatus venaticus)
Crocodile
(Crocodylus niloticus)

dian rhinoceros
inoceros unicornis)
Ounce
(Snow leopard)
(Panthera unica)
Walrus
(Odobenus rosmarus)
Giant panda
(Ailuropoda melanoleuca)
Orangutan
(Pongo pygmaeus)
C OCEAN
Arctic Circle
EUROPE
ASIA
PACIFIC
OCEAN
Tropic of Cancer
FRICA
Equator
INDIAN
OCEAN
AUSTRALIA
Tropic of Capricorn
Aye-aye
(Daubentonia madagascariensis)
Arabian oryx
(Oryx leucoryx)
Tiger
(Leo tigris)
Tasmanian wolf
(Thylacinus cynocephalus)
Kiwi
(Apteryx australis)
AN DER GRINTEN'S PROJECTION

cale 1:180 000 000

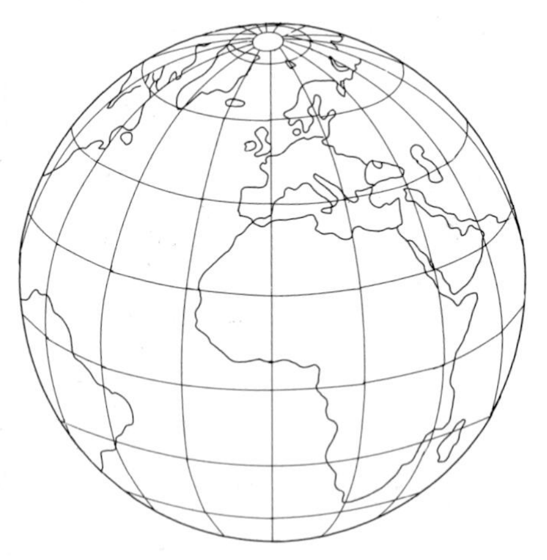

INDEX

A

Aachen **52** E 4
Aalen **53** F 5
Aạ Sumayḥ **92** D 3
Aba **91** F 4
Abaco Island **105** G 2
Abadab, Jabal **88** F 5
Ābādān **61** E 3
Ābādeh **61** F 3
Abadla **86** E 2
Abaetetuba **109** J 4
Abagnar Qi **71** G 2
Abaiang **82** C 2
Abakaliki **91** F 4
Abakan **68** F 5
Abalak **91** F 2
Abancay **110** B 3
Abant Silsilesi **58** D 2
Abariringa **82** D 3
Abarqu **61** F 3
Abarqu, Kavir-e **61** F 3
Abatskoye **63** O 4
Abay **63** O 6
Abaza **68** F 5
Abbai **92** F 2
Abbāsābād **61** G 1
Abbeville **56** D 1
Abbot Ice Shelf **115**
'Abd al Kūrī **93** J 2
Abdulino **62** K 5
Abéché **91** J 3
Abemama **82** C 2
Abengourou **90** D 4
Abeokuta **90** E 4
Aberdeen (S.D., U.S.A.) **102** G 2
Aberdeen (U.K.) **52** C 3
Aberdeen Lake **99** RS 3
Aberystwyth **52** C 4
Abhā' **89** G 5
Abhar **61** E 1
Abidjan **90** CD 4
Abilene **102** FG 5
Abkit **69** T 3
Åbo **55** H 3
Abong Abong, Gunung **74** A 3
Abong Mbang **91** G 5
Abrantes **56** B 4
'Abrī **88** E 4
Abruzzo **57** F 3
Abū ad Duhūr **60** B 2
Abū al Bukhush **61** F 4
Abū 'Alī **61** E 4
Abu Dhabī **61** FG 4
Abufari **109** F 5
Abū Ḥadrīyah **66** D 5
Abū Ḥamad **88** E 5
Abū Jifān **61** E 4
Abū Kamāl **60** C 2
Abū Maṭariq **88** D 6
Abū Mūsa' **61** G 4
Abunā (Brazil) **110** C 3
Abūqrīn **87** J 2
Abū Qumayyis, Ra's **61** F 4
Abu Road **72** B 3
Abū Sunbul **88** E 4
Abuya Myeda **93** FG 2
Abū Ẓaby **89** J 4
Abū Ẓaby (United Arab Emirates) **61** FG 4
Abū Zanīmah **60** A 3
Abyad, Ra's al **60** BC 5
Abyār 'Alī **60** C 4
Abydos **88** E 3
Ābyek **61** F 2
Açailândia **109** J 4
Acaponeta **104** AB 3
Acapulco **104** B 4
Acarai, Serra **109** G 3
Acaraú **111** HJ 1
Acari **111** J 2
Acarigua **108** E 2
Accomac **103** L 4
Accra **90** DE 4
Achao **113** B 7
Achar **112** E 5
Achayvayam **69** VW 3
Achelóos **58** B 3
Achinsk **68** F 4
Acklins Island **105** H 3
Acongagua, Cerro **112** BC 5
Acorizal **110** E 3–4
Acre (Brazil) **108** D 5
Acre (Brazil) **110** C 3
Acre (Israel) **60** B 2
Acri **57** G 4
Adaba **93** F 3
Adak (AK, U.S.A.) **98** B 5
Adak (Sweden) **54** G 2
'Adale **93** H 4
Adam, Mount **113** DE 9
Adamantina **111** F 5
Adamaoua **91** G 4
Adams Bridge **72** CD 6
Adamstown **83** G 4
Adana **60** B 1
Adapazarı **58** D 2
Adare, Cape **115**
Adavale **79** GH 4
Aḍ Ḍafrah **61** F 5
Ad Dahnā' **61** DE 4
Ad Dammām **61** EF 4
Ad Dār al Ḥamrā' **66** B 5
Ad Darb **89** G 5
Ad Dawādimī **60** D 4
Ad Dawḥah **61** F 4
Ad Dawr **60** D 2
Ad Dayr **60** A 4
Ad Dibdibah **61** E 3
Ad Dilam **61** E 5
Ad Dindar **88** E 6
Addis Ababa **93** F 3
Addis Zemen **93** F 2
Ad Dīwanīyah **61** D 3
Ad Duwaym **88** E 6
Adelaide Island **115**
Adelaide Peninsula **99** S 2
Adelaide River **78** E 1
Adélie Coast **115**
Aden **89** H 6
Adige **57** F 2
Adıgüzel Barajı **58** C 3
Adirondack Mountains **103** M 3
Adi Ugri **93** F 2
Adıyaman **59** E 3
Admiralty **98** L 4
Admiralty Islands **80** E 2
Admiralty Mountains **115**
Ado **90** E 4
Ado Ekiti **91** F 4
Adok **92** E 3
Adrano **57** F 4
Adrar **86** E 3
Adrar des Iforas **90** E 1–2
Adré **91** J 3
Adriatic Sea **57** FG 3
Adwa **93** F 2
Adzhar **59** F 2
Adzopáe **90** D 4
Aegean Sea **58** C 3
Afao, Mont **87** G 3
Afghanistan **67** GH 4
Afif **60** D 4–5
Afikpo **91** F 4
Afmadōw **93** G 4
Afognak **98** G 4
African Islands **93** J 5
Afyonkarahisar **58** D 3
Agabah, Khalij al **60** B 3
Agadez **91** F 2
Agadir **86** CD 2
Agana **82** A 2
Agapitovo **63** R 2
Agartala **73** F 3
Agata **68** F 2
Agats **75** J 5
Agattu **98** A 5
Agawa Bay **100** L 6
Agboville **90** CD 4
Agdary **68** L 3
Agen **56** D 3
Agepsta **59** F 2
Agha Jārī **61** EF 3
Agordat **93** F 1
Agra **72** C 2
Ağrı **59** F 3
Agrigento **57** F 4
Agrihan **82** A 1
Agrinion **58** B 3
Agto **101** R 2
Água Clara **111** F 5
Aguadulce **108** BC 2
Águas Formosas **111** HJ 4
Agulhas, Cape **94** C 6
Aguscalientes **104** B 3
Ahaggar **87** FG 4
Ahe **83** F 3
Ahmadabad **72** B 3
Ahmadnagar **72** BC 4
Ahome **102** E 6
Ähtävänjoki **54** H 3
Ahvāz **61** E 3
Ahvenanmaa **55** GH 3
Aḥwar **89** H 6
Aihui **69** N 6
Ailinginae **82** BC 2
Ailinglapalap **82** C 2
Aillik **101** Q 4
Ailuk **82** C 2
Aim **69** O 4
Aïn Amenas **87** G 3
Aïn Amguel **87** FG 4
Aïn Beïda **87** G 1
Aïn Ezzane **87** H 4
Aïn Tiguelguemine **87** F 3
Aioun el Atrouss **86** D 5
Aïr **91** F 2
Airao **109** F 4
Aitape **80** D 2
Aitutaki **83** E 4
Aix-en-Provence **57** DE 3
Aiyaion Pélagos **58** C 3
Aizuwakamatsu **71** M 3
Ajaccio **57** E 3
Aj Bogd Uul **70** BC 2
'Ajmān **61** G 4
Ajmer **72** B 2
Ajo, Cabo de **56** C 3
Akademii, Zaliv **69** P 5
Ak Dağ **58** C 3
Akespe **66** G 1
Akharnai **58** B 3
Akhisar **58** C 3
Akhtubinsk **62** J 6
Akhtyrka **62** FG 5
Akimiski **101** L 5
Akita **71** L 3
Akkabak **67** G 1
Akkajaure **54** G 2
'Akko **60** B 2
Aklavik **98** K 2
Akmenrags **55** H 4
Akobo **92** E 3
Akola **72** C 3
Akosombo Dam **90** E 4
Akpatok **101** O 3
Ákra Akritas **58** B 3
Akra Arnauti **60** A 2

Ákra Maleás **58** B 3
Ákra Spátha **58** B 3
Ákra Taínaron **58** B 3
Akritas, Ákra **58** B 3
Akron **103** K 3
Aksaray **59** D 3
Aksay Kazakzu Zizhixian **70** B 3
Aksehir **58** D 3
Aksha **68** K 5
Akshiy **67** G 1
Aksu (China) **67** L 2
Aksu (Turkey) **58** D 3
Aktash **67** H 3
Aktasty **63** M 5
Aktogay **63** P 6
Aktyubinsk **63** L 5
Akure **91** F 4
Akureyri **54** B 2
Ala, Monti di **57** E 3
Alabama **103** J 5
Alabama River **103** J 5
Al Abyaḍ, Ra's **87** G 1
Alaçam Dağları **58** C 3
Alachakh **69** P 4
Aladağ **59** F 3
Alagoas **111** J 2
Alagoinhas **111** J 3
Alagon **56** C 3
Alajuela **104** F 5
Alakurtti **54** K 2
Al 'Alamayn **88** D 2
Al Amādīyah **60** D 1
Alamagan **82** A 1
Al 'Amārah **61** E 3
Alamogordo **102** E 5
Alamos **102** E 6
Ålands hav **55** G 3–4
Alanya **59** D 3
Alaotra, Lac **95** H 3
Alapayevsk **63** M 4
Al' Aqabah **60** B 3
Al 'Aqaylah **87** J 2
Al 'Arabiyah as Su'udiyah **60** CD 4
Al'Arabiyah as Su'udiyah **89** GH 4
Al 'Arīsh **60** A 3
Al ʿArmah **61** DE 4
Al Arṭāwīyah **61** D 4
Al 'Āshūrīyah **66** C 4
Alaska **98** FH 2
Alaska Peninsula **98** E 4
Alaska Range **98** GH 3
Alatyr' **62** J 5
Al 'Awaynāt **87** H 3
Al'Awsajīyah **60** D 4
Al ʿAyn **61** G 4
Alazani **59** G 2
Alba **57** E 3
Al Bāb **60** B 1
Albacete **56** C 4
Al Badī' **89** H 4
Al Bahrah **61** E 3
Al Baḥr al Mayyit **60** B 3
Alba Iulia **58** B 1
Albanel, Lac **101** N 5
Albania **58** AB 2
Albano Laziale **57** F 3
Albany (Australia) **78** B 5
Albany (GA, U.S.A.) **103** K 5
Albany (N.Y., U.S.A.) **103** M 3
Albany (Ontario, Can.) **100** L 5
Al Barkāt **87** H 4
Al Basrah **61** E 3
Al Batin **61** E 3
Al Bāṭinah **89** K 4
Albatross Point **81** Q 8
Al Bayḍā' **87** K 2
Alberta **99** OP 5
Albert Nile **92** E 4
Albertville **57** E 2
Albi **56** D 3
Al Bid' **60** B 3
Albina **109** H 2
Al Bi'r **60** B 3
Al Birkah **66** C 6
Alborán **56** C 4
Ålborg **55** F 4
Al Brayqah **87** JK 3
Albu Ali **59** F 4
Al Buḥayrah al Murrah al Kubrā **60** A 3
Albuquerque **102** E 4–5
Albury **79** H 6
Alcalá **56** C 3
Alcalá **56** B 4
Alcântara **109** K 4
Alcántara, Embalse de **56** B 4
Alcaraz, Sierra de **56** C 4
Alcázar de San Juan **56** C 4
Alciéni **91** G 6
Alcira **56** C 4
Alcolea del Pinar **56** C 3
Alcoy **56** C 4
Aldabra Islands **93** H 6
Aldan **69** O 3
Aldan **69** N 4
Aldanskoye Nagor'ye **69** MN 4
Aleg **86** C 5
Alegrete **112** E 4
Aleksandriya (Ukraine, U.S.S.R.) **62** FG 6
Aleksandrovsk **63** M 4
Aleksandrovskiy **68** L 5
Aleksandrovsk-Sakhalinskiy **69** Q 5
Alekseyevka (Kazakhstan, U.S.S.R.) **63** O 5
Alekseyevo **69** R 1
Alençon **56** D 2
Aleppo **60** B 1
Aléria **57** E 3
Alès **56** D 3
Alessandria **57** E 3
Ålestrup **55** E 4
Ålesund **54** E 3
Aleutian Islands **98** AC 4
Aleutian Islands **98** AC 5
Aleutian Range **98** F 4
Alexander Archipelago **98** K 4
Alexander Island **115**
Alexandra **80** PQ 10
Alexandra Falls **99** O 3
Alexandria (Egypt) **88** DE 2
Alexandria (LA, U.S.A.) **103** H 5
Alexandria (MD, U.S.A.) **103** L 4
Alexandria (Romania) **58** BC 2
Alexandroúpolis **58** C 2
Aleysk **63** Q 5
Al Fāshir **88** D 6
Al Fatḥah **66** C 3
Al Fayyūm **88** DE 3
Al Fuḥayḥīl **61** E 3
Al Fujayrah **61** G 4
Al Furat **59** F 3–4
Al Fuwayrit **61** F 4
Algama **69** N 4
Alganskaya **69** WX 3
Algarve **56** B 4
Algeciras **56** B 4
Algeria **86–87** EF 3
Al Ghazālah **60** C 4
Alghero **57** E 3
Algiers **87** F 1
Al Ḥadhālīl **60–61** D 3
Al Hadīthah **60** CD 2
Al Hamād **60** C 2–3
Al Hamrā' **60** C 5
Al Ḥanākīyah **60** C 4
Al Ḥanīsh al Kabīr **89** G 6
Al Ḥarrah **60** BC 2
Al Harrah **60** C 3
Al Ḥasa **60** B 3
Al Hasā' **61** E 4
Al Hasakah **60** C 1
Al Ḥasan **60** D 2
Al Ḥawwārī **87** K 4
Al Ḥayy **61** DE 2
Al Hijāz **88** F 3
Al Hijaz (Saudi Arabia) **60** B 4
Al Ḥillah **61** D 2
Al Ḥillah **61** E 5
Al Ḥudaydah **89** G 6
Al Hufrah **60** BC 3–4
Al Hufūf **61** E 4
Al Hūj **60** C 3
Al Ḥusayḥiṣah **88** E 6
Al Ḥuwaymī **89** H 6
Alīābād **61** G 3
Aliákmon **58** B 2
Ali Bayramly **66** DE 3
Alicante **56** C 4
Alice River **79** H 3
Alice Springs **78** E 3
Aligarh **72** C 2
Al Iglim al Janūbīyah **92** DE 3
Alīgūdarz **61** E 2
Alījūq, Kūh-e **61** F 3
Al ʿIraq **60** D 2
Al 'Irq **87** K 3
Ali Sabjeh **93** G 2
Al ʿIsāwīyah **60** B 3
Al Iskandarīyah **88** DE 2
Aliskerovo **69** U 2
Al Ismāʿīlīyah **60** A 3
Aliwal North **94** D 6
Al Jafr **60** B 3
Al Jāfūrah **61** F 4–5
Al Jaghbūb **87** K 3
Al Jahrah **61** E 3
Al Jalāmīd **60** C 3
Al Jawf **60** C 3
Al Jaylī **88** E 5
Al Jazā'ir **87** F 1
Al Jazīrah **59** F 3–4
Al Jiwā' **61** FG 5
Al Jīzah **88** DE 2
Al Jubayl **66** DE 5
Al Jubaylah **61** E 4
Al Jumaymah **66** C 5
Al Junaynah **88** C 6
Al Karak **60** B 3
Al Karnak **88** E 3
Al Kāẓimīyah **60** D 2
Al Khalīl **60** B 3
Al Khāliṣ **61** D 2
Al Kharijah **88** DE 3
Al Kharj **61** E 5
Al Kharṭūm **88** EF 5
Al Kharṭūm Baḥrī **88** EF 5
Al Khaṣab **61** G 4
Al Khidr **61** D 3
Al Khubar **61** F 4
Al Khufayfīyah **61** D 4
Al Khunfah **60** C 3
Al Kir'ānah **61** F 4
Al Kūfah **60** D 2
Al Kumayt **61** E 2–3
Al Kuntillah **60** B 3
Al Kūt **61** D 2
Al Kuwayt **61** E 3
Al Labbah **60** C 3
Al Lādhiqīyah **88** EF 1
Al Lagowa **88** D 6
Allahabad **72** D 2
Allakh-Yun' **69** P 3
Allentown **103** L 3
Alleppey **72** C 6
Al Līfīyah **66** C 4
Al Liṣāfah **66** D 5
Al Lussuf **66** C 4
Alma-Ata **67** K 2
Almada **56** B 4
Al Madīnah **60** C 4
Al Mafraq **60** B 2
Al Maḥallah al Kubrā **88** E 2
Al Mahrah **89** J 5
Al Majann **61** F 5
Al Makhaylī **87** K 2
Al Manadīr **61** G 5
Al Manāmah **61** F 4
Al Manāqil **88** E 6
Al Manṣūrah **88** E 2
Al Maqṭā' **61** G 4
Al Marj **87** K 2
Al Mawṣil **60** D 1
Al Mayyāh **60** D 4
Almeirim **109** H 4
Almenara **111** HJ 4
Almendra, Embalse de **56** B 3
Almeria **56** C 4
Al'met'yevsk **62** K 4–5
Al Minyā **88** DE 3
Almirante Brown **115**
Almoustarat **90** D 2
Al Mubarraz **61** E 4
Al Mudawwarah **60** B 3
Al Mughayrā' **66** B 5

Al Muharraq **61** F 4
Al Mukallā **89** HJ 6
Al Murabbā' **60** D 4
Al Musayjīd **66** BC 6
Al Musayyib **60** D 2
Al Muwaylih **60** B 4
Al Nasser **60** A 4
Alofi **82** D 4
Alongshan **69** M 5
Alor, Pulau **75** F 5
Alor Setar **74** AB 2
Alpena **103** K 2
Alphonse **93** J 6
Alpi Carniche **57** F 2
Alpi Dolomitiche **57** F 2
Alpine **102** F 5
Al Qaḑārif **88** F 6
Al Qaḑīmah **89** F 4
Al Qāhirah **88** E 2
Al Qalībah **60** B 3
Al Qāmishlī **60** C 1
Al Qanţarah **60** A 3
Al Qaṭīf **61** E 4
Al Qaţrānī **60** B 3
Al Qaṭrūn **87** H 3
Al Qayʿīyah **60** D 4
Al Qayrawān **87** GH 1
Al Qayşūmah (Saudi Arabia) **66** C 5
Al Qayşūmah (Saudi Arabia) **66** D 5
Al Qunaytirah **60** B 2
Al Qunfudhah **89** FG 5
Al Qurayyah **88** F 3
Al Qurnah **61** E 3
Al Qusayr **60** B 4
Al Qūşūrīyah **60** D 5
Al Qutayfah **60** B 2
Al Quwārah **66** C 5
Al Quwayīyah **61** D 4
Al Shagra **61** F 4
Altamira **109** H 4
Altamont **102** B 3
Alta Shany **67** M 1
Altay (China) **67** M 1
Altay (Mongolia) **68** G 6
Altay (U.S.S.R.) **63** RS 5
Altiplanicie Mexicana **104** AB 2
Altmark **53** F 4
Alto - Alentejo **56** B 4
Alto Garças **111** F 4
Alton **103** H 4
Alto Parnaíba **109** J 5
Alto Río Senguerr **113** BC 7–8
Alto Turi **109** J 4
Altun Shan **70** AB 3
Alturas **102** B 3
Altus **102** FG 5
Altynasar **67** G 1
Al Ubayyid **88** DE 6
Al Ugşur **60** A 4
Al Urayq (Saudi Arabia) **60** C 3
Al Urdun **60** B 3
Al 'Uwayqīlah **60** CD 3
Al 'Uzayr **61** E 3
Alva (OK, U.S.A.) **102** G 4
Alvano, Kūh-e **61** E 2
Alvorado **111** G 3
Älvsbyn **54** H 2
Al Wajh **60** B 4
Alwar **72** C 2
Al Warīʿah **89** H 3
Al Widyān **60** C 3
Alxa Zuoqi **70** DE 3
Alygdzher **68** G 5
Alys-Khaya **69** P 2
Alytus **55** H 5
Amada **88** E 4
Amadjuak Lake **101** NO 2–3
Amakinskiy **68** K 1
Amambaí **111** EF 5
Amami-ō-shima **71** JK 5
Amangel'dy **63** N 5
Amanzimtoti **95** E 6
Amapá **109** H 3
Amarillo **102** F 4
Amaro Leite **111** G 3
Amarti **93** G 2
Amasya **59** E 2
Amazar **68** LM 5
Amazonas **108–109** EF 4
Amazonas **109** H 4
Ambala **72** C 1
Ambam **91** G 5
Ambarchik **69** U 2
Ambato **108** C 4
Ambikapur **72** D 3
Ambilobe **95** H 2
Ambohitralanana **95** J 3
Ambon **75** G 4
Ambositra **95** H 4
Ambovombe **95** H 5
Ambre, Cap d' **95** HJ 2
Ambrim **82** C 4
Ambrym **81** J 5
Ambur **72** C 5
Amchitka Pass **98** AB 5
Amdo **70** B 4
American Highland **115**
American Samoa **82** D 3
Amery Ice Shelf **115**
Ames **103** H 3
Amga **69** O 3
Amguema **98** B 2
Amguid **87** G 3
Amhara **93** F 2
Amiens **56** D 2
Amindivi Islands **72** B 5
Amirante Islands **93** J 6
Amlia **98** C 5
'Ammān **60** B 3
Ammarfjället **54** G 2
Amo **68** H 3
Āmol **61** F 1
Amorgos **58** C 3
Amos **101** M 6
Amoy **71** G 6
Amravati **72** C 3
Amritsar **72** C 1
Amsā'ad **87** K 2
Amsterdam (Netherlands) **52** DE 4
Amsterdam (N.Y., U.S.A.) **103** M 3
Amu-Dar'ya **67** G 2
Amukta Pass **98** C 5
Amundsen Gulf **99** N 1
Amundsen-Scott **115**
Amundsen Sea **115**
Amuntai **74** E 4
Amur **69** P 5
Amysakh **68** L 2
Anabarskoye Ploskogor'ye **68** J 1–2
Anaco **109** F 2
Anadoli **58–59** CD 3
Anadyr **69** WX 3
Anadyr **98** A 3
Anadyrskaja Nizmennost **69** X 2
Anadyrskiy Zaliv **69** Y 3
Anadyrskoye Ploskogor'ye **69** VW 2
Ānah **60** C 2
Anaimalai Hills **72** C 5
Anakapalle **72** D 4
Anamur **60** A 1
Anamur Burun **60** A 2
Anamuryum **59** D 3
Anantapur **72** C 5
Anapa **59** E 2
Anápolis **111** G 4
Anār **61** G 3
Añatuya **112** D 4
Anchorage **98** H 3
Ancohuma **110** C 4
Ancona **57** F 3
Ancud **113** B 7
Anda **71** J 1
Andalucía **56** BC 4
Andaman Islands **73** F 5
Andaman Sea **73** G 5–6
Andarab **67** H 3
Andenes **54** G 2
Anderson (IN, U.S.A.) **103** J 3–4
Anderson (N.W.T., Can.) **98** M 2
Anderson (S.C., U.S.A.) **103** K 5
Andes Mountains **107** C 2–6
Andfjorden **54** G 2
Andhra Pradesh **72** C 4
Andīmeshk **61** E 2
Andiria Burun **59** D 3
Andirlangar **67** L 3
Andiyskiy Khrebet **59** G 2
Andizhan **67** J 2
Andkhui **67** GH 3
Andong **71** J 3
Andorra **56** D 3
Andorra la Vella **56** D 3
Andöya **54** G 2
Andradina **111** F 5
Andreanof Islands **98** BC 5
Andriba **95** H 3
Andropov **62** G 4
Ándros **58** BC 3
Andros Island **105** G 3
Andújar **56** C 4
Andyngda **68** L 2
Anéfis **90** E 2
Anegada Passage **105** K 4
Aneto, Pico de **56** D 3
Angar **75** H 4
Angara **68** F 4
Angarsk **68** H 5
Angatau **83** F 4
Angaul **68** GH 5
Angeles **75** HJ 1
Angel Falls **109** F 2
Ängelholm **55** F 4
Ångermanälven **54** G 3
Angers **56** C 2
Angical **111** GH 3
Angijak Island **101** P 2
Angikuni Lake **99** RS 3
Angkor **73** H 5
Anglesey **52** BC 4
Angmagssalik **114**
Angoche **95** G 3
Angol **113** B 6
Angola **94** BC 2
Angoulême **56** D 2
Angu **92** C 4
Anguilla **105** K 4
Anhua **70** F 5
Anhui **71** G 4
Aniak **98** F 3
Aniakchak National Monument and Preserve **98** F 4
Animas Peak **102** E 5
Anjou **56** CD 2
Anjouan **95** GH 2
Ankang **70** E 4
Ankara **59** D 2
Ankazobe **95** H 3
Anlong **70** E 5–6
Anlu **70** F 4
Ann, Cape **115**
Annaba **87** G 1
An Nabk **60** B 2
An Nabk Abū Qasr **66** BC 4
An Nafūd **60** C 3
An Nāḩiyah **89** G 2
Annai **109** G 3
An Najaf **60** D 2–3
An' Nakhi **60** AB 3
Annam **73** J 4–5
Annandale **79** H 3
Anna Plains **78** C 2
Annapolis **103** L 4
Annapurna **72** D 2
Ann Arbor **103** K 3
An Nāsirīyah **61** E 3
Annecy **57** E 2
Annobón **91** F 6
An Nu'ayrīyah **61** E 4
An Nuhūd **88** D 6
Anori **109** F 4
Anqing **71** G 4
Anshan **71** H 2
Anshun **70** DE 5
Ansongo **90** DE 2
Anta **110** B 3
Antakya **59** E 3
Antalya Kőrfezi **58** D 3
Antananarivo **95** H 3
Antarctic Peninsula **115**

Antequera **56** C 4
Antigua and Barbuda **105** K 4
Antillas Mayores **105** HJ 4
Antiope **82** D 4
Antipodes Islands **115**
Antlät **87** K 2
Antofagasta **110** B 5
Antofagasta de la Sierra **112** C 4
Antongil, Baie d' **95** HJ 3
Antonio de Biedma **113** CD 8
Antonovo **66** E 1
Antsirabe **95** H 3
Antsiranana **95** HJ 2
Antsohihy **95** H 2
Antwerpen **52** D 4
Anuradhapura **72** D 6
Anxi **70** C 2
Anxiang **70** F 5
Anyang **70** FG 3
Anzhero-Sudzhensk **63** RS 4
Aomori **71** M 2
Aosta **57** E 2
Aoudaghost **86** CD 5
Aouinat Legraa **86** D 3
Aoulef el Arab **86–87** F 3
Apaporis **108** DE 3–4
Apataki **83** F 4
Apatity **54** K 2
Apatzingán **104** B 4
Apeldoorn **52** E 4
Api, Tanjung **74** C 3
Apia **82** D 3
Aporé **111** F 4
Appalachian Mountains **103** KM 2–4
Appenno Lucano **57** G 3–4
Appenno Tosco-Emiliano **57** F 3
Appleton **103** J 3
Apsheronsk **59** E 2
Apucarana **111** F 5
Apure **108** E 2
Apurimac **110** B 3
Aqār 'Atabah **87** H 3
Aqdā **61** F 2
Aquidauana **110** E 5
'Arabah, Wādi al **60** B 3
Arabestān **61** E 3
Arabian Sea **117**
Aracaju **111** J 3
Aracati **111** J 1
Araçatuba **111** FG 5
Aracena, Sierra de **56** B 4
Araçuai **111** H 4
Arad **58** B 1
Arada **91** J 2
'Arādah **61** F 5
Arafura Sea **75** HJ 5
Aragarças **111** F 4
Aragon **56** C 3
Araguacema **109** HJ 5
Aragua de Maturín **109** F 2
Araguaia **109** J 5
Araguaiana **111** F 4
Araguaína **109** J 5
Araguari **111** G 4
Araguatins **109** J 5
Arak (Algeria) **87** F 3
Arāk (Iran) **61** E 2
Arakaka **109** G 2
Arakan Yoma **73** FG 3–4
Aral Sea **66** F 2
Aral'sk **67** G 1
Aral'skoye More **66–67** FG 2
Aramac **79** H 3
Arandai **75** H 4
Aranjuez **56** C 3–4
Aranos **94** B 4
Aranuka **82** C 3
Araouane **90** D 2
Arapiraca **111** J 2–3
Araquara **111** G 5
Arauá **111** J 3
Arauca **108** D 2
Arauco **113** B 6
Aravalli Range **72** B 2–3
Araxá **111** G 4
Arbatax **57** E 4
Archer River National Park **79** G 1
Archipelago Kerimbas **95** G 2
Archipiélago de Colón **108** B 6
Archipiélago de la Reina Adelaida **113** A 9
Archipiélago de los Chonos **113** AB 7–8
Arco **102** D 3
Arcos **56** B 4
Arctic Ocean **114**
Arctic Red River **98** L 2
Arctowski **115**
Ardabīl **66** D 3
Ardakān **61** F 2
Årdal **54** E 3
Ard as Sawwān **60** B 3
Ardennes **52** E 4
Ardestan **61** F 2
Arecibo **105** J 4
Areia Branca **111** J 1
Arenápolis **110** E 3
Arendal **55** E 4
Arequipa **110** B 4
Arere **109** H 4
Arezzo **57** F 3
Arga **69** R 2
Argan **70** A 2
Argentina **113** CD 6
Arges **58** C 2
Argolíkós Kólpos **58** B 3
Argungu **91** EF 3
Argyle, Lake **78** D 2
Ar Horqin Qi **71** H 2
Århus **55** F 4
Arica (Chile) **110** B 4
Arica (Colombia) **108** D 4
Ariguaní **108** C 1
Arīhā **60** B 2
Arinos **110** E 3
Aripuanā **109** F 5
Aripuanā **109** FG 5
Ariquemes **109** F 5
Ariripina **111** HJ 2
Arizona (Argentina) **113** C 6
Arizona (U.S.A.) **102** D 5
Arjona **108** C 1
Arka **69** Q 3
Arkalyk **63** N 5
Arkansas **103** H 4
Arkansas City **103** G 4
Arkansas River **102–103** FH 4–5
Arkhangel'sk **62** H 3
Arkhara **69** O 6
Arklow **52** B 4
Arles **57** D 3
Arlington (OR, U.S.A.) **102** C 2
Arlington (TX, U.S.A.) **103** G 5
Arlington (VA, U.S.A.) **103** L 4
Arlit **91** F 2
Arly **90** E 3
Armant **88** E 3
Armavir **59** F 1
Armenia **108** C 3
Armeniya **59** F 2
Armidale **79** J 5
Armstrong **100** K 5
Armyansk **59** D 1
Arnauti, Akra **60** A 2
Arnawai **67** J 3
Arnhem **52** E 4
Arnhem, Cape **79** F 1
Aroab **94** B 5
Arorae **82** C 3
Arquipélago dos Bijagós **90** A 3
Ar Radīsīyah Baḥrī **60** A 4
Ar Rahad **88** E 6
Arraias **111** G 3
Ar Ramādī **60** D 2
Ar Ramlah **60** B 3
Arran **52** B 3
Ar Raqqah **60** C 2
Arras **56** D 1
Ar Rass **60** D 4
Ar Rawḍatayn **61** E 3
Ar Rayḥānī **61** G 5
Ar Rifā'ī **66** D 4
Ar Rimāl **89** J 4
Ar Riyāḍ **61** E 4
Ar Rub' al Khālī **89** HJ 4–5
Ar Ruṣāfah **66** B 3
Ar Ruṣayriṣ **88** E 6
Ar Ruṭbah **60** C 2
Ar Ruways (Qatar) **61** F 4
Ar Ruways (United Arab Emirates) **61** F 4
Års **55** E 4
Arsen'yev **71** K 2
Årskogen **54** G 3
Arsuk **101** S 3
Arteaga **104** B 4
Artem **71** K 2
Artemisa **104** F 3
Artic Circle **54** AB 2
Artigas **112** E 5
Artoli **88** E 5
Artybash **63** R 5
Artyk **69** R 3
Arua **92** E 4
Aruanā **111** F 3
Aruba, Isla **108** E 1
Arunachal **73** F 2
Arun Qi **69** M 6
Aruppukkottai **72** C 6
Arusha **93** F 5
Arvada **102** E 4
Arvayheer **70** D 1
Arvika **55** F 4
Arys' **67** H 2
Arzamas **62** H 4
Asahikawa **71** LM 2
Asamakka **91** F 2
Asansol **72** E 3
Asba Tafari **93** G 3
Ascensión **110** D 4
Ascoli Piceno **57** F 3
Aselle **93** F 3
Asha **63** L 5
Ashdod **60** B 3
Asheville **103** K 4
Ashgelon **60** B 3
Ashkhabad **66** FG 3
Ash Shabakah **60** D 3
Ash Sharqāt **60** D 2
Ash Shatrah **61** E 3
Ash Shiḥr **89** HJ 6
Ash Shinafiyah **61** D 3
Ash Shu'aybah **66** C 5
Ash Shu'bah **61** D 3
Ash Shumlūl **61** E 4
Ash Shwayrif **87** H 3
Ashtabula **103** KL 3
Ashuanipi **101** O 5
Ashuanipi Lake **101** O 5
Asinara **57** E 3
Asino **63** RS 4
Asir, Ra's **93** J 2
Asmara **93** F 1
Aspermont **102** F 5
Aspiring, Mount **80** P 9
Assab **93** G 2
Aş Şadr **61** G 4
Aş Şaḥrā' al Gharbīyah **88** D 3
Aş Şaḥrā' al Janūbīyah **88** DE 4
Aş Saḥrā' an Nūbiyah **88** EF 4
Aş Şahrā' ash Sharqīyah **60** AB 4
As Salamīyah **61** E 4
Aş Şāliḥīyah **60** C 2
As Sālimīyah **61** E 3
As Salmān **61** D 3
As Salt **60** B 2
Assam **73** F 2
As Samāwah **61** D 3
As Sarir **87** K 3
As Silā **61** F 4
Assiniboia **99** Q 6
Assis **111** F 5
Assisi **57** F 3
As Subū' **88** E 4
Aş Şulb **61** E 4
Aş Şummān **61** DE 4
Assur **60** D 2
As Suwaydā' **60** B 2
As Suways **60** A 3
Astakh **69** P 2
Astipálaia **58** C 3
Astrakhan **66** DE 1

Asturias **56** B 3
Asuncion (Mariana Is.) **82** A 1
Asunción (Paraguay) **112** E 3–4
Aswān **60** A 4
Aswan High Dam **60** A 5
Asyūṭ **88** E 3
Atacama, Desierto de **110** C 5
Atacama, Salar de **110** C 5
Atafu **82** D 3
Atambua **75** F 5
Atangmik **101** R 3
Atar **86** C 4
Atas Bogd Uul **70** C 2
Atasu **63** O 6
'Aṭbarah **88** E 5
Aṭbarah **88** EF 5
Atbasar **63** N 5
Athens (GA, U.S.A.) **103** K 5
Athens (Greece) **58** B 3
Athínai **58** B 3
Ath Thumāmī **61** D 4
Ati **91** H 3
Atico **110** B 4
Atikokan **100** J 6
Atikonak Lake **101** P 5
Atka **98** C 5
Atka (U.S.S.R.) **69** S 3
Atkarsk **62** H 5
Atlanta **103** JK 5
Atlantic City **103** M 4
Atlantic Ocean **116**
Atlas el Kebir **86** DE 2
Atlas Mountains **86** DF 2
Atlin **98** L 4
Ätran **55** F 4
Atrato **108** C 2
Atsy **75** J 5
At Tafīlah **60** B 3
Aṭ Ṭā'if **89** G 4
Attawapiskat **100** KL 5
Attawapiskat **100** L 5
At Tawīl **60** C 3
Aṭ Ṭaysīyah **60** D 3–4
Aṭ Ṭīb, Ra's **87** H 1
Attikamagen Lake **101** O 5
Attu **98** A 5
At Turayf **60** C 3
At Turbah **89** G 6
Atuel **113** C 6
Atura **92** E 4
Aua **82** A 3
Auas Mountains **94** B 4
Auburn **103** LM 3
Auckland **81** Q 8
Auckland Islands **115**
Aude **56** D 3
Augathella **79** H 4
Augsburg **53** F 5
Augusta (AR, U.S.A.) **103** H 4
Augusta (GA, U.S.A.) **103** K 5
Augusta (ME, U.S.A.) **103** N 3
Augustus, Mount **78** B 3
Auki **82** B 3
Aur **82** C 2
Aurangaband **72** C 4
Aurillac **56** D 3
Aurora **102** F 4
Aus **94** B 5
Ausangate, Nevado **110** B 3
Aust-Agder **55** E 4
Austin (MN, U.S.A.) **103** H 3
Austin (TX, U.S.A.) **102** G 5
Austin, Lake **78** B 4
Australia **78–79** CG 3
Australian Alps **79** H 6
Australian Capital Territory **79** H 6
Austria **57** F 2
Austvågöy **54** F 2
Auvézère **56** D 2
Auxerre **56** D 2
Auyuittuq National Park **101** OP 2
Avalon Peninsula **101** R 6
Avanavero **109** G 3
Avarua **83** E 4
Avaz **66** FG 4
Avdhira **58** C 2
Āvej **61** E 2
Avellaneda **112** E 5
Averöya **54** E 3
Avesta **55** G 3
Avignon **57** DE 3
Ávila **56** C 3
Avilés **56** B 3
Avola **57** G 4
Awara Plain **93** G 4
Awash **93** G 2
Awash **93** G 3
'Awaynat Wanīn **87** H 3
Awbārī **87** H 3
Awjilah **87** K 3
Axel Heiberg Island **114**
Axios **58** B 2
Ayabaca **108** BC 4
Ayacucho **110** AB 3
Ayaguz **63** Q 6
Ayan **69** P 4
Ayanaka **69** V 3
Ayava **68** H 4
Ayaviri **110** BC 3
Aydın **58** C 3
Ayers Rock – Mount Olga National Park **78** E 4
Áyion Óros **58** B 2
Aylmer Lake **99** Q 3
'Aynabo **93** H 3
'Ayn al Baydā' **60** BC 2
'Ayn al Ghazāl **87** K 4
Ayni **67** H 3
'Ayn Sukhnah **60** A 3
Ayon **69** V 1
Ayr (Australia) **79** H 2
Ayr (U.K.) **52** C 3
Aysary **63** O 5
Āzādshahr **61** G 1
Azamgarh **72** D 2
Azare **91** G 3
Azbine **91** F 2
Azerbaydzhan **66** D 2
Aznā **61** E 2
Azores **86** A 1
Azoum **91** J 3
Azov **59** E 1
Azovskoye More **59** E 1
Aztec ruins **102** E 4
Azul **113** E 6
Az Zallāq **61** F 4
Az Zargā' **61** F 4
Az Zarqā' **60** B 2
Az Zāwiyah **87** H 2
Az Zilfī **61** D 4
Az Zugar **89** G 6

B

Baba Burnu **58** D 2
Baba Burun **58** C 3
Bābā Heydar **61** F 2
Babahoyo **108** BC 4
Babai Gaxun **70** D 2
Bāb al Māndab **89** G 6
Babanūsah **88** D 6
Babar, Kepulauan **75** G 5
Babine Lake **99** M 5
Babo **75** H 4
Bābol **61** F 1
Babol Sar **61** F 1
Babushkin **68** J 5
Babylon **60** D 2
Bacabal **111** GH 1
Bacan, Pulau **75** G 4
Bacău **58** C 1
Back **99** S 2
Bād **61** F 2
Badajoz **56** B 4
Badalona **56** D 3
Badanah **60** C 3
Baden-Baden **53** E 5
Badiyat ash Shām **60** BC 2
Badoumbé **90** B 3
Badr Ḥunayn **60** C 5
Badulla **72** D 6
Badzhal **69** OP 5
Bafatá **90** B 3
Baffin Bay **114**
Baffin Island **101** NO 2
Bafia **91** G 5
Bafoussam **91** G 4
Bāfq **61** G 3
Bafra **59** E 2
Bāft **61** G 3
Bagadzha **68** L 3
Bagalkot **72** C 4
Baga Sola **91** GH 3
Bagdarin **68** K 5
Bagé **112** F 5
Baghdād **60** D 2
Bāghin **61** G 3
Baghlan **67** H 3
Bagua **108** C 5
Baguio **75** J 1
Baguirmi **91** H 3
Bahama Islands **105** H 3
Bahar Dar **93** F 2
Bahawalpur **67** J 5
Bahía (Argentina) **113** C 8
Bahía (Brazil) **111** H 3
Bahía Blanca **113** D 6
Bahía Blanca **113** D 6
Bahía de Campeche **104** CD 4
Bahía de Caráquez **108** B 4
Bahía Grande **113** C 9
Bahía Kino **102** D 6
Bahía Laura **113** CD 8
Bahía Rosario **102** C 6
Bahías, Cabo dos **113** CD 8
Bahía Sebastián Vizcaíno **102** D 6
Bahrain **61** F 4
Baḥr al Abyaḍ **88** E 6
Baḥr al Azraq **88** E 6
Baḥr al Jabal **92** E 3
Baḥr ar Rimāl al 'Aẓīm **88** CD 3
Baía de Setúbal **56** B 4
Baia Mare **58** B 1
Baião **109** J 4
Baicheng (Man. China) **71** H 1
Baicheng (Sink. Uig. China) **67** L 2
Baie aux Feuilles **101** O 4
Baie d'Antongil **95** HJ 3
Baie-des-Moutons **101** Q 5
Bailang **68** M 6
Baile Átha Cliath **52** B 4
Bailundo **94** B 2
Baimuru **80** D 3
Baing **75** F 6
Baingoin **72** E 1
Baiquan **69** N 6
Bairiki **82** C 2
Bairin Zuoqi **71** GH 2
Baixo-Alentejo **56** B 4
Baiyü **70** C 4
Baja **58** A 1
Baja California Norte **102** C 5
Baja California Sur **102** CD 6
Bakadzhitsite **58** C 2
Bakel **90** B 3
Baker **82** D 2
Baker Lake (N.W.T., Can.) **99** S 3
Baker Lake (N.W.T., Can.) **99** S 3
Bakersfield **102** C 4
Bakhta **63** RS 3
Bakhtegān, Daryācheh-ye **61** FG 3
Bakony **58** A 1
Bakouma **92** C 3
Baku **66** DE 2
Balabac Strait **74** E 2
Balabakk, Ra's **60** B 2
Baladīyat 'Adan **89** H 6
Balaghat **72** D 3
Balakhta **68** F 4
Balakovo **62** J 5
Bala Murghab **67** G 3
Balasore **72** E 3
Balaton **58** A 1
Balclutha **80** PQ 10
Balde **112** C 5
Bald Head **78** B 6
Baldy Peak **102** E 5
Bale **93** G 3
Balearic Islands **56** D 3
Baleia, Ponta da **111** J 4
Baley **68** L 5
Bali **74** D 5
Balıkesir **58** C 3
Balintang Channel **75** J 1

Balkan Mountains **58** C 2
Balkhash **63** OP 6
Balkhash, Ozero **63** P 6
Balladonia **78** C 5
Ballarat **79** G 6
Ballard, Lake **78** C 4
Balleny Islands **115**
Ballina **79** J 4
Balranald **79** G 5
Balsas **109** J 5
Balsas, Rio **104** B 4
Baltic Sea **55** GH 4
Baltimore **103** L 4
Baltiskaja Grjada **55** HJ 4–5
Baluchistan **66–67** G 5
Bam **66** F 5
Bamako **90** C 3
Bamba **90** D 2
Bambari **92** C 3
Bambesa **92** D 4
Bambesi **92** E 3
Bamenda **91** FG 4
Bamingui **92** C 3
Bamiyan **67** H 4
Bampūr **67** G 5
Banaba **81** J 2
Banalia **92** D 4
Banana **79** J 3
Banās, Ra's **60** B 5
Banās, Ra's **88** F 4
Bancroft **101** M 6
Banda **72** D 2
Banda Aceh **74** A 2
Bandar Abbas **61** G 4
Bandar-e-Anzalī **66** DE 3
Bandar-e Chārak **66** E 5
Bandar-e Deylam **66** E 4–5
Bandar-e Khomeynī **61** E 3
Bandar-e Lengeh **61** G 4
Bandar-e Māqām **61** F 4
Bandar-e Moghūyeh **61** FG 4
Bandar-e Rig **61** F 3
Bandarlampung **74** C 5
Bandarpunch **72** C 1
Bandar Seri Begawan **74** D 3
Bandar Shāh **61** E 1
Banda Sea **75** GH 5
Bandau **74** E 2
Band Bonī **66** F 5
Bandeira **111** H 5
Bandeirante **111** FG 3
Bandırma **58** C 2
Bandundu **92** B 5
Bandung **74** C 5
Banes **105** GH 3
Banff National Park **99** O 5
Banfora **90** CD 3
Bangalore **72** C 5
Bangassou **92** C 4
Bangeta, Mount **80** E 3
Banggai, Kepulauan **75** F 4
Bangko **74** B 4
Bangkok **73** H 5
Bangladesh **73** F 3
Bangor (ME, U.S.A.) **103** N 3
Bangor (N. Ireland, U.K.) **52** B 4
Bangui **92** B 4
Banhine National Park **95** E 4
Banihal Pass **67** K 4
Banī Mazār **88** DE 3
Banī Suwayf **88** E 3
Bāniyās (Lebanon) **60** B 2
Bāniyās (Syria) **60** B 2
Banja Luka **57** G 3
Banjarmasin **74** DE 4
Banjul **90** A 3
Ban Kniet **73** J 5
Banks Island (N.W.T., Can.) **99** N 1
Banks Island (Queensland, Austr.) **79** G 1
Banks Islands **81** J 4
Banks Peninsula **81** Q 9
Banks Strait **80** L 9
Ban Me Thuot **73** J 5
Bannu **67** J 4
Banská Bystrica **53** G 5
Banyo **91** G 4
Banyuwangi **74** D 5
Banzare Coast **115**
Banzart **87** GH 1
Baoding **70** FG 3
Baoji **70** E 4
Baoqing **71** K 1
Baoshan **70** CD 5
Baotou **70** E 2
Baqen **70** B 4
Baʿqūbah **61** D 2
Barabinsk **63** P 4
Barabinskaya Step' **63** P 5
Baracaldo **56** C 3
Bārah **88** E 6
Barahona **105** H 4
Barakkul' **63** N 5
Baramula **67** J 4
Baran **72** C 2
Barangbarang **75** EF 5
Baranof **98** K 4
Baranovichi **55** J 5
Barão de Capanema **110** E 3
Barão de Melgaco **110** D 3
Barbados **105** K 5
Barcaldine **79** H 3
Barcellona **57** FG 4
Barcelona (Spain) **56** D 3
Barcelona (Venezuela) **109** F 2
Barcelos **109** F 4
Bardawil, Sabkhat al **60** A 3
Bārḍēre **93** G 4
Bardeskan **66** F 3
Bardufoss **54** G 2
Barēda **93** J 2
Bareilly **72** C 2
Barentsovo More **62** GJ 1
Barents Sea **114**
Barentu **93** F 1
Bårgå **54** G 2
Barga **72** D 1
Barguzin **68** J 5
Barhaj **72** D 2
Bari **57** G 3
Barīdi, Ra's **60** B 4
Barīm **89** G 6
Barinas **108** E 2
Baring, Cape **99** O 2
Barisal **73** F 3
Barisan, Pegunungan **74** B 4
Barito, Sungai **74** D 4
Barkā' **89** K 4
Barkam **70** D 4
Barkly Tableland **79** F 2
Barlee, Lake **78** B 4
Barletta **57** G 3
Barmer **72** B 2
Barnaul **63** Q 5
Barnes Ice Cap **101** N 1–2
Barong **70** C 4
Barotseland **94** C 3
Barquisimeto **108** DE 1
Barra (Bahía, Brazil) **111** H 3
Barra (U.K.) **52** B 3
Barracão do Barreto **109** G 5
Barra do Corda **109** J 5
Barragem da Rocha de Galé **56** B 4
Barra Head **52** B 3
Barranca **108** C 4
Barrancabermeja **108** D 2
Barrancas **109** F 2
Barranquilla **108** C 1
Barreiras **111** G 3
Barreirinhas **111** H 1
Barreiro **56** B 4
Barreiros **111** JK 2
Barren **73** F 5
Barren Lands **99** QS 2
Barretos **111** G 5
Barrie **101** LM 7
Barrow (AK, U.S.A.) **98** F 1
Barrow (Argentina) **113** E 6
Barrow (Rep. of Ireland) **52** B 4
Barrow, Point **98** FG 1
Barrow Island **78** A 3
Barsi **72** C 4
Bartica **109** G 2
Bartlesville **103** G 4
Bāruni **72** E 2
Bāsa'īdū **61** G 4
Basauri **56** C 3
Basel **57** E 2
Bashi Haixia **71** H 6
Basilan City **75** F 2
Basílio **112** F 5
Baskol' **63** P 5
Basra **61** E 3
Bassas da India **95** FG 4
Bassein **73** F 4
Basse Terre **105** K 4
Bassinde Rennes **56** C 2
Bass Strait **80** KL 8
Bastak **61** G 4
Bastia **57** E 3
Bata **91** F 5
Batagay-Alyta **69** NO 2
Batama (U.S.S.R.) **68** H 5
Batamshinskiy **63** L 5
Batang **70** C 4
Batangas **75** F 1
Batang Hari **74** B 4
Bataysk **59** EF 1
Batemans Bay **79** J 6
Batha **91** H 3
Bathalha **56** B 4
Bathurst (Canada) **101** OP 6
Bathurst (N.S.W., Austr.) **79** H 5
Bathurst, Cape **98** LM 1
Bathurst Inlet **99** PQ 2
Bathurst Inlet **99** Q 2
Bathurst Island (N.T., Austr.) **78** D 1
Bathurst Island (The Arctic) **114**
Batin, Wadi al **61** DE 3
Batkanu **90** B 4
Bātlā q-e Gavkhūnī **61** F 2
Batman **59** F 3
Batna **87** G 1
Batoka **94** D 3
Batomga **69** P 4
Baton Rouge **103** H 5
Båtsfjord **54** J 1
Battambang **73** H 5
Battle Creek **103** J 3
Batu **93** F 3
Batui **75** F 4
Batumi **59** F 2
Batu Puteh, Gunung **74** B 3
Baturité **111** J 1
Baubau **75** F 5
Bauchi **91** F 3
Baures **110** D 3
Bauru **111** FG 5
Baús **111** F 4
Bavaria **53** F 5
Bavispe **102** E 5
Bawdwin **73** G 3
Baxoi **70** C 4
Bayamo **105** G 3
Bayan-Adraga **68** K 6
Bayan-Aul **63** P 5
Bayanbulag **68** G 6
Bayandzurh **68** J 6
Bayanga **92** B 4
Bayan Har Shankou **70** C 4
Bayanhongor **68** H 6
Bayan Obo **70** E 2
Bayāz **66** F 4
Bayāzeh **61** G 2
Bayburt **59** EF 2
Bay City (MI, U.S.A.) **103** K 3
Baydaratskaya Guba **63** N 2
Bay de Verde **101** R 6
Bayern **53** F 5
Bayjī **60** D 2
Baykal'skiy Khrebet **68** J 4–5
Baykit **68** G 3
Bay of Bengal **72–73** EF 4
Bay of Biscay **56** C 2–3
Bay of Fundy **101** O 6–7
Bay of Plenty **82** C 5
Bayonne **56** C 3
Bayovar **108** B 5
Bayram-Ali **67** G 3
Bayreuth **53** F 5
Bayrūt **60** B 2
Baytown **103** H 6
Bazarnyy Syzgan **62** J 5
Bazaruto National Park **95** F 4
Bazhong **70** E 4

Bear Island **114**
Beata, Cabo **105** H 4
Beatton River **99** NO 4
Beatty **102** C 4
Beaufort (Malaysia) **74** E 2
Beaufort (U.S.A.) **103** K 5
Beaufort Sea **98** JL 1
Beaufort West **94** C 6
Beaumont **103** H 5
Beausejour **99** S 5
Beauvais **56** D 2
Beaver (Sask., Can.) **99** Q 5
Beaver (UT, U.S.A.) **102** D 4
Beawar **72** BC 2
Beberibe **111** J 1
Béchar **86** E 2
Bedourie **79** F 3
Be'er Sheva **60** B 3
Beeville **102** G 6
Bega **79** HJ 6
Begejski Kanal **58** B 1
Begna **55** E 3
Behbehān **61** F 3
Behshar **61** F 1
Bei'an **69** N 6
Beibu Wan **73** J 3
Beida **87** K 2
Beihai **70** E 6
Beijing **71** G 2
Beipiao **71** H 2
Beira **95** F 3
Beirut **60** B 2
Bei Shan **70** C 2
Beitbridge **94** DE 4
Beitstad **54** F 3
Beitun **67** M 1
Beja **56** B 4
Bejaïa **87** FG 1
Bekdash **66** E 2
Békéscsaba **58** B 1
Bekopaka **95** G 3
Bela **67** H 5
Belau **75** HJ 2
Bela Vista (Brazil) **110** E 5
Bela Vista (Mozambique) **95** E 5
Belaya Kalitva **59** F 1
Belaya Tserkov **62** F 5–6
Belcher Islands **101** L 4
Belebey **62** K 5
Belém (Amazonas, Brazil) **108** E 4
Belém (Pará, Brazil) **109** J 4
Belén **108** C 3
Belep, Îles **82** B 4
Beleuli **66** F 2
Belfast **52** B 4
Belfield **102** F 2
Belfort **57** E 2
Belgaum **72** BC 4
Belgium **52** DE 4
Belgorod **62** G 5
Belgorod-Dnestrovskiy **58** CD 1
Belgrade **58** B 2
Beli **91** G 4
Belikh **60** C 1
Belitung, Pulau **74** C 4
Belize **104** E 4
Belize City **104** E 4
Bel'kachi **69** O 4
Bell **101** LM 5
Bella Bella **99** M 5
Bella Coola **99** M 5
Bellary **72** C 4
Belle Ile **56** C 2
Belleville (IL, U.S.A.) **103** J 4
Belleville (KS, U.S.A.) **102** G 4
Belleville (Ontario, Can.) **101** M 7
Bellevue **102** B 2
Bellin **101** N 3
Bellingham **102** B 2
Bellingshausen **115**
Bellingshausen Sea **115**
Bello **108** C 2
Belluno **57** F 2
Bell Ville **112** D 5
Bellyk **68** F 5
Belmonte **111** J 4
Belmopan **104** E 4
Belogorsk (U.S.S.R.) **69** N 5
Belogor'ye **63** N 3
Belo Horizonte (Minas Gerais, Brazil) **111** H 4–5
Belo Horizonte (Pará, Brazil) **109** H 5
Beloit **103** J 3
Belo Monta **109** H 4
Belorechensk **59** FG 2
Belorussiya **55** J 5
Belorusskaya **55** J 5
Belovo **63** R 5
Beloyarovo **69** NO 5
Beloye More **62** G 2
Belt'sy **58** C 1
Belush'ya Guba **62** KL 1
Belush'ya Guba **114**
Belyy **62** F 4
Bemidji **103** G 2
Bena Dibile **92** C 5
Benalla **79** H 6
Benares **72** D 2
Bend **102** B 3
Bender Bäyla **93** J 3
Bendery **58** C 1
Bendigo **79** GH 6
Benevento **57** FG 3
Bengal **72** E 3
Bengbu **71** G 4
Benghazi **87** J 2
Bengkulu **74** B 4
Benguela **94** A 2
Beni (Bolivia) **110** C 3
Beni (Zaire) **92** D 4
Benidorm **56** CD 4
Beni Mellal **86** D 2
Benin **90** E 3–4
Benin City **91** EF 4
Beni Ounif **86** E 2
Benjamin Constant **108** D 4
Ben Nevis **52** BC 3
Benson **102** D 5
Bentiaba **94** A 2
Benue **91** F 4
Benxi **71** HJ 2
Beograd **58** B 2
Beraketa **95** H 4
Berati **58** A 2
Berau, Teluk **75** H 4
Berbera **93** H 2
Berbérati **92** B 4
Berchogur **66** FG 1
Berdichev **55** J 6
Berdigestyakh **69** MN 3
Berdyansk **59** E 1
Berekum **90** D 4
Berens River **99** S 5
Berezniki **62** KL 4
Berezovka (Russia, U.S.S.R.) **63** Q 4
Berezovo **63** N 3
Berezovskiy **63** LM 5
Bergamo (Italy) **57** EF 2
Bergamo (Turkey) **58** C 3
Bergen (F.R.G.) **53** F 4
Bergen (Norway) **55** DE 3
Bergerac **56** D 3
Bergö **54** H 3
Bergviken **54** G 3
Berhampore **72** E 3
Berhampur **72** DE 4
Bering Land Bridge National Preserve **98** E 2
Beringovskiy **69** XY 3
Bering Sea **65** UV 3–4
Bering Sea **114**
Bering Strait **98** CD 2–3
Berkakit **69** M 4
Berkeley **102** B 4
Berkner Island **115**
Berlevåg **54** J 1
Bermejo (Argentina) **112** D 4
Bermejo (Argentina) **112** C 5
Bermuda Islands **105** K 1
Bern **57** E 2
Bernasconi **113** D 6
Bernburg **53** F 4
Berne **57** E 2
Berner Alpen **57** E 2
Bernina **57** E 2
Bertolínia **111** H 2
Bertoua **91** G 5
Besalampy **95** G 3
Besançon **57** E 2
Besar, Gunung **74** E 4
Beskidy Zachodny **53** GH 5
Beslan **59** F 2
Besna Kobila **58** B 2
Bessarabiya **58** C 1
Bestobe **63** O 5
Beswick **78** E 1
Bethlehem **94** D 5
Béthune **56** D 1
Betong **73** H 6
Bet-Pak-Dala **63** NO 6
Betroka **95** H 4
Beyānlū **61** E 1
Bey Dağları **58** CD 3
Beyla **90** C 4
Beyra **93** H 3
Beyşehir Gölü **58** D 3
Béziers **56** D 3
Bhadrakh **72** E 3
Bhadravati **72** C 5
Bhagalpur **72** E 3
Bhamo **73** G 3
Bhandara **72** CD 3
Bharuch **72** B 3
Bhatinda **72** BC 2
Bhatpara **72** E 3
Bhavnagar **72** B 3
Bhilwara **72** BC 2
Bhopal **72** C 3
Bhopalpatnam **72** D 4
Bhuban **72** E 3
Bhubaneswar **72** E 3
Bhumiphol Dam **73** GH 4
Bhusawal **72** C 3
Bhutan **73** F 2
Biak (Indonesia) **75** F 4
Biak (New Guinea) **75** J 4
Biak, Pulau **75** J 4
Biała Podlaska **53** H 4
Białystok **53** H 4
Biankouma **90** C 4
Biaora **72** C 3
Biarritz **56** C 3
Biberach **53** EF 5
Bicuari National Park **94** AB 3
Bida **91** F 4
Bidar **72** C 4
Bidzhan **69** O 6
Bié **94** B 2
Biebrza **53** H 4
Biel **57** E 2
Bielefeld **53** E 4
Bielsko-Biała **53** G 5
Bien Hoa **73** J 5
Bienville, Lac **101** N 4
Bifoum **91** G 6
Big Bend National Park **102** F 6
Biger **68** G 6
Bighorn River **102** E 2
Bight of Bangkok **73** H 5
Bight of Benin **90** E 4
Bigi **92** C 4
Big Spring **102** F 5
Big Trout Lake **100** K 5
Bihač **57** G 3
Bihar **72** DE 2
Bijapur **72** C 4
Bijeljina **57** G 3
Bijiang **70** C 5
Bikaner **72** B 2
Bikar **82** C 2
Bikin **69** O 6
Bikini **82** B 2
Bilaspur **72** D 3
Bilbao **56** C 3
Bili **92** D 4
Billings **102** E 2
Bilma, Grand Erg de **91** GH 2
Biloela **79** J 3
Bilogora **57** G 2
Biloxi **103** J 5
Binaiya, Gunung **75** G 4
Binder **68** K 6
Bindura **95** E 3
Bingara **79** J 4
Binghamton **103** L 3

Binjai **74** A 3
Binnaway **79** H 5
Bintan, Pulau **74** B 3
Bintulu **74** D 3
Bira **69** P 6
Birao **92** C 2
Biratnagar **72** E 2
Bi'r Bū Zurayyq **87** K 3
Bi'r Fu'ād **88** D 2
Birjand **66** F 4
Birkat Nasser **60** A 5
Birkenhead **52** C 4
Birksgate Range **78** DE 4
Bîrlad **58** C 1
Birmingham (AL, U.S.A.) **103** J 5
Birmingham (U.K.) **52** C 4
Bir Moghreim **86** C 3
Bi'r Nasīf **60** C 4
Birnie **82** D 3
Birnin Kebbi **91** EF 3
Birnin Kudu **91** F 3
Birobidzhan **69** O 6
Bir Ounane **90** D 1
Bir Rhoraffa **87** G 2
Bi'r Safājah **60** AB 4
Bi'r Shalatayn **88** F 4
Birsilpur **72** B 2
Birsk **62** L 4
Biru **70** B 4
Biscoe Islands **115**
Bishop's Falls **101** Q 6
Biskra **87** G 2
Bismarck **102** F 2
Bismarck Archipelago **80–81** EF 2
Bismarck Range **80** DE 2–3
Bismarck Sea **80** EF 2
Bissau **90** A 3
Bistrița **58** BC 1
Bitchana **93** F 2
Bitkiné **91** H 3
Bitlis **59** F 3
Bitola **58** B 2
Bitterfontein **94** B 6
Bitter Lake (Egypt) **60** A 3
Bitterroot Range **102** D 2–3
Biu **91** G 3
Biyang **70** F 4
Biysk **63** R 5
Bizerta **87** GH 1
Bjelašnica **58** A 2
Bjerkvik **54** G 2
Björkö **54** H 3
Björnöya **114**
Blackall **79** GH 3
Blackburn, Mount **98** HJ 3
Black Hills **102** F 3
Blackpool **52** C 4
Black River Falls **103** H 3
Black Sea **59** DE 2
Blackwell **102** G 4
Blåfjellhatten **54** F 3
Blagoevgrad **58** B 2
Blagoveshchensk **69** NO 5
Blaine **103** H 2
Blantyre **95** E 3
Blåskavlen **54** E 3
Blåvands Huk **55** E 4
Blekinge **55** FG 4
Blenheim **82** C 5
Blida **87** F 1
Bloemfontein **94** CD 5
Blois **56** D 2
Blönduós **54** AB 2
Bloomington (IL, U.S.A.) **103** J 3
Bloomington (IN, U.S.A.) **103** J 4
Bloomington (MN, U.S.A.) **103** H 3
Blosseville Coast **114**
Bluefields **104** F 5
Blue Ridge **103** KL 4
Bluff Knoll **78** B 5
Blumenau **112** FG 4
Blythe **102** D 5
Blytheville **103** J 4
Bo **90** B 4
Boa Vista (Cape Verde) **90** B 6
Boa Vista (Roraima, Brazil) **109** F 3
Bobai **70** EF 6
Bobo Dioulasso **90** D 3
Bobruysk **55** J 5
Boby, Pic **95** H 4
Boca del Rio **102** E 6
Bôca do Acre **108** E 5
Bocage Vendéen **56** C 2
Bocaiúva **111** H 4
Boca Raton **103** L 6
Bochum **53** E 4
Bodaybo **68** K 4
Bodélé **91** H 2
Boden **54** H 2
Bodensee **57** E 2
Bodö **54** F 2
Bo Duc **73** J 5
Boende **92** C 5
Boffa **90** B 3
Boggeragh Mountains **52** B 4
Bogor **74** C 5
Bogoroditsk **62** G 5
Bogotá **108** D 3
Bogra **72** E 2–3
Boguchany **68** G 4
Bogué **86** C 5
Bo Hai **71** GH 3
Bohemia **53** F 5
Böhmerwald **53** F 5
Bohol **75** F 2
Bohol Sea **75** F 2
Boiaçu **109** F 4
Boise **102** C 3
Boise City **102** F 4
Bojnūrd **66** F 3
Bojuro **112** F 5
Bokatola **92** B 5
Boké **90** B 3
Boknafjorden **55** E 4
Bokora Game Reserve **92** E 4
Bokpyin **74** A 1
Bokungu **92** C 5
Bolan Pass **67** H 5
Bole (China) **67** L 2
Bole (Ghana) **90** D 4
Bolesławiec **53** G 4
Bolgatanga **90** D 3
Boli **71** K 1
Bolia **92** B 5
Bolívar (Argentina) **113** D 6
Bolívar (Colombia) **108** C 3
Bolivia **110** CD 4
Bollon **79** H 4
Bologna **57** F 3
Bologoye **62** F 4
Bologur **69** O 3
Bolombo **92** C 5
Bolsena, Lago di **57** F 3
Bol'shaya Glushitsa **62** K 5
Bol'sheretsk **69** T 5
Bol'shezemel'skaya Tundra **62** KM 2
Bolshoy Kavkaz **59** F 2
Bol'shoy Nimnyr **69** MN 4
Bol'shoy Shantar, Ostrov **69** P 4–5
Bolsón de Mapimi **104** B 2
Bolton **52** C 4
Bolu **59** D 2
Bolzano **57** F 2
Boma **91** G 7
Bombay **72** B 4
Bomberai **75** H 4
Bom Jesus **111** H 2
Bom Jesus da Lapa **111** H 3
Bömlo **55** DE 4
Bomongo **92** B 4
Bom Retiro **112** G 4
Bona, Mount **98** J 3
Bonaparte Archipelago **78** C 1
Bonavista Bay **101** R 6
Bondo **92** C 4
Bondowoso **74** D 5
Bonete, Cerro **112** C 4
Bongor **91** H 3
Bonifacio, Strait of **57** E 3
Bonin Islands **65** R 7
Bonito **110** E 5
Bonn **53** E 4
Bonners Ferry **102** C 2
Bonobono **74** E 2
Boola **90** C 4
Boothby, Cape **115**
Boothia Peninsula **99** T 1
Bophuthatswana **94** C 5
Boquillagas del Carmen **104** B 2
Bor **58** B 2
Bora-Bora **83** EF 4
Borah Peak **102** D 3
Borås **55** F 4
Borasambar **72** D 3
Borāzjān **61** F 3
Borba **109** G 4
Bordeaux **56** CD 3
Bordertown **79** G 6
Bordj Fly Sainte Marie **86** E 3
Bordj Messouda **87** G 2
Börgefjellet **54** F 2
Borislav **53** H 5
Borisoglebsk **62** H 5
Borisov **55** J 5
Borispol **62** F 5
Bo River **92** D 3
Borja (Peru) **108** C 4
Borja (Yugoslavia) **58** A 2
Borkou **91** H 2
Borlänge **55** FG 3
Borneo **74** DE 3
Bornholm **55** F 5
Bornu **91** G 3
Borohoro Shan **67** L 2
Boroko **75** F 3
Borolgustakh **68** M 2
Borovichi **62** FG 4
Borroloola **79** F 2
Börselv **54** HJ 1
Borsippa **60** D 2
Boru **69** Q 1
Borūjen **61** F 3
Borūjerd **61** E 2
Borzya **68** L 5
Bōsāso **93** H 2
Bose **70** E 6
Boshan **71** G 3
Boshnyakovo **69** Q 6
Boshuslän **55** F 4
Bosna **57** G 3
Bosporus **58** C 2
Bossangoa **92** B 3
Bossembele **92** B 3
Bossemptélé II **92** B 3
Bossier City **103** H 5
Bostandyk **62** J 6
Boston **103** MN 3
Botletle **94** C 4
Botoşani **58** C 1
Bo Trach **73** J 4
Botswana **94** CD 4
Botucatu **111** G 5
Bouaflé **90** C 4
Bouaké **90** D 4
Bouar **92** B 3
Bou Arfa **86** E 2
Boubandjida **91** GH 4
Boubandjida National Park **91** GH 4
Bou Djéhiba **90** D 2
Bougainville **81** G 3
Bougainville Reef **79** H 2
Bou Garfa **86** D 3
Bougouni **90** C 3
Bouïra **87** F 1
Bou Izakarn **86** D 3
Boulanouar **86** B 4
Boulder (U.S.A. Colorado) **102** E 3
Boulder (West Australia) **78** C 5
Boulia **79** F 3
Boulouli **90** C 2
Bouna **90** D 4
Boundiali **90** C 4
Boundou **90** B 3
Boun Neua **73** H 3
Bountiful **102** D 3
Bounty Islands **115**
Bourem **90** D 2
Bourg **57** E 2
Bourges **56** D 2
Bourgogne **57** DE 2

Bou Rjeima **86** C 5
Bourke **79** H 4–5
Bournemouth **52** C 4
Bou Saâda **87** F 1
Bouvet Island **115**
Bowen (Argentina) **112** C 5
Bowen (Australia) **79** H 2
Bowling Green **103** J 4
Bowman **102** F 2
Bowman Bay **101** MN 2
Boxing **71** G 3
Boyabo **92** B 4
Boyne **52** B 4
Boyuibe **110** D 5
Bozok Platosu **59** DE 3
Brač **57** G 3
Bradenton **103** K 6
Bradford **52** C 4
Bradshaw **78** E 2
Brady **102** G 5
Braga **56** B 3
Bragança (Brazil) **109** J 4
Bragança (Portugal) **56** B 3
Bragina **69** X 3
Brahmaputra **73** F 2
Brai **101** M 2
Brăila **58** C 1
Brăk **87** H 3
Brampton **101** L 7
Brandberg **94** A 4
Brandenburg **53** F 4
Brandon **99** S 5–6
Brandvlei **94** BC 6
Brantford **101** L 7
Brasil, Planalto do **111** H 4
Brasiléia **110** C 3
Brasília **111** G 4
Braşov **58** C 1
Brassey, Mount **78** E 3
Bratislava **53** G 5
Bratsk **68** H 4
Bratskoye Vodokhranilishche **68** H 4
Bratslav **58** C 1
Bratul Chilia **58** C 1
Braunschweig **53** F 4
Brawley **102** CD 5
Brazil **110–111** EG 3
Brazo Casoquiare **108** E 3
Brazzaville **91** GH 6
Brčko **57** G 3
Brecknock, Península **113** B 9
Breda **52** D 4
Bredbyn **54** G 3
Breiðafjörður **54** A 2
Brejo **111** H 1
Brekken **54** F 3
Bremangerlandet **54** D 3
Bremen **53** E 4
Bremerhaven **53** E 4
Brenner **57** F 2
Brescia **57** F 2
Brest **56** C 2
Bretagne **56** C 2
Breves **109** H 4
Brevoort Island **101** P 3
Brewster, Kap **114**
Brewton **103** J 5
Brezhnev **62** K 4
Bridgeport **103** M 3
Bridger Peak **102** E 3
Bridgetown (Australia) **78** B 5
Bridgetown (Barbados) **105** KL 5
Brighton **52** D D 4
Brindisi **57** G 3
Brisbane **79** J 4
Bristol **52** C 4
Bristol Bay **98** EF 4
Bristol Channel **52** C D 4
British Columbia **99** MN 4–5
Britstown **94** C 6
Brive **56** D 2
Brno **53** G 5
Broadus **102** EF 2
Broadview **99** R 5
Brochet **99** R 4
Broken Hill **79** G 5
Brokhovo **69** ST 4
Brokopondo **109** G 3
Brönnöysund **54** F 2
Brookings **103** G 3
Brooks Range **98** FH 2
Brookton **78** B 5
Broome **78** C 2
Browne Range Nature Reserve **78** CD 3
Brownfield **102** F 5
Brownsville **103** G 6
Brownwood **102** G 5
Bruce, Mount **78** B 3
Bruce Crossing **103** J 2
Brugge **52** D 4
Brumado **111** H 3
Brunei **74** D 2
Brusilovka **62** KL 5
Brusque **112** G 4
Bruxelles **52** D 4
Bryan **103** G 5
Bryan Coast **115**
Bryansk **62** F 5
Bryanskoye **59** G 2
Bryne **55** E 4
Brzeg **53** G 4
Būbīyān **61** E 3
Bucaramanga **108** D 2
Buchanan **90** B 4
Bucharest **58** C 2
Buckingham Bay **79** F 1
Buckland **98** EF 2
Buco Zau **91** G 6
Bu Craa **86** C 3
Bucureşti **58** C 2
Budapest **58** AB 1
Budennovsk **59** F 2
Búðardalur **54** A 2
Buenaventura (Colombia) **108** C 3
Buenaventura (Mexico) **102** E 6
Buenavista **102** E 7
Buenos Aires **112** DE 5–6
Buenos Aires, Lago **113** B 8
Buffalo (N.Y., U.S.A.) **103** L 3
Buffalo (OK, U.S.A.) **102** G 4
Buffalo (S.D., U.S.A.) **102** F 2
Buffalo (WY, U.S.A.) **102** E 3
Buffalo Lake **99** OP 3
Buffalo Narrows **99** Q 4
Bug **53** H 4
Buga **108** C 3
Bugorkan **68** J 3
Bugöynes **54** J 2
Bugt **69** M 6
Bugul'ma **62** K 5
Buhayrat al Asad **59** E 3
Bujumbura **92** D 5
Buka **81** F 3
Bukadaban Feng **70** B 3
Bukavu **92** D 5
Bukhara **67** G 3
Bukit Gandadiwata **75** EF 4
Bukit Kambuno **75** EF 4
Bukit Masurai **74** B 4
Bukittinggi **74** AB 3–4
Bukoba **92** E 5
Bukukun **68** K 6
Būl, Kūh-e **61** F 3
Bulawayo **94** D 3–4
Buldana **72** C 3
Bulgan **68** H 6
Bulgaria **58** C 2
Bullahār **93** G 2
Bulo Berde **93** H 4
Bulungu **92** B 5
Bumba **92** C 4
Bumbulan **75** F 3
Bunbury **78** B 5
Bunda **92** E 5
Bundaberg **79** J 3
Bunda Bunda **79** G 3
Bundesrepublik Deutschland **53** EF 5
Bundooma **78** E 3
Bunia **92** DE 4
Buorkhaya, Guba **69** O 1
Buorkhaya, Mys **69** O 1
Buqayq **61** E 4
Buran **63** R 6
Bura'o **93** H 3
Burayda **60** D 4
Buraydah **89** G 3
Burdur **58** D 3
Burdwan **72** E 3
Bureinskiy, Khrebet **69** O 5
Bureya **69** O 5
Burgakhcha **69** Q 3
Burgas **58** C 2
Burgaski zaliv **58** C 2
Burgeo **101** Q 6
Burgersdorp **94** D 6
Burgfjället **54** FG 3
Burgos (Mexico) **104** C 3
Burgos (Spain) **56** C 3
Burhanpur **72** C 3
Burin Peninsula **101** QR 6
Burkhala **69** RS 3
Burkina **90** DE 3
Burlington (CO, U.S.A.) **102** F 4
Burlington (IA, U.S.A.) **103** H 3
Burlington (N.Y., U.S.A.) **103** M 3
Burma **73** FG 3
Burmantovo **63** M 3
Burnie **80** L 9
Burns **102** C 3
Burnu **58** D 3
Burqin **67** M 1
Burra **79** F 5
Bursa **58** C 2
Bur Sa'id **60** A 3
Būr Sūdān **88** F 5
Buru **75** G 4
Burundi **92** DE 5
Buşayrah **60** C 2
Būshehr **61** F 3
Bushman Land **94** BC 5
Businga **92** C 4
Busira **92** B 5
Buskerud **55** E 3
Busu Melo **92** C 4
Butang Group **73** G 6
Butaritari **82** C 2
Butembo **92** D 4
Butha Qi **69** M 6
Butte **102** D 2
Butt of Lewis **52** B 3
Button Bay **99** T 4
Button Islands **101** P 3
Butuan **75** G 2
Bu Tu Suay **73** J 5
Buy **62** H 4
Büyük Ağrı Dağı **59** F 3
Buzachi, Poluostrov **66** E 1–2
Buzău **58** C 1
Buzuluk **62** K 5
Byblos **60** B 2
Bydgoszcz **53** G 4
Bygdeå **54** H 3
Bygdeträsket **54** GH 3
Bykovo **62** J 3
Bykovskiy **69** NO 1
Bylot Island **114**
Byrd Station **115**
Byro **78** B 4
Byske **54** H 3
Byskeälven **54** GH 2
Bytom **53** G 4
Byuchennyakh **69** QR 3

C

Caaguazu **112** E 4
Cáatingas **111** GH 2–3
Caazapa **112** E 4
Cabanatuan **75** J 1
Cabezas **110** D 4
Cabimas **108** D 1
Cabinda **91** G 6–7
Cabo Barbas **86** B 4
Cabo Beata **105** H 4
Cabo Bojador **86** BC 3
Cabo Catoche **104** E 3
Cabo Corrientes **108** C 2
Cabo das Correntes **95** F 4
Cabo de Ajo **56** C 3
Cabo de Creus **56** D 3
Cabo de Finisterre **56** B 3
Cabo de Formentor **56** D 3
Cabo de Gata **56** C 4
Cabo de Hornos **113** CD 10

Cabo de la Nao **56** D 4
Cabo Delgado **95** G 2
Cabo de Palos **56** C 4
Cabo de Salinas **56** D 4
Cabo de Santa Maria (Mozambique) **95** EF 5
Cabo de Santa Maria (Portugal) **56** B 4
Cabo de São Roque **111** JK 2
Cabo de São Vicente **56** B 4
Cabo dos Bahías **113** CD 8
Cabo Frio **111** H 5
Cabo Gracias a Dios **104** F 4–5
Cabo Norte **109** J 3
Cabo Orange **109** H 3
Cabo Ortegal **56** B 3
Caborca **102** D 5
Cabo San Antonio (Argentina) **113** E 6
Cabo San Antonio (Cuba) **104** EF 3
Cabo San Diego **113** C 9
Cabo San Lucas **102** E 7
Cabo Santa Elena **104** E 5
Cabo Trafalgar **56** B 4
Cabot Strait **101** Q 6
Cabo Verde **90** AB 6
Cabrera **56** D 4
Cabrera, Sierra de la **56** B 3
Cabruta **108** E 2
Caçador **112** F 4
Čačak **58** AB 2
Caceres (Brazil) **110** E 4
Cáceres (Spain) **56** B 4
Cachi, Nevado de **110** C 5
Cachimbo **109** H 5
Cachimbo, Serra do **109** G 5
Cachoeira **111** J 3
Cachoeira Alta **111** F 4
Cachoeira do Sul **112** F 5
Cachoeiro de Itapemirim **111** HJ 5
Caconda **94** B 2
Cacula **94** A 2
Cadi, Sierra del **56** D 3
Cadiz (Philippines) **75** F 1
Cádiz (Spain) **56** B 4
Cadiz, Golfo de **56** B 4
Caen **56** C 2
Caetite **111** H 3
Cagayan de Oro **75** F 2
Cagayan Islands **75** F 2
Cagliari **57** E 4
Caguas **105** J 4
Caia **95** EF 3
Caibarién **105** G 3
Caico **111** J 2
Caicos Islands **105** H 3
Cailloma **110** B 4
Cairns **79** H 2
Cairo **88** E 2
Caiundo **94** B 3
Cajamarca **108** C 5
Cajazeiras **111** J 2
Cajuapara **109** J 4
Calabar **91** F 4
Calabozo **108** E 2
Calabria **57** G 4
Calabro, Apennino **57** G 4
Calafate **113** B 9
Calais **52** D 4
Calama **110** C 5
Calamar **108** D 3
Calamian Group **75** E 1
Cala Ratjada **56** D 4
Calatayud **56** C 3
Calatrava, Campo de **56** C 4
Calbayog **75** FG 1
Calçoene **109** H 3
Calcutta **72** E 3
Caldas **108** C 2
Caldera **112** B 4
Caleta Olivia **113** C 8
Calgary **99** P 5
Cali **108** C 3
Calicut **72** BC 5
California **102** BC 4
Calilegua **110** CD 5
Callao **110** A 3
Caltanissetta **57** F 4
Calvi **57** E 3
Camagüey **105** G 3
Camaná **110** B 4
Camapuã **111** F 4
Camaquã **112** F 5
Camarat, Cap **57** E 3
Camargo **110** C 5
Camarones **113** CD 7
Camaxilo **94** B 1
Cambodia **73** HJ 5
Cambrai **56** D 1
Cambrian Mountains **52** C 4
Cambridge (MA, U.S.A.) **103** MN 3
Cambridge (U.K.) **52** D 4
Cambridge Bay **99** QR 2
Cameia National Park **94** C 2
Cameron **103** H 2
Cameroon **91** FG 4
Cameroon, Mont **91** F 5
Cametá **109** HJ 4
Camiranga **109** J 4
Camiri **110** D 5
Camocim **111** H 1
Camooweal **79** F 2
Camorta **73** F 6
Campana, Isla **113** A 8
Campbell Island **115**
Campbellton **101** O 6
Camp Century **114**
Campeche **104** D 4
Campeche, Bahia de **104** CD 4
Campecne **104** DE 4
Campidano **57** E 4
Campina Grande **111** J 2
Campinas **111** G 5
Campo **91** F 5
Campo Corral **108** DE 2
Campo de Calatrava **56** C 4
Campo Formoso **111** H 3
Campo Gallo **112** D 4
Campo Grande **111** F 5
Campo Maior **111** H 1
Campos (Brazil) **111** GH 3–4
Campos (Brazil) **111** H 5
Cam Ranh **73** JK 5
Camrose **99** P 5
Ca Na **74** C 1
Canada **98–101**
Canadian River **102** F 4
Çanakkale **58** C 2
Canakkale Boğazı **58** C 2–3
Canal de la Mona **105** J 4
Canal do Norte **109** H 3
Canal du Midi **56** D 3
Canale de Sicilia **57** F 4
Canale di Malta **57** F 4
Cananea **102** DE 5
Canary Islands **86** B 3
Canaveral, Cape **103** KL 6
Canavieiras **111** J 4
Canberra **79** H 6
Canchas **112** BC 4
Candeias **111** J 3
Candelaria **104** D 4
Canéla **111** H 3
Cangamba **94** C 2
Cangombé **94** B 2
Cangyuan **70** C 6
Cangzhou **71** G 3
Canindé **111** J 1
Çankırı **59** D 2
Cannanore **72** BC 5
Cannes **57** E 3
Canning Basin **78** C 2
Cann River **79** H 6
Canoas **112** F 4
Canora **99** R 5
Canosa **57** G 3
Canso **101** P 6
Cantabrian Mountains **56** BC 3
Cantaura **109** F 2
Canterbury Bight **82** C 5
Can Tho **73** J 6
Canto do Buriti **111** H 2
Canton **103** K 3
Canton (China) **70** F 6
Capanema **109** J 4
Capão Bonito **111** G 5
Cap Camarat **57** E 3
Cap Corse **57** E 3
Cap de Fer **87** G 1
Cap de Gaspé **101** P 6
Cap de la Hague **56** C 2
Cap-de-la-Madeleine **101** N 6
Cape Adare **115**
Cape Agulhas **94** C 6
Cape Ann **115**
Cape Arid **78** C 5
Cape Arid National Park **78** C 5
Cape Arnhem **79** F 1
Cape Baring **99** O 2
Cape Bathurst **98** LM 1
Cape Bauld **101** QR 5
Cape Boothby **115**
Cape Breton Island **101** Q 6
Cape Canaveral **103** KL 6
Cape Catastrophe **79** F 5–6
Cape Chapman **99** U 2
Cape Charles **103** L 4
Cape Chelyuskin **114**
Cape Chidley **101** P 3
Cape Churchill **99** T 4
Cape Coast **90** DE 4
Cape Cod **103** N 3
Cape Columbine **94** B 6
Cape Comorin **72** C 6
Cape Cretin **80** E 3
Cape Croker **78** E 1
Cape Cross **94** A 4
Cape d'Ambre,Cape Bobraomby **95** HJ 2
Cape Darnley **115**
Cape Dennison **115**
Cape Dorchester **101** M 2
Cape du Couedic **79** F 6
Cape Dyer **101** P 2
Cape Engaño **75** J 1
Cape Farewell **81** Q 9
Cape Fear **103** L 5
Cape Finniss **78** E 5
Cape Flattery **102** AB 2
Cape Freels **101** R 6
Cape Fria **94** A 3
Cape Grim **80** K 9
Cape Harrison **101** Q 5
Cape Hatteras **103** LM 4
Cape Henrietta Maria **101** L 4
Cape Herluf Trolle **101** T 3
Cape Horn **113** CD 10
Cape Howe **79** J 6
Cape Jaffa **79** F 6
Cape Kellett **99** M 1
Cape Krusenstern National Monument **98** E 2
Cape Lambert **81** F 2
Cape Lambton **99** MN 1
Cape Leeuwin **78** A 5
Cape Lévêque **78** C 2
Capelinha **111** H 4
Cape Lisburne **98** D 2
Cape Londonderry **78** D 1
Cape Lookout **103** L 5
Cape Low **99** UV 3
Cape Maria van Diemen **81** PQ 7
Cape Melville**79** GH 1
Cape Mendocino **102** AB 3
Cape Mercy **101** P 3
Cape Meredith **113** D 9
Cape Mohican **98** CD 3
Cape Morris Jesup **114**
Cape Naturaliste **78** A 5
Cape Negrais **73** F 4
Cape Newenham **98** DE 4
Cape Norvegia **115**
Cape of Good Hope **94** B 6
Cape Otway **79** G 6
Cape Palmas **90** C 5
Cape Poinsett **115**
Cape Prince Alfred **99** M 1
Cape Prince of Wales **98** D 2
Cape Providence **80** OP 10
Cape Province **94** CD 6
Cape Race **101** R 6
Cape Raper **101** O 2
Cape Ray **101** Q 6
Cape Rodney **80** E 4

Cape Sable (Canada) **101** O 7
Cape Sable (FL, U.S.A.) **103** K 6
Cape Saint Francis **94** CD 6
Cape Saint George **81** F 2–3
Cape Saint Lucia **95** E 5
Cape San Blas **103** J 6
Cape Scott **78** D 1
Cape Smith **101** LM 3
Cape Town **94** B 6
Cape Van Diemen **78** D 1
Cape Verde **90** AB 6
Cape Wessel **79** F 1
Cape Wrath **52** BC 3
Cape Yakataga **98** J 4
Cape York **79** G 1
Cape York Peninsula **79** G 1
Cape Zhelaniya **114**
Cap Ferret **56** C 3
Cap-Haïtien **105** H 3–4
Cap Hopes Advance **101** O 3
Capitán Arturo Prat **115**
Cap Lopez **91** F 6
Cap Masoala **95** J 3
Capo Carbonara **57** E 4
Capo Circeo **57** F 3
Capo Gallo **57** F 4
Capoompeta **79** J 4
Capo Palinuro **57** FG 4
Capo Passero **57** G 4
Capo San Marco **57** E 4
Capo Santa Maria di Leuca **57** G 4
Capo Spartivento **57** E 4
Capo Testa **57** E 3
Capri **57** F 3
Capricorn Channel **79** J 3
Caprivi Game Park **94** C 3
Caprivi Strip **94** C 3
Cap Saint-André **95** G 3
Cap Sainte-Marie,Cap Vohimena **95** GH 5
Cap Timiris **86** B 5
Cap Vert **90** A 3
Cap Wolstenholme **101** M 3
Caquetá **108** D 4
Caracal **58** B 2
Caracarai **10** F 3
Caracas **108** E 1
Carahue **113** B 6
Carajás, Serra dos **109** H 4–5
Caratinga **111** H 4
Carauari **108** E 4
Carazinho **112** F 4
Carballo **56** B 3
Carbonara, Capo **57** E 4
Carbonia **57** E 4
Carcassonne **56** D 3
Cárdenas **105** F 3
Cardiff **52** C 4
Cardigan **52** C 4
Careiro **109** G 4
Carey, Lake **78** C 4
Caribbean Sea **105** GJ 4
Caribou Mountains **99** O 4
Carinhanha **111** H 3
Cariparé **111** G 3
Caritianas **109** F 5
Carletonville **94** D 5
Carlisle **52** C 4
Carnarvon (Australia) **78** A 3
Carnarvon (S. Africa) **94** C 6
Carnegie **78** C 4
Carnegie, Lake **78** C 4
Car Nicobar **73** F 6
Carnot **92** B 3
Carolina **109** J 5
Caroline **83** EF 3
Caroline Islands **82** AB 2
Carondelet **82** D 3
Carpathians **58** BC 1
Carpâţii Meridionali **58** B 1–2
Carpentaria Gulf of **79** F 1
Carpina **111** J 2
Carrick-on-Shannon **52** B 4
Carrillo **104** B 2
Carrizal **108** D 1
Carrizozo **102** E 5
Çarşamba **59** D 3
Carson City **102** C 4
Cartagena (Colombia) **108** C 1
Cartagena (Spain) **56** C 4
Cartago (Costa Rica) **104** F 6
Caruaru **111** J 2
Carvoeiro **109** F 4
Casablanca **86** D 2
Casbas **113** D 6
Cascade Range **102** B 2–3
Cascavel **111** F 5
Caserta **57** F 3
Casey **115**
Casino **79** J 4
Casma **108** C 5
Casper **102** E 3
Caspian Sea **66** DE 2–3
Cassiar Mountains **98** M 4
Cassino **57** F 3
Castanhal **109** J 4
Castaño **112** C 5
Castellón **56** CD 4
Castelo de Vide **56** B 4
Castelvetrano **57** F 4
Castilla (Chile) **112** B 4
Castilla (Peru) **108** BC 5
Castilla la Nueva **56** C 3–4
Castilla la Vieja **56** C 3
Castillos **112** F 5
Castlegar **99** O 6
Castor **99** P 5
Castres **56** D 3
Castries **105** K 5
Castro **113** B 7
Catalão **111** G 4
Cataluna **56** D 3
Çatalzeytin **59** D 2
Catamarca **112** CD 4
Catanduanes **75** FG 1
Catanduva **111** G 5
Catania **57** G 4
Catanzaro **57** G 4
Catastrophe, Cape **79** F 6
Catbalogan **75** FG 1
Cateel **75** G 2
Catinzaco **112** C 4
Cat Island **105** GH 3
Catoche, Cabo **104** E 3
Catrilo **113** D 6
Catrimani **109** F 3
Catwick Islands **73** J 5–6
Caucasus Mountains **59** F 2
Cauquenes **113** B 6
Caura **109** F 2
Cavalcante **111** G 3
Caxias (Amazonas, Brazil) **108** D 4
Caxias (Maranhão, Brazil) **111** H 1
Caxias do Sul **112** FG 4
Caxito **94** A 1
Cayenne **109** H 3
Cayman Islands **105** FG 4
Ceará **111** HJ 1
Ceballos **104** B 2
Cebollar **112** C 4
Cebu **75** F 2
Čechy **53** F 4
Cedar Falls **103** H 3
Cedar Lake **99** RS 5
Cedar Rapids **103** H 3
Cedros, Isla **102** C 6
Celaya **104** B 3
Celebes **75** EF 4
Celebes Sea **75** F 3
Celje **57** FG 2
Celle **53** F 4
Celtic Sea **52** B 4
Central, Cordilera (Colombia) **108** C 2–3
Central, Cordillera (Peru) **108** C 5
Central African Republic **92** BC 3
Central Arctic District **99** PR 1
Central Kalahari Game Reserve **94** C 4
Central Makran Range **67** GH 5
Centralno Tungusskoye Plato **68** GH 3–4
Central Range **80** D 2–3
Central Siberian Plateau **68** GK 3
Cereal **99** P 5
Ceres **111** FG 4
Cerf **93** J 6
Cerro Aconcagua **112** BC 5
Cerro Agua Caliente **104** A 2
Cerro Ángel **104** B 3
Cerro Blanco **102** E 6
Cerro Bonete **112** C 4
Cerro Champaquí **112** D 5
Cerro Chirripó **104** F 6
Cerro de la Encantada **102** CD 5
Cerro del Toro **112** C 4
Cerro de Pasco **110** A 3
Cerro de Tocorpuri **110** C 5
Cerro Galán **112** C 4
Cerro Grande **104** B 3
Cerro Las Casilas **102** E 7
Cerro Las Minas **104** E 4–5
Cerro Marahuaca **108** E 3
Cerro Mariquita **104** C 3
Cerro Mohinora **102** E 6
Cerro Murallón **113** B 8
Cerro Nuevo Mundo **110** C 5
Cerro Ojos del Salado **112** C 4
Cerro San Valentín **113** B 8
Cerro Ventana **102** E 7
Cerro Yavi **108** E 2
Cerro Yucuyácua **104** C 4
Cerro Yumari **108** E 3
Cesano **57** F 3
České Budějovice **53** F 5
Českézemě **53** G 5
Ceuta **86** D 1
Ceva-i-Ra **82** C 4
Cévennes **56** D 3
Ceyhan (Turkey) **59** E 3
Ceyhan (Turkey) **59** E 3
Ceylanpınar **60** C 1
Ceylon **72** D 6
Chaca **110** B 4
Chachapoyas **108** C 5
Chad **91** HJ 3
Chādegān **61** F 2
Chadobets **68** GH 4
Chagai Hills **67** G 5
Chagda **69** O 4
Chagdo Kangri **72** D 1
Chaghcharān **67** GH 4
Chagos Archipelago **65** K 10
Chagyl **66** F 2
Chahah Burjak **67** G 4
Chah Bahār **67** G 5
Chaiyaphum **73** H 4
Chakari **94** D 3
Chake Chake **93** FG 6
Chakhansur **67** G 4
Chala **110** B 4
Chalbi Desert **93** F 4
Chalhuanca **110** B 3
Challapata **110** C 4
Challenger Deep **77** D 1
Châlons-sur-Marne **57** D 2
Chalon-sur-Saône **57** DE 2
Chālūs **61** F 1
Chaman **67** H 4
Chamba **72** C 1
Chambery **57** E 2
Chamical **112** C 5
Chamoli **72** CD 1
Champagne **57** DE 2
Champaquí, Cerro **112** D 5
Champdoré, Lac **101** O 4
Chañaral **112** B 4
Chanco **113** B 6
Chandigarh **72** C 1
Chandler **101** P 6
Chandmanī **70** C 1
Chandpur **73** F 3
Chandrapur **72** C 3–4
Chanf **67** G 5
Changara **95** E 3
Changchun **71** J 2
Changde **70** F 5
Changji **67** M 2
Chang Jiang **70–71** EG 4
Changling **71** H 2
Changsha **70** F 5
Changwu **70** E 3
Changzhi **70** F 3

Channel Islands **102** C 5
Channel Islands (U.K.) **52** C 5
Chaoyang (Guangdoug, China) **70** G 6
Chaoyang (Liaoning, China) **71** GH 2
Chapayev-Zheday **68** L 3–4
Chapleau **100** L 6
Chapman, Cape **99** U 2
Chapoma **62** GH 2
Chapra **72** DE 2
Chara **68** L 4
Charagua **110** D 4
Charcot Island **115**
Chard **99** P 4
Chardzhou **67** G 3
Chari **91** H 3
Charity **109** G 2
Charkabozh **62** K 2
Charleroi **52** DE 4
Charlesbourg **101** N 6
Charles Peak **78** C 5
Charleston (S.C., U.S.A.) **103** L 5
Charleston (W.V., U.S.A.) **103** K 4
Charleville **79** H 4
Charlotte **103** KL 4
Charlottesville **103** L 4
Charlottetown **101** P 6
Charlton (Australia) **79** G 6
Charlton (Canada) **101** LM 5
Charters Towers **79** H 2–3
Chartres **56** D 2
Charyshskoye **63** Q 5
Chasel'ka **63** Q 2
Chatanga **68** K 6
Châteauroux **56** D 2
Châtellerault **56** CD 2
Chatham **81** S 9
Chatham (Ontario, Can.) **103** K 3
Chattanooga **103** J 5
Chaumont **57** DE 2
Chau Phu **73** HJ 5
Chaves (Brazil) **109** H 4
Chaves (Portugal) **56** B 3
Chayatyn, Khrebet **69** P 5
Chaykovskiy **62** KL 4
Chazhegovo **62** K 3
Cheb **53** F 4
Cheboksary **62** J 4
Cheduba **73** F 4
Chegga **87** G 2
Chegytun **98** C 2
Cheju **71** J 4
Cheju-do **71** J 4
Chekhov **69** Q 6
Chekunda **69** O 5
Chekuyevo **62** G 3
Chelforó **113** C 6
Chelkar **66** F 1
Chełm **53** H 4
Chelmuzhi **62** G 3
Chelyabinsk **63** M 4
Chenachane **86** E 3
Chengde **71** G 2
Chengdu **70** DE 4
Chenxi **70** EF 5
Chenzhou **70** F 5
Chepen **108** C 5
Chepes **112** C 5
Cherbourg **56** C 2
Cherchell **87** F 1
Cheremkhovo **68** H 5
Cherepovets **62** G 4
Cherkassy **62** EF 6
Cherkessk **59** F 2
Chernigov **62** EF 5
Chernovtsy **58** C 1
Chernyakhovsk **55** H 5
Chernyshevskiy **68** K 3
Chernyye Zemli **59** G 1
Chernyy Ostrov **68** F 3
Cherskiy Range **69** Q 2
Cherskogo, Khrebet **69** P 1–2
Chervonograd **55** H 5
Chervonoznamenka **58** CD 1
Chesapeake Bay Bridge-Tunnel **103** LM 4
Chesterfield Inlet **99** TU 3
Chesterfield Islands **82** B 4
Chetumal **104** E 4
Cheulik **69** P 2
Cheyenne **102** F 3
Chhatarpur **72** C 3
Chiang Kham **73** H 4
Chiang Mai **73** G 4
Chiang Rai **73** G 4
Chiang Saen **73** H 3
Chiapas **104** D 4
Chiavari **57** E 3
Chiayi **71** H 6
Chiba **71** M 3
Chibagalakh **69** PQ 2
Chibit **63** R 5
Chibougamau **101** N 6
Chicago **103** J 3
Chicapa **94** C 1
Chichagof **98** K 4
Chicheng **71** G 2
Chiclayo **108** B 5
Chico **113** C 7
Chicoutimi **101** N 6
Chidley, Cape **101** P 3
Chifeng **71** G 2
Chiganak **63** O 6
Chigorodó **108** C 2
Chigubo **95** E 4
Chihuahua **102** EF 6
Chik Ballapur **72** C 5
Chikhacheva **69** R 1
Chilabombwe **94** D 2
Childress **102** F 5
Chile **113** B 5–6
Chilete **108** C 5
Chilipa de Alvarez **104** C 4
Chillán **113** B 6
Chiloé, Isla de **113** B 7
Chilpancingo **104** BC 4
Chilwa, Lago **95** F 3
Chimbay **66** F 2
Chimborazo **108** C 4
Chimbote **108** C 5
Chimkent **67** H 2
Chin **73** F 3
China **70** DF 4
Chinandega **104** E 5
Chincha Alta **110** A 3
Chindu **70** C 4
Chindwin **73** FG 3
Chinese Wall **70** E 3
Chingola **94** D 2
Chinguetti **86** C 4
Chinju **71** J 4
Chipata **95** E 2
Chirchik **67** HJ 2
Chiriguaná **108** D 2
Chiriquí, Golfo de **108** B 2
Chishui **70** E 5
Chita **68** K 5
Chitado **94** A 3
Chitato **94** C 1
Chitina **98** HJ 3
Chitipa **95** E 1
Chitral **67** J 3
Chittagong **73** F 3
Chittaurgarh **72** BC 3
Chittoor **72** C 5
Chivasso **57** E 2
Chivay **110** B 4
Chizha **62** H 2
Chkalovo **63** O 5
Chobe National Park **94** C 3
Choele Choel **113** CD 6
Choggia **57** F 2
Choiseul **81** G 3
Chojnice **53** G 4
Cholet **56** C 2
Choluteca **104** E 5
Chomutov **53** F 4
Chona **68** J 3
Chon Buri **73** H 5
Ch'ŏngjin **71** JK 2
Ch'ŏngju **71** J 3
Chongqing **70** E 5
Chŏnju **71** J 3
Chonos, Archipiélago de los **113** AB 7–8
Chon Thanh **73** J 5
Chorzów **53** G 4
Chosica **110** A 3
Chos Malal **113** BC 6
Chotanagpur **72** DE 3
Chott Melrhir **87** G 2
Choum **86** C 4
Choybalsan **68** K 6
Christchurch **82** C 5
Christmas Island **74** C 6
Chubut **113** C 7
Chudskoye Ozero **55** J 4
Chukar **68** L 3
Chukchi Sea **114**
Chuken **69** P 6
Chukotsk Peninsula **114**
Chukotsk Range **114**
Chulak-Kurgan **67** HJ 2
Chulasa **62** J 3
Chula Vista **102** C 5
Chulym **63** QR 4
Chumikan **69** OP 5
Chumphon **73** GH 5
Ch'unch'ŏn **71** J 3
Chuquibamba **110** B 4
Chuquicamata **110** C 5
Chur **57** E 2
Churchill (Man., Can.) **99** ST 4
Churchill (Man., Can.) **99** T 4
Churchill, Cape **99** T 4
Churchill Falls **101** P 5
Churchill Lake **99** Q 4
Churchill Mountains **115**
Churu **72** C 2
Churuguara **108** E 1
Churún Merú **109** F 2
Chusovoy **63** L 4
Chusovskoy **62** L 3
Chute-des-Passes **101** NO 6
Chutes de Katende **92** C 6
Chutes de Livingstone **92** A 6
Chutes Ngaliema (Stanley Falls) **92** D 4
Chuxiong **70** D 5
Chuyengo **68** HJ 3
Cianjur **74** C 5
Cícero Dantas **111** J 3
Ciechanów **53** H 4
Ciego de Ávila **105** G 3
Ciénaga **108** D 1
Cienfuegos **105** F 3
Cieza **56** C 4
Cihanbeyli Platosu **59** D 3
Cilo Dağı **59** F 3
Cimarron River **102** G 4
Çimen Dağı **59** E 3
Cîmpia Bărăganului **58** C 1–2
Cîmpia Burnazului **58** C 2
Cîmpina **58** C 1
Cinca **56** D 3
Cincinatti **103** K 4
Cinto, Monte **57** E 3
Circeo, Capo **57** F 3
Circle **98** J 2
Cirebon **74** C 5
Cirque Mountain **101** P 4
Ciskei **94** D 6
Citta del Vaticano **57** F 3
Ciudad Acuña **104** B 2
Ciudad Bolívar **109** F 2
Ciudad Camargo **102** E 6
Ciudad del Carmen **104** D 4
Ciudad de Rio Grande **104** B 3
Ciudad Guayana **109** F 2
Ciudad Guzmán **104** B 4
Ciudad Hidalgo **104** BC 4
Ciudad Juárez **102** E 5
Ciudad Madero **104** C 3
Ciudad Mante **104** C 3
Ciudad Obregón **102** E 6
Ciudad Río Bravo **104** C 2
Ciudad-Rodrigo **56** B 3
Ciudad Valles **104** C 3
Ciudad Victoria **104** C 3
Civitanova Marche **57** F 3
Civitavecchia **57** F 3
Cizre **59** F 3
Claire, Lake **99** P 4
Claire Coast **115**
Clanwilliam **94** BC 6
Clarke Range **79** H 2–3
Clarksburg **103** KL 4

Clarksville **103** J 4
Clay Belt **100** LM 5
Clearwater **103** K 6
Clermont **79** H 3
Clermont-Ferrand **56** D 2
Cleveland (OH, U.S.A.) **103** K 3
Cleveland, Mount **102** D 2
Clinton **99** N 5
Clinton-Colden Lake **99** Q 3
Cloncurry **79** FG 3
Clorinda **112** E 4
Cloud Peak **102** E 3
Clovis **102** F 5
Cluj-Napoca **58** B 1
Cmi Drim **58** B 2
Cnossus **58** C 3
Coahuila **104** B 2
Coal River **99** M 4
Coari **109** F 4
Coast Mountains **98–99** LM 4–5
Coast of Labrador **101** QP 4–5
Coast Range (Queensland, Austr.) **79** J 4
Coast Range (U.S.A.) **102** B 3–4
Coats Island **99** V 3
Coats land **115**
Coatzacoalcos **104** D 4
Cobar **79** H 5
Cobija **110** C 3
Cobquecura **113** B 6
Coburg **53** F 4
Cocachacra **110** B 4
Cochabamba **110** CD 4
Cochin **72** C 6
Cochrane **113** B 8
Cocklebiddy **78** D 5
Coco Islands **73** F 5
Codó **111** H 1
Cody **102** E 3
Coetivy **93** JK 6
Coeur d'Alene **102** C 2
Coff's Harbour **79** J 5
Coihaique **113** B 8
Coimbatore **72** C 5
Coimbra **56** B 3
Cojimies **108** B 3
Cojutepeque **104** E 5
Colatina **111** HJ 4
Cold Bay **98** E 5
Col de Perthus **56** D 3
Colesberg **94** D 6
Colima **104** B 4
Collier Bay **78** C 2
Collier Ranges National Park **78** B 3
Collines du Perche **56** D 2
Collinson Peninsula **99** R 1–2
Cololo, Nevado **110** C 4
Colombia **108** D 3
Colombo **72** C 6
Colón (Cuba) **105** F 3
Colón (Panamá) **108** C 2
Colón, Archipiélago de **108** B 6
Colona **78** E 5
Colonia Las Heras **113** C 8
Colorado (Argentina) **113** D 6
Colorado (U.S.A.) **102** EF 4
Colorado Plateau **102** DE 4
Colorado River (AZ, U.S.A.) **102** D 5
Colorado River (TX, U.S.A.) **103** G 5–6
Colorado Springs **102** F 4
Columbia (MO, U.S.A.) **103** H 4
Columbia (S.C., U.S.A.) **103** K 5
Columbia (WA, U.S.A.) **102** BC 2
Columbia, Mount **99** O 5
Columbia Falls **102** D 2
Columbia Mountains **99** NO 5
Columbia Plateau **102** C 3
Columbine, Cape **94** B 6
Columbus (IN, U.S.A.) **103** J 4
Columbus (MS, U.S.A.) **103** K 5
Columbus (OH, U.S.A.) **103** K 4
Columbus (TX, U.S.A.) **103** G 6
Colville Lake **99** MN 2
Comalcalco **104** DE 4
Comandante Luis Piedrabuena **113** CD 8–9
Combarbala **112** B 5
Combermere Bay **73** F 4
Commander Islands **114**
Committee Bay **99** U 2
Como **57** E 2
Comodoro Rivadavia **113** C 8
Comorin, Cape **72** C 6
Comoros **95** G 2
Compiègne **56** D 2
Conakry **90** B 4
Conceição do Araguaia **109** HJ 5
Concepción (Bolivia) **110** D 4
Concepción (Chile) **113** B 6
Concepción (Paraguay) **110** E 5
Concepción del Oro **104** B 3
Concepción del Uruguay **112** E 5
Concord **103** M 3
Concórdia (Amazonas, Brazil) **108** E 4
Concordia (Argentina) **112** E 5
Condon **102** C 2
Conejo **102** D 7
Congo **91** H 6
Connaught **52** B 4
Connecticut **103** M 3
Conrad **102** D 2
Conselheiro Lafaiete **111** H 5
Con Son **73** J 6
Constanţa **58** C 2
Constantine **87** G 1
Contamana **108** D 5
Contwoyto Lake **99** PQ 2
Conway Reef → Ceva-i-Ra **82** C 4
Cook **78** E 5
Cook, Mount **82** C 5
Cook, Strait **82** C 5
Cookes Peak **102** E 5
Cook Inlet **98** G 3
Cook Islands **82** E 3
Cook Mountains **115**
Cook Strait **81** QR 9
Cooktown **79** H 2
Copenhagen **55** F 4
Copiapó **112** BC 4
Copperbelt **94** D 2
Coqên **72** E 1
Coquimbo **112** B 5
Coral Harbour **99** UV 3
Coral Sea **82** B 3–4
Coral Sea Islands Territory **79** HJ 1–2
Corcaigh **52** B 4
Cordillera Cantábrica **56** BC 3
Cordillera Central (Colombia) **108** C 2–3
Cordillera Central (Peru) **108** C 5
Cordillera Central (Philippines) **75** J 1
Cordillera Occidental (Colombia) **108** C 2–3
Cordillera Occidental (Peru) **110** BC 3–4
Cordillera Oriental (Bolivia) **110** CD 3–5
Cordillera Oriental (Colombia) **108** CD 2–3
Cordillera Real (Ecuador) **108** C 4
Córdoba (Argentina) **112** D 5
Córdoba (Mexico) **104** C 4
Córdoba (Spain) **56** BC 4
Corfu **58** AB 3
Corigliano Calabro **57** G 4
Corinth (Greece) **58** B 3
Corinto **111** H 4
Cork **52** B 4
Çorlu **58** C 2
Cornelio **102** D 6
Cornélio Procópio **111** F 5
Corner Brook **101** Q 6
Cornwall **101** M 6
Coro **108** DE 1
Coroatá **111** H 1
Corocoro **110** C 4
Coromandel Coast **72** D 5
Coromandel Peninsula **81** R 8
Coronation Gulf **99** P 2
Coronel **113** B 6
Coronel Fabriciano **111** H 4
Coronel Oviedo **112** E 4
Coronel Pringles **113** D 6
Coropuna, Nevado **110** B 4
Corpus Christi **103** G 6
Corrente **111** GH 3
Correntes, Cabo das **95** F 4
Correntina **111** GH 3
Corrientes **112** E 4
Corrientes, Cabo **108** C 2
Corse **57** E 3
Corse, Cap **57** E 3
Corsica **57** E 3
Çoruh **59** F 2
Çoruh Dağları **59** F 2
Çorum **62** E 2
Corumbá **110** E 4
Corunna **56** B 3
Corvallis **102** B 3
Cosenza **57** G 4
Cosmoledo Group **93** H 6
Costa Blanca **56** C 4
Costa Brava **56** D 3
Costa de la Luz **56** B 4
Costa del Azahar **56** D 3
Costa del Sol **56** C 4
Costa de Mosquitos **104** F 5
Costa Dorada **56** D 3
Costa Rica **104** EF 6
Costa Verde **56** B 3
Cotabato **75** F 2
Cotagaita **110** CD 5
Coteau du Missouri **102** FG 2
Côte d'Argent **56** C 3
Côte d'Azur **57** E 3
Cotonou **90** E 4
Cotopaxi **108** C 4
Cottbus **53** F 4
Cotulla **102** G 6
Council Bluffs **103** GH 3
Courland **55** H 4
Coventry **52** C 4
Covington **103** JK 4
Cowell **79** F 5
Cowra **79** H 5
Coxim **111** F 4
Cox's Bazar **73** F 3
Cracow **53** GH 4
Cradock **94** D 6
Craiova **58** B 2
Cranbrook **78** B 5
Crary Mountains **115**
Cratéus **111** HJ 2
Crato **111** J 2
Crawford **102** F 3
Creil **56** D 2
Cremona **57** F 2
Cres **57** F 3
Crescent City **102** AB 3
Crete **58** C 3
Creus, Cabo de **56** D 3
Creuse **56** D 2
Criciúma **112** G 4
Crimea **59** D 1
Cristmas Island **83** E 2
Cristóbal, Colón Pico **108** D 1
Croatia **57** G 2
Crockett **103** GH 5
Croker, Cape **78** E 1
Croker Island **78** E 1
Crooked Island **105** H 3
Crooked Island Passage **105** GH 3
Crookston **103** G 2
Cross, Cape **94** A 4
Crotone **57** G 4
Crowell **102** G 5
Crown Prince Frederik Island **99** U 2
Crowsnest Pass **99** OP 6

Cruz Alta **112** F 4
Cruz del Eje **112** CD 5
Cruzeiro do Oeste **111** F 5
Cruzeiro do Sul **108** D 5
Cruz Grande **104** C 4
Crystal Brook **79** F 5
Cuamba **95** F 2
Cuando Cubango **94** BC 3
Cuango **94** B 1
Cuanza **94** B 1–2
Cuanza Norte **94** AB 1
Cuanza Sul **94** AB 2
Cuauhtémoc **102** E 6
Cuba **105** FG 3
Cubango **94** B 3
Cucurpe **102** D 5
Cúcuta **108** D 2
Cuddalore **72** CD 5
Cuddapah **72** C 5
Cudi Dağı **59** F 3
Cuenca (Ecuador) **108** C 4
Cuenca (Spain) **56** C 3–4
Cuencamé de Ceniceros **104** B 3
Cuiabá **110** E 4
Cuito Cuanavale **94** B 3
Cu Lao Hon **73** JK 5
Culiacán **102** E 7
Cumaná **109** F 1
Cumbal **108** C 3
Cumberland **103** L 4
Cumberland Peninsula **101** OP 2
Cumberland Plateau **103** JK 4
Cumberland Sound **101** OP 2–3
Cunani **109** H 3
Cunene (Angola) **94** A 3
Cunene (Angola) **94** B 3
Cuneo **57** E 3
Cunnamulla **79** H 4
Cupica **108** C 2
Curaçao, Isla **108** E 1
Curacautin **113** B 6
Curdimurka **79** F 4
Curicó **113** B 5–6
Curimatá **111** H 2–3
Curitiba **112** FG 4
Curtis **82** D 5
Curtis Island **79** J 3
Curuça **109** J 4
Curumu **109** H 4
Curupuru **109** K 4
Curvelo **111** H 4
Cushing, Mount **99** M 4
Cuttack **72** E 3
Cuvette **91** H 6
Cuxhaven **53** E 4
Cuya **110** B 4
Cuyo Islands **75** F 1
Cuzco **110** B 3
Cyangugu **92** D 5
Cyclades **58** BC 3
Cypress Hills **99** PQ 6
Cyprus **59** D 3
Cyrenaica **87** JK 3
Czechoslovakia **53** G 5
Częstochowa **53** GH 4

D

Dabat **93** F 2
Dabbāgh, Jabal **60** B 4
Dabola **90** B 3
Dacca **72** F 3
Dadali **82** B 3
Dadanawa **109** G 3
Daet **75** F 1
Dafeng **71** H 4
Dagabur **93** G 3
Dagana **91** H 3
Dagi **69** Q 5
Dagur **70** C 3
Dahabān **66** B 6
Da Hinggan Ling **71** GH 1–2
Dahlak Archipelago **93** FG 1
Dahongliutan **67** KL 3
Dahra **90** AB 2
Dahūk **60** D 1
Daintree River National Park **79** G 2
Dairen **71** H 3
Daitō-shotō **71** K 5
Dajarra **79** F 3
Dakar **90** A 3
Dakha **72** F 3
Dakhla **86** B 4
Dakovica **58** B 2
Dala **94** BC 2
Dalälven **55** G 3
Dalaman **58** C 3
Dalandzadgad **70** DE 2
Dalarna **55** F 3
Da Lat **73** J 5
Dalby **79** J 4
Dali **70** D 5
Dallas **103** G 5
Dall Lake **98** E 3
Dalmā' **61** F 4
Dal'negorsk **71** L 2
Dal'nerechensk **71** KL 1
Dal'nyaya **69** Q 6
Daloa **90** C 4
Dalsland **55** F 4
Dalstroy **69** P 3
Daltonganj **72** DE 3
Dalwallinu **78** B 5
Daly River **78** E 1
Daly Waters **78** E 2
Daman **72** B 3
Damanhūr **88** DE 2
Damara **92** B 3
Damaraland **94** B 4
Damascus **88** F 2
Damascus (Syria) **60** B 2
Damāvand **61** F 2
Dāmghan **61** FG 1
Damoh **72** C 3
Dampier **78** B 3
Danakil Plain **93** G 2
Danané **90** C 4
Da Nang **73** J 4
Danba **70** D 4
Dandarah **88** E 3
Dandong **71** H 2–3
Danghe Nanshan **70** CD 3
Dangjin Shankou **70** BC 3
Dangshan **71** G 4
Danmark **55** E 4
Danmarks Havn **114**
Dan Sai **73** H 4
Danube **58** C 1
Danville **103** L 4
Dan Xian **70** E 7
Dao Xian **70** F 5
Dapoli **72** B 4
Da Qaidam **70** C 3
Dar'ā **60** B 2
Dārāb **66** E 5
Dāran **61** F 2
Darāw **60** A 4
Darband **66** F 4
Darbhanga **72** E 2
Dardanelles **58** C 3
Dar el Beida **86** C 2
Dar es Salaam **93** F 6
Dārfūr **88** C 6
Darganata **67** G 2
Dargaville **81** Q 8
Darién **108** C 2
Darjeeling **72** E 2
Darlag **70** CD 4
Darling Downs **79** H 4
Darling Range **78** B 5
Darling River **79** G 5
Darlington **52** C 4
Darmstadt **53** E 5
Darnah **87** K 2
Darnley, Cape **115**
Dar Rounga **92** C 2–3
Dartmoor **52** C 4
Dartmouth **101** P 7
Darvaza **66** F 2
Darweshan **67** G 4
Darwin **78** E 1
Daryācheh-ye Bakhtegān **61** FG 3
Daryācheh-ye Namak **61** F 2
Daryācheh-ye Orūmīyeh **61** D 1
Daryācheh-ye Tashk **61** FG 3
Daryā-ye Māzandarān **66** E 3
Dasht-e Kavīr **61** FG 2
Dasht-e Lūt **61** G 2
Dasht-e Naomid **66–67** G 4
Date **71** M 2
Datia **72** C 2
Datong (Qin. China) **70** D 3
Datong (Ziz. China) **70** F 2
Datta **69** Q 6
Dāuarzan **66** F 3
Daugava **55** H 4
Daugav'pils **55** J 4
Daung Kyun **73** G 5
Dauphin **99** R 5
Dauphiné **57** E 3
Dauphin Lake **99** S 5
Daurskoye **68** F 4
Davangere **72** C 5
Davao **75** G 2
Dāvar Panāh **67** G 5
Dāvarzan **61** G 1
Davenport **103** HJ 3
David **108** B 2
Davis (Antarctica) **115**
Davis (CA, U.S.A.) **102** B 4
Davis Inlet **101** P 4
Davis Sea **115**
Davis Strait **101** Q 2
Dawhat as Salwā **61** F 4
Dawson **98** K 3
Dawson Creek **99** N 4
Dawu **70** D 4
Dayangshu **69** M 6
Dayong **70** EF 5
Dayrūt **88** DE 3
Dayton **103** K 4
Daytona Beach **103** KL 6
Dazhu **70** E 4
Dazjā **61** G 2
De Aar **94** C 6
Dead Sea **88** EF 2
Dead Sea (Jordan) **60** B 3
Deán Funes **112** CD 5
Dease Lake **98** L 4
Dease Strait **99** Q 2
Death Valley **102** C 4
Death Valley National Monument **102** C 4
Débo, Lac **90** D 2
Deboyne Island **81** F 4
Debra Birhan **93** F 3
Debra Markos **93** F 2
Debra Zeit **93** F 3
Debrecen **58** B 1
Decatur (AL, U.S.A.) **103** J 5
Decatur (IL, U.S.A.) **103** J 4
Deccan **72** CD 3–5
Decepción **115**
Dechang **70** D 5
Dédougou **90** D 3
Dedza **95** E 2
Deering, Mount **78** D 3
Deer Lake **101** Q 6
Dêgê **70** C 4
de Gras, Lac **99** P 3
Deh Bīd **61** F 3
Dehdez **61** F 3
Dehlorān **66** D 4
Dehra Dun **72** C 1
Deh Shū **67** G 4
Dej **58** B 1
De Kalb **103** J 3
Delaware **103** M 4
Del Campillo **112** D 5
Del City **102** G 4
Delegate **79** H 6
Delgado, Cabo **95** G 2
Delgerhaan **68** HJ 6
Delgerhet **70** F 1
Delgertsogt **70** E 1
Delhi **72** C 2
Deličal Dağı **58** C 2–3
Delicias **102** E 6
Delījān **61** F 2
Delphi **58** B 3
Delta Dunării **58** CD 1
Delta Junction **98** HJ 3
Demba **92** C 6
Dembia **92** C 3
Dempo, Gunung **74** B 4
Dem'yanovka **63** N 5
Dem'yanskoye **63** N 4

Denali National Park and Preservative **98** GH 3
Denau **67** H 3
Den Helder **52** D 4
Denison **103** G 5
Denizli **58** C 3
Denkou **70** E 2
Denmark **55** E 4
Denmark Strait **114**
Dennison, Cape **115**
Denpasar **74** D 5
Denton **103** G 5
D'Entrecasteaux Islands **81** F 3
Denver **102** F 4
Deogarh **72** D 3
Deoghar **72** E 3
Deolali **72** B 4
Depósita **109** F 3
Deqing **70** F 6
Derbent **66** D 2
Derby (Australia) **78** C 2
Derby (U.K.) **52** C 4
Derdap **58** B 2
Dergachi **62** J 5
Dermott **103** H 5
Derudeb **88** F 5
Deryabino **63** Q 1
Derzhavinsk **63** N 5
Désappointement, Îles du **83** F 3
Desengaño, Punta **113** C 8
Desierto de Atacama **110** C 5
Desierto de Sechura **108** B 5
Des Moines **103** H 3
Desolación, Isla **113** AB 9
Desrouches, Île **93** J 6
Dessau **53** F 4
Dessye **93** FG 2
Detroit **103** K 3
Détroit de Jaques-Cartier **101** P 6
Détroit d'Honguedo **101** OP 6
Deutsche Bucht **53** E 4
Deutsche Demokratische Republik (D.D.R.) **53** F 4
Deva **58** B 1
Devil's Island **109** H 2
Devils Lake **102** G 2
Devon Island **114**
Devonport **82** A 5
Devrez **59** D 2
Deyang **70** D 4
Dezfūl **61** E 2
Dez Gerd **61** F 3
Dezhou **71** G 3
Dhahab **60** B 3
Dhamār **89** G 6
Dhamtari **72** D 3
Dharwar **72** B 4
Dhaulagiri **72** D 2
Dhelfoí **58** B 3
Dhíavlos Zakínthou **58** B 3
Dhirfis Óros **58** B 3
Dhoraji **72** B 3
Dhule **72** B 3
Diable, Île du **109** H 2
Diaca **95** F 2
Diamantina (Minas Gerais, Brazil) **111** H 4
Diamantina (Queensland, Austr.) **79** G 3
Diamantina Lakes **79** G 3
Diamond Jenness Peninsula **99** OP 1
Dianjiang **70** E 4
Dibrugarh **73** FG 2
Dicle **66** C 3
Didiéni **90** C 3
Didyma **58** C 3
Diéma **90** C 3
Dieppe **56** D 2
Dihang **70** C 5
Dijlāh **61** D 2
Dijon **57** E 2
Dıkmen Dağı **59** D 2
Dikson **114**
Dilaram **67** G 4
Di Linh **74** C 1
Dilj **57** G 2
Dilling **88** D 6
Dilolo **94** C 2
Dimashq **60** B 2
Dimbokro **90** D 4
Dimitrovgrad **58** C 2
Dimitrovgrad (U.S.S.R.) **62** JK 5
Dimona **60** B 3
Dinagat **75** G 1
Dinajpur **72** E 2
Dinara Planina **57** G 3
Dinder National Park **88** F 6
Dindigul **72** C 5
Dingbian **70** E 3
Dingxi **70** DE 3
Dingxian **70** FG 3
Dinokwe **94** D 4
Dionísio Cerqueira **112** F 4
Diourbel **90** A 3
Dipkarpas **60** B 2
Dipolog **75** F 2
Diré **90** D 2
Diredawa **93** G 3
Dirico **94** C 3
Dirk Hartog Island **78** A 4
Disappointment, Lake **78** C 3
Dishnā **60** A 4
Disko **114**
Disko Bugt **114**
Disna **55** J 4
District of Fort Smith **99** P 3
District of Inuvik **98** LM 2
District of Keewatin **99** SU 2–3
Distrito Federal **111** G 4
Diu **72** B 3
Dīvāndareh **61** E 1
Divinopolis **111** GH 5
Divo **90** C 4
Dixon Entrance **98** L 5
Diyālā **61** D 2
Diyarbakır **59** F 3
Djanet **87** G 4
Djelfa **87** F 2
Djibouti **93** G 2
Djibouti **93** G 2
Djougou **90** E 4
Dneprodzerzhinsk **59** D 1
Dnepropetrovsk **59** E 1
Dneprovskiy Liman **58** D 1
Dnestr **58** C 1
Doba **91** H 4
Dobreta Turnu Severin **58** B 2
Dobrogea **58** C 2
Dobrowolski **115**
Dobrudžansko Plato **58** C 2
Dodecanese **58** C 3
Dodge City **102** F 4
Dodoma **93** FG 6
Dogger Bank **52** D 4
Dogondoutchi **91** EF 3
Doguéraoua **91** F 3
Doğu Karadeniz Dağlari **59** EF 2
Doha **61** F 4
Dohad **72** B 3
Doi Inthanon **73** G 4
Doilungdêqen **73** F 1–2
Dôle **57** E 2
Dolo **93** G 4
Dolores **113** E 6
Dolphin and Union Strait **99** OP 2
Doma Peaks **80** D 3
Dom Aquino **111** F 4
Dombås **54** E 3
Dominica **105** K 4
Dominican Republic **105** J 3–4
Dompu **75** E 5
Don (U.S.S.R.) **62** H 6
Don Benito **56** B 4
Dondo **95** EF 3
Dondra Head **72** D 6
Donegal Bay **52** B 4
Donegal Mountains **52** B 4
Donetsk **59** E 1
Donetskiy Kryazh **59** EF 1
Dongara **78** B 4
Dongchuan **70** D 5
Dongfang **70** E 7
Dong Hai **71** HJ 5
Dongning **71** JK 2
Dongo **94** B 2
Dongoura **90** BC 3
Dongping **71** G 3
Dongsheng **70** EF 3
Dongting Hu **70** F 5
Dong Ujimqin Qi **71** G 1
Dongxiang **70** FG 5
Dönna **54** F 2
Doramarkog **70** C 4
Dordrecht **52** D 4
Dori **90** D 3
Dornogovĭ **70** EF 2
Döröö Nuur **68** F 6
Dortmund **53** E 4
Dosso **90** E 3
Dothan **103** J 5
Douala **91** FG 5
Douentza **90** D 3
Douglas (AZ, U.S.A.) **102** E 5
Douglas (U.K.) **52** C 4
Douglas (WY, U.S.A.) **102** EF 3
Doumbouene **91** J 3
Dourados **111** F 5
Douro **56** B 3
Dover **52** D 4
Dovrefjell **54** E 3
Dowlatābād **66** F 5
Dow Rūd **61** E 2
Dow Sar **61** E 2
Drakensberg **94** D 5–6
Drake Passage **115**
Drake Strait **113** CD 10
Dráma **58** B 2
Drammen **55** F 4
Drau **57** F 2
Drava **57** G 2
Dresden **53** F 4
Dreux **56** D 2
Drini **58** B 2
Drogobych **53** H 5
Drumheller **99** P 5
Drummondville **101** N 6
Druzhnaya **115**
Druzhnaya II **115**
Dryden **100** J 6
Drysdale River National Park **78** D 2
Dschang **91** F 4
Duaringa **79** HJ 3
Dubawnt Lake **99** R 3
Dubayy **61** G 4
Dubbo **79** H 5
Dublin **52** B 4
Dubna **62** G 4
Dubno **55** J 5
Dubovskoye **59** F 1
Dubrovitsa **55** J 5
Dubrovnik **57** G 3
Dubrovnoye **63** NO 4
Dubuque **103** H 3
Duc de Gloucester, Îles du **83** F 4
Ducie **83** G 4
du Couedic, Cape **79** F 6
Dudhi **72** D 3
Dudinka **63** R 2
Dudley **52** C 4
Duékoué **90** C 4
Duero **56** C 3
Duff Islands **82** C 3
Dugi Otok **57** F 3
Duisburg **52** E 4
Duitama **108** D 2
Dukān **61** D 2
Dukhān **61** F 4
Dukou **70** D 5
Dukwe **94** D 4
Dulan **70** C 3
Dulga-Kyuyel' **68** K 3
Duluth **103** H 2
Dūmā **60** B 2
Dumaguete **75** F 2
Dumfries **52** C 3
Dumont d'Urville **115**
Dumpu **82** A 3
Dumyāt **88** E 2
Duna **58** A 1
Dunántúl **58** A 1
Dunaujváros **58** A 1

Dunav **58** B 2
Dunbar (Australia) **79** G 2
Dunbar (U.K.) **52** C 3
Dundalk **52** B 4
Dundalk Bay **52** B 4
Dundas Peninsula **99** P 1
Dundee **52** C 3
Dundgovĭ **70** E 1
Dunedin **81** Q 10
Dunhua **71** J 2
Dunhuang **70** B 2
Dunkerque **52** D 4
Dunkwa **90** D 4
Dún Laoghaire **52** B 4
Dunmarra **78** E 2
Dunqulah al 'Ordi **88** DE 5
Duolun **71** G 2
Durack Range **78** D 2
Dura Europos **60** C 2
Durance **57** E 3
Durango (CO, U.S.A.) **102** E 4
Durango (Mexico) **104** AB 3
Duratón **56** C 3
Durban **95** E 5
Durg **72** D 3
Durgapur **72** E 3
Durham **103** L 4
Durmā **61** E 4
Duroy **68** L 5
Durresi **58** A 2
D'Urville Sea **115**
Dushan **70** E 5
Dushanbe **67** H 3
Düsseldorf **52** E 4
Dutch Harbor **98** D 5
Duwayhin **66** E 6
Duye **92** D 4
Düzce **58** D 2
Dvina, Severnaya **62** H 3
Dwarka **72** A 3
Dyadmo **68** J 4
Dyrhólaey **54** B 3
Dyurmen'tobe **67** GH 1
Dzerzhinsk **62** H 4
Dzhagdy, Khrebet **69** O 5
Dzhalinda **69** M 5
Dzhambul **67** J 2
Dzhankoy **59** D 1
Dzhanybek **62** J 6
Dzhelinde **68** K 1
Dzhetygara **63** M 5
Dzhezkazgan **63** N 6
Dzhigudzhak **69** ST 3
Dzhirgatal' **67** J 3
Dzhugdzhur, Khrebet **69** OP 4
Dzhunkun **68** K 3
Dzhusaly **67** GH 1
Dzugdzhur Range **69** PQ 4

E

Eagle **98** J 3
Eagle Pass **102** FG 6
Eagle Peak **102** BC 3
East Antarctica **115**
East Cape **81** R 8
East China Sea **71** HJ 5
Easter Island **83** H 4
Eastern Ghats **72** CD 3–5
East Falkland **113** E 9
East London **94** CD 6
Eastmain **101** M 5
East Point **103** JK 5
Eastport **103** N 3
East Siberian Sea **114**
Eau Claire **103** H 3
Eauripik **82** A 2
Ebe **69** Q 3
Eberswalde **53** F 4
Eboli **57** G 3
Ebolowa **91** G 5
Ebon **82** C 2
Ebyakh **69** S 2
Ech Cheliff **87** F 1
Echmiadzin **59** F 2
Echo Bay **99** O 2
Écija **56** B 4
Ecuador **108** B 4
Edéa **91** FG 5
Edel Land **78** A 4
Edgeöya **114**
Edinburgh **52** C 3
Edirne **58** C 2
Edmonds **102** B 2
Edmonton **99** OP 5
Edremit **58** C 3
Edwards Plateau **102** FG 5–6
Efaté **81** J 5
Efes **58** C 3
Egersund **55** E 4
Egilsstaðir **54** C 2
Eglab Dersa **86** E 3
Egmont, Mount **81** Q 8
Eğridir Gölü **58** D 3
Egvekinot **98** B 2
Egypt **60** A 4
Egypt **88** DE 4
Eiao **83** F 3
Eidfjord **55** E 3
Eifel **52** E 4
Eights Coast **115**
Eighty Mile Beach **78** BC 2
Eire **52** B 4
Eirunepé **108** D 5
Eisenach **53** F 4
Eisenhüttenstadt **53** FG 4
Ejin Qi **70** D 2
Ekibastuz **63** P 5
Ekoli **92** C 5
Ekwan **100** L 5
El Aaiún **86** C 3
El Adeb Larache **87** G 3
El Alamo **102** C 5
Elat **60** B 3
Elâzığ **59** E 3
Elba **57** F 3
El'ban **69** P 5
El Banco **108** D 2
Elbasani **58** B 2
El Bayadh **87** F 2
Elbe **53** F 4
Elbeyli **59** E 3
Elbląg **53** G 4
Elbrus **59** F 2
'El Būr **93** H 4
Elburz Mountains **61** F 1
El Cajon **102** C 5
El Cerro **110** D 4
Elche **56** C 4
El Cuy **113** C 6
Elda **56** C 4
'El Ḍēre **93** H 4
El Difícil **108** D 2
El Diviso **108** C 3
El Djouf **86** CD 4
El Dorado (AR, U.S.A.) **103** H 5
Eldorado (Argentina) **112** EF 4
El Dorado (KS, U.S.A.) **103** G 4
El Dorado (Mexico) **102** E 7
El Dorado (Venezuela) **109** F 2
Eldoret **92** EF 4
Elektrostal' **62** GH 4
Elemi Triangle **92** EF 4
El Encanto **108** D 4
Elephant Island **115**
Elesbão Veloso **111** H 2
El Escorial **56** C 3
Eleuthera Island **105** G 2
El Fasher **88** CD 6
El Ferrol del Candillo **56** B 3
El'gakan **69** M 4
Elghena **93** F 1
El Goléa **87** F 2
Elgon, Mount **92** EF 4
'El Ḥamurre **93** H 3
El Homr **87** F 3
Elisenvaara **54** JK 3
Elista **59** F 1
Elizabeth **79** F 5
El Jadida **86** D 2
Elk **53** H 4
Elk City **102** G 4
Elkhart **103** J 3
Elko **102** C 3
Ellef Ringnes Island **114**
Ellensburg **102** BC 2
Ellesmere Island **114**
Ellice Islands **82** C 3
Elliot (Australia) **78** E 2
Elliot (South Africa) **94** D 6
Elliot, Mount **79** H 2
Ellsworth Land **115**
Ellsworth Mountains **115**
El Maestrazgo **56** CD 3
El Maitén **113** B 7
El Medo **93** G 3
El Messir **91** H 2
Elmhurst **103** J 3
Elmira **103** L 3
El Mirador **104** DE 4
El Mreiti **86** D 4
El Obeid **88** DE 6
El Oued **87** G 2
El Paso **102** E 5
El Progreso **104** E 4
El Puerto **102** D 6
El Puerto de Santa Maria **56** B 4
El Salto **104** A 3
El Salvador **104** DE 5
El Sueco **102** E 6
El Tigre **109** F 2
El Tránsito **112** B 4
El Tunal **112** D 3–4
Eluru **72** D 4
El Valle **108** C 2
Elvas **56** B 4
Elvira **108** D 5
Ely **102** D 4
Emamrud **61** G 1
Emamshar **66** F 3
Emba **66** F 1
Embalse de Alcántara **56** B 4
Embalse de Almendra **56** B 3
Embalse del Ebro **56** C 3
Embalse de Mequinenza **56** C 3
Embarcación **110** D 5
Embarras Portage **99** P 4
Emden **53** E 4
Emel'dzak **69** N 4
Emerald **79** H 3
Emi **68** G 5
Emi Koussi **91** HJ 2
Empalme **102** D 6
Empedrado **112** E 4
Ems **53** E 4
Encarnación **112** E 4
Enda Salassie **93** F 2
Ende **75** F 5
Enderbury **82** D 3
Enderby Land **115**
Endicott Mountains **98** GH 2
Engaño, Cape **75** J 1
Engel's **62** J 5
Enggano, Pulau **74** B 5
England **52** D 4
English Channel **52** BC 4–5
Engozero **54** K 2
Enid **102** G 4
Eniwetok **82** B 2
Enkan **69** Q 4
Enköping **55** G 4
Enmore **109** G 2
Ennadai **99** R 3
Ennedi **91** J 2
Enontekiö **54** H 2
Enrekang **75** EF 4
Enschede **53** E 4
Ensenada **102** C 5
Enshi **70** EF 4
Entebbe **92** E 4
Entre Rios **109** H 5
Enugu **91** F 4
Enugu Ezike **91** F 4
Enurmino **98** C 2
Envigado **108** CD 2
Envira **108** D 5
Épernay **56** D 2
Ephesus **58** C 3
Epi **81** J 5
Épinal **57** E 2
Équateur **92** BC 4
Equatoria **92** DE 3–4
Equatorial Guinea **91** F 5
Erbīl **60** D 1
Érd **58** A 1
Erechim **112** F 4
Ereentsav **68** L 6
Ereğli **59** D 3
Erenhot **70** F 2

Eresma **56** C 3
Erfurt **53** F 4
Erg Brusset **91** FG 2
Erg Chech **86** E 3–4
Erg de Ténéré **91** FG 2
Erg Iguidi **86** DE 3
Ergun He **68** M 5
Ergun Zuoqi **69** M 5
Eriba **88** F 5
Eric **101** O 5
Erie **103** K 3
Erie, Lake **103** K 3
'Erigâbo **93** H 2
Erikub **82** C 2
Erimbet **67** G 2
Eritrea **93** FG 2
Ermelo **94** DE 5
Ernest Legouvé **83** E 5
Erode **72** C 5
Erongo **94** B 4
Erongo Mountains **94** B 4
Erozionnyy **69** R 2
Errego **95** F 3
Erromanga **82** C 4
Erromango **81** J 5
Ertai **67** N 1
Erzgebirge **53** F 4
Erzincan **59** E 3
Erzurum **59** F 3
Erzurum-Kars Yaylâsı **59** F 2
Esbjerg **55** E 4
Escanaba **103** J 2
Eschan **69** R 3
Escondido **102** C 5
Escuintla **104** D 5
Esfahan **61** F 2
Eskilstuna **55** G 4
Eskimo Point **99** T 3
Eskişehir **58** D 3
Eslamabad **61** E 2
Eslöv **55** F 4
Esmeralda, Isla **113** A 8
Esmeraldas **108** BC 3
España **56** C 4
Esperance Bay **78** C 5
Esperanza (Antarctica) **115**
Espinal (Bolivia) **110** E 4
Espinal (Colombia) **108** D 3
Espinar **110** B 3
Espírito Santo **111** HJ 4
Espiritu Santo **82** BC 4
Esplanada **111** J 3
Espoo (Esbo) **55** H 3–4
Esquel **113** B 7
Essaouira **86** CD 2
Essen **53** E 4
Essendon, Mount **78** C 3
Estados, Isla de los **113** D 9
Estância **111** J 3
Estelí **104** E 5
Esteros **110** D 5
Estevan **99** R 6
Estoniya **55** HJ 4
Estrecho de Gibraltar **56** B 4
Estrecho de le Maire **113** CD 9–10
Estrecho de Magallanes **113** B 9
Estrêla, Serra de **56** B 3
Estremadura **56** B 4
Estrondo, Serra do **109** J 5
Esztergom **58** A 1
Ethiopia **93** FG 3
Ethiopian Plateau **93** FG 3
Etna **57** FG 4
Etosha National Park **94** B 3
Etosha Pan **94** B 3
Eugene **102** B 3
Eugenia, Punta **102** C 6
Eugmo **54** H 3
Eungella National Park **79** HJ 3
Euphrates **60** C 2
Eureka **102** B 3
Everest, Mount **72** E 2
Everett **102** B 2
Everett Mountains **101** O 3
Everglades National Park **103** K 6
Évora **56** B 4
Evreux **56** D 2
Evvoia **58** B 3
Ewasse **81** F 3
Executive Committee Range **115**
Exeter **52** C 4
Exmouth **78** A 3
Extremadura **56** B 4
Eyre **78** D 5
Eyre Peninsula **79** F 5
Eysturoy **52** A 1
Ezop, Gora **69** S 3

F

Fabala **90** C 4
Fabriano **57** F 3
Fada **91** J 2
Faenza **57** F 3
Faeroe Islands **52** A 1
Făgăraş **58** BC 1
Fairbanks **98** GH 3
Fair Isle **52** C 3
Fairmont (W.V., U.S.A.) **103** L 4
Fairview **79** G 2
Faisalabad **67** J 4
Faizabad (Afghanistan) **67** J 3
Faizabad (India) **72** D 2
Fakaina **83** F 4
Fakaofo **82** D 3
Fakarava **83** F 4
Faku **71** H 2
Falagh **92** E 3
Falkenberg **55** F 4
Falkland Islands **113** DE 9
Falkland Sound **113** DE 9
Fallon **102** C 4
Fall River **103** M 3
Falls City **103** G 3
Falmouth **52** B 4
Falster **55** G 4
Falun **55** G 3
Famagusta **59** D 3
Fana **90** C 3
Fangataufa **83** F 4
Fangzheng **71** JK 1
Faraday **115**
Faradje **92** D 4
Farafangana **95** H 4
Farah **67** G 4
Farallon de Medinilla **82** A 1
Farallon de Pajaros **82** A 1
Faranah **90** B 3
Faraulep **82** A 2
Farewell, Cape **81** Q 9
Fargo (N.D., U.S.A.) **102** G 2
Faridpur **72** E 3
Färjestaden **55** G 4
Farmington (N.M., U.S.A.) **102** E 4
Fårö **55** G 4
Faro (Brazil) **109** G 4
Faro (Portugal) **56** B 4
Farquhar Group **93** J 7
Fārs **61** F 3
Fartak, Ra's **89** J 5
Fasā **61** F 3
Fasano **57** G 3
Fastov **62** E 6
Fataka **82** C 3
Fatehgarh **72** CD 2
Făurei **58** C 1
Faxaflói **54** A 3
Faxälven **54** G 3
Faya-Largeau **91** HJ 2
Fayetteville (AR, U.S.A.) **103** H 4
Fayetteville (N.C., U.S.A.) **103** KL 5
Faysh Khābur **60** D 1
Fayu **82** B 2
Fazilka **72** B 1
Fdérik **86** C 4
Fear, Cape **103** L 5
Feathertop, Mount **79** H 6
Federal Republic of Germany **53** E 4
Federated States of Micronesia **82** AB 2
Fehmarn **53** F 4
Feijó **108** D 5
Feira de Santana **111** J 3
Feklistova, Ostrov **69** P 4–5
Felipe Carrillo Puerto **104** E 4
Fengcheng **71** HJ 2
Fengjie **70** EF 4
Fengqing **70** CD 6
Fengshui Shan **69** M 5
Feni Islands **81** F 2
Fenoarivo Atsinanana **95** HJ 3
Fensfjorden **54** DE 3
Fenyang **70** F 3
Feodosiya **59** DE 1
Fer, Cap de **87** G 1
Ferfer **93** H 3
Fergana **67** J 2
Fergus Falls **103** G 2
Fergusson **81** F 3
Ferjukot **54** A 3
Ferkéssédougou **90** C 4
Fernando de Noronha Island **107** G 3
Fernandópolis **111** F 5
Fernando Póo → Bioko **91** F 5
Ferrara **57** F 3
Ferreira Gomes **109** H 3
Fès **86** E 2
Fethiye **58** C 3
Fezzan **87** HJ 3
Fianarantsoa **95** H 4
Fierras **54** G 2
Fiji **82** C 4
Fiji Islands **82** C 4
Filadélfia **110** E 5
Filchner Ice Shelf **115**
Fimbul Ice Shelf **115**
Fimi **92** B 5
Findlay **103** K 3
Finisterre, Cabo de **56** B 3
Finke **78** E 4
Finke, Mount **78** E 5
Finke Gorge National Park **78** E 3
Finland **54** J 3
Finnmark **54** H 2
Finnmarksvidda **54** H 2
Finnsnes **54** G 2
Finnveden **55** F 4
Finspång **55** G 4
Fiordland National Park **80** P 9–10
Fırat **59** E 3
Firenze **57** F 3
Firminy **56** D 2
Firozabad **72** CD 2
Firth of Forth **52** C 3
Fīrūzābād **66** E 5
Fīrūz Kūh **61** F 2
Fisher Strait **99** UV 3
Fishguard **52** B 4
Fiskenæsset **101** R 3
Fitzcarrald **110** B 3
Fitzgerald River National Park **78** B 5
Fitzroy Crossing **78** CD 2
Fitzroy River (Queensland, Austr.) **79** HJ 3
Fitzroy River (Western Australia) **78** C 2
Fizi **92** D 5
Flagstaff **102** D 4
Flamenco **112** B 4
Flåsjön **54** G 3
Flattery, Cape **102** AB 2
Flensburg **53** E 4
Flinders Chase National Park **79** F 6
Flinders Passage **79** H 2
Flinders Range **79** F 5
Flinders Ranges National Park **79** FG 5
Flinders River **79** G 2
Flin Flon **99** R 5
Flint (Kiribati) **83** E 3
Flint (MI, U.S.A.) **103** K 3
Flisa **55** F 3
Floraville (Queensland, Austr.) **79** F 2
Florence (AL, U.S.A.) **103** J 5
Florence (Italy) **57** F 3
Florencia **108** CD 3

Flores (Guatemala) **104** E 4
Flores (Indonesia) **75** F 5
Flores, Laut **75** E 5
Flores Sea **75** EF 5
Floriano **111** H 2
Floriano Pleixoto **108** E 5
Florianópolis **112** G 4
Florida (Cuba) **105** G 3
Florida (U.S.A.) **103** KL 6
Floridablanca **108** D 2
Florida Keys **103** L 6–7
Florö **54** E 3
Fluk **75** G 4
Fly River **80** D 3
Foci del Po **57** F 3
Focşani **58** C 1
Foggia **57** G 3
Fogo **90** B 7
Foleyet **100** L 6
Folkstone **52** D 4
Fond du Lac **103** J 3
Fonte Boa **108** E 4
Fonte do Pau-d'Agua **110** E 3
Fonualei **82** D 4
Forbes **79** H 5
Förde **54** E 3
Forêt d'Ecouves **56** C 2
Forín Linares **110** D 5
Forkas **90** E 3
Forli **57** F 3
Formentera **56** D 4
Formentor, Cabo de **56** D 3–4
Formosa **111** G 4
Formosa (Taiwan) **71** H 6
Formosa, Serra **111** EF 3
Formosa Strait **71** GH 5–6
Formoso **112** E 4
Fornæs **55** F 4
Forrest **78** D 5
Forsayth **79** G 2
Forsnäs **54** G 2
Forssa **55** H 3
Fortaleza **111** J 1
Fort Chimo **101** NO 4
Fort Chipewyan **99** PQ 4
Fort Collins **102** EF 3
Fort-de-France **105** K 5
Fort Dodge **103** H 3
Fort Frances **100** J 6
Fort Franklin **99** N 2
Fort George **101** M 5
Forth, Firth of **52** C 3
Fortin Coronel Eugenio Garay **110** D 5
Fortín Ingavi **110** DE 4
Fortín Madrejón **110** E 5
Fortín Ravelo **110** D 4
Fortín Suárez Arana **110** D 4
Fort Lauderdale **103** L 6
Fort Liard **99** N 3
Fort Mackay **99** P 4
Fort McMurray **99** P 4
Fort Miribel **87** F 3
Fort Morgan **102** F 3
Fort Myers **103** K 6
Fort Nelson **99** N 4
Fort Norman **99** M 3
Fort Peck Dam **102** E 2
Fort Peck Lake **102** E 2
Fort Pierce **103** KL 6
Fort Portal **92** DE 4
Fort Providence **99** O 3
Fort Randell Dam **102** FG 3
Fort Resolution **99** P 3
Fort Rupert **101** M 5
Fort Saint John **99** N 4
Fort Severn **100** K 4
Fort Shevchenko **66** E 2
Fort Simpson **99** N 3
Fort Smith **103** H 4–5
Fort Stockton **102** F 5
Fortune Bay **101** Q 6
Fort Vermilion **99** O 4
Fort Wayne **103** J 3
Fort Wellington **109** G 2
Fort William **52** BC 3
Fort Worth **102** G 5
Forveaux Strait **82** C 6
Foshan **70** F 6
Fosna **54** F 3
Foso **90** D 4
Fossano **57** E 3
Fossil Bluff **115**
Fougamou **91** G 6
Fougères **56** C 2
Fouladou **90** AB 3
Foumban **91** G 4
Fourmies **56** D 1
Four Mountains, Islands of **98** CD 5
Fouta Djallon **90** B 3
Fouta Ferlo **90** B 2
Foveaux Strait **80** P 10
Fowlers Bay **78** E 5
Foxe Basin **99** VW 2
Foxe Channel **101** M 3
Foxe Peninsula **101** M 3
Fox Islands **98** D 5
Foz do Breu **108** D 5
Franca **111** G 5
France **56** CD 2
Franceville **91** G 6
Francisco de Orellana (Ecuador) **108** C 4
Francisco de Orellana (Peru) **108** D 4
Francisco Escárcega **104** D 4
Francistown **94** D 4
Francs Peak **102** E 3
Frankfurt am Main **53** E 4
Franklin Mountains **99** MN 2–3
Franklin Strait **99** S 1
Franz Josef Land **114**
Fraser **99** N 5
Fraser or Great Sandy Island **79** J 4
Fraser Plateau **99** N 5
Fredericia **55** EF 4
Fredericton **101** O 6
Frederik IX-Land **101** R 2
Frederiksdal **101** S 3
Frederikshåb **101** R 3
Frederikshavn **55** EF 4
Fredrika **54** G 3
Fredrikstad **55** F 4
Freetown **90** B 4
Freiburg **53** E 5
Fréjus **57** E 3
French Guiana **109** H 3
French Polynesia **83** EF 4
Fresnillo **104** B 3
Fresno **102** BC 4
Freycinet Peninsula **80** L 9
Fria, Cape **94** A 3
Friesland **52–53** E 4
Frio, Cabo **111** H 5
Frisian Islands **52** E 4
Frobisher Bay **101** O 3
Frobisher Lake **99** Q 4
Frolovo **62** H 6
Fronteiras **111** H 2
Front Range **102** E 3–4
Fröya **54** E 3
Frunze **67** J 2
Fu'an **71** G 5
Fuding **71** H 5
Fuerte Olimpo **110** E 5
Fuerteventura **86** C 3
Fujian **71** G 5
Fujin **69** O 6
Fukui **71** L 3
Fukuoka **71** JK 4
Fukushima (Japan) **71** LM 2
Fukushima (Japan) **71** M 3
Fukuyama **71** K 3–4
Funafuti **82** CD 3
Funchal **86** B 2
Funiu Shan **70** F 4
Funtua **91** F 3
Fuqing **71** GH 5
Furancungo **95** E 2
Furmanovka **67** J 2
Furmanovo **62** JK 6
Furneaux Group **82** A 5
Fürth **53** F 5
Fury and Hecla Strait **100** KL 1
Fusagasugá **108** D 3
Fushun **71** HJ 2
Fusong **71** J 2
Futuna (Vanuatu) **82** C 4
Futuna (Wallis and Futuna) **82** D 3
Fuxin **71** H 2
Fuyang **70** G 4
Fuyuan **70** D 5
Fuyun **67** M 1
Fuzhou **71** GH 5
Fyn **55** F 4

G

Gabela **94** A 2
Gabès **87** H 2
Gabon **91** FG 6
Gaborone **94** CD 4
Gabriel Strait **101** O 3
Gach Sārān **61** F 3
Gadag **72** C 4
Gadame **92** E 3
Gadsden **103** J 5
Gaeta **57** F 3
Gaferut **82** A 2
Gagnoa **90** C 4
Gagnon **101** O 5
Gahkom **61** G 3
Gaimán **113** C 7
Gainesville **103** K 6
Gairdner, Lake **79** F 5
Gakarosa **94** C 5
Gakona **98** H 3
Galán, Cerro **112** C 4
Galanino **68** F 4
Galápagos Islands **108** B 6
Galathea Deep **82** D 5
Galaţi **58** C 1
Galatina **57** G 3
Galdhöpiggen **54** E 3
Galena **98** F 3
Galesburg **103** HJ 3
Galicia (Poland) **53** H 5
Galicia (Spain) **56** B 3
Galimyy **69** ST 3
Gālka'yo **93** H 3
Galle **72** CD 6
Gallinas, Punta **108** D 1
Gällivare **54** H 2
Gallo, Capo **57** F 4
Gallup **102** E 4
Galole **93** F 5
Galveston **103** H 6
Galvez **112** D 5
Galway **52** B 4
Gamba **91** F 6
Gambia **90** AB 3
Gambier Islands **83** FG 4
Gamboma **91** H 6
Gamboola **79** G 2
Ganāveh **61** F 3
Gandadiwata, Bukit **75** EF 4
Gandhi Sagar Dam **72** C 3
Gandía **56** CD 4
Ganetti **88** E 5
Ganga **72** E 2
Gangan **113** C 7
Gangapur **72** C 2
Gangdisê Shan **72** DE 1
Ganges **72** E 3
Ganina Gar' **68** F 4
Gannett Peak **102** E 3
Gansu **70** DE 3
Ganta **90** C 4
Ganzhou **70** FG 5
Gao **90** D 2
Gao'an **70** FG 5
Gaona **112** D 4
Gaoping **70** F 3
Gaoua **90** D 3
Gaoual **90** B 3
Gaozhou **70** EF 6
Gap **57** E 3
Garanhuns **111** J 2
Garbokaray **68** G 5
Garbosh, Kūh-e **61** EF 2
Garda, Lago di **57** F 2
Gardaneh-ye Āvej **61** E 2
Gardaneh-ye Kandovān **61** F 1
Gardaneh-ye Khāneh Sorkh **61** G 3
Gardemoen **55** F 3
Gargano, Promontorio del **57** G 3

Garissa **93** FG 5
Garmisch-Partenkirchen **53** F 5
Garmsar **61** F 2
Garonne **56** D 3
Garoua **91** G 4
Garoua Boulai **91** GH 4
Garöwe **93** H 3
Garri, Kūh-e **61** E 2
Garry Lake **99** R 2
Garwa **72** D 3
Gary **103** J 3
Garze **70** C 4
Gascogne **56** CD 3
Gascoyne Junction **78** B 3–4
Gashagar **91** G 3
Gashua **91** G 3
Gaspé **101** OP 6
Gassi Touil **87** G 2
Gastello, Iméni **69** R 3
Gästrikland **55** G 3
Gata, Sierra de **56** B 3
Gatchina **55** JK 4
Gates of the Arctic National Park and Preserve **98** G 2
Gauhati **73** F 2
Gauja **55** H 4
Gausta **55** E 4
Gavanka **69** T 4
Gávdhos **58** B 4
Gave de Pau **56** C 3
Gävle **55** G 3
Gävlebukten **55** G 3
Gaya **72** E 3
Gayndah **79** J 4
Gaza Strip **60** AB 3
Gazelle Peninsula **81** F 2
Gaziantep **59** E 3
Gaziantep Yaylası **59** E 3
Gazimurskiy Zavod **68** L 5
Gazıpaşa **60** A 1
Gbarnga **90** C 4
Gdańsk **53** G 4
Gdynia **53** G 4
Gearhart Mountain **102** B 3
Gedi **93** F 5
Gediz **58** C 3
Geelong **79** G 6
Geigar **88** E 6
Geilo **55** E 3
Gejiu **70** D 6
Gela **57** F 4
Gelendzhik **59** E 2
Gelsenkirchen **53** E 4
Gemena **92** B 4
Gemsbok National Park **94** C 4–5
General Acha **113** D 6
General Alvear **113** C 6
General Belgrano II **115**
General Belgrano III **115**
General Bernardo O'Higgins **115**
General Madariaga **113** E 6
General Pico **113** D 6
General Roca **113** C 6
General San Martin **115**
General Santos **75** G 2
Genève **57** E 2
Gengma **70** C 6
Genoa **57** E 3
Genova **57** E 3
Genova, Golfo di **57** E 3
Gent **52** D 4
George **101** O 4
Georgetown (Gambia) **90** B 3
Georgetown (Guyana) **109** G 2
George Town (Malaysia) **74** AB 2
Georgetown (Queensland, Austr.) **79** G 2
George Town (Tasmania, Austr.) **82** A 5
George V Coast **115**
George VI Sound **115**
Georgia **103** K 5
Georgia (U.S.S.R.) **59** F 2
Georgian Bay **101** L 6
Georgiu-Dezh **62** G 5
Georgiyevka **63** Q 6
Georgiyevsk **59** F 2
Georg von Neumayer **115**
Gera **53** F 4
Geraldton **78** A 4
Gerâs, Serra do **56** B 3
Gerasimovka **63** O 4
German Democratic Republic **53** F 4
Germi **61** G 2
Gerona **56** D 3
Gêrzê **72** D 1
Gesoa **80** D 3
Getafe **56** C 3
Getz Ice Shelf **115**
Geyik Dağı **59** D 3
Ghadāmis **87** G 2
Ghana **90** D 4
Ghanzi **94** C 4
Ghardaïa **87** F 2
Gharib, Ra's **60** A 3
Gharyān **87** H 2
Ghazzah **60** B 3
Gheorghe Gheorghiu-Dej **58** C 1
Ghimbi **92** F 3
Ghudāf, Wādī al **60** D 2
Gibraltar **56** B 4
Gibraltar, Estrecho de **56** BC 4
Gibson Desert **78** C 3
Gifu **71** L 3
Giglio **57** F 3
Gijon **56** B 3
Gila Bend **102** D 5
Gila River **102** D 5
Gilbert Islands **82** C 2–3
Gilbert River **79** G 2
Gilbués **109** J 5
Giles **78** D 4
Gilgandra **79** H 5
Gillam **99** T 4
Gillette **102** E 3
Gingin **78** B 5
Ginir **93** G 3
Gioia **57** G 3
Giresun **59** E 2
Girne **59** D 3
Gironde **56** C 2
Gisborne **81** R 8
Gitarama **92** DE 5
Giuba → Juba **93** G 4
Giza **88** DE 3
Gizhiga **69** U 3
Gizhiginskaya Guba **69** T 3
Gjiri i Vlorë **58** A 2
Gjögur **54** B 2
Gjövik **55** F 3
Glacier Bay National Park and Preserve **98** K 4
Gladstone **79** J 3
Glasgow **52** C 3
Glazov **62** K 4
Glen Canyon National Recreation Area **102** D 4
Glendale **102** D 5
Glendive **102** F 2
Glenhope **81** Q 9
Glennallen **98** H 3
Glenrothes **52** C 3
Glenwood Springs **102** E 4
Glittertind **54** E 3
Gliwice **53** G 4
Głogów **53** G 4
Gloucester (MA, U.S.A.) **103** MN 3
Gloucester (U.K.) **52** C 4
Glubokoye **55** J 4
Glukhov **62** F 5
Goa **72** B 4
Gobabis **94** B 4
Gobi **70** EF 2
Gochas **94** B 4
Godār-e Sorkh **61** G 2
Godar-i-Shah **67** G 5
Godavari **72** D 4
Gods Lake **99** T 5
Godthåb **101** R 3
Godwar **72** B 2
Goéland, Lac au **101** M 5–6
Goiânia **111** FG 4
Goiás (Brazil) **111** G 3
Goiás (Brazil) **111** F 4
Goksu **59** D 3
Göksu **59** E 3
Golan Heights **60** B 2
Golcuk **58** C 2
Gold Coast (Australia) **79** J 4
Gold Coast (Ghana) **90** DE 5
Golden Hinde **99** M 6
Goldsboro **103** L 4
Goldsworthy **78** BC 3
Golets Skalistyy, Gora **69** O 4
Golf de Lion **56–57** D 2
Golfe de Saint-Malo **56** C 2
Golfito **104** F 6
Golfo de Cadiz **56** B 4
Golfo de California **102** DE 5–7
Golfo de Chiriquí **108** B 2
Golfo de Guayaquil **108** B 4
Golfo de Honduras **104** E 4
Golfo de los Mosquitos **108** B 2
Golfo de Panamá **108** C 2
Golfo de Penas **113** AB 8
Golfo de Tehuantepec **104** CD 4
Golfo de Valencia **56** D 4
Golfo de Venezuela **108** D 1
Golfo di Genova **57** E 3
Golfo di Salerno **57** F 3
Golfo di Squillace **57** G 4
Golfo di Taranto **57** G 3
Golfo San Jorge **113** C 8
Golfo San Matías **113** D 7
Gölgeli Dağları **58** C 3
Golmud **70** B 3
Golovin **98** E 3
Golovnino **71** MN 2
Golubovka **63** O 5
Goma **92** D 5
Gombe **91** G 3
Gomel **62** F 5
Gomera **86** B 3
Goméz Palacio **104** B 2
Gonābād **66** F 4
Gonaïves **105** H 4
Gonam **69** O 4
Gonâve, Ile de la **105** H 4
Gonbad-e Qābus **66** EF 3
Gonda **72** D 2
Gondar **93** F 2
Gondia **72** CD 3
Gongbo' gyamda **70** BC 5
Gonghe **70** D 3
Gongpoquan **70** C 2
Goodnews Bay **98** E 4
Goondiwindi **79** HJ 4
Goose Bay **101** P 5
Gora Denezhkin Kamen' **63** LM 3
Gora Ezop **69** S 3
Gora Fisht **59** E 2
Gora Golets-Inyaptuk **68** K 4
Gora Golets-Skalistyy **68** LM 4
Gora Golets Skalistyy **69** O 4
Gora Kamen **68** FG 2
Gora Khil'mi **69** S 1
Gora Khoydype **63** N 2
Gorakhpur **72** D 2
Gora Konzhakovskiy Kamén **63** LM 4
Gora Kovriga **62** J 2
Gora Kuytun **63** R 6
Gora Medvezh'ya **69** P 6
Gora Munku-Sardyk **68** GH 5
Gora Narodnaya **63** LM 3
Gora Nelkuchan **69** P 3
Gora Pobeda **69** R 2
Gora Sokhor **68** J 5
Gora Syuge-Khaya **69** OP 2
Gora Taklaun **69** Q 3
Gora Tel'pos-Iz **63** LM 3
Gora Yamantau **63** L 5
Góra Zamkowa **53** H 4
Gorda **102** B 4
Gordion **59** D 3
Gordon **103** H 2
Gordon Downs **78** D 2
Gorgān **61** G 1
Gori **59** F 2

Gorki **63** N 2
Gor'kiy **62** H 4
Görlitz **53** F 4
Gorlovka **59** E 1
Gorna Oryakhovitsa **58** C 2
Gorno-Altaysk **63** QR 5
Gornozavodsk **69** Q 6
Gornyak **63** Q 5
Goroka **80** E 3
Goromay **69** Q 5
Gorongosa **95** E 3
Gorongosa National Park **95** EF 3
Gorontalo **75** F 3
Gory Byrranga **68** GH 1
Goryn' **55** J 5
Gory Putorana **68** FH 2
Gory Ulutau **67** H 1
Gorzów Wielkopolski **53** G 4
Goshogawara **71** LM 2
Gossi **90** D 2
Göta kanal **55** F 4
Götaland **55** FG 4
Göteborg **55** F 4
Gothenburg **55** F 4
Gotland **55** G 4
Gotska Sandön **55** GH 4
Göttingen **53** EF 4
Goulburn **79** H 5
Goulimime **86** C 3
Gouré **91** G 3
Gourma **90** E 3
Gourma-Rarous **90** D 2
Gouro **91** H 2
Gove Peninsula **79** F 1
Governador Valadares **111** H 4
Goya **112** E 4
Gozo **57** F 4
Graaff Reinet **94** C 6
Gračac **57** G 3
Gradaús, Serra dos **109** H 5
Grafton **79** J 4
Graham **98** L 5
Graham Land **115**
Grahamstown **94** D 6
Grain Coast **90** BC 4–C 5
Grajaú **109** J 5
Grampian Mountains **52** C 3
Granada (Nicaragua) **104** E 5
Granada (Spain) **56** C 4
Granby **101** N 6
Gran Canaria **86** BC 3
Gran Chaco **110** D 5
Grand Bassam **90** D 4
Grand Canyon **102** D 4
Grand Canyon National Park **102** D 4
Grand Coulee Dam **102** C 2
Grande, Bahía **113** C 9
Grande Comore **95** GH 2
Grande Prairie **99** NO 4
Grand Erg de Bilma **91** GI 2
Grand Erg Occidental **86–87** EF 2–3
Grand Erg Oriental **87** G 2–3
Grand Forks **102** G 2
Grandin, Lake **99** O 3
Grand Island **102** G 3
Grand Junction **102** E 4
Grand Marais **103** HJ 2
Grand Passage **81** H 5
Grand Rapids (Man., Can.) **99** S 5
Grand Rapids (MI, U.S.A.) **103** JK 3
Grand Rapids (MN, U.S.A.) **103** H 2
Grand Teton **102** D 3
Granite City **103** J 4
Granite Peak (MT, U.S.A.) **102** E 2
Granite Peakh (NV., U.S.A.) **102** C 3
Granja **111** H 1
Granön **54** G 3
Gran Sasso d'Italia **57** F 3
Grants Pass **102** B 3
Granville Lake **99** R 4
Gräsö **55** G 3
Grave, Pointe de **56** C 2
'S-Gravenhage **52** D 4
Gravina **57** G 3
Grayling **103** K 3
Graz **57** FG 2
Great Artesian Basin **79** G 3–4
Great Australian Bight **78** DE 5
Great Barrier **82** C 5
Great Barrier Island **81** R 8
Great Barrier Reef **79** H 1–2
Great Basin **102** C 3–4
Great Bear Lake **99** NO 2
Great Dividing Range **79** HJ 3–4
Greater Antilles **105** GH 4
Great Exuma Island **105** G 3
Great Falls **102** D 2
Great Fisher Bank **52** D 3
Great Inagua Island **105** H 3
Great Indian Desert **72** B 2
Great Karroo **94** C 6
Great Nicobar **73** F 6
Great Plains **102** FG 2–4
Great Salt Lake **102** D 3
Great Salt Lake Desert **102** D 3
Great Sandy Desert **78** C 3
Great Slave Lake **99** P 3
Great Victoria Desert **78** DE 4
Great Victoria Desert Nature Reserve **78** D 4
Greece **58** B 3
Greeley **102** F 3
Green Bay **103** J 3
Green Coast **115**
Green Islands **82** B 3
Greenland **114**
Greenland Sea **114**
Greenock **52** BC 3
Green River (Papua New Guinea) **80** D 2
Green River (UT, U.S.A.) **102** DE 4
Green River (WY, U.S.A.) **102** DE 3
Greensboro (GA, U.S.A.) **103** K 5
Greensboro (N.C., U.S.A.) **103** L 4
Greenvale **79** GH 2
Greenville (Liberia) **90** C 5
Greenville (MS, U.S.A.) **103** HJ 5
Greenville (S.C., U.S.A.) **103** K 5
Gregory, Lake **79** F 4
Gregory Range **79** G 2
Greifswald **53** F 4
Grenada **105** K 5
Grenoble **57** E 2
Greymouth **81** Q 9
Grey Range **79** G 4
Grim, Cape **80** K 9
Grimsby **52** CD 4
Grímsey **54** B 2
Grimshaw **99** O 4
Grímsstaðir **54** B 2
Grimstad **55** E 4
Grindavik **54** A 3
Griquatown **94** C 5
Grmeč **57** G 3
Grodno **55** H 5
Gröndalen **54** F 3
Grong **54** F 3
Groningen **52** E 4
Groote Eylandt **79** F 1
Grootfontein **94** B 3
Groot Vloer **94** BC 5
Groot Winter Berg **94** D 6
Grosseto **57** F 3
Group, Actaeon **83** F 4
Groznyy **59** G 2
Grudziądz **53** G 4
Grünau **94** B 5
Gruñidera **104** B 3
Gruziya **59** F 2
Grytviken **115**
Guadalajara (Mexico) **104** B 3
Guadalajara (Spain) **56** C 3
Guadalcanal **81** G 3
Guadalquivir **56** C 4
Guadalupe **56** B 4
Guadalupe **104** C 2
Guadalupe, Isla de **102** C 6
Guadalupe, Sierra de **56** B 4
Guadeloupe **105** KL 4
Guadeloupe Passage **105** K 4
Guadiana **56** B 4
Guajará Mirim **110** CD 3
Gualeguaychú **112** E 5
Guam **82** A 2
Guaminí **113** D 6
Guanare **108** E 2
Guandacol **112** C 4
Guangde **71** GH 4
Guangdong **70** F 6
Guanghua **70** F 4
Guangshan **70** G 4
Guangxi Zhuangzu Zizhiqu **70** EF 6
Guangyuan **70** E 4
Guangzhou **70** F 6
Guantánamo **105** H 3
Guan Xian **70** D 4
Guapí **108** C 3
Guaporé **110** D 3
Guaqui **110** C 4
Guarapuava **112** F 4
Guarda **56** B 3
Guardal **56** C 4
Guarenas **108** E 1
Guasave **102** E 6
Guasipati **109** F 2
Guatemala **104** DE 4
Guatemala City **104** DE 5
Guaviare **108** E 3
Guayabal **108** E 2
Guayaquil **108** C 4
Guayaquil, Golfo de **108** B 4
Guayaramerin **110** C 3
Guaymallén **112** C 5
Guba **94** D 2
Guba (U.S.S.R.) **62** F 3
Guba Buorkhaya **69** NO 1
Gubakha **63** L 4
Gubkin **62** G 5
Gudbrandsdalen **54** F 3
Gudermes **59** G 2
Gudur **72** CD 5
Guelta Zemmur **86** C 3
Guéné **90** E 3
Güera **86** B 4
Guéra **91** H 3
Guéréda **91** J 3
Guernsey **52** C 5
Guerrero **104** BC 4
Gügerd, Kūh-e **61** F 2
Gughe **93** F 3
Guguan **82** A 1
Guiana Highlands **109** FH 3
Guiding **70** E 5
Guidjiba **91** G 4
Guijá **95** E 4
Guildford **52** C 4
Guilin **70** F 5
Guinan **70** D 3
Guinea **90** BC 3
Guinea-Bissau **90** AB 3
Güines **105** F 3
Guiratinga **111** F 4
Guisanbourg **109** H 3
Guixi **71** G 5
Gui Xian **70** EF 6
Guiyang **70** E 5
Guizhou **70** E 5
Gujarat **72** B 3
Gujranwala **67** J 4
Gujrat **67** J 4
Gulbarga **72** C 4
Gulf of Aden **89** H 6
Gulf of Alaska **98** HJ 4
Gulf of Boothia **99** T 1
Gulf of Bothnia **54** GH 3
Gulf of Carpentaria **79** F 1
Gulf of Chihli **71** GH 3
Gulf of Finland **55** H 4
Gulf of Guinea **91** EF 5
Gulf of Khambhat **72** B 3–4
Gulf of Kutch **72** A 3

Gulf of Maine **103** N 3
Gulf of Mannar **72** C 6
Gulf of Martaban **73** G 4
Gulf of Mexico **104** DE 2
Gulf of Ob **63** O 2
Gulf of Oman **89** K 4
Gulf of Papua **80** DE 3
Gulf of Riga **55** H 4
Gulf of Saint Lawrence **101** P 6
Gulf of Sirt **87** J 2
Gulf of Suez **60** A 3
Gulf of Thailand **73** H 5
Gulf of Tonkin **73** J 3–4
Gulf of Venice **57** F 2–3
Gulfport **103** J 5
Gulf Saint Vincent **79** F 5–6
Gulgong **79** HJ 5
Gulin **70** E 5
Gulistan **67** H 2
Gulu **92** E 4
Guna **72** C 3
Güneydoğu Toros lar **59** EF 3
Gungu **92** B 6
Guntur **72** CD 4
Gunung Abong Abong **74** A 3
Gunung Besar **74** E 4
Gunung Binaiya **75** G 4
Gunung Dempo **74** B 4
Gunung Kerinci **74** B 4
Gunung Kinabalu **74** E 2
Gunung Kwoka **75** H 4
Gunung Leuser **74** A 3
Gunung Lokilalaki **75** F 4
Gunung Maling **75** F 3
Gunung Mulu **74** DE 3
Gunung Mutis **75** F 5
Gunung Saran **74** D 4
Gunung Sorikmerapi **74** A 3
Gunung Tahan **74** B 3
Guoyang **70** G 4
Gurban Obo **70** F 2
Gurbantünggüt Shamo **67** M 1–2
Gurgan **61** G 1
Gürlevik Dağı **59** E 3
Gurskoye **69** P 5
Gurupá **109** H 4
Gurupí **111** G 3
Gurvanbulag **68** HJ 6
Gur'yev **66** E 1
Gusau **91** F 3
Guyana **109** G 3
Guyenne **56** C 3
Guzar **67** H 3
Güzelhisar **58** C 3
Gwalior **72** C 2
Gwelo **94** D 3
Gya La **72** DE 2
Gyangzê **72** E 2
Gydanskiy Poluostrov **63** P 1–2
Gympie **79** J 4
Gyöngyös **58** B 1
Győr **57** G 2
Gypsum Point **99** OP 3
Gyula **58** B 1

H

Haanja Kõrgustik **55** J 4
Ha'apai Group **82** D 4
Haapsalu **55** H 4
Haarlem **52** D 4
Habana **105** F 3
Habay **99** O 4
Hābbāniyah **60** D 2
Hachinohe **71** M 2
Ḩadd, Ra's al **89** KL 4
Hadejia **91** F 3
Hadejia **91** G 3
Hadera **60** B 2
Hadilik **67** M 3
Hadley Bay **99** Q 1
Ḩaḑramawt **89** H 5
Ḩafar al Bāţin **89** H 3
Ḩafīrat al 'Aydā **60** C 4
Ḩafīt **61** G 4–5
Hāfūn, Ra's **93** J 2
Hagemeister **98** E 4
Hagfors **55** F 3
Hague, Cap de la **56** C 2
Haicheng **71** H 2
Haifa **60** B 2
Haifeng **70** G 6
Haikang **70** EF 6
Haikou **70** F 6–7
Ḩā'il **60** C 4
Hailar **68** L 6
Hailin **71** J 2
Hailun **69** N 6
Hailuoto **54** H 2
Hainan Dao **70** F 7
Haines **98** K 4
Haines Junction **98** K 3
Hai Phong **73** J 3
Haïti **105** H 4
Ḩajārah, Saḩrā' al **89** GH 2–H 3
Ḩājjīābād **66** F 5
Ḩajjīābād-e Māsīleh **61** F 2
Hakkâri Dağları **59** F 3
Hakodate **71** M 2
Halab **60** B 1
Ḩalā'ib **88** F 4
Ḩalbā **60** B 2
Halden **55** F 4
Hale, Mount **78** B 4
Ḩalī **89** G 5
Halifax **101** P 7
Hall **98** C 3
Halland **55** F 4
Hallat' Ammār **60** B 3
Hall Beach **99** V 2
Halle **53** F 4
Halley Bay **115**
Hallingskarvet **55** E 3
Hall Islands **82** B 2
Hall Peninsula **101** O 3
Halls Creek **78** D 2
Halmahera, Laut **75** G 4
Halmstad **55** F 4
Hälsingeskogen **54** G 3
Hälsingland **54** G 3
Halti **54** H 2
Ḩālūl **61** F 4

Hamadān **61** E 2
Ḩamāh **60** B 2
Hamamatsu **71** L 4
Hamar **55** F 3
Hamburg **53** F 4
Häme **54** HJ 3
Hämeenlinna **54** HJ 3
Hamelin Pool **78** A 4
Hamersley Range **78** B 3
Hamersley Range National Park **78** B 3
Hamhŭng **71** J 2–3
Hami **70** B 2
Hamilton (New Zealand) **81** R 8
Hamilton (Ontario, Can.) **101** M 7
Hamilton (Victoria, Austr.) **79** G 6
Hamm **53** E 4
Hammar, Hawr al **61** E 3
Hammerfest **54** H 1
Hammond **103** J 3
Hammur Koke **93** F 3
Hampden **81** Q 10
Hamrīn, Jabal **60–61** D 2
Hamuku **75** HJ 4
Hanak **60** B 4
Hanang **92** EF 5
Hanceville **99** N 5
Hanchuan **70** F 4
Handan **70** F 3
Handeni **93** F 6
Hanegev **60** B 3
Hanggin Houqi **70** E 2
Hangu **71** G 3
Hangzhou **71** H 4
Hankoniemi **55** H 4
Hannover **53** E 4
Hanöbukten **55** FG 4
Ha Noi **73** HJ 3
Hanover **94** C 6
Hanover, Islas **113** AB 9
Hanstholm **55** E 4
Hao **83** F 4
Haparanda **54** H 2
Hara **68** J 6
Ḩaraḑh **61** E 4
Harar **93** G 3
Harare **95** E 3
Hararge **93** GH 3
Harazé **91** J 4
Harbin **71** J 1
Hardangerfjorden **55** E 3–4
Hardangerjökulen **55** E 3
Hardangervidda **55** E 3
Hardin **102** E 2
Hargeysa **93** G 3
Hari, Batang **74** B 4
Ḩarib **89** H 6
Hari Kurk **55** H 4
Ḩārim **60** B 1
Härjedalen **54** F 3
Harlingen **103** G 6
Härnösand **54** G 3
Harrat al 'Uwayrid **60** B 4
Harrat Ithnayn **60** C 4
Harrington Harbour **101** Q 5

Harrisburg **103** L 3
Harrismith **94** DE 5
Harrison, Cape **101** Q 5
Harrison Bay **98** G 1
Harstad **54** G 2
Hartford **103** M 3
Hartlepool **52** C 4
Hartz Mountains National Park **80** KL 9
Har Us Nuur **68** F 6
Harvey **102** G 2
Haryana **72** C 2
Harz **53** F 4
Hasalbag **67** K 3
Hassan **72** C 5
Hassi Bel Guebbour **87** G 3
Hassi Messaoud **87** G 2
Hastings (NE, U.S.A.) **102** G 3
Hastings (New Zealand) **81** R 8
Hat Hin **73** H 3
Ha Tinh **73** J 4
Hattiesburg **103** J 5
Hatutu **83** F 3
Hat Yai **73** H 6
Hauberg Mountains **115**
Haugesund **55** DE 4
Haukipudas **54** J 2
Hauraki Gulf **81** QR 8
Hauterive **101** O 6
Haut-Zaïre **92** CD 4
Havana **105** F 3
Havern **54** G 3
Havre **102** E 2
Havre-Saint-Pierre **101** P 5
Hawaii **83** E 1
Hawaiian Islands **83** E 1
Ḩawallī **61** E 3
Hawke Harbour **101** Q 5
Hawr al Hammar **61** E 3
Hawrān, Wādī **60** C 2
Hawr as S'adīyah **61** E 2
Hay **79** G 5
Hay River **99** O 3
Hayyā **88** F 5
Hazarajat **67** H 4
Hazar Gölü **59** E 3
Hearst **100** L 6
Hebei **71** G 3
Hebel **79** H 4
Hebi **70** F 3
Hebron **101** P 4
Hecate Strait **98** L 5
Hechi **70** E 6
Hechuan **70** E 4–5
Hedmark **54** F 3
Hefa **60** B 2
Hefei **71** G 4
Hegang **69** O 6
Heidelberg **53** E 5
Heidenheim **53** F 5
Heilbronn **53** E 5
Heilong Jiang **69** O 6
Heilongjiang **71** JK 1
Heimaey **54** A 3
Heimahe **70** C 3
Hejaz **60** B 4
Hekla **54** B 3

Helagsfjället **54** F 3
Helena **102** D 2
Hellas **58** B 3
Hells Canyon **102** C 2
Helmeringhausen **94** B 5
Helong **71** JK 2
Helsingborg **55** F 4
Helsingfors **55** J 3–4
Helsingör **55** F 4
Helsinki **55** J 3–4
Henan **70** F 4
Henbury **78** E 3
Henderson **83** G 4
Hendījan **61** E 3
Hengduan Shan **70** CD 5
Heng Xian **70** E 6
Hengyang **70** F 5
Henik Lakes **99** S 3
Henrietta Maria, Cape **101** L 4
Henryetta **103** G 4
Henzada **73** FG 4
Heraklia **60** C 1
Herat **67** G 4
Herberton **79** H 2
Hereford **52** C 4
Herlen He **68** L 6
Herluf Trolle, Cape **101** T 3
Hermiston **102** C 2
Hermit Islands **82** A 3
Hermon, Mount **60** B 2
Hermosillo **102** DE 6
Herning **55** E 4
Herzliyya **60** B 2
He Xian **70** F 6
Ḥeydarābād **61** D 1
Heze **70** FG 3
Hialeah **103** K 6
Hidalgo **104** C 3
Hidalgo del Parral **102** EF 6
Hidcolândia **111** FG 4
Hierro **86** B 3
High Level **99** O 4
High Prairie **99** O 4
Higuerote **108** E 1
Hiiumaa **55** H 4
Hillsboro **103** G 5
Hilo **83** E 1
Himachal Pradesh **72** C 1
Ḥimā Ḍarīyah, Jabal **60** C 4
Himalayas **72** CE 1–2
Hims **60** B 2
Hinchinbrook Island **79** H 2
Hindu Kush **67** HJ 3–4
Hinganghat **72** C 3
Hingol **67** H 5
Hinnöya **54** G 2
Hinton **99** O 5
Hirara **71** J 6
Hirfanlı Barajı **59** D 3
Hirhafok **87** G 4
Hirosaki **71** LM 2
Hiroshima **71** K 4
Hirtshals **55** E 4
Hismā **60** B 3
Hispaniola **105** HJ 4
Hitachi **71** M 3
Hitra **54** E 3
Hiva Oa **83** F 3
Hjälmaren **55** G 4
Hjelmsöya **54** H 1
Hmeenselk **54** H 3
Ho **90** E 4
Hoa Binh **73** HJ 3
Hoachanas **94** B 4
Hoare Bay **101** P 2
Hobart **80** L 9
Hobbs **102** F 5
Hoburgen **55** G 4
Hobyā **93** H 3
Ho Chi Minh **73** J 5
Hodda **93** J 2
Hodeida **89** G 6
Hodh **86** D 5
Hofsá **54** B 2
Hofsjökull **54** B 2
Hōfu **71** K 4
Hoggar **87** F 4
Hohhot **70** F 2
Hoima **92** E 4
Hokitika **82** C 5
Hokkaidō **71** M 2
Hokmābād **66** F 3
Holanda **110** C 3
Holguín **105** G 3
Holland **103** J 3
Hollick-Kenyon Plateau **115**
Hollywood (CA, U.S.A.) **102** C 5
Hollywood (FL, U.S.A.) **103** L 6
Holstebro **55** E 4
Holyhead **52** C 4
Homāyūnshahr **61** F 2
Hombori Tondo **90** D 3
Home Bay **101** O 2
Homosassa **103** K 6
Honavar **72** B 5
Honduras **104** E 5
Hönefoss **55** F 3
Hong Kong **70** FG 6
Hongliuhe **70** BC 2
Hongor **70** F 1
Hongyuan **70** D 4
Honiara **81** G 3
Honningsvåg **54** J 1
Honolulu **83** E 1
Hon Panjang **73** H 6
Honshū **71** KL 3
Hood Point **78** BC 5
Hoover Dam **102** D 4
Hope, Point **98** D 2
Hopes Advance, Cap **101** O 3
Hopin **73** G 3
Hordaland **55** E 3
Horizon Deep **82** D 4
Horlick Mountains **115**
Hormuz, Strait of **61** G 4
Horn, Cape **113** CD 10
Hornavan **54** G 2
Hörnefors **54** G 3
Horn Islands **82** D 3
Hornos, Cabo de **113** CD 10
Horn Plateau **99** O 3
Horqin Youyi Qianqi **71** H 1
Horsens **55** EF 4
Horsham **79** G 6
Hosalay **59** D 2
Hose Mountains **74** D 3
Hoseynīyeh **61** E 3
Hospet **72** C 4
Hospitalet **56** D 3
Hoste, Isla **113** C 10
Hotagen **54** F 3
Hotan **67** K 3
Hotazel **94** C 5
Hoting **54** G 3
Hot Springs **103** H 5
Hottah Lake **99** O 2
Houma (China) **70** F 3
Houma (LA, U.S.A.) **103** H 6
Houston **103** G 5
Hovd (Mongolia) **68** F 6
Hovd (Mongolia) **70** D 2
Hövsgöl Nuur **68** H 5
Howe, Cape **79** J 6
Howland **82** D 2
Howrah **72** E 3
Hoxud **70** A 2
Hox Xil Shan **70** AB 3–4
Hoy **52** C 3
Hrvatska **57** G 2
Hsinchu **71** H 6
Huacho **108** C 6
Hua Hin **73** GH 5
Huaibin **70** FG 4
Huainan **71** G 4
Huairen **70** F 3
Huajuapan de León **104** C 4
Huallaga **108** C 5
Huambo (Angola) **94** B 2
Huambo (Angola) **94** B 2
Huanan **71** K 1
Huancabamba **108** C 5
Huancavelica **110** A 3
Huancayo **110** A 3
Huangchuan **70** G 4
Huang Hai **71** H 3
Huangshi **70** F 4
Huang Xian **71** GH 3
Huangyan **71** H 5
Huangzhong **70** D 3
Huánuco **108** C 5–6
Huara **110** C 4
Huaral **110** A 3
Huaraz **108** C 5
Huarmey **108** C 6
Huascarán, Nevado **108** C 5
Huasco **112** B 4
Huashixia **70** C 3
Huayllay **110** A 3
Hubei **70** F 4
Hubli **72** C 4–5
Huckitta **78** F 3
Hudat **93** F 4
Ḥuddur Hadama **93** G 4
Huder **69** M 6
Hudiksvall **54** G 3
Hudson Bay **99** R 5
Hudson Bay **100** KL 3–4
Hudson River **103** M 3
Hudson's Hope **99** N 4
Hudson Strait **101** NO 3
Hue **73** J 4
Huelva **56** B 4
Huesca **56** C 3
Hughenden **79** G 3
Hugo **103** GH 5
Hŭich'on **71** J 2
Huihe **68** L 6
Huíla (Angola) **94** AB 2
Huila (Colombia) **108** C 3
Huilai **70** G 6
Huili **70** D 5
Huimin **71** G 3
Huize **70** D 5
Hulayfā' **60** C 4
Huld **70** E 1
Hull **101** M 6
Huma **69** N 5
Humaitá (Amazonas, Brazil) **109** F 5
Humaitá (Paraguay) **112** E 4
Humay **110** A 3
Húnaflói **54** A 2
Hunan **70** F 5
Hunchun **71** K 2
Hunedoara **58** B 1
Hungary **58** A 1
Hŭngnam **71** J 3
Hunjiang **71** J 2
Hunsur **72** C 5
Hunter **82** C 4
Huntington **103** K 4
Huntsville (AL, U.S.A.) **103** J 5
Huntsville (Ontario, Can.) **101** M 6
Huntsville (TX, U.S.A.) **103** GH 5
Hunyuan **70** F 3
Huocheng **67** KL 2
Huon **82** B 4
Huon Gulf **80** E 3
Huo Xian **70** F 3
Huron **102** G 3
Hurst **103** G 5
Husum **53** E 4
Hutag **68** H 6
Hutchinson **102** G 4
Hvar **57** G 3
Hveragerði **54** A 3
Hyargas Nuur **68** F 6
Hyden **78** B 5
Hyderabad (India) **72** CD 4
Hyderabad (Pakistan) **67** H 5
Hyères, Iles d' **57** E 3
Hyesan **71** J 2
Hyvinkää **55** H 3

I

Iaçu **111** H 3
Ialomiţa **58** C 2
Iaripo **109** H 3
Iaşi **58** C 1
Ibadan **91** E 4
Ibagué **108** C 3
Ibaiti **111** FG 5
Ibarra **108** C 3
Iberville, Lac d' **101** N 4
Ibestad **54** G 2
Ibi **91** F 4
Ibitiara **111** H 3
Ibiza (Spain) **56** D 4

Íbiza (Spain) **56** D 4
Ibotirama **111** H 3
Ibrīm **88** E 4
Icá (Amazonas, Brazil) **108** E 4
Ica (Peru) **110** A 3
Icana **108** E 3
Içel **59** D 3
Iceland **54** A 2
Iceland **54** A 3
Ichera **68** J 4
Ichinskaya Sopka **69** ST 4
Ico **111** J 2
Icy Cape **98** E 1
Idaho **102** CD 3
Idaho Falls **102** D 3
Idfū **88** E 4
Idhān Awbārī **87** H 3
Idhān Murzuq **87** H 4
Ídhi Óros **58** BC 3
Ídhra **58** B 3
Idlib **60** B 2
Idre **54** F 3
Ifalik **82** A 2
Ifanadiana **95** H 4
Ife **91** E 4
Igarka **63** R 2
Iglesias **57** E 4
Ignace **100** J 6
Ignashino **69** M 5
İğneada **58** C 2
Iguaçu **112** F 4
Iguala **104** C 4
Iguassú Falls **112** F 4
Iguatu **111** J 2
Ihosy **95** H 4
Ihtamir **68** H 6
Iivaara **54** J 2
Ijebu Ode **91** EF 4
Ijsselmeer **52** E 4
Ijuí **112** F 4
Ikaría **58** C 3
Ikerre **91** F 4
Ikot Ekpene **91** F 4
Ilaferh **87** F 4
Ilagan **75** J 1
Ilam **61** E 2
Ilbenge **69** M 3
Ile-à-la-Crosse **99** Q 4
Ilebo **92** C 5
Île d'Anticosti **101** P 6
Ile de France **56** D 2
Ile de la Gonâve **105** H 4
Île de la Madeleine **101** P 6
Ile de Ré **56** C 2
Ile des Noefs **93** J 6
Ile des Pins **81** J 6
Ile d'Oléron **56** C 2
Ile d'Ouessant **56** B 2
Île du Diable **109** H 2
Ile d'Yeu **56** C 2
Iles Chesterfield **82** B 4
Îles de Los **90** B 4
Iles d'Hyères **57** E 3
Îles du Désappointement **83** F 3
Îles du Duc de Gloucester **83** F 4
Îles du Roi Georges **83** F 3
Iles Glorienses **95** H 2
Îles Palliser **83** F 4
Ile Tidra **86** B 5
Ilha de Maracá **109** HJ 3
Ilha de Marajó **109** HJ 4
Ilha Grande **108** E 4
Ilha Santa Carolina **95** F 4
Ilhéus **111** J 3
Iliamna **98** G 4
Iliamna Lake **98** F 4
Ilichevsk **58** D 1
Ilimsk **68** H 4
Ilinskiy **69** Q 6
Illapel **112** B 5
Illimani, Nevado **110** C 4
Illinois **103** J 3–4
Illizi **87** G 3
Ilo **110** B 4
Iloilo **75** F 1
Ilots de Bass **83** F 4
Ilubabor **92** EF 3
Ilyichovsk **58** D 1
Ima **68** L 4
Imām al Hamzah **61** D 3
Imandra, Ozero **54** K 2
Imatra **54** J 3
Imbituba **112** G 4
Iméni Gastello **69** R 3
Iméni Mariny **69** QR 3
Imgytskoye Boloto **63** O 4
Imperatriz **109** J 5
Imphal **73** F 3
Imtonzha **69** NO 2
Inagua Island, Great **105** H 3
Inarijarvi **54** J 2
In Azaoua **91** F 1
In Bogd Uul **70** CD 1
İnce Burnu **59** D 2
Inch'ŏn **71** J 3
Inchôpe **95** E 3
Independence **103** H 4
India **72** CD 3
Indiana **103** J 3
Indianapolis **103** J 4
Indian Harbour **101** Q 5
Indian Ocean **117**
Indias Occidentales **105** H 3
Indigirka **69** R 2
Indigirskaya Nizmennost' **69** QR 2
Indispensable Reefs **82** B 3
Indispensable Strait **81** H 3–4
Indonesia **74–75** OG 4
Indore **72** C 3
Indus **67** H 6
İnegöl **58** C 2
In Gall **91** F 2
Ingoda **68** K 5
Ingrid Christensen Coast **115**
Ingul **59** D 1
Inhambane **95** F 4
Inharrime **95** F 4
Inhumas **111** FG 4
Inirida **108** E 3
Inkerman **79** G 2
Inn **53** F 5
Inner Hebrides **52** B 3
Inner Mongolia **70** E 2–3
Innisfail **79** H 2
Innokent'yevka **69** P 6
Innsbruck **57** F 2
Inoucdjouac **101** M 4
In Salah **87** F 3
Insulă Sacalin **58** CD 2
Inta **63** L 2
Intletovy **63** P 3
Inuvik **98** L 2
Invercargill **80** P 10
Inverness **52** C 3
Investigator Strait **79** F 6
Inya **63** R 5
Iolotan **67** G 3
Iona National Park **94** A 3
Ionian Islands **58** A 3
Ionian Sea **58** A 3
Ionioi Nísoi **58** A 3
Iónion Pélagos **58** AB 3
Íos **58** C 3
Iowa **103** H 3
Iowa City **103** H 3
Ipameri **111** G 4
Ipatinga **111** H 4
Ipiales **108** C 3
Ipiaú **111** J 3
Ípiros **58** B 3
Ipixuna **108** D 5
Ipoh **74** B 3
Iporá **111** F 4
Ipswich (Australia) **79** J 4
Ipswich (U.K.) **52** D 4
Ipu **111** H 1
Iquapé **111** G 5
Iquique **110** B 5
Iquitos **108** D 4
Iracoubo **109** H 2
Irafshan **67** G 5
Iráklion **58** C 3
Iran **66** EF 4
Iran, Pegunungan **74** D 3
Irapuato **104** B 3
Iraq **60** D 2
Irbid **60** B 2
Irbit **63** M 4
Irebu **92** B 5
Irecê **111** H 3
Irgiz **67** G 1
Irian Jaya **75** HJ 4
Iriba **91** J 2
Iringa **93** F 6
Iriomote-jima **71** HJ 6
Iriona **104** EF 4
Iriri **109** H 4
Irish Sea **52** BC 4
Irkutsk **68** HJ 5
Iron Gate **58** B 2
Iron Knob **79** F 5
Írq al Idrīsī **87** K 4–5
'Irq al Maẓhur **60** D 4
Irrawaddy **73** G 3–4
Irrawaddy, Mouths of the **73** FG 4
Irtuia **109** J 4
Irtysh **63** N 4
Irtysh **63** O 5
Irún **56** C 3
Isa, Mount **79** F 3
Isabela **108** B 6
Isangi **92** C 4
Ischia **57** F 3
Iscia Baidoa → Isha Baydabo **93** G 4
Iseyin **90** E 4
Isfendiyar Dağlari **59** D 2
Isherton **109** G 3
Ishigaki **71** HJ 6
Ishikhly **66** D 3
Ishim **63** N 4
Ishim **63** O 4
Ishimskaya Step' **63** O 5
Ishinomaki **71** M 3
Išiklar Daği **58** C 2
Isil'kul **63** O 5
Isinga **68** K 5
Isiro **92** D 4
İskenderun **59** E 3
İskenderun Kßrfezi **59** E 3
Iskitim **63** Q 5
Isla Ángel de la Guarda **102** D 6
Isla Aruba **108** E 1
Isla Campana **113** A 8
Isla Cedros **102** C 6
Isla Curaçao **108** DE 1
Isla de Chiloé **113** B 7
Isla de Cozumel **104** E 3
Isla de Guadelupe **102** C 6
Isla de la Juventud **104** F 3
Isla del Maíz **104** F 5
Isla de los Estados **113** D 9
Isla Desolación **113** AB 9
Isla Esmeralda **113** A 8
Isla Grande de Tierra del Fuego **113** C 9
Isla Hoste **113** C 10
Islamabad **67** J 4
Isla Malpelo **108** B 3
Ísland **54** A 3
Island Lake **99** T 5
Islands of Four Mountains **98** CD 5
Isla Santa Inés **113** B 9
Islas Baleares **56** D 3–4
Islas Canarias **86** B 3
Islas Hanover **113** AB 9
Isla Tiburon **102** D 6
Isla Tobago **109** F 1
Isla Trinidad **109** F 1
Islay **52** B 3
Isle of Man **52** C 4
Isle of Wight **52** C 4
Isles of Scilly **52** B 5
Isole Eolie o Lipari **57** F 4
Isole Ponziane **57** F 3
Isosyöte **54** J 2
Isparta **58** D 3
Israel **60** B 3
Israel **88** E 2
Issano **109** G 2
İstanbul **58** C 2
İstanbul Boğazi **58** C 2
Isteren **54** F 3
Isthmus of Kra **73** G 5
Istmo de Tehuantepec **104** D 4

Isto, Mount **98** J 2
Istra **57** F 2
Itaberaba **111** H 3
Itabira **111** H 4
Itabuna **111** J 3
Itagüí **108** C 2
Itaituba **109** G 4
Itajaí **112** G 4
Italia **57** FG 3
Italy **57** F 3
Itambé **111** H 4
Itaperucu Mirim **111** H 1
Itaperuna **111** H 5
Itapetinga **111** J 4
Itapipoca **111** J 1
Itapiranga **109** G 4
Itapiúna **111** J 1
Itarsi **72** C 3
Itaúnas **111** J 4
Itbāy **60** AB 4
Itbāy **88** EF 3–4
Itchen Lake **99** P 2
Iténez **110** D 3
Ithaca **103** L 3
Itháki **58** B 3
Ithnayn, Harat **60** C 4
Itivdleg **101** R 2
Ituberá **111** J 3
Ituiutaba **111** FG 4
Itumbiara **111** FG 4
Iturama **111** F 4
Iturbe **110** C 5
Itzehoe **53** EF 4
Iul'tin **98** B 2
Ivalojoki **54** J 2
Ivanhoe **79** GH 5
Ivano-Frankovsk **62** D 6
Ivanovo **62** H 4
Ivigtut **101** S 3
Ivory Coast **90** CD 4
Ivory Coast **90** CD 5
Ivrea **57** E 2
Iwaki **71** M 3
Iwo **91** E 4
Iwo Jima **65** R 7
Iwŏn **71** J 2
Ixiamas **110** C 3
İzmir **58** C 3
İzmir Körfezi **58** C 3
İzmit **58** CD 2
Izu-shotō **71** M 4–5

J

Jabal Abadab **88** EF 5
Jabal al Bishrī **88** F 1
Jabal al Humara **88** E 5
Jabal al Lawz **88** F 3
Jabal an Nabī Shu'ayb **89** G 5
Jabal as Ḩasāwinah **87** H 3
Jabal ash Shaykh **60** B 2
Jabal at Tubayq **60** B 3
Jabal Dabbāgh **60** B 4
Jabal Hajhir **93** J 2
Jabal Hamātah **60** B 4
Jabal Hamoyet **88** F 5
Jabal Hamrīn **60–61** D 2
Jabal Ḩimā Ḑarīyah **60** C 4
Jabal Ibrāhīm **89** G 4
Jabal Kātrīna **60** AB 3
Jabal Katul **88** D 6
Jabal Lotuke **92** E 4
Jabal Lubnān **60** B 2
Jabal Marrah **88** CD 6
Jabal Oda **88** F 4
Jabalpur **72** CD 3
Jabal Ṣabīr **89** G 6
Jabal Shā'ib al Banāt **60** A 4
Jabal Shammar **60** CD 4
Jabal Ţuwayq **61** D 4
Jabālyah **60** B 3
Jablah **60** B 2
Jablanica **57** G 3
Jabung, Tanjung **74** B 4
Jacareacanga **109** G 5
Jaciara **111** F 4
Jaciparaná **109** F 5
Jackpot **102** D 3
Jackson (MS, U.S.A.) **103** HJ 5
Jackson (TX, U.S.A.) **103** J 4
Jackson, Mount **115**
Jacksonville (FL, U.S.A.) **103** K 5
Jacksonville (TX, U.S.A.) **103** GH 5
Jacobabad **67** H 5
Jacobina **111** H 3
Jacona **104** B 3–4
Jadal **91** E 2
J.A.D. Jensens Nunatakker **101** S 3
Jādū **87** H 2
Jaén **56** C 4
Jaffa, Cape **79** F 6
Jaffa → Tel Aviv-Yafo **88** E 2
Jaffna **72** D 6
Jagdalpur **72** D 4
Jaguarão **112** F 5
Jaguarari **111** J 3
Jaguariaíva **111** FG 5
Jaguaribe **111** J 2
Jahrom **61** F 3
Jaina **104** D 3
Jaipur **72** C 2
Jakarta **74** C 5
Jakobshavn **114**
Jakobstad **54** H 3
Jalaid Qi **71** H 1
Jalapa Enríquez **104** CD 4
Jalgaon **72** BC 3
Jalībah **61** E 3
Jalisco **104** B 3
Jalón **56** C 3
Jaluit **82** C 2
Jalūlā' **61** D 2
Jama **108** B 4
Jamaica **105** G 4
Jamāme **93** G 4
Jamari **109** F 5
Jambi **74** B 4
James **102** G 3
James Bay **101** L 5
James Ross Strait **99** S 1–2
Jamestown (N.D., U.S.A.) **102** G 2
Jamestown (N.Y., U.S.A.) **103** L 3
Jamiltepec **104** C 4
Jammu **67** K 4
Jammu and Kashmir **67** K 4
Jamnagar **72** AB 3
Jamsah **60** A 4
Jamshedpur **72** DE 3
Jämtland **54** F 3
Jandaia **111** FG 4
Jandaq **66** EF 4
Janesville **103** J 3
Janjira **72** B 4
Jan Mayen Island **114**
Janos **102** E 5
Januária **111** H 4
Japan **71** L 3
Japurá **108** E 4
Jarabulus **60** C 1
Jaramillo **113** C 8
Jarbah **87** H 2
Jardine River National Park **79** G 1
Jarrahdale **78** B 5
Jarud Qi **71** H 2
Jarvis **83** E 3
Jasikan **90** E 4
Jasper **103** H 5
Jasper National Park **99** O 5
Jastrzebie Zdrój **53** G 5
Jászberény **58** AB 1
Jataí **111** F 4
Jatobal **109** HJ 4
Jaú **111** G 5
Jauja **110** A 3
Java **74** C 5
Java Sea **74** CD 5
Jawa **74** CD 5
Jaya, Puncak **75** J 4
Jayapura **80** D 2
Jazā'ir Farasān **89** G 5
Jazā'ir Khurīyā Murīya **89** K 5
Jazīrat **60** B 4
Jbel Toubkal **86** D 2
Jeci **95** F 2
Jefferson, Mount (NV, U.S.A.) **102** C 4
Jefferson City **103** H 4
Jēkabpils **55** J 4
Jekkevarre **54** GH 2
Jelenia Góra **53** G 4
Jelgava **55** H 4
Jelow Gir **61** E 2
Jequié **111** H 3
Jequitinhonha **111** HJ 4
Jerada **86** E 2
Jeremoabo **111** J 3
Jerez de la Frontera **56** B 4
Jerome **102** CD 3
Jersey **52** C 5
Jerusalem **60** B 3
Jeypore **72** D 4
Jhang Sadar **67** J 4
Jhansi **72** C 2
Jhelum **67** J 4
Jiamusi **71** K 1
Jiang'an **70** DE 5
Jianghua **70** F 5
Jiangmen **70** F 6
Jiangsu **71** GH 4
Jiangxi **70** FG 5
Jiangyou **70** D 4
Jianyang **71** G 5
Jiaozuo **70** F 3
Jiayu **70** F 5
Jiayuguan **70** C 3
Jiddah **89** FG 4
Jieyang **70** G 6
Jigzhi **70** D 4
Jijiga **93** G 3
Jilib **93** G 4
Jilin **71** HJ 2
Jimāl, Wādi **60** B 4
Jimma **93** F 3
Jinan **71** G 3
Jincheng **70** F 3
Jingdezhen **71** G 5
Jingning **70** E 3
Jing Xian **70** E 5
Jingyuan **70** DE 3
Jinhua **71** GH 5
Jining **71** G 3
Jinja **92** E 4
Jinkouhe **70** D 5
Jinping **70** D 6
Jinsha **70** E 5
Jinsha Jiang **70** D 5
Jinshan **71** H 4
Jin Xian **71** H 3
Jinxiang **71** G 3–4
Jinzhou **71** H 2
Jiparaná **109** F 5
Jipijapa **108** B 4
Jishou **70** EF 5
Jisr ash Shughūr **60** B 2
Jiu **58** B 2
Jiujiang **70** G 5
Jiuquan **70** C 3
Jixi **71** K 1
João Pessoa **111** K 2
Jodhpur **72** B 2
Joensuu **54** JK 3
Jōetsu **71** L 3
Johannesburg **94** DE 5
John O'Groat's **52** C 3
Johnsons Crossing **98** L 3
Johnston **82** D 1
Johnstown **103** L 3
Johor Baharu **74** B 3
Joinvile **112** G 4
Joinville Island **115**
Jokkmokk **54** H 2
Jolo **75** F 2
Jonesboro **103** HJ 4
Jonglei **92** E 3
Jönköping **55** FG 4
Jonquière **101** N 6
Joplin **103** H 4
Jordan **60** B 2–3
Jordan **60** B 3
Jordan **88** F 2
Jorhat **73** F 2
Jos **91** F 4
Joseph Bonaparte Gulf **78** D 1
Joseph Lake **101** O 5

Jos Sodarso, Pulau **75** J 5
Jostedalsbreen **54** E 3
Jotunheimen **54** E 3
Juan de Nova **95** G 3
Juan Fernández Islands **107** B 6
Juárez **113** E 6
Juàzeiro **111** H 2
Juàzeiro do Norte **111** J 2
Jūbā **92** E 4
Jubayl **60** B 2
Jubayt **88** F 5
Júcar **56** C 4
Juchitan de Zaragoza **104** D 4
Juiz de Fora **111** H 5
Juktån **54** G 2
Juliaca **110** B 4
Julia Creek **79** G 3
Julianatop **109** G 3
Julianehåb **101** S 3
Jumanggoin **70** C 4
Junagadh **72** B 3
Jun Bulen **71** G 1
Junction **102** G 5
Jundiaí **111** G 5
Juneau **98** L 4
Junee **79** H 5
Junggar Pendi **67** M 1
Junín **112** D 5
Jūniyah **60** B 2
Jun Xian **70** F 4
Juoksengi **54** H 2
Jura **52** B 3
Jurado **108** C 2
Jurien Bay **78** A 5
Jūrmala **55** H 4
Juruá **108** E 4
Juruena **110** E 3
Juruti **109** G 4
Jutaí **108** E 4
Jutland **55** E 4
Juva **54** J 3
Juventud, Isla de la **104** F 3
Ju Xian **71** G 3
Jūyom **61** F 3
Juzur Qarqannah **87** H 2
Jylland **55** EF 4
Jyväskylä **54** J 3

K

Kabaena, Pulau **75** F 5
Kabalo **92** D 6
Kaban'ya **69** P 6
Kabba **91** F 4
Kåbdalis **54** G 2
Kabinda **92** CD 6
Kabīr Kūh **61** E 2
Kabo **92** B 3
Kabompo **94** C 2
Kabondo Dianda **92** D 6
Kabud Rāhang **61** E 2
Kabul **67** HJ 4
Kabwe **94** D 2
Kachikattsy **69** NO 3
Kachin **73** G 2
Kachug **68** J 5
Kadirli **59** E 3
Kadiyevka **59** E 1
Kadoma **94** D 3
Kâduglī **88** D 6
Kaduna **91** F 3
Kaédi **86** C 5
Kafue **94** D 2
Kafue **94** D 3
Kafue National Park **94** D 3
Kafura **92** E 5
Kagoshima **71** JK 4
Kagul **58** C 1
Kahemba **92** B 6
Kahoolawe **83** E 1
Kahramanmaras **59** E 3
Kai, Kepulauan **75** H 5
Kaifeng **70** FG 4
Kaikoura **81** Q 9
Kaili **70** E 5
Kailu **71** H 2
Kaimur Range **72** D 3
Kainantu **80** E 3
Kainji Dam **91** EF 4
Kainji Reservoir **91** E 3
Kaintragarh **72** DE 3
Kairouan → Al Qayrawān **87** GH 1
Kaiserslautern **53** E 5
Kai Xian **70** E 4
Kaiyuan **70** D 6
Kajaki Dam **67** H 4
Kakhovka **59** D 1
Kakhovskoye Vodokhranilishche **59** DE 1
Kākī **61** F 3
Kakinada **72** D 4
Kakisa **99** O 3
Kaktovik **98** J 1
Kalabagh **67** J 4
Kalach **62** H 5
Kalachinsk **63** OP 4
Kalahari **94** C 4
Kalahari Gemsbok National Park **94** BC 5
Kalai-Khumb **67** J 3
Kalajoki **54** H 3
Kalámai **58** B 3
Kalaong **75** F 2
Kalbarri National Park **78** A 4
Kaldbakur **54** A 2
Kalehe **92** D 5
Kalemie **92** CD 6
Kalevala **54** K 2
Kalewa **73** F 3
Kalga **68** L 5
Kalgoorlie **78** C 5
Kalimantan **74** DE 3
Kalinin **62** FG 4
Kaliningrad **55** H 5
Kalisz **53** G 4
Kalixälven **54** H 2
Kallsjön **54** F 3
Kalmar **55** G 4
Kalmykovo **66** E 1
Kaloko **92** D 6
Kalole **92** D 5
Kalsubai **72** B 4
Kaltag **98** F 3
Kaluga **62** FG 5
Kamaishi **71** M 3
Kamanjab **94** B 3
Kamarān **89** G 5
Kamaria Falls **109** FG 2
Kambal'naya Sopka **69** T 5
Kamchatka **69** T 4
Kamchatka Peninsula **114**
Kamenets-Podolskiy **58** C 1
Kamenjak, Rt **57** F 3
Kamen-na-Obi **63** PQ 5
Kamensk-Ural'skiy **63** M 4
Kamet **72** D 1
Kamina **92** D 6
Kamkaly **67** J 2
Kamloops **99** N 5
Kamnrokan **68** K 4
Kampala **92** E 4–5
Kampar **74** B 3
Kampar, Sungai **74** B 3
Kampot **74** B 1
Kampuchea **73** HJ 5
Kamsack **99** R 5
Kamyshin **62** HJ 5
Kanaaupscow **101** M 5
Kanaga **98** B 5
Kananga **92** C 6
Kanangra Boyd National Park **79** HJ 5
Kanazawa **71** KL 3
Kanchipuram **72** CD 5
Kandagach **66** F 1
Kandahar **67** H 4
Kandalaksha **54** K 2
Kandalakshskaya Guba **54** K 2
Kandangan **74** DE 4
Kandavu **82** C 4
Kande **90** E 4
Kandi **90** E 3
Kandy **72** D 6
Kandychan **69** RS 3
Kanem **91** GH 3
Kangalassy **69** N 3
Kangan **61** F 4
Kangar **74** B 2
Kangaroo Island **79** F 6
Kangāvar **61** E 2
Kangchenjunga **72** E 2
Kangding **70** D 5
Kangean, Kepulauan **74** E 5
Kangeeak Point **101** P 2
Kanggye **71** J 2
Kangmar **72** DE 1
Kangnŭng **71** JK 3
Kango **91** G 5
Kangping **71** H 2
Kangynin **98** B 2
Kaniama **92** C 6
Kaniet Islands **82** A 3
Kankan **90** C 3
Kankesanturai **72** D 5–6
Kankossa **86** C 5
Kanmaw Kyun **73** G 5
Kannapolis **103** K 4
Kano **91** F 3
Kanovlei **94** B 3
Kansas **102** G 4
Kansas City **103** H 4
Kansk **68** FG 4
Kantang **73** G 6
Kantaralak **73** HJ 5
Kantchari **90** E 3
Kanye **94** CD 4
Kaohsiung **71** GH 6
Kaolack **90** A 3
Kaoma **94** C 2
Kaouar **91** G 2
Kapanga **92** C 6
Kapatu **95** E 1
Kap Brewster **114**
Kapchagay **67** K 2
Kapchagayskoye Vodokhranilishche **67** K 2
Kap Farvel **101** T 4
Kapfenberg **57** G 2
Kapingamarangi **82** B 2
Kapiri Moposhi **94** DE 2
Kapisigdlit **101** RS 3
Kapona **92** D 6
Kaposvár **58** A 1
Kapsukas **55** H 5
Kapustoye **54** K 2
Karabekaul **67** GH 3
Karabük **59** D 2
Karabutak **66** F 1
Karachi **67** H 6
Kara Dağ **59** D 3
Karaga **69** U 4
Karaganda **63** OP 6
Karagüney Dağları **59** DE 2
Karaikkudi **72** C 6
Karaj **61** F 2
Kara-Kala **66** F 3
Karakelong, Pulau **75** G 3
Karakoram **67** JK 3–4
Karakorum Shankou **67** JK 3–4
Karaköse **59** F 3
Karalundi **78** B 4
Karam **68** J 4
Karamagay **67** M 1
Karaman **59** D 3
Karamay **67** LM 1
Karasburg **94** B 5
Kara Sea **114**
Karasjåkka **54** H 2
Karasu (Turkey) **59** F 2–3
Karasu-Aras Dağları **59** F 3
Karasuk **63** P 5
Karatal **63** P 6
Karatau **67** J 2
Karathuri **73** G 5
Karatogay **66** F 1
Karaton **66** E 1
Karaul **63** Q 1
Karaulkel'dy **66** EF 1
Karazhingil **63** O 6
Karbalā' **60** D 2
Kardhitsa **58** B 3
Kärdla **55** H 4
Kareliya **54** K 3
Karen **73** G 4
Karesuando **54** H 2
Karganay **69** X 2
Kargat **63** Q 4
Kargopol' **62** G 3
Kari **91** G 3

Kariba Dam **94** D 3
Karibib **94** B 4
Karikal **72** CD 5
Karimata, Selat **74** C 4
Karimganj **73** F 2
Karisimbi **92** D 5
Karjala **54** K 3
Karkār **80** E 2
Karkas, Kūh-e **61** F 2
Karkinitskiy Zaliv **59** D 1
Karleby **54** H 3
Karlik Shan **70** BC 2
Karl-Marx-Stadt **53** F 4
Karlovac **57** G 2
Karlovy Vary **53** F 4
Karlshamn **55** FG 4
Karlskoga **55** FG 4
Karlskrona **55** G 4
Karlsruhe **53** E 5
Karlstad (MN, U.S.A.) **103** G 2
Karlstad (Sweden) **55** F 4
Karmöy **55** DE 4
Karnataka **72** BC 4
Karong **73** F 2
Karonga **95** E 1
Kárpathos **58** C 3
Kars **59** F 2
Karsakpay **67** H 1
Karshi **67** H 3
Karskiye Vorota, Proliv **62–63** L 1
Karskoye More **63** LM 1
Kars Platosu **59** F 2
Kartal **58** C 2
Kartaly **63** LM 5
Karufa **75** H 4
Karwar **72** B 5
Kasai **92** B 5
Kasai Occidental **92** C 6
Kasai Oriental **92** C 5–6
Kasaji **94** C 2
Kasama **95** E 2
Kasba Lake **99** R 3
Kāshān **61** F 2
Kashi **67** K 3
Kashken Teniz **63** O 6
Kāshmar **66** F 3
Kasimov **62** H 5
Kaskelen **67** K 2
Kas Kong **73** H 5
Kasongo **92** D 5
Kásos **58** C 3
Kaspiyskiy **59** G 1
Kaspiyskoye More **66** D 1
Kassalā **88** F 5
Kassándra **58** B 2
Kassel **53** E 4
Kastamonu **59** D 2
Kasungu **95** E 2
Katako-Kombe **92** CD 5
Katangli **69** Q 5
Katawaz **67** H 4
Katende Falls **92** C 6
Katerini **58** B 2
Katherine **78** E 1
Katherine Gorge National Park **78** E 1
Kathiawar **72** B 3
Kathīri **89** H 5
Kathmandu **72** E 2
Katihar **72** E 2
Katmai National Park and Preserve **98** G 4
Katowice **53** G H 4
Kātrīna, Jabal **60** AB 3
Katrineholm **55** G 4
Katsina **91** F 3
Kattegat **55** F 4
Katyl'ga **63** P 4
Kauai **83** E 1
Kaufbeuren **53** F 5
Kaunas **55** H 5
Kauno Marios **55** H 5
Kavalerovo **71** KL 2
Kavála **58** B 2
Kavar **61** F 3
Kavendou, Mont **90** B 3
Kavīr, Dasht-e **61** FG 2
Kavir-e Abarqu **61** F 3
Kavir-e Namak **61** G 1
Kawa **88** E 5
Kawich Peak **102** CD 4
Kawm Umbū **88** E 4
Kaya **90** D 3
Kayah **73** G 4
Kayak **98** J 4
Kayala **54** K 3
Kayan **74** E 3
Kayes **90** B 3
Kaynar **63** P 6
Kayseri **59** DE 3
Kazachinskoye **68** J 4
Kazakhskiy Melkosopochnik **63** NP 6
Kazakhstan **67** FH 1
Kazan' **62** JK 4
Kazan Islands **65** QR 7
Kazanlŭk **58** C 2
Kazanskoye **63** NO 4
Kazbek **59** F 2
Kaz Dağı **58** C 3
Kāzerūn **61** F 3
Kazymskaya **63** N 3
Kazymskiy Mys **63** MN 3
Kazzān ar Ruṣayriṣ **88** E 6
Keams Canyon **102** D 4
Keban Gölü **59** E 3
Kebbi **91** E 3
Kebnekaise **54** G 2
Kediat Idjil **86** C 4
Kediri **74** D 5
Kédougou **90** B 3
Keetmanshoop **94** B 5
Kefa **93** F 3
Kefallinía **58** B 3
Keimoes **94** C 5
Keitele **54** J 3
Keith **79** FG 6
Keketa **80** D 3
Kelang **74** B 3
Keli Hājī Ibrāhīm **61** D 1
Kelkit **59** E 2
Kellett, Cape **99** M 1
Kellog (U.S.S.R.) **63** R 3
Kellogg **102** C 2
Kelloselkä **54** J 2
Kelsey **99** S 4
Kelsey Bay **99** MN 5
Keluang **74** B 3
Kem' **54** K 3
Ké Macina **90** CD 3
Kemerovo **63** QR 4
Kemi **54** HJ 2
Kemijärvi **54** J 2
Kemijoki **54** J 2
Kemkra **69** P 4
Kempendyayi **68** LM 3
Kemps Bay **105** G 3
Kempsey **79** J 5
Kenai **98** G 3–4
Kenai Fjords National Park **98** H 4
Kenai Mountains **98** G 3–4
Kenai Peninsula **98** GH 4
Kencha **69** PQ 3
Kendari **75** F 4
Kenhardt **94** C 5
Kenitra **86** D 2
Keniut **69** X 3
Kenmare **102** F 2
Kennedy Range National Park **78** B 3
Keno Hill **98** L 3
Kenora **100** KJ 6
Kentau **67** H 2
Kent Peninsula **99** Q 2
Kentucky **103** JK 4
Kentucky Lake **103** J 4
Kenya **93** F 4–5
Kenya, Mount **93** F 5
Kepe **54** K 2
Kepulauan Anambas **74** C 3
Kepulauan Aru **75** HJ 5
Kepulauan Babar **75** GH 5
Kepulauan Banggai **75** F 4
Kepulauan Kai **75** H 5
Kepulauan Kangean **74** E 5
Kepulauan Leti **75** G 5
Kepulauan Lingga **74** BC 3–4
Kepulauan Mentawai **74** AB 4
Kepulauan Natuna **74** C 3
Kepulauan Riau **74** B 3
Kepulauan Sangihe **75** G 3
Kepulauan Sula **75** FG 4
Kepulauan Talaud **75** G 3
Kepulauan Tanimbar **75** H 5
Kepulauan Tenggara **75** G 5
Kepulauan Togian **75** F 4
Kepulauan Tukangbesi **75** F 5
Kerama-rettō **71** J 5
Kerch **59** E 1
Kerchenskiy Proliv **59** E 1–2
Kerekhtyakh **69** N 3
Kerema **80** E 3
Kerempe Burnu **59** D 2
Keren **93** F 1
Keret', Ozero **54** K 2
Keriske **69** O 2
Kerki **67** GH 3
Kérkira **58** AB 3
Kermadec Islands **82** D 4–5
Kermān **66** F 4
Kermanshāh **61** E 2
Kermānshāhān **61** G 3
Kerme Körfezi **58** C 3
Kerzaz **86** E 3
Kestenga **54** K 2
Ketoy, Ostrov **69** S 6
Keul' **68** H 4
Keurusselkä **54** HJ 3
Kewanee **103** J 3
Keyano **101** N 5
Key West **103** L 7
Kezhma **68** H 4
Khabarovsk **69** P 6
Khabr, Kūh-e **61** G 3
Khabūr **60** C 1
Khachmas **66** D 2
Khafjī, Ra's al **61** E 3
Khaipur **67** H 5
Khairpur **67** J 5
Khakhea **94** C 4
Khakriz **67** GH 4
Khalesavoy **63** PQ 3
Khalīj al 'Aqabah **60** B 3
Khalīj al 'Aqabah **88** E 3
Khalīj as Suways **60** A 3
Khalīj Maṣīrah **89** K 5
Khalīj Qābis **87** H 2
Khálki **58** C 3
Khalkidhiki **58** B 2
Khalkis **58** B 3
Khambhat, Gulf of **72** B 3–4
Khamgaon **72** C 3
Khampa **68** L 3
Khampa **69** M 3
Khamseh **61** E 1
Khanabad **67** HJ 3
Khandwa **72** C 3
Khandyga **69** P 3
Khanglasy **63** M 3
Khanh Hung **73** HJ 6
Khani **68** M 4
Khánia **58** B 3
Khanpur **67** J 5
Khān Shaykhūn **60** B 2
Khantau **67** J 2
Khanty-Mansiysk **63** NO 3
Khanyangda **69** Q 4
Khanyardakh **69** N 3
Khao Lang **73** G 6
Khao Luang **73** G 6
Khao Sai Dao Tai **73** H 5
Khappyrastakh **69** M 4
Khara **68** G 5
Kharagpur **72** E 3
Kharan **67** GH 5
Kharānaq **61** G 2
Kharānaq, Kūh-e **61** G 2
Kharik **68** H 5
Khārk **61** F 3
Kharkov **62** G 5
Kharoti **67** H 4
Kharstan **69** Q 1
Khasavyurt **59** G 2
Khash (Afghanistan) **67** G 4
Khāsh (Iran) **67** G 5
Khash Desert **67** G 4
Khashm Mishraq **66** D 6
Khaskovo **58** C 2
Khatanga **68** H 1
Khatangskiy Zaliv **68** JK 1

Khataren **69** T 3
Khatyrka **69** X 3
Khawr al Fakkān **61** G 4
Khaybar **60** C 4
Khaybar, Harrat **60** C 4
Khazzān Jabal al Awliyā' **88** E 5–6
Khe Bo **73** HJ 4
Khenifra **86** D 2
Kherpuchi **69** P 5
Khersan **61** F 3
Kherson **59** D 1
Kheta **68** G 1
Kheta **68** H 1
Kheyrābād **66** EF 5
Khibiny **54** K 2
Khíos **58** C 3
Khíos **58** C 3
Khirbat Isriyah **60** BC 2
Khmel'nitskiy **62** E 6
Khodzheyli **66** F 2
Khoe **69** P 6
Khok Kloi **73** G 6
Kholmsk **69** Q 6
Khomeyn **61** F 2
Khongo **69** S 3
Khon Kaen **73** H 4
Khor Anghar **93** G 2
Khorāsān **66** F 4
Khorat Plateau **73** H 4
Khordogoy **68** L 3
Khoronnokh **68** LM 2
Khorramābād **61** E 2
Khorramshahr **61** E 3
Khorsābād **60** D 1
Khosrowābād **61** E 3
Khrebet Bureinskiy **69** O 5
Khrebet Chayatyn **69** P 5
Khrebet Cherskogo **69** P 1–2
Khrebet Dzhagdy **69** O 5
Khrebet Dzhugdzhur **69** OP 4
Khrebet Khugdyungda **68** G 2
Khrebet Kolymskiy **69** SU 3
Khrebet Koryakskiy **69** VW 3
Khrebet Nuratau **67** H 2
Khrebet Pay-Khoy **63** M 2
Khrebet Sette Daban **69** PQ 3–4
Khrebet Suntar Khayata **69** PQ 3
Khrebet Turana **69** O 5
Khudzhakh **69** R 3
Khugdyungda, Khrebet **68** G 2
Khulkhuta **59** G 1
Khulna **72** E 3
Khurayş **61** E 4
Khurayt **88** D 6
Khurr, Wādī al **60** C 3
Khurramshahr **61** E 3
Khursanīyah **61** E 4
Khuzdar **67** H 5
Khūzestān **61** E 3
Khvāf **66** FG 4
Khvojeh, Kūh-e **61** E 2
Khvor **61** G 2
Khvormūj **61** F 3
Khvoy **66** D 3
Kiambi **92** D 6
Kiantajärvi **54** J 2
Kibangou **91** G 6
Kibwezi **93** F 5
Kichi Kichi **91** H 2
Kidal **90** E 2
Kidira **90** B 3
Kiel **53** F 4
Kielce **53** H 4
Kieta **81** G 3
Kiffa **86** C 5
Kigali **92** E 5
Kigilyakh **69** P 1
Kigoma **92** D 5
Kihnu **55** H 4
Kikiakki **63** Q 3
Kikladhes **58** BC 3
Kikori **82** A 3
Kikwit **92** B 6
Kilambé **104** E 5
Kilbuck Mountains **98** F 3
Kilchu **71** J 2
Kil'din, Ostrov **54** K 2
Kili **82** C 2
Kılıç Dağları **58** C 3
Kilimanjaro **93** F 5
Kilindini **93** F 5
Kilis **59** E 3
Kiliya **58** C 2
Killarney **52** AB 4
Killeen **102** G 5
Killinek **101** O 3
Killini Óros **58** B 3
Kilmarnock **52** C 3
Kilmez **62** K 4
Kil'mez' **62** K 4
Kilosa **93** F 6
Kilpisjärvi **54** H 2
Kilp-Javr **54** K 2
Kilwa **92** D 6
Kilwa Masoko **93** F 6
Kimball, Mount **98** J 3
Kimbe Bay **81** F 3
Kimberley (South Africa) **94** CD 5
Kimberley (Western Australia) **78** D 2
Kimberley Plateau **78** D 2
Kimch'aek **71** JK 2
Kimito **55** H 3
Kimparana **90** CD 3
Kinabalu, Gunung **74** E 2
Kinchega National Park **79** G 5
Kinda **92** C 6
Kindia **90** B 4
Kindu **92** D 5
King **80** K 8
King Christian IX Land **114**
King Christian X Land **114**
King Frederik VI-Coast **114**
King Frederik VIII Land **114**
Kingissepp (Estoniya, U.S.S.R.)**55** H 4
King Leopold Ranges **78** CD 2
Kingman (AZ, U.S.A.) **102** D 4
Kingman (Pacific Ocean, U.S.A.) **82** E 2
Kingoonya **79** F 5
Kingsmill Group **82** C 3
King Sound **78** C 2
Kings Peak **102** DE 3
Kingsport **103** K 4
Kingston (Canada) **101** M 7
Kingston (Jamaica) **105** G 4
Kingston (Norfolk Is., Austr.) **82** C 4
Kingston-upon-Hull **52** C 4
Kingstown **105** K 5
Kingsville **102** G 6
King William Island **99** S 2
King Williams Town **94** D 6
Kinkala **91** G 6
Kinmaw **73** F 4
Kinnairds Head **52** C 3
Kinoosao **99** R 4
Kinshasa **92** B 5
Kipaka **92** D 5
Kipushi **94** D 2
Kirakira **82** B 3
Kirbey **68** H 2
Kirbey **68** K 2
Kirensk **68** J 4
Kirghiz Steppe **63** LM 6
Kirgiziya **67** JK 2
Kirgiz Step' **66–67** FH 1
Kiribati **82** DE 3
Kırıkhan **59** E 3
Kırıkkale **59** D 3
Kirillovka **59** E 1
Kirimati **83** E 2
Kirishi **55** K 4
Kirkenes **54** J 2
Kirkjubæjarklaustur **54** B 3
Kırklareli **58** C 2
Kirkpatrick, Mount **115**
Kirksville **103** H 3
Kirkūk **60** D 2
Kirkwall **52** C 3
Kirkwood **103** H 4
Kirov **62** JK 4
Kirov **62** FG 5
Kirovabad **66** D 2
Kirovakan **59** FG 2
Kirovo Chepetsk **62** K 4
Kirovograd **59** D 1
Kirovsk **54** K 2
Kırşehir **59** D 2–3
Kiruna **54** H 2
Kisangani **92** D 4
Kishinev **58** C 1
Kisii **92** E 5
Kısılırmak **59** D 2
Kiska **98** A 5
Kislovodsk **59** F 2
Kismāyu **93** G 5
Kisoro **92** DE 5
Kissidougou **90** BC 4
Kisumu **92** E 5
Kita **90** C 3
Kitakyushū **71** JK 4
Kitale **92** F 4
Kitami **71** M 2
Kitchener **101** L 7
Kitgum **92** E 4
Kíthira **58** B 3
Kithnos **58** B 3
Kitwe **94** D 2
Kiunga **80** D 3
Kivak **98** C 3
Kivijärvi **54** HJ 3
Kiviōli **55** J 4
Kivu **92** D 5
Kiyev **62** F 5
Kizel **63** L 4
Kızıl Dağ **59** D 3
Kızılırmak **62** E 3
Kizlyar **59** G 2
Kizlyarskiy Zaliv **59** G 2
Kizyl-Arvat **66** F 3
Kizyl-Atrek **66** E 3
Kjöllefjord **54** J 1
Klagenfurt **57** FG 2
Klaipėda **55** H 4
Klamath Falls **102** B 3
Klarälven **55** F 3
Klerksdorp **94** D 5
Klintsy **62** F 5
Klit **55** E 4
Kłodzko **53** G 4
Klotz, Lac **101** NO 3
Kluane National Park **98** K 3
Klukhorskiy Pereval **59** F 2
Klyuchr **69** U 4
Knosós **58** C 3
Knox Coast **115**
Knoxville **103** K 4
Knud Rasmussen Land **114**
Kōbe **71** KL 3–4
Köbenhavn **55** F 4
Kobenni **86** CD 5
Koblenz **53** E 4
Koboldo **69** O 5
Kobrin **55** H 5
Kobroor, Pulau **75** H 5
Kobuk **98** F 2
Kobuk Valley National Park **98** F 2
Koca Çal **59** D 3
Kocaeli **58** CD 2
Kocasu **58** C 3
Koch **101** M 2
Ko Chang **73** H 5
Kōchi **71** K 4
Kochikha **68** G 1
Kodi **75** E 5
Kodiak **98** G 4
Kodiak Island **98** G 4
Kodima **62** H 3
Kodžha Balkan **58** C 2
Kōes **94** B 5
Koforidua **90** D 4
Kohistan **67** J 3
Kohlu **67** H 5
Kohtla-Järve **55** J 4
Kokalaat **67** GH 1
Kokand **67** HJ 2
Kokchetav **63** N 5
Kokkola **54** H 3
Kokomo **103** J 3
Kokpekty **63** Q 6
Koksoak **101** O 4
Kokstad **94** D 6
Koktuma **63** Q 6

Ko Kut **73** H 5
Kola **54** K 2
Kolai **67** J 3
Kola Peninsula **62** G 2
Kolar **72** C 5
Kolar Gold Fields **72** C 5
Kolbachi **69** M 5
Kolbio **93** G 5
Kolding **55** E 4
Kolesovo **69** S 1
Kolhapur **72** B 4
Koli **54** J 3
Kolkasrags **55** H 4
Kollumúli **54** C 2
Köln **53** E 4
Kołobrzeg **53** G 4
Kolombangara **81** G 3
Kolomna **62** GH 4
Kolomyya **58** C 1
Kolpakovsky **69** T 5
Kolpashevo **63** QR 4
Koluton **63** N 5
Kolwezi **94** D 2
Kolyma **69** TU 2
Kolyma Range **69** U 3
Kolymskaya **69** UV 2
Kolymskaya Nizmennost' **69** ST 2
Kolymskiy, Khrebet **69** SU 3
Kolymskoye Nagor'ye **69** S 3
Kolyvan' **63** Q 5
Komárno **53** G 5
Komba **92** C 4
Kombolchia **93** FG 2
Komelek **69** O 3
Kommunarsk **59** E 1
Komotini **58** C 2
Kompas Berg **94** C 6
Kompong Cham **73** J 5
Kompong Chhnang **73** HJ 5
Kompong Som **73** H 5
Kompot **75** F 3
Komsomol'sk-na-Amure **69** P 5
Kona **90** D 3
Kondakova **69** T 2
Kondinin **78** B 5
Kondoa **93** F 5
Kondon **69** P 5
Kondut **78** B 5
Konevo **62** GH 3
Kong Frederik VI-Kyst **101** T 3
Kongola **94** C 3
Kongolo **92** D 6
Kongor **92** E 3
Kongsvinger **55** F 3
Konin **53** G 4
Konkan **72** B 4
Konkudera **68** K 4
Konosha **62** H 3
Konotop **62** F 5
Konstantinovka **59** E 1
Konstanz **53** E 5
Kontagora **91** F 3
Kontcha **91** G 4
Kontiomäki **54** J 3
Konya **59** D 3
Konya Ovası **59** D 3
Kooch Bihar **72** E 2
Kootenay National Park **99** OP 5
Kópasker **54** B 2
Kopeysk **63** M 5
Ko Phangan **73** H 6
Ko Phuket **73** G 6
Köping **55** G 4
Korba **72** D 3
Korça **58** B 2
Korčula **57** G 3
Kordestān **61** E 2
Kord Kūy **61** G 1
Korea Strait **71** J 4
Korenovsk **59** E 1
Korfovskiy **69** P 6
Korhogo **90** C 4
Korinthiakos Kólpos **58** B 3
Kórinthos **58** B 3
Koriolei **93** G 4
Kōriyama **71** M 3
Korkodon **69** ST 3
Korla **67** M 2
Kormakiti Bur **60** A 2
Koro **82** C 4
Köroğlu Dağları **59** D 2
Korosten **55** J 5
Koro Toro **91** H 2
Korovin Volcano **98** C 5
Korsakov **69** Q 6
Korsfjorden **55** DE 3
Korshunovo **68** K 4
Koryakskiy Khrebet **69** VW 3
Kos **58** C 3
Kosa Fedotova **59** E 1
Košice **53** H 5
Kosŏng **71** J 3
Kosovska Mitrovica **58** B 2
Kossou, Lac de **90** CD 4
Kostino **63** R 2
Kostroma **62** H 4
Koszalin **53** G 4
Kota **72** C 2
Kotabumi **74** BC 4
Kota Kinabalu **74** DE 2
Kotel'nich **62** J 4
Kotel'nikovo **59** F 1
Kotel'nyy, Ostrov **69** P 1
Kotikovo **69** QR 6
Kotka **55** J 3
Kotlas **62** J 3
Kotlik **98** E 3
Kotovsk **58** CD 1
Kotu Group **82** D 4
Kotuy **68** H 1
Kotzebue Sound **98** E 2
Koudougou **90** D 3
Koulen **73** HJ 5
Koumac **81** H 6
Koumbi-Saleh **86** D 5
Koundara **90** B 3
Koundian **90** B 3
Koungheul **90** AB 3
Kourou **109** H 2
Koutous **91** FG 3
Kouvola **54** J 3
Kova **68** H 4
Kovac **58** A 2
Kovel' **55** H 5
Kovrizhka **69** U 3
Kovrov **62** GH 4
Kowloon **70** FG 6
Kowt-e-Ashrow **67** H 4
Koyuk **98** E 2
Koyukuk **98** F 2
Kozáni **58** B 2
Kozlu **59** D 2
Kozyrevsk **69** TU 4
Kragujevac **58** B 2
Krakow **53** GH 4
Kraljevo **58** B 2
Kramfors **54** G 3
Kranj **57** F 2
Krasino **62** K 1
Krasnaya Yaranga **98** C 2
Kraśnik **53** H 4
Krasnodar **59** EF 1–2
Krasnogorsk **69** Q 6
Krasnoje Selo **55** JK 4
Krasnokamsk **62** KL 4
Krasnotur'insk **63** M 4
Krasnoural'sk **63** M 4
Krasnovodsk **66** E 2
Krasnoyarsk **68** F 4
Krasnoyarskiy **63** L 5
Krasnyy Chikoy **68** J 5
Krasnyy Luch **59** E 1
Kremenchug **62** FG 6
Kresti **62** F 4
Krestovka **62** K 2
Kresty **68** E 1
Kribi **91** F 5
Krichev **62** F 5
Krishna **72** C 4
Kristiansand **55** E 4
Kristianstad **55** F 4
Kristiansund **54** E 3
Kristineberg **54** G 2
Kristinehamn **55** F 4
Kristinestad **54** H 3
Kríti **58** B 3
Kritikón Pélagos **58** BC 3
Krivoy Rog **59** D 1
Krk **57** F 2
Krnov **53** G 4
Krokom **54** F 3
Kronotsi **69** U 5
Kronotskaya Sopka **69** TU 5
Kronshtadt **55** J 4
Kroonstad **94** D 5
Kropotkin **59** F 1
Krosno **53** H 5
Krotoszyn **53** G 4
Kruger National Park **95** E 4
Krugersdorp **94** D 5
Krung Thep **73** H 5
Kruševac **58** B 2
Krutinka **63** O 4
Kryazh Kula **69** O 2
Krym (Ukraine, U.S.S.R.) **59** D 1
Krymsk **59** E 1
Krymskiye Gory **59** D 2
Ksabi **86** E 3
Ksar Chellala **87** F 1
Ksar el Boukhari **87** F 1
Ksar Torchane **86** C 4
Ksen'yevka **68** L 5
Kuala Lumpur **74** B 3
Kuala Terengganu **74** B 2
Kuamut **74** E 2
Kuantan **74** B 3
Kuban' **59** E 1–2
Kubenskoye, Ozero **62** G 4
Kudus **74** D 5
Kudymkar **62** KI 4
Kufstein **57** F 2
Kūh-e ʿAlīābād **61** F 2
Kūh-e Alījūq **61** F 3
Kūh-e Alvano **61** E 2
Kūh-e Būl **61** F 3
Kūh-e Dīnār **61** F 3
Kūh-e Garbosh **61** EF 2
Kūh-e Garri **61** E 2
Kūh-e Gūgerd **61** F 2
Kūh-e Karkas **61** F 2
Kūh-e Khabr **61** G 3
Kūh-e Khāīz **61** F 3
Kūh-e Kharānaq **61** G 2
Kūh-e Khvojeh **61** E 2
Kūh-e Kūkalār **61** F 3
Kūh-e Masāhīm **61** G 3
Kūh-e Safīd **61** E 2
Kūh-e Sorkh **61** G 2
Kūhestak **66** F 5
Kūh-e Tābask **61** F 3
Kūhhā-ye Qorūd **61** F 2–3
Kūhhā-ye-Sabalān **66** D 3
Kūhha ye Zagros **61** EF 2–F 3
Kuikkavaara **54** J 3
Kui Nua **74** AB 1
Kuito **94** B 2
Kuivaniemi **54** J 2
Kujani Game Reserve **90** D 4
Kuji **71** M 2
Kula Kangri **73** F 2
Kulakshi **66** EF 1
Kulaneh **67** G 5
Kul'chi **69** P 5
Kulgera **78** E 4
Kulinda **68** J 3
Kullen **55** F 4
Kul'sary **66** E 1
Kulundinskaya Step' **63** P 5
Kulyab **67** HJ 3
Kuma (Russia, U.S.S.R.) **59** G 2
Kumai, Teluk **74** D 4
Kumamoto **71** K 4
Kumanovo **58** B 2
Kumasi **90** D 4
Kumba **91** F 5
Kumbakonam **72** CD 5
Kumdah **89** H 4
Kumertau **62** KL 5
Kūnas **67** L 2
Kunashir **71** N 2
Kunda Hills **72** C 5
Kunduz **67** H 3
Kunene **94** A 3
Kungälv **55** F 4
Kungrad **66** F 2
Kungu **92** B 4
Kungur **62** L 4

Kunlun Shan **67** KM 3
Kunlun Shankou **70** B 3
Kunming **70** D 5
Kunsan **71** J 3
Kuntuk **69** R 4
Kununurra **78** D 2
Kuop **82** B 2
Kuopio **54** J 3
Kuoqiang **70** A 3
Kuorboaivi **54** J 2
Kuoyka **68** LM 1
Kupang **75** F 6
Kupreanof **98** L 4
Kupyansk **62** G 6
Kuqa **67** L 2
Kura **59** G 2
Kurashiki **71** K 3–4
Kurdufān **88** DE 6
Kŭrdžhali **58** C 2
Kure **71** K 4
Kurgan **63** N 4
Kurgan-Tyube **67** H 3
Kuria **82** C 2
Kuria Muria Islands **89** K 5
Kuril Islands **69** S 6
Kurilovka **62** J 5
Kuril'skiye Ostrova (U.S.S.R) **69** RS 6
Kurmuk **88** E 6
Kurnool **72** C 4
Kursk **62** G 5
Kurşunlu Dağı **59** E 3
Kuruman (South Africa) **94** C 5
Kuruman (South Africa) **94** C 5
Kurunegala **72** D 6
Kurupka **98** C 3
Kurzeme **55** H 4
Kuşada Körfezi **58** C 3
Kusaie **82** B 2
Kushchevskaya **59** E 1
Kushiro **71** MN 2
Kushka **67** G 3
Kushmurun **63** MN 5
Kuskokwim **98** E 3
Kuskokwim Bay **98** E 4
Kuskokwim Mountains **98** FG 3
Kustanay **63** M 5
Kūstī **88** E 6
Kut **61** E 3
Kütahya **58** C 3
Kutai, Sungai **74** E 4
Kutaisi **66** C 2
Kutch **72** AB 3
Kutch, Gulf of **72** A 3
Kutch, Rann of **72** AB 3
Kutno **53** G 4
Kuvango **94** B 2
Kuwait **61** E 3
Kuwait **61** E 3
Kuybyshev **62** K 5
Kuybyshev **63** PQ 4
Kuybyshevo **69** R 6
Kuybyshevskoye Vodokhranilishche **62** J 5
Kuygan **63** O 6
Kūysanjaq **66** C 3
Kuytun, Gora **63** R 6
Kuyucuk Dağı **58** D 3
Kuyumba **68** G 3
Kuznetsk **62** J 5
Kvænangen **54** H 1
Kvalöy **54** G 2
Kvalöya **54** H 1
Kvarner **57** F 2–3
Kvarnerič **57** F 3
Kverkfjol **54** B 3
Kvichak Bay **98** F 4
Kvikkjokk **54** G 2
Kwajalein **82** C 2
Kwakoegron **109** G 2
Kwangju **71** J 3
Kwethluk **98** E 3
Kwoka, Gunung **75** H 4
Kyakhta **68** J 5
Kyancutta **79** F 5
Kyaukme **73** G 3
Kyeintali **73** F 4
Kyle of Lochalsh **52** B 3
Kynnefjell **55** F 4
Kyōto **71** KL 3
Kyrbykan **69** N 3
Kyren **68** H J 5
Kyrgyday **69** M 3
Kyrta **62** L 3
Kyrynniky **68** L 3
Kyshtovka **63** P 4
Kyshtym **63** M 4
Kystatam **68** M 2
Kytalyktakh **69** OP 2
Kyuekh-Bulung **68** KL 2
Kyushe **66** F 1
Kyūshū **71** K 4
Kyustendil **58** B 2
Kyusyur **69** N 1
Kyzas **63** RS 5
Kyzultau **63** O 6
Kyzyl **68** FG 5
Kyzyldyykan **67** H 1
Kyzylkum, Peski **67** G 2
Kyzyluy **67** H 1
Kzyl-Orda **67** H 2
Kzyltu **63** O 5

L

La Banda **112** D 4
Labbezenga **90** E 2
Labé **90** B 3
Labengke, Pulau **75** F 4
Labinsk **59** F 2
Labrador **101** NP 4
Labrador City **101** O 5
Labrador Sea **101** QR 4
Lábrea **109** F 5
Labuhanbajo **75** EF 5
Labytnangi **63** N 2
Lac Alaotra **95** H 3
Lac Albanel **101** N 5
Lac à l'Eau-Claire **101** MN 4
La Carlota **112** D 5
Lac au Goéland **101** M 5–6
Lac Bienville **101** N 4
Laccadive Islands **72** B 5
Lac Caniapiscau **101** O 5
Lac Champdoré **101** O 4
Lac Débo **90** CD 2
Lac de Gras **99** P 3
Lac de Kossou **90** CD 4
Lac d'Iberville **101** N 4
La Ceiba **104** E 4
Lacepede Bay **79** F 6
Lachlan River **79** GH 5
La Chorrera **108** BC 2
Lac Klotz **101** NO 3
Lac la Martre **99** O 3
Lac la Ronge **99** R 4
Lac Léman **57** E 2
Lac Mai-Ndombe **92** B 5
Lac Maunoir **99** MN 2
Lac Minto **101** N 4
Lac Mistassini **101** N 5
Lac Moero **92** D 6
Lac Naococane **101** N 5
La Coronilla **112** F 5
La Coruña **56** B 3
La Crosse **103** H 3
La Cruz **102** E 7
Lac Sakami **101** M 5
Lac Seul **100** J 5
Lac Upemba **92** D 6
La Digue **93** K 5
Ladoga, Lake **54** K 3
La Dorada **108** D 2
Ladozhskoye Ozero **54** K 3
Ladysmith **94** D 5
Lae (Marshall Is.) **82** C 2
Lae (Papua New Guinea) **80** E 3
Læsö **55** F 4
La Estrada **56** B 3
Lafayette (IN, U.S.A.) **103** J 3
Lafayette (LA, U.S.A.) **103** H 5–6
Lafia **91** F 4
Lafiagi **91** EF 4
La Fría **108** D 2
Lagarto **111** J 3
Laghouat **87** F 2
Lagoa dos Patos **112** F 5
Lago Agrio **108** C 4
Lagoa Mangueira **112** F 5
Lagoa Mirim **112** F 5
Lago Buenos Aires **113** B 8
Lago Cabora Bassa **95** E 3
Lago Chilwa **95** F 3
Lago de Maracaibo **108** D 1–2
Lago de Nicaragua **104** EF 5
Lago de Poopó **110** C 4
Lago di Bolsena **57** F 3
Lago Maggiore **57** E 2
Lago O'Higgins **113** B 8
Lago Posadas **113** B 8
Lago Rogagua **110** C 3
Lagos **90** E 4
Lago Titicaca **110** C 4
Lago Viedma **113** B 8
La Grande **102** C 2
La Gran Sabana **109** F 2–3
Laguna **112** G 4
Laguna Madre **103** G 6
Laguna Mar Chiquita **112** D 5
Laguna Merín **112** F 5
Lagunas (Chile) **110** BC 5
Lagunas (Peru) **108** C 5
Lagune Ndogo **91** G 6
Lagune Nkomi **91** F 6
Lagunillas **110** D 4
La Habana **105** F 3
Lāhījān **66** E 3
Lahore **67** J 4
Lahti **54** J 3
Lai **91** H 4
Lainioälven **54** H 2
Lajes **112** FG 4
La Junta (Bolivia) **110** D 4
La Junta (Mexico) **102** E 6
Lake Abaya **93** F 3
Lake Abitibi **101** M 6
Lake Albert (Zaire/Uganda) **92** E 4
Lake Amadeus **78** E 3
Lake Argyle **78** D 2
Lake Athabasca **99** Q 4
Lake Austin **78** B 4
Lake Baikal **68** J 5
Lake Ballard **78** C 4
Lake Bangweulu **94** D 2
Lake Barlee **78** B 4
Lake Carey **78** C 4
Lake Carnegie **78** C 4
Lake Chad **91** G 3
Lake Charles **103** H 5
Lake City **103** K 5
Lake Claire **99** P 4
Lake Clark National Park and Preserve **98** FG 3
Lake Dall, **98** E 3
Lake Disappointment **78** C 3
Lake Edward **92** D 5
Lake Erie **103** K 3
Lake Eyasi **92** E 5
Lake Eyre **79** F 4
Lake Eyre Basin **79** F 4
Lake Francis Case **102** FG 3
Lake Gairdner **79** F 5
Lake Grandin **99** O 3
Lake Gregory **79** FG 4
Lake Huron **103** K 3
Lake Itchen, **99** P 2
Lake Kariba **94** D 3
Lake Kivu **92** D 5
Lake Kyoga **92** E 4
Lakeland **103** K 6
Lake Lefroy **78** C 5
Lake Mackay **78** D 3
Lake Malawi **95** EF 2
Lake Manitoba **99** S 5
Lake Maurice **78** E 4
Lake Mc Leod **78** A 3
Lake Melville **101** Q 5
Lake Michigan **103** J 3
Lake Moore **78** B 4
Lake Mweru **92** D 6
Lake Nash **79** F 3
Lake Nasser **60** A 5
Lake Nasser (Egypt) **88** E 4
Lake Natron **93** F 5
Lake Nipigon **100** K 6
Lake Nipissing **101** LM 6
Lake Nyasa **95** EF 2

Lake Oahe **102** FG 2
Lake of the Ozarks **103** H 4
Lake of the Woods **100** H 6
Lake Okeechobee **103** K 6
Lake Onega **62** FG 3
Lake Ontario **103** L 3
Lake Powell **102** DE 4
Lake Rebecca **78** C 4–5
Lake River **101** L 5
Lake Rukwa **92** E 6
Lake Saint Lucia **95** E 5
Lake Sakakawea **102** F 2
Lake Stefanie **93** F 4
Lake Superior **103** J 2
Lake Tana **93** F 2
Lake Tanganyika **92** DE 6
Lake Taupo **81** R 8
Lake Torrens **79** F 5
Lake Turkana (Lake Rudolf) **93** F 4
Lake Victoria **92** E 5
Lake Volta **90** DE 4
Lake Winnipeg **99** S 5
Lake Winnipegosis **99** RS 5
Lakewood **102** E 4
Lakon **81** J 4
Lakonikos Kólpos **58** B 3
Lakselv **54** J 1–2
Lakshadweep **72** B 5
Lalara **91** G 5
Lâleli Geçidi **59** E 3
La Ligua **112** B 5
La Linea **56** B 4
Lalitpur **72** C 3
La Loche **99** Q 4
La Mancha **56** C 4
La Manche **52** C 5
Lamar **102** F 4
La Mariscala **112** F 5
La Marmora **57** E 4
Lamarque **113** C 6
Lamas **108** C 5
Lambaréné **91** F 6
Lambayeque **108** B 5
Lambert, Cape **81** F 2
Lambert Glacier **115**
Lamberts Bay **94** B 6
La Merced **112** C 4
Lamezia Terme **57** G 4
Lamía **58** B 3
Lamington National Park **79** J 4
La Montaña **110** B 2–3
La Mosquitia **104** F 4–5
Lamotrek **82** A 2
Lampang **73** G 4
Lamu **93** G 5
Lancang Jiang **70** C 6
Lancang Jiang **70** D 6
Lancaster (CA, U.S.A.) **102** C 5
Lancaster (U.K.) **52** C 4
Lanciano **57** F 3
Land's End **52** B 4
Landshut **53** F 5
Landskrona **55** F 4
Landsort **55** G 4
Landsortsdjupet **55** G 4
Langjökull **54** AB 3
Langkon **74** E 2
Langöya **54** F 2
Langry **69** Q 5
Lang Son **73** J 3
Langzhong **70** E 4
Lansing **103** JK 3
Lanzarote **86** C 3
Lanzhou **70** DE 3
Laoag **75** J 1
Laon **56** D 2
La Oroya **110** A 3
Laos **73** HJ 4
Laouni **87** G 4
Lapa **112** G 4
La Palma (Canary Islands) **86** B 3
La Palma (Panama) **108** C 2
La Paragua **109** F 2
La Paz (Argentina) **112** C 5
La Paz (Bolivia) **110** C 4
La Paz (Mexico) **102** D 7
La Piedad **104** B 3
Lapland **54** H 2
La Plata **112** E 5–6
Lappajärvi **54** H 3
Lappi **54** J 2
Laptev Sea **114**
Lapua **54** H 3
L'Aquila **57** F 3
Lār **61** G 4
Larache **86** D 1
Laramie Mountains **102** E 3
Larantuka **75** F 5
Laredo **102** G 6
Lārestān **61** G 4
La Ribera **56** C 3
La Rioja (Argentina) **112** C 4
La Rioja (Spain) **56** C 3
Lárisa **58** B 3
Larkana **67** H 5
Larlomkriny **63** O 4
Larnaca **60** A 2
Larne **52** B 4
La Rochelle **56** C 2
La Roche-sur-Yon **56** C 2
La Romana **105** J 4
La Ronge **99** Q 4
Larrey Point **78** B 2
Larsen Ice Shelf **115**
La Salina **102** D 5
Lās 'Ānōd **93** H 3
Las Cejas **112** D 4
Lās Dāred **93** H 2
La Serena (Chile) **112** B 4
La Serena (Spain) **56** B 4
La Seyne-sur-Mer **57** E 3
Las Flores **113** E 6
Lāsh-e Joveyn **67** G 4
Lashio **73** G 3
Lashkar Gāh **67** GH 4
Las Lajas **113** BC 6
Las Palmas **86** BC 3
La Spezia **57** EF 3
Las Plumas **113** C 7
Las Tablas **108** B 2
Las Vegas **102** C 4
Latady Island **115**
Latakia **60** B 2
Lätäseno **54** H 2
Latgales Augstiene **55** J 4
Latviya **55** J 4
Laughlin Peak **102** F 4
Lau Group **82** D 4
Lauhanvuori **54** H 3
Launceston **82** A 5
La Unión **113** B 7
Laurentian Scarp **101** M 6
Lauria **57** G 3
Lausanne **57** E 2
Laut, Pulau **74** E 4
Laut Arafura **75** HJ 5
Laut Bali **74** E 5
Laut Banda **75** GH 5
Laut Flores **75** E 5
Laut Halmahera **75** G 4
Laut Jawa **74** CD 4
Laut Maluku **75** G 3
Laut Seram **75** G 4
Laut Sulawesi **75** EF 3
Laut Timor **75** GH 5
Laval (France) **56** C 2
Laval (Quebec, Can.) **101** N 6
Lāvān **61** F 4
La Vega **105** H 4
Lavka Integralsoyuza **69** VW 2
Lawra **90** D 3
Lawton **102** G 5
Laydennyy, Mys **62** J 2
La Zarca **104** B 2
Lazarev **69** Q 5
Lāzeh **61** F 4
Leavenworth **103** GH 4
Lebanon **88** EF 2
Lebanon (Lebanon) **60** B 2
Lebanon (PA, U.S.A.) **103** L 3
Lebedin **62** F 5
Lebu **113** B 6
Lebyazh'ye **63** P 5
Lecce **57** G 3
Lechang **70** F 5
Le Creusot **57** D 2
Leeds **52** C 4
Leeuwarden **52** DE 4
Leeward Islands (French Polynesia) **83** E 4
Leeward Islands (West Indies) **105** K 4
Leganés **56** C 3
Legaspi **75** F 1
Legnago **57** F 2
Legnano **57** E 2
Legnica **53** G 4
Legune **78** D 2
Le Havre **56** CD 2
Leicester **52** C 4
Leichardt River **79** F 2
Leiden **52** DE 4
Leipzig **53** F 4
Leirvik **55** E 4
Leiyang **70** F 5
Leka **54** F 2
Lékana **91** G 6
Leksozero, Ozero **54** K 3
Leleque **113** B 7
Le Maire, Estrecho de **113** CD 9–10
Léman, Lac **57** E 2
Le Mans **56** D 2
Le Mars **103** G 3
Lemieux Islands **101** P 3
Lemmenjoki **54** J 2
Lemmon **102** F 2
Lemoro **75** F 4
Lena **68** J 4
Lendery **62** F 3
Leninabad **67** HJ 2–3
Leninakan **59** F 2
Leningrad **55** K 4
Leningradskaya **115**
Leninogorsk **62** K 5
Leninogorsk **63** Q 5
Leninsk-Kuznetskiy **63** QR 5
Len'ki **63** Q 5
Lenkoran' **66** D 3
Lensk **68** K 3
Lentini **57** G 4
Leon (Mexico) **104** B 3
León (Nicaragua) **104** E 5
León (Spain) **56** B 3
Leonardville **94** B 4
Leonora **78** C 4
Leopold and Astrid Coast **115**
Lepsy **63** P 6
Le Puy **56** D 2
Lerfroy, Lake **78** C 5
Lérida (Colombia) **108** D 3
Lérida (Spain) **56** D 3
Léros **58** C 3
Lerum **55** F 4
Lerwick **52** C 2
Leskovac **58** B 2
Les Landes **56** C 3
Lesnaya **69** U 4
Lesosibirsk **68** F 4
Lesotho **94** D 5
Lesozavodsk **71** KL 1
L'Esperance Rock **82** D 5
Lesser Antilles **105** K 4–5
Lesser Slave Lake **99** OP 4
Lesser Sunda Islands **75** FG 5
Lestijoki **54** H 3
Lésvos **58** C 3
Leszno **53** G 4
Lethbridge **99** P 6
Lethem **109** G 3
Leti, Kepulauan **75** G 5
Leticia **108** D 4
Letsok-aw Kyun **73** G 5
Leuser, Gunung **74** A 3
Levante, Riviera di **57** E 3
Levis **101** N 6
Levkás **58** B 3
Lewis **52** B 3
Lewiston (ID, U.S.A.) **102** C 2
Lewiston (ME, U.S.A.) **103** N 3
Lexington **103** K 4
Lhari **70** B 4
Lhasa **73** F 2
Lhazhong **72** E 1
Liancheng **70** G 5
Lianjiang **70** EF 6
Lian Xian **70** F 6

Lianyin **69** M 5
Lianyungang **71** GH 4
Liao He **71** H 2
Liaoning **71** H 2
Liaoyuan **71** HJ 2
Liard **99** N 3
Liard River **99** M 4
Liberal **102** F 4
Liberia **90** BC 4
Liberia **104** E 5
Libya **87** HK 3
Libyan Desert **88** CD 3–4
Licata **57** F 4
Lichinga **95** F 2
Lida (U.S.S.R.) **55** J 5
Lidköping **55** F 4
Liechtenstein **57** EF 2
Liege **52** E 4
Lieksa **54** K 3
Lienart **92** D 4
Lienz **57** F 2
Liepāja **55** H 4
Lievestuoreenjärvi **54** J 3
Lifou **81** J 6
Ligurian Sea **57** E 3
Lihir Group **82** B 3
Lihou Reef and Cays **79** J 2
Lijiang **70** D 5
Likasi **94** D 2
Likiep **82** C 2
Likouala **91** H 5
Lille **56** D 1
Lilongwe **95** E 2
Lima (OH, U.S.A.) **103** K 3
Lima (Peru) **110** A 3
Lima (Portugal) **56** B 3
Limassol **59** D 4
Limay Mahuida **113** C 6
Limerick **52** B 4
Limfjorden **55** E 4
Limningen **54** F 3
Limnos **58** C 3
Limoeiro **111** JK 2
Limoges **56** D 2
Limon (CO, U.S.A.) **102** F 4
Limón (Costa Rica) **104** F 5
Limousin **56** D 2
Limpopo **95** E 4
Linakhamari **54** K 2
Linares (Chile) **113** B 6
Linares (Mexico) **104** C 3
Linares (Spain) **56** C 4
Lincang **70** CD 6
Lincoln (NE, U.S.A.) **103** G 3
Lincoln (U.K.) **52** C 4
Lincoln Sea **114**
Lindau **53** EF 5
Linden **109** G 2
Lindesnes **55** E 4
Lindi **93** F 6–7
Line Islands **83** E 2–3
Linfen **70** F 3
Lingayen **75** H 1
Lingga, Kepulauan **74** B 3–4
Lingomo **92** C 4
Lingyuan **71** G 2
Linhares **111** J 4
Linhe **70** E 2
Linhpa **73** G 2
Linjanti **94** C 3
Linköping **55** G 4
Linkou **71** JK 1
Linosa **57** F 4
Lins **111** G 5
Lintao **70** D 3
Linxi **71** G 2
Linxia **70** D 3
Linyi **71** G 3
Linz **57** F 2
Lipa **75** F 1
Lipari **57** G 4
Lipetsk **62** GH 5
Lipin Bor **62** G 3
Lisala **92** C 4
Lisboa **56** B 4
Lisbon (Portugal) **56** B 4
Lisburn **52** B 4
Lisburne, Cape **98** D 2
Lishui **71** GH 5
Lisichansk **62** G 6
Lisieux **56** D 2
Lithinon, Ákra **58** B 4
Lithuania **55** H 4
Litke **69** Q 5
Litovko **69** P 6
Little Abaco Island **105** G 2
Little Andaman **73** F 5
Little Colorado River **102** D 4
Little Desert National Park **79** G 6
Little Grand Rapids **99** ST 5
Little Nicobar **73** FG 6
Little Rock **103** H 5
Litva **55** H 4
Liuzhou **70** EF 6
Livengood **98** H 2
Liverpool **52** C 4
Livingston (MT, U.S.A.) **102** DE 2
Livingstone **94** D 3
Livingstone Falls **91** G 7
Livoniya **55** J 4
Livorno **57** EF 3
Liwale **93** F 6
Liwonde **95** F 2–3
Li Xian (Hunan China) **70** F 5
Li Xian (Sichuan China) **70** D 4
Lizard **52** BC 5
Lizarda **109** J 5
Ljubelj **57** F 2
Ljungby **55** F 4
Ljusnan **54** F 3
Llallagua **110** C 4
Llano Estacado **102** F 5
Llanos **108** DE 2–3
Llanos de Moxos **110** CD 4
Llullaillaco, Volcán **110** C 5
Lobito **94** A 2
Locarno **57** E 2
Loch Lomond **52** C 3
Loch Ness **52** C 3
Lockhart River Mission **79** G 1
Lod **60** B 3
Lodja **92** C 5
Lodwar **92** F 4
Łodz **53** G 4
Lofoten **54** F 2
Logan, Mount **98** J 3
Logroño **56** C 3
Lohjanjärvi **55** H 3
Lohjanselkä **55** H 3
Loholoho **75** F 4
Loire, Val de **56** D 2
Loja **108** C 4
Lokan tekojärvi **54** J 2
Lokilalaki, Gunung **75** F 4
Lökken **54** E 3
Lokshak **69** O 5
Loks Land **101** P 3
Lolland **55** F 5
Lomami **92** C 4–5
Loma Mountains **90** B 4
Lomas **110** B 4
Lomas de Zamora **112** DE 6
Lomblen, Pulau **75** F 5
Lombok **74** E 5
Lomé **90** E 4
Lomonosov **55** J 4
Lompoc **102** B 5
Łomz'a **53** H 4
Loncoche **113** B 6
London (Canada) **101** L 7
London (U.K.) **52** CD 4
Londonderry (Chile) **113** B 10
Londonderry (U.K.) **52** B 3
Londonderry, Cape **78** D 1
Londrina **111** F 5
Long Beach (CA, U.S.A.) **102** C 5
Long Beach (WA, U.S.A.) **102** AB 2
Long Island (Papua New Guinea) **80** E 2–3
Long Island (The Bahamas) **105** GH 3
Longjiang **69** M 6
Longlac **100** K 6
Longmont **102** E 3
Long Range Mountaines **101** Q 5–6
Longreach **79** G 3
Long Valley **102** D 5
Longview (TX, U.S.A.) **103** GH 5
Longview (WA, U.S.A.) **102** B 2
Longxi **70** D 3
Long Xian **70** E 4
Long Xuyen **73** J 5
Longyan **70** G 5
Longzhou **70** E 6
Lookout, Cape **103** L 5
Lopatka **69** T 5
Lop Buri **73** H 5
Lopcha **69** M 4
Lop Nur **70** B 2
Lopphavet **54** H 1
Lopydino **62** K 3
Lorca **56** C 4
Lord Howe Island **79** K 5
Lordsburg **102** E 5
Lorestan **61** E 2
Loreto (Colombia) **108** D 4
Loreto (Maranhão, Brazil) **109** JK 5
Loreto (Mexico) **102** D 6
Lorient **56** C 2
Lorraine **57** E 2
Los Alamos **102** E 4
Los Ángeles (Chile) **113** B 6
Los Angeles (U.S.A.) **102** BC 5
Losap **82** B 2
Los Blancos **110** D 5
Los Gatos **102** B 4
Lošinj **57** F 3
Los Lagos **113** B 6
Los Lavaderos **104** C 3
Los Mochis **102** E 6
Lospalos **75** G 5
Los Teques **108** E 1
Lost Trail Pass **102** D 2
Los Vilos **112** B 5
Lot **56** D 3
Lota **113** B 6
Lotta **54** J 2
Loubomo **91** G 6
Louga **90** A 2
Louisiade Archipelago **79** J 1
Louisiana **103** H 5
Louis Trichardt **94** D 4
Louisville **103** J 4
Loukhi **62** F 2
Loum **91** FG 5
Lövånger **54** H 3
Loveč̌h **58** B 2
Lovelock **102** C 3
Loviisa **55** J 3
Lovozero **54** L 2
Low, Cape **99** UV 3
Lowa **92** D 5
Lowell **103** M 3
Lower California **102** D 6
Lowestoft **52** D 4
Loyalty Islands **81** J 6
Loyalty Islands **82** C 4
Loyoro **92** E 4
Luacano **94** C 2
Lualaba **92** D 5
Luanda **94** A 1
Luando (Angola) **94** B 2
Luando (Angola) **94** B 2
Luando Reserve **94** B 2
Luang Prabang **73** H 4
Luangwa **95** E 2
Luangwa Valley Game Reserve **95** E 2
Luanshya **94** D 2
Luapala **94** D 2
Luba **91** F 5
Lubalo **94** B 1
Lubang Islands **75** EF 1
Lubango **94** A 2
Lubao **92** D 6
Lubbock **102** F 5
Lübeck **53** F 4
Lubefu **92** CD 5
Lublin **53** H 4
Lubnān, Jabal **60** B 2
Lubny **62** F 6
Lubumbashi **94** D 2
Lucas **110** E 3

Lucea **105** G 4
Lucena **56** C 4
Lučenec **53** G 5
Lucera **57** G 3
Lucero **102** E 5
Lüchun **70** D 6
Lucknow **72** D 2
Lucusse **94** C 2
Lüda **71** H 3
Ludhiana **72** BC 1
Ludogorie **58** C 2
Ludvika **55** G 3
Ludwigshafen **53** E 5
Luebo **92** C 6
Lüeyang **70** E 4
Lufeng **70** G 6
Luga **55** J 4
Lugano **57** E 2
Luganville **82** C 4
Lugenda **95** F 2
Lugnvik **54** G 3
Lugo **56** B 3
Lugoj **58** B 1
Lugovoy **67** J 2
Luhuo **70** D 4
Luiana **94** C 3
Luimneach **52** B 4
Luís Correia **111** H 1
Luiza **92** C 6
Lukashkin Yar **63** PQ 3
Lukolela **92** B 5
Luleå **54** H 2
Luleälven **54** H 2
Lüleburgaz **58** C 2
Lumbala Kaquengue **94** C 2
Lumbala N'guimbo **94** C 2
Lumding **73** F 2
Lumsden **80** P 10
Lunda Norte **94** BC 1
Lunda Sul **94** C 2
Lundazi **95** E 2
Lüneburg **53** EF 4
Lunkho **67** J 3
Luntai **67** L 2
Luochuan **70** E 3
Luofu **92** D 5
Luoisiade **82** B 3
Luoyang **70** F 4
Luoyuan **71** GH 5
Lupane **94** D 3
Lupeni **58** B 1
Luputa **92** C 6
Lūq **93** G 4
Lusaka **94** D 3
Lusambo **92** C 5
Lushui **70** C 5
Lusk **102** F 3
Lūt, Dasht-e **61** G 2
Luton **52** C 4
Lutsk **55** J 5
Luxembourg **52** DE 5
Luxi (Junnan China) **70** C 6
Luxi (Junnan China) **70** D 6
Luxor **60** A 4
Luza **62** J 3
Luzern **57** E 2
Luzhai **70** E 6
Luzhou **70** E 5
Luzhskaya Vozvyshennost' **55** HJ 4
Lvov **53** H 5
L'vovka **63** P 4
Lyakhovskiye Ostrova **69** P 1
Lynchburg **103** L 4
Lynd **79** G 2
Lynn Lake **99** RS 4
Lynx Lake **99** Q 3
Lyon **57** E 2
Łyso Gory **53** H 4
Lyubertsy **62** G 4

M

Ma'ān **60** B 3
Maarianhamina (Mariehamn) **55** H 3–4
Ma'arrat an Nu'mān **59** E 3–4
Maastricht **52** E 4
Mabaruma **109** G 2
Mabote **95** E 4
Ma'būs Yūsuf **87** K 3
Macadam Plains **78** B 4
Macaíba **111** J 2
Macao **70** F 6
Macapá **109** H 3
Macará (Peru) **108** C 4
Macas **108** C 4
Macau **111** J 2
Macauley **82** D 4–5
Macdonnell Ranges **78** E 3
Maceió **111** JK 2
Macerata **57** F 3
Machala **108** C 4
Machevna **69** W 3
Machilipatnam **72** D 4
Machupicchu **110** B 3
Macia **95** E 5
Mackay, Lake **78** D 3
Mackenzie **98** LM 2
Mackenzie Bay **98** K 2
Mac Kenzie Bay **115**
Mackenzie King Island **114**
Mackenzie Mountains **98–99** LM 2–3
Mackenzie River **79** H 3
Mackinaw City **103** K 2
Macocola **94** B 1
Macomia **95** FG 2
Mâcon (France) **57** DE 2
Macon (GA, U.S.A.) **103** K 5
Macquarie Island **115**
Mac Robertson Land **115**
Madagascar **95** H 3
Madā'in Şāliḩ **66** B 5
Madang **80** E 3
Madaoua **91** F 3
Madd, Ra's Abū **60** B 4
Madeira (Brazil) **109** F 4–5
Madeira (Portugal) **86** B 2
Madeleine, Île de la **101** P 6
Madeniyet **63** P 6
Madetkoski **54** J 2
Madhya Pradesh **72** CD 3
Madimba **92** B 5
Madingo-Kayes **91** G 6
Madison **103** HJ 3
Madiun **74** D 5
Madoi **70** C 4
Madrakah **66** BC 6
Madrakah, Ra's al **89** K 5
Madras **72** D 5
Madre de Dios **110** C 3
Madre Oriental, Sierra **104** BC 2–3
Madrid **56** C 3
Madrona, Sierra **56** C 4
Madura, Pulau **74** D 5
Madurai **72** C 6
Madyan **60** B 4
Maebashi **71** L 3
Maevatanana **95** H 3
Maéwo **81** J 5
Mafeteng **94** D 5
Mafia Island **93** G 6
Magadan **69** S 4
Magallanes, Estrecho de **113** B 9
Magangue **108** D 2
Magaria **91** F 3
Magdagachi **69** N 5
Magdalena **108** D 1–2
Magdeburg **53** F 4
Magellan, Strait of **113** BC 9
Mageröya **54** J 1
Maggiore, Lago **57** E 2
Magnitogorsk **63** L 5
Magyarország **58** A 1
Mahābād **66** D 3
Mahabharat Range **72** E 2
Mahabo **95** GH 4
Mahadday Wëyne **93** H 4
Mahajan **72** B 2
Mahajanga **95** H 3
Mahalapye **94** D 4
Mahanoro **95** H 3
Maharashtra **72** BC 4
Maha Sarakham **73** H 4
Mahatsanary **95** G 5
Mahbés **86** CD 3
Mahbubnagar **72** C 4
Mahd adh Dhahab **66** C 6
Mahḑah **61** G 4
Mahdia **109** G 2
Mahenge **93** F 6
Mahesana **72** B 3
Mahia Peninsula **81** R 8
Mahkene **54** F 3
Mahmūdābād **61** F 1
Mahmud-Raqi **67** H 4
Mahón **56** D 4
Mahuva **72** B 3
Maiana **82** C 2
Maiduguri **91** G 3
Maimana **67** GH 3
Mai-Ndombe, Lac **92** B 5
Maine **103** N 2
Mainland (Orkney Is., U.K.) **52** C 3
Mainland (Shetland Is., U.K.) **52** C 2
Maintirano **95** G 3
Mainz **53** E 5
Maio **90** B 6
Maipú **113** E 6
Maipuco **108** D 4
Maitengwe **94** D 4
Maitland **79** J 5
Maíz, Isla del **104** F 5
Majuro **82** C 2
Makale **93** FG 2
Makambako **92** EF 6
Makarikari **94** CD 4
Makarikha **63** LM 2
Makarov **69** Q 6
Makat **66** E 1
Makaw **70** C 5
Makedhonía **58** B 2
Makedonija **58** B 2
Makeyevka **59** E 1
Makgadikgadi Pan **94** CD 4
Makhachkala **66** D 2
Makinsk **63** O 5
Makkah **89** G 4
Makó **58** B 1
Makokou **91** G 5
Makran **66–67** G 5
Makri **72** D 4
Maksimovka **71** L 1
Mākū **59** F 3
Makurdi **91** F 4
Makushino **63** N 4
Makuyuni **93** F 5
Makwa **82** BC 3
Malabar Coast **72** BC 5–6
Malabo **91** F 5
Málaga **56** C 4
Malagasy Republic **95** H 3
Malaimbandy **95** H 4
Malaita **81** H 3
Malakāl **92** E 3
Malakula **81** J 5
Malang **74** D 5
Malanje **94** B 1
Malao **81** J 5
Mälaren **55** G 4
Malargue **113** C 6
Malaspina **113** C 7
Malatya **59** E 3
Malatya Dağları **59** E 3
Malāwi **61** E 2
Malawi **95** E 2
Malawi National Park **95** E 2
Malaybalay **75** FG 2
Malāyer **61** E 2
Malaysia **74** BD 2
Malden **83** E 3
Maldives **72** B 6
Maldonado **112** F 5
Malegaon **72** BC 3
Malei **95** F 3
Malek **92** E 3
Malekula **82** C 4
Maleyevo **68** G 4
Malhada **111** H 3
Mali **90** CD 2–3
Mali Kyun **73** G 5
Malindi **93** G 5
Maling, Gunung **75** F 3
Malin Head **52** B 3
Mallaig **52** B 3
Mallani **72** B 2
Mallery Lake **99** S 3
Mallorca **56** D 4

Malmö **55** F 4
Maloelap **82** C 2
Malozemel'skaya Tundra **62** JK 2
Malpelo, Isla **108** B 3
Malta **57** F 4
Malta **102** E 2
Maluku **75** G 4
Malung **55** F 3
Maly Kavkaz **59** FG 2
Malyy Lyakhovskiy, Ostrov **69** Q 1
Malyy Yenisey **68** FG 5
Mama **68** K 4
Mamagota **81** FG 3
Mambasa **92** D 4
Mambéré **92** B 3–4
Mamoré **110** C 3
Mamou **90** B 3
Mamuju **75** E 4
Mamuno **94** C 4
Man **90** C 4
Manacapuru **109** F 4
Manado **75** F 3
Managua **104** E 5
Manaka **81** Q 9
Manakara **95** H 4
Manama **61** F 4
Mananara **95** H 3
Manapouri **82** C 6
Manas **67** M 2
Manaus **109** FG 4
Manchester **52** C 4
Manchuria **71** HJ 2
Máncora **108** B 4
Mand **61** F 3
Mandal **55** E 4
Mandalay **73** G 3
Mandal-Ovoo **70** D 2
Mandasor **72** B 3
Mandera **93** G 4
Mandeville **105** G 4
Mandiana **90** C 3
Mandimba **95** F 2
Mandji **91** G 6
Mandla **72** CD 3
Mandor **74** C 3
Mandvi **72** A 3
Manfredonia **57** G 3
Manga (Minas Gerais, Brazil) **111** H 3
Manga (Niger/Chad) **91** GH 3
Mangaia **83** E 4
Mangalore **72** B 5
Mangnai **70** B 3
Mangoky **95** G 4
Mangole, Pulau **75** G 4
Mangueira, Lagoa **112** F 5
Mangut **68** K 6
Manhan **68** F 6
Manhattan **103** G 4
Manicaland **95** E 3
Manicore **109** F 5
Manicouagan **101** O 5
Maniganggo **70** CD 4
Manihi **83** F 3
Manipur **73** F 3
Manisa **58** C 3
Manistique **103** J 2
Manitoba **99** S 5
Manitoba, Lake **99** S 5
Manitowoc **103** J 3
Manizales **108** C 2
Manjil **61** E 1
Mankato **103** H 3
Manlay **70** E 2
Manmad **72** BC 3
Mannheim **53** E 4–5
Manning **99** O 4
Manoa **108** E 5
Manono **92** D 6
Manra **82** D 3
Manresa **56** D 3
Mansa **94** D 2
Mansel Island **101** L 3
Mansfield **103** K 3
Manta **108** B 4
Mantecal **108** E 2
Mantova **57** F 2
Manú **110** B 3
Manuae **83** E 4
Manuangi **83** F 4
Manuel Urbano **108** DE 5
Manukau **82** C 5
Manus **80** E 2
Manychskaya Vpadina **59** F 1
Manyoni **92** E 6
Manzanillo (Cuba) **105** G 3
Manzanillo (Mexico) **104** B 4
Manzhouli **68** L 6
Manzil Bū Ruqaybah **87** G 1
Manzurka **68** J 5
Mao **105** H 4
Maoke, Pegunungan **75** J 4
Maoming **70** F 6
Mapaga **75** EF 4
Mapai **95** E 4
Mapi **75** J 5
Maple Creek **99** Q 6
Mapuera **109** G 4
Maputo **95** E 5
Maquela do Zombo **94** B 1
Maquinchao **113** C 7
Maraá **108** E 4
Marabá **109** HJ 5
Maracá, Ilha de **109** HJ 3
Maracaibo **108** D 1
Maracaibo, Lago de **108** D 1–2
Maracaju **111** F 5
Maracay **108** E 1
Marādah **87** J 3
Maradi **91** F 3
Marāgheh **66** D 3
Marahuaca, Cerro **108** E 3
Marajó, Ilha de **109** HJ 4
Maramba **94** D 3
Marānd **66** D 3
Maranhão **111** GH 2
Marañón **108** C 4
Marão, Serra do **56** B 3
Marathon **100** K 6
Marawī **88** E 5
Marbella **56** C 4
March **57** G 2
Marche **57** F 3
Marche, Plateaux de la **56** D 2
Mar Chiquita, Laguna **112** D 5
Mar del Plata **113** E 6
Mardin **59** F 3
Mardin Eşigi **59** F 3
Maré **81** J 6
Marēg **93** H 4
Marganets **59** D 1
Margaret River **78** A 5
Margaritovo **71** KL 2
Margilan **67** J 2
Margyang **72** E 1–2
Mari (Burma) **73** G 2
Mari (Papua New Guinea) **80** D 3
Maria (Tuamotu Is.) **83** F 4
Maria (Tubai Is.) **83** E 4
Mariana Islands **82** A 1
Marianao **105** F 3
Maria Theresa **83** E 5
Mariato, Punta **108** B 2
Maria van Diemen, Cape **81** Q 7
Maribor **57** FG 2
Maricourt **101** N 3
Marie Byrd Land **115**
Mariental **94** B 4
Mariestad **55** F 4
Marietta **103** JK 5
Mariinsk **63** R 4
Mariinskoye **69** Q 5
Marília **111** G 5
Maringa **111** F 5
Mariny, Iméni **69** R 3
Marion (IN, U.S.A.) **103** J 3
Marion (OH, U.S.A.) **103** K 3
Marion Reef **79** J 2
Mariu **80** D 3
Marīyyah **61** F 5
Märjamaa **55** HJ 4
Marka **93** GH 4
Markha **68** M 3
Marko **54** G 2
Markovo **63** R 3
Marlin **103** G 5
Marmara **58** C 2
Marmara Denizi **58** C 2
Marmaris **58** C 3
Marne **56** D 2
Maroa **108** E 3
Maroni **109** H 3
Maroua **91** GH 3
Marovoay **95** H 3
Marowijne **109** H 3
Marqadah **59** F 3
Marquesas Islands **83** F 3
Marquette **103** J 2
Marrakech **86** D 2
Marree **79** F 4
Marrero **103** HJ 6
Marrupa **95** F 2
Marsa al' Alam **60** B 4
Marsabit National Reserve **93** F 4
Marsala **57** F 4
Marsa 'Umm Ghayj **60** B 4
Marseille **57** E 3
Marsfjllet **54** G 2
Marshall Islands **82** BC 2
Marshalltown **103** H 3
Marsh Harbour **105** G 2
Marta **57** F 3
Martaban, Gulf of **73** G 4
Martigues **57** DE 3
Martinique **105** K 5
Martinique Passage **105** K 5
Martin Vaz Islands **107** H 5
Martre, Lac la **99** O 3
Marutea **83** F 4
Mary **67** G 3
Maryborough **79** J 4
Maryland **103** L 4
Marystown **101** QR 6
Maryville **103** H 3
Masāhīm, Kūh-e **61** G 3
Masai Steppe **93** F 5
Masaka **92** E 5
Masākin **87** H 1
Masan **71** J 3
Masasi **95** F 2
Masaya **104** E 5
Masbate **75** F 1
Mascarene Islands **95** K 6
Maseru **94** D 5
Mashhad **66** FG 3
Mashīz **61** G 3
Mashonaland **95** E 3
Masindi **92** E 4
Maşīrah **89** K 4
Masjed Soleymān **61** E 3
Maskanah **60** B 2
Masoala, Cap **95** J 3
Masohi **75** G 4
Mason City **103** H 3
Masqat **89** K 4
Massachusetts **103** M 3
Massafra **57** G 3
Massangena **95** E 4
Massau **81** EF 2
Massava **63** M 3
Massawa **93** FG 1
Masset **98** L 5
Massif Central **56** D 2–3
Massif du Pelvoux **57** E 2
Massif du Tsaratanana **95** H 2
Massinga **95** F 4
Masteksay **66** E 1
Mastuj **67** J 3
Mastung **67** H 5
Mastūrah **66** B 6
Masvingo **95** E 4
Maşyāf **60** B 2
Matabeleland **94** D 3–4
Matadi **92** A 6
Matagalpa **104** E 5
Matagami **101** M 6
Matagorda Island **103** G 6
Mataiva **83** F 3
Matam **90** B 2
Matara **72** CD 6
Matarani **110** B 4
Mataranka **78** E 1
Matatiele **94** D 6
Matatila Dam **72** C 2
Mata-Utu **82** D 3
Matay **63** P 6

Matehuala **104** B 3
Matera **57** G 3
Mathura **72** C 2
Matla **72** E 3
Mato Grosso **110–111** EF 3
Mato Grosso (Mato Grosso, Brazil) **110** E 3
Matozinhos **56** B 3
Mátra **58** A 1
Matrūh **88** D 2
Matsudo **71** M 3
Matsue **71** K 3
Matsuyama **71** K 4
Matterhorn (NV, U.S.A.) **102** CD 3
Matterhorn (Switzerland) **57** E 2
Matthew **82** C 4
Matu **74** D 3
Matua, Ostrov **69** S 6
Maturín **109** F 2
Matyushkinskaya **63** PQ 4
Maubeuge **56** D 1
Maués **109** G 4
Maui **83** E 1
Mauke **83** E 4
Maun **94** C 4
Mauna Kea **83** E 1
Maunoir, Lac **99** MN 2
Maupihaa **83** E 4
Mauralasan **74** E 3
Maurice, Lake **78** E 4
Mauritania **86** BD 5
Mauritius **95** K 5
Mavasjaure **54** G 2
Mawson **115**
Mawson Coast **115**
Maxcanu **104** D 3
Mayaguana Island **105** H 3
Mayagüez **105** J 4
Mayāmey **61** G 1
Mayd **93** H 2
Maydān **61** D 2
Maykop **59** F 2
Maymakan **69** P 4
Mayna **68** F 5
Maynas **108** C 4
Mayo, Mountains of **52** B 4
Mayor-Krest **69** Q 2
Mayotte **95** H 2
May Pen **105** G 4
Maysk **63** P 4
Mayumba **91** FG 6
Mayya **69** O 3
Mazabuka **94** D 3
Mazar **67** K 3
Mazar-i-Sharif **67** H 3
Mazatenango **104** D 5
Mazatlán **104** A 3
Mazomeno **92** D 5
Mazong Shan **70** C 2
Mazowsze **53** H 4
Mazury **53** H 4
Mbabane **95** E 5
Mbakaou Reservoir **91** G 4
Mbala **95** E 1
Mbale **92** E 4
Mbalmayo **91** G 5
Mbamba Bay **95** E 2
Mbandaka **92** B 4
Mbanga **91** FG 5
M'banza Congo **94** AB 1
Mbanza-Ngungu **92** B 6
Mbeya **92** E 6
Mbinda **91** G 6
Mbini **91** F 5
Mbokou **92** D 3
Mbour **90** A 3
Mbuji-Mayi **92** CD 6
McAllen **102** G 6
McCammon **102** D 3
McComb **103** H 5
McCook **102** F 3
McKean **82** D 3
McKeesport **103** L 3
McKinley, Mount **98** G 3
Mc Leod, Lake **78** A 3
M'Clintock Channel **99** R 1
M'Clure Strait **99** O 1
Mc Murdo **115**
Mc Murdo Sound **115**
Meadow Lake **99** Q 5
Meaux **56** D 2
Mecca **89** G 4
Mecklenburg **53** F 4
Mecklenburger Bucht **53** F 4
Medan **74** A 3
Medanosa, Punta **113** CD 8
Medellín **108** CD 2
Medelpad **54** G 3
Medford **102** B 3
Medgidia **58** C 2
Mediaş **58** B 1
Medicine Bow **102** E 3
Medicine Hat **99** P 5
Medigan **63** R 5
Medina **60** C 4
Mediterranean Sea **56** CE 4
Mednogorsk **63** L 5
Medvezhiy Var **68** F 1
Meekatharra **78** B 4
Meerut **72** C 2
Mega (Ethiopia) **93** F 4
Mega (Indonesia) **75** H 4
Megasani Hill **72** E 3
Meghalaya **73** F 2
Megra **62** H 2
Meguinenza, Embalse de **56** CD 3
Mehrīz **61** G 3
Mehtar-Lam **67** J 4
Meiganga **91** G 4
Meissen **53** F 4
Mei Xian **70** G 6
Mejillones **110** BC 5
Mékambo **91** G 5
Meknès **86** D 2
Mekong **73** HJ 4–5
Mekongga, Gunung **75** F 4
Melaka **74** B 3
Melanesia **81** FJ 2–3
Melbourne (Australia) **79** G 6
Melbourne (FL, U.S.A.) **103** KL 6
Melchor Ocampo **104** B 4
Melendiz Dağı **59** D 3
Meletsk **68** F 4
Meleuz **62** KL 5
Melfort **99** QR 5
Melilla **86** E 1
Melimoyo, Monte **113** B 7
Melitopol' **59** E 1
Melo **112** F 5
Meltaus **54** H 2
Melun **56** D 2
Melville **99** R 5
Melville, Cape **79** G 1
Melville, Lake **101** Q 5
Melville Bay **114**
Melville Hills **99** N 2
Melville Island (Australia) **78** E 1
Melville Island (Canada) **96** G 2
Melville Peninsula **99** UV 2
Melyuveyem **69** W 3
Memmingen **53** EF 5
Memphis (Egypt) **88** E 3
Memphis (TN, U.S.A.) **103** J 4
Mena **62** F 5
Ménaka **90** E 2
Mendoza (Argentina) **112** C 5
Mendoza (Peru) **108** C 5
Mengcheng **71** G 4
Mengene Dağı **59** F 3
Menghai **70** CD 6
Mengzi **70** D 6
Menihek Lakes **101** O 5
Meningie **79** FG 6
Menkere **68** M 2
Menongue **94** B 2
Menorca **56** D 3
Mentawai, Kepulauan **74** A 4
Mentese **58** C 3
Menyuan **70** D 3
Menza **68** J 6
Menzies **78** C 4
Menzies, Mount **115**
Mepistskaro **59** F 2
Meppen **53** E 4
Meråker **54** F 3
Merano **57** F 2
Merced **102** BC 4
Mercedes (Argentina) **112** E 4
Mercedes (Argentina) **112** C 5
Mercedes (Uruguay) **112** E 5
Merchants Bay **101** P 2
Mercy, Cape **101** P 3
Meredith, Cape **113** D 9
Merefa **62** G 6
Merenga **69** ST 3
Mergui **73** G 5
Mergui Archipelago **73** G 5
Meriç **58** C 2
Mérida (Mexico) **104** DE 3
Mérida (Spain) **56** B 4
Mérida (Venezuela) **108** D 2
Meridian **103** J 5
Mérignac **56** C 2
Merikarvia **54** H 3
Merín, Laguna **112** F 5
Merredin **78** B 5
Merritt Island **103** KL 6
Merseburg **53** F 4
Mersin **59** D 3
Meru Game Reserve **93** F 4–5
Merzifon **59** E 2
Mesabi Range **103** H 2
Mesopotamia **60–61** D 2–3
Messina **57** FG 4
Messiniakós Kolpós **58** B 3
Messo **63** P 2
Mesters Vig **114**
Meta **108** DE 2
Meta Incognita Peninsula **101** O 3
Metairie **103** H 5–6
Metán **112** D 4
Metangula **95** EF 2
Metemma **92** F 2
Metéora-monastery **58** B 3
Metlakatla **98** L 4
Metu **92** F 3
Metz **57** E 2
Meuse **57** E 2
Mexicali **102** CD 5
Mexican Hat **102** E 4
Mexico **104** AB 2
México City **104** BC 4
Meymeh **61** F 2
Mezen' **62** H 2
Mezhdurechenskiy **63** N 4
Miami **103** K 6
Miami Beach **103** L 6
Miāndowāb **61** D 1
Mīaneh (Iran) **61** E 1
Mianyang **70** DE 4
Miarinarivo **95** H 3
Miazz **63** LM 5
Michigan **103** JK 2–3
Michigan, Lake **103** J 3
Michoacán **104** B 4
Michurinsk **62** G 5
Micronesia **82** BC 2
Middelburg **94** DE 5
Middle Andaman **73** F 5
Midi, Canal du **56** D 3
Midland (MI, U.S.A.) **103** JK 3
Midland (TX, U.S.A.) **102** F 5
Midžor **58** B 2
Miekojärvi **54** HJ 2
Mielec **53** H 4
Mieres **56** B 3
Migiurtinia **93** HJ 2
Mijdaḥah **89** H 6
Mikha Tskhakaya **59** F 2
Mikhaylovgrad **58** B 2
Mikhaylovka **62** H 5
Mikinai **58** B 3
Mikindani **95** FG 2
Mikino **69** U 3
Míkonos **58** C 3
Milagro **108** C 4
Milan **57** E 2
Milando Reserve **94** B 1
Milange **95** F 3
Milano **57** E 2
Milâs **58** C 3
Milazzo **57** FG 4
Milcan Tepe **59** E 3
Mildura **79** G 5

Mile **70** D 6
Miles **79** HJ 4
Miles City **102** EF 2
Milford Haven **52** B 4
Milgun **78** B 3–4
Mili **82** C 2
Milk River **102** E 2
Millau **56** D 3
Millevaches, Plateau de **56** D 2
Mílos **58** B 3
Milparinka **79** G 4
Milwaukee **103** J 3
Mina **68** F 5
Mīnā' 'Abd Allāh **61** E 3
Minahassa Peninsula **75** F 3
Minas **112** F 5
Mīnā' Sa'ūd **61** E 3
Minas Gerais **111** GH 4
Minas Novas **111** H 4
Minatitlán **104** D 4
Minbya **73** F 3
Mincha **112** B 5
Mindanao **75** FG 2
Mindelo **90** B 6
Mindoro **75** F 1
Mindoro Strait **75** EF 1
Mineiros **111** F 4
Mineral'nyye Vody **59** F 2
Minerva Reefs **82** D 4
Minfeng **67** L 3
Mingary **79** G 5
Mingechaur **66** D 2
Mingshui **71** J 1
Mingteke **67** K 3
Minho **56** B 3
Ministro João Alberto **111** F 3
Minna **91** F 4
Minneapolis (KS, U.S.A.) **102** G 4
Minneapolis (MN, U.S.A.) **103** GH 3
Minnesota **103** GH 2
Minot **102** F 2
Minqin **70** D 3
Minqing **71** G 5
Minsin **73** G 2
Minsk **55** J 5
Minto **82** B 2
Minto, Lac **101** N 4
Minusinsk **68** F 5
Min Xian **70** D 4
Miquelon **101** M 6
Mirabad **67** G 4
Miramichi Bay **101** P 6
Miranda **110** E 5
Miranda de Ebro **56** C 3
Miri **74** D 3
Miriam Vale **79** J 3
Mirim, Lagoa **112** F 5
Mirnyy **115**
Mirpur Khas **67** H 5
Mirtóon Pélagos **58** B 3
Mirzapur **72** D 2–3
Mish'āb, Ra's al **61** E 3
Mishan **71** K 1
Miskolc **58** AB 1
Misool, Pulau **75** H 4
Mişr **88** DE 4
Mişrātah **87** H 2
Mişrātah, Ra's **87** J 2
Mississippi **103** HJ 5
Mississippi Delta **103** J 6
Mississippi River **103** H 5
Missoula **102** D 2
Missouri **103** H 4
Missouri River **102–103** GH 3–4
Mistassini, Lac **101** MN 5
Misti, Volcán **110** B 4
Misty Fjords National Monument **98** L 4
Mitchell **102** G 3
Mitchell River **79** G 2
Mitilíni **58** C 3
Mitra **91** F 5
Mitú **108** D 3
Mitumba, Monts **92** D 5–6
Miyako **71** M 3
Miyakonojō **71** K 4
Miyako-rettō **71** H 6
Miyaly **66** E 1
Mizdah **87** H 2
Mizen Head **52** AB 4
Mizoram **73** F 3
Mizuho **115**
Mizusawa **71** M 3
Mjölby **55** G 4
Mjösa **55** F 3
Mkata **93** F 6
Mkomazi **93** F 5
Mkomazi Game Reserve **93** F 5
Mkushi **94** DE 2
Mladá Boleslav **53** FG 4
Mljet **57** G 3
Moab **102** E 4
Moamba **95** E 5
Moba **92** D 6
Mobaye **92** C 4
Mobile **103** J 5
Mobridge **102** F 2
Moçambique **95** G 3
Mochudi **94** D 4
Mocímboa da Praia **95** G 2
Moctezuma (Mexico) **102** E 6
Moctezuma (Mexico) **104** B 3
Mocuba **95** F 3
Modena (Italy) **57** F 3
Modena (NV., U.S.A.) **102** D 4
Moero, Lac **92** D 6
Mogadishu **93** H 4
Mogadouro, Serra do **56** B 3
Mogaung **73** G 2
Mogilev **55** JK 5
Mogilev Podol'skiy **58** C 1
Mogogh **92** E 3
Mogoyn **68** G 6
Mogoytui **68** KL 5
Moguqi **69** M 6
Mohe **69** M 5
Moheli **95** G 2
Mohikan, Cape **98** D 3
Mohon Peak **102** D 5
Mohoro **93** F 6
Mointy **63** O 6
Mo i Rana **54** F 2
Mojave Desert **102** C 4
Mojiang **70** D 6
Mokp'o **71** J 4
Mokra Gora **58** AB 2
Moldava **58** C 1
Moldava **58** C 1
Moldaviya **58** C 1
Molde **54** E 3
Moldefjorden **54** E 3
Mole Game Reserve **90** D 4
Molepolole **94** CD 4
Mollendo **110** B 4
Molodechno **55** J 5
Molodezhnaya **115**
Molokai **83** E 1
Molopo **94** C 5
Mombasa **93** FG 5
Mombetsu **71** M 2
Momboyo **92** B 5
Momskiy Khrebet **69** QR 2
Monaco **57** E 3
Monaghan **52** B 4
Monapo **95** G 2
Monarch Mountain **99** M 5
Monasterio de Montserrat **56** D 3
Monastery of Saint Catherine **60** AB 3
Monchegorsk **54** K 2
Mönchen-Gladbach **52** E 4
Monclova **104** B 2
Moncton **101** O 6
Mondo **91** H 3
Mondragone **57** F 3
Monfalcone **57** F 2
Monga **92** C 4
Mong Hpayak **73** G 3
Monghyr **72** E 2–3
Mongolia **68** GJ 6
Mongolo **68** J 2
Mongu **94** C 3
Mönhhaan **70** F 1
Monkira **79** G 3
Monou **91** J 2
Monreal del Campo **56** C 3
Monroe (LA, U.S.A.) **103** H 5
Monroe (MI, U.S.A.) **103** K 3
Monrovia **90** B 4
Mons **52** D 4
Mont Afao **87** G 3
Montague **98** H 4
Montana **102** DE 2
Montauban **56** D 3
Montbeliard **57** E 2
Mont Blanc **57** E 2
Mont Cameroon **91** F 5
Montceau-les-Mines **56** D 2
Mont-de-Marsan **56** C 3
Monte Alegre **109** H 4
Monte Binga **95** E 3
Monte Carlo **57** E 3
Monte Cinto **57** E 3
Monte Claros **111** H 4
Montecristi **105** H 3–4
Montecristo **57** F 3
Monte Cristo **110** D 3
Monte d'Oro **57** E 3
Montego Bay **105** G 4
Montejinnie **78** E 2
Monte Melimoyo **113** B 7
Montemoreos **104** C 2
Monte Negro Falls **94** A 3
Montepuez **95** F 2
Monte Quemado **112** D 4
Monterado **74** C 3
Monterey **102** B 4
Montería **108** C 2
Montero **110** D 4
Monterrey **104** B 2
Montes Altos **109** J 5
Montes de Toledo **56** C 4
Montesilvano **57** F 3
Montes Universales **56** C 3
Montevideo **112** EF 5–6
Montgomery **103** J 5
Monti di Ala **57** E 3
Mont Kavendou **90** B 3
Mont Lozére **56** D 3
Montluçon **56** D 2
Mont Panié **81** H 6
Mont Pelat **57** E 3
Montpelier (VT, U.S.A.) **103** M 3
Montpéllier **56** D 3
Montréal **101** N 6
Montreux **57** E 2
Montrose **102** E 4
Monts d'Aubrac **56** D 3
Montserrat **105** K 4
Monts Mitumba **92** D 5–6
Monts Nimba **90** C 4
Monts Notre-Dame **101** O 6
Monts Otish **101** N 5
Monts Tamgak **91** F 2
Monts Timétrine **90** DE 2
Mont Tahat **87** G 4
Mont Tembo **91** G 5
Mont Ventoux **57** E 3
Monza **57** E 2
Moonie **79** J 4
Mooraberree **79** G 4
Moore, Lake **78** B 4
Moorhead **103** G 2
Moorlands **79** FG 6
Moose Jaw **99** Q 5
Moosonee **101** L 5
Mopti **90** D 3
Moquegua **110** BC 4
Mora **55** F 3
Moradabad **72** CD 2
Moramanga **95** H 3
Morane **83** F 4
Moratuwa **72** CD 6
Morava (Czechoslovakia) **53** G 5
Morava (Western Australia) **78** B 4
Morava (Yugoslavia) **58** B 2
Morawhanna **109** G 2
Moray Firth **52** C 3
Moree **79** H 4
More Laptevykh **68** MN 1
Morelia **104** B 4
Morena, Sierra **56** BC 4
Moreno **108** C 5

Möre og Romsdal **54** E 3
Moresby **98** L 5
Mori **70** B 2
Morioka **71** M 3
Mornington Island **79** F 2
Morobe **82** A 3
Morocco **86** D 2
Morogoro **93** F 6
Moro Gulf **75** F 2
Morombe **95** G 4
Mörön **68** H 6
Morón (Cuba) **105** G 3
Morón (Spain) **56** B 4
Morón (Venezuela) **108** E 1
Morondava **95** G 4
Moroni **95** G 2
Moroshechnoye **69** T 4
Morotai, Pulau **75** G 3
Morozovsk **59** F 1
Morro de Môco **94** AB 2
Mors **55** E 4
Morshansk **62** H 5
Mörsil **54** F 3
Mortlock Islands **82** B 2
Morwell **79** H 6
Moselle **57** E 2
Moshi **93** F 5
Mosjöen **54** F 2
Moskal'vo **69** Q 5
Moskenesöya **54** F 2
Moskva **62** FG 4
Mosquera **108** C 3
Mosquitos, Costa de **104** F 5
Mosquitos, Golfo de los **108** B 2
Moss **55** F 4
Mosselbaai **94** C 6
Mossendjo **91** G 6
Mossoró **111** J 2
Mostaganem **86** EF 1
Mostar **57** G 3
Mosul **89** G 1
Motala **55** G 4
Motihari **72** DE 2
Motril **56** C 4
Motykleyka **69** RS 4
Moudjéria **86** C 5
Moul **91** G 2
Moulins **56** D 2
Moulmein **73** G 4
Moundou **91** H 4
Mount Adam **113** DE 9
Mountains of Mayo **52** B 4
Mount Aspiring **80** P 9
Mount Augustus **78** B 3
Mount Balbi **81** F 3
Mount Bangeta **80** E 3
Mount Blackburn **98** HJ 3
Mount Bona **98** J 3
Mount Brassey **78** E 3
Mount Bruce **78** B 3
Mount Brukkaros **94** B 5
Mount Carter **79** G 1
Mount Cleveland **102** D 2
Mount Columbia **99** O 5
Mount Cook **81** Q 9
Mount Cushing **99** M 4
Mount Dalrymple **79** H 3
Mount Deering **78** D 3
Mount Demavend **61** F 2
Mount Douglas **79** H 3
Mount Egmont **81** Q 8
Mount Elbert **102** E 4
Mount Elgon **92** EF 4
Mount Elliot **79** H 2
Mount Essendon **78** C 3
Mount Everest **72** E 2
Mount Feathertop **79** H 6
Mount Finke **78** E 5
Mount Forel **114**
Mount Gambier **79** FG 6
Mount Godwin Austin **67** K 3
Mount Hale **78** B 4
Mount Hermon (Lebanon) **60** B 2
Mount Hood **102** B 2–3
Mount Hutton **79** H 4
Mount Isa **79** F 3
Mount Isto **98** J 2
Mount Jackson (Antarctica) **115**
Mount Jackson (Australia) **78** BC 5
Mount Jefferson **102** C 4
Mount Kenya **93** F 5
Mount Kimball **98** J 3
Mount Kirkpatrick **115**
Mount Livermore **102** F 5
Mount Logan **98** J 3
Mount Magnet **78** B 4
Mount Marcus Baker **98** H 3
Mount McKinley **98** G 3
Mount Menzies **115**
Mount Morgan **79** J 3
Mount Mowbullan **79** J 4
Mount Nurri **79** H 5
Mount Nyiru **93** F 4
Mount Oglethorpe **103** K 5
Mount Olympus **102** AB 2
Mount Omatako **94** B 4
Mount Ord **78** D 2
Mount Ossa **80** L 9
Mount Pulog **75** J 1
Mount Queen Bess **99** N 5
Mount Rainier **102** B 2
Mount Ratz **98** L 4
Mount Robson **99** NO 5
Mount Roosevelt **99** M 4
Mount Shasta **102** B 3
Mount Shenton **78** C 4
Mount Sir James MacBrian **98** M 3
Mount Sunflower **102** F 4
Mount Tama **94** A 2
Mount Taylor **102** E 4
Mount Victoria **73** F 3
Mount Victoria (Papua New Guinea) **82** A 3
Mount Vsevidof **98** D 5
Mount Waddington **99** MN 5
Mount Whitney **102** C 4
Mount Wilhelm **80** D 3
Mount Wilson **102** E 4
Mount Wrightson **102** D 5
Moura **109** F 4
Moussoro **91** H 3
Mouths of the Amazon **109** J 3
Mouths of the Danube **58** CD 1–2
Mouths of the Ganges **72–73** EF 3
Mouths of the Indus **67** H 6
Mouths of the Irrawaddy **73** FG 4
Mouths of the Mekong **73** J 5–6
Mouths of the Orinoco **109** FG 2
Movas **102** E 6
Mowbullan, Mount **79** J 4
Moxico **94** BC 2
Moxos, Llanos de **110** CD 4
Moyale **93** F 4
Moyobamba **108** C 5
Mozambique **95** EF 3
Mozambique Channel **95** FG 2–4
Mozdok **59** FG 2
Mozharka **68** F 5
Mozyr' **55** J 5
Mpanda **92** E 6
Mpika **95** E 2
Msata **93** F 6
Mtsensk **62** G 5
Mtwara **95** G 2
Muang Nan **73** H 4
Muang Ngao **73** GH 4
Muang Phrae **73** H 4
Muang Ubon **72** H 4
Muar **74** B 3
Muaraenim **74** B 4
Muara Teweh **74** D 4
Mubarak **61** G 4
Mubi **91** G 3
Muchinga Escarpment **95** E 2
Mucojo **95** G 2
Mudanjiang **71** JK 2
Muddy Gap **102** E 3
Mufulira **94** D 2
Muganskaya Step' **66** D 3
Muhagiriya **88** D 6
Muhammad, Ra's **60** B 4
Muḥammad Qawl **88** F 4
Mühlhausen **53** F 4
Mühlig-Hofmann Mountains **115**
Muhulu **92** D 5
Mui Bai Bung **73** H 6
Muite **95** F 2
Mukachevo **58** B 1
Mukur **66** EF 1
Mukur **67** H 4
Mulan **71** J 1
Mulanje **95** F 3
Mulata **93** G 3
Mulchén **113** B 6
Mulegé **102** D 6
Mulgrave Island **80** D 4
Mulhacén **56** C 4
Mulhouse **57** E 2
Mull **52** B 3
Mullaittivu **72** D 6
Mullaley **79** HJ 5
Muller, Pegunungan **74** D 3
Mullet Peninsula **52** A 4
Mullewa **78** B 4
Mulligan River **79** F 4
Mulobezi **94** D 3
Multan **67** J 5
Multanovy **63** O 3
Mulu, Gunung **74** DE 3
Mulym'ya **63** N 3
Mumra **66** D 1
Muna, Pulau **75** F 5
München **53** F 5
Muncie **103** JK 3
Mundar **69** R 2
Munday **102** G 5
Münden **53** E 4
Munhango **94** B 2
Munich **53** F 5
Munkhafaḍ al Qaṭṭārah **88** D 3
Munster **52** B 4
Münster **53** E 4
Muntii Rodnei **58** B 1
Munugudzhak **69** TU 3
Munzur Silsilesi **59** EF 3
Muojärvi **54** J 2
Muong Hiem **73** H 3
Muong Khoua **73** H 3
Muong Sing **73** H 3
Mupa National Park **94** B 3
Mura **57** G 2
Murallón, Cerro **113** B 8
Murana **75** H 4
Muranga **93** F 5
Murashi **62** J 4
Murat **59** F 3
Murchison River **78** AB 4
Murcia **56** C 4
Murdo **102** FG 3
Mureş **58** B 1
Muriaé **111** H 5
Murilo **82** B 2
Murjek **54** H 2
Murmansk **54** K 2
Murmashi **54** K 2
Murom **62** H 4
Muromtsevo **63** P 4
Muroran **71** M 2
Murray Bridge **79** F 6
Murray River **79** G 5
Murrumbidgee River **79** H 5
Murukta **68** H 2
Mururoa **83** F 4
Murwara **72** D 3
Muş **59** F 3
Musala **58** B 2
Musan **71** JK 2
Musandam Peninsula **61** G 4
Muscat **89** K 4
Musgrave **79** G 1
Musgrave Ranges **78** E 4
Mushāsh al 'Ashāwī **61** E 4
Mūsiān **61** E 2
Muskegon **103** JK 3
Muskogee **103** GH 4
Mussende **94** B 2
Mustafa **69** P 3
Mūṭ **88** D 3
Mutanda **94** D 2

Mutarara **95** F 3
Mutare **95** E 3
Mutoray **68** H 3
Mutshatsha **94** CD 2
Mutsu-wan **71** M 2
Mu Us Shamo **70** E 3
Muynak **66** F 2
Muzaffarnagar **72** CD 2
Muzaffarpur **72** DE 2
Muzhi **63** M 2
Muztag **67** L 3
Muztag **67** M 3
Mvomero **93** F 6
Mwanza **92** E 5
Mweka **92** C 5
Mwinilunga **94** CD 2
Myakit **69** S 3
Myaundzha **69** R 3
Mycenae **58** B 3
Myingyan **73** G 3
Myitkyina **73** G 2
Myitta **73** G 5
Myittha **73** G 3
Mymensingh **73** F 3
Mýrdalsjökull **54** B 3
Myrtle Beach **103** L 5
Mys Aniva **69** Q 6
Mys Buorkhaya **69** O 1
Mys Duga-Zapadnaya **69** R 4
Mys Kanin Nos **62** H 2
Mys Kril'on **69** Q 6
Mys Kronotskiy **69** U 4–5
Mys Kurgalskiy **55** J 4
Mys Laydennyy **62** J 2
Mys Lopatka **69** T 5
Mys Navarin **69** X 3
Mys Olyutorskiy **69** VW 4
Mysore **72** C 5
Mysovaya **69** T 2
Mys Peschanyy **66** E 2
Mys Pitsunda **59** F 2
Mys Sarych **59** D 2
Mys Shipunskiy **69** TU 5
Mys Svatoy Nos **69** P 1
Mys Svyatoy Nos **62** GH 2
Mys Taran **55** GH 4–5
Mys Tarkhankut **59** D 1
Mys Taygonos **69** U 3
Mys Terpeniya **69** QR 6
Mys Tolstoy **69** T 4
Mys Uengan **63** MN 1
Mys Yelizavety **69** Q 5
Mys Yuzhnyy **69** ST 4
My Tho **73** J 5

N

Naandi **92** D 3
Naba **73** G 3
Na Baek **73** H 4
Nabk al Gharbī **60** B 3
Nābul **87** H 1
Nābulus **60** B 2
Nachana **72** B 2
Nadiad **72** B 3
Nador **86** E 1
Nadym **63** O 2
Næstved **55** F 4
Naftshahr **61** D 2
Nafuce **91** F 3
Nafūd al 'Urayq **60** D 4
Nafūd as Sirr **66** CD 5–6
Nafūd as Surrah **66** C 6
Naga **75** F 1
Naga Hills **73** FG 2
Nagaland **73** FG 2
Nagano **71** L 3
Nagaoka **71** L 3
Nagasaki **71** J 4
Nagaur **72** B 2
Nagda **72** C 3
Nagercoil **72** C 6
Nago **71** J 5
Nagornyy **69** N 4
Nagoya **71** L 4
Nagpur **72** C 3
Nagqu **70** B 4
Nagykanizsa **58** A 1
Naha **71** J 5
Nahanni National Park **99** M, N 3
Nahariyya **60** B 2
Nahāvand **61** E 2
Nahr an Nīl **60** A 4
Nā'ın **61** F 2
Nain **101** P 4
Nairobi **93** F 5
Najafābād **61** F 2
Najd **60** CD 4
Najin **71** K 2
Najrān **89** GH 5
Nakhichevan' **66** CD 3
Nakhodka **71** K 2
Nakhon Ratchasima **73** H 5
Nakhon Sawan **73** G 4
Nakhon Si Thammarat **73** GH 6
Nakina **100** K 5
Nakuru **93** F 5
Nalayh **68** J 6
Nal'chik **59** F 2
Nālūt **87** H 2
Namak, Kavir-e **61** G 1
Namanga **93** F 5
Namangan **67** J 2
Namapa **95** G 2
Namaqualand **94** B 5
Namatanai **81** F 2
Nambour **79** J 4
Nam Can **73** J 6
Nam Dinh **73** HJ 3
Nametil **95** F 3
Namib Desert **94** AB 4–5
Namib Desert Park **94** AB 4
Namibe **94** A 3
Namibe Reserve **94** A 3
Namibia **94** AB 4
Namjagbarwa Feng **70** C 5
Namkham **73** G 3
Namlea **75** G 4
Namling **72** E 2
Namoi River **79** H 5
Namoluk **82** B 2
Namonuito **82** A 2
Namorik **82** C 2
Nampala **90** C 2
Nampula **95** FG 3
Namru **72** D 1
Namsang **73** G 3
Namsen **54** F 2–3
Namsos **54** F 3
Namtsy **69** NO 3
Namu **82** C 2
Namuli **95** F 3
Namur **52** E 4
Namy **69** O 2
Nancha **69** NO 6
Nanchang **70** G 5
Nanchong **70** E 4
Nancy **57** E 2
Nanda Devi **72** D 1
Nander **72** C 4
Nandyal **72** C 4
Nanfeng **70** G 5
Nanga Parbat **67** J 3–4
Nangatayap **74** D 4
Nangong **70** FG 3
Nang Xian **70** B 5
Nanjiang **70** E 4
Nanjing **71** GH 4
Nan Ling **70** EF 5
Nanning **70** E 6
Nanping (Fujian, China) **71** G 5
Nanping (Gansu, China) **70** DE 4
Nansei-shotō **71** J 5
Nantes **56** C 2
Nanton **99** P 5
Nantong **71** H 4
Nanumanga **82** C 3
Nanumea **82** C 3
Nanuque **111** HJ 4
Nanyang **70** F 4
Nanyuki **93** F 4
Nanzhang **70** F 4
Naococane, Lac **101** NO 5
Napata **88** E 5
Napier **81** R 8
Napier Mountains **115**
Naples **57** F 3
Napo **108** D 4
Napoli **57** F 3
Nara (Japan) **71** L 4
Nara (Mali) **90** C 2
Naranjos **104** C 3
Narasun **68** K 5
Narathiwat **73** H 6
Narayanganj **73** F 3
Narbonne **56** D 3
Nares Strait **114**
Narew **53** H 4
Narmada **72** C 3
Närpes **54** H 3
Narrabri **79** HJ 5
Narrogin **78** B 5
Narsinghgarh **72** C 3
Narssaq **101** S 3
Narva **55** J 4
Narvik **54** G 2
Narwietooma **78** E 3
Naryn **68** G 5
Näsåker **54** G 3
Nashville **103** JK 4
Näsijärvi **54** H 3
Nasik **72** B 3
Nāṣir **92** E 3
Nassau **105** G 2
Nasser, Birkat **88** E 4
Nasser, Lake **88** E 4
Nässjö **55** FG 4
Nata **94** D 4
Natal (Brazil) **111** JK 2
Natal (South Africa) **94–95** E 5
Natashquan **101** P 5
Natchez **103** H 5
Natitingou **90** E 3
Natividade **111** G 3
Natkyizin **73** G 5
Natron, Lake **93** F 5
Natuna, Kepulauan **74** C 3
Naturaliste, Cape **78** A 5
Naupe **108** C 5
Nauru **81** J 2
Nauru **82** C 3
Naushki **68** J 5
Nauta **108** D 4
Navarino **113** C 10
Navarra **56** C 3
Navia **56** B 3
Navojoa **102** DE 6
Navolok **62** G 3
Nawabshah **67** H 5
Náxos **58** C 3
Nayarit **104** B 3
Nāy Band **61** F 4
Nāy Band, Ra's-e **61** F 4
Nayoro **71** M 2
Nazaré **56** B 4
Nazareth **108** C 5
Nazca **110** A 3
Naze **71** J 5
Nazerat **60** B 2
Nazilli **58** C 3
Ndali **90** E 4
Ndélé **92** C 3
Ndendé **91** G 6
Ndola **94** D 2
Neagh, Lough **52** B 4
Néapolis **58** B 3
Near Islands **98** A 5
Nebit-Dag **66** E 3
Nebolchi **62** F 4
Nebraska **102** FG 3
Nechako Reservoir **99** M 5
Necochea **113** E 6
Nédéley **91** H 2
Nedong **73** F 2
Neftelensk **68** J 4
Nefteyugansk **63** O 3
Negage **94** AB 1
Negelli **93** F 3
Negombo **72** C 6
Negonengo **83** F 4
Negra, Punta **108** B 5
Negrais, Cape **73** F 4
Negritos **108** B 4
Negros **75** F 1–2
Nehāvand **61** E 2
Nehe **69** MN 6
Neijiang **70** DE 5
Nei Monggol Zizhiqu **70** DG 2
Neiva **108** CD 3

Nejd (Saudi Arabia) **60** CD 5
Nekemt **93** F 3
Nelemnoye **69** S 2
Nel'kan **69** P 4
Nelkuchan, Gora **69** P 3
Nellore **72** D 5
Nel'ma **69** P 6
Nelson **81** Q 9
Nelson Island **98** D 3
Nelspruit **95** E 5
Néma **86** D 5
Nemunas **55** H 4
Nemuro **71** N 2
Nendo **81** J 4
Nenjiang **69** MN 6
Nepa **68** J 4
Nepal **72** DE 2
Nepeña **108** C 5
Nerchinsk **68** L 5
Nerekhta **62** H 4
Neringa-Nida **55** H 4
Neriquinha **94** C 3
Nesbyen **55** E 3
Néstos **58** B 2
Netanya **60** B 2
Netherlands **52** D–E 4
Netherlands Antilles **105** K 4
Nettilling Lake **101** NO 2
Nettuno **57** F 3
Neuchâtel **57** E 2
Neuquén **113** C 6
Nevada (U.S.A.) **102** C 4
Nevada, Sierra (Spain) **56** C 4
Nevado Ausangate **110** B 3
Nevado Cololo **110** C 4
Nevado Coropuna **110** B 4
Nevado de Cachi **110** C 5
Nevado de Colima **104** B 4
Nevado Huascarán **108** C 5
Nevado Illimani **110** C 4
Nevado Sajama **110** C 4
Nevado Salluyo **110** C 3
Nevado Yerupajá **110** A 3
Never **69** M 5
Nevers **56** D 2
Nevinnomyssk **59** F 2
Nevşehir **59** D 3
Nev'yansk **63** M 4
New Albany **103** J 4
New Amsterdam **109** G 2
Newark (N.J., U.S.A.) **103** M 3
Newark (OH, U.S.A.) **103** K 3
New Bedford **103** M 3
New Bern **103** L 4
New Britain **81** F 3
New Brunswick **101** O 6
Newburgh **103** LM 3
New Caledonia **81** H 6
Newcastle (N.S.W., Austr.) **79** J 5
Newcastle (WY, U.S.A.) **102** EF 3
Newcastle-upon-Tyne **52** C 3
Newcastle Waters **78** E 2
New England **103** MN 3
Newenham, Cape **98** DE 4
Newfoundland **101** PQ 5
Newfoundland **101** QR 6
New Georgia **81** G 3
New Glasgow **101** P 6
New Guinea **80** E 3
New Hanover **81** F 2
New Haven **103** M 3
New Hebrides **81** J 5
New Iberia **103** H 6
New Ireland **81** F 2
New Ireland **82** AB 3
New Liskeard **103** K 2
Newman **78** B 3
New Meadows **102** C 2
New Mexico **102** E 5
New Orleans **103** J 5–6
New Plymouth **81** Q 8
Newport (OR, U.S.A.) **102** AB 3
Newport (U.K.) **52** C 4
Newport Beach **102** C 5
New Providence Island **105** G 3
Newry **78** D 2
New Siberian Islands **114**
New South Wales **79** GH 5
New Stuvahok **98** F 4
Newtonabbey **52** B 4
New York (N.Y., U.S.A.) **103** M 3
New York (U.S.A.) **103** L 3
New Zealand **81** RS 9
Neya **62** H 4
Neyriz **61** G 3
Neyshābūr **66** F 3
Nezhin **62** F 5
Ngamiland **94** C 3
Ngamring **72** E 2
Ngangla Ringco **72** DE 1
Nganglong Kangri **72** D 1
Ngatik **82** B 2
Ngidinga **92** B 6
Ngoc Linh **73** J 4
Ngoko **91** H 5
Ngoring **70** C 3
Nguara **91** H 3
Ngwane **95** E 5
Nhambiquara **110** E 3
Nha Trang **73** JK 5
Niagara Falls **103** L 3
Niamey **90** E 3
Niamtougou **90** E 3
Niangara **92** D 4
Nia-Nia **92** D 4
Nianzishan **69** M 6
Nias, Pulau **74** AB 3
Niassa **95** F 2
Nicaragua **104** EF 5
Nicaragua, Lago de **104** EF 5
Nice **57** E 3
Nichalakh **69** QR 1
Nicobar Islands **73** F 6
Nicocli **108** C 2
Nicosia **59** D 3
Nicosia (Cyprus) **60** A 2
Nicoya, Península de **104** E 6
Nicuadala **95** F 3
Nidelva **55** E 4
Niedersachsen **53** EF 4
Niedre Tauern **57** F 2
Niellé **90** C 3
Niemba **92** D 6
Nieuw Amsterdam **109** H 2
Nieuw Nickerie **109** G 2
Nieuwoudtville **94** BC 6
Niğde **59** DE 3
Niger **91** FG 2
Niger **91** F 4
Niger Delta **91** F 5
Nigeria **91** EG 4
Nihau **83** E 1
Nihiru **83** F 4
Niigata **71** L 3
Nijmegen **52** E 4
Nikel **54** K 2
Nikk **90** E 4
Nikolayev **58** D 1
Nikolayevka **63** N 5
Nikolayevsk-na-Amure **69** PQ 5
Nikoleyeva **55** JK 4
Nikol'sk **62** J 4
Nikol'skiy **67** H 1
Nikopol **59** D 1
Nīkpey **61** E 1
Nikšic **58** A 2
Nikumaroro **82** D 3
Nile (Egypt) **60** A 4
Nimba, Monts **90** C 4
Nimbe **91** F 5
Nimes **56** D 3
Nimule **92** E 4
Nincheng **71** G 2
Ninety Mile Beach **79** H 6
Nineveh **60** D 1
Ningbo **71** H 5
Ningde **71** G 5
Ningdu **70** G 5
Ningxia Huizu Zizhiqu **70** E 3
Ninigo Group **82** A 3
Nioro du Sahel **90** C 2
Niort **56** C 2
Niout **86** D 5
Nipigon **100** K 6
Nipigon, Lake **100** K 6
Nipissing, Lake **101** LM 6
Nippur **89** H 2
Nis **58** B 2
Nisāb **89** H 6
Nísoi **58** B 3
Niterói **111** H 5
Nitiya **69** P 4
Nitra **53** G 5
Niuafo'ou **82** D 4
Niuato Putapu **82** D 4
Niue **82** D 4
Niulakita **82** C 3
Niutao **82** C 3
Nizamabad **72** C 4
Nizhneangarsk **68** JK 4
Nizhne-Ozernaya **69** UV 4
Nizhneudinsk **68** G 5
Nizhnevartovskoye **63** PQ 3
Nizhneye Karelina **68** J 4
Nizhniy Pyandzh **67** H 3
Nizhniy Tagil **63** M 4
Nizhnyaya Omka **63** O 4
Nizhnyaya Poyma **68** G 4
Nizhnyaya Tunguska **68** F 3
Nizhnyaya Voch' **62** K 3
Nizhnyaya Zolotitsa (Nizhnyaya) **62** H 2
Nizina Podlaska **53** H 4
Nizip **60** B 1
Njunes **54** G 2
Njutånger **54** G 3
Nkayi **91** G 6
Nkhata Bay **95** E 2
Nkolabona **91** G 5
Nkomi, Lagune **91** F 6
Nkongsamba **91** G 4–5
Nkurenkuru **94** B 3
Noatak National Preserve **98** F 2
Noefs, Ile des **93** J 6
Nogales **102** DE 5
Nogayskiye Step' **59** G 2
Noginsk **62** G 4
Nokrek Peak **73** F 2
Nomad **82** A 3
Nome **98** D 3
Nonacho Lake **99** Q 3
Nong Khai **73** H 4
Nonouti **82** C 3
Nordaustlandet **114**
Nordfriesische Inseln **53** E 3–4
Norðoyar **52** A 1
Nordkapp **54** J 1
Nordkinn **54** J 1
Nord-Kvaloy **54** G 1
Nordland **54** EF 2
Nordostrundingen **114**
Nordöyane **54** E 3
Nordreisa **54** H 2
Nordsjßn **55** E 4
Nord-Tröndelag **54** F 3
Nordvik **68** K 1
Norfolk (NE, U.S.A.) **102** G 3
Norfolk (VA, U.S.A.) **103** L 4
Norfolk Islands **82** C 4
Norge **54** EF 2
Nori **63** O 2
Noril'sk **63** R 2
Norman **102** G 4
Normanby Island **79** J 1
Normandie **56** CD 2
Normanton **79** G 2
Norra Storfjället **54** G 2
Norrbotten **54** GH 2
Norrköping **55** G 4
Norrland **54** FG 3
Norrtälje **55** G 4
Norseman **78** C 5
Norsjö **54** G 3
Norsk **69** O 5
Norte, Canal do **109** H 3
Northam **78** B 5
Northampton **52** C 4
North Andaman **73** F 5
North Battleford **99** Q 5
North Bay **101** M 6
North Bend **102** AB 3
North Cape **82** C 5
North Carolina **103** L 4

North Cascades National Park **102** BC 2
North Channel **52** B 3–4
North Dakota **102** FG 2
Northeast Cape **98** D 3
Northeast Providence Channel **105** G 2
Northern Cook Islands **82** E 3
Northern Indian Lake **99** S 4
Northern Ireland **52** B 4
Northern Mariana Islands **82** B 1
Northern Territory **78** E 2–3
North Fork Pass **98** K 3
North Geomagnetic Pole **114**
North Highlands **102** BC 4
North Island **81** Q 8
North Korea **71** K 2
North Lakhimpur **73** F 2
North Las Vegas **102** C 4
North Little Rock **103** H 5
North Magnetic Pole **114**
North Minch **52** B 3
North Platte (Nebraska U.S.A.) **102** F 3
North Platte (Nebraska U.S.A.) **102** F 3
North Point **80** L 8
North Pole **114**
North Sea **52** D 3
North Slope **98** FH 2
North Uist **52** B 3
Northumberland Islands **79** J 3
Northumberland Strait **101** P 6
North West Cape **78** A 3
North West Highlands **52** BC 3
Northwest Territories **99** NT 2
Norton Sound **98** DE 3
Norway **54** F 2
Norwegian Sea **54** DE 2–3
Norwich **52** D 4
Noshiro **71** L 2
Nosovaya **62** K 2
Nosratābād **66** F 5
Nossob **94** BC 5
Nosy-Bé **95** H 2
Noteć **53** G 4
Nótioi Sporádhes **58** C 3
Notodden **55** E 4
Noto-hantō **71** L 3
Notre Dame Bay **101** QR 6
Nottingham (Canada) **101** MN 3
Nottingham (U.K.) **52** C 4
Nouadhibou **86** B 4
Nouakchott **86** B 5
Nouméa **81** J 6
Nouvelle-Calédonie **81** H 6
Nova Cruz **111** JK 2
Nova Iguaçu **111** H 5
Nova Mambone **95** F 4
Novara **57** E 2
Nova Scotia **101** OP 7
Nova Vida **110** D 3
Novaya Kakhovka **59** D 1
Novaya Kazanka **62** J 6
Novaya Zemlya **62** KL 1
Novgorod **55** K 4
Novgorodka **55** J 4
Novi Ligure **57** E 3
Novillero **104** A 3
Novi Pazar **58** AB 2
Novi Sad **58** A 1
Novoaltaysk **63** QR 5
Novobiryusinskiy **68** G 4
Novograd-Volynskiy **55** J 5
Novo Hamburgo **112** FG 4
Novokazalinsk **67** G 1
Novokocherdyk **63** M 5
Novokuznetsk **63** R 5
Novolazarevskaya **115**
Novomoskovsk **62** G 5
Novopavlovskoye **68** K 5
Novopokrovskaya **59** F 1
Novopolotsk **55** J 4
Novorossiysk **59** E 2
Novorybnoye **68** HJ 1
Novoshakhtinsk **62** H 6
Novosibirsk **63** QR 4
Novosibirskiye Ostrova → New Siberian Islands **61** QR 2
Novotroitskoye **67** JK 2
Novoyeniseysk **68** FG 4
Novoye Ust'ye **69** Q 4
Novvy Bug **59** D 1
Novy Uzen' **66** E 2
Novyy Karymkary **63** N 3
Novyy Port **63** O 2
Novyy Tanguy **68** H 4
Nowa Sól **53** FG 4
Nowbarān **61** E 2
Nowdesheh **61** E 2
Nowgong **73** F 2
Nowra **79** J 5
Now Shahr **61** F 1
Nowy Sacz **53** H 5
Nsukka **91** F 4
Ntui **91** G 5
Nuatja **90** E 4
Nūbiyah **88** DE 5
Nueltin Lake **99** S 3
Nueva Esperanza **110** CD 4
Nueva Galia **113** CD 6
Nueva Gerona **104** F 3
Nueva León **104** BC 2
Nueva Lubecka **113** BC 7
Nueva Rosita **104** B 2
Nueve de Julio **113** D 6
Nuevo Casas Grandes **102** E 5
Nuevo Laredo **104** BC 2
Nuevo Mundo, Cerro **110** C 5
Nuevo Rocafuerte **108** C 4
Nugāl **93** H 3
Nuguria Islands **82** B 3
Nui **82** C 3
Nukey Bluff **79** F 5
Nukhayb **60** D 2
Nuku'alofa **82** D 4
Nukufetau **82** C 3
Nuku Hiva **83** F 3
Nukulaelae **82** D 3
Nukumanu Islands **82** B 3
Nukunau **82** C 3
Nukunonu **82** D 3
Nukuoro **82** B 2
Nukus **66** FG 2
Nullarbor Plain **78** DE 5
Numan **91** G 4
Numbulwar Mission **78** EF 1
Numfor, Pulau **75** H 4
Numto **63** O 3
Nungnain Sum **71** G 1
Nunivak Island **98** D 3–4
Nunlygran **98** B 2
Nuntherungie **79** G 5
Nunyamo **98** C 2
Nuoro **57** E 3
Nuqrah **60** C 4
Nuratau, Khrebet **67** H 2
Nuremberg **53** F 5
Nurhak Daği **59** E 3
Nūrī **88** E 5
Nuristan **67** J 3
Nürnberg **53** F 5
Nurri, Mount **79** H 5
Nushki **67** H 5
Nutak **101** P 4
Nuupas **54** J 2
Nuwaybi'al Muzayyinah **60** B 3
Nyabéssan **91** G 5
Nyakanazi **92** E 5
Nyaksimvol' **63** M 3
Nyala **88** CD 6
Nyamlell **92** D 3
Nyandoma **62** H 3
Nyazepetrovsk **63** L 4
Nyda **63** O 2
Nyika Plateau **95** E 2
Nyima **72** E 1
Nyiregyháza **58** B 1
Nyiru, Mount **93** F 4
Nyköbing **55** F 5
Nyköping **55** G 4
Nylstroom **94** D 4
Nymagee **79** H 5
Nyurba **68** L 3
Nzega **92** E 5
Nzerékoré **90** C 4

O

Oahe, Lake **102** F 2
Oahe Dam **102** F 3
Oahu **83** E 1
Oakbank **79** G 5
Oakland **102** B 4
Oakley **102** F 4
Oak Ridge **103** K 4
Oates Coast **115**
Oaxaca **104** C 4
Oaxaca de Juárez **104** C 4
Oba **100** L 6
Obala **91** G 5
Oban **52** B 3
Obeh **67** G 4
Óbidos **109** GH 4
Obihiro **71** M 2
Obil'noye **59** FG 1
Obluch'ye **69** O 6
Obodovka **58** C 1
Obruk Platosu **59** D 3
Obshchiy Syrt **62** K 5
Obskaya Guba **63** O 1–2
Ocala **103** K 6
Ocaña **108** D 2
Occidental, Cordillera **108** C 2–3
Oconee River **103** K 5
Odawara **71** L 3–4
Ödemiş **58** C 3
Odendaalsrus **94** D 5
Odense **55** EF 4
Oder **53** F 4
Odessa **102** F 5
Odessa (U.S.S.R.) **58** D 1
Odienné **90** C 4
Odorheiu Secuiesc **58** C 1
Odra **53** FG 4
Odzala National Park **91** GH 5
Oeiras **111** H 2
Oeno **83** G 4
Offenbach **53** E 4–5
Oficina **109** F 2
Ogaden **93** GH 3
Ōgaki **71** L 3
Ogallala **102** F 3
Ogbomosho **91** EF 4
Ogden **102** D 3
Ogilvie Mountains **98** JK 2
Oglat Beraber **86** E 2
Ogoki **100** K 5
Ogooué **91** G 6
Ograzden **58** B 2
O'Higgins, Lago **113** B 8
Ohio **103** K 3
Ohio River **103** K 4
Ohopoho **94** A 3
Ohrid **58** B 2
Oiapoque **109** H 3
Ōita **71** K 4
Ojo de Agua **112** D 4
Ojos del Salado, Cerro **112** C 4
Okaba **75** J 5
Okahandja **94** B 4
Okak Islands **101** P 4
Okapa **80** E 3
Okara **67** J 4
Okavango **94** C 3
Okavango Swamp **94** C 3
Okavarumendu **94** B 4
Okayama **71** K 3–4
Okeanskoye **69** T 5
Okeechobee, Lake **103** K 6
Okha (U.S.S.R.) **69** Q 5
Okhotsk **69** Q 4
Okhotskiy Perevoz **69** P 3
Okhotskoye More **69** QS 4
Okinawa-jima **71** JK 5
Oki-shotō **71** K 3
Oklahoma **102–103** G 4
Oklahoma City **103** G 4
Okondja **91** G 6
Okstindan **54** F 2
Oktemberyan **59** F 2
Oktyabrskiy **62** KL 5

Oktyabr'skiy (U.S.S.R.) **68** F 5
Oktyabr'skiy (U.S.S.R.) **69** N 4
Oktyabr'skoye **63** N 3
Öland **55** G 4
Olanga **54** JK 2
Olavarría **113** DE 6
Olbia **57** E 3
Old Bahama Channel **105** G 3
Oldenburg **53** E 4
Olenegorsk **54** K 2
Olenëk **68** M 1
Olenëk **68** K 2
Olenëkskiy Zaliv **68** LM 1
Olenevod **69** WX 3
Oléron, Ile d' **56** C 2
Ölgiy **68** F 6
Olifants **95** E 4
Olimarao **82** A 2
Olimbia **58** B 3
Olimbia (Greece) **58** B 3
Olimbos**58** B 2–3
Olinda **111** K 2
Ollagüe, Volcán **110** C 5
Olmos **108** C 5
Olomouc **53** G 5
Olonets **54** K 3
Oloyskiye Gory **69** U 2
Olsztyn **53** H 4
Olt **58** B 2
Olympia **102** B 2
Olympia (Greece) **58** B 3
Olympus **58** B 3
Olympus, Mount **102** B 2
Olyutorka **69** V 3
Olyutorskiy **69** VW 3
Omaha **103** G 3
Oman **89** JK 4–5
Omatako, Mount **94** B 4
Omboué **91** F 6
Omchali **66** E 2
Ömnögovĭ **70** DE 2
Omolon **69** T 2
Omolon **69** U 2
Omsk **63** O 4
Omutinskiy **63** N 4
Omutninsk **62** K 4
Onawa **103** G 3
Ondangwa **94** B 3
Ondo **91** E 4
Öndörhaan **68** K 6
Onega **62** G 3
Ongole **72** D 4
Onilahy **95** G 4
Onitsha **91** F 4
Onkuchakh **68** KL 2
Ono-i-Lau Islands **82** CD 4
Onon **68** L 5
Onotoa **82** C 3
Onslow **78** B 3
Ontario **102** C 3
Ontario, Lake **103** L 3
Ontojärvi **54** J 3
Ontong Java **82** B 3
Oodnadatta **79** F 4
Ooldea **78** E 5
Oostende **52** D 4
Opasatika **100** L 6
Opis **60** D 2
Opobo **91** F 5
Opole **53** G 4
Oporto **56** B 3
Oppland **54** E 3
Oradea **58** B 1
Oran **86** E 1
Orange (France) **57** D 3
Orange (TX, U.S.A.) **103** H 5
Orange, Cabo **109** H 3
Orange Free State **94** D 5
Oranje **94** B 5
Orapa **94** D 4
Orcadas **115**
Ord, Mount **78** D 2
Ord River **78** D 2
Ordu **59** E 2
Ordynskoye **63** Q 5
Ordzhonikidze **59** FG 2
Örebro **55** FG 4
Oregon **102** BC 3
Orel **62** G 5
Orem **102** D 3
Orenburg **62** K 5
Orense **56** B 3
Öresund **55** F 4
Organ Peak **102** E 5
Orgeyev **58** C 1
Orhon Gol **68** HJ 6
Oriental, Cordillera (Bolivia) **110** CD 3–5
Oriental, Cordillera (Colombia) **108** CD 2–3
Orihuela **56** C 4
Orillia **101** M 7
Orinduik **109** F 3
Orinoco (Colombia) **108** E 3
Orinoco (Venezuela) **108** E 2
Orissa **72** DE 3
Orissaare **55** H 4
Oristano **57** E 3–4
Orivesi **54** J 3
Oriximiná **109** G 4
Orizaba **104** C 4
Orkanger **54** E 3
Orkney **94** D 5
Orkney Islands **52** C 3
Orlando **103** K 6
Orléans **56** D 2
Ormara **67** GH 5
Ormoc **75** FG 1
Ornö **55** G 4
Örnsköldsvik **54** G 3
Oro, Monte d' **57** E 3
Orocué **108** D 3
Oroluk **82** B 2
Orona **82** D 3
Oroqen Zizhiqi **69** M 5
Oroquieta **75** F 2
Oroville **102** C 2
Orsa **54** F 3
Orsa Finnmark **54** F 3
Orsha **55** JK 5
Orsk **63** L 5
Ortegal, Cabo **56** B 3
Orto-Ayan **69** NO 1
Ortonville **103** G 2
Orūmīyeh **59** F 3
Oruro **110** C 4
Osa **68** H 5
Ōsaka **71** L 4
Osakarovka **63** O 5
Osceola **103** H 3
Osh **67** J 2
Oshakati **94** AB 3
Oshkosh **103** J 3
Oshogbo **91** EF 4
Oshtoran Kūh **61** E 2
Osijek **57** G 2
Osinovka **63** Q 6
Oskarshamn **55** G 4
Oskoba **68** H 3
Oslo **55** F 4
Oslofjorden **55** F 4
Osmanabad **72** C 4
Osmaneli **58** D 2
Osmaniye **59** E 3
Osnabrück **53** E 4
Osorno **113** B 7
Osoyoos **99** O 6
Ost Berlin **55** F 5
Ost Berlin **55** F 5
Österdalälven **54** F 3
Österdalen **54** F 3
Östergötland **55** G 4
Östersund **54** FG 3
Östhavet **54** JK 1
Ostrava **53** G 5
Ostroda **53** GH 4
Ostrołeka **53** H 4
Ostrov (Russia, U.S.S.R.) **55** J 4
Ostrova Chernyye Brat'ya **69** S 6
Ostrov Bol'shoy Begichev **68** KL 1
Ostrov Bol'shoy Shantar **69** P 4–5
Ostrov Feklistova **69** P 4–5
Ostrov Iturup **69** R 6–7
Ostrov Ketoy **69** S 6
Ostrov Kil'din **54** KL 2
Ostrov Kolguyev **62** J 2
Ostrov Kotel'nyy **69** P 1
Ostrov Malyy Lyakhovskiy **69** Q 1
Ostrov Matua **69** S 6
Ostrovnoye (U.S.S.R.) **69** U 2
Ostrov Onekotan **69** ST 6
Ostrov Paramushir **69** ST 5
Ostrov Rasshua **69** S 6
Ostrov Shiashkotan **69** S 6
Ostrov Simushir **69** S 6
Ostrov Urup **69** S 6
Ostrov Vaygach **63** L 1–2
Ostrov Zav'yalova **69** RS 4
Ostrowiec Świetokrzyski **53** H 4
Ostrow Wielkopolski **53** G 4
Ōsumi-shotō **71** JK 4
Otaru **71** M 2
Otavalo **108** C 3
Otavi **94** B 3
Otepää Kõrgustik **55** J 4
Otjozondu **94** B 4
Otradnoye **69** T 5
Otta **54** E 3
Ottawa **101** MN 6
Ottawa River **101** M 6
Ottumwa **103** H 3
Otway, Cape **79** G 6
Otwock **53** H 4
Ouachita Mountains **103** GH 5
Ouadane **86** C 4
Ouadda **92** C 3
Ouaddaï **91** J 3
Ouad Naga **86** BC 5
Ouagadougou **90** DE 3
Ouahigouya **90** D 3
Oualam **90** E 3
Ouanda-Djallé **92** C 3
Ouangolodougou **90** D 4
Ouargla **87** G 2
Ouarzazate **86** D 2
Oubangui **91** H 5
Oudtshoorn **94** C 6
Oued Zem **86** D 2
Ouessant, Ile de **56** B 2
Ouesso **91** H 5
Ouezzane **86** DE 2
Ouham **91** H 4
Oujda **86** E 2
Oulu **54** J 2
Oulujärvi **54** J 3
Oum Chalouba **91** J 2
Oum Hadjer **91** H 3
Ounianga **91** J 2
Ouricuri **111** J 2
Ourinhos **111** G 5
Outapi **94** A 3
Outer Hebrides **52** B 3
Outjo **94** B 4
Outokumpu **54** J 3
Ouvéa **81** J 6
Ouyen **79** G 5–6
Ovalle **112** B 5
Ovamboland **94** AB 3
Oviedo **56** B 3
Owensboro **103** J 4
Owerri **91** F 4
Owo **91** F 4
Oxford **52** C 4
Oyem **91** G 5
Oyo **90** E 4
Oyón **110** A 3
Oysurdakh **69** S 2
Ozamiz **75** F 2
Ozark Plateau **103** H 4
Ózd **58** B 1
Ozernovskiy **69** T 5
Ozero Balkhash **63** OP 6
Ozero Baykal **68** J 5
Ozero Chany **63** P 5
Ozero Chervonoye **55** J 5
Ozero Dadynskoye **59** FG 1
Ozero Il'men **55** K 4
Ozero Imandra **54** K 2
Ozero Keret' **54** K 2
Ozero Kubenskoye **62** G 4
Ozero Leksozero **54** K 3
Ozero Manych Gudilo **59** F 1
Ozero Nyuk **54** K 3
Ozero Osvejskoje **55** J 4
Ozero Pyaozero **54** K 2

Ozero Sasykkol' **63** Q 6
Ozero Segozero **54** K 3
Ozero Seletyteniz **63** O 5
Ozero Sevan **59** G 2
Ozero Syamozero **54** K 3
Ozero Taymyr **68** H 1
Ozero Tengiz **63** N 5
Ozero Verkhneye Kuyto **54** K 3
Ozero Zaysan **63** Q 6

P

Paarl **94** B 6
Paavola **54** J 3
Pacaraima, Sierra **109** F 3
Pacasmayo **108** BC 5
Pachiza **108** C 5
Pachuca **104** C 3–4
Pacific Ocean **116**
Padang **74** B 4
Padang, Pulau **74** B 3
Padangpanjang **74** AB 4
Padangsidempuan **74** A 3
Paddle Prairie **99** O 4
Paderborn **53** E 4
Padilla **110** D 4
Padova **57** F 2
Padre Island **103** G 6
Paducah **103** J 4
Pag **57** FG 3
Pagan **82** A 1
Pago-Pago **82** D 3
Pagri **72** E 2
Päijänne **54** J 3
Paisley **52** BC 3
Paita **108** B 4–5
Pakin **82** B 2
Pakistan **67** H 5
Pakokku **73** FG 3
Pak Phanang **73** H 6
Pakse **73** J 4
Pakwach **92** E 4
Palacios **103** G 6
Palangkaraya **74** D 4
Palanpur **72** B 3
Palapye **94** D 4
Palatka **69** RS 3
Palauk **73** G 5
Palaw **73** G 5
Palawan **74–75** E 2
Palawan Passage **74–75** E 1–2
Palca **110** C 4
Palembang **74** BC 4
Palencia **56** C 3
Palenque **104** D 4
Palermo **57** F 4
Palestine **60** B 2–3
Paletwa **73** F 3
Pali **72** B 2
Paljakka **54** J 3
Palk Strait **72** C 5–6
Pallastunturit **54** H 2
Palliser, Cape **81** R 9
Palma **56** D 4
Pal Malmal **81** F 3
Palmares **111** JK 2
Palmar Sur **104** F 6
Palma Soriano **105** G 3
Palm Bay **103** KL 6
Palmeira dos Indios **111** J 2
Palmeirais **111** H 2
Palmer **115**
Palmer Archipelago **115**
Palmer Land **115**
Palmerston **82** E 4
Palmerston North **81** R 9
Palmira **108** C 3
Palmyra (Pacific Ocean, U.S.A.) **82** E 2
Palmyra (Syria) **60** C 2
Palmyras Point **72** E 3
Palo Alto **102** B 4
Paloich **88** E 6
Palopo **75** F 4
Palo Santo **112** E 4
Paltamo **54** J 3
Palu (Indonesia) **75** E 4
Palu (Turkey) **59** EF 3
Pamekasan **74** D 5
Pamir **67** JK 3
Pamlico Sound **103** L 4
Pampa **102** F 4
Pampas **112–113** D 5–6
Pamplona **56** C 3
Pan, Tierra del **56** B 3
Panaji **72** B 4
Panama **108** C 2
Panamá, Golfo de **108** C 2
Panama Canal **108** B 2
Panama City **103** J 5
Panay **75** F 1
Pandamatenga **94** D 3
Pandharpur **72** BC 4
Pandivere Kõrgustik **55** J 4
Panevežys **55** HJ 4
Panggoe **82** B 3
Panjao **67** H 4
Panjgur **67** G 5
Panorama **111** F 5
Pantanal de São Lourénço **110** E 4
Pantanal do Río Negro **110** E 4
Pantelleria **57** F 4
Pan Xian **70** DE 5
Paoua **92** B 3
Pápa **58** A 1
Papeete **83** F 4
Papenburg **53** E 4
Papey **54** C 3
Paphos **59** D 4
Papua, Gulf of **80** DE 3
Papua New Guinea **80** E 2–3
Papua New Guinea **82** AB 3
Pará **109** GH 5
Parabel **63** Q 4
Paracatu **111** G 4
Paracel Islands **73** K 4
Paraguai **110** E 5
Paraguarí **112** E 4
Paraguay **110** DE 5
Paraguay **112** E 4
Paraíba **111** J 2
Parakou **90** E 4
Paramaribo **109** GH 2
Paramirim **111** H 3
Paraná (Argentina) **112** DE 5
Paraná (Brazil) **111** F 5
Paranaguá **112** G 4
Paranam **109** G 2
Paranavai **111** F 5
Parangaba **111** J 1
Paraoa **83** F 4
Paratinga **111** H 3
Parbig **63** Q 4
Parc National de la Boucle De Baoule **90** C 3
Parc National de la Komoé **90** D 4
Parc National de Sinianka-Minia **91** H 3
Parc National de Taï **90** C 4
Parc National de Wonga Wongué **91** F 6
Parc National de Zakouma **91** H 3
Parc National du Bamingui-Ban-goran **92** BC 3
Parc National du Niokolo Koba **90** B 3
Parcs Nationaux du "W" **90** E 3
Pardo **111** H 4
Pardubice **53** G 4
Parecis, Serra dos **110** D 3
Parepare **75** E 4
Parima, Sierra **109** F 3
Parinari **108** D 4
Pariñas, Punta **108** B 4
Parintins **109** G 4
Paris (France) **56** D 2
Paris (TX, U.S.A.) **103** G 5
Parkano **54** H 3
Parker **102** D 5
Parkersburg **103** K 4
Parlakimidi **72** D 4
Parlakote **72** D 4
Parma **57** F 3
Parnaíba **111** H 1
Parnamirim **111** J 2
Parnarama **111** H 2
Parnassós Óros **58** B 3
Pärnu **55** H 4
Parpaillon **57** E 3
Parral **113** B 6
Parry Islands **114**
Parry Peninsula **99** MN 2
Partille **55** F 4
Partizansk **71** K 2
Paryang **72** D 2
Parys **94** D 5
Pasadena **102** C 5
Pascagoula **103** J 5
Pas de Calais **52** D 4
Pasni **67** G 5
Paso de Indios **113** C 7
Paso del Limay **113** BC 7
Paso de los Libres **112** E 4
Paso de los Vientos **105** H 3–4
Paso de San Francisco **112** C 4
Paso Río Mayo **113** B 8
Passau **53** F 5
Passo Fundo **112** F 4
Passos **111** G 5
Pasto **108** C 3
Pastos Bons **111** H 2
Patagonia **113** BC 7–9
Patan (India) **72** B 3
Patan (Nepal) **72** DE 2
Paterson **103** LM 3
Pathankot **72** C 1
Patiala **72** C 1–2
Pativilca **108** C 6
Patkaglik **67** M 3
Patna **72** E 2
Patnagarh **72** D 3
Patos **111** J 2
Patos, Lagoa dos **112** F 5
Patos de Minas **111** G 4
Pátrai **58** B 3
Patras **58** B 3
Patrïkos Kólpos **58** B 3
Patrocínio **111** G 4
Pau **56** C 3
Pau d'Arco **109** J 5
Paulina Peak **102** B 3
Paulistana **111** H 2
Paulo Afonso **111** J 2
Pauls Valley **103** G 5
Pavlodar **63** P 5
Pavlof Volcano **98** E 4
Pavlovka **63** O 5
Paxson **98** H 3
Payakumbuh **74** B 3–4
Paynes Find **78** B 4
Paysandú **112** E 5
Payturma **68** F 1
Pazardžik **58** B 2
Peace River **99** P 4
Peaked Mountain **103** N 2
Pearl **103** J 5
Peary Land **114**
Pebane **95** F 3
Pebas **108** D 4
Peć **58** B 2
Pechora **62** K 2
Pechorskoye More **62** KL 2
Pecos **102** F 5
Pecos Plains **102** F 5
Pecos River **102** F 5
Pécs **58** A 1
Pedernales **109** F 2
Pedro Afonso **109** J 5
Pedro de Valdivia **110** BC 5
Pedro Juan Caballero **110** E 5
Peera Peera Poolanna Lake **79** F 4
Pegu **73** G 4
Pegunungan Barisan **74** B 4
Pegunungan Maoke **75** J 4
Pegunungan Muller **74** D 3
Pegunungan Schwaner **74** D 4
Pegu Yoma **73** G 3–4
Pehuajó **113** D 6
Peixe **111** G 3
Pekalongan **74** CD 5
Pekanbaru **74** B 3
Pekin **103** HJ 3

Peking **71** G 3
Pelat, Mont **57** E 3
Pelješac **57** G 3
Pelly **98** L 3
Pelly Bay **99** U 2
Pelly Crossing **98** K 3
Pelly Mountains **98** L 3
Peloponnese **58** B 3
Pelopónnisos **58** B 3
Pelotas **112** F 5
Pelvoux, Massif du **57** E 3
Pemangkat **74** C 3
Pematangsiantar **74** A 3
Pemba **95** G 2
Pemba Island **93** FG 6
Pembina **102** G 2
Penas, Golfo de **113** AB 8
Pendembu **90** B 4
Penedo **111** J 3
Penglai **71** GH 3
Península Brecknock **113** B 9
Península de Nicoya **104** E 6
Península de Taitao **113** AB 8
Península Valdés **113** D 7
Péninsule de Gaspé **101** OP 6
Peninsule d'Ungava **101** MN 4
Penisola Salentina **57** G 3
Penninechain **52** C 4
Pennsylvania **103** L 3
Penny Ice Cap **101** O 2
Penong **78** E 5
Penrhyn **83** E 3
Pensacola **103** J 5
Pensacola Mountains **115**
Pentecoste **82** C 4
Pentecôte **81** J 5
Penza **62** H 5
Penzhinskaya Guba **69** U 3
Penzhinskiy Khrebet **69** U 3
Peoria **103** J 3
Perche, Collines du **56** D 2
Pereira **108** C 3
Pereval Yablonitse **58** BC 1
Pergamino **112** D 5
Pergamon **58** C 3
Périgueux **56** CD 2
Perm **62** L 4
Pernambuco **111** J 2
Perpignan **56** D 3
Perryville **98** F 4
Persepolis **61** F 3
Persevarancia **110** D 3
Persia **66** EF 4
Persian Gulf → The Gulf **61** F 4
Perth (Australia) **78** B 5
Perth (U.K.) **52** C 3
Perthus, Col de **56** D 3
Peru **108** C 5
Perugia **57** F 3
Pervomaysk (Ukraine, U.S.S.R.) **58** D 1
Pervomayskiy **62** H 3
Pervoural'sk **63** L 4
Pesaro **57** F 3
Pescara **57** F 3
Peschanyy, Mys **66** E 2
Peshawar **67** J 4
Peski Karakumy **66–67** FG 3
Peski Kyzylkum **67** GH 2
Peski Sary Ishikotrau **63** P 6
Peski Taukum **67** JK 2
Pessac **56** C 3
Petaluma **102** B 4
Petare **108** E 1
Petauke **95** E 2
Petén **104** DE 4
Peterborough (Ontario, Can.) **101** M 7
Peterborough (South Australia) **79** F 5
Peter I Island **115**
Petersburg (VA, U.S.A.) **103** L 4
Petites Pyrénées **56** D 3
Petorca **112** B 5
Petra **88** F 2
Petra Azul **111** H 4
Petrel **115**
Petrila **58** B 1
Petrodvorets **55** J 4
Petrolina **111** H 2
Petropavlovsk **63** NO 4–5
Petropavlovsk-Kamchatskiy **69** ST 5
Petrópolis **111** H 5
Petrova Gora **57** G 2
Petrovsk **62** J 5
Petrovsk-Zabaykal'skiy **68** J 5
Petrozavodsk **62** FG 3
Peureulak **74** A 3
Pevek **114**
Pforzheim **53** E 5
Phalodi **72** B 2
Phaltan **72** BC 4
Phatthalung **73** H 6
Phenix City **103** J 5
Phet Buri **73** G 5
Philadelphia **103** M 4
Philae **88** E 4
Philippines **75** G 1
Philippine Trench **75** G 1–2
Phillipsburg **102** G 4
Phitsanulok **73** H 4
Phnom Aural **74** B 1
Phnom Penh **73** H 5
Phoenix **102** D 5
Phoenix Islands **82** D 3
Phuket **73** G 6
Phuoc Le **73** J 5
Phu Set **73** J 4
Phu Vinh **73** J 5–6
Piacenza **57** EF 2–3
Piara Açu **109** H 5
Piatra Neamţ **58** C 1
Piauí **111** H 2
Pibor Post **92** E 3
Picardie **56** D 2
Pic Boby **95** H 4
Pichanal **110** D 5
Pichilemu **113** B 5
Pickle Lake **100** J 5
Pico Cristóbal Colón **108** D 1
Pico de Aneto **56** D 3
Pico Rondón **109** F 3
Picos **111** H 2
Pico Tamacuarí **108** E 3
Pidurutalagala **72** D 6
Piedras Negras **104** B 2
Piedra Sola **112** E 5
Pielinen **54** J 3
Pierre **102** FG 3
Piešt'ány **53** G 5
Pietarsaari **54** H 3
Pietermaritzburg **94** DE 5
Pietersburg **94** D 4
Pigué **113** D 6
Pihtipudas **54** J 3
Pikelot **82** A 2
Pikhtovka **63** Q 4
Pik Kommunizma **67** J 3
Pik Pobedy **67** KL 2
Piła **53** G 4
Pilão Arcado **111** H 3
Pilar (Alagoas, Brazil) **111** J 2
Pilar (Paraguay) **112** E 4
Pilcomayo **110** DE 5
Pilot Peak **102** D 3
Pil'tun **69** Q 5
Pim **63** O 3
Pimenta Bueno **110** D 3
Pimental **109** G 4
Pimentel **108** B 5
Pinaki **83** F 4
Pínar del Río **104** EF 3
Pindaíba **111** F 3
Pindaré Mirim **109** J 4
Pindhos Óros **58** B 2–3
Pine Bluff **103** H 5
Pine Island Bay **115**
Pine Pass **99** N 4
Pinerolo **57** E 2–3
Pinetown **95** E 5
Pingdingshan **70** FG 4
Pingdu **71** H 3
Pingelap **82** B 2
Pingle **70** EF 6
Pingliang **70** E 3
Pingluo **70** E 3
Pingquan **71** G 2
Pingtung **71** H 6
Pingwu **70** DE 4
Pingxiang (China) **70** E 6
Pingxiang (Jiangxi, China) **70** F 5
Pingyang **71** H 5
Pingyao **70** F 3
Pinheiro **109** J 4
Pinnaroo **79** G 6
Pinrang **75** E 4
Pins, Île des **82** C 4
Pinsk **55** J 5
Pinyug **62** J 3
Piotrków Trybunalski **53** G 4
Piracicaba **111** G 5
Piracuruca **111** H 1
Piraiévs **58** B 3
Pirapora **111** H 4
Pires do Río **111** G 4
Pirin **58** B 2
Piripiri **111** H 1
Pirot **58** B 2
Piru **75** G 4
Pisa **57** F 3
Pisac **110** B 3
Pisagua **110** B 4
Pisco **110** A 3
Písek **53** F 5
Pishan **67** K 3
Pitalito **108** C 3
Pitcairn **83** G 4
Piteå **54** H 2
Piteşti **58** B 2
Pit-Gorodoko **68** FG 4
Pitkyaranta **54** K 3
Pitt **82** D 5
Pittsburgh **103** L 3
Pium **111** G 3
Pjórsá **54** B 3
Placentia Bay **101** QR 6
Placetas **105** G 3
Plaine des Flandres **56** D 1
Planalto Central **111** G 4
Planalto do Brasil **111** H 4
Planalto do Mato Grosso **110–111** EF 3–4
Plasencia **56** B 3–4
Plateau de Millevaches **56** D 2
Plateau du Djado **91** G 1
Plateau du Tademaït **87** F 3
Plateau Laurentien **101** NQ 5
Plateau of Tibet **72** DE 1
Plateaux **91** GH 6
Plateaux de la Marche **56** D 2
Plato Ustyurt **66** EF 2
Platte River **102** FG 3
Plaza Huincul **113** C 6
Pleasanton **102** G 6
Pleiku **73** J 5
Plentywood **102** EF 2
Pleven **58** BC 2
Ploče **57** G 3
Płock **53** GH 4
Ploieşti **58** C 2
Plovdiv **58** B 2
Plymouth **52** C 4
Plzeň **53** F 5
Po **57** F 3
Pobedy, Pik **67** KL 2
Pocatello **102** D 3
Pocklington Reef **81** G 4
Poconé **110** E 4
Poços de Caldas **111** G 5
Podgornoye **63** Q 4
Podgornyy **69** R 6
Podol'sk **62** G 4
Podosinovets **62** J 3
Podresovo **63** N 4
Pod'yelanka **68** H 4
Pofadder **94** BC 5
Pogibi **69** Q 5
Pohjanmaa **54** J 3
Poinsett, Cape **115**
Point Arena **102** B 4
Point Barrow **98** FG 1
Point Conception **102** B 5
Point Culver **78** CD 5
Point D'Entrecasteaux **78** AB 5
Pointe-à-Pitre **105** K 4
Pointe de Grave **56** C 2

Pointe de Penmarch **56** BC 2
Pointe Louis-XIV **101** L 5
Pointe Noire **91** G 6
Point Hope **98** D 2
Point Lake **99** P 2
Poitiers **56** D 2
Poitou **56** CD 2
Pojeierze Pomorskie **53** G 4
Pojezierze Mazurskie **53** H 4
Pokrovsk **69** N 3
Pola de Siero **56** B 3
Poland **53** G 4
Polar Plateau **115**
Polatlı **59** D 3
Pole of Inaccessibility **115**
Polesie Lubelskie **53** H 4
Polesye **55** J 5
Polgovskoye **63** N 4
Polist' **55** K 4
Pollensa **56** D 4
Polotsk **55** J 4
Polska **53** G 4
Polson **102** D 2
Poltava **62** FG 6
Poluostrov Buzachi **66** F 1
Poluostrov Kamchatka **69** S 4–5
Poluostrov Kanin **62** HJ 2
Poluostrov Kol'skiy **62** G 2
Poluostrov Koni **69** S 4
Poluostrov Rybachiy **54** K 2
Poluostrov Taymyr **68** FH 1
Poluostrov Yamal **63** NO 1
Polyarnik **98** B 2
Polyarnyy Ural **63** MN 2
Polynesia **83** EG 2–4
Pombal **111** J 3
Pomerania **53** FG 4
Pomio **82** B 3
Pommersche Bucht **53** F 4
Pomona **102** C 5
Pompei **57** F 3
Pompeyevka **69** O 6
Ponape **82** B 2
Ponca City **103** G 4
Ponce **105** J 4
Pondicherry **72** CD 5
Ponente, Rivera di **57** E 3
Ponferrada **56** B 3
Ponoy **62** H 2
Ponta da Baleia **111** J 4
Ponta do Padrão **94** A 1
Ponta Grossa **112** F 4
Ponta Porã **111** EF 5
Ponte Nova **111** H 5
Pontevedra **56** B 3
Pontianak **74** C 4
Pontine Mountains **59** EF 2
Poochera **78** E 5
Pool **91** H 6
Poole **52** C 4
Poopó **110** C 4
Poopó, Lago de **110** C 4
Poorman **98** F 3
Popayán **108** C 3
Poplar Bluff **103** H 4
Popokabaka **92** B 6
Popondetta **80** E 3
Porangatu **111** FG 3
Porbandar **72** A 3
Porco **110** C 4
Pori **54** H 3
Porirua **81** R 9
Porjus **54** H 2
Porlamar **109** F 1
Porpoise Bay **115**
Porsangerhalvöya **54** HJ 1
Porsgrunn **55** EF 4
Portage la-Prairie **99** S 5
Port Alberni **99** N 6
Port Alice **99** M 5
Port Arthur (Tasmania, Austr.) **80** L 9
Port Arthur (TX, U.S.A.) **103** H 6
Port Augusta **79** F 5
Port au Prince **105** H 4
Port Blair **73** F 5
Port Blandford **101** R 6
Port Darwin (Falkland Is., U.K.) **113** E 9
Port Darwin (N.T., Austr.) **78** DE 1
Port Elizabeth **94** D 6
Port Gentil **91** F 6
Port Harcourt **91** F 4–5
Port Hardy **99** M 5
Port Hedland **78** B 3
Port Hope Simpson **101** QR 5
Port Huron **103** K 3
Portile de Fier **58** B 2
Port Keats **78** DE 1
Port Láirge **52** B 4
Portland (ME, U.S.A.) **103** N 3
Portland (OR, U.S.A.) **102** B 2
Portland (Victoria, Austr.) **79** G 6
Portlaoise **52** B 4
Port Lincoln **79** F 5
Port Loko **90** B 4
Port-Louis **95** K 6
Port Moller **98** E 4
Port Moresby **80** E 3
Port Nelson **99** T 4
Port Nolloth **94** B 5
Port-Nouveau-Québec **101** OP 4
Pôrto Alegre **112** FG 5
Porto Amboim **94** A 2
Pôrto Artur **111** F 3
Pôrto de Moz **109** H 4
Pôrto Esperidião **110** E 4
Port of Spain **109** F 1
Pôrto Grande **109** H 3
Pôrto Jofre **110** E 4
Pörtom **54** H 3
Pôrto Murtinho **110** E 5
Pôrto Nacional **111** G 3
Porto Novo **90** E 4
Pôrto Santana **109** H 4
Pôrto Santo **86** B 2
Pôrto Seguro **111** J 4
Pôrto Valter **108** D 5
Porto-Vecchio **57** E 3
Pôrto Velho **109** F 5
Portoviejo **108** BC 4
Portree **52** B 3
Port Said **60** A 3
Port Saint Johns **94** DE 6
Port Saunders **101** Q 5
Portsmouth (N.H., U.S.A.) **103** MN 3
Portsmouth (OH, U.S.A.) **103** K 4
Portsmouth (U.K.) **52** C 4
Portsmouth (VA, U.S.A.) **103** L 4
Portugal **56** B 3
Portugalete **56** C 3
Port Wakefield **79** F 5
Porvenir **113** BC 9
Posadas **112** E 4
Posht-e Badam **61** G 2
Positos **110** D 5
Posse **111** G 3
Postavy **55** J 4
Poste-de-la-Baleine **101** M 4
Poste Maurice Cortier **87** F 4
Postmasburg **94** C 5
Posto Cunambo **108** CD 4
Potapovo **63** R 2
Potenza **57** G 3
Potgietersrus **94** D 4
Poti (Gruziya, U.S.S.R.) **59** F 2
Potiskum **91** G 3
Potosi **110** C 4
Potrerillos **112** BC 4
Potsdam **53** F 4
Pou Bia **73** H 4
Povenets **62** F 3
Póvoa de Varzim **56** B 3
Powell, Lake **102** D 4
Požarevac **58** B 2
Poza Rica de Hidalgo **104** C 3
Poznan **53** G 4
Pozo Almonte **110** C 5
Prado **111** J 4
Prague **53** FG 4–5
Praha **53** FG 4–5
Praia **90** B 7
Prainha **109** FG 5
Praslin **93** K 5
Prato **57** F 3
Praya **74** E 5
Prepansko jezero **58** B 2
Presidencia Roque Sáenz-Peña **112** D 4
Presidente Dutra **111** H 2
Presidente Prudente **111** F 5
Presnogor'kovka **63** N 5
Preston **52** C 4
Pretoria **94** D 5
Priazovskaya Vozvyshennost' **59** E 1
Pribilof Islands **98** D 4
Příbram **53** F 5
Prichernomorskaya Nizmennost' **59** D 1
Prieska **94** C 5
Prikaspiyskaya Nizmennost **66** DE 1
Prikubanskaya Nizmennost' **59** E 1
Prilep **58** B 2
Priluki **62** H 3
Primavera **115**
Primeira Cruz **111** H 1
Primorsk **55** J 3
Primorsko-Akhtarsk **59** E 1
Prince Albert **99** Q 5
Prince Albert Mountains **115**
Prince Albert National Park **99** Q 5
Prince Albert Peninsula **99** O 1
Prince Albert Sound **99** OP 1
Prince Charles Island **101** LM 2
Prince Charles Mountains **115**
Prince Edward Island (Canada) **101** P 6
Prince Edward Islands (Antarctica) **115**
Prince George **99** N 5
Prince of Wales Island (AK, U.S.A.) **98** L 4
Prince of Wales Island (Canada) **99** S 1
Prince of Wales Island (Queensland, Austr.) **79** G 1
Prince of Wales Strait **99** O 1
Prince Patrick Island **114**
Prince Rupert **98** L 5
Princess Astrid Coast **115**
Princess Charlotte Bay **79** G 1
Princess Martha Coast **115**
Princess Ragnhild Coast **115**
Princess Royal Island **98** M 5
Prince William Sound **98** H 3
Príncipe **91** F 5
Pripet Marshes **55** J 5
Pripyat' **55** J 5
Pristina **58** B 2
Prizren **58** B 2
Prokhladnyy **59** F 2
Prokhorkino **63** P 4
Prokop'yevsk **63** R 5
Proliv Karskiye Vorota **62–63** L 1
Proliv Nevel'skogo **69** Q 5
Prome **73** G 4
Promontoire Portland **101** LM 4
Promontorio del Gargano **57** G 3
Propria **111** J 3
Protochnoye **63** N 3
Provence **57** E 3
Providence **103** M 3
Providence, Cape **80** P 10
Provideniya **98** C 3
Prudhoe Bay **98** H 1
Prut **58** C 1
Prydz Bay **115**
Przheval'sk **67** K 2
Pshish **59** E 2
Pskov **55** J 4
Pskovskoye Ozero **55** J 4
Ptich **55** J 5
Pucallpa **108** D 5
Pucheng **71** G 5
Pudasjärvi **54** J 2

Puebla **104** C 4
Pueblo **102** F 4
Pueblo Hundido **112** C 4
Puelches **113** CD 6
Puente Alto **112** BC 5
Puente-Genil **56** C 4
Puerto Aisén **113** B 8
Puerto Angel **104** C 4
Puerto Asis **108** C 3
Puerto Ayacucho **108** E 2
Puerto Baquerizo Moreno **108** B 6
Puerto Barrios **104** E 4
Puerto Cabello **108** E 1
Puerto Cabezas **104** F 5
Puerto Carreño **108** E 2
Puerto Chicama **108** BC 5
Puerto Coig **113** C 9
Puerto Colombia **108** C 1
Puerto Cortés **104** E 4
Puerto Cumarebo **108** E 1
Puerto Deseado **113** CD 8
Puerto de Somport **56** C 3
Puerto de Villatoro **56** B 3
Puerto Escondido **104** C 4
Puerto Esperanza **112** F 4
Puerto Estrella **108** D 1
Puerto Heath **110** C 3
Puerto Juárez **104** E 3
Puerto la Cruz **109** F 1
Puerto Leguizamo **108** D 4
Puerto Lempira **104** F 4
Puerto Limón **108** D 3
Puertollano **56** C 4
Puerto Madryn **113** C 7
Puerto Magdalena **102** D 7
Puerto Maldonado **110** C 3
Puerto Montt **113** B 7
Puerto Natales **113** B 9
Puerto Nuevo **108** E 2
Puerto Padilla **110** B 3
Puerto Páez **108** E 2
Puerto Patillos **110** B 5
Puerto Patiño **110** C 4
Puerto Plata **105** HJ 4
Puerto Portillo **108** D 5
Puerto Princesa **75** E 2
Puerto Rico (Argentina) **112** F 4
Puerto Rico (U.S.A.) **105** J 4
Puerto Rondón **108** D 2
Puerto Siles **110** C 3
Puerto Suárez **110** E 4
Puerto Vallarta **104** AB 3
Puerto Varas **113** B 7
Puerto Verlarde **110** D 4
Puerto Villamizar **108** D 2
Puerto Villazón **110** D 3
Puerto Wilches **108** D 2
Puerto Williams **113** BC 9–10
Pugachev **62** JK 5
Pukapuka (Cook Is.) **82** DE 3
Pukapuka (French Polynesia) **83** F 3
Pukaruha **83** FG 4
Pukatawagan **99** RS 4
Pukch'ŏng **71** J 2
Puksoozero **62** H 3
Pula **57** F 3
Pulap **82** A 2
Pulau Alor **75** F 5
Pulau Bacan **75** G 4
Pulau Bangka **74** C 4
Pulau Belitung **74** C 4
Pulau Biak **75** J 4
Pulau Bintan **74** B 3
Pulau Enggano **74** B 5
Pulau Jos Sodarso **75** J 5
Pulau Kabaena **75** F 5
Pulau Kai Besar **75** H 5
Pulau Karakelong **75** G 3
Pulau Kobroor **75** H 5
Pulau Labengke **75** F 4
Pulau Laut **74** E 4
Pulau Lomblen **75** F 5
Pulau Madura **74** D 5
Pulau Mangole **75** G 4
Pulau Misool **75** H 4
Pulau Morotai **75** G 3
Pulau Muna **75** F 5
Pulau Nias **74** A 3
Pulau Numfor **75** H 4
Pulau Padang **74** B 3
Pulau Roti **75** F 6
Pulau Salawati **75** H 4
Pulau Selaru **75** H 5
Pulau Selayar **75** F 5
Pulau Siberut **74** A 4
Pulau Simeulue **74** A 3
Pulau Taliabu **75** F 4
Pulau Trangan **75** H 5
Pulau Waigeo **75** H 3
Pulau Wetar **75** G 5
Pulau Wokam **75** H 5
Pulau Yamdena **75** H 5
Pulau Yapen **75** J 4
Puławy **53** H 4
Pullman **102** C 2
Pulog, Mount **75** J 1
Pulozero **54** K 2
Pulusuk **82** A 2
Puna de Atacama **110** C 5–6
Puncak Jaya **75** J 4
Pune **72** B 4
Punjab **67** J 4
Punkaharju **54** J 3
Puno **110** B 4
Punta Alta **113** D 6
Punta Arenas **113** B 9
Punta Desengaño **113** C 8
Punta Eugenia **102** C 6
Punta Fijo **108** D 1
Punta Gallinas **108** D 1
Punta Gorda (Belize) **104** E 4
Punta Gorda (Nicaragua) **104** F 5
Punta Mariato **108** B 2
Punta Medanosa **113** CD 8
Punta Negra **108** B 5
Punta Pariñas **108** B 4
Punta Prieta **102** D 6
Puntarenas **104** EF 6
Punta Rieles **110** E 5
Puqi **70** F 5
Pur **63** P 2
Purdy Islands **82** A 3
Purnia **72** E 2
Purus **109** F 4
Puruvesi **54** J 3
Pusan **71** JK 3
Pushchino **69** T 5
Pushkin **55** K 4
Pushkino **62** J 5
Pustoretsk **69** U 3
Putao **73** G 2
Putorana, Gory **68** FH 2
Putumayo **108** D 4
Puulavesi **54** J 3
Puyang **70** G 3
Puy de Sancy **56** D 2
Puyo **108** C 4
Pweto **92** D 6
Pyaozero, Ozero **54** K 2
Pyatigorsk **59** F 2
Pyatistennoy **69** TU 2
Pyawbwe **73** G 3
Pyhäjoki **54** HJ 3
Pyhätunturi **54** J 2
Pyinmana **73** G 4
P'yŏngyang **71** HJ 3
Pyrénées **56** CD 3
Pyshchug **62** J 4

Q

Qābis **87** H 2
Qā'emshahr **61** F 1
Qafşah **87** G 2
Qagcaka **72** D 1
Qahremānshahr **61** E 2
Qaidam Pendi **70** BC 3
Qala-Nau **67** G 3
Qālat **67** H 4
Qal' at Dīzah **61** D 1
Qal'at Şāliḩ **61** E 3
Qal' at Sukkar **61** E 3
Qalīb ash Shuyūkh **61** E 3
Qamalung **70** CD 4
Qamdo **70** C 4
Qamīnis **87** J 2
Qanāt as Suways **60** A 3
Qapqal **67** L 2
Qarah Dagh **59** F 3
Qardo **93** H 3
Qasr-e Shīrīn **61** DE 2
Qaşr Farāfirah **88** D 3
Qatar **61** F 4
Qatrūyeh **61** G 3
Qāyen **66** F 4
Qayyārah **60** D 2
Qazvīn **66** DE 3
Qeshm **61** G 4
Qeshm **61** G 4
Qeys **61** F 4
Qezel Owzan **61** E 1
Qezi'ot **60** B 3
Qian'an **71** H 2
Qiaowan **70** C 2
Qidong **71** H 4
Qiemo **67** M 3
Qift **60** A 4
Qijiang **70** E 5
Qijiaojing **70** B 2
Qila Saifullah **67** H 4
Qilian Shan **70** CD 3
Qimen **71** G 5
Qinā **60** A 4
Qina, Wādī **60** A 4
Qingdao **71** H 3
Qinggang **71** HJ 1
Qinghai **70** C 3
Qinghai Hu **70** D 3
Qingjiang (Jiangsu, China) **71** GH 4
Qingjiang (Jiangxi, China) **70** FG 5
Qing Zang Gaoyuan **72** DE 1
Qinhuangdao **71** GH 3
Qinling Shan **70** E 4
Qinzhou **70** E 6
Qionghai **70** F 7
Qionglai **70** D 4
Qiqiar **68** M 5
Qiqihar **69** MN 6
Qira **67** L 3
Qirjat Yam (Israel) **60** B 2
Qitai **70** AB 2
Qitaihe **71** K 1
Qiyang **70** F 5
Qog Ul **71** G 2
Qolleh-ye Damāvand **61** F 2
Qom **61** F 2
Qomsheh **61** F 2–3
Qorud, Kuhha-ye **61** F 2–3
Qoşbeh-ye Naşşār **61** E 3
Qotbābād **61** G 4
Quang Ngai **73** J 4
Quanhov **70** E 5
Quan Phu Quoc **73** H 5
Quanzhou **71** GH 6
Qu'Appelle **99** R 5
Quartu Sant' Elena **57** E 4
Qūchān **66** F 3
Québec **101** MO 5
Québec **101** N 6
Quebracho Coto **112** D 4
Queen Charlotte Islands **98** KL 5
Queen Charlotte Sound **98** LM 5
Queen Elizabeth Islands **114**
Queen Fabiola Mountains **115**
Queen Mary Coast **115**
Queen Maud Gulf **99** R 2
Queen Maud Land **115**
Queen Maud Mountains **115**
Queensland **79** GH 3
Queenstown (South Africa) **94** D 6
Queenstown (Tasmania, Austr.) **80** L 9
Quelimane **95** F 3
Quembo **94** B 2
Que Que **94** D 3
Querétaro **104** BC 3
Queshan **70** F 4
Quesnel **99** N 5
Quetta **67** H 4
Quevedo **108** C 4
Quezaltenango **104** DE 5
Quibala **94** B 2
Quibdó **108** C 2

Quiçama National Park 94 A 1–2
Quiculungo 94 B 1
Quillabamba 110 B 3
Quillacollo 110 C 4
Quillaicillo 112 B 5
Quillota 112 B 5
Quilon 72 C 6
Quimilí 112 D 4
Quimper 56 C 2
Quincy 103 H 4
Quines 112 C 5
Qui Nhon 73 JK 5
Quintana Roo 104 E 3–4
Quito 108 C 4
Quixadá 111 J 1
Qujing 70 D 5
Qulansiyah 93 J 2
Qulbān Layyah 61 E 3
Qurnat aş Şawdā' 60 B 2
Qūs 60 A 4
Qusaybah 66 C 4
Qusum 70 B 5
Qu Xian 71 GH 5

R

Raab 57 G 2
Raahe 54 H 3
Rába (Hungary) 58 A 1
Raba (Indonesia) 75 E 5
Rabak 88 E 6
Rabat 86 D 2
Rabaul 82 B 3
Rabyānah 87 K 4
Rach Gia 73 HJ 5–6
Racine 103 J 3
Radhanpur 72 B 3
Radisson 101 M 5
Radom 53 H 4
Radomsko 53 G 4
Rae 99 O 3
Ra's-e Nāy Band 61 F 4
Raevavae 83 F 4
Rafaela 112 D 5
Rafah 60 B 3
Rafha' 60 D 3
Rafsanjān 61 G 3
Raga 92 D 3
Rahimyar Khan 67 J 5
Raiatea 83 E 4
Raichur 72 C 4
Raiganj 72 E 2
Raigarh 72 D 3
Rainbow Peak 102 C 3
Rainier, Mount 102 B 2
Rainy Lake 100 J 6
Raipur 72 D 3
Rajada 111 H 2
Rajahmundry 72 D 4
Rajakoski 54 J 2
Rajapalaiyam 72 C 6
Rajasthan 72 BC 2
Rajgarh 72 C 3
Rajkot 72 AB 3
Raj Nandgaon 72 D 3
Rajshahi 72 E 3
Rakahanga 82 E 3
Rakitnoye 55 J 5
Rakulka 62 HJ 3
Raleigh 103 L 4
Ralik Chain 82 C 2
Ramādah 87 H 2
Ramapo Deep 65 R 6
Ramea 101 Q 6
Rāmhormoz 61 E 3
Ramlat Hagolan 60 B 2
Ramlat Rabyānah 87 JK 4
Rampur 72 CD 2
Ramree 73 F 4
Ramsgate 52 D 4
Rancagua 112 B 5
Ranchi 72 DE 3
Randers 55 F 4
Randijaure 54 G 2
Rangoon 73 FG 4
Rangpur 72 E 2
Rankin Inlet 99 T 3
Rann of Kutch 72 AB 3
Rantauprapat 74 AB 3
Ranua 54 J 2
Raoul 82 D 4
Rapa 83 F 4
Rapa Nui 83 H 4
Rapid City 102 F 3
Raraka 83 F 4
Rarotonga 83 E 4
Ra's Abū Madd 60 B 4
Ra's Abū Qumayyis 61 F 4
Ra's al Abyad 60 BC 5
Ra's al Abyaḍ 87 G 1
Ra's al Khafjī 61 E 3
Ra's al Khaymah 61 G 4
Ra's al Madrakah 89 K 5
Ra's al Mish'āb 61 E 3
Ra's ash Shaykh 60 B 3
Ra's Asir 93 J 2
Ra's as Saffānīyah 61 E 3
Ra's aṭ Ṭīb 87 H 1
Ra's az Zawr 61 E 4
Ra's Ba'labakk 60 B 2
Ra's Banās 60 B 5
Ra's Barīdī 60 B 4
Ras Dashan 93 F 2
Ra's Fartak 89 J 5
Ra's Ghārib 60 A 3
Ra's Hāfūn 93 J 2
Rasht 66 D 3
Raskoh 67 GH 5
Ra's Miṣrātah 87 J 2
Ra's Muhammad 60 B 4
Rasshua, Ostrov 69 S 6
Rasskazovo 62 H 5
Rastigaissa 54 J 1
Råstojaure 54 H 2
Ratak Chain 82 C 2
Ratangarh 72 B 2
Rat Buri 73 G 5
Rat Islands 98 A 5
Ratlam 72 BC 3
Ratnagiri 72 B 4
Ratnapura 72 D 6
Ratta 63 Q 3
Raufarhöfn 54 BC 2
Raukela 72 DE 3
Raúl Leoni, Represa 109 F 2
Rauma 54 H 3
Raupelyan 98 C 2
Ravahere 83 F 4
Ravānsar 61 E 2
Rāvar 61 G 3
Ravenna 57 F 3
Ravenshoe 79 GH 2
Rāwah 66 C 4
Rawaki 82 D 3
Rawalpindi 67 J 4
Rawāndūz 66 C 3
Rawlinna 78 D 5
Rawlins 102 E 3
Rawson 113 D 7
Raychikhinsk 69 NO 6
Raymond 102 B 2
Rāzān 61 E 2
Razdan 59 F 2
Razgrad 58 C 2
Ré, Ile de 56 C 2
Reading 52 C 4
Real, Cordillera 108 C 4
Realico 112 D 5
Reao 83 G 4
Rebbenesöy 54 G 1
Rebecca, Lake 78 C 5
Reboly 62 F 3
Recife 111 K 2
Récifs d'Entrecasteaux 82 B 4
Reconquista 112 DE 4
Red Bluff 102 B 3
Red Deer 99 P 5
Red Deer River 99 P 5
Redding 102 B 3
Redenção da Gurguéia 111 H 2
Red Lake 100 J 5
Redoubt Volcano 98 G 3
Red River (LA, U.S.A.) 103 H 5
Red River (MN, U.S.A.) 103 G 2
Red Sea 60 B 4
Red Sea 89 FG 4–5
Red Water 99 P 5
Reef Islands 82 BC 3
Regensburg 53 F 5
Reggane 86 EF 3
Reggio di Calabria 57 G 4
Reggio nell'Emilia 57 EF 3
Reghin 58 B 1
Regina (Brazil) 109 H 3
Regina (Canada) 99 R 5
Registan 67 GH 4
Rehoboth 94 B 4
Reims 56 D 2
Reina Adelaida, Archipiélago de la 113 A 9
Reindeer Lake 99 R 4
Reinoksfjellet 54 G 2
Reitoru 83 F 4
Rekinniki 69 U 3
Reliance 99 Q 3
Remansão 109 HJ 4
Remanso 111 H 2
Rembang 74 D 5
Renascença 108 E 4
Renfrew 101 M 6
Rengo 112 B 5
Rennell 81 H 4
Rennes 56 C 2
Rennie Lake 99 Q 3
Reno 102 BC 4
Renton 102 B 2
Replot 54 H 3
Represa Raúl Leoni 109 F 2
Republic of Ireland 52 B 4
Republic of South Africa 94 BD 6
Repulse Bay 99 U 2
Requena 108 D 5
Réservoir Baskatong 101 MN 6
Réservoir Cabonga 101 M 6
Réservoir Decelles 101 M 6
Réservoir Gouin 101 MN 6
Réservoir Pipmouacan 101 N 6
Reshteh-ye Kūhhā-ye Alborz 61 F 1
Resistencia 112 DE 4
Reşiţa 58 B 1
Resolution Island 101 P 3
Réunion 95 HK 6
Reus 56 D 3
Revilla Gigedo Islands 97 G 8
Rewari 72 C 2
Rey 61 F 2
Reykjahlíð 54 B 2
Reykjanes 54 A 3
Reykjavik 54 A 3
Reynosa 104 C 2
Rezé 56 C 2
Rēzekne 55J 4
Rhein 52 E 4
Rhinelander 103 J 2
Rhinmal 72 B 2
Rhodes 58 C 3
Rhodope Mts 58 BC 2
Rhondda 52 C 4
Rhône 57 D 3
Rías Altas 56 B 3
Rías Bajas 56 B 3
Riau, Kepulauan 74 B 3
Ribeirão Prêto 111 G 5
Riberalta 110 C 3
Richard's Bay 95 E 5
Richland 102 C 2
Richmond (Queensland, Austr.) 79 G 3
Richmond (VA, U.S.A.) 103 L 4
Richmond Hill 101 LM 7
Riding Mountain National Park 99 RS 5
Rietavas 55H 4
Riga 55 H 4
Rihand Dam 72 D 3
Riiser-Larsen Ice Shelf 115
Riiser-Larsen Peninsula 115
Rijau 91 F 3
Rijeka 57 F 2
Riley 102 CD 3
Rimatara 83 E 4
Rimini 57 F 3
Rimnicu Sărat 58 C 1
Rîmnicu Vîlcea 58 B 1–2
Rimouski 101 O 6

Rinchinlhümbe **68** G 5
Rinconada **110** C 5
Ringgold Isles **82** D 4
Ringvassöy **54** G 2
Ríobamba **108** C 4
Río Branco (Acre, Brazil) **108** E 5
Río Branco (Roraima, Brazil) **109** F 3
Río Bravo del Norte **102** EF 5–6
Río Chico **113** C 8
Río Claro **111** G 5
Río Colorado **113** D 6
Río Cuarto **112** CD 5
Rio das Mortes **111** F 3
Río de Janeiro **111** H 5
Río de la Plata **112** E 5–6
Rio de Oro **86** BC 4
Río Gallegos **113** C 9
Río Grande (Argentina) **113** C 9
Río Grande (Bahía, Brazil) **111** H 3
Río Grande (Brazil) **111** G 4–5
Río Grande (Río Grande do Sul, Brazil) **112** F 5
Rio Grande (TX, U.S.A.) **102** G 6
Rio Grande de Santiago **104** B 3
Río Grande do Norte **111** J 2
Río Grande do Sul **112** EF 4
Río Grande o'Guapay **110** D 4
Rioja **108** C 5
Río Lagartos **104** E 3
Riom **56** D 2
Río Mulatos **110** C 4
Río Negro (Argentina) **113** D 6–7
Río Negro (Brazil) **109** F 4
Ríosucio **108** C 2
Río Turbio Mines **113** B 9
Río Verde **111** F 4
Río Verde de Mato Grosso **111** F 4
Rissa **54** E 3
Ritzville **102** C 2
Rivadavia **112** BC 4
Rivas **104** E 5
Rivera (Argentina) **113** D 6
Rivera (Uruguay) **112** E 5
Riverside **102** C 5
Riviera di Levante **57** E 3
Riviera di Ponente **57** E 3
Rivoli **57** E 2
Riwoqê **70** C 4
Riyādh **61** E 4
Rize **59** F 2
Rizhao **71** GH 3
Rizhskiy Zaliv **55** H 4
Rjuven **55** E 4
Rkiz **86** B 5
Roanne **56** D 2
Roan Plateau **102** E 4
Robāt-e Khān **61** G 2
Robert Butte **115**
Robinson River **79** F 2
Robore **110** E 4
Robson, Mount **99** NO 5
Rocha **112** F 5
Rocha de Galé, Barragem da **56** B 4
Rochefort **56** C 2
Rocher River **99** P 3
Rocher Thomasset **83** F 3
Rochester (MN, U.S.A.) **103** H 3
Rochester (N.Y., U.S.A.) **103** L 3
Rockefeller Plateau **115**
Rockford **103** J 3
Rockhampton **79** HJ 3
Rock Hill **103** K 5
Rock Island **103** H 3
Rockport **102** B 4
Rock Springs **102** E 3
Rocky Mount **103** L 4
Rocky Mountains **99** MP 4–6
Rodeo **104** B 2
Rodez **56** D 3
Ródhos **58** C 3
Rodina **68** FG 4
Rodney, Cape **80** E 4
Rodopi **58** BC 2
Roebourne **78** B 3
Roebuck Bay **78** C 2
Roes Welcome Sound **99** U 2–3
Rogagua, Lago **110** C 3
Rogaland **55** E 4
Rogers Peak **102** D 4
Rohtak **72** C 2
Rolla **102** G 2
Rolleston **79** H 3
Roma (Italy) **57** F 3
Roma (Queensland, Austr.) **79** H 4
Romaine **101** P 5
Roman **58** C 1
Romania **58** BC 1
Romanovka **68** K 5
Romans-sur-Isère **57** E 2
Rome **102** C 3
Rome (Italy) **57** F 3
Romny **62** F 5
Romsdal **54** E 3
Roncador, Serra do **111** F 3
Ronda **56** C 4
Rondane **54** EF 3
Rondón, Pico **109** F 3
Rondonia (Brazil) **110** D 3
Rondônia (Brazil) **110** D 3
Rondonópolis **111** F 4
Rongan **70** E 5
Ronge, Lac la **99** R 4
Rongelap **82** C 2
Rongerik **82** C 2
Rongjiang **70** E 5
Rong Xian **70** F 6
Rönne **55** F 4
Ronneby **55** G 4
Ronne Ice Shelf **115**
Roosevelt, Mount **99** M 4
Roosevelt Island **115**
Roper River **78** E 1
Roraima (Brazil) **109** F 3
Roraima (Venezuela) **109** F 2
Röros **54** F 3
Rosario (Argentina) **112** D 5
Rosário (Maranhão, Brazil) **111** H 1
Rosario (Mexico) **104** A 3
Rosario, Bahía **102** C 6
Rosario de Lerma **112** C 4
Roseau **105** K 4
Roseburg **102** B 3
Rosenheim **53** F 5
Rosetown **99** Q 5
Rosignol **109** G 2
Roşiori de Vede **58** C 2
Roskilde **55** F 4
Roslavl' **62** F 5
Rossano **57** G 4
Ross Ice Shelf **115**
Ross Island **115**
Rosslare **52** B 4
Rosso **86** B 5
Rossosh **62** GH 5
Ross River **98** L 3
Ross Sea **115**
Rostock **53** F 4
Rostov **62** G 4
Rostov-na-Donu **59** EF 1
Roswell **102** EF 5
Rota **82** A 2
Rothera **115**
Roti, Pulau **75** F 6
Rotorua **81** R 8
Rotterdam **52** D 4
Rotuma **82** C 3
Rouen **56** D 2
Rovaniemi **54** J 2
Rovdino **62** H 3
Rovereto **57** F 2
Rovigo **57** F 2
Rovno **55** J 5
Rowley **101** M 2
Roxas **75** F 1
Roy Hill **78** C 3
Röyrvik **54** F 3
Rozhdestvenskoye **62** J 4
Roztocze **53** H 4
Rtishchevo **62** H 5
Rt Ploča **57** G 3
Ruacana Falls **94** AB 3
Ruaha National Park **92** E 6
Ruapehu **81** R 8
Rubtsovsk **63** Q 5
Ruby **98** G 3
Rudall River National Park **78** C 3
Rudbar **67** G 4–5
Rudnyy **63** M 5
Rufiji **93** F 6
Rufino **112** D 5
Rufisque **90** A 3
Rügen **53** F 4
Ruhr **53** E 4
Ruijin **70** G 5
Rujm al Mudhari **66** B 4
Rumādah **89** G 6
Rum Jungle **78** E 1
Rumphi **95** E 2
Rundu **94** B 3
Rungwa **92** E 6
Ruoqiang **70** A 3
Rupert **101** M 5
Rurrenabaque **110** C 3
Rurutu **83** E 4
Rusakovo **69** U 4
Ruse **58** C 2
Rushan (U.S.S.R.) **67** J 3
Russas **111** J 1
Russkaya (Antarctica) **115**
Russkaya (U.S.S.R.) **71** L 1
Rustavi **59** G 2
Rustenburg **94** D 5
Rutenga **95** E 4
Ruvuma **95** FG 2
Ruwenzori National Park **92** DE 5
Ruzayevka **62** H 5
Ružomberok **53** GH 5
Rwanda **92** DE 5
Ryazan' **62** GH 5
Ryazhsk **62** GH 5
Rybachiy, Poluostrov **54** K 2
Rybach'ye **67** K 2
Rybnik **53** G 4
Rybnitsa **58** C 1
Ryn Peski **62** J 6
Ryukyu Islands **71** J 5
Rzeszów **53** H 4

S

Sa'ādatābād **61** F 3
Saalfeld **53** F 4
Saarbrücken **53** E 5
Saaremaa **55** H 4
Saariselkä **54** J 2
Šabac **58** A 2
Sabadell **56** D 3
Sabah **74** E 2
Sabanalarga **108** C 1
Sabaya **110** C 4
Sabhā **87** H 3
Sabinas **104** B 2
Sabkhat al Bardawīl **60** A 3
Sable, Cape (Canada) **101** O 7
Sable, Cape (FL., U.S.A.) **103** K 6
Sable Island **101** P 7
Sabonkafi **91** F 3
Sabrina Coast **115**
Sabzevār **66** F 3
Sachsen **53** F 4
Sachs Harbour **99** N 1
Sacramento **102** BC 4
Sacramento Mountains **102** E 5
Sacramento Valley **102** B 3–4
Şa'dah **89** G 5
Sad Bi'Ar **60** B 2
Saddlede **54** F 3
Sa Dec **74** C 1
Sadiya **73** G 2
Sad Kharv **61** G 1
Sadon **66** C 2
Sado-shima **71** L 3
Sæból **54** A 2
Şafāqis **87** GH 2

Saffānīyah, Ra's as **61** E 3
Safi **86** D 2
Safīd, Kūh-e **61** E 2
Safonovo (U.S.S.R.) **62** J 2
Safonovo (U.S.S.R.) **62** F 4
Şafwān **61** E 3
Saga **72** DE 2
Sagaing **73** FG 3
Sagar **72** C 3
Sagastyr **69** N 1
Sage **102** D 3
Saglouc **101** M 3
Sagres **56** B 4
Sagua la Grande **105** G 3
Sagunto **56** C 4
Sagwon **98** GH 2
Sahagún **108** CD 2
Sahara **86–87** HK 4
Saharanpur **72** C 2
Sahiwal **67** J 4
Sahlābad **66** F 4
Şaḩrā' al Ḩajārah **60–61** D 3
Sahuayo de Diaz **104** B 4
Sa'īdābād **61** G 3
Said Bundas **92** CD 3
Saigon **73** JK 5
Saihan Toroi **70** CD 2
Saiki **71** KL 4
Saimaa **54** J 3
Saindak **67** G 5
Sāīn Dezh **61** E 1
Saint Alban's **101** QR 6
Saint-André, Cap **95** G 3
Saint Anthony **101** QR 5
Saint Arnaud **79** G 6
St. Austell **52** BC 4
Saint-Brieuc **56** C 2
Saint Cloud **103** GH 2
Saint Croix **105** JK 4
Saint-Denis (France) **56** D 2
Saint-Denis (Réunion) **95** HK 6
Saint-Dizier **57** E 2
Saint-Elie **109** H 3
Saintes **56** C 2
Sainte-Thérèse **101** N 6
Saint-Étienne **56** D 2
Saint Francis, Cape **94** CD 6
St. Gallen **57** E 2
Saint George (Queensland, Austr.) **79** H 4
Saint George (UT, U.S.A.) **102** D 4
Saint George, Cape **81** F 2
Saint-Georges **101** NO 6
Saint George's **105** K 5
Saint George's Channel (Papua New Guinea) **81** F 2–3
Saint George's Channel (Un. Kingdom) **52** B 4
Saint Helena **84** B 6
Saint Jean **101** N 6
Saint Jérôme **101** N 6
Saint-John **101** O 6
Saint John's (Antigua) **105** K 4
Saint Johns (AZ, U.S.A.) **102** E 5
Saint John's (Canada) **101** R 6
Saint Joseph **103** H 4
Saint Kitts-Nevis **105** K 4
Saint Lawrence Island **98** C 3
Saint Lawrence River **101** O 6
Saint Léonard **101** O 6
Saint Louis (MO, U.S.A.) **103** HJ 4
Saint-Louis (Senegal) **90** A 2
Saint Lucia **105** K 5
Saint Lucia, Lake **95** E 5
Saint-Malo **56** C 2
Saint Marys **80** L 9
St. Marys (AK, U.S.A.) **98** E 3
Saint Matthias Group **81** EF 2
St. Moritz **57** F 2
Saint-Nazaire **56** C 2
Saint Paul (MN, U.S.A.) **103** H 3
Saint-Paul (Réunion) **95** HK 6
St. Peter and St. Paul Rocks **107** G 2
Saint Petersburg **103** K 6
Saint Pierre et Miquelon **101** Q 6
Saint-Quentin **56** D 1–2
Saint-Thomas **101** L 7
Saint Vincent **105** K 5
Saint Vincent, Gulf **79** F 6
Saint Vincent Passage **105** K 5
Saipan **82** A 1
Sajama, Nevado **110** C 4
Sakākah **60** C 3
Sakami, Lac **101** M 5
Sakaraha **95** G 4
Sakarya **58** D 2
Sakata **71** L 3
Såkevare **54** G 2
Sakhalin **69** QR 5
Sakhalinskiy Zaliv **69** Q 5
Sakht Sar **61** F 1
Saksaul'skiy **67** G 1
Salaca **55** HJ 4
Salada **104** B 2
Salado **112** D 4
Salado **113** C 6
Salaga **90** D 4
Salālah **89** J 5
Salamá **104** D 4
Salamanca **56** B 3
Salamat **91** J 3
Salar de Atacama **110** C 5
Salar de Uyuni **110** C 5
Salavat **62** KL 5
Salaverry **108** C 5
Salawati, Pulau **75** H 4
Sala y Gómes **83** H 4
Saldanha **94** B 6
Sale (Australia) **79** H 6
Salé (Morocco) **86** D 2
Şāleḩābād **61** E 2
Salekhard **63** N 2
Salem (India) **72** C 5
Salem (OR, U.S.A.) **102** B 3
Salerno **57** F 3
Saletekri **72** D 3
Salida **102** E 4
Salihli **58** C 3
Salina (KS, U.S.A.) **102** G 4
Salina (UT, U.S.A.) **102** D 4
Salinas (CA, U.S.A.) **102** B 4
Salinas (Ecuador) **108** B 4
Salinas de Hidalgo **104** B 3
Salinas Grandes **112** CD 4–5
Salinópolis **109** J 4
Salisbury **101** MN 3
Salling **55** E 4
Salluyo, Nevado **110** C 3
Salmas **59** F 3
Salmon Mountains **102** B 3
Salon-de-Provence **57** E 3
Salonga National Park **92** C 5
Salonica **58** B 2
Salpausselkä **54** J 3
Sal'sk **59** F 1
Salso **57** F 4
Salta **110** CD 5
Saltdalselva **54** G 2
Saltillo **104** B 2–3
Salt Lake **79** F 3
Salt Lake City **102** D 3
Salto **112** E 5
Salt Range **67** J 4
Salumbar **72** B 3
Salvador **111** J 3
Salwā **61** F 4
Salwá Baḩrī **60** A 4
Salween **73** G 4
Salzach **57** F 2
Salzburg **57** F 2
Salzgitter **53** F 4
Samagaltay **68** G 5
Samak, Tanjung **74** C 4
Samangan **67** H 3
Samar **75** G 1
Samarkand **67** H 3
Sāmarrā' **60** D 2
Samarskoye **63** Q 6
Samaúma **108** E 5
Sambaliung **74–75** E 3
Sambalpur **72** DE 3
Sambava **95** J 2
Sambor **74** C 1
Sambor (Russia, U.S.S.R.) **53** H 5
S. Ambrosio Island **107** C 5
Samfya **94** DE 2
Samka **73** G 3
Sam Neua **73** H 3
Samoa Islands **82** D 3
Samokov **58** B 2
Sámos **58** C 3
Samothraki **58** C 2
Sampit **74** D 4
Samsang **72** D 1
Samsun **59** E 2
Samthar **72** C 2
Samus' **63** QR 4
Samut Prakan **73** H 5
Samut Songkhram **73** H 5
San'ā' **89** GH 5
Sanae **115**
Sanaga **91** G 5
Sanandaj **61** E 2
San Andrés **105** F 5
San Andrés Tuxtla **104** CD 4
San Angelo **102** F 5
San Antonia de Cortés **104** E 4–5
San Antonio (Chile) **112** B 5
San Antonio (TX., U.S.A.) **102** G 6
San Antonio, Cabo (Argentina) **113** E 6
San Antonio, Cabo (Cuba) **104** EF 3
San Antonio Oeste **113** D 7
Sanāw **89** J 5
San Bernardino **102** C 5
San Bernardo **112** BC 5
San Borja **110** C 3
San Carlos (Nicaragua) **104** F 5
San Carlos (Philippines) **75** F 1
San Carlos de Bariloche **113** BC 7
San Carlos del Zulia **108** D 2
San Casme **112** E 4
San Cristóbal (Argentina) **112** D 5
San Cristóbal (Dominican Rep.) **105** HJ 4
San Cristobal (Solomon Is.) **81** H 4
San Cristóbal (Venezuela) **108** D 2
San Cristobal, Isla **108** B 6
San Cristóbal de las Casas **104** D 4
Sancti Spíritus **105** G 3
Sandakan **74** E 2
Sandaré **90** B 3
Sand Hills **102** F 3
San Diego **102** C 5
San Diego, Cabo **113** C 9
San Dimitri Point **57** F 4
Sandnes **55** DE 4
Sandnesssjöen **54** F 2
Sandoa **92** C 6
Sandon **59** F 2
San Dona di Piave **57** F 2
Sandoy **52** A 1
Sandviken **55** G 3
Sandykachi **67** G 3
Sandy Lake **100** J 5
San Felípe (Chile) **112** B 5
San Felípe (Colombia) **108** E 3
San Felipe (Venezuela) **108** E 1
San Fernando (Chile) **113** B 5
San Fernando (Mexico) **104** C 3
San Fernando (Spain) **56** B 4
San Fernando (Trinidad and Tobago) **109** F 1
San Fernando de Apure **108** E 2
San Fernando de Atabapo **108** E 3
San Francisco (Argentina) **112** D 5

San Francisco (CA., U.S.A.) **102** B 4
San Francisco, Paso de **112** C 4
San Francisco del Rincón **104** B 3
San Francisco de Macorís **105** HJ 4
Sangar **69** N 3
Sangatolon **69** R 3
Sangha **91** GH 5
Sangihe, Kepulauan **75** G 3
Sangli **72** BC 4
San Gregorio **113** B 9
Sanhe **68** M 5
San Ignacio (Bolivia) **110** C 3
San Ignacio (Paraguay) **112** E 4
Sanikiluaq **101** M 4
San Isidro **112** DE 5
San Jacinto **108** C 2
San Javier **110** D 4
Sanjawi **67** H 4
San Joaquín **110** D 3
San Joaquin River **102** BC 4
San Jorge, Golfo **113** C 8
San Jose (CA, U.S.A.) **102** B 4
San José (Costa Rica) **104** F 6
San José de Chiquitos **110** DE 4
San José de Jáchal **112** C 5
San José del Cabo **102** E 7
San José del Guaviare **108** D 3
San José de Mayo **112** E 5
San Juan (Argentina) **112** C 5
San Juan (Dominican Rep.) **105** H 4
San Juan (Peru) **110** A 4
San Juan (Puerto Rico) **105** J 4
San Juan Bautista Tuxtepec **104** C 4
San Juan del Norte **104** F 5
San Julián **113** C 8
San Justo **112** D 5
Sankt Gotthard-Pass **57** E 2
Sankt Pölten **57** G 2
Sankt Veit an der Glan **57** F 2
Sankuru **92** C 5
San Lorenzo **108** C 3
Sanlúcar de Barrameda **56** B 4
San Lucas, Cabo **102** E 7
San Luis (Argentina)**112** C 5
San Luís (Venezuela) **108** E 1
San Luis Obispo **102** B 4
San Luis Potosí **104** BC 3
San Luis Río Colorado **102** D 5
San Marino **57** F 3
San Martín (Colombia) **108** D 3
San Martín de los Andes **113** BC 7
San Mateo **102** B 4
San Matías **110** E 4
San Matías, Golfo **113** D 7
San Miguel (Bolivia) **110** D 3
San Miguel (El Salvador) **104** E 5
San Miguel de Allende **104** BC 3
San Miguel de Huachi **110** C 4
San Miguel del Padrón **105** FG 3
San Miguel de Tucumán **112** C 4
Sannār **88** E 6
San Nicolás (Argentina) **112** DE 5
San Nicolás (Mexico) **104** B 2
Sannikova **114**
Sanok **53** H 5
San Onofre **108** C 2
San Pablo **113** C 9
San Pedro (Argentina) **110** D 5
San Pedro (Mexico) **104** B 2
San Pedro (Paraguay) **110** E 5
San Pedro de Arimena **108** D 3
San Pedro Sula **104** E 4
San Quintin **102** C 5
San Rafael **112** C 5
San Remo **57** E 3
San Salvador (El Salvador) **104** E 5
San Salvador (Watling Is.) **105** GH 3
San Salvador de Jujuy **110** C 5
Sansanding **90** C 3
San Sebastian (Argentina) **113** C 9
San Sebastián (Spain) **56** C 3
San Severo **57** G 3
Santa Ana (CA, U.S.A.) **102** C 5
Santa Ana (El Salvador) **104** DE 5
Santa Ana (Mexico) **102** D 5
Santa Ana (Solomon Is.) **81** H 4
Santa Barbara (CA, U.S.A.) **102** B 5
Santa Bárbara do Sul **112** F 4
Santa Catalina **112** C 4
Santa Catarina **112** FG 4
Santa Clara (CA, U.S.A.) **102** B 4
Santa Clara (Cuba) **105** F 3
Santa Clara (Mexico) **102** E 6
Santa Clotilde **108** D 4
Santa Cruz (Argentina) **113** C 9
Santa Cruz (Bolivia) **110** D 4
Santa Cruz (CA, U.S.A.) **102** B 4
Santa Cruz, Isla (Ecuador) **108** B 6
Santa Cruz de Mudela **56** C 4
Santa Cruz de Tenerife **86** BC 3
Santa Cruz do Sul **112** F 4
Santa Cruz Islands **81** J 4
Santa Elena **108** B 4
Santa Fé (Argentina) **112** DE 5
Santa Fe (N.M., U.S.A.) **102** EF 4
Santa Filomena **109** J 5
Santa Helena **109** JK 4
Santa Inés, Isla **113** B 9
Santa Isabel **82** B 3
Santa Isabel (Argentina) **113** C 6
Santa Isabel (Solomon Is.) **81** G 3
Santa Maria (CA., U.S.A.) **102** B 4
Santa Maria (Portugal) **86** A 1
Santa María (Río Grande do Sul, Brazil) **112** F 4
Santa Maria, Cabo de **56** B 4
Santa Maria di Leuca, Capo **57** G 4
Santa Maria dos Marmelos **109** F 5
Santa Marta **108** D 1
Santana do Livramento **112** EF 5
Santander (Colombia) **108** C 3
Santander (Spain) **56** C 3
Sant' Antioco **57** E 4
Santarém **109** H 4
Santa Rita (Colombia) **108** D 3
Santa Rita (Venezuela) **108** E 2
Santa Rosa (Argentina) **113** CD 6
Santa Rosa (CA, U.S.A.) **102** B 4
Santa Rosa (N.M., U.S.A.) **102** F 5
Santa Rosa (Río Grande do Sul, Brazil) **112** F 4
Santa Rosalia **102** D 6
Santa Sylvina **112** DE 4
Santa Teresa **111** G 3
Santiago (Chile) **112** BC 5
Santiago (Haiti) **105** HJ 4
Santiago (Panamá) **108** B 2
Santiago, Cerro **105** F 6
Santiago da Cacém **56** B 4
Santiago de Compostela **56** B 3
Santiago de Cuba **105** G 4
Santiago del Estero **112** CD 4
Santo André **111** G 5
Santo Ângelo **112** F 4
Santo Antão **90** A 6
Santo António de Jesus **111** HJ 3
Santo Antônio do Içá **108** E 4
Santo Domingo (Dominican Rep.) **105** J 4
Santo Domingo (Mexico) **102** D 6
Santos **111** G 5
Santo Tomás **104** F 5
Santo Tomé de Guayana **109** F 2
San Valentín, Cerro **113** B 8
São Borja **112** E 4
São Carlos **111** G 5
São Domingos **111** G 3
São Felix **111** F 3
São Felix do Xingu **109** H 5
São Francisco **111** HJ 2
São Francisco do Sul **112** G 4
São João **111** G 5
São João del Rei **111** GH 5
São João do Piauí **111** H 2
São José do Río Prêto **111** FG 5
São José dos Campos **111** FG 5
São Leopoldo **112** FG 4
São Luís **111** H 1
São Mateus **111** J 4
São Miguel **86** A 1
São Miguel do Araguaia **111** FG 3
Saône **57** D 2
São Nicolau **90** B 6
São Paulo (Brazil) **111** FG 5
São Paulo (Brazil) **111** G 5
São Paulo de Olivença **108** E 4
São Raimundo Nonato **111** H 2
São Romão **111** G 4
São Roque, Cabo de **111** HJ 2
São Sebastião **111** GH 5
São Tiago **90** B 6
São Tomé **91** F 5
São Tomé and Principe **91** F 5
São Vicente (Cape Verde) **90** A 6
São Vicente (São Paulo, Brazil) **111** G 5
São Vicente, Cabo de **56** B 4
Sape **75** E 5
Sapele **91** F 4
Sapporo **71** LM 2
Sapulut **74** E 3
Sāqand **61** G 2
Saqqez **61** E 1
Sara Buri **73** H 5
Sarafjagār **61** F 2
Sarajevo **57** G 3
Saraktash **62** L 5
Saralzhin **66** E 1
Saran' **63** O 6
Saran, Gunung **74** D 4
Saranpaul' **63** M 3
Saransk **62** J 5
Sarapul **62** KL 4
Sarasota **103** K 6
Saratok **74** D 3
Saratov **62** HJ 5
Sarawak **74** D 3
Saraya **59** E 3
Sarco **112** B 4
Sar Dasht **61** D 1
Sardegna **57** E 3
Sardinia **57** E 3

Sarek National Park **54** G 2
Sarektjåkkå **54** G 2
Sargasso Sea **105** JK 2
Sargodha **67** J 4
Sarh **91** H 4
Sārī **66** E 3
Sarigan **82** A 1
Sarıoğlan **59** E 3
Sarīr Tibistī **87** J 4
Sariwon **71** HJ 3
Sarkand **63** P 6
Sarmi **75** J 4
Sarmiento **113** C 8
Sarnia **100–101** L 7
Saroako **75** F 4
Saronikos Kólpos **58** B 3
Saros Kőrfezi **58** C 2
Saroto **63** NO 2
Sarpinskaya Nizmennost' **59** G 1
Sartyn'ya **63** M 3
Šarva **58** A 2
Sarvestān **61** F 3
Saryassiya **67** H 3
Saryg-Sep **68** G 5
Sary-Ozek **67** K 2
Sary-Tash **67** J 3
Sasaram **72** D 3
Sasebo **71** J 4
Saskatchewan **99** Q 5
Saskatoon **99** Q 5
Saskylakh **68** KL 1
Sason Dağları **59** F 3
Sasovo **62** H 5
Sassari **57** E 3
Sassuolo **57** F 3
Sastre **112** D 5
Sasykkol', Ozero **63** Q 6
Satara (U.S.S.R.) **69** NO 2
Satawal **82** A 2
Satawan **82** B 2
Satipo **110** B 3
Satka **63** L 4
Satna **72** D 3
Satpura Range **72** BC 3
Sattahip **74** B 1
Satu Mare **58** B 1
Sauce **112** E 5
Sauda **55** E 4
Sauda Nathil **61** F 4
Saudi Arabia **89** GH 4
Sault Sainte Marie **100** L 6
Saumarez Reef **79** J 3
Saurimo **94** BC 1
Sava **58** AB 2
Savai'i **82** D 3
Savannah **103** K 5
Savannakhet **73** HJ 4
Savant Lake **100** JK 5
Save **95** E 4
Sāveh **61** F 2
Savo **54** J 3
Savoie **57** E 2
Savonselkä **54** J 3
Sawākin **88** F 5
Sawbā **92** E 3
Sawdirī **88** D 6
Sawhāj **88** E 3
Sawu Laut **75** F 5
Saydā **60** B 2
Sayḥūt **89** J 5
Saynshand **70** F 2
Saywūn **89** H 5
Sazin **67** J 3
Sbaa **86** E 3
Scafell Pike **52** C 4
Scaife Mountains **115**
Scammon Bay **98** DE 3
Scarborough **52** C 4
Schefferville **101** O 5
Schenectady **103** M 3
Schleswig **53** EF 4
Schleswig-Holstein **53** E 4
Schouten Islands **80** DE 2
Schwaner, Pegunungan **74** D 4
Schwarzwald **53** E 5
Schwatka Mountains **98** F 2
Schwedt **53** F 4
Schweinfurt **53** F 4
Schwenningen **53** E 5
Schwerin **53** F 4
Sciacca **57** F 4
Scicli **57** F 4
Scilly, Isles of **52** B 5
Scoresby Sound **114**
Scoresbysund **114**
Scotia Sea **115**
Scotland **52** C 3
Scott (Antarctica) **115**
Scott, Cape(Canada) **98** LM 5
Scott, Cape (N.T., Austr.) **78** D 1
Scott Island **115**
Scottsdale (AZ., U.S.A.) **102** D 5
Scottsdale (Tasmania, Austr.) **80** L 9
Seabra **111** H 3
Sea of Azov **59** E 1
Sea of Crete **58** BC 3
Sea of Japan **71** KL 3
Sea of Marmara **58** C 2
Sea of Okhotsk **69** R 4
Seattle **102** B 2
Sebastián Vizcaino, Bahía **102** D 6
Sebkha Azzel Matti **86** EF 3
Sebkha Mekerrhane **87** F 3
Sebkha Oumm ed Droûs Telli **86** CD 4
Sebkha Tah **86** C 3
Sebkhet Oumm ed Droûs Guebli **86** C 4
Sechura **108** B 5
Sechura, Desierto de **108** B 5
Sedan **57** D 2
Seddenga **88** DE 4
Seeheim **94** B 5
Sefadu **90** B 4
Sefrou **86** E 2
Segesta **57** F 4
Segezha **54** K 3
Ségou **90** C 3
Segovia **56** C 3
Segozero, Ozero **54** K 3
Segre **56** D 3
Seguam **98** C 5
Seguin **102** G 6
Segura **56** C 4
Seiland **54** H 1
Seine **56** D 2
Seke **92** E 5
Sekoma **94** C 4
Sekondi-Takoradi **90** D 5
Selaru, Pulau **75** H 5
Selassi **75** H 4
Selatan, Tanjung **74** D 4
Selat Karimata **74** C 4
Selat Mentawai **74** A 4
Selat Salue Timpaus **75** F 4
Selawik **98** F 2
Selayar, Pulau **75** F 5
Seldovia **98** G 4
Selemdzhinsk **69** O 5
Selenge (Mongolia) **68** HJ 6
Selenge (Zaire) **92** B 5
Selgon **69** P 6
Selinunte **57** F 4
Selizharovo **62** F 4
Seljord **55** E 4
Selkirk Mountains **99** O 5–6
Selma **103** J 5
Selous Game Reserve **93** F 6
Selvagens, Ilhas **86** B 2
Selvānā **59** F 3
Selvas **108–109** EF 5
Selwyn Lake **99** R 3–4
Selwyn Mountains **98** LM 3
Semarang **74** D 5
Sembé **91** G 5
Semiozernoye **63** M 5
Semipalatinsk **63** Q 5
Semisopochnoi **98** AB 5
Semitau **74** D 3
Semmering **58** A 1
Semnān **61** F 2
Semporna **75** E 3
Senador Pompeu **111** HJ 2
Sena Madureira **108** E 5
Sendai **71** M 3
Sêndo **70** C 4
Sénégal **90** B 2
Senegal **90** AB 3
Senftenberg **53** F 4
Senhor do Bonfim **111** H 3
Senja **54** G 2
Senjavin Grop**82** B 2
Senneterre **101** M 6
Sens **56** D 2
Senta **58** A 1
Sentinel Peak **99** N 5
Seoni **72** C 3
Seoul **71** J 3
Sepik **82** A 3
Sepik River **80** D 2
Sept-Îles **101** O 5
Şerafettin Dağları **59** F 3
Serakhs **67** G 3
Seram **75** G 4
Seram, Laut **75** GH 4
Serang **74** C 5
Serdobsk **62** HJ 5
Seremban **74** B 3
Serengeti National Park **92** EF 5
Sergino **63** N 3
Sergipe **111** J 3
Seroglazovka **59** G 1
Serov **63** M 4
Serowe **94** D 4
Serpa **56** B 4
Serpukhov **62** G 5
Serra Acarai **109** G 3
Serra Bonita **111** G 4
Serra da Estrêla **56** B 3
Serra do Cachimbo **109** G 5
Serra do Estrondo **109** J 5
Serra do Marao **56** B 3
Serra do Mogadouro **56** B 3
Serra do Navio **109** H 3
Serra do Roncador **111** F 3
Serra dos Carajás **109** H 4–5
Serra dos Gradaús **109** H 5
Serra dos Parecis **110** D 3
Serra do Tombador **110** E 3
Serra Formosa **111** EF 3
Serrai **58** B 2
Serra Talhada **111** J 2
Serrezuela **112** C 5
Serrinha **111** J 3
Serrota **56** BC 3
Seruai **75** J 4
Serule **94** D 4
Sesfontein **94** A 3
Sesheke **94** CD 3
Sesibi **88** DE 4
Seskarö **54** H 2
Sestroretsk **55** JK 3
Séte **56** D 3
Sete Lagoas **111** H 4
Sétif **87** G 1
Settat **86** D 2
Sette Daban, Khrebet **69** P 3
Setúbal **56** B 4
Setúbal, Baía de **56** B 4
Seumanyam **74** A 3
Sevarujo **110** C 4
Sevastopol' **59** D 2
Sever **69** V 3
Severnaya Dvina **62** H 3
Severnaya Zemlya **114**
Severnoye **63** P 4
Severn River **100** K 4
Severnyy Anyuyskiy Khrebet **69** UW 2
Severodvinsk **62** G 3
Severomorsk **54** KL 2
Severo Sibirskaya Nizmennost' **68** FK 1
Sevier Desert **102** D 4
Sevilla **56** B 4
Sevrey **70** D 2
Seward (AK, U.S.A.) **98** H 3
Seward (NE, U.S.A.) **102** G 3
Seward Peninsula **98** E 2
Sewell **112** BC 5
Seychelles **93** J 6
Seyhan **59** E 3
Seymchan **69** S 3
Sfax **87** GH 2
S. Félix Island **107** B 5

Shaanxi **70** EF 4
Shaba **92** CD 6
Shache **67** K 3
Shackleton Ice Shelf **115**
Shackleton Range **115**
Shaddādī **59** F 3
Shadrinsk **63** MN 4
Shaffhausen **57** E 2
Shahdol **72** D 3
Shaḥḥāt **87** K 2
Shahjahanpur **72** CD 2
Shahmīrzad **61** F 2
Shahr Kord **61** F 2
Shahtinsk **63** O 6
Shā'ib al Banāt, Jabal **60** A 4
Sha'īb Hasb **60** D 3
Shakhrisyabz **67** H 3
Shakhterskiy **69** XY 3
Shakhty **59** F 1
Shaki **90** E 4
Shalgiya **63** O 6
Shalkar **62** K 5
Shām, Jabal ash **89** K 4
Shamattawa **99** T 4
Shambe **92** E 3
Shāmīyah **60** C 2
Shammar, Jabal **60** CD 4
Shamrock **102** F 4
Shams **61** G 3
Shan **73** G 3
Shandan **70** D 3
Shandī **88** E 5
Shandong **71** GH 3
Shandong Bandao **71** H 3
Shangcheng **70** FG 4
Shangdu **70** F 2
Shanghai **71** H 4
Shanghang **70** G 5–6
Shangqiu **70** G 4
Shangrao **71** G 5
Shangzhi **71** J 1–2
Shanh **68** H 6
Shankou **70** B 2
Shannon **52** B 4
Shannon, Mouth of the **52** A 4
Shanshan **70** B 2
Shantarskiye Ostrova **69** P 4
Shantou **70** G 6
Shanxi **70** F 3
Shaoguan **70** F 6
Shaowu **71** G 5
Shaoxing **71** GH 5
Shaoyang **70** F 5
Shaqrā' **89** H 6
Sharāf **66** C 4
Shark Bay **78** A 4
Sharm ash Shaykh **60** AB 4
Shary **66** C 5
Shashamanna **93** F 3
Shashi **70** F 4
Shasta, Mount **102** B 3
Shatt al Arab **61** E 3
Shaṭṭ al Jarīd **87** G 2
Shaviklde **59** G 2
Shawinigan **101** N 6
Shaybārā **60** B 4
Shaykh, Ra's ash **60** B 3
Shaykh Ṣa'd **61** E 2
Shaykh' Uthmān **89** H 6
Shchara **55** J 5
Shchel'yayur **62** KL 2
Shchuchinsk **63** N 5
Sheboygan **103** J 3
Shedin Peak **99** M 4
Sheffield **52** C 4
Shekhawati **72** C 2
Sheki **66** D 2
Shelburne **101** OP 7
Shelby **102** D 2
Sheldon Point **98** D 3
Shelikof Strait **98** G 4
Shellharbour **79** J 5
Shenandoah National Park **103** L 4
Shendam **91** F 4
Shenmu **70** F 3
Shenton, Mount **78** C 4
Shenyang **71** HJ 2
Shepetovka **55** J 5
Sherbro Island **90** B 4
Sherbrooke **101** N 6
Sheridan **102** E 3
Sherridon **99** RS 4
Shetland Islands **52** CD 2
Shevchenko **66** E 2
Shevli **69** O 5
Sheya **68** L 3
Sheyang **71** H 4
Sheyenne River **102** G 2
Shibarghan **67** GH 3
Shibazhan **69** MN 5
Shīb Kūh **61** F 3–4
Shijiazhuang **70** FG 3
Shikarpur **67** H 5
Shikoku **71** K 4
Shilka **68** L 5
Shilkan **69** R 4
Shilla **72** C 1
Shillong **73** F 2
Shimanovsk **69** N 5
Shimizu **71** L 4
Shimoga **72** BC 5
Shingshal **67** JK 3
Shiping **70** D 6
Shipunovo **63** Q 5
Shiquanhe **72** C 1
Shirabad **67** H 3
Shirase Glacier **115**
Shīrāz **61** F 3
Shire **95** E 3
Shirikrabat **67** G 2
Shīr Kūh **61** FG 3
Shishaldin Volcano **98** DE 5
Shishou **70** F 5
Shiveluch, Sopka **69** U 4
Shivpuri **72** C 2
Shizuoka **71** L 4
Shkodra **58** AB 2
Sholapur **72** C 4
Shoptykul' **63** P 5
Shorawak **67** H 4–5
Shoshone **102** D 3
Shoshoni **102** E 3
Shouguang **71** G 3
Showa **115**
Show Low **102** DE 5
Shqiperia **58** AB 2
Shreveport **103** H 5
Shrewsbury **52** CD 4
Shuangliao **71** H 2
Shuangyashan **71** K 1
Shucheng **71** G 4
Shuicheng **70** DE 5
Shule **67** K 3
Shumagin Islands **98** F 4–5
Shumerlya **62** J 4
Shuo Xian **70** F 3
Shurinda **68** K 4
Shūshtar **66** D 4
Shuwak **88** F 6
Siahan Range **67** GH 5
Sīah-Chashmeh **59** F 3
Siargao **75** G 2
Šiauliai **55** H 4
Sibay **63** L 5
Šibenik **57** G 3
Siberut, Pulau **74** A 4
Sibirskoye Nizmennost' **63** NQ 3
Sibiti **91** G 6
Sibiu **58** B 1
Sibolga **74** A 3
Sibsagar **73** FG 2
Sibu **74** D 3
Sibuyan Sea **75** F 1
Sicasica **110** C 4
Sichote-Alin **69** P 6
Sichuan **70** CE 4
Sicilia **57** F 4
Sicilia, Canale de **57** F 4
Sicily **57** F 4
Sicuani **110** B 3
Siderno **57** G 4
Sidi-bel-Abbès **86** EF 1–2
Sidon **60** B 2
Siedlce **53** H 4
Siegen **53** E 4
Siena **57** F 3
Sierra Colorada **113** C 7
Sierra de Alcaraz **56** C 4
Sierra de Aracena **56** B 4
Sierra de Gata **56** B 3
Sierra de Gredos **56** B 3
Sierra de Guadarrama **56** C 3
Sierra de Gúdar **56** C 3
Sierra de la Cabrera **56** B 3
Sierra del Cadí **56** D 3
Sierra Leone **90** B 4
Sierra Madre **104** D 4
Sierra Madre del Sur **104** BC 4
Sierra Madre Oriental **104** BC 2–3
Sierra Madrona **56** C 4
Sierra Mojada **104** B 2
Sierra Morena **56** BC 4
Sierra Nayarit **104** B 3
Sierra Nevada (CA., U.S.A.) **102** BC 3–4
Sierra Nevada (Spain) **56** C 4
Sierra Pacaraima **109** F 3
Sierra Parima **109** F 3
Sierra Vizcaíno **102** D 6
Sífnos **58** B 3
Sighetu Marmaţiei **58** B 1
Signy Island **115**
Siguiri **90** C 3
Siirt **59** F 3
Sikar **72** C 2
Sikasso **90** C 3
Sikerin **69** Q 2
Sikkim **72** E 2
Siktyakh **69** N 2
Silchar **73** F 3
Silesia **53** G 4
Silet **87** F 4
Silifke **59** D 3
Siliguri **72** E 2
Silistra **58** C 2
Siljan **55** FG 3
Silkleborg **55** E 4
Siltou **91** H 2
Silver City **102** E 5
Sil'yeyaki **69** Q 1
Simanggang **74** D 3
Simav **58** C 2–3
Simenga **68** J 3
Simeulue, Pulau **74** A 3
Simferopol' **59** D 2
Simla **72** C 1
Simojärvi **54** J 2
Simplicio Mendes **111** H 2
Simpson Desert **79** F 3
Simpson Desert National Park **79** F 4
Simrishamn **55** FG 4
Sīnā' **60** A 3
Sinai (Egypt) **60** A 3
Sināwan **87** H 2
Sincelejo **108** C 2
Sind **67** H 5
Sinda **69** P 6
Singapore **74** B 3
Singaraja **74** E 5
Singida **92** E 5
Singleton **79** J 5
Sinjaja **55** J 4
Sinjār **59** F 3
Sinkiang Uighur **67** L 3
Sinnamary **109** H 2
Sinop **59** E 2
Sinskoye **69** N 3
Sintang **74** D 3
Sinŭiju **71** HJ 3
Sioux City **103** G 3
Sioux Falls **103** G 3
Siping **71** H 2
Sipiwesk **99** S 4
Siple Station **115**
Siracusa **57** G 4
Sir Edward Pellew Group **79** F 2
Sireniki **98** BC 3
Siret **58** C 1
Sīrgān **67** G 5
Sirino **57** G 3
Sir James MacBrian, Mount **98** M 3
Sirsa **72** C 2
Sirt **87** J 2
Sisak **57** G 2

Sisophon **73** H 5
Sisseton **102** G 2
Sistema Iberico **56** C 3
Sistemas Béticos **56** C 4
Sistig-Khem **68** G 5
Sitapur **72** D 2
Sittwe **73** F 3
Sivaki **69** N 5
Sıvas **59** E 3
Sivash **59** DE 1
Siverek **59** E 3
Sīwah **88** D 3
Siwalik Range **72** CD 1–2
Siwan **72** D 2
Si Xian **71** G 4
Sjælland **55** F 4
Sjövegan **54** G 2
Skagen **55** F 4
Skagern **55** F 4
Skagerrak **55** EF 4
Skagway **98** K 4
Skåne **55** F 4
Skarsöy **54** E 3
Skarstind **54** E 3
Skarżysko-Kamienna **53** H 4
Skeldon **109** G 2
Skeleton Coast Park **94** A 3
Skellefteå **54** H 3
Skellefteälven **54** G 2
Skien **55** E 4
Skierniewice **53** H 4
Skiftet **55** H 3
Skikda **87** G 1
Skikotsu **71** N 2
Skíros **58** B 3
Skjoldungen **101** T 3
Sklad **68** M 1
Skópelos **58** B 3
Skopi **58** C 3
Skopje **58** B 2
Skövde **55** F 4
Skye **52** B 3
Slantsy **55** J 4
Śląsk **53** G 4
Slatina **58** B 2
Slave Coast **90** E 4
Slave River **99** P 3–4
Slavgorod **63** P 5
Slavonski Brod **57** G 2
Slavuta **55** J 5
Slavyansk **62** G 6
Sligo **52** B 4
Sliven **58** C 2
Slobodka **58** C 1
Slobodskoy **62** K 4
Slonim **55** J 5
Slovakia **53** H 5
Slovechno **55** J 5
Slovensko **53** H 5
Sluch' **55** J 5
Słupşk **53** G 4
Slutsk **55** J 5
Småland **55** G 4
Smallwood Réservoir **101** P 5
Smidovich **114**
Smirnykh **69** Q 6
Smith **99** P 4
Smokey Dome **102** CD 3
Smoky Cape **79** J 5
Smoky Hill River **102** FG 4
Smöla **54** E 3
Smolensk **62** F 5
Smooth Rock Falls **101** L 6
Snake River **102** C 2
Snezhnoye **69** W 2
Snoul **74** C 1
Snowdon **52** C 4
Snowdrift **99** PQ 3
Sobolevo **69** T 5
Sobral **111** HJ 1
Sochi **59** E 2
Society Islands **83** EF 4
Socorro **102** E 5
Sodankylä **54** J 2
Soddu **93** F 3
Söderhamn **54** G 3
Södermanland **55** G 4
Södertälje **55** G 4
Sofia **58** B 2
Sofiya **58** B 2
Sofiysk **69** O 5
Sofiysk **69** PQ 5
Sofporog **54** K 2
Sogamoso **108** D 2
Sogndalsfjöra **54** E 3
Sogn og Fjordane **54** E 3
Sog Xian **70** B 4
Söke **58** C 3
Sokhor, Gora **68** J 5
Sokodé **90** E 4
Sokółka **53** H 4
Sokolov **53** F 4
Sokosti **54** J 2
Sokoto **91** EF 3
Solberg **54** G 3
Soldatovo **69** V 3
Soledad **108** D 1
Soligorsk **55** J 5
Solikamsk **62** KL 4
Sol'-Iletsk **62** L 5
Solimões **108** E 4
Solitaire **94** B 4
Solomon Islands **81** G 3
Solomon Islands **82** B 3
Solomon Sea **81** F 3
Solomon Sea **82** B 3
Solov'yevsk **68** L 5
Solyanka **68** M 3
Somalia **93** GH 3–4
Somerset **79** G 1
Somme **56** D 1
Sonakh **69** P 5
Songea **95** F 2
Song Hong **73** H 3
Songhua Jiang **71** J 1
Songkhla **73** H 6
Songnim **71** J 3
Songo **95** E 3
Sonid Youqi **70** F 2
Sonid Zuoqi **70** F 2
Sonmiani Bay **67** H 5
Sonneberg **53** F 4
Sonoita **102** D 5
Sonoma Peak **102** C 3
Sonora **102** D 6
Sonoran Desert **102** D 5
Sonqor **66** D 4
Sonsonate **104** DE 5
Sopka Shiveluch **69** U 4
Sopochnaya Karga **68** DE 1
Sopron **58** A 1
Sopur **67** J 4
Sora **57** F 3
Soria **56** C 3
Sorikmerapi, Gunung **74** A 3
Sorkh, Kūh-e **61** G 2
Sorkheh **61** F 2
Sor Mertvyy Kultuk **66** E 1
Sorong **75** H 4
Soroti **92** E 4
Söröya **54** H 1
Sör Rondane Mountains **115**
Sorsatunturi **54** J 2
Sorsele **54** G 2
Sorsogon **75** F 1
Sortavala **54** K 3
Sör-Tröndelag **54** F 3
Sosnogorsk **62** KL 3
Sosnovyy Bor **63** Q 3
Sosyka **59** EF 1
Sotra **55** D 3
Sotsial **63** P 6
Souanké **91** GH 5
Soudan **79** F 3
Sŏul **71** HJ 3
Soumenselkä **54** H 3
Soure **109** J 4
Souris River **99** R 6
Sousa **111** J 2
Sousse **87** H 1
Southampton **52** C D 4
Southampton Island **99** UV 3
South Andaman **73** F 5
South Australia **78–79** E 4
South Bend (IN, U.S.A.) **103** JK 3
South Bend (WA, U.S.A.) **102** B 2
South Carolina **103** K 5
South China Sea **74** CD 2
South Dakota **102** FG 3
South East Cape **80** L 9
Southend **99** R 4
Southend-on-Sea **52** D 4
Southern Alps **82** C 5
Southern Cook Islands **83** E 4
Southern Cross **78** B 5
Southern Uplands **52** C 3
Southern Yemen **89** HJ 5–6
South Geomagnetic Pole **115**
South Georgia **115**
South Island **80** P 9
South Korea **71** JK 3
South Magnetic Pole **115**
South Orkney Islands **115**
South Platte River **102** F 3
South Pole **115**
South Sandwich Islands **115**
South Saskatchewan **99** PQ 5
South Shetland Islands **115**
South Shields **52** C 3
South Uist **52** B 3
South Wellesley Islands **79** FG 2
Southwest Cape **80** P 10
Soven **112** C 5
Sovetsk **62** J 4
Sovetskaya Gavan' **69** PQ 6
Sovetskaya Rechka **63** QR 2
Soya Strait **65** R 5
Sozimskiy **62** K 4
Spain **56** BC 4
Spanish Town **105** G 4
Spartanburg **103** K 5
Spartí **58** B 3
Spassk Dal'niy **71** K 2
Spearfish **102** F 3
Spence Bay **99** T 2
Spencer Gulf **79** F 5
Spicer Islands **101** M 2
Spitsbergen **114**
Split **57** G 3
Spokane **102** C 2
Spooner **103** H 2
Springbok **94** B 5
Springdale **103** H 4
Springfield (CO, U.S.A.) **102** F 4
Springfield (IL, U.S.A.) **103** HJ 4
Springfield (MA, U.S.A.) **103** M 3
Springfield (MO, U.S.A.) **103** H 4
Springfield (OR, U.S.A.) **102** B 3
Springs **94** D 5
Squillace, Golfo di **57** G 4
Srbija **58** B 2
Sredinnyy Khrebet **69** TU 4–5
Sredna Gora **58** BC 2
Srednekolymsk **69** S 2
Sredne Sibirskoye Ploskogor'ye **68** FK 2–3
Sredniy **69** S 4
Srednyaya Itkana **69** U 3
Sremska Mitrovica **58** A 1–2
Srikakulam **72** DE 4
Sri Lanka **72** D 6
Srinagar **67** K 4
Staaten River National Park **79** G 2
Stadlandet **54** D 3
Stafford **52** C 4
Stalowa Wola **53** H 4
Stamford **103** M 3
Standerton **94** D 5
Stanke Dimitrov **58** B 2
Stanley **113** E 9
Stanley Falls **92** D 4
Stanley Mission **99** R 4
Stanovka **63** O 4
Stanovoy Khrebet **68** LN 4
Stanovoy Nagor'ye **68** KL 4
Stara Planina **58** BC 2
Staraya Russa **55** K 4
Staraya Vorpavla **63** N 3
Stara Zagora **58** C 2
Starbuck **83** E 3
Stargard Szczecinski **53** G 4
Starodub **62** F 5
Starogard Gdanski **53** G 4

Staryy Oskol **62** G 5
Staten Island **113** D 9–10
Stavanger **55** DE 4
Stavropol' **59** F 1
Stavropolka **63** N 5
Stavropol'skaya Vozvyshennost' **59** F 1
Steen River **99** O 4
Stefansson Island **99** Q 1
Steinkjer **54** F 3
Steinkopf **94** B 5
Stellenbosch **94** BC 6
Stenon **58** C 3
Stepanakert **66** D 3
Sterlitamak **62** KL 5
Steubenville **103** K 3
Stevenson Entrance **98** G 4
Stewart (AK, U.S.A.) **98** M 4
Stewart (Canada) **98** KL 3
Stewart (New Zealand) **80** P 10
Stewart Crossing **98** K 3
Stewart Island (New Zeeland) **80** P 10
Stewart Island (Solomon Islands) **82** B 3
Steyr **57** F 2
Stillwater **103** G 4
Stip **58** B 2
Stirling Range National Park **78** B 5
Stjördal **54** F 3
Stockholm **55** G 4
Stockton **102** BC 4
Stockton Plateau **102** F 5
Stöde **54** G 3
Stoke-on-Trent **52** C 4
Stokksnes **54** BC 3
Stony Rapids **99** Q 4
Stony River **98** FG 3
Storån **54** G 3
Storavan **54** G 2
Stord **55** E 4
Storkerson Peninsula **99** Q 1
Stornoway **52** B 3
Storsjön **54** F 3
Storuman **54** G 2
Storvigelen **54** F 3
Stöttingfjället **54** G 3
Strait of Belle Isle **101** Q 5
Strait of Bonifacio **57** E 3
Strait of Dover **52** D 4
Strait of Gibraltar **56** B 4
Strait of Hormuz **89** K 3
Strait of Magellan **113** BC 9
Strait of Makassar **74** E 4
Strait of Malacca **74** B 3
Straits of Florida **103** KL 6–7
Stralsund **53** F 4
Strand **94** B 6
Stranraer **52** B 4
Strasbourg **57** E 2
Stratford **102** F 4
Straubing **53** F 5
Streaky Bay **78** E 5
Strelka-Chunya **68** H 3
Stretto de Messina **57** G 4
Streymoy **52** A 1
Strömsund **54** G 3
Stryy **53** H 5
Stung Treng **73** J 5
Sturt Desert **79** G 4
Sturt National Park **79** G 4
Stuttgart **53** E 5
Styr' **55** J 5
Subayhah **66** B 5
Suceava **58** C 1
Sucre **110** D 4
Sudan **88** DE 6
Sudbury **101** L 6
Suddie **109** G 2
Sudety **53** G 4
Suðuroy **52** A 1
Suez **60** A 3
Suez Canal **60** A 3
Şuḩār **89** K 4
Sühbaatar **70** F 1
Suhl **53** F 4
Suide **70** EF 3
Suining **71** G 4
Suir **62** F 3
Suizhong **71** H 2
Sukaraja **74** D 4
Sukhana **68** L 2
Sukhona **62** H 4
Sukhumi **59** F 2
Sukkertoppen **101** R 2
Sukkur **67** H 5
Suksukan **69** S 3
Sula, Kepulauan **75** FG 4
Sulaimāniya **61** D 2
Sulaiman Range **67** H 4–5
Sulanheer **70** E 2
Sulawesi **75** EF 4
Sulawesi, Laut **75** F 3
Sulb **88** DE 4
Sulima **90** B 4
Suliskongen **54** G 2
Sullana **108** BC 4
Sultan Dağları **58–59** D 3
Sulu Archipelago **75** EF 2–3
Sulu Sea **75** EF 2
Sumarokovo **63** R 3
Sumatera **74** AB 3–4
Sumaúma **109** G 5
Šumava **53** F 5
Sumba **75** EF 5
Sumbawa **74** E 5
Sumbawanga **92** E 6
Sumbe **94** A 2
Sümber **70** E 1
Sumburgh Head **52** C 3
Sumgait **66** DE 2
Summel **59** F 3
Summit Lake **99** N 4
Sumperk **53** G 5
Sumter **103** L 5
Sumy **62** G 5
Suna **92** EF 6
Sunderland **52** C 4
Sündıren Dağları **58** D 3
Sundsvall **54** G 3
Sunflower, Mount **102** F 4
Sungai Barito **74** D 4
Sungai Kampar **74** B 3
Sungai Kutai **74** E 4
Sungai Mamberamo **75** J 4
Sunndalsfjorden **54** E 3
Suntar Khayata, Khrebet **69** PQ 3
Suokonmäki **54** H 3
Suolahti **54** J 3
Suomenselkä **54** J 3
Suomi **54** J 3
Suoyarvi **62** F 3
Superior **103** H 2
Süphan Daği **59** F 3
Suquṭrā **93** J 2
Şūr **60** B 2
Surabaya **74** D 5
Surakarta **74** CD 5
Surat (India) **72** B 3
Surat (Queensland, Austr.) **79** H 4
Suratgarh **72** B 2
Surat Thani **73** GH 6
Surendranagar **72** AB 3
Surgut **63** O 3
Surgutikha **63** R 3
Surin **73** H 5
Surinam **109** G 3
Sūrīyah **60** BC 2
Surud Ad **93** H 2
Survey Pass **98** FG 2
Susa **61** E 2
Susah **87** H 1
Susques **110** C 5
Susuman **69** R 3
Sutlej **67** J 4–5
Sutton **98** H 3
Sutun'ya **69** NO 2
Suva **82** C 4
Suva Gora **58** B 2
Suva Planina **58** B 2
Suvorov **82** E 3
Suwałki **53** H 4
Suways, Qanat as **60** A 3
Suwon **71** J 3
Suzhou **71** GH 4
Suzun **63** Q 5
Svalbard **114**
Svartisen **54** F 2
Svealand **55** FG 4
Sveg **54** F 3
Svendborg **55** F 4–5
Sverdlovsk **63** M 4
Sverige **54** G 3
Svetlogorsk (Belorussiya, U.S.S.R.) **55** J 5
Svetlograd **59** F 1
Svetlyy **69** N 4
Svetozarevo **58** B 2
Svobodnyy **69** N 5
Svolvœr **54** F 2
Swain Reefs **79** J 3
Swains **82** D 3
Swakopmund **94** A 4
Swan River **99** R 5
Swansea **52** C 4
Swaziland **95** E 5
Sweden **54** G 3
Swellendam **94** C 6
Świdnik **53** H 4
Swift Current **99** Q 5
Swinoujście **53** FG 4
Switzerland **57** E 2
Syadaykharvuta **63** OP 2
Syalakh **69** MN 2
Syangannakh **69** R 2
Syðri-Hagangur **54** B 2
Sydney (Canada) **101** Q 6
Sydney (N.S.W., Austr.) **79** J 5
Syktyvkar **62** JK 3
Sylhet **73** F 3
Syracuse (N.Y., U.S.A.) **103** L 3
Syr-Dar'ya **67** H 2
Syria **60** BC 2
Syria **88** F 2
Syrian Desert **60** C 2
Syuge-Khaya, Gora **69** P 2
Syurkum **69** Q 5
Syzran **62** J 5
Szczecin **53** F 4
Szczecinek **53** G 4
Szeged **58** A 1
Székesféhérvár **58** A 1
Szekszárd **58** A 1
Szentes **58** AB 1
Szolnok **58** B 1
Szombathely **58** A 1

T

Taarom **79** HJ 4
Tabacal **110** D 5
Tabaqah **60** C 2
Tabarqah **59** E 3
Tabas **61** G 2
Tabasco **104** D 4
Tabatinga **108** E 4
Tabelbala **86** E 3
Tabelbalet **87** G 3
Tabeng **73** HJ 5
Tabiteuea **82** C 3
Tabla **90** E 3
Table Mountain **94** B 6
Tábor **53** F 5
Tabor (U.S.S.R.) **69** R 1
Tabora **92** E 6
Tabou **90** C 5
Tabrīz **66** D 3
Tabuaeran **83** E 2
Tabūk **60** B 3
Tacheng **67** L 1
Tacloban **75** F 1
Tacna **110** B 4
Tacoma **102** B 2
Tacuarembó **112** EF 5
Tademaït, Plateau du **87** F 3
Tadoule Lake **99** S 4
Tadzhikistan **67** HJ 3
Taegu **71** J 3
Taejŏn **71** J 3
Tagama **91** F 2
Taganrog **59** E 1
Taganrogskiy Zaliv **59** E 1
Tagounite **86** D 3
Taguatinga **111** G 3
Taguenout Hagguerer **90** D 1
Tagula Island **79** J 1
Tahan, Gunung **74** B 3

Tahat, Mont **87** G 4
Tahiti **83** EF 4
Tahoe, Lake **102** C 4
Tahoua **91** EF 3
Tahrūd **66** F 5
Tahtali Dağlari **59** E 3
Tahuata **83** F 3
Taibus Qi **70** FG 2
Taichung **71** H 6
Tailai **71** H 1
Taimba **68** G 3
Tainan **71** GH 6
Taipei **71** H 6
Taiping **74** B 3
Taipu **111** J 2
Taitao, Península de **113** AB 8
Taitung **71** H 6
Taivalkoski **54** J 2
Taiwan **71** H 6
Taiyuan **70** F 3
Ta'izz **89** G 6
Tajito **102** D 5
Tájo **56** B 4
Tajrīsh **61** F 2
Tajumulco, Volcán **104** D 4
Tak **73** G 4
Takāb **61** E 1
Takamatsu **71** KL 4
Takatshwane **94** C 4
Takeo **74** B 1
Takestan **61** E 1
Takhta-Bazar **67** G 3
Takht-e Soleiman **61** F 1
Takijuq Lake **99** P 2
Takla Landing **99** M 4
Takla Makan **67** L 3
Taklaun, Gora **69** Q 3
Taklimakan Shamo **67** LM 3
Takua Pa **74** A 2
Talak **91** EF 2
Talakan **69** O 6
Talandzha **69** O 6
Talara **108** B 4
Talaud, Kepulauan **75** G 3
Talavera de la Reina **56** C 3–4
Talawdī **88** E 6
Talaya (U.S.S.R.) **68** G 4
Talaya (U.S.S.R.) **69** S 3
Talca **113** B 6
Talcahuano **113** B 6
Taldy-Kurgan **63** PQ 6
Talence **56** C 3
Tālesh **66** D 3
Taliabu, Pulau **75** FG 4
Talimardzhan **67** H 3
Taliqan **67** HJ 3
Taliwang **74** E 5
Talkalakh **60** B 2
Talkeetna Mountains **98** H 3
Tall Afar **60** D 1
Tallahassee **103** K 5
Tall aş Şuwār **60** C 2
Tallinn **55** J 4
Tall Kayf **60** D 1
Tall Kūshik **60** C 1
Talo **93** F 2
Taltal **112** B 4
Tamale **90** D 4
Tamanrasset **87** G 4
Tamaulipas **104** C 3
Tambacounda **90** B 3
Tambalan **74** E 3
Tambisan **75** E 2
Tambo **79** H 3
Tambov **62** H 5
Tamch **68** F 6
Tamchaket **86** C 5
Tame **108** D 2
Tamel Aike **113** BC 8
Tamgak, Monts **91** F 2
Tamil Nadu **72** C 5
Tampa **103** K 6
Tampere **54** H 3
Tampico **104** C 3
Tamu **73** F 3
Tamworth **79** J 5
Tana (Kenya) **93** F 5
Tana (Norway) **54** J 1
Tana (Vanuatu) **82** C 4
Tanaga **98** A 5
Tanami **78** DE 2
Tanami Desert **78** E 2
Tanami Desert Wildlife Sanctuary **78** E 3
Tanana **98** G 2
Tanana River **98** H 3
Tanch'ŏn **71** JK 2
Tandaho **93** G 2
Tandil **113** E 6
Tane-ga-shima **71** K 4
Tanga **93** F 5–6
Tang-e Karam **61** F 3
Tanger **86** D 1
Tanggula Shan **70** AB 4
Tanggula Shankou **70** B 4
Tanghe **70** F 4
Tangmai **70** C 4
Tangshan **71** G 3
Tangyuan **71** J 1
Tanimbar, Kepulauan **75** H 5
Tanjung, Jabung **74** C 4
Tanjung Api **74** C 3
Tanjungbalai **74** AB 3
Tanjung Samak **74** C 4
Tanjung Selatan **74** D 4
Tanjungselor **74** E 3
Tanjung Vals **75** J 5
Tannu Ola **68** F 5
Ţanţā **88** E 2
Tan Tan **86** C 3
Tanzania **92** EF 6
Tao'an **71** H 1–2
Taolanaro **95** H 5
Taoudenni **90** D 1
Taoyuan **71** H 5
Tapachula **104** D 5
Tapajós **109** GH 4
Tapurucuara **108** E 4
Taquari (Brazil) **110** E 4
Taquari (Brazil) **111** F 4
Tara (U.S.S.R.) **63** OP 4
Tarābulus (Lebanon) **60** B 2
Ţarābulus (Libya) **87** HJ 2
Taracua **108** E 3
Tarakan **74** E 3
Tarakki **67** H 4
Taranto **57** G 3
Taranto, Golfo di **57** G 3–4
Tarapoto **108** C 5
Tarasovo **62** J 2
Tarata **110** C 4
Tarauacá **108** D 5
Tarawa **82** C 2
Tarbes **56** D 3
Taree **79** J 5
Tareya **68** F 1
Ţarīf **61** F 4
Tarija **110** D 5
Tarim Liuchang **70** A 2
Tarin Kowt **67** GH 4
Tarko-Zale **63** PQ 3
Tarkwa **90** D 4
Tarlac **75** J 1
Tarma **110** A 3
Tarn **56** D 3
Tarnobrzeg **53** H 4
Tarnów **53** H 4
Taroudant **86** D 2
Tarragona **56** D 3
Tarrasa **56** D 3
Tarsū Mūsā **87** J 4
Tarsus **60** B 1
Tart **70** B 3
Tartagal **110** D 5
Tartu **55** J 4
Tartus **60** B 2
Tarutung **74** A 3
Tashakta **63** R 6
Tashauz **66** F 2
Tashk, Daryācheh-ye **61** FG 3
Tashkent **67** H 2
Tashtagol **63** R 5
Tasman Bay **81** Q 9
Tasmania **80** KL 9
Tasman Sea **82** B 5
Tassili N-Ajjer **87** G 3
Tas-Tumus **69** O 1
Tasūj **59** G 3
Tatabánya **58** A 1
Tatakoto **83** F 4
Tatarbunary **58** C 1
Tatarsk **63** P 4
Tatarskiy Proliv **69** Q 6
Tatry **53** H 5
Taubaté **111** GH 5
Taumaturgo **108** D 5
Taunggon **73** G 3
Taungup **73** F 4
Taunton **52** C 4
Tauranga **81** R 8
Taurus Mountains **59** DE 3
Tavatuma **69** T 3
Tavda **63** N 4
Taverner Bay **101** N 2
Tavolara **57** E 3
Tavoy **73** G 5
Tawau **74** E 3
Tawitawi Group **75** F 2
Ţawūq **60** D 2
Tawzar **87** G 2
Taxco de Alarcón **104** BC 4
Taxkorgan **67** K 3
Tayga **63** QR 4
Taylor **98** DE 2
Taymā' **60** C 4
Taymyr **68** F 2
Taymyr, Ozero **68** H 1
Tayshet **68** G 4
Taytay **75** E 1
Taz **63** P 2
Taza **86** E 2
Tāzah Khurmātū **60** D 2
Tazovskoye **63** P 2
Tbilisi **59** FG 2
Tcholliré **91** G 4
Teba **75** J 4
Tébessa **87** G 1
Tebingtinggi **74** A 3
Tebulos Mta **59** G 2
Tecer Dağlari **59** E 3
Tecka **113** B 7
Tecomán **104** B 4
Tecuci **58** C 1
Tedzhen **66** FG 3
Teeside **52** C 4
Tefé **109** F 4
Tegal **74** C 5
Tegre **93** FG 2
Tegucigalpa **104** E 5
Tegyul'te-Tërde **69** O 3
Teheran → Tehrān **66** DE 3
Tehran **61** F 2
Tehuacán **104** C 4
Teiga Plateau **88** D 5
Tejo **56** B 4
Tekeli **67** K 2
Tekes **67** L 2
Tekirdağ **58** C 2
Telanaipura **74** B 4
Tel Aviv-Yafo **60** B 2–3
Telegraph Creek **98** LM 4
Telemaco Borba **111** FG 5
Telemark **55** E 4
Telén **113** C 6
Teles Pires **109** G 5
Teli **68** F 5
Tell al 'Amārna **88** E 3
Tello **112** C 5
Telok Anson **74** B 3
Tel'pos-Iz, Gora **63** L 3
Telukbatang **74** CD 4
Teluk Berau **75** H 4
Teluk Bone **75** F 4
Teluk Cendrawasih **75** HJ 4
Teluk Kumai **74** D 4
Teluk Tomini **75** F 4
Témacine **87** G 2
Tematangi **83** F 4
Tembenchi **68** G 3
Tembo **92** B 6
Tembo, Mont **91** G 5
Temirtau **63** O 5
Temiscaming **101** M 6
Temoe **83** G 4
Tempa **114**
Temple **103** G 5
Temuco **113** B 6
Tena **108** C 4
Tenali **72** D 4
Tenasserim **73** G 4–5
Tenere **91** FG 1–2
Ténéré, Erg de **91** G 2

Tenerife **86** B 3
Ténès **87** F 1
Tengchong **70** C 5
Tenggara, Kepulauan **75** G 5
Tengiz, Ozero **63** N 5
Teniente Marsh **115**
Teniente Matienzo **115**
Tenke (U.S.S.R.) **68** L 3
Tennant Creek **78** EF 2
Tennessee **103** J 4
Tenojoki **54** J 2
Teófilo Otoni **111** H 4
Tepatitlán **104** B 3
Tepic **104** AB 3
Teraina **83** E 2
Teramo **57** F 3
Tercan **59** F 3
Terceira **86** A 1
Terek **59** G 2
Teresina **111** H 2
Teressa **73** F 6
Terhazza **86** D 4
Termez **67** H 3
Terni **57** F 3
Ternopol' **62** E 6
Terpugovo **63** N 4
Terrace **98** M 5
Terracina **57** F 3
Terracy Bay **100** K 6
Tessalit **90** E 1
Tessenei **93** F 2
Testa, Capo **57** E 3
Tete **95** E 3
Tétouan **86** D 1
Tetovo **58** B 2
Tevere **57** F 3
Teverya **60** B 2
Têwo **70** D 4
Texarkana **103** H 5
Texas **102** FG 5
Texas City **103** G 6
Teya **68** F 3
Teykovo **62** GH 4
Teyuareh **67** G 4
Tezpur **73** F 2
Thailand **73** GH 4
Thakhek **73** HJ 4
Thames **52** C 4
Thana **72** B 4
Thangoo **78** C 2
Thanh Hoa **73** HJ 4
Thanjavur **72** CD 5
Thap Sakae **73** GH 5
Thar Desert **72** B 2
Thargomindah **79** G 4
Tharthār, Wādī ath **60** D 2
Thásos **58** BC 2
Thaton **73** G 4
The Alps **57** EF 2
The Bahamas **105** GH 2–3
Thebes **60** A 4
The Everglades **103** K 6
The Gambia **90** A 3
The Granites **78** DE 3
The Hague **52** D 4
The Johnston Lakes **78** BC 5
The Pas **99** R 5
Thermaïkos Kólpos **58** B 2–3
Thessalía **58** B 3
Thessaloníki **58** B 2
The Wash **52** D 4
Thiès **90** A 3
Thimphu **72** E 2
Thio (Ethiopia) **93** G 2
Thio (New Caledonia) **81** J 6
Thíra **58** C 3
Thompson **99** S 4
Thompson Falls **102** CD 2
Thon Buri **73** GH 5
Thonon **57** E 2
Thraki **58** BC 2
Thrakion Pélagos **58** BC 2
Three Forks **102** D 2
Three Kings Islands **81** PQ 7
Three Pagodas Pass **73** G 4
Thule **114**
Thunder Bay **100** K 6
Thung Song **73** GH 6
Thurston Island **115**
Thy **55** E 4
Tiandong **70** E 6
Tiangua **111** H 1
Tianjin **71** G 3
Tianjun **70** CD 3
Tianmen **70** F 4
Tiantai **71** H 5
Tiaret **87** F 1
Tiber **57** F 3
Tibesti **91** H 1
Tibet **72** E 1
Tichla **86** B 4
Tidjkdja **86** C 5
Tidra, Ile **86** B 5
Tieli **71** J 1
Tielongtan **67** K 4
Tientsin **71** G 3
Tierra de Campos **56** BC 3
Tierra del Pan **56** B 3
Tigil **69** T 4
Tigris **60** D 2
Tiguent **86** B 5
Tihāmat **89** G 5
Tijuana **102** C 5
Tikal **104** E 4
Tikhoretsk **59** F 1
Tikhvin **62** FG 4
Tilburg **52** DE 4
Tilichiki **69** V 3
Tillabéri **90** E 3
Tillamook **102** B 2
Timanskiy Kryazh **62** J 2–K 3
Timaru **81** Q 9
Timashevskaya **59** EF 1
Timbauba **111** J 2
Timétrine **90** D 2
Timétrine, Monts **90** D 2
Timia **91** F 2
Timir-Atakh-Tas **69** S 2
Timişoara **58** B 1
Timkapaul' **63** M 3
Timmins **101** L 6
Timmoudi **86** E 3
Timor **75** G 5
Timor, Laut **75** G 6
Timor Sea **75** GH 5
Timote **113** D 6
Tinaca Point **75** G 2
Tindouf **86** D 3
Tinfouchy **86** DE 3
Tingmiarmiut **101** T 3
Tingri **72** E 2
Tinian **82** A 2
Tini Wells **88** C 6
Tinogasta **112** C 4
Tínos **58** C 3
Tinsukia **73** G 2
Ti-n Zaouâtene **87** F 4
Tirân **60** B 4
Tirana **58** AB 2
Tiraspol' **58** CD 1
Tire **58** C 3
Tirgovişte **58** C 1–2
Tîrgu Jiu **58** B 1
Tîrgu Mureş **58** BC 1
Tîrnăveni **58** B 1
Tirol **57** F 2
Tirso **57** E 3
Tiruchchirappalli **72** CD 5
Tirunelveli **72** C 6
Tirupati **72** CD 5
Tiruvannamalai **72** C 5
Tisdale **99** R 5
Tisza **58** B 1
Tiszántúl **58** B 1
Titicaca, Lago **110** C 4
Titograd **58** A 2
Titovo Užice **58** AB 2
Titov Veles **58** B 2
Titusville **103** K 6
Tiveden **55** F 4
Tizatlan **104** C 4
Tizimín **104** E 3
Tiznit **86** CD 3
Tjåhumas **54** G 2
Tkhach **59** F 2
Tkvarcheli **59** F 2
Tlemcen **86** E 2
Toamasina **95** HJ 3
Tobago, Isla **109** F 1
Toba & Kakar Ranges **67** H 4
Tobermorey **79** F 3
Tobol **63** N 4
Tobol **63** M 5
Tobol'sk **63** NO 4
Tobseda **62** K 2
Tocantinia **109** J 5
Tocantins **109** J 4
Tocapilla **110** B 5
Tocorpuri, Cerro de **110** C 5
Togiak **98** E 4
Togian, Kepulauan **75** F 4
Togni **88** F 5
Togo **90** E 4
Togtoh **70** F 2
Togyz **67** G 1
Tohma **59** E 3
Toijala **54** H 3
Tok **98** J 3
Tokara-rettō **71** J 4–5
Tokat **59** E 2
Tokelau Islands **82** D 3
Tokko **68** L 4
Tokmak (U.S.S.R.) **59** E 1
Tokmak (U.S.S.R.) **67** K 2
Toksun **67** M 2
Toktogul **67** J 2
Toku-no-shima **71** J 5
Tokur **69** O 5
Tokushima **71** KL 4
Tōkyō **71** L 3
Tolbukhin **58** C 2
Toledo(OH, U.S.A.) **103** K 3
Toledo (Spain) **56** C 4
Toledo, Montes de **56** C 4
Toli **67** L 1
Toliara **95** G 4
Tolima **108** CD 3
Toltén **113** B 6
Toluca **104** BC 4
Tol'yatti **62** J 5
Tomakomai **71** M 2
Tomaszów Mazowiecki **53** H 4
Tomatlán **104** AB 4
Tombador, Serra do **110** E 3
Tombigbee River **103** J 5
Tombouctou **90** D 2
Tomé **113** B 6
Tomelloso **56** C 4
Tomini, Teluk **75** F 4
Tomkinson Ranges **78** D 4
Tomma **54** F 2
Tommot **69** N 4
Tompa **68** JK 4
Tomsk **63** R 4
Tonantins **108** E 4
Tondano **75** G 3
Tonekābon **61** F 1
Tonga **82** D 4
Tonga (Sudan) **92** E 3
Tonga Islands **82** D 4
Tongariro National Park **81** QR 8
Tongatapu Group **82** D 4
Tongchuan **70** E 3
Tonghai **70** D 6
Tonghe **71** J 1
Tonghua **71** J 2
Tongliao **71** H 2
Tongoy **112** B 5
Tongren (Guizhou, China) **70** E 5
Tongren (Qinghai, China) **70** D 3
Tongtian He **70** C 4
Tongyu **71** H 2
Tonj **92** D 3
Tonk **72** C 2
Tonle Sap **73** H 5
Tonopah **102** C 4
Tönsberg **55** F 4
Toompine **79** G 4
Toowoomba **79** J 4
Topeka **103** G 4
Topolinyy **69** P 3
Topozero, Ozero **54** K 2
Toraya **110** B 3
Torbat-e Heydarīyeh **66** FG 2–3
Torbay **52** C 4
Torbino **62** F 4
Torey **68** H J 5

Tori **92** E 3
Torino **57** E 2
Torneälven **54** H 2
Torneträsk **54** GH 2
Toro, Cerro del **112** C 4
Torom **69** P 5
Toronto **101** M 7
Toropets **62** F 4
Tororo **92** E 4
Toros Dağlari **59** D 3
Torquato Severo **112** F 5
Torrelavega **56** C 3
Torrens, Lake **79** F 5
Torrens Creek **79** H 3
Torrente **56** C 4
Torreón **104** B 2–3
Torres Strait **79** G 1
Torrington **102** F 3
Tortkuduk **63** O 5
Tortosa **56** D 3
Torud **61** G 2
Toruń **53** G 4
Toscana **57** F 3
Tosontsengel **68** G 6
Tostuya **68** K 1
Totma **62** H 4
Totness **109** G 2
Totoras **112** D 5
Totten Glacier **115**
Tottori **71** K 3
Touggourt **87** G 2
Toulon **57** E 3
Toulouse **56** D 3
Toungoo **73** G 4
Touraine **56** D 2
Tourcoing **56** D 1
Tourine **86** C 4
Tours **56** D 2
Towakaima **109** G 2
Townsend **102** D 2
Townsville **79** H 2
Toyama **71** L 3
Toygunen **98** C 2
Toyohashi **71** L 4
Toyota **71** L 3
Trabzon **59** E 2
Trafalgar, Cabo **56** B 4
Trâghan **87** HJ 3
Trang **73** G 6
Trangan, Pulau **75** H 5
Transantarctic Mountains **115**
Transilvania **58** B 1
Transkei **94** D 6
Transtrandsfjällen **54** F 3
Transvaal **94** D 5
Trapani **57** F 4
Traun **57** F 2
Treinta y Tres **112** EF 5
Trelew **113** CD 7
Trelleborg **55** F 4
Tremonton **102** D 3
Trenčin **53** G 5
Trenel **113** D 6
Trenque Lauquen **113** D 6
Trento **57** F 2
Trenton **103** M 3
Trepassey **101** R 6
Tres Arroyos **113** D 6
Tres Cerros **113** C 8
Tres Esquinas **108** CD 3
Três Lagoas **111** F 5
Tres Puentes **112** BC 4
Treviso **57** F 2
Triabunna **80** L 9
Trialetskiy Khrebet **59** F 2
Trichur **72** C 5
Trier **52** E 5
Trieste **57** F 2
Trikala **58** B 3
Trincomalee **72** D 6
Trindade Island **107** G 5
Trinidad (Bolivia) **110** D 3
Trinidad (CA, U.S.A.) **102** B 3
Trinidad (Colombia) **108** D 2
Trinidad (Cuba) **105** G 3
Trinidad (Uruguay) **112** E 5
Trinidad, Isla **109** F 1
Trinidad and Tobago **109** FG 1
Trinity Islands **98** G 4
Trinkitat **88** F 5
Tripoli **60** B 2
Tripoli (Libya) **87** H 2
Tripolitania **87** HJ 2
Tripura **73** F 3
Trivandrum **72** C 6
Trnava **53** G 5
Trobriand or Kiriwina Islands **81** F 3
Trois-Pistoles **101** O 6
Trois Rivières **101** N 6
Troitsk (U.S.S.R.) **63** M 5
Troitsk (U.S.S.R.) **68** F 4
Troitsko-Pechorsk **62** KL 3
Trollhättan **55** F 4
Trollhetta **54** E 3
Tromelin **85** H 6
Troms **54** G 2
Tromsö **54** G 2
Trondheim **54** F 3
Troodos **59** D 4
Trout Peak **102** E 3
Trout River **101** Q 6
Troy **103** J 5
Troy (Turkey) **58** C 3
Troyan **58** BC 2
Troyez **56** D 2
Troy Peak **102** C 4
Trucial Coast (United Arab Emirates) **61** FG 4
Trujillo (Peru) **108** C 5
Trujillo (Venezuela) **108** D 2
Truk Islands **82** B 2
Truro **101** P 6
Trust Territory of the Pacific Islands **82** AB 2
Truth or Consequences **102** E 5
Truva **58** C 3
Trysilfjellet **54** F 3
Tsavo National Park **93** F 5
Tselinograd **63** NO 5
Tsenhermandal **68** JK 6
Tsenogora **62** J 3
Tsentralno Tungusskoye Plato **68** H 3–4
Tsetseg **68** F 6
Tsetserleg **68** G 6
Tshane **94** C 4
Tshesebe **94** D 4
Tshikapa **92** C 6
Tsiafajavona **95** H 3
Tsimlyanskoye Vodokhranilishche **59** F 1
Tsingtao **71** H 3
Tsipanda **69** OP 4
Tsjokkarassa **54** HJ 2
Tskhinvali **59** F 2
Tsodilo Hills **94** C 3
Tsuchiura **71** M 3
Tsumeb **94** B 3
Tsumkwe **94** C 3
Tsuruoka **71** L 3
Tuamotu Archipelago **83** FG 4
Tuan **73** H 3
Tuapse **59** E 2
Tuba **68** H 4
Ţubal, Wādī aţ **60** C 2
Tubarão **112** G 4
Tubayq, Jabal at **60** B 3
Ţubruq **87** K 2
Tubuaï **83** F 4
Tubuai Islands **83** EF 4
Tucano **111** J 3
Tucavaca **110** E 4
Tucson **102** D 5
Tucumcari **102** F 4
Tucuruí **109** HJ 4
Tufi **82** A 3
Tuguegarao **75** J 1
Tugur **69** P 5
Tukangbesi, Kepulauan **75** F 5
Tuktoyaktuk **98** L 2
Tukzar **67** H 3
Tula **104** C 3
Tula (U.S.S.R.) **62** G 5
Tulancingo **104** C 3–4
Tulbagh **94** B 6
Tulcán **108** C 3
Tulcea **58** C 1
Tulchin **58** C 1
Tuloma **54** K 2
Tulsa **103** GH 4
Tuluá **108** C 3
Tulun **68** H 5
Tumaco **108** C 3
Tumany **69** T 3
Tumat **69** PQ 1
Tumbes **108** B 4
Tumd Youqi **70** F 2
Tumeremo **109** F 2
Tūmū **87** H 4
Tunas **111** G 5
Tunduru **95** F 2
Tunga **91** F 4
Tungsten **98** M 3
Tunguska, Nizhnyaya **68** F 2
Tungus-Khaya **69** N 3
Tūnis **87** G 1
Tunisia **87** GH 1
Tunja **108** D 2
Tununak **98** D 3
Tunxi **71** G 5
Tuöroyri **52** A 1
Tuostakh **69** P 2
Tuotuo Heyan **70** B 4
Tupã **111** F 5
Tupelo **103** J 5
Tupiza **110** C 5
Tuquan **71** H 1
Tura (U.S.S.R.) **68** H 3
Turakh **68** MN 1
Turana, Khrebet **69** O 5
Turanskaya **66** F 2
Turanskaya Nizmennost **66–67** FG 2
Turbo **108** C 2
Tūreh **61** E 2
Tureia **83** F 4
Turgay **67** G 1
Turgayskaya Dolina **63** M 5–6
Turgayskaya Stolovaya Strana **63** M 5
Türgen Uul **68** F 6
Tŭrgovishte **58** C 2
Turgutlu **58** C 3
Turhal **59** E 2
Turin **57** E 2–3
Turkestan **67** H 2
Turkey **59** DE 3
Turkey **60** AB 1
Türkiye **59** DE 3
Turkmeniya **66** F 3
Turks and Caicos Islands **105** HJ 3
Turks Islands **105** H 3
Turku **55** H 3
Turnu Măgurele **58** BC 2
Turpan **70** A 2
Tursha **62** J 4
Turukhansk **63** RS 2
Turukta **68** L 3
Tuscaloosa **103** J 5
Tuticorin **72** C 6
Tutonchany **68** FG 3
Tutubu **92** E 6
Tutuila **82** D 3
Tuvalu **82** D 3
Ţuwayq, Jabal **61** D 4
Tuxpan de Rodríguez Cano **104** C 3
Tuxtla Gutiérrez **104** D 4
Tuz Gölü **59** D 3
Tūz Khurmātū **61** D 2
Tuzla **57** G 3
Tyan'-Shan' **67** JK 2
Tychy **53** G 4
Tygda **69** N 5
Tyler **103** G 5
Tynda **69** M 4
Tynset **54** F 3
Tyre **60** B 2
Tyrma **69** O 5
Tyrrhenian Sea **57** F 3–4
Tyubelyakh **69** Q 2
Tyukalinsk **63** O 4
Tyumen' **63** MN 4
Tyungulyu **69** O 3
Tzaneen **94** DE 4

U

Uad el Jat **86** C 3
Ua Huka **83** F 3
Uatumá **109** G 4
Uauá **111** J 2
Uaupés **108** E 4
Ubá **111** H 5
Ubangi **92** B 4
'Ubayyid, Wādī al **60** CD 2
Ubeda **56** C 4
Uberaba **111** G 4
Uberlândia **111** G 4
Ubolratna Dam **73** H 4
Ubombo **95** E 5
Ubort' **55** J 5
Ucayali **108** D 5
Uch-Aral **63** Q 6
Uch Kuduk **67** GH 2
Udachnaya **68** K 2
Udaipur **72** B 3
Udanna **69** Q 2
Uddevalla **55** F 4
Uddjaure **54** G 2
Udgir **72** C 4
Udine **57** F 2
Udipi **72** B 5
Udon Thani **73** H 4
Udskoye **69** O 5
Udzha **68** L 1
Uele **92** C 4
Uelen **98** C 2
Uel'Kal' **98** AB 2
Uelzen **53** F 4
Ufa **62** L 4–5
Ugalla **92** E 6
Ugalla River Game Reserve **92** E 6
Uganda **92** E 4
Uglegorsk **69** Q 6
Ugoyan **69** N 4
Ugulan **69** T 3
Ugumun **68** L 2
Ugun **69** N 4
Uherské Hradiště **53** G 5
Uil **66** E 1
Uis Mine **94** AB 4
Uitenhage **94** DE 6
Ujae **82** C 2
Ujelang **82** B 2
Ujiji **92** D 6
Ujjain **72** C 3
Ujung **75** E 5
Ujung Pandang **75** E 4–5
Uka **69** U 4
Ukelayat **69** WX 3
Ukhta **62** K 3
Ukmergė **55** HJ 4
Ukraina **62** FG 6
Ukrainka **54** K 5–6
Uktym **62** J 3
Ukwaa **92** E 3
Ulaanbaatar **68** J 6
Ulaga **69** O 2
Ulan Bator **68** J 6
Ulan-Ude **68** J 5
Ularunda **79** H 4
Uleåborg **54** J 3
Ulety **68** K 5
Ulhasnagar **72** B 4
Uliastay **68** G 6
Uliga **82** C 2
Ullapool **52** B 3
Ulovo **69** S 1
Ulsan **71** JK 3
Ulster **52** B 4
Ulu **88** E 6
Uludağ **58** C 3
Ulutau, Gory **67** H 1
Ul'yanovsk **62** J 5
Uma **68** M 5
Uman' **58** D 1
Umanak **114**
Umari **75** J 4
Umba **54** K 2
Umboi **80** E 3
Umbria **57** F 3
Umeå **54** H 3
Umm al Qaywayn **61** G 4
Umm Durmān **88** E 5
Umm Lajj **60** B 4
Umm Ruwābah **88** E 6
Umm Urūmah **60** B 4
Umnak **98** D 5
Umtata **94** D 6
Umuarama **111** F 5
Umvuma **95** E 3
Unaí **111** G 4
Unalakleet **98** E 3
Unalaska **98** D 5
Unayzah (Jordan) **60** B 3
'Unayzah (Saudi Arabia) **60** D 4
Ungava Bay **101** O 4
União do Vitória **112** F 4
Unimak **98** E 5
Union of Soviet Socialist Republics **65** HP 4
United Arab Emirates **61** FG 5
United Kingdom **52** DC 3
United States **102–103**
Unity **99** Q 5
Universales, Montes **56** C 3
Unst **52** C 2
Uoyan **68** K 4
Upata **109** F 2
Upemba, Lac **92** D 6
Upemba National Park **92** D 6
Upernavik **114**
Upington **94** C 5
Upolu **82** D 3
Upper Red Lake **103** GH 2
Uppland **55** G 3
Uppsala **55** G 4
Urak **69** Q 4
Ural **66** E 1
Ural Mountains **63** LM 2–4
Ural'sk **62** K 5
Urandangie **79** F 3
Urandi **111** H 3
Uranium City **99** Q 4
Uraricoera **109** F 3
Ura Tyube **67** H 3
Urayq, Natud al **60** D 4
Urbano Santos **111** H 1
Uren **62** J 4
Urewera National Park **81** R 8
Urfa (Turkey) **59** E 3
Urfa Platosu **59** E 3
Urgench **66** FG 2
Uribia **108** D 1
Uromi **91** F 4
Ur Suq ash Shuyūkh **61** DE 3
Ursus **53** H 4
Uruaçu **111** G 3
Uruapan **104** B 4
Urucará **109** G 4
Uruçuí **111** H 2
Uruguaiana **112** E 4–5
Uruguay **112** EF 5
Uruguay **112** EF 5
Urumchi **67** M 2
Ürümqi **67** M 2
Uruqnay **112** E 5
Uryupinsk **62** H 5
Uşak **58** C 3
'Ushayrah **61** DE 4
Ushuaia **113** C 9
Üsküdar **58** C 2
Ussuriysk **71** K 2
Ust'-Bol'sheretsk **69** ST 5
Ust'-Chayka **68** J 3
Ust'-Ilimsk **68** H 4
Ustinov **62** K 4
Ust-Kada **68** H 5
Ust'-Kamchatsk **69** U 4
Ust'-Kamenogorsk **63** QR 5–6
Ust'-Karenga **68** L 5
Ust'-Karsk **68** L 5
Ust'-Khayryuzovo **69** ST 4
Ust'-Kulom **62** K 3
Ust'-Kut **68** J 4
Ust-Labinsk **59** EF 1
Ust'-Nera **69** Q 3
Ust'-Olenëk **68** LM 1
Ust'-Ozernoye **63** RS 4
Ust'-Pit **68** F 4
Ust'-Port **63** Q 2
Ust'-Sugoy **69** S 3
Ust'-Tatta **69** O 3
Ust'-Tym **63** Q 4
Ust'-Ura **62** H 3
Ust'-Urgal **69** O 5
Ust'-Us **68** F 5
Ust'-Usa **62** L 2
Ust'-Uyskoye **63** M 5
Ustuyurt, Plato **66** F 2
Ust'-Vyyskaya **62** J 3
Ust'Yuribey **63** NO 2
Usu **67** L 2
Usulután **104** E 5
Usumacinta, Rio **104** D 4
Utah **102** D 4
Utah Lake **102** D 4
Utata **68** H J 5
Utēs **63** P 5
Utesiki **69** W 2
Utiariti **110** E 3
Utica **103** M 3
Utirik **82** C 2
Utrecht **52** DE E 4
Utrera **56** B 4
Uttyakh **69** O 2
Uuldza **68** K 6
Uusimaa **55** J 3
Uvarovo **62** H 5
Uvinza **92** DE 6
Uvs Nuur **68** F 5
Uwayrid, Harrat al **60** B 4
Uxituba **109** G 4
Uyaly **67** G 2
Uyandi **69** Q 2
Uyega **69** Q 3
Uyuni **110** C 5
Uyuni, Salar de **110** C 5
Uzbekistan **67** GH 2
Uzbel Shankou **67** J 3
Uzhgorod **58** B 1
Uzhur **63** R 4
Uzunköprü **58** C 2

V

Vaal **94** C 5
Vaasa **54** H 3
Vác **58** A 1
Vacaria **112** FG 4
Vadodara **72** B 3
Vadsö **54** J 1
Vaduz **57** E 2
Vágar **52** A 1
Vaghena **81** G 3
Vairaatea **83** F 4
Vaitupu **82** C 3
Vakarevo **69** W 3
Valachia **58** BC 2
Valcheta **113** C 7
Valday **62** F 4
Val de Loire **56** D 2
Valdepeñas **56** C 4
Valdés, Península **113** D 7
Valdez **98** H 3
Valdivia **113** B 6
Val-d'Or **101** M 6
Valdosta **103** K 5
Valença **111** J 3
Valenca do Piauí **111** H 2
Valence **57** DE 2–3
Valencia (Spain) **56** CD 4
Valencia (Venezuela) **108** E 2
Valentine **102** F 3
Valera **108** D 2
Valga **55** J 4
Valjevo **58** AB 2
Valladolid (Mexico) **104** E 3
Valladolid (Spain) **56** C 3
Vall de Uxó **56** C 4
Valle de la Pascua **108** E 2
Valledupar **108** D 1
Valle Grande **110** D 4
Vallenar **112** BC 4
Valletta **57** F 4
Valleyview **99** O 4
Valparaíso **112** B 5
Vals, Tanjung **75** J 5
Vammala **54** H 3
Van **59** F 3
Vanavara **68** H 3
Vancouver **99** N 6
Vancouver Island **99** M 6
Vanda **115**
Vanderbijlpark **94** D 5

Vanderhoof **99** N 5
Van Diemen, Cape **78** D 1
Van Diemen Gulf **78** E 1
Vanduzi **95** E 3
Vänern **55** F 4
Van Gölü **59** F 3
Vangunu **81** G 3
Vanikolo Islands **81** J 4
Vanikoro Island **82** C 3
Vankarem **98** B 2
Vannes **56** C 2
Vanoua Lava **81** J 4
Vanrhynsdorp **94** B 6
Vanua Levu **82** C 4
Vanuatu **81** J 5
Vanuatu **82** B 3
Vanzhil'kynak **63** QR 3
Varanasi **72** D 2
Varangerfjorden **54** K 1–2
Varangerhalvöya **54** JK 1
Varaždin **57** G 2
Varberg **55** F 4
Vardö **54** K 1
Vardofjällen **54** FG 2
Varginha **111** GH 5
Varkaus **54** J 3
Värmland **55** F 4
Varna (Bulgaria) **58** C 2
Värnamo **55** F 4
Varsinais Suomi **55** H 3
Var'yegan **63** P 3
Vashnel **63** N 3
Vasiss **63** O 4
Vassdalsegga **55** E 4
Västerås **55** G 4
Västerbotten **54** G 3
Västergötland **55** F 4
Västervik **55** G 4
Vasto **57** F 3
Västra Granberget **54** H 2
Vasyugan **63** P 4
Vaticano, Citta Del **57** F 3
Vatnajökull **54** B 3
Vatoa **82** D 4
Vättern **55** F 4
Vatyna **69** W 3
Vaughn **102** E 5
Vaupés **108** D 3
Vava'u Group **82** D 4
Växjö **55** FG 4
Vayvida **68** FG 3
Vazhgort **62** J 3
Veadeiros **111** G 3
Vefsna **54** F 2
Vega **54** F 2
Vegreville **99** P 5
Vejle **55** E 4
Velež **57** G 3
Vélez-Málaga **56** C 4
Velikiye Luki **55** K 4
Velikiy Ustyug **62** HJ 3
Veliko Tŭrnovo **58** C 2
Vella Lavella **81** G 3
Vellore **72** CD 5
Velsk **62** H 3
Vel't **62** K 2
Vemor'ye **69** Q 6
Venado Tuerto **112** D 5
Venda **95** E 4
Venezia **57** F 2
Venezuela **108–109** EF 2
Venezuela, Golfo de **108** D 1
Vengerovo **63** P 4
Venice **57** F 2
Venta **55** H 4
Ventoux, Mont **57** E 3
Ventspils **55** H 4
Ventura **102** C 5
Venustiano Carranza **104** D 4
Vera **112** DE 4
Veracruz **104** CD 4
Veraval **72** AB 3
Verbania **57** E 2
Verdalsöra **54** F 3
Verdun **57** E 2
Vereeniging **94** D 5
Verkhn'aya Salda **63** M 4
Verkhneimbatskoye **63** RS 3
Verkhneural'sk **63** LM 5
Verkhnevilyuyskt **68** LM 3
Verkhneye Kuyto,Ozero
54 K 3
Verkhnyaya Amga **69** NO 4
Verkhnyaya Vol'dzha **63** PQ 4
Verkhoyansk **69** O 2
Verkhoyanskiy Khrebet
69 N 2–P 3
Verkhoyansk Range **69** N 2
Vermilion Bay **100** J 5
Vermont **103** M 3
Verona **57** F 2
Vérroia **58** B 2
Versailles **56** D 2
Vershina **63** M 3
Vershino-Shakhtaminskiye
68 L 5
Vest-Agder **55** E 4
Vesterålen **54** FG 2
Vestfirðir **54** A 2
Vestfjorden **54** F 2
Vestvågöy **54** F 2
Vesuvio **57** F 3
Vetlanda **55** G 4
Vetrenyy **69** R 3
Viacha **110** C 4
Viborg **55** E 4
Vibo Valentia **57** G 4
Vicecommodoro Marambio
115
Vicenza **57** F 2
Vichada **108** E 3
Vichy **56** D 2
Vicksburg **103** HJ 5
Victoria (Australia) **79** G 6
Victoria (Canada) **99** N 6
Victoria (Chile) **113** B 6
Victoria (Hong Kong) **70** F 6
Victoria (Seychelles) **93** JK 5
Victoria (TX, U.S.A.) **103** G 6
Victoria, Mount (Burma)
73 F 3
Victoria, Mount (Papua New
Guinea) **82** A 3
Victoria de Durango **104** B 3
Victoria de las Tunas **105** G 3
Victoria Falls **94** D 3
Victoria Island **99** PQ 1
Victoria Land **115**
Victoria River **78** E 2
Victoria Strait **99** R 2
Victoria West **94** C 6
Vicuña Mackenna **112** D 5
Vidin **58** B 2
Vidisha **72** C 3
Vidsel **54** H 2
Viduša **57** G 3
Vidzemes Augstiene **55** J 4
Viedma **113** D 7
Viedma, Lago **113** B 8
Vieng Pou Kha **73** H 3
Vienna **57** G 2
Vienne **57** DE 2
Vientiane **73** H 4
Vientos, Paso de los
105 H 3–4
Vierzon **56** D 2
Vietnam **73** JK 5
Vifosa **58** B 2
Vigan **75** J 1
Vigevano **57** E 2
Vigo **56** B 3
Viiala **54** H 3
Vijayawada **72** D 4
Vikna **54** F 3
Vila **81** J 5
Vila Conceição **109** F 3
Vilanculo **95** F 4
Vila Nova de Gaia **56** B 3
Vila Velha (Amapá, Brazil)
109 H 3
Vila Velha (Espírito Santo,
Brazil) **111** HJ 5
Vıldız Dağları **58** C 2
Vilhena **110** D 3
Villa Abecia **110** CD 5
Villa Bella **110** C 3
Villach **57** F 2
Villa Constitución **112** D 5
Villa Coronado **104** B 2
Villa Dolores **112** C 5
Villa Frontera **104** B 2
Villagarcia de Arosa **56** B 3
Villaguay **112** E 5
Villahermosa **104** D 4
Villa Huidobro **112** D 5
Villa Ingavi **110** D 5
Villalonga **113** D 6
Villa María **112** D 5
Villa Mazán **112** C 4
Villa Montes **110** D 5
Villanova y Geltrú **56** D 3
Villa Ocampo **104** AB 2
Villareal de las Enfants
56 CD 4
Villa Regina **113** C 6
Villarreal de los Infantes
56 CD 4
Villarrica (Chile) **113** B 6
Villarrica (Paraguay) **112** E 4
Villatoro, Puerto de **56** B 3
Villa Unión **112** C 4
Villavicencio **108** D 3
Villazón **110** C 5
Villefranche **57** DE 2
Villena **56** C 4
Vilnius **55** J 5
Vilyuy **69** MN 3
Vilyuyskoye Plato **68** J 2
Vilyuyskt **68** M 3
Viña del Mar **112** B 5
Vindhya Range **72** BC 3
Vinh **73** J 4
Vinh Giat **73** JK 5
Vinh Linh **73** J 4
Vinh Loi **73** J 6
Vinkovci **57** G 2
Vinnitsa **62** E 6
Vinson Massif **115**
Virac **75** F 1
Virandozero **62** FG 3
Viranşehir **59** F 3
Virden **99** R 6
Virgem da Lapa **111** H 4
Virginia (South Africa) **94** D 5
Virginia (U.S.A.) **103** L 4
Virginia Beach **103** LM 4
Virginia Falls **99** N 3
Virgin Islands **105** JK 4
Virrat **54** H 3
Virtsu **55** H 4
Virtul Gutii **58** B 1
Visayan Sea **75** F 1
Visby **55** G 4
Viscount Melville Sound
99 P 1
Vishakhapatnam **72** DE 4
Vista Alegre **109** F 3
Vistula **53** G 5
Vitebsk **55** K 4
Vitiaz Strait **80** E 3
Viti Levu **82** C 4
Vitim **68** K 4–5
Vitimskoye Ploskogor'ye
68 K 5
Vitória (Espírito Santo, Brazil)
111 HJ 5
Vitória (Pará, Brazil) **109** H 4
Vitoria (Spain) **56** C 3
Vitória da Conquista **111** H 3
Vittorio Veneto **57** F 2
Vivorata **113** E 6
Vizianagaram **72** D 4
Vladimir **62** H 4
Vladimir **71** L 2
Vladimirovka **62** K 5
Vladimir-Volynskiy **55** H 5
Vladivostok **71** K 2
Vlissingen **52** D 4
Vlorë **58** A 2
Vltava **57** F 2
Vogan **90** E 4
Voghera **57** E 2
Voi **93** F 5
Voinjama **90** C 4
Volcán Citlaltépetl **104** C 4
Volcán Llullaillaco **110** C 5
Volcán Miravalles **104** EF 5
Volcán Misti **110** B 4
Volcán Ollagüe **110** C 5
Volcán Popocatéptl **104** C 4
Volcán Tajumulco **104** D 4
Volga **62** J 5

Volgo-Balt (I.V. Lenin) Kanal **62** FG 3
Volgodonsk **59** F 1
Volgograd **62** H 6
Volkhau **54** K 4
Volkhov **55** K 4
Volochayevka **69** O 6
Vologda **62** GH 4
Volokon **68** J 4
Volos **58** B 3
Vol'sk **62** J 5
Volta **90** E 4
Volta Redonda **111** GH 5
Volynskoye Polesye **55** J 5
Volzhsk **62** J 4
Volzhskiy **62** J 6
Vopnafjörður **54** C 2
Vórioi Sporádhes **58** B 3
Vorkuta **63** MN 2
Vormsi **55** H 4
Voronezh **62** GH 5
Voroshilovgrad **59** EF 1
Võrts Järv **55** J 4
Võru **55** J 4
Vosges **57** E 2
Voss **55** E 3
Vostochnaya Litsa **62** G 2
Vostochnyy Sayan **68** G 5
Vostok (Antarctica) **115**
Vostok (Kiribati) **83** E 3
Votkinsk **62** K 4
Voyampolka **69** T 4
Vozhega **62** H 3
Voznesensk **58** D 1
Vozvyshennost' Karabil' **67** G 3
Vran **57** G 3
Vranje **58** B 2
Vratsa **58** B 2
Vršac **58** B 1
Vryburg **94** C 5
Vryheid **95** E 5
Vsetin **53** G 5
Vsevidof, Mount **98** D 5
Vsevolozhsk **55** K 3
Vukovar **57** G 2
Vung Tau **73** J 5
Vuoksa **54** J 3
Vyaltsevo **62** H 4
Vyatskiye Polyany **62** K 4
Vyazemskiy **69** OP 6
Vyaz'ma **62** F 4
Vyborg **54** J 3
Vychegda **62** J 3
Vygozero, Ozero **62** G 3
Vyksa **62** H 4
Vyngapur **63** P 3
Vysotsk **55** J 3
V'yuny **63** Q 4

W

Wabowden **99** S 5
Wabrah **66** D 5
Waco **103** G 5
Wad **67** H 5
Waddān **87** J 3
Waddington, Mount **99** M 5
Wādi al 'Arabah **60** B 3
Wādī al Bātin **61** DE 3
Wādī al Ghudāf **60** D 2
Wādi al Khurr **60** C 3
Wādī al 'Ubayyid **60** CD 2
Wādī ath Tharthār **60** D 2
Wādī at Ṭubal **60** C 2
Wādī Ḥalfa' **88** E 4
Wādī Hawrān **60** C 2
Wādī Jimāl **60** B 4
Wādī Qina **60** A 4
Wadley **103** K 5
Wad Madanī **88** EF 6
Wafrah **66** D 5
Wagga Wagga **79** H 6
Wagin **78** B 5
Wah **67** J 4
Wahai **75** G 4
Wāhāt al Khārijah **88** E 3–4
Waigeo, Pulau **75** H 4
Waingapu **75** F 5
Wajir **93** G 4
Wakayama **71** L 4
Wake **82** C 1
Wakkanai **71** M 1
Wałbrzych **53** G 4
Waldia **93** F 2
Wales **52** C 4
Walewale **90** D 3
Walgett **79** H 4–5
Wallaroo **79** F 5
Wallis **82** D 3
Wallis and Futuna **82** CD 3
Walnut Ridge **103** H 4
Walvis Bay **94** A 4
Wanaaring **79** G 4
Wanaka **82** C 5
Wandel Sea **114**
Wanganui **81** R 8
Wangka **73** G 5
Wangqing **71** J 2
Wan Hsa-la **73** G 3
Wankie **94** D 3
Wankie National Park **94** D 3
Wanxian **70** E 4
Warangal **72** CD 4
Warbumi **75** H 4
Warburton Mission **78** D 4
Waren **75** J 4
Warner Peak **102** C 3
Warner Robins **103** K 5
Warragul **79** H 6
Warren **103** K 3
Warrenton **94** C 5
Warri **91** F 4
Warrnambool **79** G 6
Warrumbungle Range **79** H 5
Warsaw **53** H 4
Warszawa **53** H 4
Warta **53** G 4
Warwick **79** J 4
Wasatch Range **102** D 3–4
Washington (D.C., U.S.A.) **103** L 4
Washington (U.S.A.) **102** BC 2
Wasua **80** D 3
Wasum **81** E 3
Watampone **75** F 4
Waterberg **94** B 4
Waterford **52** B 4
Waterloo **103** H 3
Waterton Lakes National Park **99** OP 6
Watertown **103** LM 3
Watheroo **78** B 5
Watrous (Canada) **99** QR 5
Watrous (N.M., U.S.A.) **102** F 4
Watsa **92** D 4
Watson Lake **98** LM 3
Wauchope **79** J 5
Wausau **103** J 3
Wave Hill **78** E 2
Wāw **92** D 3
Wawotobi **75** F 4
Waycross **103** K 5
Wayland **103** K 4
Weagamow Lake **100** J 5
Webbe Shibeli **93** G 3
Weddel Sea **115**
Weichang **71** G 2
Weiden **53** F 5
Weifang **71** GH 3
Weimar **53** F 4
Weining **70** D 5
Weipa **79** G 1
Wejherowo **53** G 4
Welkom **94** D 5
Wellesley Islands **79** F 2
Wellington (New Zealand) **81** R 9
Wellington, Isla (Chile) **113** AB 8
Wells (NV, U.S.A.) **102** C 3
Wels **57** F 2
Wendeng **71** H 3
Wenshan **70** DE 6
Wentworth **79** G 5
Wenzhou **71** H 5
Wepener **94** D 5
Weser **53** E 4
Wesleyville **101** R 6
Wessel, Cape **79** F 1
West Antarctica **115**
Westbank **60** B 2
West Berlin **55** F 5
West Berlin **55** F 5
West Cape **82** C 6
Western Australia **78** C 3–4
Western Ghats Kerala **72** BC 4–5
Western Sahara **86** C 4
Western Samoa **82** D 3
West Falkland **113** D 9
West Ice Shelf **115**
West Indies **104** HJ 3
West Indies **105** HJ 3
Westlock **99** P 5
West Memphis **103** H 4–5
West Palm Beach **103** L 6
West Plains **103** H 4
Westport **81** Q 9
Westree **101** L 6
West Siberian Plain **63** OQ 3
West Wirginia **103** K 4
West Wyalong **79** H 5
West Yellowstone **102** D 3
Wetar, Pulau **75** G 5
Wetaskiwin **99** P 5
Wete **93** FG 5
Wewak **80** D 2
Weyburn **99** R 6
Whale Cove **99** T 3
Whangarei **81** Q 8
Wheatland **102** F 3
Wheeler Peak **102** E 4
Wheeling **103** KL 4
Whitecourt **99** O 5
Whitehaven **52** C 4
Whitehorse **98** KL 3
White Mountain Peak **102** C 4
White Nile **88** E 6
White Pass **98** L 4
White River **100** L 6
White Russia **55** J 5
White Sea **62** G 2
Whitewood **79** G 3
Whitmore Mountains **115**
Wholdaia Lake **99** QR 3
Wichita **102** G 4
Wichita Falls **102** G 5
Wick **52** C 3
Wickenburg **102** D 5
Wien **57** G 2
Wiener Neustadt **57** G 2
Wieprz **53** H 4
Wiesbaden **53** E 4
Wilhelm, Mount **80** D 3
Wilhelmshaven **53** E 4
Wilkes-Barre **103** L 3
Wilkes Land **115**
Willcox **102** E 5
Willemstad **108** E 1
Willeroo **78** E 2
Williams **102** D 4
Williams Lake **99** N 5
Williamsport **103** L 3
Williston (South Africa) **94** C 6
Williston (U.S.A.) **102** F 2
Williston Lake **99** N 4
Wilmington (DE, U.S.A.) **103** L 4
Wilmington (N.C., U.S.A.) **103** L 5
Wilowmore **94** C 6
Wilson **103** L 4
Wilson Bluff **78** D 5
Wilsons Promontory **79** H 6
Windhoek **94** B 4
Windsor **103** K 3
Windward Islands (French Polynesia) **83** F 4
Windward Islands (Lesser Antilles) **105** L 4–5
Winisk **100** K 4
Winisk River **100** K 5
Winneba **90** D 4
Winnemucca **102** C 3
Winnipeg **99** S 6
Winnipeg, Lake **99** S 5
Winnipegosis, Lake **99** RS 5
Winona **103** H 3
Winslow (AZ., U.S.A.) **102** DE 4
Winslow (Kiribati) **82** D 3

Winston-Salem **103** K 4
Winterthur **57** E 2
Wisconsin **103** HJ 2
Wiseman **98** G 2
Wisła **53** G 4
Wismar **53** F 4
Wittenberg **53** F 4
Wittenberge **53** F 4
Włocławek **53** G 4
Wokam, Pulau **75** H 5
Woleai **82** A 2
Wollastone Lake **99** R 4
Wollaston Lake **99** R 4
Wollaston Peninsula **99** OP 2
Wollongong **79** J 5
Wolverhamton **52** C 4
Wonju **71** J 3
Wŏnsan **71** J 3
Wonthaggi **79** GH 6
Wood Buffalo National Park **99** OP 4
Woodlark **81** F 3
Wood River Lakes **98** F 4
Woodstock (Queensland, Austr.) **79** G 2
Woodward **102** FG 4
Woomera **79** F 5
Wooramel **78** A 4
Worcester (South Africa) **94** BC 6
Worcester (U.K.) **52** C 4
Worchester (MA, U.S.A.) **103** M 3
Worland **102** E 3
Wosi **75** G 4
Wotho **82** BC 2
Wotje **82** C 2
Wrangel Island **114**
Wrangell **98** L 4
Wrangell Saint Elias National Park and Preserve **98** J 3
Wrigley **99** N 3
Wrocław **53** G 4
Wuchuan **70** E 5
Wudaoliang **70** B 3
Wudu **70** D 4
Wugang **70** F 5
Wugong **70** E 4
Wuhai **70** E 3
Wuhan **70** FG 4
Wuhu **71** G 4
Wūjang **72** D 1
Wukari **91** F 4
Wuliang Shan **70** D 6
Wun Rog **92** D 3
Wuppertal **53** E 4
Wurung **79** G 2
Würzburg **53** F 5
Wutunghliao **70** D 5
Wuvulu **82** A 3
Wuwei **70** D 3
Wuxi **71** H 4
Wuxing **71** H 4
Wuyiling **69** N 6
Wuyuan **70** E 2
Wuzhi Shan **70** E 7
Wuzhong **70** E 3
Wuzhou **70** F 6
Wynbring **78** E 5
Wyndham **78** D 2
Wyoming **102** E 3
Wyoming Peak **102** DE 3
Wyperfeld National Park **79** G 6
Wysoczyzna Ciechanowska **53** GH 4

X

Xainza **72** E 1
Xai-Xai **95** E 5
Xambioá **109** J 5
Xangongo **94** AB 3
Xánthi **58** B 2
Xanthos **58** C 3
Xapecó **112** F 4
Xapuri **110** C 3
Xayar **67** L 2
Xenia **103** K 4
Xiaguan **70** D 5
Xiamen **71** G 6
Xi'an **70** EF 4
Xiangfan **70** F 4
Xiangshan **71** H 5
Xiangtan **70** F 5
Xiangyin **70** F 5
Xianju **71** H 5
Xianyang **70** E 4
Xiao'ergou **69** M 6
Xiao Hinggan Ling **69** N 5–6
Xiapu **71** H 5
Xichang **70** D 5
Xigazê **72** E 2
Xiliao He **71** H 2
Ximiao **70** D 2
Xin Barag Zuoqi **68** L 6
Xingcheng **71** GH 2
Xingdi **70** A 2
Xingren **70** E 5
Xingtai **70** F 3
Xingu **109** H 4
Xing Xian **70** EF 3
Xingxingxia **70** C 2
Xingyi **70** D 5–6
Xining **70** D 3
Xinjiang Uygur Zizhiqu **67** KM 2
Xinjin (Liaoning, China) **71** H 3
Xinjin (Sichuan, China) **70** D 4
Xinlitun **69** N 5
Xin Xian **70** F 3
Xinxiang **70** FG 3
Xinyang **70** F 4
Xinyi **71** G 4
Xinyuan **67** L 2
Xique-Xique **111** H 3
Xiushui **70** F 5
Xiuyan **71** H 2
Xiwu **70** C 4
Xixiang **70** E 4
Xizang Zizhiqu **72** DE 1
Xpuhil **104** E 4
Xuanhan **70** E 4
Xuanhua **70** F 2
Xuanwei **70** D 5
Xuchang **70** FG 4
Xuguit Qi **68** LM 6
Xümatang **70** C 4
Xuwen **70** F 6
Xuyong **70** DE 5
Xuzhou **71** G 4

Y

Yablonovyy Khrebet **68** JL 5
Yabrūd **60** B 2
Yacuiba **110** D 5
Yadgir **72** C 4
Yagoua **91** GH 3
Yagradagze Shan **70** C 3
Yakima **102** BC 2
Yakmach **67** G 5
Yakoma **92** C 4
Yakrik **67** L 2
Yakumo **71** LM 2
Yakutat **98** K 4
Yakutsk **69** N 3
Yala (Sri Lanka) **72** D 6
Yala (Thailand) **73** H 6
Yalgoo **78** B 4
Yalnızçam Dağları **59** F 2
Yalong Jiang **70** D 4–5
Yalta **59** D 2
Yalutorovsk **63** MN 4
Yamagata **71** LM 3
Yamal Peninsula **63** NO 1
Yambio **92** D 4
Yambol **58** C 2
Yamburg **63** OP 2
Yamdena, Pulau **75** H 5
Yamoussoukro **90** C 4
Yamuna **72** D 2
Yana **69** P 1
Yan'an **70** E 3
Yanartaş Dağları **58** CD 3
Yanbu' **60** C 4
Yanchang **70** EF 3
Yandrakinot **98** C 2
Yangambi **92** CD 4
Yangjiang **70** F 6
Yangquan **70** F 3
Yangtze Kiang **70** C 4
Yangtze Leiang **71** G 4
Yang Xian **70** E 4
Yanhe **70** E 5
Yanhuqu **72** D 1
Yankton **102** G 3
Yano-Indigirskaya Nizmennost **69** PR 1
Yanov Stan **63** Q 2
Yanqi Huizu Zizhixian **67** LM 2
Yanshou **71** J 1
Yanskiy Zaliv **69** OP 1
Yantai **71** H 3
Yaoundé **91** G 5
Yapen, Pulau **75** J 4
Yapura **108** D 4
Yaraka **79** G 3
Yaranga **69** X 3
Yaransk **62** J 4
Yari **108** D 3
Yarlung Zangbo Jiang **70** B 5
Yarmouth **101** O 7
Yaroslavl' **62** G 4
Yarram **79** H 6
Yarroto **63** O 2
Yartsevo **63** RS 3
Yarumal **108** CD 2
Yashkino **69** P 5
Yasnyy **69** N 5
Yaté-Village **81** J 6
Yathkyed Lake **99** S 3
Yatsushiro **71** JK 4
Yavi, Cerro **108** E 2
Yawng-hwe **73** G 3
Ya Xian **70** E 7
Yazd **61** G 3
Yazdān **67** G 4
Yaz-ed Khvāst **61** F 3
Yecheng **67** K 3
Yedoma **62** H 3
Yeeda River **78** C 2
Yefremov **62** G 5
Yegorlykskaya **59** F 1
Yei **92** E 4
Yelabuga **62** K 4
Yelets **62** G 5
Yelizarovo **63** N 3
Yelizovo **69** T 5
Yellowhead Pass **99** O 5
Yellowknife **99** P 3
Yellow Sea **71** H 4
Yellowstone National Park **102** D 3
Yellowstone river **102** EF 2
Yelovka **69** U 4
Yelvertoft **79** F 3
Yemanzhelinsk **63** M 5
Yematan **70** C 3
Yemen **89** GH 5
Yengisar **67** K 3
Yengo **91** H 5
Yengue **91** F 5
Yenice **59** E 3
Yenisey **63** R 2
Yenisey, Malyy **68** FG 5
Yeniseyskiy Kryazh **68** F 3–4
Yepoko **63** OP 2
Yercha **69** R 2
Yerema **68** J 3
Yerevan **59** FG 2
Yergeni **59** F 1
Yermak **63** P 5
Yerofey-Pavlovich **69** M 5
Yeropol **69** V 2
Yertom **62** J 3
Yerupajá, Nevado **110** A 3
Yerushalayim **60** B 3
Yesil **63** N 5
Yeşilırmak **59** E 2
Yessentuki **59** F 2
Yetman **79** J 4
Yeu, Ile d' **56** C 2
Yevpatoriya **59** D 1
Yeya **59** E 1
Yeysk **59** E 1
Yi'an **69** N 6
Yibin **70** D 5
Yichang **70** F 4
Yichun **69** N 6
Yidu **70** F 4
Yıldız Dağı **59** E 2

Yilehuli Shan **69** MN 5
Yiliang **70** D 6
Yinchuan **70** E 3
Yingde **70** F 6
Yingkou **71** H 2
Yining **67** L 2
Yirga Alem **93** F 3
Yitulihe **69** M 5
Yiyang **70** F 5
Ylikitka **54** J 2
Yllastuntun **54** H 2
Yoboki **93** G 2
Yogyakarta **74** CD 5
Yokohama **71** LM 3–4
Yokosuka **71** LM 3–4
Yokote **71** LM 3
Yola **91** G 4a
Yolombo **92** C 5
Yonago **71** K 3
Yŏngan **71** JK 2
Yongchang **70** D 3
Yong deng **70** D 3
Yongren **70** D 5
Yonkers **103** M 3
Yonne **56** D 2
York (PA, U.S.A.) **103** L 4
York (U.K.) **52** C 4
York (Western Australia) **78** B 5
Yorke Peninsula **79** F 5
Yorkton **99** R 5
Yosemite National Park **102** BC 4
Yoshkar Ola **62** J 4
Yŏsu **71** J 4
Young **79** H 5
Youngstown **103** KL 3
Yozgat **59** D 3
Ytyk-Kel' **69** O 3
Yuanping **70** F 3
Yucatán Peninsula **104** E 3–4
Yucheng **71** G 3
Yuci **70** F 3
Yudoma **69** P 4
Yuexi **70** D 5
Yueyang **70** F 5
Yugorskiy Poluostrov **63** M 2
Yugoslavia **57** G 3
Yukagirskoye Ploskogor'ye **69** ST 2
Yukon **98** EF 3
Yukon-Charley Rivers National Preserve **98** J 2–3
Yukon Flats **98** H 2
Yukon Flats National Monument **98** H 2
Yukon Plateau **98** K 3
Yukon River **98** J 2
Yukon Territory **98** KL 3
Yulin (China) **70** EF 6
Yulin (Shaanxi, China) **70** E 3
Yuma **102** F 3
Yumari, Cerro **108** E 3
Yumen **70** C 3
Yumenzhen **70** C 2
Yunaska **98** C 5
Yunling Shan **70** C 5
Yunnan **70** D 6
Yunxiao **71** G 6
Yuriby **63** P 1
Yurimaguas **108** C 5
Yurty **69** U 4
Yushan (China) **71** G 5
Yushan (Taiwan) **71** H 6
Yushnoye **69** Q 6
Yuxi **70** D 6
Yu Xian **70** FG 2–3
Yuzhno-Sakhalinsk **69** Q 6
Yuzhnyy Bug **58** CD 1

Z

Zabarjad **60** B 5
Zabol **67** G 4
Zabrze **53** G 4
Zacapu **104** B 4
Zacatecas **104** B 3
Zadar **57** G 3
Zadetkale Kyun **73** G 5
Zadran **67** H 4
Za'faranah **60** A 3
Żag **86** D 3
Zāgheh-ye Bālā **61** E 2
Zagorsk **62** G 4
Zagreb **57** G 2
Zagros, Kūhha ye **61** EF 2
Zagros Mountains (Iran) **61** F 3
Zāhedān **67** G 5
Ẓāhirah **61** G 5
Zahlah **60** B 2
Zaire **92** BD 5
Zaire (Angola) **94** A 1
Zakamensk **68** H J 5
Zakharov **69** O 3
Zākhū **66** C 3
Zákinthos **58** B 3
Zalābiyah (Syria) **60** C 2
Zalaegerszeg **58** A 1
Ẓalim **89** G 4
Zaliv Akademii **69** P 5
Zaliv Kara-Bogaz Gol **66** E 2
Zaliv Shelikhova **69** T 3–4
Zaliv Terpeniya **69** Q 6
Zallah **87** J 3
Zamakh **89** H 5
Zambeze **95** E 3
Zambezi **94** C 2
Zambia **94** D 2
Zamboanga **75** F 2
Zamora (Ecuador) **108** C 4
Zamora (Spain) **56** B 3
Zamość **53** H 4
Zanesville **103** K 4
Zanjān **66** D 3
Zanthus **78** C 5
Zanul'e **62** K 3
Zanzibar **93** FG 6
Zanzibar Island **93** FG 6
Zaouatallaz **87** G 4
Zaoyang **70** F 4
Zaozernyy **68** FG 4
Zaozhuang **71** G 4
Zaragoza **56** C 3
Zarand (Iran) **61** F 2
Zarand (Iran) **66** F 4
Zárate **112** E 5
Zaraza **108** E 2
Zard Kūh **61** F 2
Zarechensk **54** K 2
Zarghun **67** H 4
Zaria **91** F 3
Zaruma **108** C 4
Zaskar Mountains **67** K 4
Zastron **94** D 6
Zatish'ye **69** T 2
Zatoka Gdańska **53** G 4
Zav'yalova, Ostrov **69** RS 4
Zāwiyat Masūs **87** K 2
Zawr, Ra's az **61** E 4
Zayü **70** C 5
Zduńska Wola **53** G 4
Zeehan **82** A 5
Zêkog **70** D 4
Zelenoborskiy **54** K 2
Zelenodol'sk **62** JK 4
Zelenokumsk **59** F 2
Zell am See **57** F 2
Žemaičiu Aukštuma **55** H 4
Žemaitija **55** H 4
Zemgale **55** HJ 4
Zemio **92** D 3
Zenica **57** G 3
Zeya **69** N 5
Zêzere **56** B 4
Zhag'yab **70** C 4
Zhailma **63** M 5
Zhaksylyk **63** O 6
Zhanabas **67** H 1
Zhanabek **63** P 6
Zhangjiakou **70** FG 2
Zhangping **71** G 5
Zhangwu **71** H 2
Zhangye **70** CD 3
Zhangzhou **71** G 5–6
Zhangzi **70** F 3
Zhanjiang **70** F 6
Zhantekets **63** Q 6
Zhao'an **70** G 6
Zhaodong **71** HJ 1
Zhaojue **70** D 5
Zhaotong **70** D 5
Zhaoyuan **71** J 1
Zhaozhou **71** HJ 1
Zharkamys **66** F 1
Zharkova **63** R 4
Zharlykamys **63** P 6
Zharma **63** Q 6
Zharyk **63** O 6
Zhdanov **59** E 1
Zhejiang **71** GH 5
Zhel'dyadyr **67** H 1
Zhelezinka **63** P 5
Zheleznodorozhnyy **62** K 3
Zheleznogorsk **62** FG 5
Zhenghe **71** G 5
Zhengzhou **70** F 4
Zhenjiang **71** GH 4
Zhenlai **71** H 1
Zhenning **70** DE 5
Zhenxiong **70** D 5
Zapadnaya Dvina **55** J 4
Zapadno **63** OP 3
Zapala **113** B 6
Zaporosh'ye **59** E 1
Zhenyuan **70** E 5
Zhigalovo **68** J 5
Zhijiang **70** E 5
Zhitomir **55** J 5
Zhlatyr **63** P 5
Zhmerinka **58** C 1
Zhongba **72** D 2
Zhongning **70** E 3
Zhongwei **70** DE 3
Zhong Xian **70** E 4
Zhongxiang **70** F 4
Zhoukouzhen **70** FG 4
Zhovtnevoye **59** D 1
Zhuanghe **71** H 3
Zhuo Xian **70** G 3
Zhupanovo **69** TU 5
Zhurban **69** N 5
Zhushan **70** EF 4
Zhuzhou **70** F 5
Zibā **60** B 4
Zielona Góra **53** G 4
Zigong **70** DE 5
Ziguinchor **90** A 3
Zihuatanejo **104** B 4
Zilair **63** L 5
Zile **62** E 2
Žilina **53** G 5
Zima **68** H 5
Zimba **94** D 3
Zimbabwe **94–95** DE 3
Zimbabwe **95** E 4
Zimi **90** B 4
Zimovniki **59** F 1
Zincirli **59** E 3
Zinder **91** F 3
Zlatoust **63** L 4
Zlatoustovsk **69** OP 5
Znamenka **59** D 1
Znojmo **53** G 5
Zoigê **70** D 4
Zolotaya Gora **69** N 5
Zomba **95** F 3
Zonga **92** B 4
Zonguldak **59** D 2
Zorritos **108** B 4
Zrenjanin **58** B 1
Zufār **89** J 5
Zugdidi **59** F 2
Zugspitze **57** F 2
Zújar **56** B 4
Zunyi **70** E 5
Zurbāṭīyah **61** D 2
Zurich **57** E 2
Zurmat **67** H 4
Zuwārah **87** H 2
Zvolen **53** G 5
Zwickau **53** F 4
Żyrardów **53** H 4
Zyryanka **69** S 2
Zyryanovsk **63** Q 6